Thinking theologically about youth ministry

Starting Right

Thinking theologically about youth ministry

Starting Right

Kenda Creasy Dean
Chap Clark
David Rahn

YOUTH
SPECIALTIES

A

ACADEMIC

ZondervanPublishingHouse
Grand Rapids, Michigan

A Division of HarperCollins*Publishers*

Starting Right: Thinking theologically about youth ministry

Copyright © 2001 by Kenda Creasy Dean, Chap Clark, and Dave Rahn
(except Chapter 14, "Theological Framework for Youth Ministry," copyright © 2001 by Robin Maas)

Youth Specialties, 300 S. Pierce St., El Cajon, CA 92020, books are published by Zondervan Publishing House, 5300 Patterson Ave. S.E., Grand Rapids, MI 49530.

Library of Congress Cataloging-In-Publication Data

Dean, Kenda Creasy, 1959-
   Starting Right : thinking theologically about youth ministry / Kenda Creasy Dean,
   Chapman Clark & David Rahn.
      p. cm.
   Includes bibliographical references and index.
   ISBN 0-310-23406-9
   1. Church work with youth. 2. Theology, Practical. I. Clark, Chap, 1954- II. Rahn,
   Dave, 1954- III. Title.

BV4446 .D37 2001
259'.23—dc21

00-043879

Unless otherwise indicated, all Scripture quotations are taken from the *Holy Bible: New International Version* (North American Edition). Copyright © 1973, 1978, 1984 by International Bible Society. Used by permission of Zondervan Publishing House.

Edited by Tim McLaughlin and Sheri Stanley
Cover and interior design by Razdezignz

Printed in the United States of America

01 02 03 04 05 06/ / 10 9 8 7 6 5 4 3 2 1

To all those who helped us start right...

Biographies

General Editors

Kenda Creasy Dean (Ph.D., Princeton Theological Seminary) teaches at Princeton Theological Seminary, where she is assistant professor of youth, church, and culture, and director of the School of Christian Education. The coauthor of *The Godbearing Life: The Art of Soul Tending for Youth Ministry*, Kenda directed the seminary's Institute for Youth Ministry until 1998.

Chap Clark (Ph.D., University of Denver) is associate professor of youth and family ministries at Fuller Theological Seminary and is director of youth ministry programs. Chap is also the executive administrator at Glendale (California) Presbyterian Church, a youth ministry volunteer for Young Life, and a consultant to schools, denominations, and parachurch organizations. His publishing credits include *The Youth Worker's Handbook to Family Ministry*, *Daughters and Dads: Building a Lasting Relationship* (coauthor), and *Four Views of Youth Ministry and the Church* (coauthor).

Dave Rahn (Ph.D., Purdue University) is professor of educational ministries at Huntington College and director of that school's Link Institute for Faithful and Effective Youth Ministry. He is coauthor of *Contagious Faith: Empowering Student Leadership in Youth Evangelism* and of a book that details the results and implications of an exhaustive study of Protestant youth ministers in America (to be published in 2001). Dave's volunteer work with Campus Life/Youth for Christ continues a streak of youth ministry that dates back to 1972.

Contributing Authors

Tony Campolo (Ph.D., Temple University) professor emeritus of sociology at Eastern College in St. Davids, Pennsylvania, the chairman of the board of that school's Institute for Urban Studies, and founder of the Evangelical Association for the Promotion of Education (devoted to the educational, medical, and economic needs of people in third-world nations). He is a popular speaker and also author of more than 25 books, including *Revolution and Renewal: How Churches Are Saving Our Cities* and *Following Jesus without Embarrassing God*.

Mark W. Cannister (Ed.D., University of Pittsburgh) is associate professor of youth ministries and Christian education at Gordon College in Wenham, Massachusetts, where he also chairs the youth ministries and missions programs and the humanities division. Mark is vice president of the North American Professors of Christian Education and serves on the board of directors of The Boston Project Ministries (an urban outreach and service ministry) and of the Youth Ministry Educators Forum. A 25-year veteran of youth ministry in both church and parachurch organizations, Mark consults with a variety of ministry organizations as well as speaks and teaches at camps, conferences, and seminars.

Patricia Davis (Ph.D., Princeton Theological Seminary) is associate professor of pastoral theology at Perkins School of Theology in Dallas, Texas, and author of two books on adolescent girls—*Counseling Adolescent Girls* and *Beyond Nice: The Spiritual Wisdom of Adolescent Girls*. A counselor for families and kids in crisis, Patricia leads workshops across the country on spirituality and adolescents.

Mark DeVries (M.Div., Princeton) is pastor to youth and their families at First Presbyterian Church in Nashville, Tennessee, where he's served for 13 years. A 21-year youth ministry veteran, he has served both as a Young Life volunteer and on church staffs. He is author of *Family-Based Youth Ministry: Reaching the Been-There, Done-That Generation*.

Mark Dodrill (Ph.D., Trinity Evangelical Divinity School) lives in Castelldefels, Spain, where he studies the interaction between culture and youth ministry as the national director of Youth for Christ and professor of Christian education and youth ministry at the Instituto Bíblico y Seminario Teológico de España. Ordained as a Baptist pastor, he leads the cell group ministry at Terrassa United Baptist Church. He is the coeditor of the GrupoJoven Collection—44 titles in youth evangelism, discipleship, and leadership training for distribution throughout the Spanish-speaking world.

Steve Gerali (D.Phil., Oxford Graduate School) serves as the chair of the youth ministry and adolescent studies department at Judson College and the director of graduate studies at Northern Baptist Theological Seminary. He is founder and director of the Chicago-based International Center for Ministry to Adolescents. As an author, lecturer (to young people as well as adults), and consultant with expertise in adolescent development and disorders, Steve draws from over 22 years of experience with preteens and adolescents as a youth pastor and clinical counselor. He conducts continuing-education seminars and workshops for many youth ministry organizations, colleges, and seminaries.

Simon Hall (M.A., Oxford University) is pastor of Revive, a new church reaching out to alternative 18-to-30-year-olds in Leeds, U.K., and tutors part-time at the Centre for Youth Ministry in Oxford. He has served as a church-based youth pastor and a street outreach worker. Simon is the editor of the *NIV Youth Bible* (non-U.S. version) and author of *Mind Games* and *Breakfast with God*.

Darrell W. Johnson (M.Div. Fuller Theological Seminary) is associate professor of pastoral theology at Regent College, Vancouver, B.C., Canada, and adjunct professor of preaching at Fuller Theological Seminary. He has pastored churches in central and Southern California, as well as in Manila, Philippines. His articles have appeared in the *Leadership Handbook* and *Quest Bible*. Until his Regent College appointment, his Sunday sermons were broadcast by the Far East Broadcasting Company into much of Asia.

Karen Jones (Ph.D., Southwestern Baptist Theological Seminary) is assistant professor of educational ministries and associate director of Link Institute for Faithful and Effective Youth Ministry at Huntington College in Huntington, Indiana. With nearly 20 years of experience as youth minister, curriculum writer, and conference speaker, she is involved in several academic and professional youth ministry organizations and has several published articles to her credit, based on her research. She is one of three researcher-writers of the Link Institute Study of Protestant Youth Ministers in America, with results to be published in 2001.

Robin Maas (Ph.D., The Catholic University of America) is professor of spirituality and the recently retired academic dean at the John Paul II Institute for Studies in Marriage and Family in Washington. Prior to her involvement with the Institute, she served as professor of Christian formation and discipleship at Wesley Theological Seminary in Washington, D.C. She is the founder and director of the Women's Apostolate to Youth (an intergenerational community for female spiritual leaders of children and youth in the Arlington, Virginia, diocese). Robin directs retreats, gives lectures, and conducts parish classes and workshops in the area of spirituality. She is the author of numerous articles in these areas (*Theology Today, Spiritual Life, The Catholic Faith, Living Light*), and her books include *The Church Bible Study Handbook, Crucified Love,* and *Spiritual Traditions for the Contemporary Church* (coeditor).

Terry McGonigal (Ph.D., Fuller Theological Seminary) is dean of the chapel and associate professor of religion at Whitworth College in Spokane, Washington, and the former director of the Institute of Youth Ministries at Fuller Theological Seminary. He has served as Seattle extension director for Fuller Theological Seminary and as western division training director for Young Life. Terry is an ordained Presbyterian minister (PCUSA).

Charles N. Neder (M.Div., Columbia Theological Seminary) is the national director of youth ministry for Presbyterians for Renewal, in addition to founding Fun in the Son, Great Escape, Son Servants, Youth Worker Equipping Conferences, and Family Life Seminars around the country—the purpose of these events being to strengthen local churches and equip their youth ministers. Chuck speaks at parenting events, participates in strategic planning with local churches, and helps churches evaluate their youth ministries, both in the United States and in Europe.

Rodger Nishioka (M.Div, McCormick Theological Seminary) is associate professor of Christian education at Columbia Theological Seminary in Decatur, Georgia, with teaching and research expertise in youth ministry, young-adult ministry, and general Christian education. Before joining the faculty of the seminary, Rodger served for 13 years as the director of youth and young adult ministry for the Presbyterian Church national offices. He has authored three books and several articles on youth ministry and is a frequent preacher and workshop leader.

Soren Oestergaard (Ph.D., University of Copenhagen) is youth secretary in the Danish Baptist Union and youth ministry lecturer at University of Copenhagen and Scandinavian Academy of Leadership and Theology.

Evelyn Parker (Ph.D., Garrett ETS/Northwestern University) is assistant professor of Christian education at Perkins School of Theology at Southern Methodist University in Dallas, Texas. She has served as director of Christian education for the Christian Methodist Episcopal Church, director of children and youth ministries at Northaven United Methodist Church, a YMCA program coordinator, and volunteer counselor to homeless teens. Evelyn's publishing credits include the forthcoming book *When Hope Seems Hopeless: Emancipatory Ministry with African American Adolescents* and the article "Karibu: A New Meaning for Hospitality" in *Midstream: An Ecumenical Journal*.

Marv Penner (D.Phil., Oxford Graduate School) chairs the youth and family ministry division at Briercrest Bible College and Seminary in Caronport, Saskatchewan, where he is professor of youth and family ministry. He directs not only the Canadian Centre for Adolescent Research, but also Youth Quake, Canada's biggest weekend campus youth event. An ordained Christian and Missionary Alliance minister and member of Youth Specialties' National Resource Seminar team, Marv trains youth workers internationally, counsels kids and their families, and writes about youth and family ministry.

Kara Eckmann Powell (Ph.D., Fuller Theological Seminary) is assistant professor at Azusa Pacific University and assistant junior high pastor at Lake Avenue Church in Pasadena, California. The general editor of Gospel Light's Pulse Junior High Curriculum series, Kara has written many books and articles for Gospel Light, Youth Specialties, Cook Communications, and *Youthworker* journal.

Don C. Richter (Ph.D., Princeton Theological Seminary) is an associate with the Valparaiso Project on the Education and Formation of People in Faith, an initiative funded by the Valparaiso University-based religion division of the Lilly Endowment. Don is responsible for managing the project Web site (*www.practicingourfaith.org*), administering the small-grants program, and coordinating the Youth and Practices Seminar. He was the founding director of Emory University's Youth Theology Institute and has taught Christian education at Emory's Candler School of Theology and Bethany Theological Seminary. Don is an ordained minister in the Presbyterian Church.

Duffy Robbins (M.Div., Gordon-Conwell Theological Seminary) chairs the youth ministry department at Eastern College and speaks to teenagers and youth workers around the world. He is ordained in the United Methodist Church, for whose *Good News* magazine he writes a column. For almost 20 years Duffy has served as associate staff with Youth Specialties, speaking at its annual National Youth Worker Conventions and on its National Resource Seminar team. He has written more than 13 books, including *Youth Ministry That Works, The Ministry of Nurture, Youth Ministry Nuts & Bolts, Memory Makers* (coauthor), and *Everyday Object Lessons for Youth Groups* (coauthor).

Ed Trimmer (Ed.D., Teachers College, Columbia University) is head of the school of religion at Pfeiffer University, where he heads the undergraduate and graduate programs in youth ministry and Christian education. Prior to this he served as a theological educator for 16 years, including two terms as acting academic dean. The author of *Youth Ministry Handbook*, Ed is a member of the advisory board of both the Youth Ministry Educators Forum and the Fellowship of Adults in Youth Ministry.

David F. White, (Ph.D., Claremont School of Theology) directs the Youth Discipleship Project at the Claremont School of Theology in Southern California, a research project exploring new approaches to youth ministry. He comes to this project with almost 30 years of experience in youth ministry (Kentucky, Mississippi, Alaska, California), having taught at Columbia Theological Seminary and served on the faculty of the Youth Theology Institute at Candler School of Theology. David has authored chapters in several religious education volumes as well as in forthcoming youth ministry volumes. He is a regular conference speaker on youth ministry topics.

Mark Yaconelli (M.A., Graduate Theological Union) is director of the Youth Ministry and Spirituality Project at San Francisco Theological Seminary, where he is adjunct professor of youth ministry. He is the founder and director of Sabbath, a one-week spiritual renewal retreat held in several locations across the U.S. Mark volunteers as director of youth ministries at Sleepy Hollow Presbyterian Church in San Anselmo, California, and is a speaker, retreat leader, and consultant for mainline congregations across North America.

Contents

(continued)

Contents (continued)

Acknowlegments

We'd like to express our appreciation to the authors who worked under our demanding time-frame. They responded with grace and skill.

—*K. C. D., C. C., D. R.*

I'm grateful for the behind-the-scenes ministries of Princeton Theological Seminary students Larisa Hamada, who offered editorial candor, wit, and insight on several chapters; and Cazden Minter, who willingly verified facts and footnotes that people said could never be found. Thanks also to Jane Neuwirth, secretary to the School of Christian Education at Princeton Theological Seminary, for her extra effort in helping contact the authors who contributed to this book.

—*K. C. D.*

Special thanks to my faculty assistants, Dawn Toloya and Michael Evans, who have spent many hours on this project. And thanks also to my research colleagues and doctoral students in the Fuller Theological Seminary Schools of Psychology and Theology, especially Dr. Jim Furrow, my *compadre* in theologically and academically caring for kids and families. Thanks to the Young Life community, who instilled in me the essential role theology plays in youth ministry. I will always be grateful. Finally, thanks to Dee, Chap, Rob, and Katie, for walking through life with me and teaching me that good theology starts at home with those you love.

—*C. C.*

Thanks to the graduate students of Huntington College who help me think theologically all the time and to the youth ministers with whom I have the privilege of serving week in and week out. You help me practice what I think.

—*D. R.*

Theological Rocks—First Things First
Kenda Creasy Dean

> Therefore everyone who hears these words of mine and puts them into practice is like a wise man who built his house on the rock. The rain came down, the streams rose, and the winds blew and beat against that house; yet it did not fall, because it had its foundation on the rock. But everyone who hears these words of mine and does not put them into practice is like a foolish man who built his house on sand. The rain came down, the streams rose, and the winds blew and beat against that house, and it fell with a great crash.
>
> —*Matthew 7:24-26*

Most of us have known our share of "beach ministries"—ministries with young people whose foundations are firmly anchored in...sand. Gangbusters one day, gone the next, these ministries just couldn't weather storms of conflict or the wet blankets of indifference. They couldn't keep up with the flood of overwhelming need, or withstand the winds of pastoral change. One day they just fell with a great crash. Or, more likely, the youth minister in charge did.

Storms, wet blankets, floods, and wind are part of ministry. Fortunately, so are sunny days, clear sinuses, and quiet, warm eddies that keep life interesting. The difference between those who thrive in youth ministry and those who collapse under its weight lies in the substance of our foundations: have we built ministry on theological bedrock, or on the shifting sand of cultural relevance? Don't get me wrong: Jesus didn't tell the parable about the wise and foolish builders to condemn the sand—and nor should the church condemn efforts to relate to culture. But beach trips and attunement to cultural change take place on the *surface* of ministry, not at its heart. The problem in this parable isn't the sand, but the *builder*: somebody who should have known better chose to forego the hard work of laying a solid foundation for the sake of quick construction, a spectacular view, and bargain prices.

You've probably heard the story, repackaged recently by management guru Stephen Covey, about the professor who one day filled an aquarium with large rocks. "Is it full?" he asked his students. Most of them nodded yes. Then he took gravel and poured it into the aquarium, letting it spill between the rocks. "Now is it full?" More cautiously, most students said yes, it was full. Then the professor poured sand into the aquarium, filling in the gaps and crevices left by the gravel. "*Now* is it full?" he asked the class. The students squirmed—but anyone could see that the aquarium was practi-

Intro

What are your theological rocks?[1] Which of your beliefs about God matter the most to you? Which ones would you say are "musts" for youth ministry? Do you have a theological conviction that serves as the hub of your beliefs and practices?

Think of an adolescent you know. If you could share only five things about God over the course of your ministry with this teenager, what would want him or her to hear you say?

Write your theological rocks here:

1.

2.

3.

4.

5.

---

1. Thanks to Ron Foster for the loan of this exercise.

cally overflowing. Then the professor took a large pitcher of water, and carefully poured it into the sand. At last, the aquarium could hold no more.[1]

I share this story with you for the same reason Stephen Covey tells it in management seminars: it's a simple illustration of *first things*. Had the professor filled the aquarium first with sand and water, the rocks—the aquarium's main substance, the "big stuff"—never would have fit. Trying to shove rocks in last would be futile (not to mention messy). Of course, that may not stop us from trying. Remember the middle high Sunday school lesson? After you checked in on the week's highs and lows, after you finished the jelly bean relay (which was more fun than expected, so it took twice as long as planned), after you told the pithy story that seemed to illustrate the day's Bible text—well, time ran out. Half the class left for choir, the other half dissolved in chaos, and (oops) the Bible lesson never quite got covered. "*Theological rocks*": *first things first.* Or what about those disruptive eighth-grade girls at the camp you ran this summer? You knew they were begging for attention, so you meant to arrange some one-on-one time with them once the school year started. But then the school year started with a vengeance. Your workload went from zero to 60 overnight. The camp director wants your input for next summer—tomorrow. You're still preparing your Thursday small group when the doorbell rings with the first arrivals, every single time. And now there's a message on your answering machine from some youth ministry publisher reminding you about the free resources your church can have *if* you show up to Saturday's training event. Girls? Oh—those girls. "*Theological rocks*": *first things first.*

Or maybe you remember a frantic phone call from a distraught mother whose son, a freshman at the local university, drank himself into alcohol poisoning at a fraternity party. You, another intern, and the pastor met them at the hospital. You brokered counseling sessions with the campus rehab center, contacted university support systems, prayed with both mother and son. In some ways, your crisis intervention skills had never been better. And yet it didn't occur to you to suggest to this helpless mother that *she* pray for her child's recovery. Nor did it cross your mind that she needed you to teach her how. "*Theological rocks*": *first things first.*

These are real stories from my own ministry, drawn from days I filled with sand and water instead of with the theological "rocks" that brought me into ministry in the first place. I wish there weren't so many of those days to choose from. Youth ministers are forever filling sacred opportunities with competence, usefulness, busyness, enthusiasm—everything *but* intentional reflection on God and how our ministries do, and do not, bear out our convictions in our practice.[2] The irony is that church professionals usually have theological commitments to spare, and yet we are more apt to develop ministry, and maybe youth ministry especially, in response to a job description or the latest barrage of parental complaints than from careful theological reflection. We seldom take time to reflect on *why* we do what we do, or *whom* we do it for—that is, unless something has gone horribly and irrevocably wrong.

---

1. Stephen Covey, and others, *First Things First: To Live, to Love, to Learn, to Leave a Legacy* (New York: Simon and Schuster, 1994), 88-90.

2. Technically, of course, it is never our ministry, but God's ministry. However, the possessive pronoun is used in this book to indicate that God entrusts certain ministries to our care, and to that extent they are indeed "ours" because God has given them to us to faithfully execute.

Geology 101

The basic premise behind this textbook is this: *Practical theological reflection*—reflection that connects what we believe about God with how we live as disciples of Jesus Christ—is the *first* task of ministry with young people. By *first*, we do not mean that practical theological reflection on youth ministry necessarily precedes everything else. All decent theology begins and ends in practice, so sequence matters little in the ongoing cycle of practical theological reflection. Such reflection comes "first" in the sense that it is primary, fundamental—basic to everything else we do and to who God calls us to be. To fail to think theologically about youth ministry, as Eugene Peterson has pointedly noted, is to risk substituting a religious career for a holy vocation.[3] To fail to name our theological priorities in ministry—our "theological rocks," if you will—tempts both vocational infidelity and professional impotence.

Those of us preparing for ministry with young people must do more than pack a pastoral bag of tricks (at worst) or ready ourselves with models, strategies, and theories relevant to young people and the world in which they live (at best). *First* we must identify our "theological rocks," the convictions about who God is and what God is about that are normative for everything we do. These are the convictions that call us to faith and that govern our ministries. Whether we realize it or not, our theological rocks affect how we develop an evening youth program, approach a sermon, handle conflict, engage parents, plan a retreat, counsel teenagers, relate to our own families. *Practical theology* is concerned with Christian action, with the way we *enact* faith in the life of discipleship and ministry in the church and in the world. Sometimes, when we begin to recognize the deep connections between our theological convictions and the way we do ministry, we change our actions. Sometimes we change our convictions instead. In either case, we engage in practical theological reflection in order to discover more faithful ways of *doing* faith.

If, upon reading this book, you begin to see threads between the way you think about God and the way you practice youth ministry, then our mission will be accomplished. Hopefully, you will also lay claim to some of your theological rocks along the way. Theological rocks may be sandstone or granite; some remain constant throughout our lives, others are smoothed by circumstance, personality, education, the Christian tradition in which we worship, our personal experience, and knowledge of God, to name a few possible streams of influence. Since youth ministers must become skilled *backdoor theologians*—people who can slip theological truth in through the cracks of everyday life, without waiting for a formal invitation to preach[4]—the *first* task of ministry must discern those theological rocks we want our lives and our ministries to proclaim. Five minutes with a teenager is a lifetime. Given such a holy window, what above all else would you want that young person to know about God?

Your timing is good

The early 21ST century is an encouraging time to enter youth ministry. Approxi-

---

3. For a provocative treatment of this thesis, see Eugene Peterson, *Working the Angles* (Grand Rapids: Eerdman's), 1987.

4. I am indebted to Ron Foster for this concept, who explains the importance of backdoor theology and theological rocks for youth ministry in our book, *The Godbearing Life: The Art of Soul-Tending in Youth Ministry* (Nashville: Upper Room, 1998), 180–181.

Year	Youth Population	Percentage of Total Global Population
1985	0.94 billion	19.40%
1995	1.03 billion	17.80%
2025	1.36 billion	16%

Youth population table (1985-2025)[1]

1. Eighty-five percent of these youth live in developing countries, and this number is expected to rise to 89 percent by 2020. The United Nations defines "youth" as anyone between the ages of 15 and 24. All statistics taken from the United Nations Division for Social Policy and Development (January 6, 1999), www.un.org/esa/socdev/unyin/q-and-a/htm.

mately one person in five is between the ages of 15 and 24 years, or 18 percent of the world's population. Although the percentage of young people will decline in the early 21ST century, in real numbers this represents an increase in the number of youth in the world (see chart).

According to one estimate, the U.S. teen population will rise in the next decade from 29 million to 36 million. "In other words," observed *Rolling Stone* recently, "resistance is futile. Teenagers are driving our culture—and they won't be giving the keys back anytime soon."[5]

Your ministry is taking root while the tectonic plates of intellectual and cultural change are still shifting, altering not only *what* people think, but *how* thinking actually happens. Discoveries like quantum physics and the arrival of the information age have sealed the tomb on modernity and toppled the reign of linear reason. Chaos theory demonstrates that science can defy prediction, hermeneutics reveals that there is no such thing as "objective" inquiry. Hyperlinks are teaching us to think in terms of connections, not closure, and the Internet smashes through old paradigms, creating relationships between both people and data that we once thought impossible.

Our culture's current interest in spirituality is the predictable consequence of these shifts—changes that have led to a period in which we find some of our most basic cultural assumptions on shifting sand. The intellectual atmosphere of the early 21ST century invites comparisons to the climate that gave rise to the Protestant Reformation, the Great Awakening, and even the Pentecostal revivals of the early 20TH century. Historians have long noted a relationship between cultural upheaval and religious revival, as times of uncertainty cause humans to turn to religion to reconstruct the cultural narrative.[6]

Perhaps, then, we should not be surprised that "God" is experiencing a popular comeback. Teenagers meet at school flagpoles for prayer, corporate executives attend seminars on spirituality, and religion is discussed openly in chat rooms and lunchrooms alike. When pollster George Gallup asked the question, "Have you had occasion to talk about your religious faith in the workplace in the past 24 hours?," 48 percent of Americans said yes.[7] MTV, VH-1, MP3, and prime time all fearlessly invoke religious imagery. Even public policy has cleared the way for religious institutions to proclaim their faith while addressing social concerns from school reform to gang violence.[8] For the first

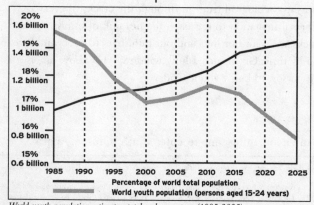

World youth population estimates: total and percentage (1985-2025)

5. "Britney Spears: Inside the Heart, Mind, and Bedroom of a Teen Dream," *Rolling Stone* (April 15, 1999), 131.

6. Thanks to church historian Douglas Strong of Wesley Theological Seminary for pointing me to this thesis. See William McLaughlin, *Revivalism, Awakenings, and Reform* (Chicago and London: University of Chicago Press), 1978 and Richard Riss, *A Survey of 20th Century Revival Movements in North America* (Peabody, Massachusetts: Hendrickson), 1988.

7. Michelle Conlin, "Religion in the Workplace: The Growing Presence of Spirituality in Corporate America," *Business Week* (November 1, 1999), 152.

8. Foremost among those public policies to take religious formation seriously is controversial political scientist John DiIulio, who describes himself as a "born-again Catholic" and who cites social science research correlating religious faith and reduced antisocial behavior in urban adolescents. See Tim Stafford, "The Criminologist Who Discovered Churches," *Christianity Today* (June 14, 1999), 35-39.

The global village of youth
If the world's youth population in
1995 consisted of a village of 100
people, here is what it would look
like:
- There would be 51 young men
  and 49 young women;
- 49 of these youthful villagers
  would live in the village center,
  51 of them in the rural outskirts;
- There would be 60 young Asians,
  15 Africans, nine Latin Americans
  and Caribbeans, and only 16
  young people from the industrialized countries of the world;
- 15 of the villagers would be illiterate; nine of these 15 illiterate
  villagers would be young women.
- 61 of the young villagers would
  be working or looking for work;
- 64 would be living off an average
  income of less than U.S. $1,000
  per year, and only 11 would be
  earning an average
  income of more
  than $10,000;
- By the end of the year, one young
  person would have contracted
  the HIV virus.[1]

1. United Nations Division for Social Policy
and Development (January 6, 1999),
www.un.org/esa/socdev/unyin/q-and-a/
village.htm.

time since 1986, church attendance among teenagers in North America is on the rise—and surpasses adult church attendance—and more teenagers today say they attend church, not because their parents tell them to, but because "they want to."[9] God is clearly "hot."

Could there be a more exciting time to enter ministry, especially ministry with young people? But wait: first things first. After all, in this philosophically unstable but spiritually fertile environment, martyrdom has also reentered the adolescent vocabulary. Nobody counted on a renewed interest in spirituality that included murder in the school library, or gunmen shooting teen worshipers in a Texas church sanctuary. Nobody counted on the fact that God calls youth ministers to pastor the Eric Harrises and Dylan Klebolds of our communities, as well as the Cassie Bernalls, Rachel Scotts, and Valeen Schnurrs. Nobody counted on the fact that, despite our high-tech, virtual reality expectations, Christianity always traffics in *visceral* reality, turning the tables—in the Temple and elsewhere—in ways we seldom anticipate. Nobody counted on the stakes of youth ministry being quite this high. But that's exactly how high they are.

And so: first things first.

Youth ministry and practical theology

Until very recently, practical theology has been altogether absent from the youth ministry equation. Youth ministry has often been conceived as a junior partner in the Christian education enterprise rather than as a pastoral calling. Clearly, Christian education is one component of our mission with young people—but it is not the only component, nor is it the primary one. Approaching youth ministry from the perspective of practical theology assumes that youth are called to take part in every practice of Christian ministry, to participate in the total mission of the church, for God calls all of us into the divine plan of salvation.

While adolescents' unparalleled spiritual openness requires intentional ministries on their behalf, youth are practical theologians by virtue of calling, not proficiency. Like you and me, youth must grapple with what it means to be a child of God on a planet marred by sin and redeemed by love. They must reflect on the activities of Christian life in order to construct a faithful one they may call their own. They must listen for and respond to God's call to them to become ministers in their own right. Their vocation is no different than our own. They simply plough different fields, with (perhaps) less practice and experience.

This book locates youth ministry squarely within the broader theological enterprise called practical theology, or theological reflection on Christian action. Because Christian action unapologetically invites God to use us to transform the world in Jesus' name, practical theology is intimately connected to the practices of ministry—which is not to say it is *limited* to the practices of professional church ministers. All Christians are called to be practical theologians, disciples whose obedience to God in the church and in the world puts our truth claims into practice. Theology that goes unnamed and

9. George H. Gallup, Jr., *The Spiritual Life of Young Americans: Approaching the Year 2000* (Princeton, New Jersey: George H. Gallup International Institute, 1999), 9–10; George Gallup, Jr., and D. Michael Lindsay, *Surveying the Religious Landscape* (Harrisburg, Pennsylvania: Morehouse Publishing, 1999), 145.

unnoticed is powerless to change lives or ministries. Practical theology assumes that we live our convictions about who God is and how God works in the world, and that we practice our theology most faithfully when we do it on purpose.

How this book works

This book is organized as an example of practical theological reflection on youth ministry and is divided into four sections reminiscent of four tasks within practical theological reflection:[10]

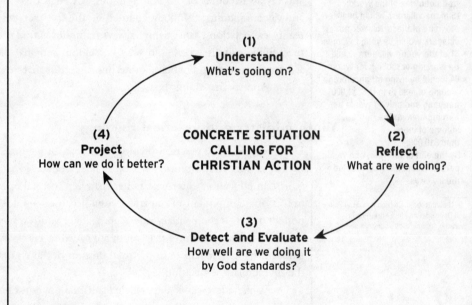

The Tasks of Practical Theology

The first section of this book explores the nature of practical theology and its significance for youth ministry, and describes how theological reflection affects the way we understand our present context for ministry with young people. This task (Understand) asks, *How can we understand a concrete situation using the theological resources of Scripture, Christian tradition (church teachings or doctrine), human reason, and sacred experience?* So the first question practical theology poses for youth ministry is *How can we describe the concrete situation in which God is calling us to act as youth ministers?*

Sections 2, 3, and 4 focus on subsequent questions of practical theology. Section 2 (Reflect) asks: *What should the practice of youth ministry look like, given the concrete situa-*

---

10. I am borrowing heavily from the methodology for practical theological reflection proposed by Don S. Browning in *A Fundamental Practical Theology: Descriptive and Strategic Proposals* (Minneapolis: Augsburg Fortress), 1991. Browning offers what is arguably the most comprehensive method for practical theological reflection available in contemporary scholarship. I am sympathetic to his effort to locate all theological reflection within the context of practical theology, but this argument lies beyond the scope of the present text.

tion described above? In this book, different authors answer this question in different ways, but together they reflect the landscape of current approaches to youth ministry.

Section 3 (Detect and Evaluate) critically defends various practices of youth ministry according to certain theological rocks or norms held by the section's authors. These authors suggest that our practices of youth ministry should be guided by theological doctrines like repentance, grace, redemption, and hope. The third task in practical theology makes explicit use of theological rocks by asking *How do we critically defend what youth ministry should be like in the concrete situation we have described?*

The fourth task in the cycle might be called Project—reconstructing youth ministry to more faithfully and self-consciously communicate the God we know, lest we format God to fit our limited vision, or shrink salvation to the shape of our ministries. This final task of practical theological reflection for youth ministry asks *What means, strategies, and forms of persuasion should we use in this concrete situation with young people that best communicate the gospel?* [11]

We have invited a number of different theological perspectives into the discussion in each section. We hope you will test these perspectives against your own, using the supplementary comments along the margins of these pages to help you practice thinking theologically about what you are reading. These marginalia are our editorial fingerprints, and like fingerprints, they give us away. You'll see my fingerprints in sections 1 and 3, Chap Clark's in section 2, and Dave Rahn's in section 4. Take us on. The marginalia are intended to muss up the theological hairs on your head, to provoke conversation and theological reflection, and—most importantly—to help you consider what your own theological foundation for youth ministry might look like. You may even stumble across some theological rocks along the way.

Who are youth?

As you explore this text, you will notice a number of terms for young people: *youth, adolescents, teenagers, students.* Although we will offer a more differentiated understanding of adolescence in chapter 2, for the most part you may consider these terms synonymous. Each of these terms has its own history, but casual usage over the past several decades has homogenized most of their differences.

Youth ministry for much of the 20TH century meant ministry with high school and, more recently, with junior high students. Today a *youth* may be any young person between the onset of puberty and fully individuated adulthood.[12] During this period in the life cycle, adolescents must acquire an *identity,* a coherent sense of self that hangs

---

11. I have adapted Browning's four basic questions of what he calls strategic practical theology—the form of practical theology most directly associated with Christian action. He places strategic practical theology within the larger enterprise of "fundamental practical theology" which has four movements: descriptive theology (describing present praxis in light of Christian faith), which is followed by historical theology (discerning normative texts and teachings that help provide a context for present praxis) and systematic theology (discerning encompassing themes in the gospel that speak to present praxis), and finally strategic practical theology (focusing on appropriate strategies for communicating the gospel in a concrete situation for ministry).

12. The term "individuation" will also receive more attention in Chapter 2, but it should not be confused with either "differentiation" (implying separateness from other human beings) or with "individualization" (a sociological term implying the priority of one's own perspective in approaching the world).

together over time and persists throughout multiple social roles.[13] Arbitrary though these boundaries for adolescence may seem, they are really quite fluid. Adolescence in the United States today often begins during late childhood (ages nine or 10) and extends through the mid-20s or sometimes later (when the young person makes enduring commitments relative to vocation and intimacy). Youth ministry, therefore, properly addresses young people in any of these stages.

A word about language

One final observation before we begin. While we have used inclusive language to refer to women and men throughout this book, we have chosen to honor individual conscience in regard to language about God. The use of pronouns for God (male or female) are consciously chosen by each author, and you may assume that these choices reflect something about the author's theological tradition and personal beliefs that he or she wishes to convey. Their choices do not necessarily reflect the convictions of those of us in the editors' seats (all of whom, by the way, understand God to be both male and female and, at the same time, to transcend gender—although we each use language differently to express this belief). We hope the different voices represented in this volume will spur your own theological reflection, not only on inclusive language, but on all matters of ministry. We want you to wonder whether your own "God-talk" with young people grows out of your conviction about who God is, or whether it is a byproduct of unexamined assumptions that—until now—you might not have even known you had.

That said, our decision not to force conformity around the issue of inclusive language says something about our own theological convictions—namely, that youth ministry includes, but goes beyond, any single theological discussion or debate. Many of us who have grown up in the United States have learned to approach language with scalpel precision, and this cultural norm makes inclusive language about God an important matter for many people in our culture. Christians growing up in other cultures may just as properly privilege other theological discussions instead. None of us has the corner on divine identity; Christians of all theological flavors need one another in order to critique and embrace possibilities about God that might not occur to us, were we without each other's differences. Youth ministry is one place our kaleidoscope church comes together to focus on a common mission: Jesus' call to the church to love young people to him so they can hear Christ's call to ministries of their own. Theological politics aside, in the end there is always more in our faith to unite than divide us. After all, every Christian calls upon the name of Jesus, and we all do so for the sake of our young. In every Christian community, of every theological tradition, from every conceivable polity, with every possible liturgical form, at the end of the day people go

---

13. The concept of "identity formation" has evolved in the 50 years since it was first popularized by the work of Erik H. Erikson. However, its basic categories still inform the way scholars and youth workers talk about adolescence, although postmodern research will undoubtedly refine its meaning for the 21ST century.

home—parents, grandparents, aunts, uncles, cousins, neighbors, and friends—people go home and pray for their children.

In so doing, perhaps we pray for ourselves.

Kenda Creasy Dean
Princeton Theological Seminary
March 25, 2000
Feast of the Annunciation of the Theotokos

Section 1

The Tasks of Practical Theology:

Understanding the Concrete Situation

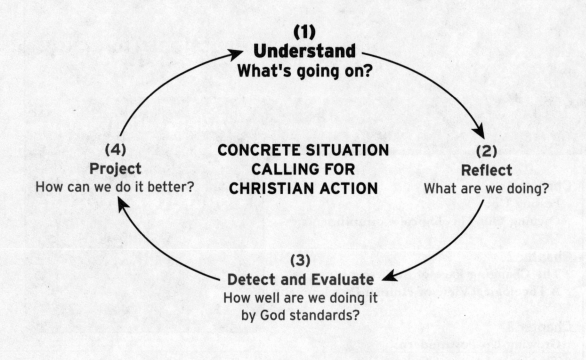

The Tasks of Practical Theology

Fessing Up: Owning Our Theological Commitments
Kenda Creasy Dean

To be a Christian at all is to be a theologian. There are no exceptions.[1]

It was during my first year of ordained ministry, while I was in my late 20s, that I learned my younger sister had multiple sclerosis. Kathy's diagnosis was the first really awful news to confront me personally, and for months I reeled under the weight of the disease and the dreams it altered. MS is a cowardly disease; it maims but it does not kill. Today, I am profoundly grateful for that fact—but at the time, all I could feel was terror of the disease's cruelty. One day, on a visit back to my seminary campus, I dumped my anguish on my former seminary advisor. "But God made your sister," Robin insisted. "God made her body..."

"Yeah," I shot back, "but when God made her, it all *worked*." And then I dissolved into a pile of sobs, right there in the middle of her office.

Robin's idea of pastoral care wasn't what they teach you in counseling class. She didn't reach for the Kleenex, do reflective listening, or give me "space." Instead, she leaned forward, looked at me straight through those hot tears, and said: "*Do you believe in God? Because you live *as if there is no God*!*"

And I cringed—because it was true.

Leaky theology

I hadn't meant to live that way, of course. After all, I was an ordained pastor, a shepherd of souls, convinced of my call and knee-deep in leading young people to Christ. When Robin shone the halogen beams of God's love onto the way I lived my life, the God-light in my eyes was so bright that everything else receded into deep space. For an instant things looked the way they look from onstage in the theater: the spotlight freezes you in time, so bright that you can't see the audience, forcing you to exist in the *now* onstage. The light in Robin's office stung my unadjusted eyes. I couldn't see through it, or around it, or beyond it. There was only light, and Jesus, and *now*.

We call them *moments of truth* for a reason. We see things differently after the light of Christ exposes us, reveals what we truly believe—even those of us vowed to ministry. It took Saul three days to see straight after the light of Christ knocked him off his high horse; personally, I'm still working on it. Until Robin challenged me to "'fess up," I hadn't realized what a practical atheist I had become. I was...I *am*...a sincere coward who confesses Christ and then runs for cover. I live like a theological schizophrenic. There is the theology I want to believe, that I think I believe, that I tell youth I

---

1. Howard W. Stone and James O. Duke, *How to Think Theologically* (Minneapolis: Fortress Press, 1996), 2.

believe, that I entered ministry *because* I believe—and then there is the theology I actually practice. The first theology is risky, radical, self-abandoning. But the second one—the theology that leaks through my life and ministry, and as a result has devastating potential to drain my actions of authenticity and power—is cautious, calculated, credible.

Christianity isn't any of those things.

A moment of truth for youth ministry

The word of the Lord came to me, saying,
    "Before I formed you in the womb I knew you, before you were born I set you apart; I appointed you as a prophet to the nations."
    "Ah, Sovereign Lord," I said, "I do not know how to speak; I am only a child!"
    But the Lord said to me, "Do not say, 'I am only a child.' You must go to everyone I send you to and say whatever I command you.
    Do not be afraid of them, for I am with you and will rescue you," declares the Lord.

—Jeremiah 1:4-8

The tragic spring of 1999 shattered our national complacency about "youth these days" and ended a century of youth ministry more often devoted to keeping young people safe and entertained than to challenging them with mature faith. After the Columbine High School massacre, stories of teen martyrs flooded the media and gripped our hearts. As youth ministers tried to regain their pastoral balance in the days and months that followed, I heard from Christian youth leaders all over the country who were haunted by the same question. It was a question asked pointedly by teens in chat rooms and churches, by parents and pastors in pews and in pulpits, by young people who have had it up to *here* with pizza and volleyball, and who are dying—literally—for something worth dying for. "Would *you* die for your faith?" they asked us. About the best most of us could manage was, "Gosh...I hope so."

The shocking congruency between the faith professed by Columbine students of many Christian traditions, and the way they lived that faith in word and deed during the shootings, stopped us dead in our tracks. Teenagers who couldn't keep a promise to clean their rooms remained faithful to Christ at gunpoint. We saw the cost of this radical discipleship in the lives it ended as well as in the lives it saved. Meanwhile—while teenagers were stockpiling explosives in a garage, posting threats on the Web and recording their deadly plans on video—Congress debated the definition of sex and school boards wondered if squirt guns merited expulsion and church leaders got themselves tied up in knots over the color of the youth room—for perhaps the millionth time this century.

Just what were we thinking?

Christians preach a God who is (thankfully) bigger than we are, and as a result our lives and our ministries always fall miserably short. This is human and inevitable; but it is also redeemable. Unless those of us in youth ministry learn to approach our calling as a *theological* enterprise, asking ourselves why we pastor youth in the ways that we do, we risk turning youth ministry into a giant *Saturday Night Live* skit:

What we say: "God sent Jesus to save the world!"
What we think: "I must save this young person from self-destructing."

What we say: "God is in control!"
What we think: "They can't run this program without me."

What we say: "Jesus loves us unconditionally."
What we think: "I can't tell them what I think or they won't like me."

What we say: "With God, nothing is impossible."
What we think: "I feel like I'm drowning in youth ministry."

Put simply, theological reflection keeps the practice of youth ministry focused on God instead of on us. It makes possible radical congruency between what we say we believe and how we conduct our lives. Without intentional theological reflection in our ministries with young people, we will all be living like atheists in no time. And the next moment of truth could be ours.

Theology: it's everywhere you are

Theology is rampant among teenagers. Perhaps that statement surprises you. We have grown accustomed to thinking of theology as academic gobbledygook, alien to adolescents and the (real) people who work with them. Think again. A few minutes of television ought to convince you: Postmodern society pelts young people with gods from every side—gods of good times, gods of good looks, gods of success, gods of excess, gods of health, gods of wealth, gods of ambition, gods of position, and countless others—all claiming salvation or your money back. Because there is no shortage of truths vying for the adolescent soul, there is no shortage of theological discussion among teenagers who must daily choose between them.[2] Theological images permeate music and movies, theological rituals find their way into gangs and families, theological assumptions work their way into the way teenagers approach proms and parents, homework and careers. *Adolescents traffic in theology every single day.* Of course, this theology may not be Christian. Chances are good that it's not even conscious. But theology infuses the air young people breathe, punctuating the practices of families, hovering in the hallways of the high school, and reverberating in the rhythms of the neighborhood.

Adolescents, therefore, take their theology quite seriously, even though they're not conscious of it. Most of their theological reflection goes unheard, unnamed, and unclaimed. They are unaware that the social studies discussion on freedom is a theological discussion. They don't realize that the way they treat an unpopular classmate reflects a doctrine of creation. They don't suspect that their impulse to sacrifice on behalf of others is an act of faith. They may treat their CDs as sacred artifacts, vaguely aware that music transports them to a mysterious "higher ground." But they often deny that music has the power to influence them—although if you try to change the radio station, you will encounter a resistance so fierce that it can only be compared to parishioners' reaction the last time you tried to update the music in church.

Most adolescents engage in *intuitive theology*—reflection about the divine-human relationship that often bypasses language and rational discourse, but that nonetheless constitutes a real part of a young person's inner life. Intuitive theology might be composed of beliefs or actions that "feel" right to a teenager, but they lack a conscious

---

Add to your glossary
- *Theology:* human reflection on who God is and how God works in the world
- *Historical theology:* reflection on the historic texts of Christian faith, such as the Bible, doctrinal documents, creeds, and confessions.
- *Systematic theology:* reflection on general themes found throughout Christian tradition, especially church teachings (doctrines).
- *Practical theology:* reflection about how God works in Christian action, in order to set forth norms and strategies for practices that faithfully participate in God's transformation to transform the church and the world.

Genius and intuitive theology
"The most beautiful and deepest experience a [human] can have is a sense of the mysterious. It is the underlying principle of religion as well as of all serious endeavour in art and in science…He who has never had this experience seems to me, if not dead, then at least blind. The sense that behind anything that can be experienced there is a something that our mind cannot grasp and whose beauty and sublimity reaches us only indirectly and as feeble reflexion, this is religiousness. In this sense I am religious. To me it suffices to wonder at these secrets and to attempt humbly to grasp with my mind a mere image of the lofty structure in all that there is."
—Albert Einstein, "My Credo," cited by William J. O'Malley, *Daily Prayers for Busy People* (Winona, Minnesota: Saint Mary's Press, 1990), 77.

---

2. This search is part of the adolescent need to establish a worldview, or personal ideology, which is an important task during adolescence. Cf. Erik H. Erikson, *Youth, Identity and Crisis* (New York: W.W. Norton, 1968); Robert Kegan, *The Evolving Self* (Cambridge, Massachusetts: Harvard University Press, 1982); David Elkind, *All Grown Up and No Place to Go* (Reading, Massachusetts: Addison-Wesley, 1984); James E. Loder, *The Logic of the Spirit* (San Francisco: Jossey-Bass, 1998). A discussion of the quest for truth among postmodern adolescents is specifically discussed in K.C. Dean, "X-Files and Unknown Gods: The Adolescent Search for Truth," *American Baptist Quarterly* (Spring 2000), in press.

Ponderable
Do you know anyone who experienced a crisis of faith during college? What challenged her or his faith? Can you explain that person's reaction developmentally?

Anselm (1033-1109) was a well-known philosopher/theologian famous for his ontological argument for the existence of God.

"If you are a theologian, pray truly; and if you pray truly, you are a theologian."
—Evagrius of Pontus, cited by Kathleen Norris, *Amazing Grace: A Vocabulary of Faith* (New York: Riverhead, 1998), 359.

structure or story that holds them together.

If the teenager has been involved in a religious community, she might have an *embedded theology*. Embedded theology comes from a religious story inherited from a faith community. The images and language from this story *ring true* for the adolescent, but she has not critically examined them.[3] Intuitive and embedded theologies are extremely vulnerable to manipulation, and they don't hold up well to scrutiny—which partly explains the crisis of faith awaiting many a devout Christian high school student who takes an embedded theology to college, only to find that critical thinking is the order of the day.[4]

The alternative to intuitive or embedded theology is *deliberate theology*—an understanding of faith that arises when a young person carefully examines his theological assumptions and practices. Deliberate theology is not simply a rational exercise in critical thinking (which would reduce theology to a cognitive operation). Above all, deliberate theology is *faith*—but it is faith seeking understanding. To use Anselm's description, it is faith that tries to figure out God, faith that can ask "why" with confidence knowing that God is not threatened by our doubt. Students with embedded theologies say, "I believe..." Students with deliberate theologies say, "I believe *because*..." Whenever a young person asks why, he edges toward deliberate faith. The "why" questions always lead us to God, even when that God is unknown.

The theological nature of adolescence

Ponderable
Ninety-five percent of American teenagers say they believe in God, and half say they attend church weekly—68 percent "because they want to." Think about the young people you know. Do these statistics ring true with your experience of ministry?[1]

1. George H. Gallup, Jr., *The Spiritual Life of Young Americans: Approaching the Year 2000* (Princeton, NJ: George H. Gallup International Institute, 1999), 3, 10.

Deliberate theological reflection lays a stable, though flexible, foundation for growing faith. Unfortunately, youth ministry has been reluctant to invite young people into this level of theological thinking. We tend to view young people as *consumers* of theology rather than as people who help *construct* religious discourse. We are far more likely to consider youth *objects* of ministry rather than *agents* of ministry; people to be ministered *unto* rather than people Jesus has called into ministry in their own right. We think teenagers need theology added to them, like antifreeze, when they really require a language that claims for Christ the unnamed quest for God that is already well underway.

The irony, of course, is that adolescents are theologians by nature, uniquely wired for theological reflection because questions about who we are in relationship to "the gods" form the spine of the human search for self. Children cannot ask theological questions because they have not yet developed the cognitive capacity for *third person perspective-taking*, or the ability to see the world through someone else's eyes. Adolescents, however, begin to develop the ability to see themselves and the world from the perspective of another—an extraordinary mental achievement that literally changes the way youth experience themselves in the world. "We do our young people a great disservice when we speak of this new power as critical thought," notes educator Sharon

3. See Howard W. Stone and James O. Duke, *How to Think Theologically* (Minneapolis: Fortress, 1996), 13-16. I have borrowed the term "embedded theology" from Stone and Duke, who prefer the term "deliberative" to "deliberate theology," which rightly preserves the rhetorical nature of this form of theological discourse.

4. The other reason for questioning faith during the college years is developmental and has to do with the fact that late adolescents have developed cognitive skills that allow them to step back and evaluate their situation from another perspective. In other words, most adolescents are most likely to be cognitively capable of a faith crisis during late adolescence.

"Believing in God is not the issue [for teenagers]; believing God matters is the issue."
—Kenda Creasy Dean and Ron Foster, *The Godbearing Life: The Art of Soul-Tending for Youth Ministry* (Nashville: Upper Room, 1998), 15.

Daloz Parks, describing the importance of third person perspective-taking for spiritual development:

> New questions can now be asked, and they can sound critical; however, the essence of this emerging power in adolescent lives is the capacity for reflection and for wondering in new ways about the relationship between the self and world. This new power is vital in the development of both the moral and the spiritual life. It allows the individual to take into account the perspective of the other—even many others. It enables the individual to come closer to participating in the perspective of God. It represents an enlargement of consciousness and an enhanced capacity for wonder.[5]

In short, third-person perspective-taking equips the adolescent with a sense of *interiority* that is altogether new—a recognition that the emerging self is composed of inward as well as external qualities. This interiority gives the adolescent "more space for becoming," as Parks puts it. It gives young people room to entertain transcendence—to consider possibilities that pull youth beyond themselves, into a larger reality that includes but is not limited to them. They begin to recognize the possibility of another point of view besides their own—including God's. They "try on" God-mode, imagining what it might be like to participate in the perspective of God. They wonder: about God, about themselves, about their purpose and place in the cosmos. Children inquire *about* God; youth inquire *after* God, seeking a relationship, a sacred trust, an anchor that remains steady in winds of change.

The roots of practical theology
Practical theology is rooted in the form of knowledge Aristotle called *phronesis*. *Phronesis*, or *practical wisdom*, is the ability to make judgments appropriate for particular, concrete situations, the kind of knowledge necessary in law or medicine. The ancient Greeks valued this kind of knowledge for the highest of Greek vocations—political leadership. They believed practical wisdom could be developed through education and through participation in praxis (see page 32).

Aristotle distinguished *phronesis* from two other kinds of knowledge: *theoria* (where we get the word "theory"), which referred to knowledge born of detached, philosophical reflection and analysis, and *poiesis*, the kind of knowledge that comes from creative technical skill.[1] If philosophy is the child of *theoria*, art is the offspring of *poiesis*.

Do you view theology as *phronesis*, *theoria*, or *poiesis*? To what aspects of Christian life does each branch of knowledge contribute? Is one form of knowledge more important than others for faith formation?

Practical theology: theological reflection on Christian action

Youth ministry practices a particular kind of deliberate theology called *practical theology*, or theological reflection on Christian action. There is no sharp line between practical theology and theology in general; as British practical theologian Paul Ballard points out, "All theology is in the service of the community of faith, and therefore all theology is essentially practical."[6] Don Browning, the most well-known American practical theologian, describes all theology as "fundamentally practical," with historical and systematic theology informing the larger practical theological enterprise.[7]

Practical theology is the kind of theological reflection that takes place when we're up to our necks in the particularities of Christian life and ministry. Unlike historical or systematic theology, which seek to discover God's truth by stepping back from Christian life and analyzing the texts, traditions, and general themes of Christianity, practical theology discovers God's *truth in and through* Christian life. Historical and sys-

1. For a concise summary of these concepts, see James Fowler, "The Emerging New Shape of Practical Theology," *Practical Theology—International Perspectives* (Frankfurt and Main: Peter Lang, 1999), 78-80.

5. Sharon Daloz Parks, "Faithful Becoming in a Complex World: New Powers, Perils, and Possibilities," Growing Up Postmodern: Imitating Christ in the Age of "Whatever," The 1998 Princeton Lectures on Youth, Church, and Culture (Princeton, New Jersey: Institute of Youth Ministry, Princeton Theological Seminary), 42.

6. Paul Ballard, "Practical Theology as the Theology of Practice," *Practical Theology—International Perspectives* (Frankfurt am Main: Peter Lang, 1999), 142.

7. See Don Browning, *A Fundamental Practical Theology* (Minneapolis: Fortress), 1991.

Praxis or practice?

Praxis is a pattern of activity in which action and ongoing reflection interpenetrate.[1] Academic internships are examples of praxis, because they involve learning through action and intentional reflection on that action simultaneously.

Practices are shared patterns of interaction in a community that have evolved to meet people's needs and serve their recurring interests in that community.[2] Practices both identify us as, and shape us into, people who belong to a particular community. Saying the Pledge of Allegiance, celebrating July 4th and voting are ways we practice being American. Abstaining from the use of electricity, wearing simple dress, using straight pins as fasteners after baptism are ways Amish Mennonites practice what it means to be Amish. Prayer, stewardship, hospitality and care, and worship are just a few of the practices of the Christian community, ways we practice our faith.

Should youth ministry be more concerned with praxis or practices? Are they truly distinct, or is praxis simply good practice?

---

1. Cf. Richard J. Bernstein, *Praxis and Action* (Philadelphia: University of Pennsylvania Press), 1971.

2. For a concise summary of these concepts, see James Fowler, "The Emerging Shape of Practical Theology," *Practical Theology—International Perspectives* (Frankfurt and Main: Peter Lang, 1999), 78-80.

tematic theology give youth ministry a broader context—a wider conversation in which the particular situation of practical theology may participate.

But practical theology is more than a matter of applying historical and systematic theology, like so much spray paint, to the surface of Christian life. Practical theology has creative force: It weaves together multiple strands of theological reflection to evoke new understandings of God in particular—concrete situations that call for action. As a result, practical theology's unique objective is reconceiving the ways we actually practice faith—reconstructing our strategies for communicating the gospel—so that they become more useful to God in the divine transformation of the world.

Put simply, practical theology is reflection about how God works in Christian action to transform people in order to set forth strategies for Christian practice that faithfully participate in that transformation. Practical theology works a little like plumbing: it connects what we confess and what we do as Christians, in order to create a clean flow—a radical congruency—between the source of Living Water and the spigot from which it flows. To that end, practical theology constantly evaluates Christian action in order to find ways to practice our faith more transparently—ways that will better communicate the gospel.

Theology from the middle of the pool

When our son was four, I decided to sign him up for swimming lessons (bad idea). We went faithfully, but Brendan steadfastly refused to get in the pool. Every week the teacher would stand waist deep in water and hold her hands out for Brendan to come to her. Nothing doing. "You come *here*," he told her emphatically, patting the edge of the pool where he was sitting. In eight weeks of swimming lessons, Brendan got *wet* twice. Maybe he had a better understanding of the pool environment—slippery floors, smell of chlorine, swarms of half-clad children and over-eager parents—but he was no closer to swimming at the end of those lessons than at the beginning.

A lot of people confuse knowledge about the faith environment with faith itself. "I'm very spiritual, but I'm not religious," they will say. What they mean is that they appreciate faith from the side of the pool, but they're not about to get wet. Christians, on the other hand, *never* think about faith from the side of the pool. The practices of Christian community are so counterintuitive—tithing, simplicity, sacraments, prayer, worship, hospitality to the stranger, and so on—that we simply can never understand God's grace in them until we *do* them. Likewise, some aspects of Jesus' love are impossible to understand until we finally put down our nets and *follow* him.

Practical theology takes place in the middle of the pool. Practical theology includes reflection before and after plunging into Christian action, just as diving requires forethought to gauge the depth of the water, and afterthought to figure out how to improve the next dive. But practical theology's primary emphasis is on the dive itself, the normative practice of Christian life. Consequently, practical theologians are people who can discern and execute a faithful dive—action that communicates the gospel faithfully and appropriately for a concrete situation.

After all, this is the objective of youth ministry: to help young people grow

Why I make Sam go to church

"Sam is the only kid he knows who goes to church—who is made to go to church two or three times a month. He rarely wants to. This is not exactly true: the truth is he never wants to go. What young boy would rather be in church on the weekends than hanging out with a friend?

"You might think, noting the bitterness, the resignation, that he was being made to sit through a six-hour Latin mass. Or you might wonder why I make this strapping, exuberant boy come with me most weeks, and if you were to ask, this is what I would say:

"'I make him because I can.' I outweigh him by nearly 75 pounds.

"But that is only part of it. The main reason is that I want to give him what I found in the world, which is to say a path and a little light to see by. Most of the people I know who have what I want—which is to say, purpose, heart, balance, gratitude, joy—are people with a deep sense of spirituality. They are people in community, who pray, or practice their faith…They follow a brighter light than the glimmer of their own candle; they are part of something beautiful."

—Anne Lamott, *Traveling Mercies* (New York: Pantheon Books, 1999), 99-100.

faith mature enough that they can use that faith—their assumptions about who God is and how God works in the world—to discern and execute faithful Christian action as disciples of Jesus Christ. If youth ministry is going to help adolescents become practical theologians, then we must begin by helping them *practice* faith, which requires *both* a relationship with Jesus Christ and opportunities for ministry *as teenagers*. Youth ministry that emphasizes evangelism, without simultaneously giving adolescents opportunities to serve in substantive ministry, eviscerates discipleship. Youth ministry that seeks Christian action without a growing relationship with Jesus reduces it to good works. Neither dimension can stand on its own as faith.

In short, if adolescents are to become practical theologians in their own right, we have to get them in the pool. And that means that you and I have to stand in the middle of the pool ourselves, practicing our faith while holding out our hands, inviting the youth we love to jump into the Christian community alongside us.

One more thing: Because this book is written for people studying for the professional ministry, many of our examples will be written from the perspective of youth leaders like you. But it is important that we not understand practical theology as something church professionals do. Jesus calls all Christians (youth included) into ministry; therefore, Jesus calls all Christians (youth included) to be practical theologians—people who try to better understand how God works in Christian action so that our practices may cooperate with God's work more fully.

God gives each of us a little flock to pastor: a congregation, a high school, a family, a group of friends who gather around a lunch table at school, the lady next door. But it would be arrogant to assume that Jesus' plans for the sheep stopped with their grateful conversion. Jesus wants the people in our flocks to become pastors of flocks as well. That means that our "flock folk" need to become aware of the theological convictions governing their lives, too (even if they aren't Christians),[8] and to be challenged to evaluate and reconstruct their practices to serve God more faithfully, freely, and fully.

Meanwhile, back at the ranch...

Add to your glossary

• *Pastor* (from Latin *pastor*, herdsman; from *pascere*, to feed): someone who feeds a flock.

Anne Jenkins is the solo pastor of a small, rural Presbyterian congregation in Montana.[9] A year into Anne's pastorate, the congregation received a windfall gift of more than a million dollars, specifically earmarked for youth programs. As a veteran youth minister, Anne was both delighted and cautious. She had spent a year trying to redirect the church's entertainment-oriented youth program toward a model of spiritual formation. The "youth program" gift was put in a temporary account until a planning committee could be formed and a long-range vision developed for the money's use. As the pastor, Anne had sole access to the account.

Meanwhile, Anne took some youth from the church on their first mission project to Mexico. A student leadership team had drafted a covenant for the trip, outlining

---

8. Even not believing in God is a conviction about God.

9. Details have been changed.

expectations for participation. Since students who are underage in the United States can legally drink in Mexico, the student leadership team decided that, as American citizens, they should abide by U.S. law and abstain from drinking in Mexico. They included a clause to this effect in the trip covenant, which also stated that anyone failing to uphold the covenant would be sent home, along with an accompanying adult. Everyone going on the trip signed the covenant.

You guessed it: early in the trip, two girls slipped out one night and got drunk. Everyone knew that the consequence of drinking was a speedy trip home to Montana, but the girls shrugged off the incident, defending their right to drink rather than repenting of their violation of the group covenant. So, Anne called the airlines and found out that the tickets would cost over $2,000, with Anne fronting the amount on her already over-burdened credit card. She phoned the girls' parents. One girl's parents refused to pick up their daughter at the airport if she came home. The other girl's mother, an active member of the youth council and a former leader of the youth program before Anne's arrival, was furious—at Anne. After planning the trip for a year, how could Anne even think of sending her daughter home? "What about forgiveness? What about a second chance? What about grace?" she demanded. Neither girls' parents said they would pay for the plane tickets.

Now, if you were Anne, what would you do? You might choose the course of action most likely to *work* (and working is a good and honorable thing), which would be basing your decision on a philosophical point of view called *pragmatism*. Since the girls' parents would not cooperate, and Anne couldn't afford $2,000 on her credit card, and the girls were not a danger to themselves or to others, a pragmatic response might be to let them finish out the trip. True, the covenant would no longer stand for anything—but just how pragmatic are covenants, anyway? Covenants are signed and broken every day. As a means of enforcing behavior, they don't really *work*.

Or you could base your decision on interpersonal harmony, choosing the course of action that would maintain relationships and create the least friction. There's certainly nothing wrong with interpersonal harmony. Anne liked being liked. She didn't want to irritate parents or parishioners, or the girls for that matter. She didn't want dissent to ruin the trip for the rest of the students. The mission project was an important part of the new direction for youth ministry she hoped to instill; if the youth could just see it through, they would know what it's like to be changed by serving others in Christ's name. True, Anne would have to swallow her anger at the girls and their parents, and maybe even deny her anger toward herself for being "played" by the girls. But maybe swallowing her own feelings would be a small price to pay for harmony on the rest of the trip.

Or perhaps you would base your position on safety by choosing the course of action that entails the least risk. Safety is critically important in youth ministry. Physical risk was not an issue in Anne's case; the girls would fly home, chaperoned. But what about the girl whose parents refused to meet her at the airport? What if the church would not reimburse Anne's credit card? What if the congregation sided with the girls' parents about Anne's decision—and in a small community with two influential parents lobbying against her, that seemed fairly likely—and began to question her judgment as their pastor? Would sending the girls home jeopardize the progress Anne had made in redirecting the youth program? All of these risks factor into a decision based on safety.

Fessing up

The praxis-theory-praxis loop
Many practical theologians consider the "praxis-theory-praxis loop" one of the features that distinguishes practical theology from other forms of theological reflection. Put simply, practical theology begins in praxis (what we *do* as Christians), moves to theory (*reflection* about what we do as Christians), and moves back to praxis (more faithful ways of doing what we do as Christians). And so the cycle continues.

Is practical theology unique in this regard? Or do you think all theology is fundamentally practical?

Anne decided to let the girls stay on the trip, mostly for pragmatic reasons—but six months later when she told me about the incident, Anne was still ruing her decision. It wasn't the choice she wanted to make, and she had spent months reflecting on why. Practical theological reflection usually works this way. Something catches us off guard, brings us up short, jolts us into searching for a new set of tools to address a situation. It didn't occur to Anne until afterward that she might have used some of the earmarked money to reimburse the cost of the plane tickets or that the parents involved had opposed her at other times when her actions differed from their former pastor's.

But what bothered Anne most was the realization that the decision had compromised some of her core theological commitments with the youth themselves. Inadvertently, Anne had undermined the very parts of the gospel story she had spent a year trying to convey to these young people. She wanted to teach about costly grace, about redemption from sin won by a price, so she had arranged a mission project that required financial sacrifice, sweat equity, a time commitment. The girls' unrepentant attitude (and that of their parents) mutated forgiveness into *cheap grace*, a facile compromise rather than an act of discipleship. As a Presbyterian, Anne especially prized the doctrine of *covenant*, representing God's unbroken promise to creation, fulfilled in Jesus Christ. In letting the girls stay, Anne had destroyed the credibility of the written covenant, and violated an unspoken covenant of trust with the student leadership team, who had risked advocating an unpopular position on drinking with their peers.

When faced with a concrete situation of ministry like Anne's, theological convictions do not normally jump out and advertise themselves. This part of practical theological reflection must be done in advance. Anne's dilemma with the girls on the Mexico trip would have been less agonizing if she had been able to approach her decision with a method of practical theological reflection in mind. This is the reason for a book like this on youth ministry: you need time and space to tease out the underlying theological convictions that are normative for your life and ministry (see "What are your theological rocks?" on page 15), both so you can intentionally construct your ministry around these convictions, and so you can evaluate practices of ministry in light of these convictions as particular situations call for Christian action in the future.

Furthermore, our theological priorities have as much to do with who we are, as with who Jesus is. You might view Anne's situation in Mexico through the lens of God's *forgiveness* and *grace*, while someone else will look at it in terms of God's *justice* and *redemption*. Not to worry; it doesn't matter from which side of the pool we jump into practical theological reflection—we still get wet. The point is that practical theological reflection leads to a *radical congruency* between the theology we espouse and the one we live. Take a look at your own faith journey, your faith tradition, your family's religious practices, the communities in your life that have partly defined you. Do they explain in any way the theological commitments you choose to emphasize? What do they say about your own relationship with Jesus Christ?

The four tasks of practical theological reflection

Practical theological reflection is a process—a spiral more than a cycle. In this spiral we move closer to the perspective of God as we reflect on norms and strategies for Christian action. This cycle of theological reflection lays the foundation for practices of faith that cooperate with God's transformation of the church and the world—a plan of salvation in which every young person, in his or her particular place and time, plays an irreplaceable part.

Practical theology differs from other forms of theological reflection in that it focuses on knowing God through concrete situations. Instead of developing pastoral theories from biblical texts, historic confessions, or church doctrine, practical theology is informed by—but goes beyond—all of this. Ultimately our practical theology for youth ministry grows out of the accumulated wisdom of hundreds of pastoral situations—not all of them our own—that eventually add up to a theory: "These are the normative ways in which I expect to practice faith with young people so they will encounter the good news of Jesus Christ in this particular ministry, in this particular time and place, that God has laid before me."

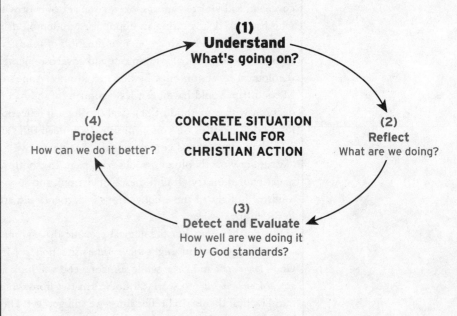

The Tasks of Practical Theology

The first task of practical theology: understand

The first section of this book focuses on the first task in practical theological reflection: *understanding the concrete situation in which we must act.* In youth ministry this means action on behalf of God's love for young people. Because God calls us to act as Christians, and not just as "good moral people," we must identify theological assumptions—and not only philosophical, developmental, sociological, or educational ones—that influence the way we practice faith. And we must bring these assumptions into conversation with the concrete situation at hand (see diagram, page 32).

For example, Anne's decision to let the girls remain on the mission project was ultimately based on philosophical, developmental, sociological reasons, and perhaps professional reasons, not theological ones. To fully understand a concrete situation calling for Christian action, youth ministry *must* take these factors into account—but we cannot stop here. Philosophically, Anne's decision "worked" in that it kept the group functioning as a whole (pragmatism). Developmentally, her decision protected young girls from risky behavior around alcohol. Sociologically, Anne's decision was consistent with the congregational culture in which she served. Professionally, it spared Anne questions about her pastoral judgment. However, without understanding the *theological* dimension of the situation, in the end human interests—and not necessarily God's interests—were ultimately served.

Historical and systematic theology are helpful in unpacking a situation theologically, and our faith traditions inevitably equip us with certain doctrinal "bookmarks"—theological assumptions that we draw on again and again. As a United Methodist, for instance, I am likely to view youth ministry through the lenses of grace, incarnation, salvation—themes emphasized by United Methodist preaching, worship, and hymnody. At the Presbyterian seminary where I teach, words like *covenant*, *vocation*, and *transformation* are all the rage—but they would rather leave the term *salvation* to the Baptists!

Even those of us without denominational affiliations can locate ourselves in streams of Christian tradition without digging too far. And as a result of our location, we practice ministry in certain ways. I've been tilting youth ministry toward sanctifying grace and holiness for years without a second thought—and I did this long before I knew words like *sanctification* and *holiness*. Every theological *thought* has been thought before. Historical and systematic theology give these streams of thought names to provide a shorthand for the church's internal discussions about who we are and what we believe.

But you can explain your theological priorities just as well—and sometimes better, where youth are concerned—without relying on a graduate course in systematic theology. Practical theology begins and ends in practice, so if you want to discover the theological assumptions you hold dear, start by examining the way you practice your faith. Go ahead—try it:

Make a list of the things you do *because you are Christian*. Include both the

---

God-talk

"When God-talk is speech that is not of this world, it is a false language. In a religion that celebrates the Incarnation—the joining together of the human and the divine—a spiritualized jargon that does not ground itself in the five senses should be anathema. But the human tendency to disincarnate language is a strong one. I used to wonder if Jesus Christ, with all of the earthy metaphors he customarily employed, would marvel at the letters my beloved grandmother Norris would send me when I was in college. Ordinary family news would fill a page or so, but then she'd turn to faith, and her language would ascend to a realm in which the words were full of ether. It seemed as if my grandmother's considerable ego had been subsumed, imperfectly, into 'Jesus' this and 'Jesus' that. The heavyweight theological words were a code I could not crack; evidently they spoke only to the saved.

"In seeking my own faith, I've had to contend mightily with the language of Christianity. I've learned that if these words are to remain viable, I must find ways to incarnate them, so as to make them accessible to believer and non-believer alike...I don't mean that pastors shouldn't speak of God, or Christ, or salvation—they'd be foolish not to. But when a sermon is little but biblical or theological language that the preacher has not troubled to digest, to incarnate, as it were, so that it might readily translate into the lives of parishioners, it is often worse than no sermon at all...God-talk is a form of idolatry, a way of making God small and manageable."
—Kathleen Norris, *Amazing Grace: A Vocabulary of Faith* (New York: Riverhead, 1998), 211-213.

Things I do because I am Christian:

-
-
-
-
-
-
-

What themes, patterns, or relationships do I notice in these actions? What do these themes, patterns, or relationships suggest about what I believe about God?

"Anyone is a disguise for God." —Albert Einstein, cited William J. O'Malley, *Daily Prayers for Busy People* (Winona, Minnesota: Saint Mary's Press, 1990), 77

kinds of things you do with young people in ministry and your personal practices of faith. Pay special attention to the things you do for God—and the ways that you do them—that bring you the most joy. Also look for those aspects of youth ministry that matter most to you—that you can't imagine ministry without.

Now look for themes and patterns that emerge from your list. For example, maybe you find yourself drawn to any action that tries to preserve the sanctity of life: you work hard so youth will respect the earth, or you protest abortion, or you introduce young people to human rights violations in Sudan, or you invest in health ministries that help teenagers take care of their bodies. What you're telling young people in these actions is that God's love for them can be discovered in the way God has made them, which is one aspect of what the church calls a doctrine of creation.

Or maybe you love the practices of contemplative spirituality. Above all, you want youth to learn to pray, and you yourself seek opportunities for confession, thanksgiving, petition, intercession, and praise. You're big on retreats, you light candles during youth meetings, and you use music behind every activity to create a *mood* that will encourage youth to focus on God. These actions tell young people that God is a mystery, holy, and awesome but approachable through the mediating structures of worship. Such actions underscore the fact that God's love for adolescents is too great to be contained by words, and is best grasped existentially in the contemplative practices of prayer and worship.

Or maybe when you look at your Christian journey, all you can see are relationships. Your most significant God-encounters have come through important Christian friends, and you find yourself doing back flips to help young people and the adult leaders establish significant Christian friendships with each other. You emphasize summer work projects, camps, and bike trips so kids will have an excuse to deepen their relationships. When you look at your calendar for ministry, it is peppered by lunch appointments, soccer practice, choir concerts (at five different high schools), and a dozen different small groups. What your actions are telling young people (besides the fact that you're probably way overscheduled) is that there is something holy about a relationship: Jesus is present wherever two or three gather in his name—God meets us through human beings. Historically, the church has called this belief the doctrine of the Incarnation—God's decision to walk among us in the human form of Jesus Christ.

The first question of practical theologians, then, is: *What's going on here? How do I understand this concrete situation in which I must act on behalf of God's love for young people?* Asking *what's going on* means listening to clues from the social sciences, too: Psychologically, what is this young person's struggle? Sociologically, what cultural factors are at work here? Educationally, what can be learned from this situation? Practical theology is always an interdisciplinary enterprise, simply because no concrete situation is one-dimensional. At the same time, practical theological reflection must raise our theological assumptions to the surface to shed God's light on wisdom from other disciplines and initiate a conversation that can lead to radical congruency between what we confess and who we are as Christians.

The other tasks of practical theology: reflect, detect and evaluate, and project
The other tasks of practical theology constitute the second, third, and fourth sections of this book. I'll be back to introduce those sections and to give you some handles for the discussion that follows.

For now, let the pages here help you better understand the concrete situation into which you have been called to ministry. God has called you, not just to any time or place, but to this time and place—"for such a time as this" (Esther 4:14)—on behalf of God's love for young people. God has deemed your ministry in this particular place and time necessary in God's transformation of the church and the world.

As you try to understand this situation, you have many disciplines that will guide you. Take into account the developmental changes that influence your understanding of this situation (Chapter 2, Chap Clark); sociological and anthropological factors that make a difference (Chapter 3, Don Richter); historical trajectories leading up to the ministry you will begin or inherit (Chapter 4, Mark Cannister); and the impact of contemporary social trends like globalization and urbanization (Chapter 5, Tony Campolo).

But don't forget to take your theological rocks with you, for they will color how you read the words that lie ahead, not to mention the way you do ministry in the weeks, months, and years that follow. You might exchange rocks as you read further, or discover that a rock that seems small when you reach down to pick it up actually reaches deep into your theological soil. Don't despair if it takes more digging than you bargained for to unearth your practical theological assumptions. Faith most easily takes root in soil where the rocks have been dug out. You may feel overwhelmed by the complexity of the concrete situations into which you have been called; maybe the particularity of practical theology makes you dizzy, and you yearn for the simplicity of one good all-encompassing theory. You may even wonder if it's possible to actually practice the theology you believe. After all, radical congruency is for martyrs, not ministers.

Or is it?

The Changing Face of Adolescence: A Theological View of Human Development
Chap Clark

[They] are passionate, irascible, and apt to be carried away by their impulses. They are slaves, too, of their passion...If the young commit a fault, it is always on the side of excess and exaggeration for they carry everything too far, whether it be their love or hatred or anything else. They regard themselves as omniscient and are positive in their assertions; this is, in fact, the reason for their carrying everything too far.[1]

—*Aristotle*

Citing the words of Aristotle and others, some people say that adolescents are the same as they have always been—free, unencumbered, wild, passionate, and disrespectful of those who have come before them (especially their parents). These people believe that adolescence has simply always been with us, and basically, when it comes to those in the midst of the transition from childhood to adulthood, things have not changed very much. But statements like these can just as easily be explained by recognizing that, out of context, remarks taken from history may not actually refer to what we postmoderns call *adolescence* at all. They may just as easily refer to young people who—then, as now—were simply upsetting the societal status quo. Notable perhaps, but not a description of the kind of adolescence that is the concern of churches and youth workers at the beginning of the 21ST century.

Other people claim that contemporary culture is changing so rapidly that our children and adolescents have been left behind by adults and have essentially been abandoned by the culture at large. These people argue that the result of this abandonment is a new generation of lost and broken young people who are struggling more than ever to find their way in the world. Still others see a bright future for the young because of the oft-reported optimistic character and values displayed by the generation known as the Millennials. This debate is currently being waged on several fronts, and the temptation for those who care about the young is to land in one camp over another.[2]

As with any generalized analysis of a complex phenomenon, all of these views have elements of truth and elements of oversimplification.[3] Youth workers are rarely afraid to jump into the philosophical fray, and also report mixed reactions regarding the state and future of adolescence. But due to the dynamic nature of our task, youth

"The question for the new century is, *How much longer will teenagers exist, at least in the form that James Dean made famous?* Twenty years, tops, is my guess. Teenagers, as classically defined, are already dying out, or at least changing into something different. The buffer zone they once inhabited is being squeezed out of existence for two reasons: children are growing up faster than ever before, and adults are growing up more slowly."

—Walter Kirn,
"Will Teenagers Disappear?"
Time (February 21, 2000), 60.

1. As quoted in N. Kiell, *The Universal Experience of Adolescence* (Boston: Beacon, 1967), 18-19.

2. Examples of these views' supporters: David A. Black, *The Myth of Adolescence* (Yorba Linda, California: Davidson Press, 1999); David Elkind, *Ties That Stress: The New Family Imbalance* (Cambridge, Massachusetts: Harvard University Press, 1994); William Strauss and Neil Howe, *The Fourth Turning* (New York: Broadway Books, 1997).

3. For a much more detailed discussion of the merits of these and other views, see, Paul H. Mussen, John J. Conger, Jerome Kagan, and James Geiwitz, *Psychological Development: A Life-Span Approach* (New York: Harper & Row, 1979), 281.

Who are these people, anyway?

We tend to use words like *adolescent, youth, teenager, student,* and sometimes *young adult* interchangeably, although these terms have had fluid meanings over the past century.

Adolescent usually refers to anyone who has reached puberty but who has not yet made the vocational, ideological, or relational commitments of young adulthood.

Until the late 20th century, *youth* simply meant anyone who was young or inexperienced, especially people in their late teens and early 20s. Today *youth* can mean anyone who is an adolescent.

Teenagers are those in the second decade of life. Recently, the media has dubbed younger teens *tweens*—a label that acknowledges a newly identified aspect of adolescence: the transition into teens.

The term *student* refers to persons in school—although it belies youth ministry's historic middle class bias in favor of educated young people. Technically, of course, students may be old or young, and the church is called to minister to all young people in the name of Jesus Christ, not just to those who are in school.

The term *young adult* was co-opted by church educators as a marketing device during the 1960s and 1970s when young people began to vanish from the pews like disappearing ink. Some denominational curricula informally adopted the term *young adult* during this period to refer to adolescents, in hopes that the term would flatter youth into increased church attendance (it didn't work).

And then there are *kids,* the term young people often use to describe themselves but that sometimes offends on the lips of adults.

Should youth ministers describe their flocks as kids? What will you call the young people you serve in ministry?

workers frequently do more reflection—sociologically, psychologically, even theologically—*on the fly* than through careful deliberation.

For the past 40 years or so, youth ministry has been the normative title describing ministry efforts targeted toward adolescents. But it is rare when a youth minister stops to ask some fundamental of questions like, Just what is a *youth*? What kind of person am I trying to minister to? What are the distinctives between the students I work with in junior high and high school and the fifth graders who will soon be joining us? Most people who directly interact with adolescents believe that the culture has shifted in dramatic ways in the late 20TH century, and the pace of cultural change shows no signs of slowing down. These cultural changes have impacted the nature of adolescence itself, to the point that anyone who cares about children and adolescents has no choice but to take a new and careful look at how a postmodern, technological, and urbanized context affects the adolescent journey.

This is all the more important as we consider the theological mandate of the youth ministry task. We *must* care about what is happening in the adolescent world. The church is called to "declare [God's] power to the next generation, [God's] might to all who are to come" (Psalm 71:18). This is the ultimate *reason* for youth ministry. This *passing on*, however, becomes increasingly difficult in a changing world and community context. For those who are committed to "declaring the Lord" to adolescents, then, this chapter presents a theological response to what we know about the adolescent journey in a rapidly changing cultural situation. It is not only the cultural environment that is changing; social rules, norms, even the process of adolescence itself are changing. To those experiencing this critical and often difficult phase of life we are called to proclaim and model the hope of the gospel and the reality of a living God who cares. To care for those in transition we must take great care to make sure what we do in our ministry takes seriously the changing landscape.

The fertile soil of this ever-changing environment, however, does not nor should it ever change the core of the call. Jesus Christ is and will always be the only relevant and redeeming presence that a person could ever experience. When it comes to youth ministry, these constants remain:

• There is a Creator-God who is on the move to find those who are lost (Luke 15:1f).
• God's heart is decisively compassionate toward children (Mark 10:13f).
• God loves people enough to invade human history via the Incarnation (Philippians 2:5–11).
• Followers of Jesus Christ are likewise called to love and pursue those whom God loves, and are therefore called to "go" into the world of the young (John 17:18).
• The message of the gospel focused on the Incarnate Word brings hope and healing to every person regardless of culture, ethnicity, or age (Romans 10:12–13).

Youth ministry, then, is the call of the church to relationally pass on the gospel to adolescents in any cultural or environmental setting. This means that we *must* know and understand, as much as possible, the population we are dealing with. Our message must never change, but in seeking to care for and reach the coming generations, our methods *must* change. This chapter focuses on understanding adolescents in a changing culture in order to best know how to change our ways of passing on the gospel to them.

At the outset it is important to note that this chapter is not primarily concerned with culture as a whole, but rather offers a focused understanding of adolescence in a changing cultural context.[4] This chapter does take the view that a wildly adaptive cultural environment requires contemporary psychosocial developmental theories and assumptions about adolescence to be reexamined and contextualized. This is not to say that the basic elements of human developmental knowledge are "up for grabs," but that how the framework of these and other related theories play out in a changing culture must be of concern to the theologically committed youth worker. These traditional theories have been and remain helpful general starting points for overview information regarding adolescent development. Youth ministry students would be well advised to learn all they can regarding different approaches to and views of human development. This chapter does not go into specific detail regarding any of the developmental theories. The point here is to understand the general issues that impact an adolescent so that theologically driven youth ministry can respond accordingly. Detailed human developmental theories are therefore outside the purview of this chapter.

What should be mentioned, however, is that many accepted developmental theories, developed primarily in the mid-20TH century, tend to view the adolescent journey as a relatively stable, predictable, and orderly—though sometimes difficult—process.[5] For the past two or three decades, researchers and theorists attempting to more fully understand human development have been challenging many of these (and other) "tidy" themes and stages of development. But postmodern culture has tossed a proverbial wrench into the gears of developmental theory. In particular, such variables as shifts in cultural values and structure; changes in the family system; new research into peer relations; gender and ethnic differences; and new ways of thinking about morality, character, and ethics have become increasingly important in describing the nature of adolescence.[6] As a result, this chapter will focus on these and other relevant cultural factors in looking at the changing face of adolescent development.

This chapter, then, is *not:*

- an annotated summary of developmental theories or themes throughout history;
- a discussion of popular assumptions regarding "today's adolescent"; or
- an attempt to create new or definitive theories of adolescent development.

---

4. The scope of this discussion is primarily limited to the North American context (although in much of the world there are far more similarities among this age group than differences).

5. As stated, this chapter is not intended to debate traditional or classic developmental theories and concepts, nor to critique historical developmental theories. Rather it is intended to provide a balanced spin on those developmental and relational issues that most directly relate to the youth ministry task and to draw together those areas of research, study, and debate that a youth worker needs to recognize and understand.

6. Some contemporary developmental theorists, for instance, have challenged many of the assumptions of developmental pioneers like Jean Piaget and Erik Erikson. For examples of a more nuanced approach to stage theory, see Robert Kegan, *The Emerging Self: Problem and Process in Human Development* (Cambridge, Massachusetts: Harvard University Press, 1982) and *In Over Our Heads: The Mental Demands of Modern Life* (Cambridge, Massachusetts: Harvard University Press, 1994).

Stages of faith?
As Chap Clark points out, "stage theories" still dominate discussions of human development. For example:
- *Jean Piaget* believed that the development of human logic followed an invariant pattern moving from sensory motor reflexes to intuitive, concrete, and finally abstract thinking.
- *Erik Erikson* identified eight stages of human psychosocial development, each marked by a developmental issue crisis that must be resolved in order to continue to the next developmental phase.
- *Lawrence Kohlberg* noted a sequential pattern of moral development in boys that culminated in an ethic of justice.
- *Carol Gilligan* observed a different pattern of moral development in girls that culminated in an ethic of care and responsibility.
- *James Fowler* posited six stages of faith that occur irrespective of religious belief system, tying faith development closely to cognitive and psychosocial development.[1]

Stage theories' relationship to faith poses special difficulties. While faith does mature over time, the question of how faith matures is unclear. Does God create us to be "hard wired" for faith to develop naturally under the right conditions, the way our intellects or our egos develop? Or does God bequeath faith by breaking through normative stages of human development, "messing up" developmental sequences by creating unexpected sacred sinews that hold us together in new ways?

Think about your own faith journey. Has it matured gradually and predictably over time? Has faith thrown a wrench into the well-oiled gears of your personal growth? Have you ever known

Instead, this chapter will focus on the following two goals related to the latest trends in adolescent research that impact youth ministry:

- to present a description of much of the recent *theoretical* and *empirical* trends in the social science literature about adolescence, and
- to offer suggestions for making youth ministry philosophical and programmatic decisions accordingly.

Defining adolescence

The term *adolescence* is derived from the Latin root word *adolescere*, "to grow up," and is most often considered to be the period from puberty to adulthood or maturity.[7] Because the concept of adolescence as a life span phase is a relatively new idea, gaining currency in the social sciences only in the last 100 years, it is sometimes considered an "invention" of society.[8] Some researchers credit the "pagan firebrand" Jean-Jacques Rousseau with introducing the new romantic ideal of free-spirited and passionate adolescence into Western society as early as the mid-18TH century.[9] By using the term *adolescere*, the French philosopher Rousseau did play a part in the eventual acknowledgment that adolescence was a new social force to be reckoned with. But in calling for societal blessing for young adults' behavior (encouraging them to delay the demands of contemporary adulthood), he was as concerned with describing sweeping cultural shifts while he observed them as he was arguing for a whole new social structure.

The earliest person to give developmental prominence to the notion of modern adolescence was G. Stanley Hall, a late 19TH-century American psychologist. As Rousseau was seemingly elevating the appropriate exuberance of young adults, Hall pointed out that adolescence was actually a phase of late childhood. Hall, who has been labeled "the father of adolescent psychology,"[10] has been credited with changing the social landscape by setting in motion new attitudes toward young people. Americans no longer thought of adolescents as "little adults," but as older children in a prolonged stage of childhood.[11] Whomever ultimately receives the credit for naming this newly emerging phase of life, by the turn of the 20TH century, adolescence had come to be accepted as sociological reality, and by the 1920s it was clear that the emerging youth subculture that was here to stay—although it was not until 1960 that there was common agreement among developmental psychologists that adolescence was a legitimate phase of the life span.[12]

7. See Louise J. Kaplan, *Adolescence: The Farewell to Childhood* (New York: Touchstone, 1984), 281, and Mussen.

8. Hans Seabold, *Adolescence: A Sociological/Psychological Analysis,* 4th ed. (New York: Prentice-Hall, 1992). In some limited theological circles the notion of adolescence as a legitimate phase of life is almost offensive, primarily because there is really no equivalent to be found in Scripture. See David Alan Black (1999) for an example of such a view.

9. Kaplan, 51.

10. Seabold, 90.

11. Kaplan, 51.

12. Seabold, 90.

anyone whose faith makes them seem wise beyond their years, or childlike and open despite a lifetime of hardship?

What do the variety of faith stories suggest about the Holy Spirit's relationship to human development?

1. For more about the developmental theorists listed here, see Barbel Inhelder and Jean Piaget, *The Growth of Logical Thinking*, A. Parsons and S. Milgram, trans. (New York: Basic Books), 1958; Erik H. Erikson, *The Life Cycle Completed: A Review* (New York: W.W. Norton), 1985; Lawrence Kohlberg, *The Philosophy of Moral Development: Moral Stages and the Idea of Justice: Essays on Moral Development 1* (San Francisco: Harper & Row), 1981; Carol Gilligan, *In a Different Voice: Psychological Theory and Women's Development* (Cambridge, Massachusetts: Harvard University Press), 1982; James Fowler, *Stages of Faith: The Psychology of Human Development and the Quest for Meaning* (San Francisco: Harper & Row), 1981.

For a less sequential understanding of cognitive development in women, see Mary Belenky, et al., *Women's Ways of Knowing: The Development of Self, Voice and Mind* (New York: Basic Books), 1986. For a more nuanced structuralist approach to cognitive development, see Robert Kegan, *The Evolving Self: Problem and Process in Human Development* (Cambridge, Massachusetts: Harvard University Press), 1982, and especially *In Over Our Heads: The Mental Demands of Modern Life* (Cambridge, Massachusetts: Harvard University Press), 1994. For a theological treatment of the relationship between faith development and human development, see James E. Loder, *The Logic of the Spirit: Human Development in Theological Perspective* (San Francisco: Jossey Bass), 1998.

It is clear from the history of adolescence that understanding and interpreting this phase of life has been developed primarily in the field of psychology. Hall was a psychologist who attempted to combine Darwinian theory with newly emergent developmental theories that correlated species evolution to species-specific development. His concept of adolescence was a key element in his developmental theory—that humans must go through a developmental process akin to the evolutionary history of the human species. To many Christians this may sound like a gross and heretical stretch of logic, and it soon ran aground among psychologists as well. But Hall's theory opened the door for developmental theorists working more directly from a psychological framework to create developmental theories and systems no longer dependent upon Darwinian biology as a basis for understanding human growth. By the 1950s, Erik Erikson and others began to see human development as a psychosocial phenomenon, having to do with more than simply the mind and genetics but also mediated and affected by social realities and relationships. Currently adolescent research and discussion is interdisciplinary, for the complex nature of the adolescent process, especially as culture changes, must take into account not *only* psychological factors, but sociological and even interaction factors as well.

Theologians have only recently acknowledged the impact of adolescence on the church, missiological theory, or systematic theology. Although youth ministry has now become a staple of theological curriculum at all levels, there is almost no theological discussion—in print or otherwise—concerning adolescence. This trend may be waning, but as with many social realities, church leadership and thinking has a great deal of catching up to do.

Today, a generally accepted definition of adolescence has been summarized by developmental psychologist John Santrock, who calls adolescence "the period of life between childhood and adulthood... (the process) lasts from roughly 10 to 13 years of age and ends at 18 to 22 years of age, (however) defining when adolescence ends is not an easy task. It has been said that adolescence begins in biology and ends in culture."[13] Santrock offers as tight a definition as the phenomenon probably allows, for the entire adolescent experience fluctuates constantly and deviates greatly according to such variables as culture, locale, and familial health and makeup. But to understand adolescence, it is important to first define its parameters—where it begins and ends, and just what it involves.

Adolescence begins in biology

As noted above, the oft-cited beginning point of adolescence is puberty. There is debate, however, over when the exact physiological changes of puberty begin, and it is even harder to define for boys than it is for girls. It is relatively accepted, for example, that puberty for girls has been reported to be slowly dropping from as late as an average of 14.5 years old a century and more ago, to as early as 11 years old today. Whether or not the numbers are precise, there is strong consensus that a trend exists—puberty is

13. J. W. Santrock, *Adolescence*, 4th ed. (Dubuque, Iowa: William C. Brown, 1990), 28-29.

Vanishing markers
Adolescent psychologist David Elkind defines *markers* as external signs of where we stand "in the stages on life's way." Markers are signs that we are growing and changing. According to Elkind, "Markers protect teenagers by helping them attain a clear self-definition, and they reduce stress by supplying rules, limits, taboos, and prohibitions that liberate teenagers from the need to make age-inappropriate decisions and choices."[1]

Elkind—like Chap—thinks that vanishing markers are reason for concern. Without markers, the distinction between adult and adolescent disappears, creating "adultified" youth (adolescents assumed to be fully competent to deal with complex adult issues) and "adolescent" adults (adults unable to individuate, and whose "self" is borrowed from whomever they are near at the moment).

What kind of markers do you notice among young people today? In the absence of socially sanctioned markers, do adolescents create their own? (If so, name some.) Or do they simply go without, and become "adultified youth," as Elkind suggests?

beginning at an increasingly younger age. The American Medical Association, the United States Centers for Disease Control,[14] and the majority of social scientists report this as demonstrable fact. [15]

Because the beginning of the adolescent phase of development has been tied to the onset of puberty, it is therefore possible to assume that the *psychological* process of adolescence is beginning at a younger age as well. In other words, 30 years ago most people considered adolescence commencing around 13 years of age. Today it is seen as occurring at roughly the same period as the reported earlier onset of puberty, or around 11 years of age. It is interesting to note that these developmental shifts have taken place in *both* the physiology impacting adolescence *and* in the psychosocial factors that influence adolescence *at the same time*. Although most researchers are convinced that earlier menses (the final evidence of female puberty) is taking place,[16] little attention has been given to the relationship between earlier menses and the psychosocial developmental process.[17] The timing of and entrance into adolescence, then, is marked by a physiological (having to do with functioning of the body) event (puberty), but is generally described and discussed as a psychological (having to do with mind and behavior) as well as sociological (having to do with relationships and human interaction) event. This is why the developmental aspect of adolescence is often referred to a *psychosocial* phenomenon.

Since most agree that the age of physiological development is declining, the question then becomes, Why is this important? For the purposes of youth ministry, if adolescence is beginning earlier than 30 years ago, then the ministry models designed during that era must be reexamined or outright rejected. The days have changed, and yet the majority of youth ministry models, philosophies, and programmatic expectations were created in the 1960s and '70s. Forty years ago a 12-year-old was a child needing the expertise of those in the field of children's ministry. Today, a 12-year-old is an adolescent needing a different ministry focus. Clearly, to take seriously the call of the youth ministry task, we must be more committed to the continual contextualization of our theology than to the perpetuation of programs, models, and philosophies that no longer are appropriate for a changing adolescent culture.

Adolescence ends in culture

When developmental theorists attempt to define the endpoint of the adolescent journey, the most common reference is made to "culture." However, across the centuries and cultures it has been far easier to demarcate the line between a child and an adult

14. See these organizations' Web sites for more information: www.ama-assn.org and www.cdc.gov.

15. Ronald Koteskey points out, "Researchers argue over how much the age of puberty has declined, but all agree that it has. People reach puberty somewhere between two and four years earlier than they did in the early 19th century." Cited in "Adolescence as a Cultural Invention," in Donald Ratcliff and James A. Davies, *Handbook of Youth Ministry* (Birmingham, Alabama: Religious Education Press, 1991), 43.

16. Reportedly due to better nutrition and body fatness available in Western cultures. V. Matkovic, and others, "Leptin Is Inversely Related to Age at Menarche in Human Females," *The Journal of Clinical Endocrinology & Metabolism* (October, 1997), 3239.

17. Youth workers have sensed this downward shift for the last few years, to the point that it has become an accepted assumption underlying youth ministry trends.

1. David Elkind, *All Grown Up and No Place to Go* (Reading, Massachusetts: Addison-Wesley, 1984), 93.

What do we mean by *maturity*?
"When we talk about a mature person, we are talking in part about the healthy sense of identity and of self developed during the teen years. The kind of parenting a teenager receives and the social climate in which he or she grows up are critical in determining what sort of self-definition he or she will attain.

"Growth by integration is conflictual, time-consuming, and laborious…[But] once growth by integration has occurred, it is difficult if not impossible to break down… People who have a strong sense of self do not lose it even under the most trying circumstances…

"Substitution is the kind of growth suggested by the well-known adage, 'When in Rome do as the Romans do.' …Such learning is not adaptive when it comes to constructing a sense of personal identity. A sense of self constructed by the simple addition of feelings, thoughts, and beliefs copied from others amounts to a patchwork self…Teenagers with a patchwork self have not developed an inner core of consistency and stability that allows them to deal with new situations in terms of past experiences."

—David Elkind,
All Grown Up and No Place to Go
(Reading, Massachusetts:
Addison-Wesley, 1984), 15-17.

than between an adolescent and an adult. Unlike adolescence, the transition between childhood and adulthood has included clear markers distinguishing these two stages of life.[18] Historically, these markers have included rites of passage and specific training for children preparing to take on adult roles in society. Once these rites and training are completed, the child is both equipped and expected to fulfill the role of an adult in his or her community.

Today the only real marker available to youth growing up in Western and urbanized societies is the process of adolescence itself. Some point to "turning 18 or 21" as chronological markers, due to the legal responsibilities and privileges associated with these ages. But few developmental theorists accept an arbitrary age standard set by a government as a cultural marker capable of ending the adolescent journey. In addition, the American judicial system, which is lowering the age of adult accountability into the early teens and lower, has essentially negated any credence this notion may have once had. If, as some historians claim, adolescence was invented "to prolong the years of childhood,"[19] the invention has succeeded to the point where the process seems now to have no end. The "inventors" failed to prescribe when the child *could* (as in, be equipped) and finally *should* (as in, be expected to) become an adult!

If, as others suggest, adolescence itself has become the marker distinguishing youth from adulthood, an assumptive leap becomes necessary: "When the process of adolescence has been completed, the young person has reached adulthood." The ambiguous endpoint of adolescence in our culture is a much larger question than this chapter can handle, but it is clearly cause for concern. When young people go through a process of "growing up into adulthood," they must also be provided with some understanding of and appreciation for the end goal. With the media's enticing encouragement, many contemporary adults are trying to live like adolescents. Adolescents, intuitively recognizing this, have little incentive to finish the process and become adults. Thus the adolescent journey continues to stretch into what centuries of human culture have considered the *adult* years.

Individuation: a key to understanding adolescent development

The primary and most basic goal of adolescence is known as *individuation*. Although there is some disagreement in social sciences regarding the exact definition, there is general consensus that *individuation* essentially means "becoming one's own person."[20] When a young person begins the process of breaking away from the role of child in the ecology of the family system, she has embarked on a journey from which there is no turning back. This is the first step into adolescence, in which a young person intuitively recognizes that she yearns to leave the relative safety and comfort of the child's role and become an interdependent, autonomous person.

---

18. David Elkind, *All Grown Up and No Place to Go: Teenagers in Crisis* (Reading, Massachusetts: Addison-Wesley, 1984).

19. David Bakan, "Adolescence in America: From Idea to Social Fact," *Daedalus* 100 (1971), 981; see also Joseph Kett, "The Invention of the Adolescent," *Rites of Passage: Adolescence in America, 1790 to the Present* (New York: Basic, 1977), 215-243.

20. James E. Loder, *The Logic of the Spirit: Human Development in Theological Perspective* (San Francisco: Jossey-Bass, 1998), 286.

Carl Jung made extensive use of this term throughout his writings. In *Psychology Types*, he states:

> The concept of individuation plays a large role in our psychology. In general, it is the process by which individual beings are formed and differentiated; in particular, it is the development of the psychological *individual* as being distinct from the general, collective psychology. Individuation, therefore, is a process of *differentiation*, having for its goal the development of the individual personality.[21]

Ponderable
Why is it important for Christians to understand individuation as more that just "separation" from others? Humans are created in the image of God, who is Triune relationship, and we gather as one interconnected body of Christ. What implications does this have for a Christian understanding of self, in light of Chap's discussion of individuation? How might Christians understand individualtion—"becoming one's own person"—in light of a theology that defines us in relationship to God and others?

The concept of individuation has many uses in social science. In philosophy, for example, the term is used as "a means of uniquely distinguishing or identifying particular items or individuals."[22] Mostly, however, individuation describes a uniquely human developmental process. Margaret S. Mahler uses the term in describing what she calls the *separation-individuation phase* of early childhood (from roughly the fifth month following birth until the 36TH month). [23] In describing the process that occurs during this time, the *separation-individuation process*, she and her team coupled the concept of individuation with separation.[24] Integrating Jung's characterization alongside several others, individuation is essentially the process of becoming a unique person. This process actually occurs over the entire lifespan, but, as Jung refers to the process, is generally initiated and primarily developed during adolescence.

Mahler describes individuation as the process whereby a person achieves a level of independence from some external control and therefore becomes somewhat self-reliant (within the context of appropriate developmental expectations). But more recently developmental psychologists have used Mahler's typology to define the adolescent process of separation and individuation. When a child begins to transition from the role of child to the role of adult, he goes through a similar process of separating from an external control figure (usually parents) in order to achieve a certain level of independence (although for an adolescent, the actual task of individuation is never fully complete, and is more about beginning the healthy journey of interdependence with others rather than actual independence).[25] It is very important to remember that this "separating" is *not* about separating from the family, for the evidence is overwhelming that adolescents *need* and generally *desire* to have a close relationship with their family system, and parents in particular. But in adolescent individuation, the child goes

---

21. Carl G. Jung. *Personality Types* (Princeton, New Jersey: Princeton University Press, 1971), 448.

22. A. C. Grayling, "Individuation," in Alan Bullock and Stephen Trombley (eds.), *The Norton Dictionary of Modern Thought* (New York: W. W. Norton & Company, 1999), 423.

23. Margaret S. Mahler, Fred Pine, and Anni Bergman, "Stages in the Infant's Separation from the Mother," in Gerald Handel and Gail G. Whitchurch (eds.), *The Psychosocial Interior of the Family,* 4th ed. (New York: Aldine De Gruyter, 1994), 419.

24. Mahler, and others, 419.

25. As Carl Jung notes, "The goal is important only as an idea; the essential thing is the opus which leads to the goal: that is the goal of a lifetime," in "The Psychology of Transference," *The Collected Works of C. G. Jung.* 20 vols. Bollinger Series XX, trans. by R. C. F. Hull, ed. by H. Read, M. Fordham, G. Adler, and Wm. McGuire (Princeton, New Jersey: Princeton University Press, Princeton, 1953-1979), par. 400.

through the process that has been described by Peter Blos as the *second separation-individuation phase.*[26] In this second separation-individuation phase, the young person separates from the *role* and *associated identity* of child and moves toward becoming her own adult, differentiated person. In describing this *second individuation*, Santrock notes:

> It is critical for adolescents to gain difference and distance from parents to transcend infantile ties to them. Individuation during adolescence is defined as a sharpened sense of one's distinctness from others, a heightened awareness of one's self-boundaries... individuation in adolescence means that individuals now take increasing responsibility for what they do and what they are, rather than depositing this responsibility on the shoulders under whose influence and tutelage they have grown up.[27]

It should be noted that empirical as well as anecdotal evidence suggests that there are differences between how girls and boys go through the process of individuation. There are arguments that suggest, for example, that girls individuate more according to relationship patterns and interactions and boys more through activities and competition.[28] There is little doubt that there are differences, and this is an important area for future research in adolescent development. As distinctive areas become more clearly studied and demonstrated, youth workers must make themselves aware of the unique markers of male and female individuation. But it is *equally* important to recognize that, while some differences surely exist between how boys and girls grow up, human development across gender lines has far more similarities. For the youth worker, recognizing these similarities is perhaps a more crucial aspect of understanding adolescent development than trying to become an expert in the nuances of adolescent male and female development.

Primarily our task in youth ministry is to approach each adolescent as a uniquely designed and gifted masterpiece of the Creator. While it is important to understand the broad developmental differences between genders and across age groups, what every child, adolescent, and young adult needs far more is the personal touch of a loving community. In youth ministry we are seeking to *theologically* as well as *developmentally* understand the unique needs and desires of every adolescent God brings to us. The most foundational understanding we must carry with us as youth workers, then, is that *both* boys and girls are created in the image of God, "male and female he created them" (Genesis 1:27). This essentially means that the basic makeup of both men and women, and therefore boys and girls, is relational, for God as a three-person unit is relational (John 1:1-3). As relational creations, adolescent women and men are called to *both* care and to need care, instinctively long to connect to others, and yearn for a connection to

---

26. Peter Blos, "The Second Individuation Process of Adolescence," in Peter Blos (ed.), *The Adolescent Passage* (New York: International Universities Press, 1979). As Laurie Kaplan notes, "Some researchers, Peter Blos chief among them, are clear to point out that while there are many similarities between the two phases there are also many differences."

27. Blos, 226.

28. Cf. Nancy Chodorow, *The Reproduction of Mothering: Psychoanalysis and the Sociology of Gender* (Berkeley, California: University of California Press, 1978).

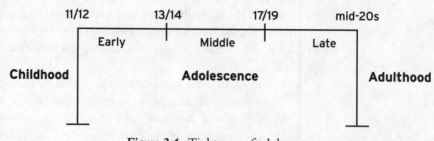

Figure 2.1. Tightrope of adolescence

the God who has created them. This theological understanding must guide us as we consider the implications of adolescent individuation.

Figure 2.1, Tightrope of Adolescence, depicts the individuation process of adolescence. The left stanchion or pole in Figure 2.1 represents the childhood phase of development. A child climbs this pole holding fast to the relationships and context of the family, relying on the family system to provide protection, security, and a sense of place. Throughout the first 10 or 11 years of life, a child's sense of self is grounded in familial relationships. As the child goes through the first separation-individuation phase (infancy through age three) until she prepares to take those first steps on the adolescent journey (represented by the tightrope model), there is an innate dependency upon the family system as a whole and the mother (or primary caretaker) in particular. [29]

During this period, a child's relationship with his or her family sets the stage for future development. This phase necessitates a child experiencing the comfort of a committed and nurturing presence, a supportive environment where a child is encouraged to explore and to experiment, and a relational setting where appropriate independence is encouraged. "For normal development to occur, the parent must walk the fine line of both encouraging independence while continuing to serve as a source of protection and nurturance. Overemphasis on either extreme can result in personality disturbances."[30] But if the phase is successfully navigated, the child will have developed the sense of security and self-concept needed to enter the second separation-individuation phase with relative confidence, which is known as adolescence. If the child does *not* successfully complete the first phase, then the adolescent phase will be affected as well.[31]

As a youth worker, occasionally we encounter an adolescent who is terribly insecure, well beyond shy. Or we may struggle with someone who is extremely aggressive or consistently inappropriate in social or program settings. Especially with early

29. There are many people that do not believe that the biological mother is any more necessary in healthy development than any other caretaker. John Bowlby (1982), credited as the first to recognize the importance of infant attachment, held this view. But his colleague Mary Ainsworth (1979) seemed to soften this it does not matter approach by taking the role of the mother more seriously. There are potent arguments on both sides and strong feelings as well.

30. Stanton L. Jones and Richard E. Butman, *Modern Psychotherapies* (Downers Grove, Illinois: InterVarsity Press, 1991), 98. In describing the kind of parenting a child needs, Alfred Adler summarized the parental role three generations ago by emphasizing that parents must take children seriously, stating that "ridicule of children is well-nigh criminal." See Adler's *Understanding Human Nature* (New York: Garden City Publishing, 1927), 69-71.

31. Kaplan, 51.

adolescents who are trying on the new clothes of individuation, these can be simple reactions to nervousness, slight social fear, or the amount of sugar they consumed before the meeting! But there are those whom we encounter who have deeper needs that youth ministry training and education has not equipped us to handle. The best route to take when confronted with someone who displays potentially significant personality or social issues is to get advice from a health professional. Every youth worker would do well to memorize the axiom, "When in doubt, refer!"

Once a child begins to pull away from the role of child in the family system, she begins to explore the next phase of life known as adolescence. This is represented on the model as a tightrope between the stanchion representing childhood (on the left side of the model) and that representing adulthood (on the right). The tightrope signifies the process of individuation, which adolescents must navigate as they pass through the second separation–individuation phase (from now on referred to simply as *individuation*). Today this commonly occurs somewhere between 10 and 12 years of age (although as previously mentioned, this may vary widely across regions, cultures, and even individual children).[32]

As noted, while the completion of individuation signals the entrance into *societal adulthood*,[33] it is much harder to specify the end of adolescence than the beginning. As Raymore asserted, "Defining the point of transition from adolescence to young adulthood can pose problems for researchers."[34] Puberty is a far more discernible and objective marker than culture. In postmodern society, successful completion of individuation and becoming an adult is such a subjective experience that it varies from person to person. There is no societal or even intuitive moment when someone has "arrived" on the threshold of adulthood. There are no classes, rites, or rituals that definitively certify an adolescent is fully individuated. Individuation is a fluid, complex, and even internal process. One way to describe the end of the adolescent journey, then, is to analyze the tasks that comprise the individuation process. When young people have successfully completed these tasks, they are psychologically and sociologically equipped to take on the roles of adulthood. In most cases, this seems to occur as early as the mid-20s to as late as 30 years old.

Changes in the timing of the adolescence process

As has been mentioned, the timing and length associated with adolescence has changed over the past century (Figure 2.2, The Changing Face of Adolescence). The remarkable fact that this table makes clear is how the adolescent journey has significantly lengthened over the years. When psychology first identified adolescence as an actual phase of life (around the turn of the 20TH century), it generally lasted only three to four years. At the turn of the century, children were not quite children when they entered the high

---

32. Mussen, and others, 281.

33. Koteskey, 43.

34. Raymore, Barber, Eccles, & Godbey, "Leisure Behavior Pattern Stability during the Transition from Adolescence to Young Adulthood," *Journal of Youth and Adolescence,* 28 (1999), 1, 82.

Years	Age entering adolescence/puberty	Age entering adulthood
Pre-1900	14	16/18
1960-1970	13	18/19
2000	11/12	mid to late 20s

Figure 2.2. The changing face of adolescence

school (made mandatory by the 1930s but creating a societal foothold earlier), but they were clearly not adults. This created the cultural environment for Hall's work that defined the life span phase.

But neither Hall nor early adherents to his views saw adolescence as a lengthy period. The markers that described this new stage of life were more related to a "not quite child, not yet adult" set of loosely defined criteria than a long, drawn-out period of one's life. Although Hall was a psychologist and attached his theory to biological factors, the majority of discussions in the 1920s and '30s were related to the high school community and subculture. "Primary school" was designed for children—six to 13 years of age, grades one through eight. The high school, designed during this period for the 14- to 19-year-old, marked the sociological beginning of adolescence. Adolescence ended there as well, for once young people finished high school they were expected to enter cultural adulthood, take up a trade, become economically responsible, and get married. Social historian Joseph Kett demonstrated that during this period, adolescence was understood as a phase experienced between 14 and 18 years of age.[35]

Then somewhere between 1950 and 1960, developmental theorists began to acknowledge adolescence as a legitimate part of the life span.[36] In doing this, they assumed a universally accepted psychological clarity over when the process of adolescence started (the onset of puberty). When puberty began at roughly 13 years of age, psychosocial adolescence began at the same time. The sociological and familial dimensions of adolescence began to appear earlier, roughly seventh grade, dragging the institution of junior high school into the adolescent mix. During the '50s and '60s, students were considered adults soon after graduation from high school. At this stage, adolescence lasted on the average from five to seven years—from the age of approximately 12 or 13 to 18 or 19. Society had clear expectations that upon graduation from high school an adolescent was to live and function as an adult. Thus the process of individuation was (relatively) ordered, controlled, and directed by the external social systems.

Today adolescence begins earlier, both in the sociological world (the advent of the middle school, where students begin entering a traditional adolescent cultural environment as young as 11 years old) and in the psychological literature. Like adolescence, adulthood is at least partially culturally determined, and begins when a culture says it does. In our culture, however, a young person is on his own to determine the outcome of the adolescent journey. No longer does society solve the adolescent dilemma for its

Will teenagers disappear in the 21st century?

This is the question columnist Walter Kirn asks in a recent *Time* special report on the millennium. Kirn suggests that adolescence is a "blip" on the historical radar screen, noting that "early 20th-century adolescents were farmers, apprentices, students and soldiers—perhaps even wives and husbands—but not teenagers."

Kirn describes teenagers as a modern luxury good. Those days, says Kirn, are rapidly coming to an end as teenagers become economically powerful, socially precocious, and legally responsible. He muses: "What will a world without teenagers look like? Like the adult world does now. Adolescents will feel the same pressures as their parents do: to succeed financially, to maintain their health, to stay on society's good side. What's more, adolescents will field these pressures using their elders' traditional techniques: spending money, taking medication, contracting for professional advice. The carefree years will become the prudent years, and the prudent years will continue throughout life."[1]

Is Kirn right? Why or why not?[1]

1. Walter Kirn, "Will Teenagers Disappear?" *Time* (February 21, 2000), 60-61.

35. Joseph F. Kett, *Rites of Passage: Adolescence in America 1790 to the Present* (New York: Basic Books, 1977).

36. Seabold, 90.

young. Indeed, no longer do the social structures and systems *either* equip the young for adulthood *or* expect the young to embrace adulthood at any prescribed point. So a contemporary adolescent does not *necessarily* need to remain an adolescent well into his or 20s. But as Lance Morrow wrote in a *Time* editorial, "No growing up occurs if there is nothing to grow up to, without the adult connection, adolescence becomes a Neverland, a Mall of Lost Children."[37] And in postmodern contemporary society, that "Neverland" can (and usually does) last as long as 15 years or more![38]

As the length of adolescence has been increasing, the field of youth ministry has been forming its own methodological axioms that drive youth ministry philosophy and practice. An example of this is how the parent-adolescent relationship is now perceived by most youth workers. As youth ministry became more programmatically sophisticated, and books were written and seminars were presented, arguments supporting the idea of parental separation during early adolescence were developed during the '60s and '70s when adolescence comprised a shorter span of time than it does today. Youth ministry leaders during these decades promoted a subtle but important misunderstanding about what occurs at the outset of the adolescent process: that adolescents want and need to separate from their families and connect to friends as soon as they begin the task of individuation. One well-known resource, originally written during this period (and still widely respected) notes: "When children reach adolescence, they want to be their own person, separate from their parents. They want to make their own choices and commitments, to be set free."[39] While statements like this are true to a point, they have been greatly exaggerated, misunderstood, and misused in the name of youth ministry, and especially early adolescent ministry.

But adolescent individuation involves separating from the *role* of child, not separating from the love, support, and nurture of the family system. In our current cultural context, the adolescent journey is a *15-year* process of separation from the role of child in the family system and individuating in terms of becoming one's own person in a larger community context. Eventually adolescents do seek to and need to connect to peers as a key component of this phase, for the very process of individuation is about learning how to connect to others, including family members. But the perception that adolescent separation requires severing primary familial relationships is rarely true and *never* ultimately healthy for an adolescent. And even the desire to separate from the *role* of child for the adolescent is more a characteristic of middle adolescence (around 13 to 19 years of age) than of early adolescence (around ages 10 to 14). An early adolescent is still *far more child than adult.* As a newcomer to individuation, the early adolescent is more concerned with issues of safety, support, stability, and "feel" than about leaving parents behind in the search for meaningful peer friendships.

In youth ministry, the difference between an early and a middle adolescent is a very important distinction. Young adolescents need to be treated with tender care and

---

37. Lance Morrow, "The Boys and the Bees: More Arguments for Abolishing Adolescence," *Time* (May 30, 1999).

38. See Barbara S. Fuhrmann, *Adolescence, Adolescents* (Boston: Little, Brown, 1986).

39. See Wayne Rice, *Junior High Ministry: A Guide to Early Adolescence for Youth Workers,* rev. ed. (Grand Rapids: Zondervan/Youth Specialties, 1997), 86. This statement is made without qualification or empirical support offered.

diligent understanding, being careful not to think they are developing faster than they are. Typically middle adolescents are more interested in exploring life on their own, but even that is seeming to wane. An increasingly lengthy adolescent process makes the concept of familial separation for the postmodern early adolescent a far different, and more difficult, experience than it was for his counterpart a century or even a generation ago. Postmodern youth workers need to be aware that in a culture where few systems and relationships are trustworthy or stable, adolescents need to know that a Christian ministry designed to serve them will do all it can to ensure an experience of stability and health.

The three key tasks of individuation— identity, autonomy, and reconnection

There is much debate over the specific tasks of the adolescent journey. Almost every perspective on human development offers its own unique lexical description of these tasks. [40] One key figure in understanding the adolescent journey was Erik Erikson who, for example, stated that the single most crucial task for adolescents is identity formation. He used the label *identity crisis* to define the adolescent experience (although *crisis* for Erikson did not necessarily dictate some sort of catastrophe in the life of an adolescent, but rather defined a normative and crucial period in the adolescent life stage that would propel her toward adulthood). As Erikson formulated his theory, he recognized that there are other important issues that come into play during adolescent individuation. But like most theorists, he was convinced that the quest for identity lay at the heart of adolescence. [41]

The range of opinions, theories, and debates about the exact definitions of and processes concerning the tasks of adolescence is far beyond the scope of this chapter. The tack I have chosen is to present three of the most important and relatively agreed-upon characteristics of every adolescent's journey. This synthesis is not intended to be a comprehensive summary of varied opinions but rather a framework for understanding some of the basic elements every young person must consider, experience, and face during the adolescent journey. Developmental psychologist John Santrock asserts: "Individuation has two main components—separateness and self-assertion." [42] He later acknowledges that there is a third component, but, as with several authors, practitioners, and theorists, he has also brought the need to reconnect with others under the umbrella of the other two components he mentions discussed here. So, to use Santrock's template, another way to describe these terms is to view adolescent individuation as a process that accomplishes three basic tasks for the adolescent:

---

40. Mussen, and others, in *Psychological Development: A Life-Span Approach*, lists five essential tasks: identity formation, biological adjustment; connection to peers, independence from family, and values/standards leading to order and consistent actions (pages 280-318). Psychologist Hans Seabold lists six markers which signal adulthood (*Adolescence: A Sociological/Psychological Analysis*, 6), and John Santrock tends to synthesize and condense various concepts into tighter but less easily defined packages (*Adolescence*, 28-29).

41. Erik Erikson, *Identity: Youth and Crisis* (New York: W. W. Norton, 1968).

42. Santrock, 387.

- The task of discovering *identity*, in answer to the question, *Who am I?*
- The task of accepting responsibility for one's life, or achieving *autonomy*, in answer to the question, *Do I matter?*
- The task of *reconnecting* in appropriate ways to others in community, in answer to the question, *How do I relate to others?*

One additional internal mechanism must be in place during this phase as a mediator of the three primary tasks. In asking the questions, *Who am I?* and *Do I matter?*, the adolescent must also continually ask a more fundamental question: *How do I know these things?* This self-reflection during the adolescent individuation process provides the internal structure for developing the confidence to trust the answers that emerge from the process. It is most often accomplished during the middle and late adolescent period where the individual tries on different selves with others in different relational settings. As the adolescent attempts to break away from reliance on his parents for self-awareness, and seeks to take a modicum of control over his life and his choices, he is also attempting to reform himself via relationships with others—primarily peers. As these converge there is a continual internal process gauging the progress the journey is making. This becomes the internalized governor to the process of adolescent individuation.[43]

Identity and autonomy for young, middle, and older adolescents

Discovering who we are and deciding to accept the person we have been created to be as we live in community, are the fundamental concerns of the human psyche.[44] Who am I? is a question directly related to our understanding of self, or our identity. As mentioned earlier, there are more similarities between boys and girls in terms of identity formation than differences.[45] Pastoral psychologist, author, and spirituality author Henri J. M. Nouwen observed that, in one way or another, we all ask, Who am I? every day.[46] How we come to answer this question will impact every other area of our life. This is especially true for adolescents, who are by definition attempting to narrow in on the essence of the identity they will refine for the remainder of their lives. To Nouwen, identity is not imposed from the outside of one's life, or even "tried on" as an internalized process of trial and error. It is, rather, discovered as we hear the voice of the God who calls us *beloved*.[47] Our identity, then, is firmly rooted in the doctrines of creation and redemption. Every child is created by God with

43. Thanks to Jim Furrow, Ph.D., who offered insight into this highly complex process.

44. For a profound discussion, see Henri J. M. Nouwen, *In the Name of Jesus* (New York: Crossroad, 1988).

45. In critiquing Erikson's male perspective of identity formation, Carol Gilligan notes that human beings are such complex creatures that identity formation has more in common across gender lines than differences: "In sum, daughters forge some percentage of their identity through interaction with world, and in some cases as much as do sons." *In a Different Voice: Psychological Theory and Women's Development* (Cambridge, Massachusetts: Harvard University Press, 1982), 13f.

46. The exact wording came from an informal conversation with him while the author was on a directed week long retreat at L'Arche in Toronto in December, 1991.

47. For more on Nouwen's view, see Henri Nouwen, *Life of the Beloved: Spiritual Living in a Secular World* (New York: Crossroad, 1992) and *Return of the Prodigal: A Meditation on Fathers, Brothers and Sons* (New York: Doubleday), 1992.

Identity: given, not found

Searching for identity is a theme as old as myths and fairy tales where young men are sent on a quest to parts unknown, in order to accomplish certain tasks necessary to receiving the reward. (In mythology young women are seldom sent to search for their true selves. Rather they find their true identities in the context of a relationship usually as a mother or a wife to the young man now home with an identity of his own).

While these stories inform our cultural consciousness in powerful ways and provide intriguing fodder for gender studies, Christians understand identity theologically. For Christians, identity—the true self—is a gift, ours by redemption, not human development. While that identity is distorted by sin, Jesus restored our relationship with God—and in so doing, he made visible once more the outline of our true identities as God's beloved.

What difference does it make for youth ministry if identity is God's gift to us and not something we must go out and find?

great care, and has been purchased by the death of the Son, Jesus Christ (Psalm 139 and Romans 8).

These fundamental facts, then, provide the ultimate answer to the question, *Who am I?,* and the key to our understanding and sense of personal identity—"I am the uniquely created, redeemed child of the living God." As one of the key components of the individuation task, youth ministry must continually and consistently reinforce this theological truth in everything we do and to every student we encounter.

Young adolescents (usually around 10 to 14 years of age) have just begun to ask the question of identity. The identity of a young adolescent is still firmly fixed within the context of the family system, although the child will at times struggle to try on new identities, even at this early stage.[48] This is expressed in the young adolescent who is happy-go-lucky one week, moody the next, an aggressive bully on Sunday morning, and a shy introvert on Wednesday night. All this is typical of the young adolescent. Early adolescence calls the youth worker to remain consistent in loving and caring for "tweens" for the unique persons *they are*, and not to be fooled by the roles and masks they wear. (This is especially true when we take into account the *Mountain Dew factor*, in which behavior bears a direct relationship upon the amount of Mountain Dew consumed immediately preceding the meeting!)

A middle adolescent (usually 13 to 19 years of age) has traversed the tightrope of adolescence to the point where family support is still present, but is seldom claimed by the adolescent as a significant point of security. There is a need for familial, and especially a father's, blessing, affirmation, and attachment, but this is mostly sought out from a *safe* relational and sociological distance.[49] A middle adolescent, for the most part, may not express a desire to spend time with her parents, but there is almost always the desire to know that parents are available if the adolescent *wants* to be with them. While conflict between parents and adolescents can be explosive throughout the entire developmental phase, usually the most difficult family conflicts occur during middle adolescence. Middle adolescents sense the need to be on their own, to discover who they are in relation to the world (i.e., peers), and to take responsibility for their own life. Problems arise when a middle adolescent longs to *please*, and wants to be acknowledged in the family as responsible—but due to the as-yet unformed self, he often stumbles. Many parents abdicate their responsibility to remain close to their children during this period, for it is easier to avoid this family tension than confront it. But a middle adolescent still *needs* parental influence, advice, nurture, and guidance. Middle adolescence calls caring youth workers to recognize and be available to assist the entire family as they navigate this period in the life cycle.

An area receiving more attention from social scientists in the last decade or so is the notion of parental attachment. Drawing on John Bowlby and Mary Ainsworth's

---

48. Erikson.

49. There is strong evidence that there is a correlation between an adolescent's relationship with his father and everything from self-esteem to problem-solving skills. See R. H. Aseltine, "A Reconsideration of Parental and Peer Influences on Adolescent Deviance," *Journal of Health and Social Behavior* 36(2) (1995), 103-121; D. Burge, C. Hammen, J. Davila, and S. E. Daley, "The Relationship between Attachment Cognitions and Psychological Adjustment in Late Adolescent Women," *Development and Psychopathology* 9(1) (1997), 151-167.

work on infant attachment[50] researchers have expanded Bowlby and Ainsworth's basic premise to point out that our need for secure attachments is not limited to the first few years of life. Although it is too soon in the research process to assert these findings with significant confidence, healthy parental attachment appears to be related to the ability to complete both the first *and* the second separation-individuation phases of life, albeit in different ways. In infant attachment theory, which has seen significant consensus in recent years, the more secure and confident a child is in her relationship with her mother, the more positive the separation-individuation phase. Using this finding as a model for the second individuation phase, adolescent attachment to parents enables the adolescent to more quickly and confidently complete adolescence, as well as fosters a healthy self-concept and sense of confidence that accompanies the adolescent into adulthood. The notion of parental attachment, then, may play a significant role in the development of adolescents.

As has been mentioned, in early adolescence the family is still the foundation of loyalty and support. Youth ministry during this phase of the adolescent journey must see its role as a *support* to the family system. In middle adolescence, parents need to be viewed as partners. Although in many cases young adolescents may want their parents to stay far away from the youth ministry, youth workers must remember that nearly all high school students still desire a safe, connected relationship with their parents and families, no matter what they may say. When this is not the case, the youth worker should carefully seek to find out why. Perhaps this is an area where the family needs help.

In contemporary culture, late adolescence is an almost developmentally unnecessary but still dominant phase of the adolescent process. An older adolescent (usually late teens to middle 20s or later) is potentially ready to enter adulthood, but almost always still needs to be taught, led, and encouraged to make the final leap into an adult role as a capable, responsible, and interdependent person in the community. But, as noted earlier, we live in a culture that seems to deify youth and youthful irresponsibility and lack of commitment. Older adolescents stand on the threshold of making their mark on society and community but are often held back by systemic and environmental factors—parents who empower sloth and financial dependency, an educational system that treats the undergraduate curriculum as barely adequate preparation for graduate school, and media and advertising industries that make a far larger profit by appealing to the young to stay young (and the old to fight aging), to name but a few.

But late adolescents are culpable as well, for the opportunities abound for jumping into adulthood and influencing social change. For many if not most, it just seems too easy to stay a kid and float until one has no choice but to grow up. A basic rule of thumb, then, for those who serve the college-aged and *young adults* completing the individuation process (who have almost, but not quite, taken on the mantle of adulthood) is to *treat them like adults* but *lead them like adolescents*.

Ponderable
Chap suggests that a number of factors impede older adolescents from making the final jump into adulthood: Do you agree that something is keeping older adolescents from joining the ranks of adulthood? If so, what? Is Chap too hard on parents, educators, and media?

---

50. As examples of their work, see M. D. S. Ainsworth, "Infant-Mother Attachment," *American Psychologist* 34 (1979), 932-937; and J. Bowlby, *Attachment and Loss*, vol. I, 2nd ed. (New York: Basic Books, 1982).

Role of parents in adolescent individuation

A relatively recent area of interest has been the role of parents in adolescent development. For Christians, this is hardly new territory; the apostle Paul provides a window into the cultural and perhaps universal role parents play in the life of a developing child (1 Thessalonians 2:7-11) in modeling human relationships. In describing how he dealt with the people in Thessalonica, Paul says, "we were gentle among you, like a mother caring for her little children" (v. 7). The statement here concerns the role of a mother, not biological packaging, and is clearly not intended to dictate rigid rules over households. Rather, Paul uses the image of a mother to describe the nurturing relationships that characterize Christian community.

Later, as the disciples matured and needed a different kind of nurturing, Paul writes, "For you know that we dealt with each of you as a father deals with his own children, encouraging, comforting and urging you to live lives worthy of God, who calls you into his kingdom and glory" (vv. 11-12). Although it would be inappropriate to understand these passages as models for human development, Paul's description of Christian care and encouragement is clearly derived from his observations of the differing needs of children as they reach varying stages of maturity.

Despite a few popular writers in recent years who have claimed that peer influence far outweighs parental influence in the overall health and life of a child and adolescent, the sheer volume of data suggest this view is simply wrong.[51] It is clear, at least from the data compiled thus far, that parents are more influential in young people's healthy development than any other single external influence. Peer influence, though powerful in its own right, runs a distant second in influence to the impact of parents, for better and for worse.

Adolescence is the stage of life during which a father takes on a more decisive role in the life of a child. This is not to say that a mother's influence decreases, per se, but that as an adolescent begins to shift into having to be more and more responsible for his own life, parents become much more background but just as developmentally important. Because mothers are most often experienced as primary attachment figures throughout childhood, fathers tend to have less impact on the day-to-day lives of their children. But a mother's role is also connected to the child's role as well, and so when a child moves through adolescence, there can develop a tension between a mother and her child. As Nancy Chodorow points out, during and following puberty, a girl "usually moves from preoccupation with her relationship to her mother to her concern with her father and males…She may feel guilty toward her mother for loving her father more."[52]

Although generally true, this may be slightly overstated, for there is little evidence that a mother's role significantly diminishes during this period. She often still represents the warmth, safety, and nurturance of the familial environment. Few doubt

---

51. I am principally referring to Judith R. Harris, *The Nurture Assumption: Why Children Turn Out the Way They Do* (New York: Free Press, 1998).

52. N. Chodorow, *The Reproduction of Mothering: Psychoanalysis and the Sociology of Gender* (Berkeley, California: University of California Press, 1978), 138.

that mothers (and primary caretakers) are important in the lives of their children throughout the life span, but a father's role takes on a new significance in that a father generally represents to an emerging adult the "real world" that he or she is approaching. Although far more understudied than the more generic distinction of *parent*, a father has shown to be a unique influence in the life of an adolescent. The following studies have demonstrated that the more strongly the adolescent perceives his attachment to his father, the more likely he is to experience the following outcomes, compared to adolescents who perceive weak father attachment:[53]

• reduced risk-taking behaviors (Burge et al., 1997; Noppe and Noppe, 1997)
• greater interpersonal competence (Schneider and Younger, 1996)
• greater self-esteem (Rice and Cummings, 1996)
• increased likelihood of identity formation (Schultheiss and Blustein, 1994)
• greater social competence (Paterson et al., 1995)
• greater career self-efficacy (O'Brien, 1996)
• increased problem-solving ability and experience (Cobb, 1996)

Again, this is *not* to say that mothers do not matter in the developmental life of an adolescent. But in a cultural environment where the role of the father is generally discounted at every turn, these are important studies.

Looking again at the Tightrope of Adolescence, but now adding the attachment component (figure 2.3), helps define the process of individuation more completely.

On the left side of the stanchion, mother (or primary caretaker) attachment represents the key relational figure in the life of the child. Underneath the tightrope itself, represented by a safety net, is father (or father figure) attachment. Underscoring all of this is the parental security factor of a stable home environment. Along with mother and father attachment, the security that comes from the perception of a secure parental couple adds one more layer of security for the child or adolescent to fall back on when needed.[54]

What about nontraditional families?

At this stage, however, it is *crucial* to recognize that even the most positive family situation is not a perfect familial situation. Single parents, grandparents, foster, and adoptive parents all have the ability to offer a child and an adolescent the kind of environment where there is love, safety, and nurture. There is no question that many households

---

53. D. Burge, C. Hammen, J. Davila, and S. E. Daley, "The Relationship between Attachment Cognitions and Psychological Adjustment in Late Adolescent Women," *Development and Psychopathology* (1997), 151-167; I. C. Noppe and L. D. Noppe, "Evolving Meanings of Death during Early, Middle, and Later Adolescence," *Death Studies* (1997), 253-275; B. H. Schneider and A. J. Younger, "Adolescent-Parent Attachment and Adolescents' Relations with Their Peers: A Closer Look," *Youth and Society* (1996), 95-108; K. G. Rice and P. N. Cummins, "Late Adolescent and Parent Perceptions of Attachment: An Exploratory Study of Personal and Social Well-Being," *Journal of Counseling and Development* (1996), 50-57; D. Schultheiss and D. L. Blusteain, "Contributions of Family Relationship Factors to the Identity Formation Process," *Journal of Counseling and Development* (1994), 159-166; J. Paterson, J. Pryor, and J. Field, "Adolescent Attachment to Parents and Friends in Relation to Aspects of Self-Esteem," *Journal of Youth and Adolescence* (1995), 365-376; K. M. O'Brien, "The Influence of Psychological Separation and Parental Attachment on the Career Development of Adolescent Women," *Journal of Vocational Behavior* (1995), 257-274; C. Cobb, "Adolescent-Parent Attachments and Family Problem-Solving Styles," *Family Process* (1996), 57-82.

54. Elkind.

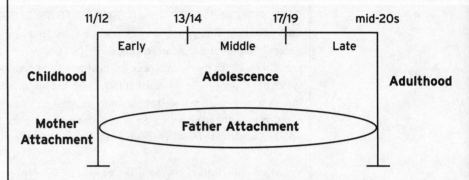

Figure 2.3. The tightrope of adolecence with attachment

where no father is present are far more conducive to healthy growth and development than many homes where a father lives. And theologically, God knows that we are fallen creatures who have allowed selfishness, stupidity, and the raw realities and circumstances of life to wreak havoc with the familial needs of children and adolescents. Therefore God has given us other people so that, no matter how good or bad our families are, we have others to rely on. This is an area where a theologically grounded youth ministry can make an impact on postmodern families. In an ideal, all-things-considered world, mothers and fathers are very important in the developmental life of an adolescent. At the same time, youth ministers must constantly seek to care for students and families who need the support that the church is called to provide. As Paul writes, "Carry each other's burdens, and in this way you will fulfill the law of Christ" (Galatians 6:2).

Adolescence through the lens of practical theology

A method for theological thinking
Chap claims that just because the Scriptures don't offer specific guidelines on how to deal with adolescents, "the church cannot sit back and allow theories of development to create a *de facto* theology of adolescent development." Why not? Should the church take its guidance from the social sciences, from theology, or both? Can the social sciences inform youth ministry or only youth work? What disciplines have been the most helpful to you for youth ministry: social sciences—like psychology, education, anthropology, sociology—or theology? Why?

Because adolescence is an invention of modernity in an urbanized culture, it is very difficult to extrapolate from the Scriptures specific guidelines for understanding and then dealing with adolescents.[55] But that certainly does not mean the church should sit back and allow theories of development to create a *de facto* theology of adolescent development. In fact the opposite is true, especially for those of us engaged in youth ministry. If you are involved in ministry, you are called to be a practical theologian, for you are making divine revelation relevant and coherent to a specific cultural setting. The task of practical theology, then, is to connect God's story to the stories of those we serve in youth ministry.

Adolescence is changing—and quickly. Puberty is starting earlier and resolving the questions of identity and autonomy later and later. This means that the concept of *youth* can no longer be limited to the two programmatic foci of North American youth ministry, junior and senior high. From fifth grade to the mid-20s, young men and women are finding themselves in a state of flux, continually on the lookout for anyone who would bless, affirm, and help them to finally land as a unique, responsible person. This is where youth ministry is at its best—recognizing the unique needs and dreams of the emerging generation—and taking it seriously enough to reach out. Because ado-

55. As an example of this attempt, see David A. Black, *The Myth of Adolescence* (Yorba Linda, California: Davidson Press, 1999).

lescents are in such an emotionally and relationally transitional state, the calling to care for them is an exciting and necessary opportunity and adventure. The transitional nature of adolescence implies, however, that youth workers must be especially diligent in making sure that youth ministry appropriately nurtures the young.

Addressing the uniqueness of adolescence cannot be limited to the sole responsibility of a youth ministry leader, team, or program. The church, as a family of "families," is called *as a community* to be the prime agent of nurturing this and any future generation. The church is not intended to be a large organization with several smaller, more specific congregations who happen to gather on a Sunday morning. The local church is instead called to be a living, connected, caring community of people who love Jesus Christ and are committed to loving and serving God in their fellowship and in the world (John 15).[56]

Youth ministry, then, is not an appendage of the body, it is rather an expression of the *whole* body caring for a specific group. Adolescents need an adult community who will love them appropriately and with great care. This is the call of the church. Young adolescents need several second families, and middle adolescents need a safe place to explore peer relationships *while* knowing that there are many others in the wings committed and available to them. Older adolescents need to know that they matter to the other adults in the community. Youth ministry is *everybody's* job!

---

56. For a detailed theological argument for this position, see Dennis Guernsey, *A New Design for Family Ministry.* David C. Cook, 1982.

Growing Up Postmodern: Theological Uses of Culture
Don C. Richter

Chapter 3

Recently I was invited to present a guest lecture on Youth and Spirituality at a local college. One of the questions I posed for discussion was this: In what ways can the Internet be a spiritual resource for teens today? I assumed that the majority of these computer-savvy college students would regard the Internet as a useful means of communication and a constructive vehicle for teen spirituality. Instead, my question provoked controversy and lively debate. Several students expressed strong conviction that the Internet is an isolating and voyeuristic medium, steeped in consumerism and detrimental to the general well-being of teenagers. "Keep kids off the Web!" they pleaded. Other students countered that the Internet offers a wealth of information—if one browses responsibly—and provides valuable ways of connecting to others, making new friends and sustaining community over great distances. These students encouraged the development of faith-oriented Web resources for youth.

A key issue this discussion surfaced for the class was how to discern appropriate technologies and teaching strategies in our educational ministry with youth. Our class discussion also pointed to some larger questions, however, which are the subject of this chapter:

• What perspectives help us understand the relationship between theology and culture in our ministry with youth?
• What guidelines do we need to help us interpret contemporary culture—including youth culture—in light of the gospel?

We'll begin by defining *theology* and *culture*, claiming that one term always points toward the other. Theology always implicates culture, and culture always lends itself to theological critique. We'll examine the role *language* plays in shaping our worldview, our theological ideas, and spirituality. We'll then examine two central themes of *Christian* theology that have implications for culture. Christian theology is grounded in the *Incarnation*—the scandalous claim that God became human and dwelt among us in the person of Jesus of Nazareth. Christian theology is given wings through our experience of *redemption*—the freedom and new life inaugurated by the death and resurrection of this same Jesus. For Christians, God's incarnation and redemptive activity color every aspect of how we understand and relate to culture and how we understand and minister with youth—including how we evaluate cultural phenomena like the Internet as a spiritual resource for teens today.

The interplay of theology and culture

Tom Beaudoin, author of *Virtual Faith,* recalls that when he first studied theology, he

The grammar of faith

Christian traditions all share a grammar, or structure, of faith in Jesus Christ. The Christian story has recognizable parts, arranged like a skeleton across which scores of faith traditions have been stretched over the centuries, each colored by its particular social and historical location. As a result, Christian traditions speak the language of faith with different theological accents, so to speak.

If the only time you've ever studied language was in English Composition or Spanish 101, it may seem strange to hear Don Richter talk about language as a bridge between theology and culture. And yet *language* refers to historically established patterns of human behavior (spoken or otherwise) that carry meaning—but that only make sense within certain communities. Language defines a culture. Until we learn a culture's language, it is alien to us. The same can be said for the language of faith. Until we learn the grammar of Christian faith, we cannot live fully as Christians. We learn that language best by immersion in the practices of a particular Christian community.

Languages do not define God, but they do frame theologies, the ways people of faith have come to talk about God over the centuries. Theological languages—those concrete patterns of believing, behaving, and communicating that enact our basic convictions about who God is and how God acts in the world—make sense only in theological communities. And while Christians do share a common language of faith, Jesus also calls us to find ways to translate this theological language so we can speak to secular culture as well. Furthermore, we must do so without corrupting the basic grammar of the Christian story.

- Think about your theological "accent." Does God-talk come easily to you? Do you steer clear of churchy words? What practices of faith seem natural to you? What actions commonly

thought he was going to be living with his "head in the clouds, floating in an airy, spiritual nothingness." He imagined returning to earth at the end of each day to find himself back in his own culture. "I was completely wrong," Beaudoin confesses.

> Theology has to do with culture because theology has to do with living religiously, which always takes place within a culture. *Theology*, by its very name, makes the great assertion that we can express a *logos* (word or reason) about a *theos* (God). Theology means "talk about" God, because it is first possible to "talk with" God, or to encounter revelation about God.[1]

We can see how theology and culture are deeply intertwined by considering how they are both dependent upon language. As Beaudoin notes:

> Whenever we use theological language, such as the phrase *kingdom of God*, our cultural concepts make it possible for us to understand what *kingdom and God* means. For us to understand even the word *theology*, a theology must take the form of terms and ideas that we can grasp, which means that it must be articulated in the language of our culture.[2]

The term *culture* refers broadly to the way of life of a society—the shared learned behavior (thinking, feeling, and acting) and its products (art, laws, customs, etc.) that distinguish one community of people from another. We swim in our culture the way fish swim in water—it surrounds us so closely that we barely notice it affecting the ways we move through the world. By sharing our culture, though, we attempt to *cultivate* children into ways of life that are important to us. New generations do not have to reinvent the wheel because the wheel is an important artifact of culture that has been handed down for thousands of years.[3]

Language is a defining feature of human culture, because every language conveys symbolic meanings and enables human knowledge to be transmitted to succeeding generations. Language marks the shift between biological and cultural existence. Individuals may utter nonsense sounds and make random motions, but when these become *communication* by means of sounds and gestures that signify shared social meanings, culture is born. How does this shift occur?

All humans are born with *linguistic capacity*. Listen to the clicks, clucks, and cooing of an infant. Gradually, they begin to take on the sounds of the spoken language the child hears. A child's linguistic capacity takes root and grows within the rich soil of a given language system. The child learns to interpret the world—to interpret reality itself—through the lens of a specific language with its vocabulary, grammar, syntax, and nuances of expression. We don't learn to speak *language in general;* we learn to speak and

---

1. Tom Beaudoin, *Virtual Faith* (San Francisco: Jossey-Bass, 1998), 29.

2. Beaudoin, 30.

3. One of the most tragic and disastrous social experiments of the past century occurred in the 1970s when the Khmer Rouge seized power in Cambodia and attempted to reinvent society by turning back the clock to "year zero" and banishing or killing all the cultural leaders of their land.

give you away as a Christian? How do you account for your particular theological accent?

• Is your theological accent so pronounced that non-Christians have trouble understanding you? Or is it so thin that no one can tell you apart from non-Christians?

comprehend a particular language.

The language we use helps us see and know certain things but may prevent us from seeing and knowing other things. Persons raised within multilingual cultures (or bilingual families) become aware at an early age that different words can be used to identify the same object. A piece of furniture consisting of a smooth flat slab fixed on legs, is not only *a table*, but can also be *der Tisch* or *la mesa*. Persons who are conversant in several languages also recognize that each language is *idiomatic*—that it has its own peculiar logic and structure and way of viewing reality. "I'm cold," I might say in English, though the equivalent German expression would translate, "It is to me cold"—two similar yet distinct ways of describing bodily experience.

Sometimes the only way to appreciate how we have been shaped by our native culture is to step out of it and view it from the perspective of a different culture. Then we realize that what we have always taken for granted as "the way things are" suddenly seems strange and maybe even arbitrary to us. We realize that our native culture has formed us in powerful ways—in some ways that are healthy and in other ways that may not be. We don't have to travel to foreign lands to have this experience, however. Leaving home and going away to college often prompts such reflection on our homes and families of origin.[4] Learning a different language can also make us keenly aware of how deeply our worldview has been shaped by our *mother tongue*—the language system that has nurtured us since infancy in the ways of our culture.

How does language link theology and culture?

Theology is like a living language, a way of communicating meaning—even ultimate meaning—to ourselves and to others. Understanding how language functions in transmitting culture has six important implications for how we understand our practical theological task with youth.

First, theological doctrines do not arrive prepackaged from on high, but are always constructed using the available tools of a particular culture.

Tool time
Because each culture brings different tools to the job, theological reflection arising in different cultural settings bring different theological truths to the surface. Can the same be said for youth and the culture they inhabit? What special tools do young people bring to the task of theological reflection? What truths might youth be able to discern in the Christian story that adults (with different tools) might overlook?

Just as an artist uses available materials for an art project, a theologian draws upon the language, imagery, and cultural forms available in the immediate environment. Recall how Jesus told parables based in the common business and sociopolitical life of first-century Palestine. Fifteen centuries later Martin Luther led a church reformation movement by translating the Bible into German and describing the gospel in ways that were publicly accessible. And four centuries after that, Martin Luther King Jr. drew from African-American cultural resources to reinterpret biblical images and proclaim a theological message that addressed his country's legacy of slavery and racial segregation. What we bring to the theological task depends upon the available tools in our cultural toolbox. If our toolbox doesn't have a hammer, we might not notice how helpful nails can be until someone arrives with a hammer and shows us how to use it.

---

4. Regardless of how this newfound awareness makes us feel, it's important for youth leaders to model charity toward their families of origin when relating to teens who are still in the process of negotiating their own leave-taking from home.

A panoramic view
Don Richter contends that if we understand the way language functions in culture, we can better grasp the way theology functions in culture as well. He outlines six ways theology operates as a kind of language for Christians:

• Theologies are not universal, but are constructed with the tools available in a given cultural context.

• Theologies both shape their host cultures and are shaped by them.

• Theologies transcend contemporary cultures by pointing to realities beyond the culture.

• Just as we are born with the innate capacity for language, we are born with an innate capacity for faith that comes into being through concrete religious practices in particular faith communities.

• Theologies are partial and may not explain the fullness of God.

• As in language, the broader our theological vocabulary, the larger our repertoire for perceiving God in the world.

Ponderable
Does the word *Whatever!* in young people's vocabulary suggest that they have a "passion for tolerance"? Does a Christian passion for tolerance extend to those who are intolerant of others?

We might spend all our time screwing in screws instead. In a similar vein, biblical scholars learn ancient Hebrew and Greek so they'll have a wider range of tools to use in interpreting Scripture. They realize that the tools we bring to a task determine in large part what we can contribute to the task. And they know that learning to use different cultural tools gives us access to different theological understandings.

Those who minister with youth need to draw upon every available tool in constructing theologies that speak to the cultural contexts of young people. The task before us is daunting: "In the first decade of the 21ST century, America can anticipate the largest generation of teenagers in its history, one even larger than the baby boomer generation that entered its teens four decades ago."[5] Good resources from the past will be available, but the theological reflection necessary to ministry in the 21ST century does not already exist on bookshelves or in seminary classrooms. Evangelizing the *millennial generation* will require the most talented, well-trained, energetic, and faithful group of adult leaders in the history of North American Christianity.[6]

Second, just as theology is profoundly shaped by its host culture, theological claims and concepts powerfully shape culture.

Even a casual observer of the North American scene would concede that the expression "religion and politics don't mix" is, from a descriptive standpoint, both inaccurate and misleading. Consider the role religious values play in shaping school curriculum (for example, evolution versus creation), in framing ethical issues surrounding abortion, and in mustering support for or opposition to capital punishment. Our convictions about God and the nature of things—in light of God's creative and redemptive activity—inevitably influence our positions regarding public policy and political decision-making.

Many teens consider their *personal faith* an important resource for participating in the wider culture. Fewer teens, though, consider *theology* a constructive resource for influencing culture. Theology gives faith a *public face*, a way to communicate our personal faith to others. Yet the face of theology that teens often witness is not pleasant to behold. At home and abroad, youth observe how theology is wielded as an ideological (and sometimes a literal) ax for chopping down all opposing positions. Youth ministry, then, must prepare teens to engage culture with a spirit—and a public face—that is generous and non-defensive. To become responsible agents in the public realm, young people must be nurtured by a passion for tolerance as well as a passion for truth. As a Quaker pacifist once put it: "Tolerance is the battlefield on which the struggle for truth is to be waged."[7]

Holding together a passion for truth and tolerance is not an easy task. It's easier

---

5. Thomas Hine, *The Rise & Fall of the American Teenager* (New York: Avon Books, 1999), 11-12. Hine bases his demographic projection on statistical data found in Youth Indicators, 1996, ed. Thomas Snyder (Washington, D.C.: National Center for Educational Statistics, U.S. Department of Education, 1996).

6. Neil Howe and William Strauss define "the millennial generation" as those born from the early 1980s through the 1990s to Baby Boomer and Generation X parents. This millennial cohort will come of age during the early decades of the new millennium. See *Thirteenth Generation: Abort, Retry, Ignore, Fail?* (New York: Vintage Books, 1993).

7. Cited on p. 113 in Jan Lochman's "Zeal for Truth and Tolerance: Spiritual Presuppositions of Christian Ministry" in the *Princeton Theological Seminary Bulletin*, vol. V, No. 2 (1984): 106-117.

to have a passion for truth or tolerance rather than for both. We've already mentioned people who have such a zeal for truth that they would rather be right than reconciled. Other people show a basic level of respect for others but have no desire to discern or live in obedience to Truth. They have an indiscriminate tolerance, an *anything goes* attitude that refuses to take a stand or be guided by principles and convictions. And then there are people who exhibit a general apathy toward both truth *and* tolerance.

Fortunately, most teenagers have zeal for both truth and tolerance. Youth leaders can familiarize teenagers with theology as a resource for influencing their host culture. When teens learn to articulate and defend their faith perspectives in public settings, when they learn to use language that is broadly accessible rather than resorting to the use of in-house slogans and private code phrases, they discover their political agency and claim their voice as *public theologians*. (See related point six below.)

Third, since theology is an activity of a living faith tradition, theology has the capacity to *transcend* or point beyond the limitations of its host culture.

My host culture tells me that day begins at sunrise and that time is best measured by digital clocks that count seconds, minutes, and hours. A theological account of time, based on my Christian faith tradition, informs me that day begins at *dusk* rather than *dawn* (see Genesis 1) and that the kind of clocks I depend on were invented by Benedictine monks to call their community to prayer at set hours during the course of a day.[8] God's idea of time has little to do with mine. Theology helps me see a truth that is obscured by the temporal limitations of my native culture.

Of course, it is possible for a theological agenda to be so thoroughly determined by the prevailing culture that precious little light can shine through its self-made prison walls. Lest we Christians be smug, we should remember that both Nazi Germany and apartheid South Africa were defended in the name of Christianity. And yet, because Christian theology is always accountable to the gospel of Jesus Christ, light will always break through even in situations of deep darkness.

Archbishop Desmond Tutu has described the gospel's illuminating power to expose and overturn the distorted, racist worldviews that were promulgated under the banner of Christianity in his homeland:

> There is a story, fairly well known, about when the missionaries came to Africa. They had the Bible as we, the natives, had the land. They said, "Let us pray," and we dutifully shut our eyes. When we opened them, why, they now had the land and we had the Bible. It would, on the surface, appear as if we had struck a bad bargain, but the fact of the matter is that we came out of that transaction a great deal better off than when we started. The point is that we were given a priceless gift in the Word of God: the gospel of salvation, the good news of God's love for us that is given so utterly unconditionally. But even more wonderful is the fact

Ponderable
Some theologians believe that our language determines what we can know. In other words, we can only know those things that we can express.[1] Is it possible to know God without having a language to describe God? Do we need a theological language before God becomes real for us?

---

1. For the best-known explanation of this perspective, see George A. Lindbeck, *The Nature of Doctrine: Religion and Theology in a Postliberal Age* (Philadelphia: Westminster Press), 1984.

---

8. See Dorothy C. Bass, *Receiving the Day: Christian Practices for Opening the Gift of Time* (San Francisco: Jossey-Bass, 2000), 15–30.

that we were given the most subversive, most revolutionary thing around. Those who may have wanted to exploit us and to subject us to injustice and oppression should really not have given us the Bible, because that placed dynamite under their nefarious schemes.[9]

When democratic change finally did occur, South African religious leaders resisted efforts to dehumanize and persecute those who had held power. "To dehumanize someone is to commit blasphemy by dishonoring the image of God in that person," Tutu proclaimed. Grounded in the power of the gospel rather than in the cultural script of revenge, South Africa established a Truth and Reconciliation Commission to undertake the painful but necessary task of beginning the healing process among all of its peoples.

We'll return below to consider the gospel's capacity to transcend and transform its host culture. For youth ministry, the implications of this culture-transcending dynamic are substantial indeed. Christian faith provides youth with critical leverage over the limited range of cultural scripts they are handed and expected to perform. These scripts are cultural expectations that ask teenagers to accept prevailing views of adolescence, casting teens in a variety of roles: *questers* on a psychological journey of self-discovery; *consumers* of culture rather than persons who help create and shape their culture; *tourists* wandering aimlessly through a period of life rather than pilgrims seeking a destination for their souls; or *exotic pagans* who have their own subculture that requires (adult) youth workers to be interpreters, field guides, and missionaries.[10]

Ministry that encourages youth to discern their *vocation*—their life calling—can free youth to be the persons God calls them to be. Cultural scripts must still be negotiated, but Christian teens can be set free within the context of these scripts to fashion their own personhood as disciples of Jesus. Learning the language of Christian faith is essential to discerning God's call, for this language invites us to step out of our socially-defined roles and pay attention to the way of abundant life God sets before us. This way of life will not be scripted or preordained, though, but will be more like improvisational theater with God onstage as a companion actor.

Fourth, just as we are born with linguistic capacity that becomes activated through learning a particular language, we are also endowed with spiritual capacity that becomes activated through our participation in particular, concrete religious practices.

It's not uncommon, especially among postmodern people, to hear someone say, "I'm a *spiritual* but not a *religious* person." Typically this means that the person appreciates religious ideas and perspectives, but chooses not to be affiliated with any specific religious tradition. What may feel like "spiritual liberation" to that individual, however, may simply be a repackaging of the values of the contemporary culture and the global

Ponderable
Why do you think our culture casts teenagers in the roles of questers, consumers, tourists, and exotic pagans? Which of these scripts do teenagers seem to play out most often in your context for ministry? Can you think of other cultural scripts we hand to young people?

---

9. Quoted in the preface of John Witte, Jr., and Johan D. van der Vyver, eds., *Religious Human Rights in Global Perspective: Religious Perspectives* (The Hague: Martinus Nijhoff Publishers, 1996), ix.

10. For an elaboration of these insights regarding cultural scripts and vocational youth ministry, see "Reconceiving Youth Ministry," which I coauthored with Doug Magnuson and Michael Baizerman, in *Religious Education* vol. 93, no. 3 (Summer 1998).

marketplace. Taking cues from my surrounding culture, for instance, I might imagine "God" as my warm-and-fuzzy cosmic security blanket, and I might dismiss evil as "uncivilized behavior" or as a failed investment strategy. Without the anchor of specific religious practices that have endured over time, individual spirituality is cast about by winds blowing from every direction. Just as human utterance becomes unintelligible apart from its mooring in specific language, the activities of human spirit lose their mooring and larger significance apart from the logic and form of religious practices.

While different faith traditions may emphasize a similar set of religious practices—worshiping, forgiving, caring for the downtrodden—the practices of each tradition point toward a distinct way of life. *The Christian way of life is characterized by shared activities that address fundamental human needs in response to and in light of God's redemptive activity in Jesus Christ for the life of the world.*[11] Christian practices address fundamental human needs and conditions, thereby involving practitioners in God's activity and purposes in the world. People who are traveling or homeless are vulnerable and in need of food, shelter, and hospitality. People who are estranged need forgiveness and reconciliation. People who are ill need renewal and healing. By offering hospitality, forgiveness, and healing, and by doing so in light of the gospel, Christians confess that we participate in God's providential care for all creation.

The danger in talking about "Christian practices" is that we might delude ourselves into thinking that our salvation has more to do with *human* initiative and goodness than with *God's* initiative and goodness toward us. As one wise preacher has put it: "By the goodness of God we have been born into this world; by the grace of God we have been sustained all the day long, even to this hour; and by the love of God, fully revealed to us in the face of Jesus Christ, we are being redeemed!"[12] Christian practices are a *means of grace* by which God sustains us all the day long throughout our earthly pilgrimage. Indeed, when we participate in a Christian practice such as *singing our lives to God*, we join our voices with the communion of saints who have been singing praises and laments to God for thousands of years.

Participating in Christian practices means becoming part of an ongoing, worldwide community—the church—that has been doing these things for 20 centuries, and that has wisdom to offer about doing them faithfully and well. Beliefs are very important, yet the primary form by which Christian faith has been transmitted—or institutionalized—from generation to generation has been through beliefs embodied as practices. In this broad sense, everyone who participates in Christian practices, in whatever setting and regardless of formal affiliation, is participating in the *institutional church*.[13] A sports analogy: someone who plays golf participates in the ongoing *institution* of golf (with all of golf's specific rules, customs, and lore) even if she doesn't belong to a golf club or association, and even when she's playing a round of golf by herself.

---

11. This definition is adapted from an unpublished essay "Life Abundant: A Theological Understanding of Christian Practices," by Dorothy Bass and Craig Dykstra (November 1999). A description of 12 Christian practices can be found in *Practicing Our Faith: A Way of Life for a Searching People*, edited by Dorothy Bass (San Francisco: Jossey-Bass, 1997).

12. Benediction attributed to the Rev. John Claypool.

13. This is admittedly a Reformed rather than Roman Catholic view of church. Catholic teaching emphasizes that being *in ekklesia* ("in the church") means being in official communion with the Church of Rome.

To join or not to join?
Don offers three reasons why a Christian should be a member of a particular, local congregation.

What do you think of Richter's reasons? Would any of these reasons be compelling for teenagers you know?

So how important is it for a Christian to be a member of a local congregation? What if I can't bring myself to join a local congregation because the members seem too hypocritical? Or what if I make an honest effort to go to church, but most of the time I feel like I'm just going through the motions? Here are guidelines to consider in response to these frequently asked questions:

- *Christians are called to life together in community.* A Christian congregation is a face-to-face, intergenerational community that links people together in a network of care and accountability. A congregation initiates members into Christian practices—especially worship—and holds members accountable over the long haul for practicing their faith on a daily basis. Congregations also provide a place for corporate solidarity in the face of immense pressures urging cultural conformity. Youth ministry is called to build bridges between teens and local congregations, and to assist youth in finding a congregational home in which their faith can be shaped and nurtured.

- *Since the days of the early church, Christians from diverse congregations have been linked by a set of common practices.* That's why Paul's letters to the congregations in Rome and Corinth were included in the Bible. The apostle Paul addressed local concerns in such a way that even today, almost 2,000 years later, congregations benefit from reflecting on their faith community in light of these letters. Paul knew that every congregation has its vices as well as virtues, and that some congregations are deeply conflicted by a spirit that seems more destructive than life-giving. Paul also trusted the Holy Spirit to blow cleansing winds of repentance and breezes of new life within Christian congregations. Youth ministry need not *romanticize* congregations, but can encourage teens to trust that the same purifying Spirit is at work among God's people today.

- *The local congregation or parish is a vital form for Christian community.* There are other settings, however, in which we can learn and participate in Christian practices. Study groups, soup kitchens, parachurch organizations, mission trips, and campus ministries are but a few of the contexts in which faith can be nurtured and enriched. Indeed, experiencing the vitality of Christian practices in a variety of settings helps us focus our spirituality and appreciate how Christian faith extends into every sphere of life. And Jesus did promise that wherever two or three are gathered in his name, he would be in the midst of them (Matthew 18:20). The task for youth ministry, then, is for youth leaders to become more deeply involved in soul-shaping practices of faith ourselves—within congregations and beyond—so that our own lives will have integrity and so that we can invite teens to join us in a *work-in-progress.*[14]

---

14. Kenda Creasy Dean and Ron Foster, *The Godbearing Life: The Art of Soul Tending for Youth Ministry* (Nashville: Upper Room Books, 1998), especially sections 3 and 4. Also, Dorothy C. Bass is editing a forthcoming book on way-of-life practices, addressed to ninth and 10th graders.

Fifth, thinking about how culture functions like a language provides a framework for living faithfully in our postmodern context.

In the *premodern* view of the medieval world, the assumption was that everyone could best understand the world by looking at it the way the church did. If everyone chanted the same hymns (in Latin!) and peered together through the stained glass window of faith, everyone would understand the world in the same way. If folks didn't happen to see the world the way the church did, well, they just needed their vision corrected—nothing a little Inquisition couldn't fix!

In reacting to this premodern worldview, the modern view insisted that people would best understand the world by speaking the common language of science and by observing reality objectively through the clear window pane of reason. The modern worldview of the Enlightenment did not believe coersion was necessary. Modernists were convinced that anyone gazing through a telescope or microscope would observe the same thing. Those who refused to see the world through the eyes of reason were simply choosing to live in ignorance, they surmised.

In reacting to the *hubris* (overconfidence) of modernism, postmodernists reject the notion that there is any objective platform from which everyone can share the same view of reality. Instead of observing through clear glass, we find ourselves viewing reality through a kaleidoscope—the image changes when viewed from different angles by different persons. Instead of using the common language of science or *Esperanto* to describe the world, we recognize how different languages provide different yet valid ways of perceiving reality.[15]

Today, some of us may choose to relate to the world primarily through stained glass and hymn singing—including an occasional Latin chant—but in a postmodern context we no longer assume that this is the *only* correct way to know reality and relate to the world. Even Christians have different ways of viewing the world, since every stained glass window is different. And though we believe that God has been revealed to us in Jesus Christ, human knowledge of divine truth is always partial and imperfect.

Culturally, we respect that all knowledge—like language—is local, intersubjective, and community-specific. Theologically, as Christians we do not presume to know how persons of other faiths are experiencing God in their lives. If we are concerned about the spiritual well-being of friends, neighbors, and strangers who are not Christian, we must make the effort to understand how *they* perceive and relate to God. We must pay careful attention to their life stories—for stories convey our hopes and fears, our joys and sorrows, our faith convictions and deep yearnings. The stories we tell about ourselves, disclose the *practices* that give our lives meaning and purpose (see above).

The challenge for youth ministry is to invite persons into communities that have been deeply formed by the *stories* (as well as practices) of Christian faith. This is not an easy task, for popular culture dismisses stories and proclaims "image is everything." Images are impressionistic and appeal to us at the gut-level of feelings and impulses.

---

15. The artificial international language of Esperanto was developed by L. Zamenhof, a Polish occulist, during the late 19th century as an attempt to homogenize European languages. Zamenhof believed that if Europeans spoke a common language, they would come to see the world in a similar way and nations would cease fighting one another.

That's why the image is king in the advertising business. Advertisements *suggest opportunities* to individuals but rarely present and defend *truth claims* that are subject to communal accountability. From an early age, children are taught to consume advertising images so that by the time they are teenagers, they have learned to be *consumers of culture* rather than *creators of culture*. Even so-called youth culture is produced primarily by adults and sold to teenagers as a commodity. The power of advertising imagery persuades teens that they must purchase their way into youthhood rather than inheriting it by virtue of their chronological status.[16]

The Christian faith story, on the other hand, teaches us that the image of God trumps any other images by which society may label us. Learning what it means to be created in the image of God requires more than reciting slogans and listening to sound bites. Youth yearn for deep familiarity with the biblical story that has been told and treasured for 2,000 years. Youth leaders need to resist moralizing and proof-texting and instead find creative ways for youth to encounter the Bible as *Scripture* (authoritative writings). We trust that the Bible will stake an authority claim on the lives of teenagers when we teach them to sing hymns of praise and psalms of lament; when we invite them to mime, paint, or sculpt a biblical scene; when we direct them in performing the role of biblical characters in plays and musicals. Simply by sharing the biblical story with teens, we provide them with a life-preserving, narrative anchor in a sea of cultural flotsam and jetsam.[17]

Communities shaped by the Christian story are characterized by *accountability and care*. The postmodern market economy appeals to our capacity *to choose* (products), but is not equipped to hold us accountable for our choices and doesn't care whether we choose wisely. Market interests actually benefit from the fragmentation of institutions such as families, schools, and congregations. The logic is simple: *Weak institutional loyalties lead to fragile relationships and a lack of trust that one will be cared for by others. Therefore, one must become self-reliant and care for oneself. The market makes available—for a price—a variety of panaceas and strategies for self-care.* Business leaders don't necessarily conspire to undermine social institutions, but they do have a vested interest in sustaining their market share in a competitive economy.

Youth ministry should strengthen and hold accountable those primary institutions that care for teens on a daily basis. We cannot afford an attitude of ironic detachment or casual disregard for the schools youth attend and the families with which they share a household. Theologically, we view these institutions as instruments of divine providence, as social structures God has provided for our nurture and well-being. Some youth ministries currently partner directly with area colleges, high schools, and middle schools. Other youth ministries advocate *family-based youth ministry* instead of age-segregated youth groups.[18]

Ponderable
Christian ethicist Paul Lehmann defined *koinonia* as "the fellowship-creating reality of Christ's presence in the world."[1] Would you say this is the same thing as Richter's "communities of accountability and care"?

1. Paul L. Lehmann, *Ethics in a Christian Context* (New York: Harper & Row, 1963), 59.

---

16. See Quentin Schultze, and others, *Dancing in the Dark* (Grand Rapids, Michigan: Eerdmans, 1991) and Jean Kilbourne, *Deadly Persuasion: The Addictive Power of Advertising* (New York: Simon & Shuster, 1999).

17. Postmodern philosophers reject "meta-narratives" that seek to organize and interpret experience under the umbrella of grand explanatory systems. In a sense, however, inviting youth to significant encounter with the "strange world of the Bible" (K. Barth) means inviting them to orient their lives in relation to the meta-narrative of Scripture, though acknowledging that not all questions are preformulated and not all answers predetermined.

18. See Mark DeVries, *Family-Based Youth Ministry* (Downers Grove, Illinois: InterVarsity Press, 1994) and Marie J. Thompson, *Family: The Forming Center* (Nashville: Abingdon, 1997).

Becoming a community of accountability and care for teenagers means helping them make wise and responsible choices within the various institutions that support them on a daily basis. In a postmodern era, we cannot expect society in general to teach teens how to live responsibly and faithfully.

Sixth, just as familiarity with different languages makes us aware of the different ways people perceive and describe the world, familiarity with the *vocabulary* of other faith traditions can help us appreciate the diversity of God's creation and the mystery of God's gracious love for all people.

Day by day, the religious landscape of North America is becoming more diverse. Most teens have friends, classmates, and e-mail correspondents of various religious backgrounds. Christian teens view persons of other faiths *not* with anthropological curiosity but with heartfelt concern for their salvation. "Sandra is my best friend at school and she is Hindu. My faith tells me that we can only be saved through faith in Jesus Christ. Does this mean that Sandra will not be saved and that she will go to hell? How can this be fair?! Sandra's a much better person than I am."

A youth leader could use this occasion to say a truthful word about how salvation is a matter of grace rather than good works, yet this would still not satisfy the more urgent concern being expressed about Sandra's well-being as my friend. Youth leaders can help teens identify the ways we are *interconnected* with others, as well as the ways in which we are *different* from one another. We can then approach our neighbors with the attitude that together, we can both learn more about the life of faith and the world around us, without surrendering our deepest convictions or requiring others to conform to ours. The ground rule for interfaith dialogue is that all partners remain both *committed* to their respective faiths and *open* to the insights of others.[19]

Christians believe that God was specifically revealed and embodied in the person of Jesus of Nazareth, whom we confess is Jesus the Christ (the Messiah). This is the good news we have received that we are eager to share with others, including persons of other faith traditions. *Testimony* means bearing witness to the truth as we have seen and heard and experienced it. Truthful speech is not coercive or manipulative but has a way of opening up space for others to add their own witness to the presence of God in the world.[20] Youth ministry should nurture teens in this practice of telling the truth to one another and to God. This requires attentive listening to the testimony of others, especially to those who live on the margins of our culture. By remaining open to the testimony of the outsider and the other, we remain open to mystery and to the new word God may have for us this very day.

We've examined the interplay between *theology* and *culture*, showing how one term always points toward the other. We've also explored the crucial role language plays in mediating both theology and culture. Many of these claims would hold for any religious tradition, but some point more directly toward Christianity. In the final section,

More ways than one?

Catholic theologian Hans Kung suggests that instead of insisting on the axiom, "There is no salvation outside the church," Christians would do better to insist: "There is salvation inside the church!"[1] Richter suggests that in a postmodern context, we can no longer assume that *our* way of knowing reality and relating to the world is the only way of doing so. "As Christians," he writes, "we do not presume to know how persons of other faiths are experiencing God in their lives."

Do you agree? Are Kung and Richter compromising Jesus' exclusive claims of salvation (cf. John 3:18; 14:6), or providing a viable alternative for sharing the Christian story in a postmodern culture? As a Christian youth minister, how do you see yourself relating to young people of other faiths?

1. Hans Kung, *The Church* (Garden City, New York: Image Books, 1976), 410.

19. See M. Thomas Thangaraj, *Relating to People of Other Religions: What Every Christian Needs to Know* (Nashville: Abingdon, 1997).

20. See the chapter of Thomas Hoyt, Jr., on the practice of "testimony" in *Practicing Our Faith*, 91-103.

we turn specifically to *Christian* theology by investigating what *incarnation* and *redemption* mean for our understanding of culture, and we identify implications for our ministry with youth.

Incarnation and redemption

Christians believe that God is not just an abstract principle or distant cosmic designer. At the heart of Christian faith is the scandalous claim that God assumed human flesh—actually became human—and dwelt among us in the person of Jesus of Nazareth. In the midst of a Greco-Roman culture that viewed *spirit* as sacred and *matter* as corrupt, Christianity was considered an abomination by many because of its blatant concern for the material world. Throughout the pages of the New Testament, we read that the early church's concern for people's spiritual well-being always required concern for their physical well-being, too. To be fair, the Jewish tradition had a significant "this-worldly" emphasis that Jesus magnified in his teaching and healing ministry. But the doctrine of the Incarnation thrust the Christian community into a radically new relationship to culture—a paradoxical relationship that continues to this day.

First, in Jesus of Nazareth, the Almighty God graciously accommodated our limited human capacities and understanding, becoming embodied in human form (a man) at a particular time and place.

Likewise, Christian faith does not come to us *out of the blue*, but always comes to us embodied through the concrete material stuff of our culture such as word, water, bread, and cup.

Jesus typically spoke to his followers in Aramaic, his native tongue. Likewise, we believe that the gospel can be mediated to us today in our native tongue. Jesus encountered folks in the midst of their daily lives and occupations. Likewise, we believe that Christ can encounter and accompany us in the midst of our concrete, individual circumstances. There's no *naked truth*, because Christian faith—like all other faiths—always wears the clothing of a particular culture. And yet, instead of designating culturally specific objects, words, and places as *sacred*, Christianity evolved as a religion that can make sacred use of any available objects, words, and places.

This points to a second feature of incarnational Christianity: Christian faith relativizes every culture it inhabits, viewing no particular culture as more special than any other.

For Islam, Arabic is the sacred language of the Koran, and Mecca is the holy city for the hajj pilgrimage. For Christianity, sacred Scripture can readily be translated into any language, and any place can become a sanctuary for experiencing the presence of God. The first Christians were Jewish, yet the early church determined that Gentile converts need not become ritually Jewish on their way to becoming Christian (Acts

The accomodation principle
Accommodation means to oblige or adjust oneself to another. Augustine described the Incarnation as God's accommodation to human limitations. Since human beings cannot adjust to God, God adjusted to human nature and became one of us. John Calvin viewed Scripture as God's gentle way of approaching human beings in a way we could grasp, since we are far too weak to handle God's undiluted revelation. Citing Augustine, Calvin noted: "We can safely follow Scripture, which walks softly, as with a mother's step, in accommodation to our weakness."[1]

Don Richter advises youth ministers to be guided by an "accommodation principle." What would ministry look like in a congregation that took accommodation to young people seriously?

1. John Calvin, *Institutes*, Book III, Chapter 21.

A Gen-Xer's open letter to the church: tell the story
Responding to churches' frustration with how to reach Gen-Xers who think truth is relative and suffering is inevitable, Xer Sarah Hinlicky writes:

"So, you're in quite a pickle: you can't tell us that the church has 'the Truth,' and we know that the church won't miraculously cure us of our misery. What do you have left to persuade us? One thing: the story. We are story people. We know narratives, not ideas. Our surrogate parents were the TV and the VCR . . . You wonder why we're so self-destructive, but we're looking for one story with staying power, the destruction and redemption of our own lives. That's to your advantage: you have the best redemption story on the market."[1]

_____

Add to your glossary
• _Paradox:_ the holding together of two contradictory views without collapsing one into the other. A paradox from physics is how light behaves as both particle and wave. The Incarnation is the central paradox of Christian faith: Jesus Christ was both human and divine at the same time.
• _Redeem:_ to buy or win back, to free from captivity, to release from blame or debt, to repair or restore.

10). God revealed to the early church that the gospel—the Good News of Jesus Christ—can be embodied in and through every culture. Indeed, the gospel has a way of infiltrating and eventually transforming every culture it inhabits.

Youth ministry must be guided by this _accommodation principle._ We must not expect teenagers to bear the primary burden of accommodating themselves to our agenda, schedule, and program design. We begin by discerning how to accommodate our ministry to the capacities and life-worlds of teenagers. This does not mean simply throwing our hands up in despair because young people in our town are already over-programmed. Accommodation first means _making room_ for youth in our hearts and minds, paying attention to where youth gather and how they spend their time, energy, and money. Youth leaders need to go where youth already are and address them within the context of their daily lives.

Today _going where youth already are_ involves forays into cyberspace as well as trips to the local mall. Responsible youth ministry will learn to make use of a wide range of cultural media for communicating gospel, including the Internet and the World Wide Web.[21] But the accommodation principle does not mean that all forms of communication with youth must be explicit and direct. Sometimes the most powerful forms of communication are _indirect._ When the scribes and Pharisees grumbled about Jesus' poor judgment in choosing dinner companions, Jesus did not launch into a lecture about the virtues of God's come-as-you-are, open-table eating policy. That would have been direct communication. Instead, Jesus told three short stories—parables—about a shepherd searching for a lost sheep, a woman searching for a lost coin, and a father longing to be reunited with his two lost sons (Luke 15). These three stories communicate indirectly to Jesus' accusers that God cares for _everyone_ who is lost, including those who are lost due to stubborn self-righteousness. Jesus invites all who "overhear the gospel"—including his disciples today—to see themselves as characters in his stories of judgment and grace and to decide how they will now live in relation to the existence possibility these stories convey.

Storytelling is a powerful vehicle for indirect communication. So are other art forms such as drama, role-play, singing, sculpting, mime, mask-making, dance, film, poetry, and silent contemplation. The key to indirect communication is not the teacher's technique, but rather the teacher's focus and intention. For example, if I mime the story of blind Bartimaeus receiving sight from Jesus (Mark 10:46-52), I must perform the mime with passionate integrity and trust the Spirit to communicate through the mime. I can't allow myself to become self-conscious about appearing foolish to my teenage audience. My direct focus is on the biblical story and on my own relationship to God whom I encounter in that story. Indirectly, my intent is to invite youth to decide for or against the new way of life—the new way of _seeing_—that this gospel proclamation reveals to them. As a teacher or youth leader, I must trust my subject matter implicitly and show radical respect for the freedom of learners to say yes or no to

_____

21. Instead of teens resorting to anonymous chat rooms, they can enjoy online "conversations" by means of a church-sponsored bulletin board or a listserv that monitors subscriptions. Likewise, youth leaders can offer young people navigational tips on Web sites that communicate the gospel effectively and help teens explore their faith convictions more deeply. And creating a group Web site can catalyze teens to give a "public face" to their faith convictions. An important caveat: Web sites must not feature photos or personal contact information for individual youths.

Unhelpful ways Christians relate to culture

Here are four common attitudes Christians hold toward "the world."

• *Christian yellow pages.* "The world is evil and corrupt, so we must band together and develop an alternate culture to insulate our young people from contact with the nonredeemed world." We are not called to insulate ourselves from others, but to go into all the world proclaiming the gospel of Jesus Christ.

• *Vaccination.* "The world may be corrupt, but since I've been inoculated by Christian faith I'm immune to the seductions of culture." Rather than being wary of the powers of darkness, we confidently assume that we are invulnerable to temptation. Our capacity for self-deception and self-justification is great; we need a faith community to hold us accountable, to help us detect, confess, and resist sin.

• *Sin's a sham.* "Persons who are enlightened by Christ come to see the world as good rather than as fallen, and come to understand sin and evil as illusions that have no power." The cosmic struggle between good and evil continues, so we do not deny the very real consequences of evil's potential to destroy and corrupt.

• *Pop culture preaches.* "Since every human culture expresses religious impulses and longings—at least implicitly—we can simply immerse ourselves in popular culture to find God." It's one thing to claim that culture has religious significance and that we can reflect on culture (including popular culture) theologically. It's another thing, however, to turn to contemporary pop culture for spiritual guidance and nourishment. Pop culture cannot "preach" unless we put it into dynamic interplay with the stories and imagery of the gospel.

what is presented, resisting my impulse to interfere with their heartfelt responses, even when their responses are not what I had hoped for.[22]

But what if teens reject the invitation or misunderstand it? That's precisely the risk God took in accommodating to humanity in Jesus Christ! God so greatly desires human freedom that God permits us to turn our backs and walk away from the fountain of new life and the table of grace. Yet even when we reject God, God still pursues us to offer us redemption. Of course, being Christian does not remove us from the world like some *Invasion of the Body Snatchers* movie. As described above, the Christian faith tradition has a complex and paradoxical relationship to culture.

What does our experience of redemption mean for the way Christian youth relate to their surrounding culture? As Christians, we are called to be *in the world but not of the world*. Being *in* but not *of* the world means that Christians experience a profound sense of freedom in whatever cultural circumstances they find themselves. It's helpful to think of Christian freedom as *freedom from* and *freedom for*. For example, Christians are called to be good citizens, to pay their taxes, and to support just laws and political leaders. Yet Christians are *free from* giving ultimate allegiance to anyone or anything but God. Knowing that God is our only true source of security frees us from anxiously trying to save and secure ourselves. This is important good news to share with teenagers who are (understandably) worried about their future prospects in a shifting global economy.

Trusting God with our lives frees us from all cultural scripts that tempt us to be less than God is calling us to be. Teenagers live in a cultural era when public space that welcomes them is becoming more limited and when the range of socially permissible behaviors for them is becoming more restrictive. Christianity's *radical* freedom provides youth with critical leverage over the limited range of cultural scripts they are handed and expected to perform. Teenagers—and all of us—need to hear the good news that we are more than the sum total of our SAT scores, our trophies, our résumés, and our net worth. The knowledge that sets us free is that we are created in the image of God; redeemed by God's accommodation to us through the incarnation of Jesus Christ; and accompanied throughout our earthly pilgrimage (and beyond) by Christ's Spirit who teaches us daily how to be in the world but not of the world. That's *real freedom*, the kind of freedom that will give young people the theological wisdom to navigate their way through culture—including the Internet—for years to come.

---

22. In *The Courage to Teach* (San Francisco: Jossey-Bass, 1998), Parker Palmer explains how good teaching is neither teacher-centered nor student-centered but subject-centered: "In a subject-centered classroom, the teacher's central task is to give the great thing [the subject] an independent voice—a capacity to speak its truth quite apart from the teacher's voice in terms that students can hear and understand. When the great thing speaks for itself, teachers and students are more likely to come into a genuine learning community, a community that does not collapse into the egos of students or teacher but knows itself accountable to the subject at its core" (118).

Youth Ministry's Historical Context: The Education and Evangelism of Young People
Mark W. Cannister

The conversion/nurture continuum
Mark Cannister's contrast between youth ministry as mission and youth ministry as education grows out of much larger theological question that has framed the church's response to young people for centuries: Is the objective of ministry with young people conversion or nurture?

Clearly, conversion and nurture are both critical. Christian history (and youth ministry is no exception) is filled with excesses and correctives:

- The Protestant Reformation emerged to protest the church's skewed view of good works, while reformers lifted up the biblical promise of salvation through faith instead.
- The Great Awakening called those disaffected by the state church's rational view of faith into revivals, where preachers urged them to give their hearts as well as their minds to God.
- After World War II, parachurch youth movements like Young Life and Youth for Christ stressed the doctrine of personal salvation, which they believed mainstream congregational youth programs had overlooked.
- Meanwhile, liberal congregational youth programs emphasized

Pinpointing the genesis of youth ministry is not as simple as one might imagine. Some would point to the Twelve as a starting point. Others would argue for the Society for Christian Endeavor, which was established in churches in 1881. Still others point to Young Life's beginnings in the early 1940s. This disparity of consensus on the history of youth ministry occurs because the field of youth ministry has never been well defined. Is youth ministry a missional discipline or an educational discipline of practical theology, or both? How should youth ministry be defined sociologically and psychologically? The way we outline the history of youth ministry is greatly dependent upon how we answer these definitional questions.

Therefore, we must make some definitional assumptions about theology and adolescence at the outset. This chapter takes the position that youth ministry concerns the period of human development sociologically defined as adolescence. It also accepts that, historically, missiology and Christian education have been considered distinct categories of practical theology. This distinction has created definitional problems. Youth ministry that does not intentionally evangelize the life stage known as *adolescence* is not genuine youth ministry. On the other hand, youth ministry that is void of educational components—both those that initiate young people into the faith and mature those who have grown up in the faith—should not be considered genuine youth ministry either. Therefore, youth ministry must include theology from both the missional and educational fields of practical theology.

Unfortunately, when studying the history of youth ministry and Christian education, it is easy to be seduced into a reductionistic paradigm that places *youth evangelism* and *youth education* at odds with each other. While it is important to understand this tension as it is revealed in history, it is equally important to reflect on the impact these issues have on contemporary youth ministry and on the history of youth ministry that is yet to be written.

A Youth Ministry Timeline for the United States[1]

1. Generational names and dates are taken from William Strauss and Neil Howe, *Generations: The History of American's Future, 1584-2069* (New York: Quill/William Morrow), 1991. The dates suggested here are more ambiguous than those suggested by Strauss and Howe, to reflect the editors' conviction that generational divides are never precise.

				1780	1785
				William Raikes starts first Sunday school in Gloucester, England	William Elliot opens first North American Sunday school in Virginia

1740s-70s The Great Awakening

1740s-1760s: The Republican Generation: preparing for democracy

1760s-1790s: The Compromise Generation: the post-heroic era

| 1740 | 1750 | 1760 | 1770 | 1780 | 1790 |

Jesus' call to youth to join in God's transformation of society, which they believed the para-church youth ministries ignored.

Historically, youth ministry—like churches and the people who populate them—has vacillated between a concern for conversion and a concern for nurture.[1] Where do you locate your own understanding of the purpose of youth ministry? Are you more likely to use conversion or nurture as a theological starting point for youth ministry?

---

1. John Westerhoff, *Will Our Children Have Faith?* (San Francisco: Harper & Row, 1976), 38.

The historical roots of Christian education

Christian education may be traced back to the apostolic church, where the apostles' primary responsibility was to educate baptismal candidates (*catechumeni*), which almost always followed immediately after Christian conversion.[1] In the second century the *Didache*, or *The Teaching of the Twelve Apostles*, appeared in the post-apostolic church as a catechetical manual for the instruction of baptismal candidates following their conversion. By the end of the second century, the Alexandrian catechetical school had become highly influential in the development of Christian education. As in the apostolic and post-apostolic church, catechetical religious instruction occurred most often following a person's conversion, as they prepared for baptism. This instruction was instituted for adults wherever Christianity reached, providing a foundational doctrinal orientation, moral education, and instruction in reading and writing.

By the middle of the fifth century, Christians were withdrawing from the moral decay of Roman culture. Monastic communities were formed that provided shelter from the cultural immorality as well as formal education, but the Great Commission of Jesus seemed to have been forgotten as Christianity became an isolated society. Coming out of the Middle Ages, the Renaissance ushered in the great intellectual awakening of the modern era. Unfortunately, this awakening was a missed opportunity for Christian education, where faith instruction faded behind the invention of the modern university. In a time of unparalleled human progress, Christian scholars chose to participate in developing secular fields of inquiry, rather than in efforts aimed at biblical correctives to a humanistic worldview. This worldview placed human reason in a position of ultimate authority, and gave rise to an educational philosophy that focused solely on the acquisition of knowledge. Some Christian theologians finally did take issue with the humanistic worldview by taking part in ecclesial reform, including the Protestant Reformation.

While a number of theologians such as John Knox in Scotland, Philip Melanchthon in Germany, and Huldreich Zwingli in Switzerland should be credited with sustaining the Protestant Reformation, it was Martin Luther and John Calvin whose thoughts and vision most directly influenced Christian education. Calvin emphasized the educational responsibility of the church and developed a philosophy of teaching for lifestyle transformation rather than simply the acquisition of knowledge.

---

1. James Reed and Ronnie Prevost, *A History of Christian Education* (Nashville: Broadman, 1993), 69-70.

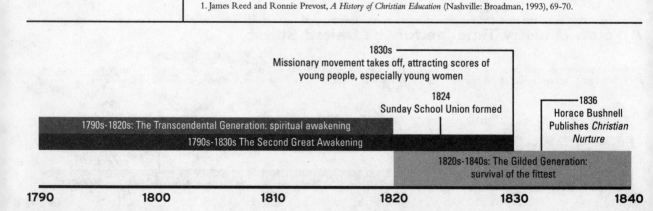

1830s — Missionary movement takes off, attracting scores of young people, especially young women

1824 Sunday School Union formed

1836 Horace Bushnell Publishes *Christian Nurture*

1790s-1820s: The Transcendental Generation: spiritual awakening

1790s-1830s The Second Great Awakening

1820s-1840s: The Gilded Generation: survival of the fittest

| 1790 | 1800 | 1810 | 1820 | 1830 | 1840 |

Luther focused on the educational responsibility of the home, the centrality of Scripture, and education of all people. The combined influence of Luther and Calvin significantly wrested Christian education from the domination of Greek philosophy and Renaissance humanism.[2]

After two centuries of humanism's intellectual influence, Robert Raikes, a man of moderate wealth and champion of the poor, determined that educating delinquent children could curb their vice and moral degeneration. In 1780 he recruited the impoverished children of Gloucester, England, to his first Sunday school. Raikes' primary objective was literacy training. However, students were also given some Christian education as they were taught to read the Bible, memorize catechisms, and required to attend worship.[3]

As the Sunday schools of Great Britain multiplied, William Elliot of Virginia opened a Sunday school in 1785 modeled after Raikes' vision, and the Sunday school movement spread across the United States. The American Sunday School Union was formed in 1824 with the goal of planting Sunday schools throughout the Mississippi Valley, which was then the western frontier of America. This work resulted in over 30,000 professions of faith throughout the Mississippi Valley. By the middle of the 1800s, the American Sunday School Union was struggling to provide oversight for the thousands of new Sunday schools planted during this period. As the Sunday School Union became divided along denominational lines, the movement's unified vision disintegrated and teaching deteriorated into oral recitations of memory verses.[4] The great exception to this was the Sunday school established in Chicago by Dwight L. Moody in 1859. Moody focused on evangelism in his Sunday school, and by 1863 enrolled over 1,500 students. Following the Civil War, Moody and a group of men known as the Illinois Band transformed the Sunday school movement into a mission of evangelical Protestantism.[5]

The Young Men's Christian Association (YMCA), which began in England in 1844, was introduced in America in 1851, followed by the YWCA in 1858. Initially the

Add to your glossary
- *Catechesis*: literally, to *echo back* (orally) or to *hand down* the beliefs and practices of Christian tradition from one generation to the next.
- *Catechumen*: a candidate for baptism in the early church, who was undergoing instruction in the beliefs and practices of Christian faith
- *Catechist*: a teacher of the Christian faith; originally, someone who instructed catechumens preparing for baptism
- *Catechism*: a form of religious instruction developed during the Reformation, in which children learned the principles of faith in question-and-answer form.

2. Reed and Prevost, 197–198.

3. Reed and Prevost, 255–258.

4. See Mark Senter, *The Coming Revolution in Youth Ministry* (Wheaton, Illinois: Victor Books, 1992).

5. Robert Lynn and Elliot Wright, *The Big Little School* (Birmingham, Alabama: Religious Education Press, 1971), 56.

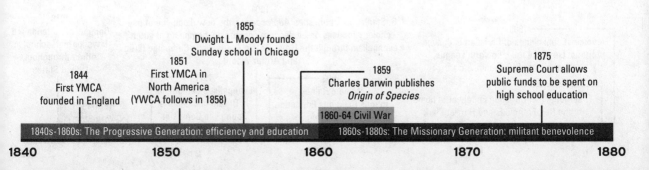

1855
Dwight L. Moody founds
Sunday school in Chicago

1851
First YMCA in
North America
(YWCA follows in 1858)

1844
First YMCA
founded in England

1859
Charles Darwin publishes
Origin of Species

1875
Supreme Court allows
public funds to be spent on
high school education

1860-64 Civil War

1840s-1860s: The Progressive Generation: efficiency and education   1860s-1880s: The Missionary Generation: militant benevolence

1840   1850   1860   1870   1880

School on Sunday

The Sunday school movement began in England during the Industrial Revolution as a way to provide an education to children who worked in the factories during the week. Since these children could not attend weekday school with wealthy young people, they met for Sunday school. Although the Bible was the primary textbook used in the Sunday schools (it was the primary text for the weekday schools as well), *catechesis*, or "handing on" the beliefs and practices of Christian tradition, was secondary to the goals of teaching reading, writing, and arithmetic.

Most of us have experienced Sunday school in quite the opposite manner. Yet more and more people are turning back to schools as contexts for Christian education. Christian colleges, the home school movement, and the increasing number of schools being started in and by churches are just a few examples of how Raikes' vision of the Sunday "school" is being reconsidered for contemporary young people.

What makes Christian education "Christian"? Should today's Christian education include liberal arts education, as it did until well into the Enlightenment? Or is Christian education properly understood as faith formation independent from a liberal arts education? Where does youth ministry fit into the education of young people?

purpose of the YMCA was "to help Christian young people retain their Christian commitments after they had moved into the urban jungles where jobs were available."[6] The evangelical spirit of the men who gathered at the YMCAs drove the organization to an evangelistic ministry that witnessed revival from 1857–1859. Over this two-year period, the churches of America received over one million converts.[7]

While the Sunday school and the YMCA became established throughout the 19TH century as vehicles for making and retaining professions of faith, Horace Bushnell was being prepared to play another role in Christian education, which would not be fully realized until after his death in 1875. While attending Yale, Bushnell's participation in a revival that swept the campus in 1831 resulted in his conversion. Bushnell entered the divinity school, from which he graduated in1833, and became pastor of the North Congregational Church in Hartford, Connecticut, where he served for 26 years.[8]

In his first few years as a pastor, Bushnell attempted to recreate the spirit of the Yale revival. The results were not encouraging. In 1836 Bushnell wrote, "The most disheartening impediment to the Christian minister is the thought that religion depends only on revivals."[9] At that point Bushnell rejected revivalism and turned to a theology of Christian nurture placing an emphasis on his thesis that "the child is to grow up Christian and never know himself as being otherwise."[10]

This phrase became the watchword of the Christian nurture movement. Although not fully embraced until the early 20TH century, the impact of Horace Bushnell's thought on Christian education is immeasurable. As Christian educators Kenneth Gangel and Warren Benson put it:

> At the first meeting of the Religious Education Association in 1903, George Albert Coe, the leading theorist in liberal Christian education circles during the first 50 years of the 20TH century, appealed to the writings of Horace Bushnell as the driving force behind that growing

---

6. Senter, 90.

7. Charles Howard Hopkins, *History of the YMCA in North America* (New York: Associated Press, 1951), 81.

8. William Adamson, *Bushnell Rediscovered* (Philadelphia: United Church Press, 1966), 13–20.

9. William Johnson, *Nature and the Supernatural in the Theology of Horace Bushnell* (Lund: CWK Gleerup, 1963), 108

10. Horace Bushnell, *Christian Nurture* (Grand Rapids: Baker Books, 1861), 10.

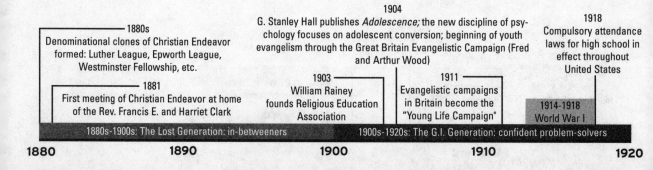

1880s
Denominational clones of Christian Endeavor formed: Luther League, Epworth League, Westminster Fellowship, etc.

1904
G. Stanley Hall publishes *Adolescence;* the new discipline of psychology focuses on adolescent conversion; beginning of youth evangelism through the Great Britain Evangelistic Campaign (Fred and Arthur Wood)

1918
Compulsory attendance laws for high school in effect throughout United States

1881
First meeting of Christian Endeavor at home of the Rev. Francis E. and Harriet Clark

1903
William Rainey founds Religious Education Association

1911
Evangelistic campaigns in Britain become the "Young Life Campaign"

1914-1918
World War I

1880s-1900s: The Lost Generation: in-betweeners

1900s-1920s: The G.I. Generation: confident problem-solvers

| 1880 | 1890 | 1900 | 1910 | 1920 |

Altar-ed states

The two greatest periods of religious revival in American history—the First Great Awakening of the 1740s-1780s, and the Second Great Awakening of the early 1800s—were primarily youth movements. Revivals not only attracted young people; they were often started by them. By the early 1800s, religious conversion was normative for teenagers across all major Protestant denominational lines.[1] When Horace Bushnell penned *Christian Nurture* in 1836, he challenged the dominant theological assumptions of his age, urging Christian nurturists to resist revivalism's emphasis on human responsibility in conversion. It took another 50 years for childrearing, education, and religion to acknowledge the importance of environment in the shaping of character—which probably explains why Bushnell's ideas were largely dismissed until after his death.

––––––––––––
1. Joseph Kett, *Rites of Passage* (New York: Basic, 1977), 64; Sidney Ahlstrom, *A Religious History of the American People*, vol. 1 (Garden City, New York: Image, 1975), 178.

Ponderable

Do you think it is possible for a child "to grow up Christian and never know himself [or herself] as being otherwise" in a pluralistic, postmodern, interfaith culture?

movement. Bushnell's theory that people could be educated into Christian faith with no need for conversion fit right in with the modern Christian education views. Bushnell's writings were not widely accepted while he was still living. But after his death, and on into the 20TH century, Horace Bushnell was and is considered one of the dominant forces in the development of Christian education as a separate discipline. Although his theological basis was questionable at best, his thesis that "a child should grow up Christian" is still one of the most critical thoughts in the field of Christian education.[11]

Bushnell's influence on the Sunday school movement was minimal in the 19TH century; raising children as if they had always been Christian seemed contrary to the prevailing evangelical spirit of the age and the Moody curriculum that viewed children as "little adults" needing conversion. As the father of the socialization approach to Christian education, Bushnell's influential offspring include liberal Christian educator George Albert Coe, conservative Lawrence O. Richards, and C. Ellis Nelson and John H. Westerhoff III in the theological middle. Each of these theorists, irrespective of theological leanings, has grounded his theory of Christian education on the concepts of Bushnellian nurture.[12] Ever since the missionary thrust of the Sunday school movement in the 19TH century, Christian education has most often been concerned with nurturing those within the church, rather than evangelizing those outside of it.[13]

The arrival of adolescence at the turn of the century

In the last quarter of the 19TH century, a sociological phenomenon occurred that created the concept of adolescence. For most of human history, the lifecycle was divided only into childhood and adulthood—the transition between these being marked by puberty. Prior to the 19TH century, puberty began as late as age 17 in women, yet over

––––––––––––
11. Kenneth Gangel and Warren Benson, *Christian Education: Its History and Philosophy* (Chicago: Moody Press), 281.

12. Lynn and Wright, 80–81.

13. See Daniel C. Stevens, "The Theology of Christian Education," in *Foundations of Ministry*, ed. Michael Anthony (Wheaton, Illinois: Victor Books, 1992).

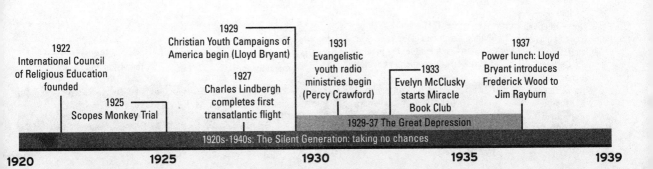

1922
International Council of Religious Education founded

1925
Scopes Monkey Trial

1929
Christian Youth Campaigns of America begin (Lloyd Bryant)

1927
Charles Lindbergh completes first transatlantic flight

1931
Evangelistic youth radio ministries begin (Percy Crawford)

1933
Evelyn McClusky starts Miracle Book Club

1937
Power lunch: Lloyd Bryant introduces Frederick Wood to Jim Rayburn

1929-37 The Great Depression

1920s-1940s: The Silent Generation: taking no chances

1920   1925   1930   1935   1939

the past 150 years the onset of puberty has fallen to age 12 or below.[14] While the age of puberty fell in most industrialized nations, the minimum legal age of marriage was being raised (from 12 to 18 in the United States.) This began to create the period of life we now call adolescence. Christian educator Ronald Koteskey notes, "For the first time people were not allowed to make adult decisions at the age of puberty."[15] Today adolescence is commonly defined as the period between puberty and economic independence.

In addition to the recession of the age of puberty and the rise of the age of marriage, in 1875 the United States Supreme Court allowed tax money to be spent on high school education. This assured that nearly all young people would extend their adolescence from puberty through high school graduation. By 1918 every state in the union had established compulsory attendance laws requiring students to attend high school through at least 16 years of age, thus delaying teenagers' entrance into the workforce.[16]

Given the assumption that youth ministry is defined as a ministry to adolescents, we would be hard pressed to demonstrate that youth ministry existed prior to the late 19TH century. The first possible youth ministry movement would have been the Society for Christian Endeavor, which is best described as a youth education movement as it was theologically based on Bushnell's theology of Christian nurture and geared for youth within the church.

Youth ministry as education: socializing youth for the church

An historical snapshot of the last quarter of the 19TH century reveals a time when the age of puberty was decreasing, the age of marriage was increasing, public high schools were multiplying, and Bushnell's theory of nurture was being embraced. It was in this context that Francis E. Clark and the Society for Christian Endeavor stepped onto the scene in 1881.

Clark, the Pastor of Williston Church in Portland, Maine, and his wife, Harriet, had been looking for a way to assist the young people of their congregational church

14. See Patricia Davis, *Counseling Adolescent Girls* (Minneapolis: Augsburg Fortress, 1996).

15. Ronald Kotesky, Understnading Adolescence (Wheaton, Illinois: Victor Books, 1987), 15

16. Edward Krug, *The Shaping of the American High School, 1920-1940*, I (Madison, Wisconsin: University of Wisconsin Press, 1972).

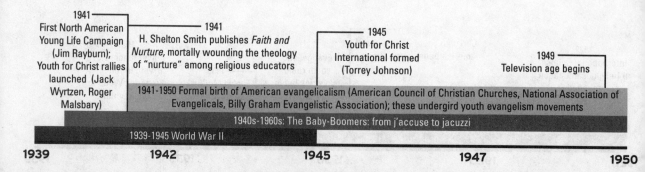

1941
First North American Young Life Campaign (Jim Rayburn); Youth for Christ rallies launched (Jack Wyrtzen, Roger Malsbary)

1941
H. Shelton Smith publishes *Faith and Nurture,* mortally wounding the theology of "nurture" among religious educators

1945
Youth for Christ International formed (Torrey Johnson)

1949
Television age begins

1941-1950 Formal birth of American evangelicalism (American Council of Christian Churches, National Association of Evangelicals, Billy Graham Evangelistic Association); these undergird youth evangelism movements

1940s-1960s: The Baby-Boomers: from j'accuse to jacuzzi

1939-1945 World War II

1939   1942   1945   1947   1950

to *continue* in their Christian faith after an initial salvation experience. Clark's vision for Christian Endeavor grew from a simple goal of maintaining the faith of the youth of his church to the broader impact that Christian Endeavor might have on the youth in other congregations as an inter-denominational fellowship. The original objective of the society was "to promote an earnest Christian life among its members, to increase their mutual acquaintance, and to make them more useful in the service to God."[17]

Membership in the society was open to young people between the ages of 13 and 30 and was divided into two classes, active and associate. The active members were required to sign a pledge that indicated they were earnest Christians willing to be held accountable for their "Christian Endeavor." Associate members were young people unwilling to call themselves Christians, but were interested in the fellowship and activities of the society.

In 1882 Clark published his first book concerning the need for and the distinctiveness of Christian Endeavor.[18] This book clearly placed the theology of Francis Clark under the influence of Horace Bushnell. Consider Clark's description of his first tome as he reflected on it 10 years after its initial publication:

> This little volume does not describe simply the methods of the Society of Christian Endeavor.
>
> As its main title indicates—"The Children and the Church"—it seeks to cover the larger ground of Christian nurture, and its central thought may be considered "growth from within, rather than conquest from without" as expressed in the chapter on Church Membership for Children.
>
> "What nation," it says, "would neglect its own children and rely for growth on conquered foreigners? Even Napoleon, king of conquest though he was, was wiser than this. Though he laid every nation under tribute to France, his constant principle was: France must depend upon the children born upon her soil for her strength and glory rather then

---

17. Francis Clark, *World Wide Endeavor: The Story of the Young People's Society for Christian Endeavor from the Beginnings and in All Lands* (Philadelphia: Gillespei, Metzgar & Kelly, 1895), 57.

18. See Francis Clark, *The Children and the Church and the Young People's Society for Christian Endeavor as a Means of Bringing Them Together* (Boston: Congregational Sunday School and Publishing Company, 1882).

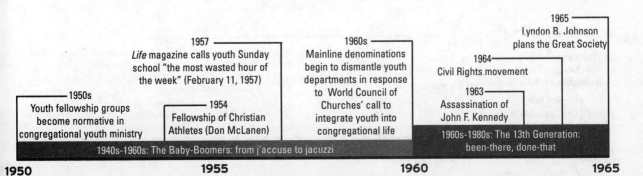

1965
Lyndon B. Johnson plans the Great Society

1957
Life magazine calls youth Sunday school "the most wasted hour of the week" (February 11, 1957)

1960s
Mainline denominations begin to dismantle youth departments in response to World Council of Churches' call to integrate youth into congregational life

1964
Civil Rights movement

1963
Assassination of John F. Kennedy

1950s
Youth fellowship groups become normative in congregational youth ministry

1954
Fellowship of Christian Athletes (Don McLanen)

1960s-1980s: The 13th Generation: been-there, done-that

1940s-1960s: The Baby-Boomers: from j'accuse to jacuzzi

1950   **1955**   **1960**   **1965**

upon the annexation of alien nations."

"No nation can long thrive by a spirit of conquest," says Dr. Bushnell. "No more can a church. There must be internal growth. Let us try if we may not train up our children in the way they should go. Simply this, if we can do it, will make the church multiply her numbers many fold more rapidly than now, with the advantage that more will be gained from without than now."

This quotation from Dr. Bushnell leads me to acknowledge my indebtedness to his most stimulating book entitled *Christian Nurture*.

Though it contains no hint of the methods of the Society of Christian Endeavor, it is the most thought-provoking and fascinating volume ever written on this subject of Christian training of children. I wish that every parent, as well as every minister, might read it.[19]

Even though the primary focus of Christian Endeavor was clearly the Christian nurture of the church's young people, there was a missional undercurrent that resulted from the class of associate membership. Evangelism in the society was not that of the pulpit pounding, finger pointing, proclamational preaching of the Great Awakenings, as there was very little preaching or instruction at society meetings. The missionary method was relational and testimonial. Christian Endeavor was open to "seekers" interested in exploring the Christian faith, but was by no means reaching out the heathens of secular society. Clark made this important distinction concerning the associate members of the society (italics mine):

> The associate membership of the society is for those who are *facing upward*, from a life of indifference and worldliness or childish carelessness, to an Alpine height of Christian devotion; *not* for those who put their hands to the plough and are looking back; *not* for those who have made a profession of their love for better things and are looking down to the flesh-pots of Egypt.[20]

---

19. Clark, *World Wide Endeavor*, 136–137.

20. Clark, *World Wide Endeavor*, 259.

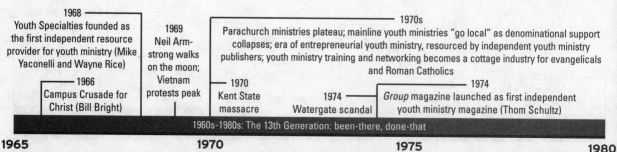

1968 — Youth Specialties founded as the first independent resource provider for youth ministry (Mike Yaconelli and Wayne Rice)

1966 — Campus Crusade for Christ (Bill Bright)

1969 — Neil Armstrong walks on the moon; Vietnam protests peak

1970 — Kent State massacre

1974 — Watergate scandal

1970s — Parachurch ministries plateau; mainline youth ministries "go local" as denominational support collapses; era of entrepreneurial youth ministry, resourced by independent youth ministry publishers; youth ministry training and networking becomes a cottage industry for evangelicals and Roman Catholics

1974 — *Group* magazine launched as first independent youth ministry magazine (Thom Schultz)

1960s-1980s: The 13th Generation: been-there, done-that

1965   1970   1975   1980

Christian Endeavor viewed associate membership as a first step to an active Christian life and required a keen interest in moving toward that end.

As Clark's ideas were popularized through books, articles, program materials, and the success of conferences and conventions, denominational groups took notice. By the turn of the century, nearly all of the major denominations had formed youth societies modeled after Christian Endeavor. Mark Senter comments on the new focus of these denominational clones of Christian Endeavor:

> The Christian Endeavor idea was designed to sustain a spiritual awakening among young people. Fulfilling the pledge kept members endeavored to discover God in what Clark considered historically proven ways. Even risking a type of legalism, which could creep into the prescribed disciplines, the founder felt the possible danger was worth the hazard. But soon after denominational societies were formed, new lives inhabited the "shell." The new societies broadened their focus to include teaching denominational loyalty, and leadership development. Though worthy objectives, these life forms used the "shell" in an increasingly different manner.[21]

In 1922, 40 denominational boards and 33 state councils of churches came together to form the International Council of Religious Education (ICRE). The ICRE had a strong liberal influence on the organizational form and theological focus of youth work. Youth society meetings also came to be dictated by denominational agendas and focused on topics concerning stewardship, social issues, and denominational distinctives, rather than studying the Bible. By 1935 both the Sunday school and the youth societies had fallen on hard times in the liberal churches. "The spiritual depression throughout the land was equal to the economic depression that gripped America from 1930 to 1937."[22]

Throughout the first quarter of the 20TH century, conservative and fundamental churches and denominations were nurturing their youth without the support of a national coalition akin to the liberal's ICRE. The single event that marked the beginning

21. Senter, 68.

22. Roy B. Zuck and Warren S. Benson (eds.), *Youth Education in the Church* (Chicago: Moody Press, 1978), 62.

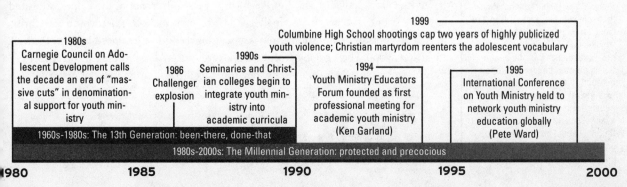

1980s
Carnegie Council on Adolescent Development calls the decade an era of "massive cuts" in denominational support for youth ministry

1986
Challenger explosion

1990s
Seminaries and Christian colleges begin to integrate youth ministry into academic curricula

1999
Columbine High School shootings cap two years of highly publicized youth violence; Christian martyrdom reenters the adolescent vocabulary

1994
Youth Ministry Educators Forum founded as first professional meeting for academic youth ministry (Ken Garland)

1995
International Conference on Youth Ministry held to network youth ministry education globally (Pete Ward)

1960s-1980s: The 13th Generation: been-there, done-that

1980s-2000s: The Millennial Generation: protected and precocious

1980   1985   1990   1995   2000

Mission: evangelism only?
Mark suggests that "missional" youth ministry primarily engages in evangelism, since its goal is "reaching youth for Christ." Of course, the church is by its very nature missionary, in that the love of God flows through the church into the world—which means that the entire church, and not just missionaries and youth ministers, is called to spread the gospel. Scottish missionary Lesslie Newbigin has defined mission as that aspect of ministry that "[crosses] the frontier between faith in Christ as Lord and unbelief."[1] But what does crossing that frontier look like?

Missiologist David Bosch pointed out that each period of Christian history has yielded a distinctive answer to that question.[2] As a result, evangelism is only one way to think about mission, just as nurture is only one way to think about Christian education. Some theologians, including Dietrich Bonhoeffer, have viewed mission as the church being alongside others, especially those in need, to await God's revelation. Others, like John Mbiti, think mission mediates Christ's salvation of the cosmos as well as of individuals. Some people equate mission with the quest for justice (Willem Visser 't Hooft) or liberation (Gustavo Guttierez, Julia Esquivel) while others discuss mission in terms of contextualization (Juan Segundo), enculturation (Laurenti Magesa), common witness (Karl Barth), or action-in-hope (Jurgen Moltmann).[3]

Many retain the connection between mission and evangelism, but redefine "evangelism" in order to avoid triumphalist connotations that separate the "saved" from the "lost." According to Sri Lankan missiologist D.T. Niles, for example, "Evangelism…is one beggar telling another beggar where to get food."[4] Mother Teresa viewed evangelization (a term sometimes equated with a broad view of evangelism) as transparency to Christ: "Let the poor, seeing you, be drawn to Christ."[5]

A missionary is one who is sent,

of the end of the conservative youth societies—and from which fundamentalism has yet to recover—was the 1925 Scopes Monkey Trial:

> This [Scopes Monkey Trial] proved to be the biggest public relations disaster of all time for fundamentalism. Fundamentalists came to be seen as intolerant, backward, and ignorant dolts who stood outside the mainstream of American culture. From that moment onward, fundamentalism became as much a cultural stereotype as a religious movement. It could not hope to win support among the educated and cultural elites within mainline Protestantism. The damage inflicted would never be undone. It was only with the emergence of a new form of evangelicalism after the Second World War that momentum and credibility were regained.[23]

As world events during the early 20TH century drew young people's attention—and young people themselves—away from young people's societies to war, economic hardship, and matters of survival, the educational curriculum of youth ministry seemed rooted in a distant past. Christian educators Donald Pugh and Milford Sholund, observing the landscape of Protestant youth work by the early 1930s, note: "The basic teachings of the Bible on the sinfulness of human nature, the atoning work of Christ on the cross, and the call to world evangelism were lacking in the purposes, plans, and programs of young people's organizations."[24]

While adolescence had come into its own during the early 20TH century, and Christian Endeavor was clearly ministering to these adolescents, this form of youth ministry was primarily concerned with children of believers since its theology was based on Bushnell's theory of nurture. Christian Endeavor and its denominational clones are best identified as the first significant *Christian education* movements for adolescents. Adolescent ministry was on the verge of being defined as far more than simply an age category of Christian education. Meanwhile, adolescents themselves seemed ripe for something new.

The youth ministry as evangelism: reaching youth for Christ

The Great Depression and World War II solidified the identity of adolescence as a new sociological phenomenon in America. By 1930 high school enrollment in America had increased to over 6.6 million students and the existence of adolescent culture could no longer be denied.[25] There was a new mission field that the mainline denominations had not recognized. But people like Arthur Wood, Lloyd Bryant, Jack Wyrtzen, Evelyn McClusky, Percy Crawford, and Jim Rayburn were keenly aware of the culture surrounding young people as they unknowingly launched a movement to reach youth for Christ.

The concept of a missional ministry to adolescents can be traced back to Fredrick and Arthur Wood. These young Irish evangelists set out in 1904 to preach the gospel across Great Britain. After seven years they came to the realization that the majority of

---

23. Alister McGrath, *An Introduction to Christianity* (Cambridge, Massachusetts: Blackwell Publishers, 1997), 331.

24. Donald Pugh and Milford Sholund, "A Historical Survey of Youth Work," in Roy B. Zuck and Warren S. Benson (eds.), *Youth Education in the Church* (Chicago: Moody Press, 1978), 62.

25. Senter, 107-109.

especially one who is sent across boundaries. The early church viewed mission as the *missio Dei* (mission of God). This made God in Jesus Christ a missionary, one sent across every boundary imaginable, across geographic, cultural and political borders, but also across the boundaries of space and time and life and death in order to bring the good news of God's salvation into the world.

In your view, what should be the objective of youth ministry "as mission"? How is this different from youth ministry "as education"? Are mission and education adequate to describe the tasks of youth ministry?

---

1. Lesslie Newbigin, *One Body, One Gospel, One World* (New York: Internationalal Missionary Council, 1958), 28.

2. David J. Bosch, *Transforming Mission* (Maryknoll, New York: Orbis Books), 1991.

3. Each of these views is represented in Norman Thomas (ed.), *Classic Texts in Mission and World Christianity* (Maryknoll, New York: Orbis Books), 1995.

4. D.T. Niles, in *Classic Texts in Mission*

5. Mother Teresa, *Total Surrender*, revised ed. (Ann Arbor, Michigan: Servant Publications, 1995), 149-150, 156.

their converts were young people. Their new vision, to focus on winning young people to Christ, was launched in 1911 with a series of Young Life Campaigns throughout Great Britain. The campaigns reached thousands of young people and expanded so fast that the National Young Life Campaign was formed and headquartered in London.

In 1929 Lloyd Bryant felt called by God to reach millions of young people in America who had no religious connections. The result was The Christian Youth Campaign of America. By 1932 these rallies attracted significant crowds in the Times Square district of New York City on Monday and Tuesday nights. The name was changed in 1935 to The Association of Christian Youth in America and the ministry was restructured on the model of the Young Life Campaign in England.

In 1931 Percy Crawford began the Young People's Church of the Air in Philadelphia and Australian evangelist Paul Guiness visited Brantford, Canada, with the mission of planting a Christian youth movement in high schools and colleges. In 1934 Oscar Gillian created the "Voice of Christian Youth" radio program to reach young people in Southern California. In 1933 Evelyn McClusky established the Miracle Book Club in Portland, Oregon, which by 1938 had planted over 1,000 clubs across the country.[26] The four goals of the Miracle Book Club were—

1. To invite high school students to salvation in Christ
2. To help converts realize and understand the true meaning of Christ living in them
3. To enable converts to successfully implement a new Christian lifestyle
4. To teach students how to become Christian conversationalist in witnessing to their peers.[27]

McClusky's clubs attracted people into leadership positions who went on to significantly impact the Youth for Christ movement. Jim Rayburn, who later established Young Life, USA served as the Miracle Book Club state director in Texas in 1940. Jack Hamilton (who later founded the Youth for Christ club programs) and Al Metsker were vice president and president, respectively, of the first Miracle Book Club chapter in Kansas City in 1941.

Unlike Christian Endeavor and the youth societies, whose primary purpose was to nurture the young people of the church, these youth ministries of the early and mid-30s focused on winning converts. The theological distinctions between revival and nurture, conversion and education, and evangelism and discipleship had come to a crossroads. In 1937 Fredrick Wood and his wife accepted the invitation of Lloyd Bryant to visit the United States. While in Texas, the Woods met a young seminarian named Jim Rayburn. With the blessing of Wood, Rayburn started the Young Life Campaign in the United States in 1941. Rayburn's initial ministry was very similar to the campaigns in Great Britain. However, by the middle of the 1940s the Young Life rallies had taken a back seat to the exploding club and camping programs.[28]

---

26. Senter, 74.

27. See Evelyn McClusky, *Torch and Sword: A Handbook for Leadership of Young People* (Richmond, California: The Miracle Book Club, 1937).

28. Melvin G. Larson, *Youth for Christ: Twentieth Century Wonder* (Grand Rapids: Zondervan, 1947), 33.

Parachurch youth movements
Many 20ᵀᴴ-century youth ministry movements focusing on evangelism were parachurch ministries.

The parachurch youth organizations that emerged in the 1940s were designed to reach young people for Christ who were not already attending church. In practice, however, these ministries have appealed primarily to church kids, who have comprised the bulk of their membership.[1] This often creates tension between parachurch and congregational youth ministries.

How do you view the relationship between parachurch and congregation-based youth ministries? What do congregations offer youth that parachurch ministries cannot, and vice versa? How will you advise students who may have to choose one over the other?

_____
1. See Mark Senter, *The Coming Revolution in Youth Ministry* (Wheaton, Illinois: Victor Books, 1992), 130; also Shirley R. Postlethwaite, "The Young Life Campaign: A Study and Evaluation," unpublished Th.M. thesis, Princeton Theological Seminary, 1956.

Also in 1941, Jack Wyrtzen launched a Tuesday morning radio broadcast called "Word of Life." His coast-to-coast broadcasts were extremely successful as they galvanized many of the youth ministries that had come before. On April 1, 1944 Wyrtzen's youth rally drew over 20,000 people in Madison Square Garden, and 10,000 were turned away. Similarly, Roger Malsbary rented a theater in Indianapolis to hold a Christian youth rally. Malsbary invited the Chicago preacher Torrey Johnson to speak at the first Indianapolis Youth for Christ rally on May 27, 1943. Soon Dick Harvey and George Wilson were holding rallies in St. Louis and Minneapolis where auditoriums were filled to capacity.

As pastor of the Midwest Bible Church in Chicago, Torrey Johnson was a significant player in the National Association of Evangelicals (NAE). Johnson assembled a vast array of talented people and on May 26, 1944, the first Chicagoland Youth for Christ rally was held in Orchestra Hall with a young local pastor named Billy Graham preaching. On October 21, 1944, a rally was held at Chicago Stadium drawing 28,000 people. The first anniversary of Chicagoland Youth for Christ was celebrated on May 30, 1945, with a rally at Soldier Field where 70,000 people assembled to hear the preaching of Percy Crawford.

From there Youth for Christ rallies sprang up across the country as advice and expertise were shared freely among directors. Speakers would comment: "It's much easier to preach in Youth for Christ meetings than any other place, as the power of the Holy Spirit is felt so much."[29] Roger Malsbary sensed the need for an international organization that would bring together those with similar convictions of winning youth for Christ. On July 29, 1945, Youth for Christ International was officially formed and Torrey Johnson was named president. The first article of the 1945 constitution "set forth the four-fold aim of Youth for Christ International:

1. To promote and help win youth for Christ everywhere
2. To encourage evangelism everywhere
3. To emphasize radiant, victorious Christian living
4. To foster international service of youth through existing agencies."[30]

As a leader in the NAE, Johnson brought to Youth for Christ the vision of Harrold Ockenga, the first president of NAE. The NAE was fully supportive of Johnson and viewed Youth for Christ not only as an evangelistic mission to unchurched youth, but also as an ally in winning adolescents away from the older liberal denominational youth societies. Youth for Christ International and the NAE were the two primary organizations that laid the foundation for evangelicalism. Commenting on the impact of this alliance, McLoughlin states—

> Because of this, and because Youth for Christ organized its rallies upon the most flamboyant lines, hiring large auditoriums or stadiums, plaster-

_____
29. Larson, 50.

30. Larson, 88.

ing the city with posters, bringing jazzy musical groups into their programs, and instilling the whole movement with the aura of an adolescent crusade for fundamentalism, the pastors of the regular churches
denounced it as divisive, emotional, and spiritually shallow. The *Christian
Century's* editor called Youth for Christ "a streamlined expression of a
traditionally conservative type of revivalism" which was "little concerned
with the social or ethical bearing of the Christian faith."[31]

Despite such criticisms, the Youth for Christ organization thrived under Johnson's leadership. His most important decision was to recruit Billy Graham as Youth for Christ's
first paid field representative in 1945, traveling and preaching at rallies throughout
North America and Great Britain. Graham had worked with Johnson in the Youth for
Christ movement for a couple years as a speaker and radio preacher while pastoring a
small church in suburban Chicago. When Graham left the church to become an itiner-
ant preacher at Youth for Christ rallies, the organization became even more aggressively
evangelistic. Graham was the spearhead for citywide revivals designed to win over converts through spiritual ecumenicalism, much to the delight of Ockenga and the NAE.[32]

At the 1949 summer convention of Youth for Christ, Harrold Ockenga proclaimed that it was time for a spiritual revival and by the spring of 1950 the president
of the NAE declared that revival was in fact breaking out across the land. The youth
evangelists were on the front lines of this spiritual awakening. Billy Graham and others
were reaching thousands of people through their evangelistic preaching. As McGrath
puts it, "Billy Graham, the most publicly visible representative of this new evangelical
style, became a well-known figure in many western societies, and a role model for a
younger generation of evangelicals."[33]

As in the case of Christian Endeavor, the success of Youth for Christ caught the
attention of the denominational church. Some denominational groups such as the Baptist Youth Movement copied the formula of Youth for Christ. Some other denominations—as well as Christian Endeavor—condemned Youth for Christ as shallow and not
church-centered. Just four months after Youth for Christ was officially formed, the
Christian Endeavor board of trustees established the Youth Marches for Christ and the
Church. This was an attempt to unite Christian agencies and churches in organizing
young people "under the banner of their faith for the highest goals of citizenship, community service, and brotherhood."[34]

The development of the Youth for Christ movement and the development of
evangelicalism cannot be separated. It is here that the theological roots of youth evangelism were developed in stark contrast to the theology of nurture upon which youth
education had been founded.

---

31. William G. McLoughlin, *Modern Revivalism* (New York: Rolland Press Co., 1959), 480.

32. McLoughlin, 487–489.

33. McGrath, 333.

34. Larson, 47.

Conclusion

As the Wood brothers, Evelyn McClusky, Roger Malsbary, Torrey Johnson, Jim Rayburn, Jack Wyrtzen, Percy Crawford, Jack Hamilton, and a host of evangelical youth ministries developed throughout the mid-20TH century, the purpose of youth ministry was to reach irreligious adolescents with the gospel of Christ. At the same time many churches and denominations, especially those affiliated with the National Council of Churches, were content to continue their youth societies, focusing on the nurture of teenagers who they claimed were being raised in the faith.

Since the end of the 19TH century, the Christian education of youth has generally been based upon the theology of nurture, primarily due to the influence of Bushnell and Coe at the end of the 19TH century. Youth evangelism grew out of revivalism and has typically been based upon a missional theology. Understanding the history of these two facets of youth ministry should be helpful in developing a more holistic theology of youth ministry for the future. As we enter the 21ST century, it is important that youth ministry become committed to turning lost adolescents into fully committed disciples of Jesus. This will require both a missional and an educational theology to frame this essential ministry of the church. Not long ago Mike Yaconelli, cofounder and president of Youth Specialties, suggested that youth ministers are not social workers or counselors or family therapists or activities coordinators or programmers. While youth ministers certainly help kids relate to their families, engage in social services, counsel, and program, youth ministry has historically been missional and educational in nature. The purpose of youth ministry according to Yaconelli is this: "Youth ministry is about bringing kids into the presence of Jesus Christ."[35]

This is the aim of the Great Commission. Youth ministry must be both missional and educational—concerned with both evangelism and discipleship. While the dichotomy between missions and education, evangelism and discipleship, youth ministry and Christian education is part of our history, it is a false theological dichotomy. The purpose of ministry to adolescents cannot be one-sided. The ultimate purpose is to get kids committed to the long and costly journey of following Jesus Christ. And those involved in the leadership of youth ministry would do well to think more deeply about the relationship of missional and educational theology to a holistic view of youth ministry as the next chapter of our history unfolds.

35. Mike Yaconelli, *The Heart of Youth Ministry*, video (Grand Rapids, Michigan: Zondervan/Youth Specialties, 1995).

5 Chapter

Reflections on Youth Ministry in a Global Context: Taking Seriously the Least of These
Tony Campolo

Global what?

When somebody mentions the "global context" for youth ministry, I think of things like mission projects in poor villages of Mexico or Haiti, or maybe the faces of children in the photos from Compassion, International who are sponsored by the youth at our church.

Actually, however, ministry in the 21st century takes place in a global context whether or not we leave home. *Globalization* is used to describe our sense that the world has become a single place, thanks to the increasingly connected nature of communication systems (like computers and the entertainment media), transportation systems (especially air travel), and economic systems (such as multinational corporations like McDonald's and Toyota).[1]

Christians are called to think and live in a way that points to the sacrificial love of Jesus Christ. In a world where globalization increasingly shapes our culture, where we know our global neighbors' faces better and better, and where the chasm between those who have what they want and those who lack what they need grows wider, youth ministry calls for prophetic discernment and risk, as well as compassionate commitment and care.

1. See Roland Robertson, *Globalization: Social Theory and Global Culture* (London: Sage), 1992. For a more readable summary of globalization theories, try Malcolm Waters, *Globalization* (London and New York: Routledge), 1995.

During the past quarter of a century, middle-class churches in general, and Christian youth groups in particular, have discovered the poor. Teenagers have *planned famines* in which they fast for one meal or a day to feel what hungry people experience as commonplace. *Short-term* mission trips to third-world countries often replace church camp on the summer agenda. Doing *something* for the homeless is just about a *must* for any suburban youth group.

The motivations behind all of this so-called social action are varied. One woman told a youth worker that she wanted to have her children see how poor people live, so that they would be more grateful for what they had. An intensely evangelistic youth pastor wanted to help the poor because that would make them more willing to listen to the salvation story. Then there was the high school cheerleader who testified that the best thing about helping the poor was how it made her feel.

Often we give little attention to what we do *to* the poor in the midst of all of this. Ivan Illich, the famous Swiss missionary to Brazil, criticized church youth groups that traveled to poor countries to help "unfortunate people." He claimed that whatever good might be done through these excursions into the world of the poor was more than negated by the assault on their dignity and the dehumanization experienced by the poor who are visited.[1]

The sacramental poor

A biblically based theology to govern encounters with the poor can help prevent such ugly exploitation of people by altruistically motivated young people who really want to help. When it comes to a theology of the poor, there are few who can match that developed by Francis of Assisi.[2] This 10th-century saint let us know in no uncertain terms that the poor were, as he called them, *sacramental*, and not just objects of pity. What Francis meant by the term *sacramental* is that the eternal Christ somehow infuses the poor so that, as we meet them face to face, we are meeting not only the poor, but encountering something of the presence of Christ. To Francis, the poor were not Christ, but he believed that Christ came through the poor to those who would look into their eyes with spiritual discernment. Even as Lutherans believe that there is a real presence of Christ in the bread and the wine in Holy Communion (though the elements still remain bread and wine), so Francis believed that, though the poor remain what they are, Christ flows through them to those who have eyes to see him and ears

1. Ivan Illich, speech for the Inter-American Student Projects, 1970.

2. An easy-to-read overview of the life and thought of St. Francis is C.K. Chesterton, *St. Francis of Assisi* (Garden City, New York: Image Books, 1957).

to hear him. Mother Teresa caught what Francis meant by this when she said, "Every time I look in to the eyes of a poor man dying of AIDS, I have this eerie awareness that Jesus is staring back at me."

Learning what Francis tried to tell us can radically transform our encounters with the poor. Young people can be delivered from condescending pity with its dehumanizing effects. Instead of pity, they can learn to encounter the poor with reverence, to ask only if they are worthy of the privilege of ministering to such a sacred people. Francis wanted us to take literally the words of Jesus who said, "whatever you did for one of the least of these...you did for me" (Matthew 25:40). It would benefit any church youth group to spend time discussing Matthew 25:31–46, because this is the passage that molded Francis' thinking about the poor. As young people study this passage, it will alter the way they perceive the poor and help them to become a servant people.

Having a Franciscan disposition when encountering the poor can motivate young people into action. Sensing Christ's suffering in the poor, they will *want* to act. And what they want to do will change them. We are mistaken if we think that change in a person comes about only through intellectual arguments. We often fail to recognize that, while what young people think and believe can determine what they do, it is equally true that what young people do can determine what they think and believe. Conversion can and does occur in the context of *praxis*.[3] Time and time again, young people give witness to having experienced Christ in a "real" way while working among the poor. For many of them, this was the first time they had a mystical encounter with Christ, and often they testify that is was through such encounters that they really became Christians.

Getting teenagers to help the poor will earn the support of almost everyone in a typical church congregation. Organizing them to build houses for Habitat for Humanity will mark up credit for the youth worker with the church's Christian education committee. Getting teenagers to participate in a march for the homeless may result in a flattering article in the town paper. But should a church youth group begin to deal with the *causes* of poverty, and start to advocate political policy changes to ameliorate the sufferings of the oppressed, the responses from the larger community might not be so positive.

Bishop Oscar Romero, the martyred leader of the Nicaraguan church, once observed: "When I feed the poor, they call me a saint. When I ask *why* the poor are poor, they call me a communist." Nevertheless, more and more Christian youth are doing just that. They are asking, "What makes the poor *poor*?" And what they find sometimes radicalizes their politics, which in turn upsets the good people of the church. Sooner or later, investigating teenagers realize that there is something very wrong with the social system, and that Christian responsibility requires that something be done about it.

Sacramental or detrimental?

Tony Campolo critiques the "condescending pity" common to many approaches to Christian outreach. Outreach undertaken for the sake of inspiring gratitude among the privileged, for the sake of priming youth for the story of salvation, or for the sake of making youth feel good about themselves assault the dignity and the humanity of the poor. Yet Campolo also suggests that when young people encounter the poor with a "Franciscan disposition," they often report a mystical encounter that leads them to becoming Christians.

Does a sacramental view of the poor empower them to be bearers of God's grace? Or does it dehumanize the poor by making them "teachable moments" for the sake of more affluent youth?

---

3. *Praxis* is a style of learning that requires reflection in the context of action. Those who apprehend truth through praxis believe that it is only when involved in existential struggles that we are capable of understanding what special interests and justifying ideologies are operative in defining the situation. For a fuller explanation of praxis in Christian thinking, see chapter 5 of Jose Miguez Bonino, *Doing Theology in a Revolutionary Situation* (Philadelphia: Fortress Press, 1975).

Youth ministry and the kingdom of God

To be faithful to all that Scripture teaches, the youth worker must lead young people to recognize that the gospel is not simply a story of individualistic salvation. The gospel is not about offering personal benefits to believers in the here and now, and pie-in-the-sky when they die. Sooner or later, the youth worker must point out that the gospel declares that the kingdom of God is at hand (Matthew 4:17). This kingdom requires justice for the poor. It is imperative that the up and coming generation recognize that the biblical Jesus was committed to the realization of a new social order *in this world*, in which the hungry will be fed; the naked will be clothed; and the poor will receive "good news" (Luke 4:18-19).

When Christ entered history, he did so to create a people through whom he could begin to change this world into the kind of world God willed for it to be when the world was created. This is why Jesus taught us to pray, "your kingdom come, your will be done, *on earth* as it is in heaven" (Matthew 6:9-13, italics added). His teachings and parables were about the kingdom, and the last things Jesus taught his disciples before ascending into heaven concerned the kingdom of God (Acts 1:3).[4]

The kingdom of God is a societal system wherein things are ordered according to God's will. In this kingdom there will be no poverty. No children will die in infancy because of a lack of nutrition and medical care; no ghetto teenagers will be blown away in gang warfare; everyone will have decent housing; and everyone will have a fair income derived from properly rewarded labor (Isaiah 65:17-25). The calling for Christian youth is to join with God in creating that kingdom here and now, while living in the expectation that at the second coming the good work initiated through them will be completed (Philippians 1:6). Becoming a Christian, therefore, is a call to social action. When young people understand this and begin to challenge injustices inherent in the dominant socioeconomic system, they are likely to experience opposition from those church members who have a vested interest in maintaining things just as they are.

The apostle Paul warns that, in any effort to transform this world into God's kingdom, we must wrestle against principalities and powers and rulers in high places (Ephesians 6:12). For many Christian young people, this may require them to become countercultural. This was not difficult to imagine in the rebellious '60s, but for many youth at the turn of the century, who seem to have become all too comfortable with our affluent, attractive, seductive American social system, acting counterculturally can be very hard to do. It may mean opposing government policies or even standing against the destructive practices of multinational corporations from which their parents earn their livings.

The apostle Paul admonishes Christians that struggling against "the principalities and powers" of society is what *spiritual warfare* is all about. When he uses that phrase, Paul is not simply talking about demonic spirits or fallen angels, but is referring to any and all superhuman forces or institutions that exercise controlling influences on human behavior.[5] For instance, the educational system is such a principality and power, in that

---

4. See A.M. Hunter, *Interpreting the Parables* (Naperville, Illinois: SCM Book Club, 1960).

5. See Albert van den Heuvel, *These Rebellious Powers* (Naperville, Illinois: SCM Book Club, 1966).

it wields great influence over the consciousness of children and teenagers. The components of the economic system, with its corporate structures and its labor unions, also may be understood as principalities and powers. Likewise, political parties and administrations deserve this designation. And certainly the media, with their awesome opinion-creating abilities, deserve to be called principalities and powers. According to theologian Hendrik Berkhof, one of Karl Barth's favorite students, all principalities and powers were ordained into existence by God. Berkhof's reading of Colossians 1:16 ("For by him all things were created: things in heaven and on earth, visible and invisible, whether thrones or powers or rulers or authorities; all things were created by him and for him.") leads us to believe that God is the creative force behind their formation. Berkhof contends that God wills all social institutions into existence. However, following Paul's teachings, Berkhof also believes that these principalities and powers have taken on a life of their own, and have become rebellious against the will of their creator. Instead of facilitating good for humanity, as God intended them to do, these principalities and powers often became instruments of demonic forces that oppress people—especially poor people. Berkhof points out that the Pauline epistles call upon us to struggle against the principalities and powers (Ephesians 6:12) and calls the church to recognize that one of its responsibilities is to bring them into subjection to Christ (Ephesians 1:22).[6]

Challenging principalities and powers: opportunities for youth ministry in a global context

Youth workers who accept this interpretation of Paul's teachings will probably challenge young people to recognize that being social activists is part of what it means to be Christian. Organizing young people to challenge educational bureaucracies that inadequately fund schools in poor neighborhoods and to attack unions that protect incompetent teachers will be seen as part of youth ministry. Calling upon young people to help elect politicians who are committed to such things as alleviating the oppression of third world countries and providing health care for the poor in the United States will be viewed as the ministry of youth workers. It does little good to sensitize young people to the sufferings of the poor or to help them see how principalities and powers create the sufferings that the poor must endure, unless we can also help young people see how they can change oppressive social structures to reflect God's justice.

Scenario: reducing third-world debt

In England, some Christian young people who wanted to challenge the principalities and powers oppressing the poor have formed an organization called SPEAK, which has lobbied for justice with various world governments. In their efforts to combat poverty, these young people have called upon the political leaders of rich countries to cancel the debts owed to them by third-world countries. They point out that, in the past, dic-

---

6. See Hendrik Berkhof, *Christ and the Powers* (Scottdale, Pennsylvania: Herald Press), 1962.

tators of poor nations often borrowed money from rich nations to finance, among other things, gigantic war machines. In many instances, these totalitarian rulers pocketed for themselves billions of dollars that were earmarked for public assistance. All of this left the general public of these third-world nations deeply in debt, and today as much as half of all the tax dollars these people pay to their governments must be spent *just to pay the interest on what they owe*. This leaves little money for education, public health, and welfare. The young people involved in SPEAK contend that only if these debts are canceled can third-world countries begin to find the resources necessary to meet the basic needs of the poor.[7]

Efforts to cancel the debts of the world's poor nations will be challenged by many in our churches. Those who demand lower taxes for middle class American families know that canceling the debts of third-world countries will interfere with having these demands met.[8] At a recent meeting of Baptist leaders, a woman declared, "If those people in Third World countries are ever going to become responsible, they must recognize that they have got some debts to pay off." Even Christians may not realize that the poor who are victimized by such debts are not the ones who incurred them.

Senario: challenging unjust welfare reform

Many Christians accepted without question the recent changes in the American welfare systems. But while some saw the government's actions as welfare reform, others saw it as welfare repeal. Some Christians were concerned that new welfare laws lacked adequate directives controlling the bloc grants made to states to help welfare recipients make the transition to holding jobs. These people contended that if single mothers were to be forced off the welfare rolls, then adequate day care must be provided for their children, and proper job training must be made available to them. To express their concerns, a group of some 40 Christian activists demonstrated on behalf of those poor young people affected by these changes, and were arrested in the rotunda of the Capitol Building in Washington, D.C.

Practicing civil disobedience in this manner seemed right to them, but to other thoughtful Christians, unlawful demonstration such as this was contrary to what Romans 13 teaches about being submissive to the government: "Everyone must submit himself to the governing authorities, for there is no authority except that which God has established. The authorities that exist have been established by God" (Romans 13:1). This is just one example of how standing against the government on behalf of the poor can be polarizing and controversial for the church. The youth worker who gets the church's young people involved in such activities might soon be out of a job.

Senario: opposing corporate abuse

At Eastern College, near Philadelphia, some young people decided to get involved in a stockholders' action against a large multinational company on behalf of the poor. These

---

7. For information on SPEAK, write to Louise Donkin, 38 St. Mary's Park, Louth, Lincolnshire, LN11 OEF, United Kingdom.

8. Christian Coalition, *Contract with the American Family* (Nashville: Moorings, 1996).

undergraduates focused on a corporation that controlled the sugar production in a small Caribbean nation. They bought stock in that corporation, and then attended stockholders' meetings to voice their concerns. They wanted the local company to raise the low wages paid to the sugar cutters and to provide medical care and education for the children who lived under the company's jurisdiction. Incredibly, after these students brought up their concerns at the annual stockholders' meeting, the corporation was responsive to their pleas. Over a five-year period, the corporation spent more than a half billion dollars to do what was right in the third-world country where it did business. But let it be known: a great deal of criticism followed these young women and men from church people who thought such action was inappropriate for Christian young people.[9]

Scenario: standing for environmental stewardship

Environmentalism is another issue that initiates a great deal of conflict within the life of the church with respect to the poor. Christian social action groups such as Evangelicals for Social Action and Target Earth have recognized the link between the plight of the poor and the destruction of the natural environment.[10] For instance, while the population of Haiti, the poorest country in the Western Hemisphere, grows exponentially, the land available to grow food for its people is diminishing drastically. Almost 70 percent of the land that was usable for growing crops just two decades ago has now been eroded and rendered infertile. Each year, an area of the Amazon rain forest the size of the state of Washington is destroyed, displacing indigenous people and contributing to an oncoming ecological disaster. Meanwhile, in the Sahel region of Africa, the process of desertification is occurring so quickly that the Sahara Desert, which is the size of the United States, is expanding southward at the rate of two miles per year.

Everybody knows that as the earth loses its capacity to support all of its people, the poor will suffer disproportionately. Young people are being educated to understand the implications of the environmental holocaust for the poor. However, many adults remain indifferent to the ecological disaster that is at hand. Some question whether the effort and expense of environmental awareness are really necessary. Some suggest that environmentalism endangers North American capitalism because its cost could render some of our industries less competitive in the world market. Still others see environmentalists' crusades as a cover-up for the New Age movement, believing environmentalism to be a satanic effort to lure young people away from the true God. Regardless of their motives, adults are aware that environmental care will require tax dollars and will restrict the *laissez faire* practices of government with regard to industries.[11]

---

9. See Anthony Campolo, "The Greening of Gulf and Western," *Eternity* (January 1981), 30–32.

10. For information about Evangelicals for Social Action, write to ESA, 10 E. Lancaster Avenue, Wynnewood, Pennsylvania, 19096. For information on Target Earth, write to Gordon Aeschliman, Target Earth, 900 Buttonwood Street, Philadelphia, Pennsylvania 19123.

11. For a fuller explanation of environmentalism from a Christian perspective, see Anthony Campolo, *How to Rescue the Earth without Worshipping Nature* (Nashville: Thomas Nelson Publishers, 1992).

A matter of lifestyle: youth ministry's challenge to the church

Finally, when dealing with concern for the poor, youth workers must get teenagers to deal with the whole question of lifestyle. A careful reading of Scripture reveals over 2,000 verses specifying that the people of God must care for the poor. Most theologians are ready to point out that *preference for the poor* should be at the heart of the church's concerns. Furthermore, most young people realize (even without the help of theologians) that being Christian involves sacrificing personal wealth to help the economically deprived. Mother Teresa stands out for them as exemplifying the lifestyle they see as authentically Christian. They realize that if they are to take Jesus seriously, they will have to do what the rich young ruler failed to do and give up much of what they have to help the poor (Mark 10:17-27). They are ready to believe that it's harder for a rich person to be part of God's kingdom than for a camel to go through the eye of a needle. When they put on a WWJD pin, they begin to sense that the Jesus they try to imitate would not buy into the affluent consumeristic lifestyle that has come to characterize their way of life.

The matter of lifestyle becomes especially difficult to handle in a world in which people in the United States, who compose 6 percent of the world's population, consume 42 percent of the earth's resources. Deep down inside, most young people know that there may be enough in the world to satisfy everyone's needs, but not enough to satisfy everyone's wants. Young people know that the artificial wants generated by the media—and which have become so important to them—can be gratified only at the expense of the poor. There is a growing recognition among young people that the Nike sneakers and bargain clothes they buy at department stores in North American shopping malls are available primarily because poor people in third-world countries are exploited laborers.

Ponderable
Is a simple lifestyle and strict obedience to the teachings of the Sermon on the Mount required of all those who call themselves followers of Jesus? How would you explain your position to a young person? How would you explain it to his or her parents? How would you explain it to the pastor who is the head of your staff?

It is in the matter of their own lifestyles that young people struggle most in dealing with their concerns for the poor. They find themselves constantly indoctrinated by media that advertise consumer items as necessary to a good life. Obtaining the products advertised on television motivates young people to stay in school. They are told that if they don't get a good education they won't get the jobs that will enable them to earn the money to buy the *stuff* they think they have to have. Herbert Marcuse, the neo-Marxist sociologist from San Diego State University, points out that, for this generation, media-created wants have become more important than real needs.[12] Many young people find themselves torn between a sense that true Christianity requires them to sacrifice luxuries and give to the poor, and a craving for the things that the culture prescribes as essential for the good life.

A tale of two cities: revelation in a consumer culture

In the final analysis, young people must choose lifestyles with respect to the poor that will have ultimate significance. In the Book of Revelation (chapters 17-21), John

---

12. See Herbert Marcuse, *One Dimensional Man* (Boston: Beacon Press, 1964).

describes two societal systems, each with its own values and way of life. First, there is *Babylon*. This refers to the dominant culture and its prescribed consumer lifestyles. Revelation 17:5 describes this system as "the great whore" because of its seductive character. According to Revelation 18, Babylon sustains itself by exploiting the earth's resources in an ecologically destructive manner that not only destroys the natural environment, but eventually consumes "the bodies and souls of men" (Revelation 18:13). The same seductive societal system is advertised in today's media, with allurements so attractive that many young people are willing to sacrifice their lives in order to have a piece of it.

Over and against Babylon, John sees an alternative societal lifestyle, which he labels *Jerusalem*. Biblical scholars generally declare that Jerusalem stands for the new social order as defined by God. Clearly outlined by the prophets, this society eliminates poverty because the people of God, who are Jerusalem's citizens, are committed to contributing to the well-being of others in accord with their abilities, and take only what meets their real needs (Acts 2:44-45).

The question youth workers must answer in this context is, "Toward which societal system are we directing young people?" Are we directing them to live out their lives in Babylon and take their places comfortably in respected professional positions within its establishment? Or are we daring enough to call young people out of Babylon to be part of the new way of life that the Bible says belongs to Jerusalem? Are we willing to plead with young people not to conform to the affluent lifestyles of Babylon, lived at the expense of the poor and oppressed, and instead embrace a radically countercultural, simple lifestyle that comes from being transformed by the power of the Holy Spirit (Romans 12:1-2)?

For disaffected teenagers in urban slums or in rural shacks, our consumer society poses a special problem. Among them is despair of ever getting the products the media has made of utmost importance to them. It is not surprising that social deviance is the consequence of a society that indoctrinates young people with messages evoking intense desire for products that they lack the legitimate means to obtain. To live in a society in which everyone receives the same media messages leads to great frustration and anger among young people who are poor. These young people's family backgrounds, education and job opportunities are so limited that little possibility exists for them to ever earn salaries that would enable them to buy the things they are made to crave. Robert Merton, one of America's foremost sociologists, contends that such a social structure dooms such young people to seek out illegitimate means for getting what has been denied to them via legitimate means.[13]

In his book *Race Matters*, Cornel West, chair of the department of American Studies at Harvard, picks up on this insight and points out that African-American youth are especially hard hit by this reality. West contends that consumer society has generated a nihilism among poor African-American teenagers that most middle class youth workers find hard to understand.[14] Poverty in a consumer society renders people

---

13. Robert Merton, *Social Theory and Social Structure* (New York: Free Press, 1968), chapters 6 and 7.

14. Cornel West, *Race Matters* (New York: Vintage Books, 1993).

1. Eugene F. Rivers III, "New Wineskins, New Models, and Visions for a New Century," *An Unexpected Prophet: What the 21ST Century Church Can Learn from Youth Ministry,* The 1999 Princeton Lectures on Youth, Church, and Culture (Princeton, New Jersey: Princeton Theological Seminary, 2000), 83–89.

"poor in spirit," and is psychologically destroying poor African-American youths who are powerless to secure what they have been made to feel they must have. It is hard—if not impossible—to encourage these alienated teenagers to embrace a biblically prescribed simple lifestyle. Not surprisingly, they are especially susceptible to a kind of religion that is based on a prosperity theology and promises wealth and power to the faithful.

When white middle-class young people begin to empathize with the poor in their own society, it can have disturbing results. As a case in point, a group of students from Eastern College (a different group from those mentioned above) became deeply involved with the homeless of nearby Philadelphia. At first, they took food and clothing to those who lived in the streets in an all-too-typical middle-class way of helping the poor. But it was not long before they began to recognize that their homeless new friends were being victimized by police who harassed them and business owners who wanted them off the streets. The students committed themselves to championing the cause of the homeless against the city's establishment. When the police tried to keep the homeless from sleeping in public places, these young people slept out on the streets with them and then were duly arrested. Some of them dropped out of school so they could give more time to helping their new friends. Some who were very talented graduates gave up professional careers to live their lives with these socially disinherited street folks. Together, these young people have rented a house in one of the most derelict sections of the city, where they live *in community* and have established a place where the homeless can come for help.

Obviously, such countercultural behavior stirs criticisms and concerns among these young people's parents, as well as unsettles many religious leaders of the city. Some youth workers have kept their youth groups away from these radical Christians, lest their young people get what they consider to be the "wrong idea" of what Christianity is all about. It is easy to see that impressionable young people might readily conclude that such a simple lifestyle and such strict obedience to the Sermon on the Mount is required of all those who call themselves *followers of Jesus.* What may be closer to the truth is that those youth workers covertly believe that these radical Christians with their simple lifestyles may be closer to consistent biblical Christianity than they are, and are embarrassed by that reality.

Connecting with the poor existentially, and reflecting on the biblical imperatives to minister to the poor, often has an impact on decisions regarding young people's life vocations. The more seriously they consider their responses to those who suffer injustice and oppression because of poverty, the more likely young people are to sense a calling that urges them to give their lives over to being advocates for the poor. Almost every youth worker who has taken a group of teenagers to work among the victims of poverty in a third-world country can tell of young people who wanted to go back as missionaries and do what they could to help. The parents of these affluent youngsters seldom welcome such vocational commitments, and negative reactions can lead to family conflicts. No wonder Jesus said, "Do not suppose that I have come to bring peace to the earth. I did not come to bring peace, but a sword. For I have come to turn a man against his father, a daughter against her mother, a daughter-in-law against her mother-in-law—a man's enemies will be the members of his own household" (Matthew 10:35-36). Youth workers just may find themselves caught between teenagers with a zeal for sacrificial service, and parents whose designs for their children's lives require establishment careers and comfortable adjustments to the dominant American socioeconomic system.

Servant leadership as a vocational goal of youth ministry

If youth workers encourage teenagers to pursue vocations in serving the poor, they should do their best to help these young people understand the ways in which *servant leadership* will be required of them. To imitate Jesus, according to Philippians 2, they must learn to "empty themselves" of their class and cultural biases and values. When Jesus came to minister to us, he set aside his power and glory, took upon himself the form of a servant, and humbled himself (Philippians 2:7-8). This is the model that must be imitated, and it is never too soon for youth workers to begin teaching teenagers that helping the poor paternalistically can be disabling and dehumanizing. Whether young people envision themselves as social workers in the urban United States, or as community-development missionaries in the third world, they should constantly be learning that there are ways of helping the poor, even well-intentioned ways, that diminish the dignity of poor people and give them a sense of powerlessness.

The Jewish Talmud outlines four ways of helping the poor:

1. The first and best way is to find or create real jobs for them. That way the poor can escape poverty with their self-respect intact. Being employed, they will have no need of a handout.
2. The second is to *make* work for the poor. The WPA programs during the Depression years that put people to work in public works projects and were invented primarily to give them work, are an example of this second best way the Talmud says to help the poor.
3. Third, the Talmud says we should *give* the poor what they need, but see to it that the poor have no idea who it was that provided for them. We need to look critically at the idea of youth groups delivering food baskets and toys to poor families at Christmas time, and then standing around to sing Christmas carols to them. It does not take much imagination to figure out what such condescending charity does to these poor families. I am not suggesting that our holiday giving be discontinued. Instead, in accord with the Talmud, I am suggesting something like leaving the Christmas gifts by the back doors of poor families, running away, then calling them on the phone to say, "There's some stuff on the back steps! It's for you! This is God!" and hanging up.

The God who sees what is done in secret will reward the givers openly (Matthew 6:3-4).

4. The fourth and least desirable way to help the poor, according to the Talmud, is the all-too-typical handouts. The poor will receive them because they are desperate, but they will resent the givers.

Given that the best way to help the poor is through job creation, there are many young people who are now planning to become missionary entrepreneurs, both in the United States and in developing countries. Some Christian colleges and universities have developed specialized academic programs to provide training in the skills needed to empower indigenous people to create small businesses and micro-industries that the poor can own and run themselves. A graduate from one such program has developed a silkscreen printing factory that employs young people who otherwise would have few job options. Another is working with the poor in Africa, helping them to operate a food processing plant. Still another has developed a program for battered women, in which battered women own and run a business that recharges used cartridges from laser printers.[15]

A survey of what youth workers have been doing recently to get teenagers to address the needs of the poor is encouraging. A suburban youth group in Ohio staffs a tutoring program in a poor section of Dayton. In Camden, New Jersey, more than 100 teenagers are involved in running summer street camping programs for at-risk children. Huge numbers of youth groups are regularly involved in fundraising activities that give financial support to ministries serving the poor. Compassion International, a child sponsorship organization that raises money to provide basic care for children in Third World countries, reports that there are thousands of high school students who are putting up the $24 a month required to support a child.[16]

There is much evidence that youth workers have had a great deal to do with all of this. In the 21ST century, the church may have to say "thank you" to youth groups for leading them to address the needs of the poor and helping to rediscover that serving the poor is a dominant theme in Scripture. And behind all of this, youth workers may well be the unsung heroes and heroines.

15. All of these people graduated from Eastern College, which has had such an MBA program in place for more than a decade. More than 100 of its graduates are presently involved in micro-economic development projects both in the United States and in Third World countries. For information, write to the Graduate Admissions Office, Eastern College, 1300 Eagle Rd., St. Davids, Pennsylvania, 19087.

16. For information and video presentations of the ministries of Compassion International, write to Compassion International, 3955 Cragwood Rd., Box 7000, Colorado Springs, Colorado, 80933.

Section 2

The Tasks of

Practical Theology:

Reflecting on

Present Practice

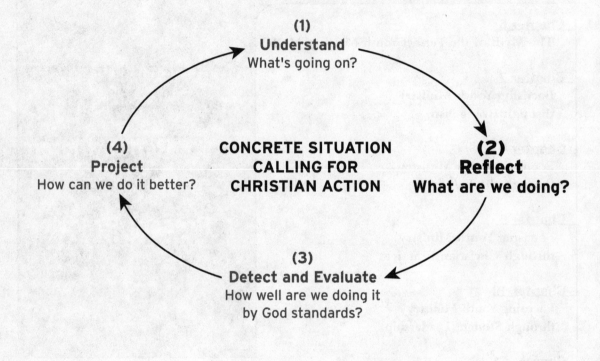

The Tasks of Practical Theology

The Tasks of Practical Theology:
Reflecting on Present Practice
Kenda Creasy Dean

Intro

The youth rally that wasn't

It seemed like such a good idea at the time. Charles Atkins, a.k.a. Christian hip-hop artist Manchild, came to seminary convinced that God had called him to a ministry of music with urban young people. So when one of his seminary professors urged him to perform at a Christian youth rally in a downtown Washington, D.C., city park, Charles cut short a stint in Latin America to do it.

The youth rally was the brainchild of the resident bishop of a large denomination, who estimated attendance would reach 5,000 people. He envisioned an event that would attract young people, especially unchurched teenagers in the neighborhood, and he turned the planning over to denominational youth staff in the area. Their job was to construct an event (in two months) that would appeal to teenagers in the city. Meanwhile, the bishop incorporated the youth rally into the schedule of a large church conference meeting at the same time in a nearby hotel, focusing on the church's care of young people. The bishop arranged for a parade of teenagers and adults to march together from the conference hotel to the park, where the 90-minute rally—complete with music, food, and speakers to attract passersby—was in full swing.

That, at least, was the plan. When Charles arrived in Washington, D.C., the night before the event, he met the denominational youth director at the conference hotel. She seemed a little apprehensive. There had been a few additions to the schedule for tomorrow, she said. First came the parade, as planned, followed by some local church youth choirs, dancers, and a steel drum band. Then some local officials might be dropping by; the bishop's office had invited several political leaders to speak, so they would need platform time, too. Then there was the motivational speaker, hired at the last minute to appeal to non-Christian youth with a non-sectarian "inspirational" message. Oh—and there were three or four local church rock bands that wanted to play at some point during the rally. The sermon would follow the bands, delivered by the seminary professor who had invited Charles, and then Charles would perform as the featured musician for the day.

Any questions?

"Yes," said Charles. "How long is this rally supposed to last?"

"Well, it might take close to two hours—a little longer than planned, but then again, the political speakers had been a surprise."

The next day, the rally unfolded as predicted. The sunny lunch hour parade of people streaming from a Washington, D.C., hotel to a park attracted lots of attention, including the press, and 30 minutes later the park was full of adults as well as youth.

The youth choirs, dancers, and steel drums were magnificent. The first political leader's message for voters was a little too long; the press shot some footage and cleared out, as the crowd thinned a little. The next civic leader spoke to parents, a little longer than necessary; youths began to grow listless, and the sun ducked behind a cloud. The third politician addressed moral decay for much longer than seemed wise; teenagers began to fade visibly from the edges of the park and the dark clouds began to cloak the sky.

Two hours and 45 minutes into the rally, when the secular motivational speaker ended his energetic pitch with his a cappella solo of "The Impossible Dream," thunder rumbled ominously. Most people started ducking for cover. Youth had vanished. The seminary professor was up to preach next. She called to the front platform any youths "still in the park"—there were about 20 of them—and prayed with them, then asked if they minded very much if she just cancelled the sermon. (They didn't mind.) One of the local rock groups performed, to "warm up the crowd" for Charles. Charles couldn't tell if the crowd looked sympathetic or just pathetic. The sky looked downright menacing.

Finally, Charles took the stage. The youth rally designed to attract 5,000 people had dwindled to about 20 teenagers and a handful of polite adults who (you could just tell) hated hip-hop music.

Now, if you were Charles, what would you do?

Reflecting on present practice

As a practical theologian, you would already be trying to make sense of the context of the youth rally. You would draw on the social sciences from the perspective of your theological convictions in order to describe the situation for ministry God had laid before you that Saturday afternoon. You might learn something from this description that modifies your theological rocks in some way, but for the most part you have simply been intent on understanding the context that calls for Christian action in this particular case.

But your theological perspective would also help you enter the second task of practical theology: reflection on present practice in youth ministry. You need to understand the youth rally *both* in light of the psychological, social, and historical climate of urban life, and in light of the way ministry is actually happening there (for better or worse). Some of this reflection happens outside the situation in which the action occurs; Charles had given careful thought to the basic purpose of the event, coordinating his music selection with the text of the sermon. But some amount of this reflection on Christian action also has to take place "in traffic," as the concrete situation unfolds. In short, the second task of *practical theology* requires reflecting on current Christian practice in this particular case. In the second task we ask, *What are we doing that faithfully represents the gospel in this concrete situation?* While the first task of practical theology (Understand) wants to know *What's going on in this concrete situation?* The second task

(Reflect) asks, *What is it that we're doing in this concrete situation—and specifically, what is it that we're doing as Christians?* The reflective task explicitly seeks to identify the practices of Christian life and ministry in a given situation, and begins to consider some of the theological assumptions that guide those practices.

Putting reflection to work

Reflecting on the practice of youth ministry at the youth rally, for instance, reveals a number of things that bear watching. In the first place, despite the rhetoric of the occasion, the rally was really *not* intended as youth ministry. As it turned out, the real planning for the event resided in the bishop's office, where the decisions to include political leaders and to invite the press were made. The bishop's office envisioned an event *about* youth, while the denominational youth director envisioned an event *for and with* youth—two objectives that competed in planning the rally.

Theologically, the bishop's office saw the event as a form of prophetic witness, and viewed its media-savvy spectacle as consistent with biblical norms of sensational prophetic practice. The denominational youth director, on the other hand, saw the rally as a pastoral event, designed to reach young people who don't normally have an opportunity to hear the good news preached in their own backyard. To her, the presence of political speeches derailed the event's significance for youth themselves.

The sequence of the rally also revealed theological assumptions behind the event. Scheduling the political leaders first might have highlighted the prophetic nature of the event, seizing an opportunity for the church to speak to public policy about youth. However, following the political speeches with a lengthy secular "inspirational" message made the event seem tailored for public consumption, not proclamation of the gospel. The conference planners assumed that straight-up Christian practice—namely preaching and praise music—would be too "churchy" (whether that meant *radical* or *boring* is unclear) to appeal to youth without church connections. Putting the secular aspects of the rally up front had the effect of preempting the sermon and the featured Christian music, the two parts of the rally that explicitly linked the event to Jesus Christ. When the seminary professor ditched the sermon—deferring to haggard attention spans as much as to the weather—the de facto preemption became official.

Now it's your turn

In this section of the book, you will reflect on current practices of youth ministry that respond to the psychological, sociological, historical, and cultural contexts to which we have been called as youth ministers. After Chap Clark reminds us that there is no such thing as a perfect model for youth ministry (chapter 6), you can take a look at what it might be like to approach youth ministry through evangelism (chapter 7, Terry McGonigal); through families (chapter 8, Mark DeVries); through Christian practices (chapter 9, Mark Yaconelli); through student leadership (chapter 10, Dave Rahn);

through critical consciousness (chapter 11, David F. White); through community (chapter 12, Kara Eckmann Powell); and through innovation (chapter 13, Soren Oestergaard and Simon Hall). These approaches are suggestive, not exhaustive. Chances are, your own approach to youth ministry is an amalgam of many of these approaches, as well as others not featured here.

As always, bring your theological rocks to the discussion as you enter this second task of *practical theological reflection*. Your experience of youth ministry and your theological priorities will predispose you to favor some approaches over others. As you begin to locate your own practice of ministry in these pages, notice how your preferred approaches to youth ministry underscore theological rocks you find important. Some of the approaches outlined here may bother you, as well. Wrestle with why this is the case: do they omit or compromise theological convictions that matter greatly in your ministry with young people? These conversations are the first steps toward giving your own practices of youth ministry theological mooring. In other words, they will help you defend your pastoral choices along the lines of your convictions about who God is and how God works in the world, rather than as reactions to peer pressure, parent pressure, pastor pressure, or simply the pressure to stay relevant.

Dancing in the rain of God

Charles had come a long way to be at this rally. He placed a high priority on the doctrine of vocation; he wanted to model for youths needing a compass in their lives his own clear sense that God had called him to use his gifts for ministry. He wanted them to know that God has called each of them to use their gifts for ministry as well. Charles believed God wanted him to promote the gospel through music to teenagers in the cities. "This wasn't exactly what I had in mind when I came here," he thought as he took the stage, scanning the weary rally audience for the remaining 20 youths. But they were youths, and this was the city, and God had given him a gift for music they could identify with. So, Charles made a decision. He brought the 20 youths from the audience up on the stage beside him, and he taught them to dance. And as the downpour began, it found Manchild singing hip-hop onstage, surrounded by a group of relieved and happy teenagers, dancing for Jesus in the rain.

The Myth of the Perfect Youth Ministry Model
Chap Clark

"If we are to keep young people involved in the church and if we are to renew our congregations, we first must acknowledge that many of our current forms of youth ministry are destructive."
—Mark Yaconelli, "Youth Ministry: A Contemplative Approach," *The Christian Century* (Web version), April 28, 1999, 2.

Ponderable
What convictions do you bring to a discussion on youth ministry models? The biases you carry will affect the way you hear others talk and write about ministry, and will ultimately impact your ability to grow beyond your personal journey.

The exasperation of the executive pastor was driven by his inability to think beyond the "proven" models:

"Show me where this *works*!"

I was in the early stages of consulting the leadership of a large church on the need for a theology of community and family life as they made decisions regarding where the ministry should *go* (a term I now know means "how we programmatically create those ministries that we 'do' in church"). The frustration level gradually crescendoed when I offered a picture, or model, of what I thought would be an appropriate course of action for this particular church given this particular time in this particular place. It was clear from the ensuing discussion that neither this executive pastor nor most of the rest of the staff and lay leaders present were even slightly interested in having to create a ministry model that fit just for them. They wanted to take what someone else had done—and done successfully—and copy it.

The truth is, however, that a local church has little in common with a company that produces or sells products that can be franchised regardless of setting or environment. And there is more to church life than can be formulated through a careful analysis of demographic or socioeconomic factors. The church is the visible, tangible expression of God's living community in the world. It is made up of ordinary, broken people who gather together in order to worship, love one another, connect, relationally share their lives, struggle with how to incarnate faith in a relatively hostile world, and be equipped and set free to serve Jesus Christ by loving those he loves. In every community and with every group of believers the expression of this family looks different, at least a little. To create an exact replica of "what works" in a different community, or family, is neither advisable nor even possible.

This chapter constitutes a call to the church to be more theologically and sociologically committed to God's unique movements in different places, with different people, and at different times than the staff and lay team described above. Models are helpful in that they enable us to see why and how others have expressed their corporate calling in their unique setting with their own unique people. But because the intent of this book is to push youth workers to think beyond the simple question of what works in order to learn how to think, act, and live theologically, it is important to let go of the need to copy and duplicate, and become men and women of prayerful thought and careful theological analysis and reflection. The goal of this entire section, then, is to enable readers to see how other youth ministry pioneers, influencers, and leaders have sought to bring the mandate of Christian mission to the adolescent community so that youth workers can use this history and these methods and tools to sculpt a unique ministry for the people to whom God has called them.

This chapter describes the power of youth ministry models (why it matters to know about, understand, and discuss other models), the history of models in youth ministry, the common threads of youth ministry models, a theological template for assessing the *appropriateness* of a given model in a given ministry context, and then closes with a plea to avoid the temptation to blindly apply *carte blanche* any model that may receive the most attention in any given year.

The power of a model

Every Christian leader must develop a balanced view of ministry models to create the kind of church community that has the flexibility to change with the environment and stay true to the biblical intent of the church. This means that our *ecclesiology*—our understanding of the theology of the church—must not always drive any programmatic expression of ministry but also be open to new *forms* of expressing our understanding of what it means to *be* the church. These models do and should come and go over time and place.

As we attempt to take the timeless truth of Scripture and contextualize it into our unique ministry setting, models are powerful in three ways: they are developed out of a response to a unique setting and need, they are organically shaped and evolve over time, and they give us hope that the gospel works in a wildly changing environment.

Models are developed out of a response to a unique setting and need.
Every model, whether involving sweeping changes or prescribing minor adjustments, began with someone asking important systemic, structural, programmatic, or strategic questions in the light of a given need or setting. There was *always* a first step in the development of a model. The pioneers of well-known ministry models seem to the rest of normal humanity as super-disciples who had an inside track on culture and ministry effectiveness. The assumption is that the inventor or initiator of a well-known model somehow came up with his "formula for success" in an error-free ministry laboratory. But in reality every single new idea for ministry that ultimately becomes packaged as a *model* began when a church or group decided that something needed to be a bit different. Almost no one sets out to develop a new, comprehensive model for everyone else to follow. Few start-up pioneers began with a vision designed to change the world— they simply set out to change *their* world. The seeds were planted in response to a unique need and setting, and the founding group moved on from there.

This is important because today most ministry leaders either do not trust themselves to create something from scratch in response to a given setting or need, or are not even willing to take the time to ask the hard questions. It is simply easier to trust the "experts." But when the model was being formulated, the experts were not yet experts! They tended to simply ask some important questions and respond accordingly.

Models are organically shaped and evolve over time.

After a new idea emerges and begins to take root, it is almost never a full-blown model. What we end up reading or hearing about is actually the result of many starts and stops, several large and small decisions and programs, and a great deal of experimentation. It is important not to be intimidated by the successes and marketing of those who peddle universal models of ministry. A model is often more stumbled upon than strategically realized, and rarely do we get to see the dark side of the evolutionary process. A new youth ministry strategy, for example, may imply that the entire ministry is based on students being set free to use their gifts and relationships. But what looks like, at least on the outside, the definitive model for a new paradigm of youth ministry fails to recognize or even mention a 10-year history of healthy adult involvement and leadership in the lives of the student leaders. In this scenario, this one fact could be the linchpin of the entire model, and yet, because of the complexity of history and setting, it is underplayed by the model's architects out of ignorance, focus, or streamlining of information.

In developing the most appropriate ministry strategies, programs, and techniques, it is vital to recognize that even the most well-known and respected model pioneers went through evolutionary stages in developing their models. This is the same for all of us, for environmental, relational, historical, and other factors will *always* make tweaking, experimenting, and changing course a fact of life. To be wed to the "finished product" of the popularized, defined model is to deny the implicit nature of model development itself.

Models give us hope that the gospel works in a wildly changing environment.

The best thing about models is that they constantly provide us with hope that the gospel matters and is relevant regardless of the cultural or environmental setting. Throughout church history, leaders devoted to one another in community have produced incredibly creative and culturally relevant ways to express the truth to a world that Jesus Christ died to redeem. Models remind us, whether or not they work for everyone today or tomorrow, that God is faithful in moving his people to be creative, passionate, and involved in bringing God's love, light, and salt to those he loves.

The history of models in youth ministry

In three major youth ministry publications, Trinity Christian educator Mark Senter III has described several different "models of youth ministry."[1] Senter lists a variety of models, most of which are technically currently employed. Nowhere does he provide the reader with the pros and cons of various models, but rather he has chosen to simply

Ponderable
What's the best youth ministry model or program you have seen or heard about? What made it good? What about it caused you to be impressed, excited, or motivated to imitate it?

---

1. See "Youth Programs," in Zuck and Benson (eds.), *Youth Education in the Church* (Chicago: Moody Press, 1978): 267–283; "Models of Youth Ministry," in Senter and Benson (eds.), *The Complete Book of Youth Ministry* (Chicago: Moody Press, 1987): 267–283; and "Basic Models of Youth Ministry" and "Emerging Models of Youth Ministry," in Senter and Dunn (eds.), *Reaching a Generation for Christ* (Chicago: Moody, 1996): 163–191, 193–214.

describe each as a viable alternative for the doing of youth ministry. Some examples of the models he describes are Christian school, competition, discipleship, and ministry. What Senter has done in the chronicling of the history of the youth ministry movement is to detail how wide and diverse the notion of youth ministry is—or at least has been. To even include the Christian school in the history of youth ministry models, for instance, is nonsensical to some and yet to others is absolutely essential.[2] And in these chapters Senter has not discussed every model of youth ministry. When all is said and done, there are dozens if not hundreds of models of youth ministry actively functioning around the world.

As Senter describes these models, he does not advocate taking a singular model and ignoring all others. The lesson this youth ministry historian has for us is to *learn from* models and utilize their strengths as tools and resources as we develop our own unique ministry expressions. As Senter states, "Youth ministers most frequently take programs from a variety of possibilities and form them into a ministry package."[3]

Perhaps the greatest youth ministry influencer of the 1980s and '90s is Duffy Robbins of Eastern College. In his book on foundational youth ministry, *Youth Ministry That Works,*[4] Robbins advocates a *funnel* concept for organizing a youth ministry program. Borrowing from the work of Dennis Miller, he offers the following funnel,[5] where programming is not so dependent on a *model* per se but rather on strategic categories of ministry focus:

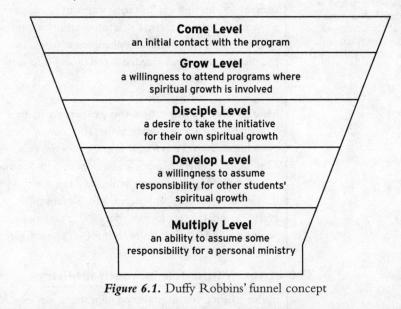

Figure 6.1. Duffy Robbins' funnel concept

2. The Christian school is a central strategy for the Seventh-day Adventist Church as well as the Reformed Church of America, to name but two. To many other groups and denominations, the Christian school movement represents a negative retreat strategy that the church must avoid at all costs. Senter's intent is to show how both of these viewpoints are part of the youth ministry world, both historically and currently.

3. "Basic Models of Youth Ministry," 189.

4. Duffy Robbins, *Youth Ministry That Works* (Wheaton, Illinois: Victor, 1991), 80.

5. Robbins, 80.

Ponderable
What is your experience with out-reach programs? Do they really attract and win those students not at all into religion? Or is it possible that even the most creative and winsome church-based programs will have a hard time attracting those adolescents that see the church as irrelevant at best or offensive at worst?

Perhaps there needs to be another level—one that recognizes the reality of a huge population of youth who will not likely respond to traditional models of youth ministry.

In this template for youth ministry programming, Robbins states:

> For a youth program to be well-rounded, accomplishing the purpose for which it was designed, there must be some type of formal or informal programming that will meet the needs of kids at each of these levels of commitment. There needs to be *Come Level* programs, geared to the student who is 'not into religion at all,' and there needs to be programs that will motivate the forward progress and growth of those at the *Grow, Disciple*, and *Develop Levels*.[6]

These two contributors to the field of youth ministry have provided the most comprehensive thinking and programming strategy to date. Both Senter's and Robbins' contributions are invaluable to understanding the basic task of parish youth ministry.

The common threads of youth ministry models

I believe that Mark Senter's contribution to the discussion on models is to see how others have viewed ministry focused on adolescents over the past 100 years. Even in his most recent chapter on models where he lists a section on the new models,[7] however, there are obviously many ways to view the task of youth ministry. Senter's work helps us to recognize that there are many viable alternatives to youth ministry other than the one that is most current with a given group, organization, church, or denomination.

Duffy Robbins, on the other hand, has most influenced the future *development* of healthy, creative, and workable youth ministry in offering a *way of thinking* about the youth ministry task (especially from the perspective of the local church). Robbins' (and others') notion of the funnel allows a youth ministry team to do exactly what Senter recommends—pick and choose the best of historical and current models in a comprehensive and holistic way. By applying a template from which to assess and deliver new programmatic, structural, or even philosophical ideas, a youth ministry can alter the forms of ministry without having to dismantle all history and structure.

In following up on Robbins' work, over the last few decades of youth ministry there have emerged two foundational components of youth ministry programming. The first is a formula for making programmatic decisions in response to a defined mission statement and identified set of student needs. The second component is exemplified by the funnel of programming. Making use of the general idea of Robbins' funnel, where students are programmatically and strategically encouraged to move downward (in the model), the Funnel of Programming offered herein provides a theological framework for deepening a student's level of interest in—and therefore, hopefully, commitment to—a deeper walk with Christ.

6. Robbins, 79–80.

7. "Emerging Models of Youth Ministry," 193-214.

There are three basic pieces to choosing programmatic and structural responses to the task of youth ministry—mission, needs, and resources.

Mission statement

The first and in some ways most important piece of the formula, spotlighted by Doug Fields in *Purpose-Driven Youth Ministry*, is the driving theological mandate of the ministry, or the *purpose* of the youth ministry task. Fields (and his senior pastor Rick Warren, *Purpose-Driven Church*) offers youth workers the "five purposes of the church" as the starting point for ministry to adolescents. This view has rightly received wide acclaim around the world in youth ministry circles. And yet, while wholeheartedly in agreement with the basic premises of the argument Fields brings, it is possible, and at times even advisable, to nuance and even more pointedly focus a mission statement than may be assumed from his strategy. Nonetheless, whatever the statement of mission you choose, it is imperative that this mission be all-encompassing enough to define and decide all youth ministry programs, strategies, and structures. A mission statement gives a *reason for doing what you do*.

For the purposes of the formula presented here, a mission statement is a compelling phrase that enables all decisions concerning structure and programming to be filtered. A mission statement, for example, that includes students' assimilation into the larger body of Christ will push the ministry to structure itself and therefore program accordingly a strategy to make this happen. If a church already has a mission statement, it is imperative that the youth ministry either maintain the *exact same statement* or be so connected as to naturally flow from the general (church) to the specific (youth ministry).

Needs of constituency

The next aspect or piece of the formula for making programmatic and structural decisions is assessing the needs of the people the ministry is designed to reach. When the issue of needs-based youth ministry is discussed, often there is little discussion beyond the surface of the kinds of needs adolescents experience. But it is important to delineate between the *felt* needs of adolescents and the *real* needs. *Felt* needs are those issues or areas that can be described by an adolescent community as being important or significant. *Real* needs, on the other hand, are those issues or areas that an adolescent community may or may not recognize as important or significant but an adult supportive community can recognize. Felt needs are comprised of issues like sexuality, dating, friendship, and choices. Real needs, conversely, could be related to such issues as studying and knowing the Bible, the intent of God related to authority, and the value of intergenerational connectedness. Both real and felt needs must be considered when designing a youth ministry structure, program, and strategy.

In addition to delineating between real and felt needs, there are also three levels to both types of needs that must be considered. The first level to be discerned involves

Ponderable

What are some of the mission or purpose statements you have seen or heard about? Have you ever been around a youth ministry program where one actually made a difference?

Felt needs, real needs

Felt needs are those issues or areas that are described by adolescents as being important or significant. Example of statements that reflect felt needs:

- I can talk about—
- I worry about—
- I think about—
- I care about—
- I often experience—

Real needs are those issues or areas that adolescents may or may not recognize as important or significant, but that supportive adults can recognize. Example of statements that reflect an outsider's view of real needs:

- Your life shows me—
- Your world reflects—
- The Bible describes (or dictates)—
- Your future demands—
- Your life needs—

the *general* needs of students. This is where cultural analysis—movies, television, Internet, music, etc.—fits in. Books, statistics, lectures, and seminars often tend to describe young people in unequivocal homogeneous "blocks." This is a helpful source of cultural and developmental analysis that must be considered, but it is not the *only* source of information that must be considered. It is just the *first*.

Figure 6.2. General needs of adolescents

The second area of consideration deals with the *specific* needs of the group of students you are attempting to reach. Often when youth ministry or culture leaders write a book or speak, they are offering general trends and attitudes among adolescent culture, usually confined to Caucasian, middle to upper-middle class adolescents, and even then in sweeping, generalized terms. But it is important to remember that because middle adolescents cluster in small groups more than ever, there are subtle yet determinative differences between groups of students. And this is especially true when one factors in economic, geographic, and ethnic differences, to name but a few.

In determining the *specific* needs of students, it is important to keep in mind *any area or issue that may influence a ministry's ability to fulfill the mission to that particular group.* For example, the majority of the students you are working with may come from relatively stable homes, and even 50 percent are home schooled. This information *must* come into play as you make programmatic and structural decisions. Conversely, if you have a group where 70 percent come from divorced homes, this will alter how you go about your work and planning. The *general* needs give you an overall picture and must be taken seriously, but an analysis of and commitment to discerning the *specific* needs of your students will allow you to be more focused and more personal as you attempt to design a program that truly impacts adolescents.

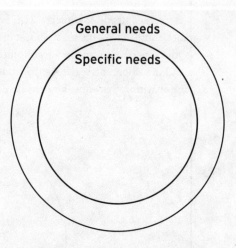

Figure 6.3. Specific needs of adolescents

There is one more area of needs to be addressed—one that is commonly overlooked in day-to-day youth ministry programming and strategic planning: the *individual* needs of *each student impacted by the ministry*. Even if a group is largely influenced by home schooled students, to use the above example, there will inevitably be a few who come from homes where parents are largely uninvolved. While it is difficult if not impossible to consistently program and structure a ministry to meet *every* student's needs, any ministry team who seeks to touch adolescents' lives in the name of Christ must be aware of and concerned about the individual issues involved. There must be an educated and strategic analysis of each students' unique needs and issues, or they will be lost through the cracks.

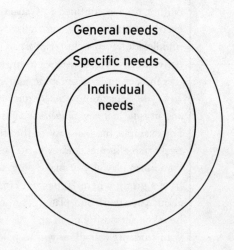

Figure 6.4. Individual needs of adolescents

Resources of constituency

The last aspect or piece of the formula for making programmatic and structural decisions is assessing the resources available that will affect the community's ability to meet the students' needs according to the mandate of the mission. This requires a broader redefinition of the term *resources*. In this formula for programmatic, structural, and strategic decision making, *resources* refers to "anything that will *positively or negatively* impact a community's ability to fulfill the stated mission according to the needs of students." In other words, a resource may not be something wholly tangible, or even measurable, but it is very real.

For example, the amount of money a church or group has available will have an impact on the programmatic and strategic decisions that have to be made. If a group decided that a key mission mandate was to introduce students to Christ in a way that was relevant and attractive to them, and the conclusion was reached that according to the needs of students it is important to be taken out of the intensity of their cultural environment, then a possible programmatic solution could be to take kids to camps where they relationally encounter the gospel in a socially unencumbered setting. On the surface this is as clean and orderly a process as possible, thus offering a rationale for the status quo.

The *danger* of this process, however, is that the final ingredient of the formula—assessing the resources of the community—is left out of the equation. In this scenario the programmatic decision to take kids to camp is decided *before* any strategic analysis of the resource *appropriateness* of the programmatic solution. Once decided, it would be in this case necessary to eventually go backward and most likely try to find the money to pull off the program, after the fact. The formula we are advocating—assessing the needs of the constituency, *then* determining any and every connected resource that will have an impact on the programmatic decision—enables the creative decision-making process to consider *all* of the factors *before* a decision has been reached. This is the process where effectiveness as well as creativity has the best chance to flourish, for decisions are not blindsided by lack of strategic consideration and appropriate data collection.

Possible resources to consider are wide-ranging. Everything from money to facility, and numbers and maturity of staff to expectations of the power structures, needs to be considered at this stage. Sometimes this is very tangible, like money or facility. At other times this is more difficult but equally as important, like with institutional or programmatic history, maturity of staff, or expectations of parents and church or organizational leadership. But every resource stone must be turned over to determine the most appropriate course of action for any ministry program, strategy, or structure.

After the resource analysis has been thoroughly accomplished, then programmatic decisions can be adopted and strategic concerns addressed. Thus the formula looks like this:

MISSION STATEMENT

↓

NEEDS + RESOURCES → PROGRAMMING

Figure 6.5. Component one—formula for programmatic decisions

There is one additional major aspect to making strategic and programmatic decisions. As mentioned above, it is vital to make choices according to the mission purpose, needs, and appropriate resources that will affect the ministry. But it is also important to recognize that students arrive at every program in very different places—developmentally, spiritually, and emotionally. For a variety of reasons, every individual student goes through unique stages of spiritual development and religious interest, and in some cases they change from week to week, especially at the upper levels of the Funnel. These initial attitudes, which are deeply personal and immensely powerful, are ultimately the most important direct factor in a youth ministry program's ability to touch a student at any meaningful level. Every veteran youth worker knows this intuitively, yet few take the time to systematically address this fact of adolescent ministry.

In synthesizing the wide variety of youth ministry programs and models of the last 40 years, there has emerged a general consensus that it is important to employ a diversity of programmatic options according to the interest level of the students who we are trying to reach. For example, if we genuinely want to strategically and programmatically care about the proverbial—

- Joshua, a slightly hyperactive, disinterested freshman boy who is forced by his stepfather to attend the youth ministry program;
- Samantha, an overly enthusiastic sophomore who knows more Bible than the senior pastor but has few friends; and
- Jon, who has always enjoyed church but as a senior feels a bit out of it with no real place to be known and to serve,

we must program differently for different levels of student interest and commitment. In other words, we must scratch where they itch, instead of trying to place the round pegs of the students that God has called us to work with into the square hole of a prepackaged *model* of ministry. This is the assumption driving the Funnel of Programming.[8]

The Funnel of Programming represents a synthesis of the most effective, historically viable, and biblically appropriate of contemporary youth ministry models. The Funnel identifies five levels of programming necessary to adequately cover the needs and desires of students in any sized youth ministry program. The five levels of student involvement and interest are Outreach Level, Entry Level, Community Building/Discipleship Level, Intimate Relationship Level, and Mentoring (or one-on-one) Level.

Outreach level

It is important to note that youth ministry Outreach Level attempts, programs, and events are distinct from Entry Level events in that an Entry Level adolescent is defined as one who would at least *show up* to a church or labeled "Christian" event or program. He or she may not be interested, connected, or involved—the student may in fact be

---

8. While the Funnel of Programming looks similar to the model found in Duffy Robbins's *Youth Ministry That Works*, there are several significant differences between the two models. I am indebted to him for spurring my thinking in this direction and for teaching me how to look at youth ministry according to students' levels. The models differ in that the Funnel of Programming mentioned here is strictly limited to a student's level of interest at any give time. One basic difference I have with Robbins's scheme is that I believe that his disciple, development, and multiply levels occur simultaneously in the Discipleship/Community Building level.

"Do we know the poor in our own family? Maybe the members of our family are not hungry for a piece of bread, maybe they're not naked or homeless, but do any of them feel unwanted or unloved?...

The Missionaries of Charity care for the crippled and unwanted, the dying and the hungry, the lepers and the alcoholics. But the poor come to all of us in many forms. Let us be sure that we never turn our backs on them, wherever we may find them. For when we turn our backs on the poor, we turn them on Jesus Christ."
—Mother Teresa, "The Poor in Our Midst," *New Covenant Magazine* (January 1977), 17.

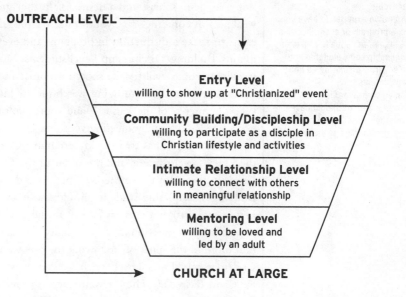

Figure 6.6. Component two—the funnel of programming

somewhat hostile—but at least that person is somewhat comfortable with the sociological environment of the church or "Christianized" setting. There are millions of adolescents in North America alone who would not, if they could help it, intentionally attend a church-sponsored event. These are Outreach students, and it is a rare Entry Level program or event that will attract or even entice them. The key words for Outreach Level programming are: *going, relationships, time, investment,* and *adventure.* These describe the essence of the task of reaching out to the severely disinterested student, the one who *will not,* for one reason or another, come to any kind of Christian meeting.

Entry level

Entry Level programming is focused on caring for the student who comes but is disinterested, bored, or disengaged. The key words in this level are: *Christ-centered, winsome, quality, relevant,* and *relational.* These five words provide a template for creating Entry Level programs and events. Adults spending time pursuing these students on their own "turf" (called *contact work*) and going where they live and move to develop trusting relationships, is a crucial point of ministry to Entry Level students. Messages that lift up Jesus Christ in a way that engages the mind and heart of the less involved is also key. When an Entry Level student leaves a program targeted to her, the response sought is something like, "That was okay, even though it was *church*!"

Community building/discipleship level

The third level of programming in the Funnel is the Community Building/Discipleship Level, which is geared toward those students with a genuine and dynamic relation-

Ponderable
In your own experience have you seen a program or event that was able to connect equally well with Discipleship Level students and with severely disinterested Entry Level students?

Do you agree or disagree that different meetings should have different goals for different interest levels of students? Is there a middle ground?

ship with Jesus Christ and a desire for further growth in their faith. The greatest weakness of contemporary youth ministry programming is that there is rarely an effort to make a distinction in programs and events between Entry Level and Community Building/Discipleship Level students. Most programs, even those with multiple weekly meetings, will try the shotgun approach to discipleship—some prayer, but not too much; some Bible study, but watch for the kid who's bored; some crazy fun, but keep the interest of the seniors—and youth ministry becomes a vain attempt at hitting every need and thereby meeting very few.

If a church has two weekly programs, one should generally be more slanted to the Entry Level student, and the other to the Community Building/Discipleship Level studnet. Not that either will be ignored when they participate (Community Building/Discipleship students should also enjoy the focus and intent of the Entry Level programs), but there is clearly a time when those who love God are given the opportunity to function as a community. The key words in this level are: *Christ-centered* (but more in the spirit of "following the one we love," rather than "check this God/man out" Entry Level focus), *worship, prayer, intergenerational, church-wide, commitment,* and *Bible study.* These seven concepts provide a template for creating Community Building/Discipleship Level programs and events. Contact work remains crucial, for teenagers and adults need to know they matter *away* from the program. But Community Building/Discipleship students are also expected to show almost as much relational initiative and investment to the community as the adult leadership.

Intimate relationship level
The fourth and fifth levels of programming in the funnel are the Intimate Relationship and Mentoring Levels. These levels of programming are geared toward those students with a genuine and dynamic relationship with Jesus Christ and a desire for further growth in their faith, as in the Community Building/Discipleship Level. These last levels take two more steps in helping the students attain a more intimate experience of faith while still under the focus of structured youth ministry.

Intimate relationships, usually programmed in some form of small group ministry, can take on a variety of expressions, but the most important component is an adult directly related with a small number (from three to eight or so) of students. This is the level on the Funnel where student leadership fits—because every student leader should still have an adult who maintains a discipleship focus on the students involved. For example, from a student's perspective, a program may have three student leadership teams (worship and music, welcoming, and activity) and three other small groups. From the adult leadership perspective, you actually have six small groups that all function a little differently, but still care for students in a more focused way than in Community Building/Discipleship Level programs where individuals can get lost.

The key words in the Intimate Relationship Level are *accountability, safety, warmth, friendship,* and *intimacy.* These five words provide a template for creating Intimate Relationship Level programs and events. Again, contact work remains crucial, for the small group leader is now a key figure in the lives of those students.

Mentoring level

The Mentoring Level is most often an informal expression of the small groups. A leader of small groups can easily function, and probably in most cases should, as a mentor of sorts. In this case a mentor is simply an older friend who knows and loves the student. This leads to the ultimate goal of the funnel of programming—every student in the program develops an intimate, growing relationship with Jesus Christ and has at least one adult who has walked through this journey with her. This is after an adolescent's segue into the larger church community. As a student is known and cared for by an adult, she is relationally drawn into the larger body via the adult. This is the ultimate goal of any youth ministry program—mature, healthy young adults who, once they have graduated from high school, are relationally and structurally assimilated into the fellowship of the body.

One note: applying the funnel of programming as a strategic framework for other programmatic or structural templates allows for any model to be employed at a given time in a given environment or setting. The model chosen is not ultimately what is important. What does matter is that students are taken seriously *where* they are in their theological and sociological journey of individuation. The Outreach Level students need friends who will pursue them; Entry Level individuals need programming that is surprisingly relevant and friendly; and the Community Building/Discipleship Level students need to be taught the truth, led into deeper commitment to and community with the greater body of Christ, drawn in to intimate relationships, and ultimately mentored by an adult who is invested in them as an individual. This is what the Funnel of Programming is designed to facilitate.

Remember, the funnel is *not* another model of youth ministry. It is a sociological, developmental, and foundationally theological *template* that enables youth workers to bring young people into the "fold of faith" in a way that honors, respects, and nurtures them while they go through this relatively wild adventure called adolescence. The following represents the theological foundation for not only the funnel of programming but for the task of youth ministry itself.

Though far from exhaustive—the following chapters of this section will provide different angles on this same theme—this brief theological look at the five levels of student interest provides the youth worker with some biblical and theological categories that will keep the youth ministry focused.

Outreach level (Colossians 4:5, 1 Peter 3:15, and 1 Thessalonians 2)

The apostle Paul not only encouraged the followers of Christ to "be wise in the way you act toward outsiders; make the most of every opportunity" (Colossians 4:5), he *lived* it. In his letter to his friends in Thessalonica, he reminded them that he and his team loved them "so much that we were delighted to share with you not only the gospel of God but our lives as well, because you had become so dear to us" (1 Thessalonians 2:8). This was the method of Jesus and the resultant method of Paul. "You know brothers, our visit to you..." begins the first verse of this same chapter, and that is what God did for us. In the Incarnation, Jesus visited us, not allowing our disinterest or behavior to hold him back or cause him to question his love for us. In Paul's ministry, he visited those who did not invite him in order to bring the visible, tangible reality of the gospel to those who were *not* seeking (for they did not yet know what their heart sought). In fact, *seeking* is the job of the church, not the job of the disinterested.

And when we go to the world of disinterested adolescents, Peter reminds us to go with "gentleness and respect." The gospel is to be presented as a peace offering, a beautiful fragrance, delivered to those who do not yet know or care about God's love for them in a way that communicates God's tender mercy and unfailing kindness. Any programmatic or strategic attempt to reach out to the least-of-these disinterested lost sheep that is not completely gentle, kind, peaceful, and respectful denies a biblical theology of evangelism and outreach.

Entry level (Mark 10:13–16)

Entry Level students are by definition disinterested to a point, but are still for some reason willing to show up. A career car salesperson knows the principle associated with this fact—showing up is 95 percent of the sale. Because these students are willing to at least walk through the door, they are thus communicating to the church, at *some level*, that they want to connect with it. Again, these are *not* Outreach students, for the true Outreach students would almost *never* show up, unless they were tricked or coerced.

Theologically this is where the developmental passages of Scripture come into play. For adolescent ministry, an Entry Level student by showing up has taken the first—and biggest—step in the process of connecting to the community of faith. They have done their part, now (in their mind) it is time for us to do ours. They are developmentally as much children as adults (even high school students) and are often "hanging back" trying to determine if they fit, if they matter, and if anyone authentically cares about them. Contrary to popular opinion, the Entry Level student is far less concerned with programmatic quality and content as she is with relational safety and meaningful connectedness. More often than not, "Boring!" means "I'm not safe!"

When the little children were brought to Jesus, and the disciples rebuked the people bringing them, the Incarnate Word became indignant. "Let the little children come to me, and do not hinder them," he told his disciples. So often our programming and strategies are more about the size of the event, the quality of the program, the content of the lesson, and the consistency of positive comments, that we lose sight of the *reason* for youth ministry—*not to hinder the little ones from coming to Jesus!* For the Entry Level kid to show up means that we have them right where God wants them, placing themselves in the vulnerable position of leaving their world and coming to ours. *Every-*

thing we do, say, and offer *must* be carefully designed and orchestrated in a way that will whisper to that student, "You are safe here, you are welcome. The King has made you his special guest at the wedding feast!"

Community building/discipleship level (John 15, Galatians 5)

Students considered to be at this level of interest have displayed a willingness to be a part of communal Christian spirituality. This means that there is an expressed desire to know and connect to Jesus Christ (John 15:1-8) *and* to know and connect to others who share this common faith. This is what Paul means when he says that "the only thing that counts is faith expressing itself through love" (Galatians 5:6). Faith (*pistis*, also translated *trust* or *belief*) is the act of the will and the heart of putting our complete trust in Jesus Christ. This level student demonstrates a *desire* to connect to the vine, to trust Christ, and to authentically follow him (in developmentally appropriate ways) via his relationships. This is where spiritual disciplines, Bible study, and instruction are functionally inserted. This is the level where relatively deep and relevant contextual and interpretational discussions take place. It is in this setting where Christian community is developed, and where singing becomes a real expression of worship and praise.

All too often Community Building/Discipleship Level students are left behind in a youth ministry program because there is simply too much energy devoted to trying to get, or keep, Entry Level students' attention. The adolescent serious about Christ, however, deserves a focused ministry that will enable the interested, even committed, student to grow to new depths of faith. Every youth ministry program designed to bring young disciples into the "adult" faith community *must* find ways to develop the two central callings of the Christian faith—a meaningful, rich connection to Christ and committed relationships within the diversity of the family of God.

Intimate relationship level (Colossians 3:13, Galatians 6:2)

The biblical record consistently calls God's people to intimate relationships. "Bear with each other" and "Carry each other's burdens" imply a *knowing* and a significant involvement with one another. In this culture, this does not come naturally—or easily. Students, especially high school students, intuitively long for intimate relationships, but have very few resources to enable that to happen at any deep level.

Generally small groups is the way we tend to address this need. But typically small group programs become essentially that—programs. Instead of being strategic and theological tools created to train young people how to connect at deep levels with others, they become one more ministry to manage. Regardless of the look of the youth ministry, God calls them (and therefore us as leaders) into long-term, authentic friendships with others in the body. This is a mandate of the family of God.

Mentoring level (Titus 2:1-8; 2 Timothy 1)

The final stage of the Funnel is to plan for each student to be personally known and loved by an adult. This most easily is a leader involved in the facilitation of the Intimate Relationships Level, but it can be anyone in a congregation or community, so long as the relationship is based on leading—by modeling and relationship—the adolescent to a deeper dependency on Christ. In Titus this is expressed as a direct admonition to older women to lead younger women, and also an implicit instruction for older men to model godly living, presumably to the younger members of the body. In Timothy we get a glimpse of the relationship that Paul had with his son in the faith. These are both examples of the Mentoring Level, and it fulfills the old adage, "Christianity is not taught, it is caught."

The myth of the perfect model—a plea

- *Pray, both individually and corporately*. In every setting and with every decision, make Jesus Christ the Lord of your program, and *not* anyone else's idea of what you should do. History, tradition, resources, expectations, and advice are all helpful and good in making large and small strategic and programmatic plans and decisions. But the Scripture is clear that God's people called to leadership must devote a great deal of time and energy to prayer.

- *Be theologically grounded and committed*. First and foremost, youth ministry must be a theological task (that is the basic purpose of this book). Avoid *any* program, strategy, or decision that you are not thoroughly convinced is the most theologically appropriate course of action you can determine for your unique situation. Whether it is in fundraising, camps and retreats, mid-week programming, student leadership, or special event planning, make sure that every person involved in your ministry can articulate the *theological rationale* for the strategy.

- *Stay open to change*. The most dangerous youth worker is the one who thinks he has arrived at knowing how to do the task of youth ministry. Whether it is resilience in the way to do it or loyalty to a specific model or a subtle arrogance due to previous successes, it is the kiss of death to theologically and sociologically sensitive youth ministry. God is always moving—and always working—regardless of the cultural shifts and changes. We must be fresh in our openness to changing the way we bring the gospel to adolescents.

- *Trust in the Incarnate God, not proven models*. Jesus Christ is the Lord and he is therefore Lord over methods, strategies, programs, and models. As long as he reigns on the throne of your ministry, his kingdom will come!

Focusing Youth Ministry through Evangelism
Terry McGonigal

Chapter 7

"Even when I am old and gray, do not forsake me, O God, till I declare your power to the next generation, your might to all who are to come."
—Psalm 71:18

"If we preach a gospel that neglects the welfare of the whole in exchange for the happiness of the individual, then the Church as a living, pulsing body is weakened as is the welfare of the family. We must recover the priority of inter-relationships."
—Dennis Guernsey, *A New Design for Family Ministry* (Elgin, Illinois: David C. Cook, 1982), 99.

In the bushland of rural Kenya Masai herdsmen welcome one another by saying, "And how are the children?" The response to this traditional greeting is, "All the children are well." For the Masai, the children are of primary importance. How they are doing is a telltale sign of the entire tribe's well-being. Roland Martinson writes, "A child is also a trust from God on behalf of the present. It is often said that if one wants to measure how constructive or how toxic a culture has become, one should look into the face of the most vulnerable. Children are among the most vulnerable in our contemporary culture. Who will speak for the children? Are our children doing well? Perhaps in the cry of the crack baby we hear the most poignant, honest evaluation of this culture."[1] Given the troubled state of most youth today, the biblical imperative to communicate the good news of God's love for every kid, everywhere, has never been more imperative.

The Bible also places great emphasis upon the importance of children and youth. Throughout the Scriptures people of faith are commanded to live in such a way that children and adolescents will experience God's love. Their communal life is evangelistic; as they live in covenant faithfulness with God and each other, the good news of God's love will draw the younger ones into the beauty and wonder of that same relationship with God.

This chapter considers the topic of youth evangelism in two distinct yet related sections. First we will develop working definitions of the terms youth ministry and evangelism. In the Old Testament, special responsibility is given to the community to 1) nurture children and adolescents in the love of God, and 2) to communicate clearly the gospel of God's rule over all creation. The second section will focus on the model of evangelism portrayed in the narratives of Jesus' ministry, especially from the gospel of Mark. We will watch Jesus as he interacts with children and adolescents who are in great need of his ministering presence. We will also hear Jesus place particular emphasis upon the community's responsibility for youth.

Evangelism and Ministry to Youth: Old Testament Priorities

The importance of youth

The Bible has a lot to say about youth, although not in exactly the same context as implied in the modern term adolescent. This distinction illustrates the essential principle of biblical interpretation that original cultural setting is primary, and application

---

1. Roland Martinson, "Getting to All God's Kids," The 1997 Princeton Lectures on Youth, Church, and Culture (Princeton, New Jersey: Institute of Youth Ministry, Princeton Theological Seminary), 28.

into contemporary situations is secondary. When sociologists use the term youth in reference to modern-day adolescents, they are naming an age/developmental category bracketed by childhood on one side and adulthood on the other. A youth is someone in the middle category—no longer a child, yet not an adult.

Used in this way, the term youth appears approximately 75 times in Scripture and is defined as "the time, with no fixed limit, beyond infancy and before a person's prime, a time of vigor and opportunity though not of judgment and maturity."[2] But the Scriptures speak about the community's responsibility for youth from a cultural context that is quite different from our own. In contrast to ancient Hebrew society, "one difficulty of contemporary adolescence is the absence of markers or rites of passage."[3] Without these clear demarcation points symbolized in ritual, how long one stays in this complicated in-between stage is a subject of much discussion among developmental experts.[4] Adding further confusion to the modern cultural discussion, the term youth ministry describes a sociological phenomenon that has developed its own distinct form of ministry only in the 20th century. This development has come about as a result of a growing cultural emphasis on the brackets between various developmental stages, with increasing emphasis of upon adolescence.[5]

In contrast, the scriptural understanding of youth is much clearer. Biblically speaking, youth are linked with the stage of childhood when dependence upon parents and community for life support, nurture, guidance, and instruction is the rule. The terms child and children are mentioned quite frequently in the Old Testament—over 550 times. The community of God's people is given special responsibility to care for the children. The parents and extended family, as well as the rest of the surrounding community, are expected to carry out their evangelistic responsibility of preparing the children and youth for the convergence of physical, spiritual, and social maturity in adulthood. They accomplish this task primarily through the daily living of the *Shema* (italics added).

> "Hear [shema], O Israel: The Lord our God, the Lord is One. Love the Lord your God with all your heart and with all your soul and with all your strength. These commandments that I give you today are to be upon your hearts. *Impress them on your children*. Talk about them when you sit at home and when you walk along the road, when you lie down and when you get up. Tie them as symbols on your hands and bind them on your foreheads. Write them on the doorframes of your houses and on your gates."
>
> —*Deuteronomy 6:4-9*

Ponderable

Is an adolescent a big child, or a young adult? McGonigal lands in the big-child category and moves theologically from this starting place. Is this where you stand? Do you agree that this an appropriate framework from which to theologically unpack the adolescent need and task? Where is an adolescent more adult than child, and what are the markers of that transition?

2. S. H. Blank, "Youth," in G.A. Buttrick (ed.), *Interpreter's Dictionary of the Bible* vol. 4 (Nashville: Abingdon, 1962), 925.

3. Dean Borgmann, *When Kumbayah Is Not Enough: A Practical Theology for Youth Ministry* (Hendrickson, Peabody, Massachusetts, 1997), 115

4. See Chapter 2 for more information on this. See also David Elkind, *All Grown Up and No Place to Go: Teenagers in Crisis* (Reading, Massachusetts; Addison-Wesley, 1984), 93-114; and B. Frank Brown/National Commission on Youth, *The Transition of Youth to Adulthood: A Bridge Too Long* (Boulder, Colorado: Westview, 1980).

5. Mark H. Senter III, *The Coming Revolution in Youth Ministry* (Wheaton, Illinois: Victor, 1992); and Sara Little, "Youth Ministry: Historical Reflections near the End of the Twentieth Century," The 1997 Princeton Lectures on Youth, Church, and Culture (Princeton, New Jersey: Institute of Youth Ministry, Princeton Theological Seminary), 11-21.

The children and youth learn of God's love for them by observing the daily model of adults and through their own interactions with adults—in the home and on the street, through the exchange of intellectual ideas and business transactions. Resting and rising, work and play, family discussion and village commerce are all permeated with one message: there is nothing more important in life than the knowledge and experience of God's love. Kids participate with adults in life together, and in the process they grow in the knowledge and appreciation of God's love, as well as God's claim upon their lives. This lifestyle of love is the primary training vehicle for the assumption of full community responsibility as an adult.

In the Old Testament, the demarcation for life's second major phase as an adult is marked by the development of physiological ability to bring forth offspring. About the time a person is biologically capable of reproduction, an important rite of passage takes place. Boys are accepted as full members of the community through full participation in the worship life of the synagogue around the age of 13. The first time he reads from Torah in the synagogue he ceases to be a boy—the child becomes a man. From that moment on, he is viewed as an adult and is expected to make his full contribution to the common good through marriage, work, and community leadership. For girls, betrothal and marriage occur at the age of physical capability for childbearing. The community recognizes this transition through rites of passage, and celebrates with the youth, now become adult, with great enthusiasm. They are ready for adult responsibility because they have been prepared for this transition through their daily nurture in the love of the community as an expression of God's love. The Shema has taken root in their hearts through the love they have received and the models they have observed. All adults bear responsibility for this training.

Evangelistic emphasis

"In the beginning" the Bible tells the story of creation. God creates a perfect universe, the heavens and the earth, by speaking every aspect of creation into existence. The first chapter of Genesis is ordered by the repetition of the refrain, "And God said" (Genesis 1:3, 6, 9, 11, 14, 20, 26, 29). The pinnacle of the narrative is the creation of humankind, male and female, in God's image (Genesis 1:26-27). Every relationship in the created order functions perfectly according to the divinely spoken intention. "God saw all that he had made, and it was very good" (Genesis 1:31; *tob me'od*—abundant, overflowing goodness).

By human disobedience sin invaded this exceedingly good creation. As a result, every kind of relationship was negatively distorted. Enmity, strife, and chaos replace harmony and order. Human relationships with God, with the physical creation, with the animal kingdom, and with each other are all broken (Genesis 3:10-24). The first evidence of this breakdown is an attack on relationships within the family—the violent murder of Abel by his brother Cain (Genesis 4:1-14). From that tragic moment to the

Evangelism is...
In many circles, the term *evangelism* has come to mean to verbally share the good news. But Terry McGonigal broadens that idea considerably when he defines evangelism as "God's activity of restoring all the created order, especially people." According to the author, evangelism is what *God* does, and we walk with and proclaim him in the saving work.

How does this definition of evangelism differ from your own? Before reading this far in the chapter, would you have described evangelism as God's work that we are invited into—or would you have said that God wants *us* to do the evangelism? As you continue reading, consider what the Bible has to say about evangelism and its implications for youth ministry.

The difficulty, danger, and disappointment of evangelism
For those across the centuries and cultures committed to being salt and light in a tasteless and dark world, difficulty, perceptions of failure, heartache, disappointment, and physical or relational danger are more often the markers of the task than emotional euphoria or visible success. There are exceptions, to be sure—but the evangelist who seeks sustenance and fulfillment from so-called effective strategies or tried-and-true formulae will in the end likely be sorely disappointed. It is the nature of evangelism. "Foxes have holes and birds of the air have nests," as Jesus himself remarked, "but the Son of Man has no place to lay his head" (Matthew 8:20).

present, children and their families have felt the effects of the Fall in horrendously painful and tragic ways.

The good news is that human rebellion, and its consequences, is not the final word. God is unwilling to allow creation to self-destruct. God will intervene and save what has been lost, and that saving intention includes all of creation. In biblical theology, God's activity of restoring all the created order, especially people, is evangelism. Those who participate with God in this work are evangelists.

The first book of the Bible describes the beginning of God's decisive action to bring about the healing and transformation of a once-perfect, now-broken creation. God starts the process of reversing the tragic and universal consequences of the Fall by selecting one person. God's call to Abraham to be an agent of blessing concludes with this seventh and climactic promise, "...all peoples on earth will be blessed through you" (Genesis 12:3). God's design is for the creation to be restored. The promise is for all. The Hebrew word for people is goyim, which means "non-Jewish people groups," "Gentiles." In order to participate with God in this evangelistic endeavor, Abraham must listen to God and go where he is sent. "The Lord had said to Abram, 'Leave your country, your people and your father's household and go to land I will show you'" (Genesis 12:1). Even though that call seems extremely vague, he obeys, and thus becomes the first evangelist. The overall trajectory of his life follows God's leading (Genesis 22:1-19), in spite of momentary lapses into self-centered sin (see Genesis 16:1-16; 20:1-18; 21:8-21). Ultimately, Abraham's participation in God's saving work is related to Jesus' incarnational saving ministry, as described by Jesus in John's gospel, "Your father Abraham rejoiced at the thought of seeing my day; he saw it and was glad" (John 8:56).

From this simple beginning the story of evangelism weaves its way through the Old Testament. There are faithful women and men who follow Abram's model, where they too participate in God's saving work, in spite of incredible difficulty, danger, and the disappointment of not seeing fulfilled in their own time the dream of God's salvation (Hebrews 11:1-40).

The prophet Isaiah picks up the theme of evangelism and uses it in unprecedented ways. Isaiah foresees the day when all interpersonal animosity and international warfare will come to an end through the establishment of the reign of one who is called "Wonderful Counselor, Mighty God, Everlasting Father, Prince of Peace" (Isaiah 9:1-7). His rule will eliminate all manner of strife in the animal kingdom and restore the divine-human relationship (Isaiah 11:1-9). The foundation of such redemptive activity is God's forgiveness of human sin (Isaiah 52:13-53:12), both Israel's (Isaiah 40:1-2), as well as the Gentile nations' (Isaiah 11:10-11).

Isaiah's vision is good news—a proclamation that must be announced. The prophet emphasizes this evangelistic activity in three different passages, each of which use the same Hebrew term basar (to announce, to participate in and proclaim God's saving activity):

You who bring good tidings [basar] to Zion,
Go up on a high mountain.
You who bring good tidings to Jerusalem,
Lift up your voice with a shout,
Lift it up, and do not be afraid;
Say to the towns of Judah,
'Here is your God!'

—Isaiah 40:9

How beautiful on the mountains
are the feet of those who bring good news, [basar]
who proclaim peace,
who bring good tidings
who proclaim salvation,
who say to Zion, "Your God reigns!"

—Isaiah 52:7

The Spirit of the Sovereign Lord is on me,
because the Lord has anointed me
to preach good news [basar]to the poor.
He has sent me to bind up the brokenhearted,
to proclaim freedom for the captives
and release from darkness for the prisoners,
to proclaim the year of the Lord's favor.

—Isaiah 61:1-2

In prophetic terms, evangelism is the proclamation of God's universal rule over all creation, seen clearly in the phrases "Here is your God" (Isaiah 40:9) and "Your God reigns!" (Isaiah 52:7). The prophet describes evangelistic ministry expressed through tender and compassionate ministry to victims of oppression, to the spiritually and materially impoverished, and to those whose life circumstances have plunged them into darkness (Isaiah 61). The good news is for all, and those who communicate God's saving message through word and in deed receive special recognition from the prophet.

These prophetic descriptions undergird the New Testament's understanding of evangelism. Isaiah's vision for evangelistic proclamation influences Paul's understanding of himself as an evangelist. The apostle quotes the first portion of Isaiah 52:7, "How beautiful on the mountains are the feet of those who bring good news," to explain his evangelistic ministry (Romans 10:15). Furthermore, Jesus reads from Isaiah 61 in the synagogue in Nazareth and then declares, "Today this Scripture is fulfilled in your hearing" (Luke 4:21). Clearly, then, the Old Testament provides the foundations for the New Testament's understanding of evangelism, especially as that endeavor focuses upon youth. In Jesus, the theme of youth evangelism comes together in a remarkable and instructive way.

Youth Evangelism: The Model of Jesus

The focal point of the divine reclamation project is Jesus Christ. The first gospel writer says it this way: "The beginning of the gospel of Jesus Christ, the Son of God" (Mark 1:1). For Mark, Jesus is the one who commences, communicates, and completes God's Good News (euangelion). "Jesus proclaims the gospel and it proclaims his story."[6] The first words spoken by Jesus in Mark's narrative affirm the centrality of the gospel, "God's good news," as the focal point of Jesus' ministry. "After John was put in prison, Jesus went into Galilee, proclaiming the good news (kerusson to euangelion) of God. 'The time has come,' he said. 'The kingdom of God is near. Repent and believe the good news (euangelio)'" (Mark 1:14–15). In his ministry Jesus fulfills Isaiah's vision of announcing the good news of God's salvation. God is at work through the Galilean preacher. God's rule over creation will be reasserted by Jesus, and this turning point means everything must change. People are called to forsake their former manner of life—to repent. They are also called to place their trust in the gospel of God's salvation—to believe the Good News. The decisive moment has come. Through Jesus, God will accomplish the work of redemption now!

But Jesus will not do it alone. Just like in the Old Testament, others are called to participate in God's saving activity. In Mark 3:13–19 Jesus gathers together an unlikely crew of helpers; two sets of brothers who have fished all their lives; one who collected taxes from the fishermen; another from an opposition party who hated tax collectors; assorted others from various Galilean communities of mixed ethnic heritage; and one who would ultimately betray him. Jesus calls them together for three distinct purposes as found in Mark 3:14:

1. That they might be with him
2. That he might send them out to preach
3. To have authority to cast out demons

Jesus' agenda is clear. The apostles will learn how to proclaim the good news of God's reign through word and in deed, and they will learn how to confront evil in such a way that God's reign is reestablished in those whose lives who have been plagued by demonic forces. How will they learn such ministry? Jesus' methodology is simple. The success of the disciples' evangelistic ministry depends on the learning that will take place as they are with Jesus. Everything depends on the model conveyed through the power of that relationship. They had better pay attention!

Ponderable
Who does the work of redemption? In other words, who builds the kingdom? Do we build the kingdom for God, or does God build his own kingdom? If God is the builder, what is our role?

---

6. C.C. Broyles, "Gospel (Good News)," *Dictionary of Jesus and the Gospels* (Downers Grove, Illinois: InterVarsity Press, 1992), 285.

First priority: being with Jesus

Mark is clear about Jesus' priorities. The most important activity for the apostolic band, and first on the list, is "being with Jesus." The gospel writers tell us that in the person of Jesus, God has come to be with us.[7] In other words, relationships are at the heart of Jesus' incarnational gospel ministry. Roland Martinson asserts that relationality is at the heart of God:

> The Triune God is three who live as one; the God who is living Creator; the God who is Jesus the Christ; the God who is Inspirator/Encourager, Holy Spirit. This one who was in the past at creation and redemption is present everywhere in the world and will be forever. The mystery: What is at the heart of God? Relationship! God said, "Let us create humankind in our own image." Man and woman, God created them. Then, at the heart of God, at the center of reality, at the core of humankind, this mystery: relationship.[8]

Jesus' closest followers will learn how to do this relational gospel ministry by being with the one who is the Incarnation of God, Jesus the Messiah. They will watch Jesus at work and in prayer. They will see him deal with people, sometimes in large groups but more often in private conversations with individuals. They will listen to him as he preaches and teaches. Through daily contact with Jesus they will learn about evangelism—why, who, what, and how.

For Jesus, ministry methods are just as important as ministry outcomes. In this gospel ministry, the disciples will represent the Creator of the universe, the Lord of all life. Their attitudes, motives, words, and actions must reflect the character and purposes of the one true God. Being with Jesus for approximately three years will change them in unimaginable ways. Before they assume the full responsibility of being evangelists, they must be evangelized themselves by being with Jesus. They simply need to keep their eyes on the one they will call "Rabbi" (teacher), their ears receptive to his teaching, and their hearts open to being changed every day, simply by "being with Jesus." Everyone involved in evangelistic youth ministry must take seriously this priority of personal spirituality—of "being with Jesus" before engaging in ministry activity.

The twofold call of being with Jesus

The night before his death, Jesus gave the disciples a clear picture of how he wanted his followers to fulfill his mission to the lost, broken, and oppressed. In John 15:1-17, Jesus presents this twofold call for disciples who would proclaim his message: love me and love each other.

In verses 1-8 Jesus emphasizes the absolutely central theme of *individual* loyalty and connection to himself—"I am the vine; you are the branches...apart from me you can do nothing" (v. 5). Each disciple, as a branch, has no power, no function, and therefore ultimately no place in God's vineyard without a healthy connection point to Jesus Christ. This is the first call of "being with Jesus"—growing out directly from a deep, intimate personal experience of him.

But that is not the *only* connection point for the disciple. In verses 9-17 Jesus goes on to say that just as individual connection is vital, so too is a commitment to *corporate* connection to others attached to the branch—"My command is this: love each other as I have loved you" (v. 12). There can be no discipleship, no fruit, no ministry, and therefore no evangelism apart from this twofold call to "be with Jesus"—to "remain" in the vine and love one another.

How does this understanding of being with Jesus line up with your experience in ministry?

Second priority: preach the Good News

As the gospel narratives make clear, Jesus has a lot of work to do to get the disciples ready for their evangelistic ministry. By being with Jesus and learning his message and his methods, they will be equipped to preach—the second priority on Jesus' agenda. And when they preach, they must communicate the right message. Everything they say about God must first be scrutinized and approved by Jesus himself. They must learn

7. Immanuel is the name the prophet Isaiah designates for this child, and Matthew applies this name to Jesus in his birth narrative (see Isaiah 7:14 and Matthew 1:23). According to John, God has come to make "his dwelling among us" (Jn. 1:14ff). The Greek verb skenoo literally means to pitch your tent, to camp with. Eugene Peterson paraphrases John 1:14 this way: "The Word became flesh and blood, and moved into the neighborhood." See *The Message: New Testament with Psalms and Proverbs* (Colorado Springs: NavPress, 1993), 219.

8. Martinson, 27.

that, in this ministry, special emphasis is placed on the importance of evangelizing children and youth.

In Mark's gospel this emphasis becomes clear in the chapters that describe Jesus' journey to Jerusalem (Mark 8:27–10:45). Twice Jesus uses young ones to counteract the misguided notions of the disciples about the nature of stature in God's kingdom and the means by which they will be included in the anticipated coming reign of Jesus. For Jesus, kids and the kingdom are linked together. Roland Martinson writes, "A child is also a trust from God. A child is *imago dei*—created in the image of God—holy ground. Getting to all God's kids is grounded in the understanding that every child is a trust from God—on behalf of God."[9] The disciples, contrary to their misguided notions of the importance of younger ones, are about to get a lesson in gospel priorities.

The first connection between kids and God's reign comes on the heels of the disciples' argument about who is the greatest among them (Mark 9:33–34). Their agenda has nothing to do with Jesus' ministry. Self-centered motives are antithetical to his purpose and proclamation. He reprimands such thinking with this response, "If anyone wants to be first, he must be the very last, and the servant of all" (Mark 9:35). Then Jesus does something remarkable.

> He put a child in the middle of the room. Then, cradling the little one
> in his arms, he said, "Whoever embraces one of these children as I do
> embraces me, and far more than me—God who sent me."
> —*Mark 9:36-37,* The Message

"The simplicity and profundity of this truth is better enacted than spoken...Children, in particular, were thought of as 'not having arrived.' They were 'the very last' (v. 35)...It is in the small and powerless that God appears to the world...The humblest act of kindness sets off a chain reaction that shakes heaven itself, for whatever is done to the little and least is done to Jesus, and whatever is done to Jesus is done to God."[10] It is difficult to overstate the importance of this acted parable. As ministry takes place with, for, and among the young, the evangelist connects with God incarnate in Jesus Christ. There is something divine about every encounter a youth worker has with an adolescent, because in some hidden and mysterious way, God is present. Can there be any stronger message regarding the priority of youth ministry?

Making the same point, the second incident is triggered once again by the disciples' misunderstanding of the primacy of youth. When the disciples chastise those who are bringing children to Jesus (Mark 10:13), apparently because of some misguided notion that there are more important people to pay attention to in this kingdom ministry, Jesus becomes "indignant."[11] Contrary to what the disciples think, Jesus asserts that children hold the keys to understanding the true nature of God's saving kingdom work.

---

9. Martinson, 28.

10. Jim Edwards, *Mark's Story of Jesus* (Grand Rapids, Michigan: Eerdmans), to press in 2001; see section on Mk. 9:33–37.

11. *Aganakteo* is used only here in all the Gospel narratives, and it means to become irate!

Don't push these children away. Don't ever get between them and me. These children are at the very center of life in the kingdom. Mark this: Unless you accept God's kingdom in the simplicity of a child, you'll never get in.

—*Mark 10:14-15,* The Message

To emphasize the point, Jesus reached out and gathered the children in his arms with an embrace of love (Mark 10:16). "He laid his hands on them, conveying that God's call was to them also. This was an appalling act. Children were expected to look to adults as models, but Jesus was asking adults to look toward children."[12]

Jesus is always open to respond to a child, for in so doing, he is teaching all who watch, including the disciples, the true nature of God's love, just as the Shema emphasizes. By being with Jesus, the disciples learn the spiritual priorities necessary to proclaim God's good news with accuracy and clarity. The lesson here is clear. Proclaiming the good news must begin with children and youth, and the one doing the proclamation needs to be aware of the gospel lessons being taught, not just to the audience, but to the preacher by the audience. In Jesus' ministry, kids take priority because in some mysterious way they are the teachers!

Third priority: confronting evil through healing power

Sometimes in the gospel narratives, evil manifests itself in physical sickness, and at other times it appears as psychological/spiritual torment. In his ministry Jesus is never satisfied simply with evangelistic proclamation. He verifies the truth of his public preaching and private discussions by confronting manifestations of evil that destroy bodies, relationships, families, and community. In particular, Mark provides several instances where young people are the primary beneficiaries of God's loving, healing power. We will focus on two of these events.

The healing of Jairus' daughter (Mark 5:21-43; Matthew 9:18-26)

A prominent synagogue leader named Jairus pleads with Jesus: "My little daughter is dying. Please come and put your hands on her so that she will be healed and live" (Mark 5:23). Jairus and his wife have sat at the bedside of their precious, beloved daughter and watched as some kind of debilitating disease has ravaged her body. Waiting and hoping and praying, they have watched the girl go from bad to worse. Mark tells us that the girl is 12 years old, junior high age, an early adolescent (v. 42).

Everyone who has been involved in youth ministry knows this kind of desperate urgency. Kids get in all kinds of trouble—some they bring on themselves, and some perpetrated by others. Sometimes the emotional trauma they feel can be released through a youth minister's willingness to listen. On other occasions, a life hangs in the balance and the leader must intervene immediately. Such is the case here.

Jesus and children = Jesus and adolescents?
Jesus' emphasis on and love for children is clear in the New Testament. But what does it mean to proclaim the gospel to adolescents who are by definition not yet adults, but clearly no longer dependent and innocent children? Where and in what ways do we need to encourage adolescents in a youth ministry context to become more *adult?*

Perhaps the content of the gospel must draw kids—who tend to seek sophistication and independence—into realizing that God values and honors a commitment to child*likeness,* as opposed to child*ishness.*

"Sympathetic suffering enters most directly into the movements of the power of God in evangelism. As a mother's face may reflect more pain than the face of her suffering child, so there is an unlimited realm of possible suffering in sympathy and burden for another. This highest and deepest suffering is born of two parents, which are love and appreciation."
—Lewis S. Chafer, *True Evangelism: Winning Souls by Prayer* (Grand Rapids, Michigan: Kregel, 1998), 105.

---

12. Mary Elizabeth Mullino Moore, "Walking with Youth: Youth Ministry in Many Cultures," The 1997 Princeton Lectures on Youth, Church, and Culture (Princeton, New Jersey: Institute of Youth Ministry, Princeton Theological Seminary), 49.

The father's plea in verse 23, "Please come and put your hands on her so that she will be healed and live" is laced with a faith that transcends the circumstances. And it creates an amazing response on the part of Jesus—he follows the man (v. 24). Up until now, in Mark's gospel, Jesus is always the one calling others to follow him. Now Jesus follows the man who has interceded on behalf of the dying girl. "Where faith comes, Jesus follows—willingly, immediately." [13]

Into this tension-filled crisis narrative, Mark inserts a second event about another person who has been waiting—far longer. A woman who has suffered for 12 years reaches out of the mob that is following Jesus and jostling him on every side. She touches Jesus and immediately she is healed. Jesus stops and looks around. He wants to meet the person who touched him—the one who has been healed. The disciples think Jesus is crazy to look for one person in the huge throng, but Jesus will not be deterred. The woman comes forward, and she tells Jesus "the whole story." [14] How long does it take for a person who has been sick for 12 years to tell all the details of her ailment including the treatments she had received, which only left her worse off physically and financially (v. 26)? A few minutes? A few hours?

Mark doesn't tell us, except to highlight the patience of Jesus, who is always willing to deal with people one at a time. That's the way God's healing ministry works (vv. 24-34). In Mark's gospel what everyone knows is that a girl's life hangs in the balance as Jesus patiently listens to the healed woman.

Their conversation is interrupted by the news that comes to Jairus, "Your daughter is dead…Why bother the teacher any more?" (Mark 5:35). Time has run out. The delay has cost the girl her life. [15] Mark says nothing about the man's response to this dreaded declaration. We can only wonder about the questions that must have raced across his mind and the sorrow that struck his heart in that moment.

What Mark does tell us is Jesus' response to this terrible and tragic news. In this grief-laced moment, Jesus engages in another aspect of evangelistic ministry. He doesn't take the news with resignation. He doesn't walk away. He stays with the father. In the face of others' suffering, the most compassionate, evangelistic, and grace-filled act is often simple physical presence. Philip Yancey, who has interviewed hundreds of suffering people, comments that in the face of suffering—

> …no one offers the name of a philosopher when I ask the question, "Who helped you most?" Most often they answer by describing a quiet, unassuming person. Someone who was there whenever needed, who listened more than talked, who didn't keep glancing down at a watch, who hugged and touched, and cried. In short, someone who was available, and came on the sufferer's terms and not their own. [16]

13. Dale Bruner, Matthew, vol. 1 (Dallas: Word, 1987), 342.

14. The Message.

15. In Matthew's narration, Jairus initially approaches Jesus with these words, "My daughter has just died. But come and put your hand on her, and she will live" (Matthew 9:18). "To say 'dead but' requires extraordinary confidence…The man does not believe that Jesus is helpless before the last and most intractable human problem" (Bruner, 341).

16. Philip Yancey, Where Is God When It Hurts? (Grand Rapids, Michigan: Zondervan, 1990), 177.

Initially, Jairus asked Jesus to come to his house. Before they were interrupted, that's where they were going, and Jesus' intention still is to honor the man's request and accompany him to his daughter. Jesus will finish that journey. The difference now is that Jesus is in the lead, supporting the grief-stricken father with his strong arms, followed by three of his disciples.[17]

The narrative reaches its climax in a collision of perspectives. By the time they get to Jairus' home, the mourners have already gathered, "crying and wailing loudly" (v. 38). In Jewish culture professional mourners were always hired to lead the community in a public expression of grief. They came to the home of the deceased immediately after expiration. On the human side, it is time to say goodbye and bury the dead girl. Despair has set in—the kind of despair experienced by everyone who has stood next to a casket and seen death's reality firsthand. Its shadow is cast over the entire setting and all involved.

But there is another reality at work here as well. Jesus provided comfort to Jairus at the announcement of his daughter's death by saying, "Don't be afraid, only believe" *(Me phobou, monon pisteue).*[18] "Fear is the universal primal response to suffering. And yet beyond doubt it is also the single great 'enemy of recovery.'"[19]

The divine perspective in this scene is quite different than the human one. When they arrive at the house, Jesus' response to the mourners reveals God's intention to bring salvation into this situation. "Why all this commotion and wailing? The child is not dead but asleep" (v. 39). The statement is met with derision, as all present laugh at Jesus (v. 40). What can Jesus do in the face of the reality that the girl is dead? Who will have the final word—death, or Jesus?

This interaction captures the constant pressure faced by everyone involved in youth ministry. The gravitational pull of the dominant cultural perspectives is so powerful that it can often seem impossible to break its power and help adolescents experience the powerful intervention of God to bring healing grace and sustaining hope. Against such a rising tide, youth ministers may be tempted to give up on the culture and try to flee its influence, hoping along the way to bring a few "saved souls" along with them.

Like the prophets that went before him, he endures the scorn and ridicule of the assembled multitude. But Jesus does not turn his back on the mocking crowd. If he had, he would have walked away from Jairus the moment his daughter was pronounced dead. Instead, Jesus steps right into the middle of this situation. He doesn't turn and run. He stays and engages the people around him. He recognizes what is going on and speaks to them in their terms. But he transcends their perspective by recognizing this moment as an opportunity to speak God's word and do God's work. What looks and smells like death on the human side, is nothing more than sleep from the divine view.

A little girl has a broken body. A mother and father have broken hearts. Surely,

---

17. "I have learned that simple availability is the most powerful force we can contribute to calm the fears of others" (Yancey, 176).

18. "Don't be afraid" is the most frequent command in the Bible, appearing over 350 times.

19. Yancey, 171. The twin commands summon forth Jairus' ongoing trust that Jesus can and will bring healing.

Jesus can endure the crowd's mocking in order to bring God's good news. In the process, he transforms the situation, and clearly communicates God's saving grace. Youth ministers must learn this same craft and become skilled and courageous practitioners of prophetic cultural analysis.[20]

Death robbing an adolescent girl of life and stabbing her parents' hearts with grief's sword is not a part of God's creation intent. This situation is evil, and the master will tolerate it no longer! Jesus does have the final word. His touch ("He took her by the hand") and his speech ("Talitha koum"—"Little girl, I say to you, get up!") bring divine salvation (v. 41). "Immediately the girl stood up and walked around (she was 12 years old). At this they were completely astonished" (v. 42).

This remarkable story contains a number of elements essential for youth evangelism, including:

- being empathic with another's crisis
- being willing to listen
- being patient
- being present with those who suffer
- being courageous to withstand culture's ridicule
- being wise in analyzing and utilizing culture for ministry purposes
- seeing adolescents in relationship to family and community
- never giving up on any person, no matter how far gone they seem

Jesus' disciples, then and now, can learn much by observing Jesus' evangelistic model.

The healing of the boy with an evil spirit (Matthew 17:14–19; Mark 9:14–21; Luke 9:37–43)

Jesus comes down the mountain from the Transfiguration event to find his disciples engaged in a heated argument with the teachers of the law (Mark 9:14). When Jesus inquires about the cause of the argument, a disappointed father reports, "Teacher, I brought my son, who is possessed by a spirit...I asked your disciples to drive out the spirit, but they could not" (vs. 17–18). In dealing with this young person, Jesus is confronted by evil in two different forms: (1) the evil spirit wreaking havoc in the boy, robbing the father of a natural loving relationship with his precious son, and (2) the evil of unbelief at work in his own followers, rendering them impotent in the face of evil. Jesus will deal with each in turn.

Like Jairus, this father is confident that Jesus has the power to bring salvation in the form of healing his child. When the boy is brought before him, the evil spirit demonstrates its power by convulsing the boy.[21] As in the previous story, Jesus knows that part of the healing process is the opportunity to talk about the nature and extent of suffering, and so he asks the question "How long has the boy been like this?" The

"It is right to recognize our responsibility to engage in aggressive evangelism. It is right to desire the conversion of unbelievers...But it is not right when we take it on us to do more than God has given us to do. It is not right when we regard ourselves as responsible for securing converts, and look to our own enterprise and techniques to accomplish what only God can accomplish. To do that is to intrude ourselves into the office of the Holy Ghost, and to exalt ourselves as the agents of the new birth... the spirit of self-reliance is a blight on evangelism."
—John Stott, *Evangelism and the Sovereignty of God* (Downers Grove, Illinois: InterVarsity Press), 29.

20. For two outstanding examples of cultural analysis aiding the cause of youth ministry, see Tony Campolo, *Growing Up in America: A Sociology of Youth Ministry* (Grand Rapids, Michigan: Zondervan/Youth Specialties, 1989); and Quentin J. Schultze (ed.), *Dancing in the Dark: Youth, Popular Culture, and Electronic Media* (Grand Rapids, Michigan: Eerdmans, 1991).

21. Matthew 17:15 describes the condition as epilepsy.

father explains that this has gone on a long time, since his birth.[22] Through four separate descriptions (vv. 18, 20, 22, 26), Mark emphasizes the extent of the boy's suffering that repeatedly threatens his life ("It has often thrown him into fire or water to kill him" v. 22.). Once again Jesus is involved in a life-and-death situation involving an adolescent. Evil is at work here, and another child's life hangs in the balance.

The dialogue that follows is a source of tremendous encouragement for everyone involved in youth ministry. How often do we face situations that seem utterly hopeless? Family dysfunction rooted so deep that it seems impossible for kids to escape its clutches; children having babies; addiction and violence; the chain seems unbreakable—the cycle endless.

The father intercedes on behalf of his beloved son. "But if you can do anything, take pity on us and help us" (v. 22). The love of a devoted father and the disciples' delegated authority are no match against the seemingly invincible evil force at work in the boy. Desperately, the father cries out to the only one left who might have a chance of saving his son. Jesus' response is one of the great words to all engaged in ministry, "If you can?...Everything is possible for him who believes" (v. 23).[23] Faced with the seemingly unstoppable cycle of evil destroying the life of this boy, Jesus points away from human impotence to divine power. The father's response can be every youth worker's prayer, "I do believe; help me overcome my unbelief!" (v. 24).

Jesus responds immediately and directly. He rebukes the evil spirit with the command to come out of the boy and leave him alone (v. 25). One last time the spirit convulses the boy, so violently that to all the onlookers the boy appears dead (v. 26). As he did with Jairus' daughter, Jesus reaches out and raises the boy to his feet, restoring him to life and to relationship with his father (v. 27). Jesus rebukes the terrifying power that has seized this boy, and overcomes evil through the power of relational love. "We, as the church, can repair the ancient ruins and become the repairers of the breach. However, we must be willing to be taken out of our comfort zone and complacency to repent and to openly embrace young people, even the super-predators, for they are God's children, too."[24]

The disciples have been on the sidelines since the beginning, embarrassed by their impotence. Now they reappear in the narrative, but only after Jesus has gone behind closed doors. Alone with him, they blurt out the question they have held since Jesus came down off the mountain and intervened in this situation. "Why couldn't we drive it out?" (v. 28). Jesus' reply strikes at the heart of spirituality for ministry, "There is no way to get rid of this kind of demon except by prayer" (v. 29, *The Message*). Ched Meyers comments—

> What is unbelief but the despair, dictated by the dominant powers, that
> nothing can really change, a despair that renders revolutionary vision

The power to believe

A dangerous assumption many youth workers carry into their jobs is that they have the power to change hearts and minds. To the contrary—youth ministers are in the faith business, and the first boundary of biblical ministry is to recognize what is our role and what is God's.

Notice this passage where the father pleads for more faith and help with unbelief (Mark 9:14-29). Our role is to point to Jesus and to walk with those who long for his touch. It is God's job to deal with unbelief. We can pray and point and care and counsel—but we must never lose sight of the limits of our ministry calling. We must let God be God.

---

22. The literal phrase, "For a long time he has been like this, from childhood," hints that this story may be about someone of adolescent age.

23. "If? There are no 'ifs' among believers. Anything can happen" (*The Message*).

24. A.G. Miller, "What Jesus Christ and African American Teenagers Are Telling the African American Church," The 1997 Princeton Lectures on Youth, Church, and Culture (Princeton, New Jersey: Institute of Youth Ministry, Princeton Theological Seminary), 44.

and practice impotent. The disciples are instructed to battle this impotence, this temptation to resignation, through prayer...(And) is not prayer the intensely personal struggle within each disciple, and among us collectively, to resist the despair and distractions that cause us to practice unbelief, to abandon or avoid the way of Jesus?"[25]

There is another "demon" at work in this story. It is the evil of unbelief, resident in the hearts of Jesus' closest followers. From this point on in Mark's gospel, Jesus emphasizes the importance of prayer as the foundation of the disciples' ability to stay on the road with Jesus and to carry out the ministry to which they've been called. (Mark 11:22-25; 14:38).[26]

The lessons from this story for evangelistic youth ministry?

- There is a time and place for theological discussion and debate, and it is not in the midst of another's crisis in suffering.
- Be patient to listen to someone's entire story of suffering.
- Intervene in seemingly hopeless situations.
- Admit doubt.
- Resist despair through the discipline of prayer.
- Pray for a perspective of hope.

The Scriptures clearly teach the biblical priority of youth evangelization. To be faithful to this calling, youth workers must live out the same priorities we have seen in the gospel of ministry of Jesus, and in the right order:

1. The need to be disciplined in the development of personal spirituality ("being with Jesus")
2. The need to be clear about the content of the gospel and its emphasis upon adolescent ministry ("preach the good news")
3. The need for courageous confrontation with personal and corporate evil that threatens the well-being of adolescents ("to cast out demons")

The only way this kind of ministry can be carried out is with a constant prayer upon the lips of everyone involved in ministry with kids—

Lord, I'm trusting you. Help me overcome my doubts of you and myself. Give me the enduring confidence that you truly are at work, especially when from my perspective it looks like virtually nothing is happening in the lives of the kids to whom I've been called by your Spirit. Transform my heartfelt fears into the courage to reach out to disinterested kids whom you love with a compassion that transcends my comprehension. I believe there is no more important calling than to invest myself in the lives of the precious kids whom you have placed upon my heart and put in the way of my life's journey. Lord, when the question is

25. Ched Meyers, *Binding the Strong Man* (Maryknoll, New York: Orbis Books, 1988), 255-256.

26. For a powerful description of the importance of prayer undergirding ministry, see Eugene Peterson, *Working the Angles* (Grand Rapids, Michigan: Eerdmans, 1987), 15-60.

asked of me, "And how are the children?" I want to be able to say,"All the children are well." Only as I am empowered by your Holy Spirit is that possible. Amen.

Focusing Youth Ministry through the Family
Mark DeVries

Several years back, I received a curious invitation. I was told that a new book was in the works, to be called, *The 10 Hottest Youth Groups in the Country*. I was honored to submit a chapter, but as I mailed it off, I realized that soon everyone would know what I had come to know so well: Our youth ministry was, in many ways, anything but hot. Nonetheless, I looked forward to receiving a copy of the book to discover the fascinating accounts of other ministries from which I was certain to learn a great deal.

That was over five years ago. And I'm still waiting.

I never heard another word from the would-be editor. The book, quite obviously, was never published. And it doesn't take a rocket scientist to figure out why: the hottest youth groups in the country, were, on closer inspection, doing a lot of little things faithfully, but certainly nothing outrageous enough to make *The 10 Hottest Youth Groups* a decent read.

Youth ministry is a messy, typically unspectacular vocation regardless of how many years we have under our belts. No matter how clear our model, how tight our evaluation system, or how much we invest in the work, it's messy—not something that can be domesticated into policies or models or procedures.

But despite my realism, I have, for more than 20 years, had one consuming passion in my work: to find the most effective ways of leading young people toward maturity in Christ (Colossians 1:28). Early in my ministry, I became aware that having a group of on fire teenagers was often not a reliable predictor of whether those students would grow to be *men and women* living with a passionate love for Christ as adults. And after years in this business, I have been disappointed again and again when some of our most committed youth group kids would head off to college and into adulthood without the sufficient spiritual infrastructure to make it as faithful disciples in the adult world.

It was in the context of these experiences that the whole notion of *family-based youth ministry*[1] began taking shape for me. And over the past five years, I have been fascinated by the broad-based groundswell of interest in this whole approach to youth ministry. In charismatic groups and to groups that are terrified of charismatics, in traditional groups and groups that despise tradition, in denominational groups and in groups that insist on calling their denomination "nondenominational," in conservative groups, liberal groups, and even in groups that have trouble finding any theological common ground, I have found youth leaders embracing the principles of family-based youth ministry.

---

1. Mark DeVries, *Family-Based Youth Ministry* (Downers Grove, Illinois: InterVarsity Press, 1994).

Ponderable
What comes to mind when you hear the phrase *family-based youth ministry?* How does it fit with your understanding of the basic task of youth ministry?

Though this vision of youth ministry has created a great deal of interest, it has also stirred up a good deal of confusion. Some see it as synonymous with abandoning all traditional youth programming. Others see it as a way to place the entire responsibility for the Christian nurture of teenagers on their own parents. And a few see it as just another good thing to add to their already overloaded job description.

This chapter will provide some clarity and perspective to those seeking to understand and hopefully engage in a family-based ministry. To simplify my explanation, I have organized my thoughts around four basic questions: Why? Who? What? How?

⌐ The *why* of focusing youth ministry through the family

"With all the kids I know who make it, there's one thing they all have in common: individual contact with an adult who cared and kept hanging in there."
—Barbara Staggers, counselor and physician at Children's Hospital Teen Clinic in Oakland, California, quoted in *Rolling Stone*, December 9, 1993

For the past decade or so, I have maintained the somewhat controversial position that youth ministry today is in crisis. When I use the word *crisis*, many are quick to point out all the positive signs in youth ministry today. They point to the many churches reporting record numbers of young people active in their programs. They remind me of all the parachurch organizations and national church ministries that have found ways of attracting unprecedented numbers to their events. And they document the staggering number of youth ministry practitioners who are drawn to national youth worker training events.

But when I speak of the crisis in youth ministry, I am not suggesting that traditional youth ministry models have failed to get students and their leaders to attend meetings. I readily admit that we have become quite proficient at *that* process. But I still insist that there is a crisis.

Observe the following markers:

George Barna's research indicates that in spite of the fact that more and more youth are participating in our programs, those teenagers are not growing up to be adults who participate in church any more than they did almost 30 years ago. In 1988, he wrote—

> Since 1970, there has been no appreciable change in the proportion of adults who attend church services at any time during the week. This is true in spite of a growing number of churches, increased church spending for advertising and promotion, and the availability of more sophisticated techniques for informing people of a church's existence.[2]

Additionally, by 1996, Barna was documenting a relatively steady decline in the levels of adult participation in church and in Christian education over the previous decade.[3]

The crisis in youth ministry is, simply put, that we have not been effective in leading our young people to mature Christian *adulthood*. Even with the massive increase in funding and training for youth ministry, even with the professionalization of youth pastors, even with the exponential increase in the number of resources available to

A controversy
Some agree with Mark DeVries on this point, and others don't. As one youth ministry vet put it, "If it ain't broke, don't fix it—and youth ministry ain't broke." Do you agree with the severity of this perspective? Has youth ministry failed in its mission to train mature disciples?

2. George Barna, *Marketing the Church* (Colorado Springs, Colorado: NavPress, 1988), 22.

3. George Barna, *Index of Leading Spiritual Indicators* (Dallas, Texas: Word, 1996), 36, 19.

those of us doing youth ministry, we are seeing no appreciable increase in the percentage of adults in our culture who are living out their faith for themselves.

By way of illustration, consider how would we evaluate an automotive production plant that brought only a small percentage of its cars off the assembly line, ready to be shipped to customers. The managers could point to the efficiency of the workers on the assembly line, the new developments in technology, or the increased morale of the staff. But if the company was not doing what it was created to do, namely, to produce cars, *crisis* would not be too strong a word to describe the situation.

If you look deep into the bowels of George Barna's *Index of Leading Spiritual Indicators*, you'll find that when thousands of believers were asked to rate what churches do best and what they do worst, "creating programs for teenagers" came in dead last.[4] And we are nearing consensus that the frightening decrease in membership in mainline denominations is directly related the failure of those denominations to retain their own young people.

We could point to any number of secondary reasons for our inability to lead our young people to mature Christian adulthood: Most youth ministries today are funded for failure, setting aside just enough money to guarantee a frustrated staff.[5] Most churches hire youth staff and recruit volunteers only for the short haul, making it sometimes impossible for youth in the church to develop friendships with durable, available adults.[6]

But I am convinced that reasons like those are only secondary causes for our failure to lead children to mature Christian adulthood. The primary cause of the current crisis in youth ministry lies in the ways that our culture (and too often our churches) has systematically isolated young people from the very relationships that are most likely to lead them to maturity. Granting our children the "privilege of being left alone,"[7] has created, in part, a wholesale epidemic of adult neglect of the next generation. This audacious claim is precisely the thesis of Patricia Hersch in her groundbreaking study of adolescence in America, called *A Tribe Apart*. She writes—

> A clear picture of adolescents, of even our own children, eludes us—not necessarily because they are rebelling, or avoiding or evading us. It is because we aren't there. Not just parents, but any adults. American society has left its children behind as the cost of progress in the workplace. This isn't about working parents, right or wrong, but an issue for society to set its priorities and to pay attention to its young in the same way it pays attention to its income.[8]

"It's one factor we haven't mentioned: our woeful inability as mainline Protestants to retain our young."
—Will Willimon, *Christianity Today,* August 17, 1997, 17-18.

4. George Barna, *Index of Leading Spiritual Indicators* (Dallas, Texas: Word, 1996), 43-44.

5. It is not particularly surprising that in the Link Institute's study of over 2,100 youth workers, only one in five expressed satisfaction with their work (*Youthworker*, November/December 1997), 50.

6. Tony Souder, the director of the Chattanooga Youth Ministry Network, told me recently that his organization just completed a study of 160 different youth ministries in his area. One of their most fascinating discoveries was that out of those 160 youth ministries surveyed, 112 (over 70 percent) had gone through key leadership transitions during a single 18-month period.

7. Patricia Hersch, *A Tribe Apart* (New York: Ballantine Books, 1998), 22.

8. Hersch, 19.

The television series "Dawson's Creek" comes as close as anything to demonstrate how *adults* perceive the teenage experience. The producers of the show (I'm guessing not an adolescent in the bunch) leave viewers with the impression that the town of Capeside would change little if there were no parents or other adults present. In the make-believe world of "Dawson's Creek," it is, in fact, the youth who are the purveyors of wisdom about their world. And those over 18 are either hopelessly out of touch or have little else to occupy their time than interfering with Dawson and his friends.

Back in the 1980s, Mihaly Csikzentmihalyi and Reed Larson, in their book, *Being Adolescent*, startled us with their report that teenagers spend less than 7 percent of their waking hours with any adults, while spending approximately half of their time with peers.[9] And today, more and more children simply fend for themselves, often under the dispassionate care of television and other technology, sometimes under the thumb of shameful abuse and neglect. Emotionally available neighbors, grandparents, teachers, or coaches are quickly moving to the endangered species list, as the pace of life topples over itself and the number of children who need care vastly outpaces the number of adults who choose to be available to them. And even many youth-friendly churches block the doors of adult worship to their teenagers, sometimes in the name of age-appropriate worship somewhere else, but more often because of a lack of willingness to speak (or sing) in language and form that youth can understand.

Though the statistics and studies on this isolation are legion, they often don't accurately depict the desperate aloneness that so many teenagers feel, an aloneness acted out in the self-destructive actions of millions each year. The following journal entry of a teenage girl writing several years ago for her high school English class portrays the pathos of this *alone* experience in all its intensity:

> No one is there...
> My wounds are green and throbbing.
> I can't scream any louder.
>
> If they were here now
> They would see
> That the beauty that was out is now in
> And the rottenness that was in is now out.
>
> But no one will come.

It is clear that young people grow to maturity in general and to maturity in Christ in particular by being around those people who have such maturity themselves. Margaret Mead, the renowned anthropologist, warned of the dangers of what she called a *co-figurative culture*—a culture in which all learning is horizontal, and little or no learning comes from an older and wiser generation.[10]

"More often than not, children are learning major value systems in life from the horizontal peer culture. The vertical structure is not there in adequate increments of time or intensity to do the job."
—Gordon MacDonald, *The Effective Father* (Wheaton, Illinois: Tyndale House, 1989), 102.

9. Mihaly Csikzentmihalyi and Reed Larson, *Being Adolescent: Conflict and Growth in the Teenage Years* (Basic Books, 1984), quoted in Quentin J. Schultze, *Winning Your Kids Back from the Media* (Downers Grove, Illinois: InterVarsity Press, 1994), 49.

10. Margaret Mead, *Culture and Commitment: A Study of the Generation Gap* (Garden City, New York: Doubleday-Natural History Press, 1970), 45.

The obvious limitation of a co-figurative culture, or what Robert Bly calls a *sibling society*, is that each generation has to re-learn (and often incorrectly) a value system that can give them coherence and meaning. And Mary Pipher (of *Reviving Ophelia* fame) even goes so far as to pinpoint this phenomenon as the cause of much of our current social ills:

> A great deal of America's social sickness comes from age segregation. If 10- to 14-year-olds are grouped together, they will form a *Lord of the Flies* culture with its competitiveness and meanness. But if 10 people ages 2 to 80 are grouped together, they will fall into a natural age hierarchy that nurtures and teaches them all. For our own mental and societal health, we need to reconnect the age groups.[11]

Cold war

Is it possible that what Mark calls "the segregation of our teenagers into their own ghetto" has become a double-edged sword? Adults seem not to know what to do with kids, and are often too preoccupied with their own lives to invest significantly in the young. Sensing this, the young tend to respond, "Okay, then, just give me my own room, money, freedom, and space, and I'll be fine. Who needs you, anyway?"

Youth workers (and committed teachers, compassionate coaches, concerned parents—those adults who truly care for kids) are often caught in the middle of this subtle relational cold war. And this is Mark's plea in this chapter: the youth ministry task is to mobilize a systemically committed barrage of adults in love with adolescents devoted to caring for kids as they are, where they are. This is the best hope of reaching a lost, forgotten, and alienated generation.

Do you agree? Is it too late?

Increasingly, the message of adult culture to its youth has become "You're on your own." And this isolation (intentional or unintentional) has placed our culture squarely atop a demographic time bomb, and more and more voices are reporting that they can hear it ticking. I am convinced, therefore, that the most chronic problem our church's youth ministries must address is the segregation of our teenagers into their own ghetto. We may assume that spending money on a youth house or a state-of-the-art youth room is exactly what our kids need. But nine times out of 10, such traditional "youth-serving" practices serve only as a quick fix, patronizing solution, resulting in even more isolation of youth from the very people they need to be around to develop a mature Christian faith. *Any approach to youth ministry in the new millennium must move beyond a myopic focus on programming and "relational ministry" done by a few enthusiastic, inexperienced, short-term, early-20s youth leaders who stay around only long enough to "wow" our kids.* Our modern fascination with the professionalization of youth ministry may have kept us blissfully ignorant of our growing proficiency at rearranging deck chairs on the Titanic. Unless our new models of ministry can help our culture restore the "generational threads that used to weave their way into the fabric of growing up,"[12] our ministries will be severely limited in their long-term effectiveness.

The *who* of focusing youth ministry through the family

> Give me a lever long enough and a prop strong enough. I can single-handed move the world.
>
> —*Archimedes*

For years we have known that the statistics are out there. Though social scientists have trouble agreeing about much of anything, most are clear in their recognition of the incomparable power (for better or for worse) of moms and dads in the faith and character formation of their children.

---

11. Mary Pipher, *USA Weekend* (March 19-21, 1999), 12.

12. Hersch, 20.

Take, for example, the results of a study done recently by the National Center on Addiction and Substance Abuse (CASA). The survey of 1,115 teenagers affirmed the crucial role that parents play in insuring that their children grow up drug-free. They found a clear link between certain types of parental behaviors and children who are likely to be free of chemical dependency. Here's a sampling of those parental habits:

- The are engaged in their teens' lives, including helping with homework or attending teens' extracurricular activities.
- They have at least five sit down meals together weekly with their families.
- They attend religious services together with their teens.
- They set curfews.
- They see drug use as dangerous and morally wrong.[13]

But those of us over 35 don't need to see the studies. The reality of our own parents' influence is all too obvious. I can still remember the day several years ago when I looked into the mirror in horror, realizing for the first time, that I looked less and less like the guy in my high school annual and more and more like my father. And I hadn't been a parent for long before I found myself saying and doing the very things my parents had said and done, even those things I had promised myself as a child that I would never do.

When I ask adults in the church to consider the influence that their parents have had on their own faith formation, the vast majority of them have little difficulty describing the immensity of that influence. And it is staggering that whenever I ask a group of Christian youth leaders how many of them came from a home in which at least one Christian parent was present, an average of 90 percent of the folks in the class raise their hands. Even in families where neither parent was a Christian, the adult children confess that they bear some undeniable marks of the value system they grew up with.

Across the nation, churches are beginning to wake up to the fact that often the most faithful, long-term leaders of youth can actually be parents of youth themselves. Here's why: No one has more long-term interest in students than their parents. In Nashville we have gone against conventional wisdom and filled our volunteer youth staff with parents. Of the more than 100 volunteers who work weekly with our teenagers, the vast majority are parents of one of the youths in the group.

But as powerful as the influence of a parent is on the faith development of child, there is another influence that can be even more powerful. The book, *Faithful Parents/Faithful Kids*, documents a study of Christian adults, a study that sought to determine the most effective faith-nurturing practices for parents. What they found was that there was no single, across-the-board practice that worked in even a slim majority of families. Some effective parents required their teenage children to attend church, but the majority did not (over 50 percent actually quit going to Sunday school in high school). Some families (25 percent) had devotions together; the majority did not. And

---

13. Mitzi Perdue, "Research Describes Drugs' Dangers and What Parents Can Do," *The Tennessean* (February 4), 98.

surprisingly few of the adults (15 percent) surveyed reported praying fairly often with their parents during the teenage years. For the researchers looking for a barn-burning discovery, the results had to be somewhat frustrating.

What the study did discover, however, *was a single faith-nurturing factor that was present in over 90 percent of those surveyed*. The authors wrote, "While we didn't come up with a sure-fire formula, one thing was obvious: *Those who stuck with their faith…had a half-dozen 'mentors' present during their growing up years*." [14] It is this influence that we must lean heavily on as our youth ministries become increasingly populated with teenagers who do not come from Christian homes.

Emmy E. Werner, from the University of California at Davis, has come to a similar, well-documented conclusion. Since 1955, she has been studying resiliency in a group of 500 Hawaiians who were born into difficult circumstances (poverty, addiction, etc.). Her work was one of small number of studies included in Radcliffe College's Landmark Studies of the 20TH Century conference this year. Her "landmark" conclusion? The strongest predictor of resilience (of children who grow up in abusive situations and then go on to live happy and productive lives) was "an adult mentor outside the immediate family—grandmother, a minister [for example]—who gave them a sense of being loved and important."[15]

As adolescents go through the acute changes of their developmental years, they are likely to go through any number of psychopathologies. But in the vast majority of cases, these imbalances do not last. During these years when the ability to offend and stumble clumsily along is so great, teenagers need adults who will know the wisdom of waiting and remaining connected as the process evolves in its own timetable.

It is only when the church and family abandon their role of helping young people navigate that passage to adulthood, that teenagers look to their friends, their music, and the media as surrogate (and often tyrannical) mentors. For too many kids, the media steps into the gap created by our cultural neglect and gives them a map of reality—telling them who they are and what they need to think about. And there they learn the frightening lie that the only ultimate arbiter of truth is oneself. Alone again. Unfortunately, it is often the students who *desperately* need mentors who have the most difficult time finding them. As Judith Wallerstein discovered in her highly acclaimed study of the children of divorce—

> Children of divorce, who need help most of all, may find it even harder than other children to find mentors…There aren't many mentors in the shopping mall. Where are modern youngsters going to find them? Of all the children in our study, only very few found and made use of mentors.[16]

---

14. Greg Johnson and Mike Yorkey, *Faithful Parents, Faithful Kids* (Wheaton, Illinois: Tyndale House, 1993), 249.

15. Monika Guttman, "Resilience," *USA Weekend* (March 5-7, 1999), 5.

16. Judith Wallerstein and Sandra Blakeslee, *Second Chances* (New York: Ticknor & Fields, 1989), 112.

What about...?
A family-focused youth ministry inherently brings at least one significant challenge, if not clear danger: what about those students whose families are not connected to the church, or who do not want to be? How can a youth ministry program resolve this in attempting to implement the issues raised in this chapter?

But there are signs of hope—islands of light—where kids are making it out of circumstances in which all the odds are stacked against them.

Consider the story of Gene Rivers.

He grew up in a neighborhood where kids going to Harvard only happened in pipe dreams and miracle stories. So one might naturally assume that after getting his Ivy League ticket out of the gang-infested world of his childhood, Gene Rivers would never look back. But now, at 48 years old, after attending both Harvard and Yale, he is beating the odds again.

He's back in his old neighborhood giving hope to a generation of would-be disposable children, providing an alternative to kids growing up in the crime-ridden streets of Dorchester—one of the poorest areas in Boston. The work of this maverick minister has caused *Newsweek*, somewhat surprisingly, to suggest that it may just be the church that holds the secret that traditional secular strategies have missed:

> Now both sides [of the political fence] are beginning to form an unlikely alliance founded on the idea that the only way to rescue kids from the seduction of the drug and gang culture is with another, more powerful set of values: *A substitute family* for young people who almost never have two parents, and maybe not even one at home. And *the only institution* with the spiritual message and the physical presence to offer those traditional values, these strange bedfellows have concluded, *is the church* (emphasis mine).[17]

The secret found in Gene Rivers' story may just hold the key to providing a lasting ministry to teenagers in our churches—suburban, rural, and urban alike. It's about churches doing the one thing they are best equipped to do: build supportive, nurturing relationships across the generations, in essence, an extended Christian family.

The "who" of family-based youth ministry, is quite simply, then, the parents and an extended Christian family of adults partnering together for the sake of the spiritual formation of the next generation. When a student makes it to mature Christian adulthood, she can almost always point either to the influence of godly parents or to the influence of at least one available, durable, non-exploitive Christian adult who modeled for them what being an adult Christian was all about. Sometimes 20-something youth directors can make this kind of long-term, ongoing investment in a handful of students, but by and large, their age-driven transience severely limits their long-term availability.

The *what* of focusing youth ministry through the family

> If we are going to learn a life of holiness in the mess of history, we are going to have to prepare for something intergenerational and think in centuries.[18]
>
> —*Eugene Peterson,* The Contemplative Pastor

---

17. John Leland with Claudia Kalb, "Savior of the Streets," *Newsweek* (June 1, 1998).

18. Eugene Peterson, *The Contemplative Pastor* (Grand Rapids, Michigan: Eerdmans, 1989), 47.

Several years ago, scientists in Canada discovered that the population of rabbits in a particular area of their country had diminished to frighteningly low levels. And loving mysteries, as scientists are want to do, these curious scholars set out to discover the cause of this dramatic shift in the rabbit population.

Their first assumption was that there must have been an illness killing off all these rabbits. But they could find no evidence of any such epidemic. Several years later, while they were still scratching their heads over the cause of the decrease in the rabbit population, they noticed an unexplainable *increase* in those same numbers.

At the same time, other scientists began to notice dramatic fluctuations in the area's fox population as well. Again, they investigated the possibility of an animal-specific disease, and again they came up with nothing. Finally, another scientist read of this quandary and offered this simple solution, one which ultimately proved to be astonishingly accurate. Having observed the relationship between the fluctuations in the rabbit and fox population, this scientist discovered an inverse relationship between these two groups. As the population of foxes increased, the number of rabbits decreased; and when the fox population decreased, the number of rabbits increased.

He postulated that as the population of rabbits multiplied, they provided an ample food supply for the foxes, resulting in an increase in the number of foxes. But as the fox population increased, they ate more of the rabbits, resulting in a decrease in the rabbit population. And the resulting lower number of available bunny meals caused a decrease in the fox population, which consequently again made it possible for the rabbits to multiply more rapidly. The cycle was self-perpetuating.[19]

When the scientists limited their focus to a single group, they were unable to discover a solution. When we attempt to "solve" the crisis in youth ministry with a myopic focus on adolescents and their problems, we will likely find ourselves coming up empty as well. When our perspective of a problem is limited to what happens *within* a specific group alone, we will of necessity ignore the problematic interactions between groups. If we become too narrowly focused "on teenagers and their problems," the solutions we are searching for will remain a mystery.

For me, family-based youth ministry is grounded in at least two texts from Scripture. The first is a passage that directs the people of God to be specifically attentive to the next generation and confirms the priority and power of vertical relationships between generations. Though the nuclear family is central to this process, it is the entire *extended family* of God's people who are commanded to take responsibility for naturally and repeatedly passing on the faith to the next generation:

> Hear, O Israel: the Lord our God, the Lord is one. Love the Lord your
> God with all your heart and with all your soul and with all your
> strength. These commandments that I give you today are to be upon
> your hearts. *Impress them on your children.* Talk about them *when you sit* at
> home and *when you walk* along the road, *when you lie down* and *when you*

---

19. William J. Lederer and Don D. Jackson, *The Mirages of Marriage* (New York: W.W. Norton & Co., 1968), 88; Mark DeVries and Nan Russell, *Bridges*, (Downers Grove: InterVarsity Press, 1995; out of print, available at www.familybasedym.com).

> get up. *Tie them* as symbols on your hands and *bind them* on your fore-
> heads. *Write them* on the doorframes of your houses and on your gates.
> —*Deuteronomy 6:4-9 [italics added]*

The second text, from the New Testament, contains a direct command to every
believer to run the race of faith well. But it is not so much the command as the context that is instructive for the vision of Family-based youth ministry. According to the
author of Hebrews, we are to run this race well because of the kinds of people by
whom we are surrounded.

> Therefore, since we are surrounded by such a great cloud of witnesses,
> let us throw off everything that hinders and the sin that so easily entan-
> gles, and let us run with perseverance the race marked out for us.
> —*Hebrews 12:1*

In Hebrews 11, we are introduced to a "hall of fame of faith," of sorts, as the author
lists 20 or so men and women who, by faith, obeyed God. And chapter 12 begins by
pulling those characters out of the history books and into our lives with a compelling
image. By way of analogy, we are asked to imagine that these men and women of faith
are in the arena surrounding us, perhaps even cheering for us as we run the race of
faith. Family-based youth ministry is about stacking the stands, surrounding kids with
an arena full of godly adults (both living and dead).

And so, rooted in these texts, I define my own approach to family-based youth
ministry in this way: Using the position of the youth ministry to access, empower, and
connect students to the most effective sources of faith formation, namely the nuclear
family and the extended family of the church.

As I have attended family conferences and discussed and explored the different
changes in family-based youth ministry, I have discovered two distinct approaches: the
family ministry model and the *youth ministry model*. The major distinction between the
two is found in the answer to a single question—What drives this ministry?

The family ministry model

If a family-based youth ministry is driven by a desire to empower families, it would
likely fit into the *family ministry model*. No one describes (and more importantly, lives
out) this model of family-based youth ministry better than my friend, Ben Freudenberg
at Concordia Lutheran Church in St. Louis. Ben's perspective (well documented in his
book, *The Family Friendly Church* [20] is that the church's primary job in youth ministry is
to *support* the ministry that rightly belongs to the family.

Programming for his ministry, therefore, is driven not by the church or the
youth ministry as much as by individual families. Ben sometimes refers to this approach
as family-centered, church-supported. In larger churches, this model of ministry would

---

20. Ber Freudenburg with Rick Lawrence, *The Family Friendly Church* (Loveland, Colorado: Group Publishing, 1998).

likely be run by a family pastor who focuses on empowering and equipping parents to fulfill the vows that many of them took for the Christian nurture of their children.

They might also spend a good deal of time on what some in family ministry refer to as *ambulance programs* (systems, like Stephen Ministry, that help people in crisis) and *guardrail programs* (including programs like Marriage Enrichment, that prevent later, larger problems in families). This approach is likely the most effective way to assist and support families, though it may be less effective in leading young people (particularly those from non-Christian or nominal Christian homes) to mature Christian adulthood.

The youth ministry model

If a family-based youth ministry is driven primarily by a desire to see young people grow to maturity in Christ, it would fit into the *youth ministry model*. Over the past few years, I have often straddled the fence of my ministerial identity, not quite sure if I was a youth pastor or a family pastor. Though many family ministers are dear friends of mine and I believe deeply in what they are doing, I have come to realize that I am, by calling and by passion, a youth pastor. And though I am committed to healthy families, it is my passion for seeing young people grow to maturity in Christ that has driven me to work with families.

In contrast to the family ministry model, the youth ministry model accesses parents and significant other adults, knowing that this approach will always be the most fruitful process for helping young people grow in Christ. The distinction is subtle yet significant. In the family ministry model, the focus is on supporting parents and families with classes, counseling, and support; while in the youth ministry model, the priority shifts to building an intergenerational faith-nurturing community for the teenagers. Both approaches can reasonably be called *family-based youth ministry*. But my particular emphasis is on the latter model.

The *how* of focusing youth ministry through the family

"I loved coming home to a place where the first three pews celebrated my coming back from college."
—Mary Price Maddox, describing her experience growing up in an intentional family-based youth ministry.

First the good news: Across the nation, youth leaders are coming to recognize that ignoring families is no longer a luxury that we can afford in youth ministry.

Now the bad news: The vast majority of youth leaders feel ill-equipped to work with adults in general and with parents in particular. In a recent Link Institute study, "working with adults" was listed near the top of the list of the hardest things about youth ministry. And similarly, "lack of parental support" was ranked very near the top of the greatest challenges.[21]

It's the same message I have heard from youth leaders all over the country: family-based youth ministry is a great idea, but show us *how* to do it.

When I talk about implementing a family-based youth ministry, it is important to understand that I am talking more about creating an ongoing ethos in the ministry (what might be called a *new normal*) than establishing any specific program or programs.

---

21. *Youthworker* (November/December, 1997), 50.

Family-based youth ministry is not, strictly speaking, a model but rather a foundation that I believe every youth ministry needs to insure its long-term impact. Therefore, the specific model of youth ministry a church chooses is almost irrelevant.

Suppose, for example, that your church wants to adopt Doug Fields' *purpose-driven* approach to youth ministry. You need not choose against family-based youth ministry in favor of purpose-driven youth ministry. Instead, you would use Doug's principles as your model for your youth ministry but undergird that program with the kind of family-based connections that will offer the structures for the long-term faith formation of your youth. Another church might choose to use the Logos model or a Peer Ministry model. Family-based principles are an imperative foundation for any of them. Regardless of the model, every ministry must find ways to build on a foundation of parents providing intentional Christian nurture for their children and students connecting to an extended Christian family of faith-full adults.

The implementation process for family-based youth ministry is, therefore, very different from implementing a specific model for a youth ministry. When implementing a family-based youth ministry, it is not necessary to put weekly or even regular programs in place all at once. As a matter of fact, the most effective implementation process takes years (it took us almost a decade) to put in place. I teach a specific long-term implementation process for family-based youth ministry that borders on being absurdly simple. Here it is—

Year One: Experiment with one family-based program.
Expect limited response.
If the program is well-received, repeat it the next year.
If the program flops, try something else the next year.
Year Two: Repeat what worked the year before (if anything).
Experiment with another family-based program.
Again, expect limited response.
Year Three: Repeat what worked the year before (if anything)
Experiment with another family-based program.
By this year, you can expect that something has been well-received.

I jokingly summarize this anybody-can-do-this, four-year process like this—
Try something. Fail.
Try something else. Fail again.
Try something else. Stumble on one thing that works.
Repeat what works. Try something else…
You get the idea.

Since my implementation process essentially involves the creation or experimentation with only *one* new family-based program a year, there is little need for hundreds of program ideas (though they are certainly out there). Instead, I have found it helpful to categorize family-based youth ministry programming into two distinct types: (1) completely new, family-based events and (2) what I call "*exfamized*" events.

In the final analysis, though, family-based programs provide only the context for healthy connections to be made. It is the caring attentiveness of the older generation to the younger that is likely to make the most significant difference in the lives of the teenagers we touch.

I recently heard the story of an altar boy in a small village, who, as he was carrying the chalice before the priest, dropped the goblet, spilling the consecrated wine all over the floor. The priest responded by backhanding the boy, striking him in the face and shouting, "Never come back here again!" The child obeyed.

In a very similar situation, another altar boy in a different church committed the very same mistake, serving before the bishop himself. But the bishop reacted very differently. He winked at the boy and whispered, "You're going to be a priest someday."

The first boy grew up to become Marshall Tito, the abusive, tyrannical head of the communist party in Yugoslavia, who reigned with an iron fist for decades. The second grew to become Archbishop Fulton J. Sheen, the Roman Catholic bishop who, in the 1950s received an Emmy for his work on television, a role in which he positively affected hundreds of thousands.

May we who form the face of youth ministry in the next century, lead and train others to lead in such a way that when our youth grow to be adults, we will know that we have invested well.

Focusing Youth Ministry through Christian Practices
Mark Yaconelli

At First Church young people are invited to attend a Sunday evening youth group meeting that involves one hour of games, 30 minutes of singing, a "message" from the youth pastor, and snacks. Down the street at Second Church, youth participate in a Sunday school class led by a local college student. Excused from worship, youth watch a video dramatization of different moral dilemmas that Christians may encounter. At Third Church there is no youth program; however, young people between the ages of 12 and 16 are encouraged to attend a six-week confirmation course taught by the senior pastor. Every Sunday afternoon students listen to presentations on the various doctrines and belief statements of the church followed by tests and homework. Those students who complete the course are invited to become members of the church.

These three churches provide different, yet not uncommon, forms of youth discipleship. Assuming there is no difference in theological teaching, what do the methods of each of these ministries communicate about the Christian experience? How do the activities (or lack of) form young people as Christians? More specifically, what *way of life* are youth "practicing" in each of these ministries?

The way of God

Youth ministry is about inviting young people into a way of life.[1] "Prepare the way of the Lord," is the cry of John the Baptist to those who will listen; and this is still the cry of every church to its children. Like John, we invite youth to repent (to turn, change direction) and walk in the way of God. From the earliest records of the biblical testament, God has called people to show their children a pattern of life that is receptive to God's love. Abraham is charged to teach his children to "keep the way of the Lord" (Genesis 18:19). Moses instructs the Jewish people that God's way is to be modeled, taught, and discussed with children (Deuteronomy 6:7; 11:19). In Proverbs, parents are reminded that their first task is to train their children in a way of life devoted to God (Proverbs 22:6).

What is the way of the Lord? For the chosen people it is the way of life (Jeremiah 21:8). It is the way of righteousness and justice offered to Abraham (Genesis 18:19), the way of perfection sung by David (2 Samuel 22:31), the road to wisdom (Proverbs 4:11), and the path of peace (Isaiah 59:8). For the Israelites, to live in God's way was to live in obedience to the commandments and ordinances given to Moses (Deuteronomy 31:29). This was a way of life not limited to a religious system or statements of belief, but rather a form of living that encompassed all the dimensions of human life; from use

---

1. The use of practices as "a way of life" is suggested by Dorothy Bass and Craig Dykstra, "Times of Yearning, Practices of Faith," *Practicing our Faith* (San Francisco: Jossey-Bass, 1997), 6.

Ponderable
Does thinking about youth ministry as "inviting young people into a way of life" resonate with you, or do you have to work at understanding what he means? How does your background and history influence your understanding of Yaconelli's message?

of time and dietary practices, to rules of business and marital conduct. For the earliest followers, God's way was described and prescribed by the laws of Moses; to be faithful was to obey God's holy law (Psalm 1).

And yet, God's way is more than right behavior—more than Sabbath observance and burnt offerings. Obedience to God's law was not the ultimate in godly living, it was simply a means. God's way, contained in the law, is the way of loving relationship. It is life lived with one's heart available to God and others. It is to walk in humility with God, acting with justice and kindness toward other human beings (Micah 6:8). All of the laws and practices of the *Torah* were designed to express and nurture these two intentions: to love God with heart, soul, and strength (Deuteronomy 6:5) and to love fellow human beings as yourself (Leviticus 19:18). Thus the way of God is undertaken as one seeks to embody and live out these two trajectories of love.

For Christians, God's way of life is made fully visible and available in Jesus Christ. As the New Testament attests, Jesus not only practices the way of the Lord, he claims to *be* the way of the Lord (John 14:6). From the first disciples into our present time, Christians claim to experience a deeper, more loving relationship with God and others through the Spirit of the living Christ. For Christians to know Christ, to live in Christ is to live in the way of the Lord. Thus, early Christians are called *The Way* (Acts 9:2) because they experienced in Jesus Christ a path that led to intimacy with God and solidarity with others.

Learning a way of life requires more than listening to inspiring messages, navigating moral quagmires, and knowing the right answers. A way of life addresses all the dimensions of human living. For Christians, it is seeking to shape all of our human capacities—heart, soul, mind, and strength (Mark 12:28-34) in conformity with Jesus Christ. If the way of Christ is living with increasing love for God and others, then there is no ending point, for "love never ends" (1 Corinthians 13:8, 13). Youth ministry cannot end at conversion or church membership. It is not complete once young people know the right answers. For any disciple, the way of Christ can never be *attained* or completed; it can only be *practiced*. Like the athlete who seeks to exercise in order to run the race, youth ministry provides a training ground—space for youth to encounter and engage the habits and disciplines, the exercises and practices, that will help them respond to the heavenly call of God in Jesus Christ (1 Corinthians 9:24-27; Philippians 3:13-14).

Christian practices

Central focus
Mark Yaconelli argues for a youth ministry that is centered in relationships and in love. Do you believe that youth ministry flows from a center of loving relationships? How does what you've seen of youth ministry programs, models, and philosophies compare to this central focus?

Christian practices are the *means* through which Christians seek to respond to God's invitations of love. They are the habits, disciplines, and patterns of life through which Christians seek communion with Christ and solidarity with others. Just as Paul invites the Ephesians to be "imitators of God," Christian practices are the way in which Christians seek to imitate the intentions and patterns of Jesus Christ (Ephesians 5:1).

All youth ministries engage youth in practices; however, not all practices within ministries with youth are beneficial or even Christian. For example, a youth ministry that engages youth solely in forms of entertainment may train youth to relate to God in passive observance. If discipleship only involves lectures on moral living, then youth may relate to God only through how well they are able to live moral lives. If youth ministry revolves around study and memorization, then God may only be known in the intellect. A youth ministry grounded in Christian practices will pay attention to the whole way of life promoted in the content and activities of the ministry. It will seek to offer youth tools and give them opportunities to practice life lived in imitation of Christ.

How do we determine if a practice is Christian? How do we know which practices form young people in the way of Christ? What does it mean to ground youth ministry in Christian practices? In order to answer these questions and better discern the nature of spiritual practices within adolescent discipleship, this chapter examines the four relationships present within every practice of faith. All Christian practices begin in *prayer*, invite personal *confession*, take place within the *worshiping community*, and bear fruit in *solidarity with the poor* in communion with the Spirit of Jesus Christ. It is our availability to love within these four relationships—God, ourselves, the faithful, and the poor—that is the hope of all faithful practices.

Prayer

Christian practices are rooted in prayer. "Prayer," writes Kenneth Leech, "is the fundamental relationship of [people] to God, a state of attention to God."[2] By drawing the attention and intention of the heart toward God, prayer separates Christian practices from self-improvement exercises. Contained within prayer are three qualities that transform all practices into habits of devotion: response, awareness, and relationship.

Response. Prayer is the conscious engagement of our relationship with God; and like the life of faith, it is the response to God's active presence.[3] Prayer is "always the second word...it is not primarily address but response."[4] Just as Abram hears the call of God and begins the journey to the Promised Land (Genesis 12:1-3); just as Moses encounters God in the burning bush and leads God's people to freedom (Exodus 3:1-6); just as Peter and the sons of Zebedee encounter Christ while they work and follow; just as Mary Magdalene encounters Christ at the tomb and proclaims his resurrection—so prayer is also first a response to the ways in which God encounters us.

"The Spirit himself intercedes for us with groans that words cannot express," writes Paul to the Romans (8:26). The biblical promise is that God is praying in us; our task is to respond, to join the conversation, to participate in God's longing within. Through the attitude of prayer, Christian practices allow not only the meditations of our hearts, but the very activities of faith, to become a response to God's desire within us.

---

2. Kenneth Leech, *Soul Friend: An Invitation to Spiritual Direction* (San Francisco: Harper, 1992), 168.

3. Marjorie J. Thompson, *Soul Feast: An Invitation to the Christian Spiritual Life* (Louisville, Kentucky: Westminster John Knox, 1995), 31.

4. Eugene Peterson, *Working the Angles: The Shape of Pastoral Integrity* (Grand Rapids, Michigan: Eerdmans, 1987), 45.

Awareness. Prayer requires that we turn our attention to God. Prayer, it can be said, is the awareness of God. It turns our heart's focus from the distractions around and within us and places it on the presence of the Holy. Through prayerful awareness, every activity becomes an opportunity to deepen our intimacy with God—every habitual practice becomes a conscious participation in God's divine activity. The awareness that prayer brings makes every Christian activity an opportunity to practice the presence of God.[5] The awareness embodied within prayer allows us to discern the benefit of a particular activity or practice—we sense our movements toward and away from God. We notice how a practice increases or diminishes our love for God and others. With the attitude of prayer, Christian living is no longer something we do *for* God, but rather life is shared with God, keeping us receptive and available to God's nurturing, even in the most demanding of spiritual disciplines.

Relationship. Finally, prayer calls attention to our relatedness to God. It is remembering that Christ is with us in this and every moment (Matthew 28:20). It is welcoming God's invitations to be known as lover, parent, and friend (John 16:27; Isaiah 66:13; John 15:15). Prayer is conscious participation in our relationship with God. It is sharing life with God just as the disciples did—walking, eating, working, serving, praying—all of life's activities done in friendship with the living Christ. Like any intimate relationship, it is the process of becoming more and more transparent before God, consciously placing our joys and disappointments, worries and anxieties before God—and then listening for God's concerns, joys, and hopes. Prayer understood as relationship transforms every Christian practice into a spiritual practice—an opportunity for growing in communion with Christ.

"Prayer is more a way of being, than an isolated act of doing";[6] prayer is the basic attitude—the primal stance required in all Christian practices. Without the awareness of prayer, spiritual practices can be destructive and aimed at our own inadequacies or sense of personal holiness. Prayer, as a way of being, directs the attention and intention of our hearts in a way that makes us malleable in the Spirit, regardless of the stiffness or dryness embodied within a chosen practice. As stated previously, this intention of the heart is the basis of God's way of life; prayer is the opening through which our heart is drawn to God.

All Christian practices are prayer in that they require that we respond to the Spirit's stirring within us, draw our awareness to God, and seek to deepen our relationship with Christ. However, although *every* Christian practice requires a prayerful stance, it's important to engage youth in practices that focus solely on our life of prayer—particularly forms of prayer that highlight the three qualities of response, awareness, and relationship. Youth need practices of conversational prayer like journaling, psalm-writing, and models of prayerful conversation. Contemplative prayer practices that rely on silence, solitude, and attention are important for helping youth develop skills for listening to God within all of their activities. Prayers like *lectio divina*, the Jesus Prayer, and the Ignatian Awareness Examen can help youth realize that there is no place where

Ponderable
According to Mark, prayer is the starting point of a program. What does this approach mean in terms of normative youth ministry programming?

---

5. See Brother Lawrence, *Practicing the Presence of God* (Springdale, Pennsylvania: Whitaker House, 1982).

6. Tilden Edwards, *Living in the Presence* (San Francisco: Harper, 1995), 11.

they can "flee from God's presence."[7] Finally, invitations to pray with Jesus as friend and companion can help youth develop a relational attitude—a companionship with the Holy that will flow into the rest of their lives.

All Christian practices require prayerful awareness; for youth ministry, prayer practices are the means by which the church helps young people turn their attention from the seductions of the marketplace and direct it toward the wonder of God. The primary task of those involved in youth ministry is the same as Peterson's requirement for parish pastors, "to keep the community attentive to God."[8] Christian practices are the tools by which this attentiveness is formed in youth.

Confession

Just as all Christian practices require the stance of prayer, so all practices invite confession. Christian practices not only create awareness of God, they also invite an interior awareness. In the New Testament people continually came into a new self-awareness in the encounter with Jesus: Peter cries, "I am a sinful man!" (Luke 5:8); Zacchaeus discovers his generosity (Luke 19:8); and Martha faces her worries and distractions (Luke 10:40). All of these self-discoveries occur in the presence of Christ. Awareness of God always brings an awareness of the self. We see this dynamic in Psalm 139 as the writer moves between meditating on God's presence, to wondering about the mystery of his own life. The subject of Christian practices is God, yet the object, or objective of spiritual practices is the self and its growth in Christ; the two are deeply intertwined. Thus Paul charges the Corinthians to examine themselves to see if they are living in faith— and then in the same verse, exclaims, "Do you not realize that Christ Jesus is in you…?" (2 Corinthians 13:5).

Confession is the movement toward humility. It is that aspect of Christian practice that seeks to have integrity before God, to drop the pretensions that are carried in public, and make oneself transparent before God. Confession not only focuses on our sins, the broken places revealed in the awareness of God's perfect light; it also is the recognition of our strengths and beauty. It is the willingness to wait and listen for God's voice of blessing, calling out to us to live as the "one he loves" (Mark 1:11). Christ tells us that the kingdom of God lives within each person (Luke 17:21), young or old, and yet, it is only as we pay attention to our interior mix of faults and blessings that this kingdom becomes a reality in our lives.

Just as prayer begins with listening to God, so confession begins with the remembrance of love.[9] Though we may engage in Christian practices for spiritual self-improvement, a practice can become shallow or an "invitation to despair"[10] if we fail to remember that our life is already held in God's open arms. Confession is self-assessment; it seeks a greater awareness of the openings and blocks to God's love. This is time in the desert, which often involves a persistent commitment to battle interior

Confession and the self-absorbed
"Confession is self-assessment," Mark writes. What happens to this understanding of confession in light of adolescent development? Mid-adolescents are by definition self-focused and often egocentric in how they view relationships. Yet confession, according to the author, "is the fundamental practice of humility." How does a youth worker take seriously this theologically valid encouragement with early and middle adolescents in a self-absorbed culture?

---

7. A good resource for these practices is Marjorie J. Thompson, *Soul Feast* (Louisville, Kentucky: Westminster John Knox, 1995); and Tilden Edwards, *Living in the Presence* (San Francisco: Harper, 1995).

8. Peterson, 2.

9. Richard Foster, *Prayer: Finding the Heart's True Home* (San Francisco: Harper, 1992), 28.

10. Thompson, 86.

demons—fear and self-loathing, pride and destructive appetites. Christian practices not only call us to notice the obstructions to God's grace, they also invite us to confess our helplessness. All Christian practices call us to wait on God, to trust in God's strength, and to recognize that Jesus Christ is Lord. Confession reminds us who God is. It is the fundamental practice of humility.

This inward journey ends in the confession that Jesus Christ is the Lord of life (Philippians 2:11). In this admission we claim our identity as disciples and make ourselves available to God's healing Spirit. Just as Jesus healed those who placed themselves unashamedly before him, so we too are invited in Christian practices to place our true selves before Christ. To confess Jesus Christ as Lord (1 John 4:15), is to recognize the power of Christ within us—it is to allow God into the doubts, anxieties, and celebrations that capture our energies. Confession is that aspect of Christian practice that continually requires us to say, "Here am I" (Isaiah 6:8); and then wait and listen for the still, small inner voice of love.

Within youth ministry, the confessional aspect of Christian practices is significant because it allows young people the space and time to reflect on their emerging identity. Practices create space between the young person's sense of self and the projections of peers, family, and the secular culture. It creates deeper integrity and connection to their true self—their identity as a person created in the image of God (Genesis 1:27). All Christian practices will have an inward dimension, a call to reflect on one's life in faith. For youth these opportunities for self-assessment are necessary for maturity and growth to take place.[11] Practices that focus on confession such as journaling, the Ignatian Awareness Examen, meditations on the Ten Commandments, spiritual friendships, spiritual assessments, prayers of confession, and other practices of self-examination help young people notice the ongoing call to live in truth and humility as the beloved of God.

The call of community

In many youth ministry contexts, the messages offered to students focuses more on the necessity of an individual's response to God than on the call of a community. But central to Mark's thesis is that any presentation of or invitation into the Christian life is to be grounded first and foremost in the context of the "worshiping community." It is also clear that community is not merely the youth group or Sunday school class, but the entire congregation.

What, if anything, have you observed of people experiencing community across programs and age groups at any level? Do young and old practice the Christian faith (as described in this chapter) together in any meaningful and regular way? What are a few practical ways a church (*your* church) can move closer to a congregationwide understanding and experience of Mark's idea of Christian practice?

Worshiping community

The context of all Christian practices is the worshiping community. "It is impossible to be a Christian in solitary splendor."[12] Solitude, silence, and other disciplines of the interior journey are never engaged without an abiding awareness of, and relationship with, the community of faith. The worshiping community "is the earth into which we sink our spiritual roots."[13] All Christian practices flow out of this holy gathering of praise, prayer, and breaking of bread. It is in the community that gathers before God that our prayers are shared and our confessions heard. Without the worshiping community, our practices become private experiences of truth, superficial exercises of pride, and subject to our own broken perspectives.

Christianity is practiced as a communal faith; in this way all spiritual practices are corporate practices—they are always in relationship with the community of faith.

---

11. Mark Yaconelli, "Ignatian Contemplation and the Process of Adolescent Spiritual Formation," unpublished thesis, San Francisco Theological Seminary, 1996.

12. Thompson, 56.

13. Monks of New Skete, *In the Spirit of Happiness* (Boston: Little, Brown and Co., 1999), 211.

The Christian practice of faith exists only within the corporate body that is made one in Christ (Colossians 3:15**)**. All Christian practices seek to unite us with the communion of saints. It is for this unity among believers for which Christ prays and the Psalmist rejoices (John 17:11; Psalms 133:1). For Dietrich Bonhoeffer, Christianity is defined as "community through Christ."[14] It is the community that carries and protects the practices of the Christian tradition for the new generations; and it is for the benefit of the community that we engage in Christian practices, to build up the body of Christ (1 Corinthians 12:7). Thus all practices of faith come out of and are returned to the common worship of God.[15]

Communal worship shapes and articulates our practices of faith—it is the most *fundamental* of all Christian practices. The whole of Christian life is expressed and experienced in the gathering before God. In the reading of Scripture, the proclamation of the gospel, the passing of peace, the sharing of prayers, the offering of gifts, the hearing of confessions, and the celebration of the sacraments dwells all the rhythms of our life before God. In worship, the meaning of Christian practices is distilled and held up for the whole community to see.[16] Worship is the expression and formation of our communal spirituality—it is the space in which all practices are refined, reformed, and held accountable to the Spirit of Christ.

Finally, it is in the worshiping community that we can experience the presence of God's Spirit. In the physical gathering of Christians for worship, we offer God to one another (Ephesians 4:1-5). God's Spirit is made available to us, through and for the community of worship (1 Corinthians 12:7-11). It is in this community that we make ourselves and our practices vulnerable to God's refinement. The experience of God within the worshiping community comforts and encourages our journey with Christ. All practices need the rejuvenation of touching God's Spirit, which is particularly available in worship before God.

For youth to learn the way of Christ, they cannot and must not be segregated or isolated from the worshiping community. Youth ministry cannot be practiced with its own particular activities and methods unless they are grounded in the rhythms and presence of the community before God. This means youth (and children) must be physically recognized as equal partners in the worship of God. It is imperative that worship incorporates and makes room for the unique gifts and abilities that are present in young people. Youth should have opportunities to lead and shape worship—to the same extent as other members—and to engage in the communal practices of faith. They must be physically present—seen, heard, and welcomed within the worship of God. If worship is the fundamental Christian practice, and the worshiping community is the container of all Christian practices, then it follows that adolescent spiritual formation must take place in the worship of God.

Equal partners?
The recent history of youth ministry is founded on the belief that kids need their own space—which is why few churches of any size and fewer that are committed to youth ministry functionally agree with Yaconelli. Where do you stand on this? Should students be encouraged to sit in their own section during congregational worship services?...lead worship a few times a year to remind the congregation they exist?... basically stay out of the way of the adult congregation, as is common to modern youth ministry? Or should we heed Yaconelli's advice and ensure that youth are "recognized as equal partners in the worship of God"?

---

14. Dietrich Bonhoeffer, *Life Together* (San Francisco: Harper, 1954), 21.

15. Dorothy C. Bass (ed.), *Practicing Our Faith* (San Francisco: Jossey-Bass, 1997), 9.

16. Bass, 9.

Solidarity with the poor

The fruit of all Christian practice is our solidarity with and sacrifice for the poor. If God's way of life is through Jesus Christ, then all Christian practices seek to break bread with the outcasts. For it is among the "least of these" that we experience communion with the Spirit of Christ (Matthew 25:40). All Christian practices are useless if they do not seek to address the poor in our midst. Those who were cast out of communities, marginalized, ignored, and forgotten—those who lacked basic necessities of food, health, and shelter—were the focus of Christ's life (Luke 4:18-19). These are the ones we seek to embrace in every practice of Christian living. Every Christian practice seeks to open our hearts and strengthen our spirits so that we may be available to those in need. It is on behalf of the needy that Christ came (Matthew 9:12-13), and so it is on behalf of the needy that we live our life in Christ.

Christian practices are only made complete in acts of service—in the washing of feet, the feeding of the hungry, and the clothing of the naked—and in every true act of sacrifice. It is as we seek to comfort the least of these in self-giving acts of love that we find the true meaning of Christian living (Matthew 25:45).

In our practice of solidarity with the poor, we are careful to avoid acts of *self-righteous service*—acts that seek to assuage guilt or gain admiration.[17] Seeking a "service experience" only separates us from the truth of our own weaknesses and the gift of Christ's presence in the underprivileged. Solidarity seeks to reveal our intimate companionship with the world's weak and broken.

To increase our solidarity with the poor we seek to practice lives of hospitality. We welcome the stranger into our homes, share the food from our table, offer a listening ear, and bear the burdens of others (Galatians 6:2). It is in the physical presence of the poor—in our presence to the needy—that God's peace is shared.[18] We recognize that in receiving the stranger, we are also receiving Christ; we are making ourselves available to Christ's spirit in the world. "Power is made perfect in weakness" (2 Corinthians 12:9); in welcoming the weak, God's power comes. In acts of hospitality we are reminded of the true Host—the one who gives us food, clothing, companionship, and life. Thus our solidarity with the poor is always a form of desire to grow in solidarity with Christ.

To receive the call to solidarity with the poor is to grow in our practice of humility—to combat our desire for separation and preferential treatment. Christian practices invite us to sit at the table of sinners and tax collectors, to embrace the leper, and speak with the Samaritans. To companion the poor is to welcome our own weakness, and live humbly before God. It is to recognize that the poor are living reminders of our own needs before God. Christian practices seek this truth: that the poverty of others is ours as well. The oppressed, hungry, homeless, and needy are not separate from us, they are our brothers and sisters—as intimate to us as our own soul. And only as we seek to love those in need will we remove the obstacles of fear and pride and make room for God to care for us.

---

17. Richard Foster, *Celebration of Discipline: The Path to Spiritual Growth* (San Francisco: Harper & Row, 1988), 128.

18. Bonhoeffer, 20.

Ponderable
How can youth ministry address Christian practices that identify with and serve the poor, the oppressed, the broken? To what degree do typical expressions of service and missions (annual mission trips, occasional assistance for and visit to the elderly, Vacation Bible School in a cross-cultural setting) achieve what Mark advocates here?

Christian practices seek to remove the cage of self-protection, safety, and self-preservation. Practices call us to live among the at-risk, to lose our life among the lost, and to share life with those who face death and destruction. Christian practices always draw us to share the cross of the ignored and forgotten. Christian practices draw us toward a life of self-giving solidarity with the poor; and it is only in this way of sacrifice and companionship with Christ—only as we share the life of the oppressed—that practices are able to set us free.

In youth ministry Christian practices must always be engaged with our awareness of the poor. We must help youth engage in experiences of service that go beyond sightseeing tours. We must create opportunities for youth to stand in the receiving line of the soup kitchen, to share the sidewalks of the homeless, to feel the suffering of the AIDS victim, and to weep with the abandoned child. Christian practices must always seek to increase our relationship and connections with the poor. We do this not only through acts of service, but by welcoming the poor into our ministries—by engaging in spiritual practices with and among the poor. We seek to find ways to make our ministries shelters for the outcasts and havens for the oppressed—in this way, every youth ministry gathering is an opportunity to help youth practice their love for/with others. Without the ongoing presence of the poor, our ministries only help insulate youth—Christianity loses its power and simply becomes a tool of culture, subject to the powers and principalities. It is only with the regular contact with the poor that Christian practices unleash the dynamic and radical power of the Good News.

In the Spirit of Jesus

Having examined the four basic elements within Christian practices, we can proceed to make some summations of how practices operate in Christian formation:

- **All four elements of Christian practices—prayer, confession, the presence of the worshiping community, solidarity with the poor—are present in any one practice.** Praying in solitude is never without an awareness of the poor. Being among the worshiping community is always an experience of prayer. Serving the poor is always within the context confessing our own weakness and gifts. If life with the poor does not contain the nourishment of prayer, or if individual confession occurs without the accountability of the worshiping community, then our practice can become broken and even destructive. Although a practice may focus on worship, it must stay in relationship with our prayer, the poor, and our own self-examination, if it is to increase our love for God and others. The way of Christ demands the tension of these four dimensions in order for us to be available to the Spirit of Christ.

- **All practices seek to grow into the image of Jesus Christ.** "We only come to know God by acting as God acts;"[19] if our actions and practices do not resemble Christ's actions, we are not engaged in a Christian practice. Thus the practices within our youth ministry are never without the remembrance of Christ. Within a community of seekers, Christ lived a life of contemplation and action, prayer and service. This is the way of love for God and love for others. To learn this rhythm, youth need to experience inward practices of prayer and confession as well as outward practices of communal worship and solidarity with the poor. This is the "way of the Lord"—the way of Christ— and it is in these practices that youth become available and vulnerable to the presence of Christ.

- **One of the revelations in the teachings of Jesus Christ is that there is nothing holy about Christian practices in and of themselves (Mark 2:27).** Jesus continually points out that engaging in good and holy practices does not guarantee good or holy disciples (Matthew 23:1-4). Christian practices only place us before God and make us available and open to God. As Quaker pastor Richard Foster writes, "by themselves they can do nothing; they can only get us to the place where something can be done."[20] Thus it is misdirected to expect that youth will have mystical encounters in prayer, conversion experiences in confession, a new sense of community in worship, and a call to service amidst the poor. Practices only make us available, remove the obstacles, and make us dependent on the work of the Spirit.

  In this way, Christian practices are only engaged in faith and obedience. We engage in practices because that is the way of Christ—all that we can bring is a desire for transformation, a desire to be renewed, and better discerning of God's will (Romans 12:2). Christian practices in no way prove or earn salvation; this is the free gift of God's grace (Ephesians 2:8). They are simply the way of sanctification—the means through which we express our discipleship—the habits in which we seek to grow into the "fullness of Christ" (Ephesians 4:13).

- **Almost any activity can become a spiritual practice.** As stated previously, Christian practices are born in prayer and made useful through the intentions of the heart. Therefore, our role in youth ministry is to help youth notice the activities and practices toward which God is calling them. Youth ministry must not only engage youth in various Christian practices, we must also help them notice the moments in life when they experience kindness, generosity, peace, joy, self-discipline, and love (Galatians 5:22). These are the moments when the Spirit of God is at work—these are the moments that can guide us as to which practices are best suited for our youth. It is the continual practice of contemplative prayer and reflection that will help youth discern the practices into which God is calling them.

---

19. Diogenes Allen, *Spiritual Theology* (Boston: Cowley Publications), 27.

20. Foster, *Celebration of Discipline*, 7.

Youth ministry and Christian practices

Youth ministry is concerned with forming youth in the way of Christ. This is the way of Christian practice. Youth ministries can best facilitate growth in conformity with Christ when they focus on helping youth experience and develop practices of faith. The Christian practices are best inherited from a practicing community. If our youth ministries are not led by intentional spiritual communities, embedded with adults who are practicing the presence of Christ, youth will simply see faith, at best, as an intellectual endeavor. Youth must have opportunities to practice the way of Christ alongside Christian adults if Christian practices are to take root. A healthy spiritual formation program not only invites youth into practices, it also offers them opportunities to reflect and understand how practices work and their connection to the life of Christ.

All activities in youth ministry need to be evaluated according to the way of life that is being promoted. Is a particular event, activity, or retreat helpful in forming youth in the image of Christ (e.g., increasing their solidarity with the poor) or does it appeal to modern consumerist desires? If we evaluate all of our youth ministry practices according to the four elements listed above, we may create ministries that are less like the activities of the culture, and thus potentially less popular and attractive to youth. However, we have to trust that as we invite youth into the way of Christ, Jesus himself will be the attraction.

In a sense, trusting the way of Christ calls youth ministers and churches to embody greater trust in Christ. Christian practices can remove the focus of youth ministry from the youth minister and the dynamic program, and place it on the presence of God. A youth ministry concerned with Christian practices will become more available to Christ and vulnerable to God's transforming spirit. In this way youth ministries can become life-giving for adults and youth as co-practitioners of faith. It is conceivable that youth ministries might become more like faith communities or spiritual retreat centers rather than places for informal spiritual conversation. For youth ministers, it is as we practice faithfulness to Christ in companionship with young people that we are no longer alone—no longer "peddlers of God's word" but can live amidst young people "as persons, sent from God and standing in his presence" (2 Corinthians 2:17 NRSV).

Pleasing God

Mark writes, "All activities in youth ministry need to be evaluated according to the way of life that is being promoted." Far too often a youth ministry program is evaluated by students' excitement, by the satisfaction of the parents, by the look of the students, by the size or growth of the group, by the breadth of activities.

To the contrary, Mark's statement offers a far more concise, clear, and theologically driven criteria than what most churches focus on. And aside from being a measure of programmatic effectiveness in a given ministry setting, this statement assumes that *everything we do*—programs, leadership, philosophy, vision, planning, communication, staffing, small groups, missions, games—must be *driven* and *boundaried* by a theology that always asks first, "Is God pleased with the lives that are being changed and the practices that being lived out in our community?"

Focusing Youth Ministry through Student Leadership
Dave Rahn

"Today's young adults, torn loose from their moorings by accelerated social change, rapid globalization, and the constant novelty of the entertainment culture, are searching for meaning and intimacy. Some of them wonder if the faith that worked for their parents' generation will work for them as well."
—Gen-X, *Christianity Today,*
April 26, 1999, 90.

"Let's face it, we're afraid of our children these days. We're scared to death of them."
—Alex Wilson, State District Attorney for Prince George County, Maryland, as quoted in Patricia H. Davis, *Counseling Adolescent Girls,* Minneapolis: Augsburg Fortress, 1996, 12.

I came to put my faith in Jesus Christ as a high school sophomore, responding immediately to the gospel the first time I really understood it. While this chapter details the theological basis for my belief in the necessity of student leadership in any youth ministry strategy—in both development and implementation—the underlying conviction driving this focus is related to my own spiritual journey. I am a product of one youth ministry's commitment to student leadership. This is less a confession than a fact that clearly taints my views. But because all of our lives, histories, and experiences uniquely come together to influence who we are and what we think, this kind of confession can be said for any of us. This said, it is the goal of this chapter to convince the reader of the importance of incorporating student leadership into any youth ministry strategy.

It was because my new friend Brent invited me to a youth group outreach that I heard about Jesus' personal love for me, and my faith took hold as I responded to that love. In trying to make sense of this new life, I leaned on Brent to literally tell me what I was supposed to believe. He stayed after me until I developed the habit of joining him at the small church where his dad was the pastor. Brent's big brother, Doug, was a year older than us and loved being adventurous in the way he leaned into his faith. I was fascinated by him and drawn to his advanced wisdom. He always led the way when our small group of 15 kids gathered in the musty basement each week for youth group. I learned about dedication, commitment, and faithfulness from these two brothers and their family.

And that's not the best of it. They got me involved in Campus Life, which led to my eventual participation in Young Life. My worldview became infested with the single-mindedness of following Christ. Before long I had owned up to my personal responsibility to grow and learn more about following Jesus. I dedicated myself to sharing my faith with my peers. During the first semester of my senior year I helped 18 of my friends come to trust in Jesus Christ. Others emerged from among this group with a passion to "make a difference." We developed and led weekly Bible studies for each other, discovering the inductive Bible study method, drawing on writers like Francis Schaffer, John Stott, and Watchman Nee, and inventing ways to increase our impact in the school. When TV newsman Edwin Newman's investigation of life in the heartland led him into our school during the spring of 1972, he had to reckon with the newly emerging "Jesus movement" that he stumbled upon. We really became impressed with ourselves when we caught our testimonies on national TV!

It would be misleading to suggest that there were no adults in this mix. Pastor Birdsall, Walt Chave (Sunday school teacher), Hank Altorfer (Young Life volunteer), Marv Kelso (Young Life staff person), and T. A. Strader (Youth for Christ director) all touched my life in powerful ways—encouraging me and teaching me. The program resources were also impressive and attractive, with 180 kids coming weekly to Young Life and 120 (largely different teens) attending Campus Life. But nobody *hung out* with me as I learned to do when I came on staff with YFC/Campus Life. Our lives intersected around the church, Young Life, and Campus Life programs we attended.

Was I a student leader? Of course I was. So were many of my friends. We never were formally labeled as such, but those adults who stayed close to us continued to look for ways to provide the support and leadership necessary for me and my friends to focus our individual walks with Christ, deepen our spiritual maturity, and guide the resultant influence we had in our peer group. We were students who made an impact in our world as others, mostly adults and the church, made an impact on us. This is what is meant by the concept, *student leaders*.

Student leadership in youth ministry is not new. Youth for Christ's Bible clubs in the '50s and early '60s were built around the premise that Christian students could and should take responsibility to reach their peers and teach one another.[1] That's why Jay Kesler, in his earliest days as a full-time staff member with YFC, could "run" more than 12 of these clubs at once.[2] The same is true of the early days of Young Life, where the students involved were called *Campaigners* because they were the peer influencers for the local Young Life Campaign, the first name of Young Life. Earlier still, Christian Endeavor was structured around the premise of students taking on leadership roles as they were led and guided by adults.[3]

The fact that these examples predate the era of parish-based professional youth ministers and pastors does not change the fact that there is nothing inherent in the *idea* of student leadership that has changed. Furthermore, as we enter a new century, there are contemporary advocates of student leadership who have refined their understanding of this model and located it at the heart of their overall approach to youth ministry. What motivates this impassioned commitment? While there are significant pragmatic considerations—it would be surprising if there were not pragmatic considerations in our postmodern culture—there is also a compelling theological framework that argues for *some type* of student leadership integrated into one's youth ministry strategy. This chapter will demonstrate the theological commitments driving youth ministries that are focused through student leadership.

But first, what exactly do we mean by *student leadership*?

Ponderable
Were you a student leader? When you were in high school, did you feel as though you had something significant to offer that was recognized by the leadership? Or did you feel left out, lost, or neglected?

1. James C. Hefley, *God Goes to High School* (Waco, Texas: Word Books, 1970), 47-57, 90-93.

2. This is based on personal conversations with Jay Kesler beginning at the time in the early 1970s when he learned that I was running a Campus Life club at one of the schools he was responsible for.

3. Dean Borgman, "A History of American Youth Ministry," in Benson and Senter (eds.), *The Complete Book of Youth Ministry* (Chicago: Moody Press, 1987), 64-66.

Three perspectives of student leadership

Long-time youth ministry leader Tiger McLuen's recent work suggests at least five different categories of student leadership.[4] In describing the focus of student leaders' activity, he presents a clear and tangible description of how these approaches differ from one another. Building on the distinctions McLuen identifies, this chapter focuses the student leadership movement in youth ministry into three distinct yet related perspectives. Each perspective, or *family*, operates with a necessary central value that has operational implications for how student leadership is actually practiced.

Student leaders in the system

The first student leadership perspective is clustered around the central value of *organizational development*. Some young persons are intentionally *enculturated* into their church's way of life so that they are ready to receive the torch of leadership when those adults currently in power pass it on.

Patrick had this kind of experience. When he was elected president of his church's youth group, he automatically became a voting member of the church's administrative board. He became involved in decision-making when the church needed to find a new pastor and was able to talk intelligently about church politics within the larger district of his denomination.

This form of student leadership is basically designed to be implemented within an organizational framework or context. This perspective draws upon the assumption that developing student leaders is necessary if the organization-as-species will continue to survive. It is designed and implemented by the adults who have as their focus the future of their churches. Students like Patrick are groomed for future church leadership by being involved in the present, formal systems of organizational leadership. This perspective can be referred to as *Student Leaders in the System*.

Student leaders in charge

Another student leadership perspective and resultant strategy involves adolescents in the *leadership* of the youth ministry program. The driving philosophy behind this perspective is the notion that when students are involved in significant leadership in the program, youth ownership is enhanced, which, presumably, leads to greater and more meaningful participation by young people.

Ponderable
If you had to choose, where on this scale would you land?

| Giving adolescents in the church adult-like authority and responsibility |⊢————————————⊣| Allowing adolescents to give input regarding church business, but ensuring that adults are the ones who make decisions |

What factors do you think should determine how much or how little real responsibility you give a church's teenagers? How does your answer fit with developmental realities and the real needs of adolescents?

Dawn was such a leader. When I met her, I was impressed by the number of activities in which she was involved and the balancing act she performed while racing from one activity to another. One of her many commitments was being a leader in her

---

4. Dennis "Tiger" McLuen and Chuck Wysong, *The Student Leadership Training Manual* (Grand Rapids, Michigan: Zondervan/Youth Specialties).

church youth group. She planned meetings that they hoped would attract her peers and help get them involved in the program. She diligently worked her way through Youth Specialties' *Ideas* volumes and other youth ministry resources. Sometimes she and the other student leaders arranged for guest speakers, but it was clear that the teens were in charge. The adult youth sponsors were given the roles of chaperones and support personnel, supplying refreshments for meetings and helping out as they were asked.

The central value for this perspective of student leadership is *program ownership*. Seasoned youth workers will easily recognize the value of having young people feel that the programs in which they're involved are, to some degree, *theirs*. They have come to appreciate an insight from management theory that if the right stakeholders do not have some sense of ownership, even the highest quality may not ensure effectiveness.[5]

As was true for Dawn, in this perspective, young people may lead virtually all of the *up-front* elements in meetings. They are given the permission and authority to take nearly unlimited initiative to plan and promote programs. It is not ultimately important if the quality and even direction of a given youth ministry program may fluctuate from year to year, dependent as it is on the changing student leadership, for the goal is to get the students to take charge. Adults as *sponsors* generally are called upon primarily to be a resource to the student leaders as they *run the show* for their peers. This perspective, then, can be labeled *Student Leaders in Charge*.

Student leaders in relationship

There is still another way to think of student leadership. Its central value is *interpersonal influence*. It recognizes the unique impact that adolescent friends have on another's life. Since authentic life transformation is often correlated with the presence of a trusted model, peer friends have a natural inroad over adults when it comes to building trusted relationships. They are, after all, *already* immersed in the same world as those we are seeking to reach, which is the first step in creating a relationship that can draw others.[6] With this perspective of student leadership, adults and teens share the partnership of the immediate youth ministry mission, dividing responsibilities according to gifts, experiences, and developmental concerns. This perspective, then, could be described as *Student Leaders in Relationship*.

Bart and Cassie are both discovering this as they look for ways to reach their friends and teammates for Christ. They are faithful in praying aggressively for their friends. They consider ways to attract them to meetings, trips, events, and conversations that will draw them to interest in Jesus Christ. They encourage one another to overcome their own natural fears and share their faith—communicating the love of Christ first with how they live, and second with their words (for praying, inviting, and telling have all been linked to effectiveness in peer evangelism[7]). Above all else they recognize that *they* are a tool that the Lord can and wants to use, and they are conscientious in their efforts to be available for God's purposes in their friends' lives.

---

5. Adapted from Norman Maier, *Problem-Solving Discussions and Conferences: Leadership Methods and Skills* (New York: McGraw-Hill, 1963), 3-9.

6. See the discussion and summary provided by Lawrence Richards, *Christian Education: Seeking to Become Like Jesus Christ* (Grand Rapids, Michigan: Zondervan, 1975), 81-85.

7. Dave Rahn and Terry Linhart, *Student Leadership & Youth Evangelism* (Loveland, Colorado: Group Publishing, 2000).

Which perspective to choose?

Ponderable
Do you frame the idea of student leadership as Dave Rahn does (student leaders in the system, in charge, and in relationship)? If not, how would you frame it? Are there any other ways to think about student leadership? Do you agree with Dave Rahn that student leaders in relationship is the most appropriate biblical perspective?

Granted, there is strategic value in each of these three approaches to student leadership. But I am convinced that the theological foundations for student leadership distribute themselves unevenly for the three different orientations. The central values of *student leaders in the system* and *student leaders in charge* are not clearly formulated through a careful study of Scripture. These two perspectives do not represent universal contexts necessary for ministry among young people. On the other hand, the biblical call of relational influence in the name of Christ—as well as the aforementioned reality of the potential impact of peer influence—make the *Student Leaders in Relationship* the most compelling perspective for a student leadership philosophy.

The next section explores the theological basis of the church's essential nature, evangelistic mission, and appropriate formation processes. It is for these theological reasons that I believe youth ministry needs to be focused through *student leaders in relationship*. As with all youth ministry philosophy and strategy, it is vital to cement student leadership practices into God's master design for the church. Let's explore this connection by asking two questions. First, is there anything in the essential nature of the church that should either commend, boundary, or restrict student leadership practices? Second, is there anything inherent in biblically prescribed organizational patterns for the church that should either commend, boundary, or restrict student leadership practices?

The church's essential nature

The church must be understood primarily as God's people— "the community of the King."[8] By affirming our belief that this is the core identity of the church, we reject a number of other options. The church is not essentially an institution—an arrangement of programs, a building, or a denomination. God's people have historically expressed their purposes in these forms, but none are essential to the nature of the church. The church is called to be a relational network of people who love God and love others.

It is indisputable that among the people of God called together in a particular place, there are almost always adolescents functioning as part of the community. Their membership and inclusion in the family of God must not be questioned because of their age. When persons put their trust in Jesus Christ they enter into a bond with all others who have done the same. This church is multicultural, intergenerational, and transcendent even if every local expression of the church does not reflect these properties. If God were to do a file-sort of the master database for the church, there would be a significant number of adolescents on the list.

Are there asterisks by their names because they are not yet adults? Are they considered—by virtue of their ages only—to be exempt from either the benefits or the responsibilities that others who belong to Christ's church receive? With the single exception of developmental appropriateness, there is little biblical evidence to support such a notion. That said, even *developmental appropriateness* is different for different eras,

Ponderable
Where in the church in general and its youth ministry in particular do you think adolescents should be monitored—or outright denied participation—by adult officials? By what criteria should a church decide when—or if—a student is ready for significant leadership responsibility?

8. Howard Snyder, *The Community of the King* (Downers Grove, Illinois: InterVarsity Press, 1977).

places, and even individuals. It is important to note, for example, that there is a huge difference between adolescents in the 1970s and in today's culture. (The age span of 13 to 19 was a big enough transitional gap, but the lengthening of adolescence today from about 10 to the early 20s is a developmental half-life![9]) Even so, the call to become *Student Leaders in Relationship* does not mean that adolescents can't participate in much if not most of the leadership responsibilities in the church. Even early adolescents should not automatically be kept out of the loop of using their gifts, energy, and talents in the body. Rather responsibility and involvement must be carefully weighed with respect to an individual's readiness.

If church members are called to demonstrate their relationship to God through their love for one another (John 13:34–35), then those members who are not yet adults are as equally invited to be included in the twofold command to love God and one another. There is a relational equality of responsibility and character for believers of *all* ages when considering biblical encouragements and instructions. We are—among other things—to honor one another (Romans 12:10), submit to one another (Ephesians 5:21), live in harmony with one another (Romans 12:16; 1 Peter 3:8), be patient with one another (Ephesians 4:2), encourage one another (1 Thessalonians 5:11; Hebrews 3:13; 10:24–25), teach one another (Romans 15:14; Colossians 3:16), and refrain from unfairly passing judgment on one another (Romans 14:13). If the Great Commission (Matthew 28:19–20) is a central task for the church, then teens also must be encouraged and equipped to appropriately play their part in making disciples. Clearly, every disciple was created to accomplish the good works prepared for us by the Lord Jesus (Ephesians 2:8–10).

If the church's essential nature is that of a collected group of diversely gifted people, united only because of our common allegiance to Jesus Christ, then those youngest members of the body must be accepted and encouraged to take their place *at the pace at which they are ready*. The biblical criteria for such readiness (i.e., the characteristics listed above, along with many others) are far more important in assessing readiness and fitness for leadership than arbitrarily delineated age restrictions. There still must be safeguards to ensure that adolescents are cared for as they move through such a crucial life stage transformation, but this does not mean all young people are automatically told they must wait to use their gifts and energy for service to the Lord.

There are those who believe that biblical "readiness" and "fitness" standards implicitly include some sort of age expectations. In what sense *can* a teen, still spending too much time in front of the sociological and developmental mirror, be ready to exercise leadership in the church? Certainly, spiritual maturity is a critical factor influencing the faithful use of everyone's gifts, and such wisdom seems to be naturally connected to the richness of experiences. It stands to reason that older folks can draw upon a greater life reservoir to build upon their history of faithfulness. But we all know persons who, in spite of their advanced age, have missed the transformational power of their experiences because they never practiced the sort of disciplined theological reflection of

The true story of First Church

What does it mean, practically and programmatically, to encourage students to "exercise leadership in the church"?

Say a church is looking for their third youth minister in two years. The last two leaders were hired by committees with as many adolescent members as adult members. In both of the previous two hires, the committee split down teenager-adult lines—and the kids won both times by swaying a single adult to their viewpoint.

The criteria for hiring was obviously different for the students and the adults, as was the emphasis of the job description in the interviews: the adults wanted someone who would recruit and train leaders, was theologically trained, had administrative savvy if not outright gifts, and would be a team player with the staff. The students? They wanted someone who was "kickback," fun, young (early 20s was the choice both times), an energetic speaker, and one who could help the youth group to "go where God wanted them to go."

So now they're looking for the *next* person to lead the youth ministry—and because the church is, as it says, "committed to youth in leadership and owning the decisions that affect them," the committee make-up remains the same. "We just didn't have good luck the last two times," a student committee member told me.

What do you think? What would you do? Why? How does one balance what Dave so passionately argues for without giving up the necessity of godly, experienced, theologically-driven adult leadership?

---

9. See chapter 2, "Theological Uses of Human Development," for a more detailed discussion of the lengthening of adolescence.

which we're talking about in this book. I want to suggest that we may also know some adolescents who are so eager and honest to be used by God that they can accelerate their maturity by the intensity of their reflective practices. Age may give persons an edge on maturity, but it is no guarantee. If we focus on adolescents' spiritual *and* developmental and psychosocial maturity when we determine their readiness to assume their roles in the body of Christ, we will be on safe ground. And since the version of leadership we are commending is about relational *influence*, we can expect that teens faithfully navigating tricky developmental issues, like individuation and the search for identity, will have the inner resources necessary to have positive ministries among their peers.

To reiterate, there is nothing in the church's nature that justifies restricting the development of teens to be *Student Leaders in Relationship*. On the contrary, this version of student leadership is naturally derived from an understanding of the church just described. I do not believe that the same could be said of either the *Student Leaders in the System* or *Student Leaders in Charge* models.

The church's organizational design

Closely connected to the organic nature of the church is the organizational form the local church takes. While biblical parameters for parish organization have obviously been wide enough to result in a variety of denominational expressions, there are some principles recognized by virtually all traditions. For example, the *function* of leadership must include equipping other members of the body of Christ to fulfill their God-ordained calling on behalf of the church's health and the world's need. Biblically identified as *elders*, there is an important empowering role that church leadership must attend to, so that we are *all* equipped for leadership-as-influence in our little corner of the world—regardless of our temperament, personality, or unique gifting. Godly adults—serving, teaching, and caring—must come alongside student leaders to assist and guide them as they seek to follow the call of God in their lives.

The Bible also teaches that every believer has been given gifts to be used on behalf of the church (Romans 14; 1 Corinthians 12-14; Ephesians 4). The Bible does *not* teach that such gifts and resulting service are hidden like time-release capsules in the lives of Christians—inoperable until they reach the age of 20 (or 40!). At the very least this suggests that we must begin early (in youth ministry), to help identify, nurture, foster, and utilize the gifts God has given the young in the church. A grave mistake many, if not most, churches make is forcing kids to wait until post-adolescence to begin to use their gifts and energy in the church, and in the world.

An evangelistically influential church needs student leadership

Because it can argued that there are few biblical restrictions on how young people (i.e., adolescents) may function in leadership roles in the church, we must consider how adolescents can be active participants in evangelizational task of the church. I have elsewhere tried to make the case that student leadership—what I have here labeled the *Student Leaders in Relationship* perspective—ought to be driven by an evangelistic vision.[10] There are three intersecting facts that contribute to my thinking.

The first fact spins out of the sheer demographics of world population growth. More than one-third of all persons in the world are either teenagers or younger. Our world population reached the six billion mark in 1999, and it should grow by another billion in just 12 years. At the turn of the century, over two billion persons were under 20 years of age.[11] It just makes sense to ask how the church will best reach this massive population group with the gospel of Jesus Christ.

The second fact is derived from missiological observations. It has long been useful for missiologists to characterize evangelism strategies in relation to their relative effectiveness. They have found that the fewer cultural or language barriers that need to be crossed by a missionary, the greater the likelihood that evangelism will be, in the words of Ralph Winter, "most potent."[12] It seems logical to assume, then, that when we encourage young people to reach out to their friends in the name of Christ, they will encounter fewer of these natural barriers than will adults. Adults can, and probably should, be partners in this ministry, so the entire spiritual responsibility for their friends does not fall to the student leader. But an adolescent can take the lead role in peer evangelism and outreach to her friends.

Finally, no one I know in ministry seriously challenges the suggestion that a tremendous percentage of significant decisions for Christ take place during the teenage years. There are certainly developmental factors at work during adolescence that can help us understand and even explain this observation. Perhaps this group simply receives more evangelistic attention than do other age groups. At any rate, it's not hard to get youth ministry veterans to agree that the teenage years are an exceptionally fruitful time for evangelism.

A recent study reflecting these factors concluded—

> "When we pull these facts together for strategic ministry reflection, the implications become pretty clear. One of the primary reasons for the existence in the church of specialized ministries to youth must be to take advantage of this evangelistic 'window of opportunity' made possible at the intersection of Demographic Growth Patterns and Adolescent Conversion Readiness. Youth evangelism must be a priority of youth ministry. By extension, the most fruitful youth evangelism will be derived from strategies that have young people telling their friends the good news of life in Jesus Christ."[13]

Peer evangelism versus adult-to-adolescent evangelism

Dave has tapped into yet another youth ministry controversy of today. On one hand, students reaching those among whom they live and move appears to be obvious to some if not most youth ministers. But there are those who believe that it is far too easy for adults to use this viewpoint as an excuse for not entering the adolescents' world. The preferable way to reach nonbelieving students, Dave concedes, is for teenagers and adults to work in concert.

What has been your experience? When you were in middle school or high school, do you think a commitment to peer evangelism would have been (or was) the most appropriate strategy for authentic and effective outreach to students? What do you think now, in retrospect?

---

10. Rahn and Linhart, Chapter 1.

11. United Nations Population Division, "World Population Prospects: The 1998 Revision," Web site.

12. R. D. Winter, "The Highest Priority: Cross-Cultural Evangelism" in Let the Earth Hear His Voice, compilation of papers presented at the 1974 International Congress on World Evangelization in Lausanne, Switzerland (Minneapolis, Minnesota: World Wide Publications, 1975), 219. Winter's designation for this type of evangelism is "E-1."

13. Rahn and Linhart.

The *Student Leaders in the System* model is inadequate at this point because it doesn't speak directly to this evangelistic priority in the church. And there is research to suggest that *Student Leaders in Charge* may actually be counterproductive to teenage evangelism effectiveness.[14] But it is also important not to overstate the strength of the *Student Leaders in Relationship* model on this point. That the church needs to strategically target evangelism efforts at young people is clear. Many students are capable of taking the responsibility for reaching their friends for Christ. In fact, when their own Christian life is marked by faithfulness and maturity, we can expect them to be even more effective than adult youth ministers may be.

But there is a caution to be considered for those who want to rush toward some sort of "kids rule" vision of ministry. While research on adolescent influence suggests teens may be expected to have an important impact on their friends, it is not as conclusive about general peer-to-peer influence among adolescents.[15] Teens do not typically seem to be well-equipped to cross the socio-cultural barriers that exist in the adolescent environment, even if those obstacles exist only within their age group. It is not hard for me to accept the notion that some adults may be better suited than student leaders to accomplish these types of evangelistic initiatives among teens. What *does* seem to be the most appropriate approach and therefore expectation for *Student Leaders in Relationship*, is for every student leader to have the benefit of an adult partner/mentor/friend to walk with in this ministry. This is the best of all worlds—mature adult leadership encouraging, equipping, and ultimately validating student leadership.

Radar trouble
Dave alludes here to peer-to-peer evangelism. Although in the context of this chapter one may assume that he would support this as the single most effective outreach methodology, he in fact takes a much softer stand. To Dave, adolescents may have a hard time crossing "sociocultural boundaries" and are therefore in need of adult partners to make a significant evangelistic impact in an adolescent community. When we make friendship evangelism the only form of outreach, those without Christian friends are left beneath the church's radar.

Biblical discipleship suggests student leadership

"Have you been discipled?" I remember the frustration I felt the first time I was asked this question. The questioner had in mind a kind of personalized faith tutorial—rigorous and disciplined—that would help me to grow up in Christ. The implications were that if I had not received such attention, there could be predictable cracks in my faith's foundation.

I have since come to appreciate the complexity and breadth of the biblical disciple-making task. The spiritual formation process that results in disciples who follow Jesus Christ, may vary considerably from person to person. The following three observations highlight these variations and also suggest the important role that students can play in helping one another become more faithful disciples of the Lord Jesus.

Not all disciple-making influence flows one-way downstream
While it is important to note that in Jesus' original disciple-making schema, he imparted his life into his followers unidirectionally, our ministry as his followers must be not to impart *our* lives, but to impart Jesus' life. Paul asked both the Corinthians (1 Corinthians 11:1) and the Philippians (Philippians 3:17, 4:9) to follow his example, but clearly he did so because he thought he could be a helpful model on their journey toward Christlikeness.

14. Rahn and Linhart.

15. For a discussion of research supporting this point, see Dave Rahn, "Reckoning with Adolescent Influence: A Sociological Perspective on Youth Ministry," *Christian Education Journal*, 3 (NS), no. 2, (1999).

The fact is that in this process of growing toward becoming more like Jesus (Romans 8:29; Colossians 2:6,7), there are many times when we benefit from those we are trying to help. The influence is mutual. Rather than seeing our impact on others rush downstream in a great current—where there is little chance for reciprocal impact—it is far better to connect to other believers in the calm waters of a gentle pond. We aren't "discipled"—the word even sounds mechanical—so much as we each contribute to the process of *helping one another become faithful disciples*. The patterns of influence in the early church were not one-way. Peter's leadership is well established, but even so he is admonished by Paul to do the right thing (Galatians 2:11-21). Paul's corrective concern in that setting also extends to Barnabas (v. 13), the person most responsible for Paul's ministerial training (Acts 9:27; 11:22-26). Even Paul's letters speak of the genuine value the believers he is writing to have had in his life (see especially Ephesians, Philippians, and 1 Thessalonians).

When we understand that we need not be "complete" before we exercise disciple-making influence on others, the possibilities for impact expand enormously. Paul wrote to this very point in his letter to the Philippians (3:7-17). He wanted his readers to know that he was trustworthy, not as a model of perfection, but as a model of dedication and commitment. An experience in my more athletic years has helped me to understand just how important this distinction is. When I climbed the Grand Tetons, I was helped tremendously by the presence of Larry, who stayed just a few steps ahead of me. He would have been of no benefit to my climb had he perched himself on top of the summit, waving ant-sized encouragement down the 3,000-foot gulf between us.

Dedicated student leaders can be sure that God will use them as positive models in others' lives, in part because they *aren't* perfect and in part because their accessibility to their friends makes them easy to walk with. Understanding the dynamics of this part of disciple-making means that Christian students can play a part in the spiritual formation of their peers that isn't as naturally available to adults. This does not mean that adults cannot play a role in the disciple-making process. It simply means that students can also play a role with their peers.

Not all disciple-making influence takes place in one-to-one contexts

This isn't hard to demonstrate from the biblical pattern. The word *disciple* is used in its singular form in the New Testament only 28 times; it's used in the plural form 266 times.[16] The dynamics of observational learning were at work as the disciples watched Peter try to walk across the water to Jesus (Matthew 14:25-31). Did they learn a faith lesson also, or was Peter the only beneficiary of the experience?

As effective as it may be to receive individual faith instruction, there may also be some drawbacks to this mentoring approach. One of them is obvious. Jesus put a primary value on the kind of loving relationships Christians ought to have with one another (John 13:35). For us to grow in the ability to truly love one another, we need

---

16. This count is derived from the *New International Version* of the Bible.

plenty of practice, coaching, and feedback. Group settings allow us to learn from others' experiences and to stretch our own relational skills.

When student leaders commit themselves to learning from one another, creating a caring atmosphere, and displaying a unity that is sustained by Christ at the center of the community, they soon discover that biblical standards for relationships are, indeed, possible in today's world. Their influence among their peers will be a by-product of such a community. These positive experiences create seeds of discontent that will eventually help to renew the church.

I know that I don't ever want to *settle* for shallow ways of relating to and helping my fellow Christians. I have worked hard to bring about positive change wherever I have worshipped. My vision for what is possible today was born in the unusual camaraderie of my high school days. It's been rooted in the theological conviction that this is supposed to be the "normal Christian life."[17] It's been encouraged by examples of the church making significant stabs of faithfulness throughout history.

Because the disciple-making process is not intended to be an individual experience, student leadership teams should be forged and cultivated. By practicing teamwork and learning how to relate to one another, these teens will grow into the responsibilities expected of them as members of the body of Christ.

Most disciple-making influence has little to do with formal curriculum

Jesus' purpose in choosing the Twelve included the call for them to "be with him" (Mark 3:14). While they were able to experience plenty of formal instruction, this group learned most in the context of a life lived in community. For example, it seems fair to conclude that Jesus' formal instruction resulting in the Lord's Prayer was a response to his followers wanting Jesus to explain his own prayer patterns (Luke 11:1-13). There is incredible learning potential contained in nonformal experiences,[18] and when we are wise to this fact, we can be more effective in our disciple-making simply by being more intentional in our normal routines.

My high school buddy Jeff had picked up a copy of a book on fasting while cruising through the Christian bookstore. I can still picture us flopped on the beds in his room, listening to Neil Young's *Harvest*, when he grabbed the book off of his nightstand and read me portions that he had marked. We started talking about what we should do about what we were learning. Eventually we decided to try a day without eating, ending our food deprivation around a Big Mac feast exactly 24 hours after we had begun. I've since learned a lot about how to improve on the quality of this discipline, but the transformational power of this experience was first unleashed in an unplanned conversation between our jamming harmonica tunes.

Student leaders have a tremendous natural advantage over adults when it comes to tapping into the potential of non-formal learning. Their time with friends is largely of this variety. When they seek to "make the most of every opportunity" (Colossians 4:5), they will raise the importance of following Christ while demonstrating his rele-

17. Watchman Nee, *The Normal Christian Life* (first printing: Bombay, India: Gospel Literature Service, 1957).

18. Richards, 60–68.

vance throughout their lives. These two factors contribute significantly to the transformational power of learning.[19]

Concluding commitments

I'm not convinced that student leadership necessarily leads to a particular programmatic model of youth ministry. Persons in church and parachurch settings, committed to small group structures, worship evangelism, or drop-in centers may each focus their youth ministries through the type of student leadership I have advocated in this chapter. Because of my theological commitments, I want to find a way to integrate the following three principles of *Student Leaders in Relationship* into my ministry strategies. (At this point, it should not be a surprise that my theological commitments don't lead me to advocate either of the other two student leader approaches.)

Adults and student leaders are partners

Even approaches to youth ministry that focus on student leadership dare not assume that adults don't play a major role. In reality, youth ministry must be a partnership. I've spent most of this chapter making the case for the kind of leadership of which students are capable. I now need to explicitly reject any model that suggests that adults aren't equally necessary to the practice of youth ministry. In fact, there is student leadership research to the contrary. We found that when adults are involved in meaningful, weekly, life-coaching relationships with teens, when they take responsibility to plan and run quality programs, when they teach Scripture, and when they model evangelism practices that student leaders are significantly more likely to be effective in reaching their friends for Christ.[20] The inclusiveness of biblical texts that lends itself to considering student leaders as capable co-ministers can't be contorted to imply that adults should now be relegated to marginal roles. Adults and teens must become partners in ministry.

Typically adults will have access to greater experiences than teens. This background is important as a source of wisdom and equips them well to coach and mentor their younger brothers and sisters in the faith. But it is also typical that teens will have access to more natural avenues of influence among their friends than adults. These opportunities are important if we're going to move forward toward an expansive vision of youth ministry. Adults and student leaders need one another, and ministry teams ought to be forged to accommodate this reality.

Maturity, faithfulness, opportunities, and gifts determine roles

I've had student leaders do a better job of following up new teen Christians than adults, even though they didn't have nearly the same quality of training. I think they were more effective simply because they were more available to the natural dimensions of the task; their relational world was the same as that of the new converts.

---

19. Dave Rahn, "Marketplace Youth Ministry," *Group* (September/October 1996), 41-44.

20. Rahn and Linhart, chapter 3.

We ought to resist being prescriptive about the roles that youth and adults play in ministry. Chances are that our criteria will be derived from our limited experiences or unfounded age biases. Rather, we must recognize that God's way of accomplishing his purposes is always through the diverse readiness of his people. Fresh strategies can be developed, used, and abandoned based upon the mix of people God has made available to do his work at a particular place and time. This is the task of a ministry team.

Student leadership contexts for effectiveness

The *Student Leaders in Charge* version of student leadership suggests that persons need to be up-front in large group meetings, and the *Student Leaders in the System* approach implies they may need to be elected to some post that gives them permission to lead. That's not how I'm coaching my freshman son these days. I want him to see his role in partnership with the adults in his life who want to help him grow and reach his friends. We pray and brainstorm over ways to take conversations deeper, build more meaningful relationships, and expose his buddies to other Christians who can add clarity to the gospel message. None of these moves has required Jason to be captain of the basketball team or president of the youth group.

In fact, the genius of Jesus' servant leadership strategy is that a slave could be expected to influence his or her master through the quality of a life well-lived and opportunistic, Spirit-led boldness. Everyone has spheres of influence that are natural to their world. Student leaders are those spiritually mature teens committed to becoming more faithful and effective in leading their friends to Christ and helping them grow in Christ.

There were occasions while growing up where my mother would salivate on her finger to rub off the nearly invisible dirt smudge on my cheek. I never remember this uninvited intrusion to my facial space as being welcome. It may be that my student leader convictions have led me to approach others like my wet-fingered mom, poised for the clean-up. While it's been an honor to champion my version of student leadership through this chapter, I sure hope readers who aren't so enthusiastic about *Student Leaders in Relationship* will forgive me if they feel anything like I did when mom started scrubbing.

Focusing Youth Ministry through Critical Consciousness
David F. White

> For our struggle is not against flesh and blood, but against the rulers, against the authorities, against the powers of this dark world and against the spiritual forces of evil in the heavenly realms.
>
> —*Ephesians 6:12*

> The Powers...have long since been identified as an order of angelic beings in heaven , or as demons flapping about in the sky. Most people have simply consigned them to the dustbin of superstition. Others sensing the tremendous potential in the concept of the Powers for interpreting social reality, have identified them without remainder as institutions, structures, and systems...The Powers are the simultaneity of an outer, visible structure and an inner, spiritual reality. The Powers properly speaking, are not just the spirituality of institutions, but their outer manifestations as well. The New Testament uses the language of power to refer now to the outer aspect, now to the inner aspect, now to both together...It is the spiritual aspect, however, that is so hard for people inured to materialism to grasp.
>
> —*Walter Wink,* Engaging the Powers

He removed the dangling pewter cross and tossed it to the dirt, taking another desperate swipe at the volleyball. I pondered the reason why Brian so easily discarded my confirmation gift of a few months earlier. I could not prevent the feeling that with it he had tossed aside the only tangible proof of his participation in the long, rigorous confirmation class of 13 junior and senior high youth. We had studied the Bible, church history, theology, and church polity together, and we had together made numerous retreats for prayer and reflection. Each youth had been assigned an adult mentor who met with them weekly to pray and discuss the journals they kept as reflections on their experiences. With other clergy staff, I had arranged significant liturgical events in which the entire faith community confirmed the progress of these youth toward full participation in the life of faith. But now, only six months beyond Easter, these newly confirmed youth rarely participated in liturgy, never achieved significant voice on church committees, sat at entirely different sides of the fellowship hall for church dinners, and were now playing volleyball outside as the adults debated the future of the church in this year's charge conference.

Ponderable
David White implies that there are systems, structures, and powers that keep youths from getting and staying involved as "active agents of the faith." Do you agree with his assessment? Is a main reason so many students drop out or lose interest in our programs due to the attitudes and structures of adult system? Or are there other more vital factors?

Twenty-two years of youth ministry, with all its problems and questions, led me to hold out much hope for this approach to educating youth in the stories, symbols, values, practices, and norms of this faith community. Instead, I found that even though we had succeeded in thoroughly enculturating youth in the symbols and stories of faith, both youth and adults had internalized the powerful and unconscious cultural assumption that youth were somehow not yet capable of being full participants in the life of the church. Although most adults of this church would happily affirm their theological conviction that youth are gifted and capable of great faith as disciples of Jesus Christ, these convictions remained in contradiction to their deeply held unconscious beliefs about youth and their capacities. It seems unfaithful to simply relegate youth to marginal congregational space in the basement or attic, to entertain them with games and parties until they someday become real adult members, or to teach them the Bible abstracted from real struggles and problems of their community. Perhaps there remains some dimension of youth ministry that could empower youth to critically engage their communities as active agents of faith.

What barriers and inhibitions prevent Brian, his friends, and their families from participating or allowing youth to participate fully in the life and mission of the church? And perhaps more importantly, is this a faithful question, relevant or central to ministry with youth, or any endeavor in Christian discipleship? These are perhaps the two most relevant questions facing youth ministry into the next century—an era in which the boundaries of adolescence are increasingly blurred, beginning earlier and extending later than any other time in history, within institutions where they have less than full power.

Clues for empowering youth

Many of the reasons youth are not empowered as full agents of faith and equipped to transform their churches and communities have to do with deep unconscious forces or powers that shape adolescent life and inform our understandings of them. Inhibitions to youth discipleship include the deep unconscious messages and cultural myths that can determine our relations with youth when we remain unreflective about them. Youth and adults who live in communities internalize the *spirits* or *powers* of those communities—the symbols, the myths, and tacit understandings, for example, about youth and their abilities. Teaching at a sheer cognitive or propositional level will not fully engage these spirits and powers that exist on an unconscious level. Often these inhibitions remain in unconscious contradiction to stated doctrines or theological assumptions. What are the sources of these spirits, forces, or powers? New Testament scholar Walter Wink argues that real spiritual force emanates from actual institutions— schools, cultures, churches, economies, families, nations, etc. He states:

There were, in the first century, both Jews and Christians who perceived
in the Roman Empire a demonic spirituality that they called Sammael

or Satan. But they encountered this spirit in the actual institutional forms of Roman life: legions, governors, crucifixions, payment of tribute, Roman sacred emblems and standards, and so forth. The spirit they perceived existed right at the heart of the empire, but their worldview equipped them to discern that spirit only by intuiting it and then projecting it out, in visionary form, as a spiritual being residing in heaven and representing Rome in the heavenly council.[1]

Wink observes that in New Testament times, people projected the felt or intuited spiritual qualities onto the screen of the universe, and perceived them as cosmic forces reigning from the sky. In the ancient worldview, a seer or prophet was able to sense the diseased spirituality of an institution or state, and then bring that spirituality to awareness by projecting it in visionary form onto the heavenly realm and depicting it as a demon on high. Our task today is to withdraw that projection from on high and locate it in the institution in which it actually resides. This requires the rigorous activity of discerning the spirits.

Discernment has a long history in the Christian church. In the early church discernment and expulsion of evil spirits was of primary importance for Christian discipleship. Records from around the third through fourth centuries from church fathers Cyril, Ambrose, Chrysostom, and Augustine reveal that candidates for Christian baptism underwent not only instruction in the Christian teachings, but rigorous examination and exorcism. Exorcism was viewed as intense work with a spiritual director for the purpose of exposing ways unwitting candidates participated in evil.[2] The assumption of such examination is that what remains unconscious within us has the power to drive behavior and attitudes, but that raising the awareness of evil allows those seeking Christian discipleship to root it out, making room for the holy to abide. In later centuries St. Ignatius Loyola explored ways of refining the practice of discernment for understanding where God is at work in the world. And in modern times, various traditions as the Mennonites and Quakers have sought ways to engage entire communities, as well as individuals, in discerning good and evil.

The modern church in general and youth ministry in particular has undervalued the role of discernment in the Christian life. In some circles proof-texting biblical references, or merely seeking impressions in prayer, or superficial conversation has fallen under the rubric of discernment. What the early church seemed to practice was instead a deep critical engagement with shadow dimensions of society and one's own internal distortions and false tendencies. Without such deep critical engagement with these shadow powers, Christian instruction can become nullified by our assimilation to dominant cultural attitudes and practices. For example, the southern United States in the 1940s and '50s deeply internalized Christian symbols, stories, doctrines, etc., yet amidst religious revival and church expansion somehow we remained oblivious to our oppressive attitudes and practices toward African-Americans. When we internalize racist struc-

The spirit world
Central to David's understanding of discernment is the belief that demonic powers are institutionally governed, instead of being personified creatures of evil from outside the visible realm. The author seems to have tacitly challenged those who fundamentally disagree with his interpretation of powers and forces.

But has he really? Regardless of what you believe about the spirit world in general and the demonic in particular, David's point in this chapter is an important one for all Christians, wherever they land on the theological spectrum: adolescents need to be freed from institutional and systemic oppression and suppression. They also need to be encouraged and taught how to read and resist the spirit powers that would seek to destroy them and hold them back from the life God has created for them.

---

1. Walter Wink, *Engaging the Powers: Discernment and Resistance in a World of Domination* (Minneapolis: Fortress Press, 1992), 7.

2. John H. Westerhoff III, *A Faithful Church: Issues in the History of Catechesis* (Wilton, Connecticut: Morehouse-Barlow, 1981), 70–76.

tures so deeply, only ruthless critical reflection and introspection can expose these distorted powers. Without discernment, what is evil can appear natural and normal. While Christian instruction is an important part of discipleship, merely instructing youth and adults lacks the rigor of deep self and social critical investigation, and risks something analogous to the 19TH-century practice of teaching the Bible to African slaves while ignoring slavery itself as an evil structure.

Youth ministry that does not engage youth in discerning and engaging the powers and principalities—the social forces that constitute their lives—risks working only in the cracks and crevasses of systems and structures that colonize more and more of life. The comparison of adolescence to slavery has more relevance than revealed at first glance. Both are ideas and practices constructed by societies and are seen by some as representing the natural state of existence, and both require critical awareness to resist their power. While many in mainline Christianity have become more aware, however incompletely, of the dangers of racism, few have become sensitized to the dangers of viewing the institution of adolescence as natural to the life cycle. Our churches and youth risk naturalizing the situation and institution of adolescence—a thoroughly social and somewhat oppressive construct.

Ponderable

David compares the social construct of slavery to that of adolescence, concluding that the essence of adolescence is something to be resisted. Elsewhere in this book, however, adolescence is perceived as a cultural invention that evolved into a "legitimate phase of the life span." The author here obviously disagrees, stating that adolescence is a "somewhat oppressive construct." Between these positions, where do you stand?

The social construction of adolescence

While there has always been a liminal stage of life in all cultures, marking the movement from childhood to adulthood, the current prolonged stage of adolescence is relatively new, emerging with force only in this century. Once upon a time prior to the 19TH century, young children worked side by side with adults—watching, learning, playing, laughing, and talking. Young people became adults as they developed physical abilities for work to sustain themselves and contribute to their families. Young people also took on adult roles much earlier in life—marriage, work, and civic concerns for the common good of their communities. With the establishment of adolescence came the modern high school, which was initially designed as a means of keeping young street urchins out of trouble and socializing new immigrants into the American language, norms, and values—with academic aims being a somewhat distant consideration. In this context, the original Christian youth group movement began in 1884 as the Christian Endeavor Movement, with mainline Protestant versions following soon after—as an attempt to find a niche for youth, whose role in this new world was still in question. As the high school and youth group movements grew, and as more and more youth were assimilated, others saw a chance to exploit youth in this new protective institutional cocoon.

Quentin Schultze of Calvin College documents the exploitative and symbiotic relationship that soon developed between youth and the entertainment media. As early as the 1920s, youth became increasingly relegated to their own private subsociety, where peer conformity dictated style—clothes, cars, partners, social activities, etc.—

Institutional cocoon—necessary precaution or restrictive exploitation?

David perceives postmodern culture, and especially Christian culture, as an exploitation of the young.

It is a serious indictment to include Christian support systems (youth ministry publishers and organizations that live off of the needs of youth ministry) in the same mix with the mainstream media, musicians, and advertisers. On the other hand, when you consider the cost of Christian-label CDs, for example, or ticket prices for outreach concerts, or the popularity of some youth speakers—when you consider factors like these, you wonder if David addresses forthrightly what most youth workers only whisper about. In any case, few on either side of this question deny that youth ministry is big business.

What do you think?

with money making it all possible.[3] Movies, cars, radios, and records all played a role in defining youth status. In fact, music has helped to define youth against their parents, family, and tradition. In each succeeding generation, music and media have driven youth and their families further and further apart. Creating markets means creating separate cultures, thus making the generations increasingly incomprehensible to each other. On this division, the entertainment industry depends. A special target of marketers is the disposable income of youth, now estimated at $2,500 per year per youth, on average.

Additionally, mainstream media portrays life as a perpetual identity crisis, compelling youth to adapt to the latest trend. Youth report that they learn how to dress, make-up their faces, talk, and act from movies and television. Yet, they confess an abiding dissatisfaction with themselves, fed by the media that depends on it for the sale of products, driving the individual back for more products to salve the wound prescribed in a consumer economy. In fact, the success of the media depends on an ongoing crisis in social authority, and can be directly attributed to diminished authority of institutions of primary care—home, church, and school, etc. The void left by these institutions among youth has been filled by the media. For example, the founders of MTV reported that in their original market research they observed two *gaps* in American adolescent life—identity and intimacy. So in packaging their program for youth, they construct an informal set in which the VJs lounge on sofas and chat with the audience as they play music videos that provide norms, values, and beliefs for a generation of youth. Similarly, engaging in what was once considered the responsibility of trusted adults, teen magazines offer advice for dating, relationships, school, and career.

Another function of entertainment media is that of *gender intensification*. In their recent book, *Generation On Hold: Coming of Age in the Late Twentieth Century*, Cote and Allahar observe that the mass media sell goods and services based upon gender identity and they report, "gender is big business." [4] For example, young women spend enormous sums of money on feminine products—make-up, clothes, perfume—to shape them into the willowy, and often emaciated, creatures they view in teen magazines and movies. At the hands of teen-oriented media, young women experience a decline in self-esteem and academic performance as they attempt to become the pleasing, largely ornamental figures who will not threaten male egos, depicted in the media. Young men likewise are killing themselves in record numbers in attempts to drink beer, drive fast, smoke cigarettes, and have casual sex, promoted as norms of maleness. Yet, these cries are not often connected to these sources for adolescent identity—the powers of the media.

Youth ministry has in many communities become a new and somewhat pervasive social force impacting the lives of youth. But youth ministry, like other forms of social activity, can take many forms for good or ill. Youth ministry may unconsciously mirror popular culture or economic and political structures—e.g., exalting celebrity

---

3. See Quentin J. Schultze, and others, *Dancing in the Dark* (Grand Rapids, Michigan: Eerdmans, 1991).

4. James E. Cote and Anton L. Allahar, *Generation On Hold: Coming of Age in the Late Twentieth Century* (New York: New York University Press, 1994), 84ff.

Christian musicians, overshadowing the gifts of youth themselves in creating music, forming youth as consumers. William Myers, for example, in his book *Black and White Styles of Youth Ministry* reveals the ways white suburban churches often internalize the root metaphors of their life context—e.g., the *corporate* metaphor, which shapes their understanding of church leadership as a hierarchically organized efficient machine.[5] Alternately, youth ministry may also reach deep into ethnic traditions and find ways of resisting corporate powers, utilizing alternate root metaphors such as *kinship*. Many African-American churches, for example, have found in their ancient traditions, practices, and metaphors resources for survival and resistance in an otherwise hostile and racist world. These root metaphors and ways we organize our lives should be a source of reflection for the church and youth ministry that seeks to be faithful to Jesus and the church's way of resisting the powers.

This glimpse of the social forces constituting contemporary adolescence, however incomplete, offers a hint of these external powers that confine the lives of historical and contemporary youth. But, the powers are not just "out there" but are also "in here." Even as racism is not simply embodied outwardly as prohibitions from drinking fountains, restaurants, and restrooms—but also exists as inner feelings and attitudes inscribed as prejudices and fears onto our very hearts; so our attitudes toward youth are not simply manifested in school and media structures and practices, but are internalized—not just by adults, but by youth themselves. Powers exist as outward structures delineating a more domesticating role for youth, while at the same time shaping our unconscious responses and relationships with youth.

The powers of the entertainment industry view youth not as a prophetic presence or gifts for the healing of the world, but as a source of bottom-line profit. And what is worse, the church has often unwittingly participated in this aggressive marketing to youth, by promoting contemporary Christian music celebrities, slick Christian youth magazines mirroring those proliferating in popular media, and acres of Christian youth products—T-shirts, CDs, tattoos, bumper stickers, key chains, Frisbees, video tapes, etc. And worse than participating in this marketing frenzy to youth, we have failed to engage them critically and equip them with the skills to see the dangers of the consumer market. Is it a matter of faith that youth buy or resist Nike shoes made with sweatshop labor in Southeast Asia? One wonders how Jesus might name the demons observed in a walk through the local shopping mall? What powers are analogous to the Roman powers of Jesus' day? What are the symbols that elicit the feelings of dread, fear, hopelessness, anger, hunger, apathy among the social world of our youth—a Nike swoosh, a drive-by shooting, a television set, the image of an emaciated supermodel?

Movements of discernment

Modern adolescent life is in many ways more complex than in earlier or more traditional cultures, requiring the church to engage and refine its practices of discernment.

In the driver's seat
Some claim the media mirrors culture, which means that the young actually drive the media. Still others believe that while the media has some influence, adolescents are extremely street smart and use the media even as the media seeks to exploit them—which produces a cycle that rapidly spirals out of control as the young both empower and feed off the media.
What do *you* think?

From a Christian youth magazine ad: "Jesus said, 'Let your light shine before men.' And [the Christian T-shirts are] a great way to shine your light."
And they will know you are my disciples by your T-shirts and your fish ornaments.

---

5. William Myers, *Black and White Styles of Youth Ministry* (New York: Pilgrim Press, 1991).

Learn to discern
It is clear where David stands on consumerism in the youth ministry culture. But his severest critique is against a youth ministry milieu that fails to help students discern the manipulative culture, both in and outside the church.

How can we help young disciples to be more discerning in how they spend their money and resist cultural pressures? What is a youth minister's responsibility to shield students from the marketing efforts of Christian youth ministry companies?

In particular, discernment in this era should include engaging the church in seeking to understand the sociocultural influence of life—the ethnic traditions, religious traditions, economic and political forces, etc. Discernment in this era should include a growing understanding of the social and cultural powers that constitute adolescent life and the ways God works in the redemption of them—and how youth might participate with God in resisting alienating cultural forces. While discernment may be shaped differently in different religious contexts and may include a wide variety of practices for raising awareness and judging, the barest understanding of discernment should include the following components: *listening*, *understanding*, *dreaming*, and *acting*.

Listening: loving God with our hearts

The guiding questions for these listening activities are—

- Where do youth themselves experience anger, frustration, sadness, tension, or anxiety within various contexts of school, home, work, church, peer relationships, etc.?
- Where do youth experience satisfaction, joy, vitality, delight, or pleasure in these and other contexts of their lives?

Listening is for the purpose of appreciating the energies that determine adolescents' lives at a very deep level—reaching below the complexity of life to attend to emotions and passions surrounding concrete situations. Passions are the spring and source from which all ethical moral choices flow—what we love and yearn for is fundamental to our understandings of right and wrong. Human passion represents ways we are touched by God and moved toward God. Yet the human heart is also restless enough to form attachments in unhealthy ways, as neurosis, addictions, prejudices, patterns, sins, or complexes that close us off from life, God, and others.

G. Simon Harak in *Virtuous Passions* recounts a story of his visit to Kingston, Jamaica, where he escorted a group of 18- to 19-year-old boys from St. George's College to meet their little brothers—a group of younger boys orphaned and from abused homes. He relates this story:

> They had all been playing soccer when Fabian, the elected leader of the young men from St. George's, came to me distraught and upset. His little brother, with whom he was trying so hard to get along, had scored a goal in the game. Everyone was excited. Fabian ran up to him and lifted his hand to clap him on the shoulder. But the boy flinched, and then cowered away from him. Fabian was stunned. "I was going to congratulate him," he kept saying to me. "I wasn't going to hurt him. What did he pull away for? I wasn't going to hurt him."...He (ultimately) discovered that every time (previously) a hand was raised to that little boy, he

had been struck. Now, even when a hand was raised in congratulation, the boy had no choice.[6]

In Harak's story the young orphan's passions had been shaped in the abusive context of his early life, and was now closed to fuller life and relationship. As illustrated in the small boy's once necessary, yet now unexamined flinching response, as long as our affective lives remain unconscious to us, our passions or our affective patterns of response have the power to determine our lives, thus closing us to God, fullness, love, and beauty.

For Christian theologians Augustine, Thomas Aquinas, and Ignatius Loyola, Christian discipleship is the process of attending to the shape of our passions and supporting or reshaping them in more completely life-giving ways. Thomas Aquinas acknowledges that God is love, and that the best way to know God is through the experience of love. According to Aquinas, God has created all of us out of the very fabric of God's own self. God shares love and being with all in the form of their simple existing and in the uniqueness of their existence. To fulfill our nature is to satisfy fully the very purpose of our being—loving and being loved—as we are caught up in the love of God. All people are drawn close to God through all others in creation.

Movements of attraction and repulsion characterize all of creation—fire is drawn to air, rocks are drawn to the earth, etc. As human beings, we have a natural passion for God and also for each other. For Aquinas there are right and wrong appetites or passions—those that draw us to each other and God, and those that repel us from each other and God, and it is vital that we discern these deep forces within us. While the example used above illuminates the way a violent family can limit the life-giving responses of a child, the process of internalizing habits, addictions, myths, and prejudices can be initiated by not only families, but individuals in relation to communities, ethnic cultures, economic and political structures, and media sources.

By exploring practical ways to attend to our emotions and passions and their surrounding situations and relationships, we can get some distance from them and are not so immediately and unreflectively determined by them. Human life and experience is a complex mixture of social and cultural forces, community and family patterns, and individual psychic dynamics—all with addictions, distortions, gifts, and graces that remain unconscious to us. And what remains unconscious to us has the power to determine our behavior. For example, anger or frustration might thus be clues about injustice to us or to our community. By attending to this anger or frustration, we may sense, however vaguely at first, the possibility that life could be other than it is. Alternately, feelings of joy or vitality could signal directions for Christian vocation or giftedness. It is these energies that make us human and suggest the possibility of being fully who we were created to be in relation to each other and God. And it is here that we can sense the Spirit's work among us—through yearnings deeper than words.

---

6. G. Simon Harak, *Virtuous Passions* (New York: Paulist Press, 1993), 1.

Ponderable
In considering your own experience, is youth ministry typically a good environment for adults to authentically listen to kids? What are some ways to help teenagers to tell their stories, to freely name their fears, and to feel safe enough to bare their souls with people they see once or twice a week in an institutional environment? Are we asking too much of teenagers? Of youth workers? Should we change how and where we do what we do?

Certainly one aim of listening to the stories and passions of youth is for the purpose of ultimately discerning where God is working—where there is life and where life is draining away—and participating in the transformation of all life for the reign of God. However, listening can in itself be understood as a healing practice, even in isolation from a full-blown discernment process with these ultimate aims. In a recent summer program at Emory University in which 60 youths from around the country were gathered to reflect on theology and engage in practical forms of Christian discipleship, the staff engineered an elaborate program of study, worship, recreation, music, service, and spiritual direction. But to the surprise of the staff, the one activity that consistently ranked highest on youth evaluations was a one-hour interview with a graduate student who was gathering research for a thesis. Rarely do youth experience the full and prolonged attention of a significant adult for the purpose of listening to them—for hearing what they love, what they hate, what their gifts are, what their families are like, what their hopes and dreams are for the future. Similarly, in a local California church when the adult staff spent months listening to the stories of youth—what makes them angry, sad, frustrated, loved, alive, joyful, connected—the youth and adults experienced a mutual conversion to each other, each feeling more understood, much less contemptuous and judgmental of each other. The mere practice of listening is healing for youth who are alienated from adults.

Some practical ways to engage youth in listening activities are the employment of small groups, drama, surveys that enable the group to go to deeper levels of discovery and discernment, using video and other popular media. There are many books and resources available to youth workers that can be invaluable in helping bring students to a more developed sense of wisdom and insight.

Understanding: loving God with our minds

The guiding questions for this movement include—

- How can we understand the causes for the various situations that cause us anger, frustration, sadness, joy, vitality, etc.?
- What are all of the possible causes for these situations that elicit emotion?

Thomas Aquinas offers an understanding of human life and intellect grounded in God. Briefly, Aquinas understands human beings as unique in that our intellect is united with a physical reality, our bodies. Like God, humans have an increased degree of freedom over rocks that must rely upon the physical nature of their being, and animals who are more free than rocks yet are largely bound by their senses and physical needs. Significantly, humans are able to think and move beyond our senses and physical being. We are capable of perceiving the Supreme Good, and able to order our particular goods in light of the Supreme Good. The vision of the Supreme Good and the power to act upon it is characteristic of human rationality. Rational beings do not blindly partake of the order of the universe but have the freedom and ability to participate in the ordering of ourselves and the universe toward God—our ultimate happiness and goal.

Aquinas' conception of the organic unity of the soul and body must not be understood as the rational repression of the body and senses. The lifelong moral project of a human being would thus be to complete and fulfill the integration of the self, so that the whole self becomes fully rational, ordered in relation to God—an integrated body, heart, mind, soul. In fact, as noted earlier, it is not the intellect that is first drawn to God—instead we find ourselves desiring or wanting God. We are drawn more profoundly by love than by knowledge. By being created in the image of God, we have implanted in our very nature the seeds of a *natural attraction* to God's own self. The human moral project is to be fully who we were created to be, fully alive and fully human, in love with God and rightly ordered in our loves in the world—with others, nature, etc. The ordering of the whole self to God is that of seeking the fullest delight—using our minds in attending to our bodies and senses and ordering our lives in ways that seek constant delight—the way to God. Our bodies and hearts are not sufficient in themselves for the task, but require the intellect for training and ordering the whole self returned to God. This ordering requires some concrete practices described below.

Observing and describing. Passions are evoked in relation to specific concrete historical circumstances. Understanding includes deliberately observing and describing the situations that evoke the emotions. It is important for those seeking God to understand the present action of their community—to name or express the present behaviors and circumstances evoking particular emotions. Until we can understand the dynamics of "what is going on" we cannot see beyond to further possibilities. Questions that are appropriate to this stage of discernment include, What is going on here? What is being done here?

Reflecting critically. Understanding a situation also means engaging questions about the social and personal dynamics that surround situations—understanding ways they are historically shaped by economic, political, and cultural forces. We live in a world so complex that cultures or traditions or social influences are rarely found in any pure state, but mingle in some form with multiple other traditions—ethnic, class, religious, pop cultural, etc. Emotions alone are not sufficient for discernment until the intellect is engaged in understanding the complexity of human situations. The appropriate questions for these understanding activities are, But why? What are the reasons why this situation has emerged in history? What are all of the aspects that determine this situation?

As we attend to our emotions, reflect upon them and the situations in which they are evoked, make judgments about them, and act faithfully in ways that honor them, we can participate in the transformation and healing of the world in God's image. Understanding these situations includes perceiving individual ways we form attachments to ideas, relationships, images, possessions, or structures that may be less than ultimate—and the defenses we utilize to defend these attachments.

Dreaming: loving God with our souls

Some have noted that the imagination is the seat of the soul. We can become disembeded from the normal structures of our lives only if we can imagine other ways of being. Dreaming should reflect an attempt to order all of one's passions and priorities in line with one's ultimate passion for God, opening us out to fuller experiences of life, self, and God. Dreaming is the step of considering one's emerging love of God in relation with the other affective attachments. Dreaming with God, through the resources of the Christian tradition, includes being reminded of our true self and being in God. The guiding questions for this movement include—

- What in the Christian tradition touches you on some deep level—what Scriptures, traditions, liturgies, stories, insights, and practices?
- How do these practices speak to the particular issues of youth unearthed in listening processes?
- How is our love for God in contradiction to our current relationships and practices in the world?
- How does our love for God require us to order our other loves, passions, and commitments in relation to God?
- How can I order my life so that I might more consistently experience love and delight?

Dreaming includes developing a vision for how the world could be other than it is, and more reflective of the reign of God in the world. Dreaming includes bringing into view the historical expressions of the Christian community, particularly those that are moving for you and your community—as expressed in Scriptures, traditions, writings, practices, liturgies, and so on. The resources of the Christian tradition offer numerous opportunities for youth and adults to remember and nurture their passion for God— through remembering the historical people of Israel and their understandings of God's work in the world, the winsome stories of Jesus Christ, the ecclesial practices of Eucharist, baptism, and confirmation, through the fellowship of the faith community, through prayer and meditation, and acts of solidarity and service with the poor and suffering of the world.

These resources of the Christian tradition should not be engaged only as an imposed framework of meaning—as rational understandings and doctrines—but as opportunities for and places where youth encounter God in fullness, glory, love, and compassion. Dreaming includes reflecting upon the promises and demands that arise from the Christian stories, relevant for conceptualizing new and more faithful ways of shaping and participating in the world. Authentic discipleship calls us beyond our present ways of acting and thinking into ways that are appropriate in light of our own lives and understandings of the Christian tradition—i.e., imagining more just ways of living that attend to the cultural and personal forces and impulses.

One practical approach for engaging youth in this stage of dreaming includes the following exercise:

1. Invite youth to prepare a story from their lives that engages them in one strong emotion—anger, frustration, sadness, etc. (Perhaps a story from the above listening movement.)
2. As each person reads her story, the one telling the story and the group members share feelings evoked for them in the telling of the story. This may spark others to tell similar stories. Participants then ask questions to tease out details and feelings.
3. Ask the group to reflect on the shared story, and the question, "Where is God in this story? Where is life?" Or "Where is God missing? Where is life draining away?"
4. Youth may make connections with songs, Bible events or verses, symbols, etc., in answer to the question above. The aim is to engage them in seeing where God is at work in their lives now, and where they can participate more deliberately with God's work, and how they can resist the powers that diminish life.

Acting: loving God with our strength

The guiding questions for this movement include—

- How does the listening to and understanding of these stories of youth—and dreaming of alternate faithful futures—call us to change any future action, or shape our behaviors in different ways?
- What kinds of communal, civic, political, or individual responses are we called to?

Reflection cannot neglect action, and neither can action neglect reflection. Discernment is an ongoing process in which actions are highlighted for reflection, and constantly refined in deliberate fashion. Human practices and processes must speak back to dreams and reflections, driving us to consider new and more adequate understandings and ways of ministry and life.

One persistent theme among youth is their yearning to *do something*. By this they are expressing a desire to engage beyond superficial social and recreational activities in order to participate in God's redemptive kingdom work in the world. They sense the need to be actors in history and to not simply be acted upon. Indeed, their desire is consistent with the God of Jesus Christ who wrought redemption not simply in an eternal sphere but within the bounds of history, space, and time. As adolescents grow, they yearn to break free from the artificial protective institutions of adolescence to engage the world as agents of faith—not simply as passive consumers. In a day when youth workers languish in often tired rituals of youth group games and pizza parties, youth themselves relish significant roles in partnership with God's Spirit in the redemption and healing of the world.

Conclusion

The church in general and youth ministry in particular has participated in the domestication of adolescents—bringing them into our institutions for our purposes. As a result, we have not only stifled them as gifted and creative children of God, but we have denied our own churches the energy, beauty, questioning, and the courageous challenge of youth—and thus a force for our own transformation. The shadow side of our cultural repression of youth has been that much of their creative energy has been channeled into exploitative, oppressive, dangerous, and unhealthy directions.

The practice of discernment engages youth and their churches in seeing the ways their understandings and behaviors need to be exposed to the light of Christ come into the world. Practices of discernment engage youth and their churches in staying attuned to God's ever-present work in the world and discovering ways they can participate in it. Those of us who have risked ourselves in work with youth have found their gifts considerable and invaluable for the church and the world. Youth have vital gifts for the adult world, drained by alienating work of much of its life. Youth have gifts of questioning for adults who have been so enculturated by social and cultural forces and have forgotten their own questions. Youth have gifts of play for adults and congregations who have forgotten that God's foundational work of creation was an act of play, and that Christ's work in the world is a playful redemption of too-serious forces. Youth have gifts for courageous historic action and can once again, as in Civil Rights movements, labor movements, peace movements, and modern movements of diversity, be at the forefront of movements of justice and peace, in the name of God. The church can risk empowering youth through engaging them in rhythms of critical discernment of the powers, or it can relegate them to volleyball games and marginal spaces in the church attic or basement.

Focusing Youth Ministry through Community
Kara Eckmann Powell

As long as I can remember I've loved football. The first football field I played on regularly was the street in front of my dad's house. My dad was almost always the quarterback, I would be the wide receiver, and my younger brother would usually play defense. My dad showed me the plays he wanted me to run by tracing post, button hook, and flare patterns on the palm of his hand, and would throw me the ball when he thought I had broken free from my brother's defensive coverage. Given that my brother was fast, this sometimes took a few minutes, but since we had no other defenders to rush my dad, he would wait patiently until I was open (or until my brother and I got cramps in our sides from all that running around). This prepared me for my debut on my first official football team. When I was 12 years old, my brother, two neighbor kids, and I formed A.F.A.S., short for Alley Football All Stars. We had plays we had practiced, we had cheers we had worked out, and when it came to game time, we scored touchdown after touchdown against the other kids in the neighborhood. That is, until mom called us in for dinner.

But even when no other teammates were around, I still loved to play. I'd hike the ball to myself, take a few step backs, throw the football high into the air, try to catch it, and then run as fast as I could for the crack in the sidewalk that marked the end zone, dodging imaginary defenders. I didn't even have to have a real ball. I was a one-woman team. And I played with gusto.

As I scan the current youth ministry horizon, I don't think I'm alone in pretending to be a one-person team. Far too many youth workers I know do it every week. They are dedicated men and women, rookies and veterans, church and parachurch workers, working creatively and diligently to make sure their youth group is welcoming, encouraging, and inspiring. And some are very good at it. But perhaps labeling these youth workers or the youth groups they lead a *team* is an overstatement.[1] What they usually are is tired individual players, on the verge of injury and near defeat. My aim in this chapter is to identify and explore the metaphor of a youth group community as a *team*. To maintain a balance between sociology, theology, and practical ministry, this aim will be accomplished through a three-step practical theology methodology, presented in Figure 12.1. Fundamental to the discipline of practical theology and this investigation of youth group community is the belief in theory-laden practices. According to Don S. Browning, a widely recognized theorist in the field of practical theology, a *theory-laden practice* is an act or behavior that emerges from a principle or set of principles, however subconsciously these principles may be held.[2] By using Brown-

Ponderable

What has been your experience with professional youth ministers? Imagine a continuum: a quiet, behind-the-scenes guide/leader on one end and a superstar hero that obviously runs the show on the other. Which have you seen most of?

In Kara's description of the Lone Ranger youth worker, she seems to assume that such a youth worker lives "on the verge of injury and near defeat." Do you agree with this? Is the Lone Ranger or the benevolent star or the one-person show, destined for injury and defeat?

---

1. By *youth group*, I mean all regularly scheduled meetings of a youth ministry, as well as the sense of belonging that is created by these meetings.

2. Don S. Browning, *A Fundamental Practical Theology* (Minneapolis, Minnesota: Fortress Press, 1991), 6.

ing's term *theory-laden practices*, I intend to eliminate the assumption that theory and practice are distinct.[3] Most, and quite possibly all, practices reflect beliefs and theories, and most, if not all, theories overflow into practices. Because of the relative lack of valid research on youth ministry, it is difficult to ascertain the exact principles that drive some of the behaviors of youth groups, youth pastors, and youth group attenders. However, in this chapter I will suggest some potential theories drawn primarily from recent social science research and secondarily from my own observations as a youth ministry practitioner.

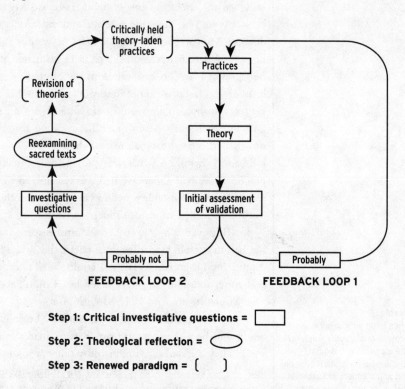

Figure 12.1. Practical theology feeback loops

Browning believes that once a religious community uncovers the theories that motivate its behaviors, it has two initial assessment options—the first of which is to accept those theories and continue with the same behaviors, illustrated in Figure 12.1 by Feedback Loop 1.[4] The second option is to begin to reflect and ask questions about the validity and appropriateness of these theories that carry over into practices, represented in Figure 12.1 by Feedback Loop 2. In this chapter, I will choose the second option and pose some investigative questions to help narrow the focus of our practical theology reflection.

The more thorough the reflection and the more provocative the investigative questions, the more likely the community is to resolve them by reexamining its sacred texts and events, diagrammed in Figure 12.1 as Step 2. Once this analysis is complete,

3. Browning, 6.

4. Browning, 6.

the community may revise its theories and practices based any newly understood norms and ideals. As Step 3 in Figure 12.1 illustrates, the practices that had been accepted and assumed to be true now become *critically held theory-laden practices* that arise from a more accurate understanding of the normative texts.[5] In this chapter, and in most youth group communities, the primary sacred text is Scripture; thus I will turn to its pages both to answer the investigative questions and to suggest a revised pattern for youth group involvement that more closely resembles Christ-centered community.

Step 1: the critical investigative questions

Although no two youth group communities are alike, some common themes have emerged in recent youth ministry research and theoretical paradigms. In this first step, I will examine the few social science studies that pertain to our exploration of the youth group as *team*, as well as comment on some of the youth group practices that seem to reflect their findings. In addition, I will suggest some theories that may be behind these empirically observed attitudes and trends. As I unearth these theories, I will pose relevant investigative questions that will shape subsequent theological analysis.

The reasons your students are coming to your youth group

Why do you think your students are coming to your youth group? If you answer that they walk in and decide to stay because of the relationships and friendships they've developed in your youth group, you're largely correct. In a 1998 randomized national telephone survey of 600 teenagers, 36 percent identified themselves as attending a church youth group "every week," 34 percent as "attending occasionally," and 30 percent as "never attending." Of the 70 percent who labeled themselves as youth group attenders, the second most important reason they gave for attending was "relationships," "friendships," and "the people there." Just ahead of friendships, students named "the opportunity to learn about faith and God" as the main reason for their involvement.[6]

While their recognition of the importance of learning is initially encouraging, the lack of statistically significant difference between the replies of youth group attenders and non-attenders regarding Christian doctrine makes the substance of their learning unclear. When asked to rate their level of agreement, a difference of less than 10 percentage points was reported between youth group attenders and non-attenders responding to the following doctrinal statements: "It doesn't matter what religious faith you associate with because they all believe the same principles and truths," "People who do not consciously accept Jesus Christ as savior will be condemned to hell," and "God created humans, but he is no longer personally involved in your life or experiences."[7] Beyond "the opportunity to learn," and "relationships," the other primary reasons teens gave for attending youth group were: "parents make them attend," "it makes them feel good, comfortable," "the teaching

Reading between the lines
As a theologically trained student, you need to make sure what you read and hear is accurate before you make programmatic or philosophical decisions. There are many individuals and organizations that are called experts, not all are necessarily on target.

While Kara does not rely on this research to make her case, the theological student must still pause and ask the question, "Is this really true?" Although you will not win any popularity contests by questioning famous and oft-cited leaders and influencers, it is nonetheless valuable to simply make sure that what someone reports as true is true.

For instance, the Barna Group reports that in a random survey 70 percent of teenagers in America attended church youth groups "occasionally." Test this statistic by finding out the number of teenagers in your town, survey church and parachurch youth groups, and do the math.

---

5. Browning, 6–8.

6. Barna Research Group, Ltd., "Teenagers Describe Their Youth Group," unpublished paper (Ventura, California: Fall 1998),

7. Barna, 13.

The role of the youth pastor

What is the actual, bottom-line job of the youth pastor? Or possibly more important vocationally, what makes for a competent and successful youth minister? The list of answers is massive, enough to frighten any sane person. And when you line up all the expectations that a professional youth worker carries on top of the written, black-and-white tasks of, the sheer weight of the role can be overwhelming.

How do you believe you line up with the various roles and expectations of the youth ministry job? In the first column prioritize what you believe to be the most important to the least (1 = critically important, to 17 = negligible)

Entertainer		
Recruiter		
Money manager		
Mentor		
Administrator		
Counselor/listener		
Worship leader		
One-on-one discipler		
Speaker		
Networker		
Trainer		
Musician		
"Captain Fun"		
Parent supporter		
Community resource		
Bible teacher		
Spiritual director/guru		

Now in the second column, prioritize your strengths in relation to the areas listed here (1 = greatest strength, to 17 = greatest weakness).

What do your responses say about you as a youth minister? Where will you need help to cover all of the bases? How will you make sure that everything is taken care of while not burning yourself out by trying to do and be too much?

and discussion," "experiencing God," and "the activities, events, retreats, and games."[8]

A second study conducted six years earlier of high school students confined to attenders of churches in the Conservative Baptist Association of Southern California partially confirms these findings, but indicates a more pervasively spiritual theme. The top five reasons given for attending Sunday school in the 486 useable instruments were later categorized and ranked as: "spiritual growth," "honor to God," "service to others," "social contact with new friends," and "identity formation." The same students responded they attended mid-week youth meetings because of spiritual growth, identity formation, cognitive interest, social stimulation through existing friendships, and integration with life.[9] It is possible that the difference between the more relational emphasis in the 1998 survey and the more spiritual theme in the 1992 survey is partially due either to the more conservative theological stance, or the geographical location of the respondents in the 1992 survey.

On a theoretical level, all of these are valid reasons for attending a church youth group. Yet many resemble those likely to be given by teens attending a wide variety of student gatherings, ranging from soccer practices and piano rehearsals to student government meetings and debate contests. While the nature of adolescent intellectual and socioemotional development leads me to expect a common set of reasons for students' attendance at any club or meeting, I would also hope that the encounter with God at youth group would be substantively different from any other meeting. Furthermore, at this point it is unclear if the reasons students come to youth group match the biblical picture of why they should come. It is quite possible, if not likely, that the Bible spells out reasons for being involved in a Christian community, such as a youth group, that students are blind to. Thus a pertinent investigative question becomes, *What are some purposes for a youth group meeting that seem to be missing from students' current understanding of their youth group involvement?*

The role of the youth pastor

The multiple vocational roles associated with the pastorate in general have been widely and repeatedly documented.[10] An empirical survey examining the more narrow category of the youth pastor reveals 11 vocational roles, including that of administrator, edu-

---

8. Barna, 13.

9. Ken Garland, unpublished paper presented at Youth Ministry Educators Forum in October 1999. The terms were defined as follows:
 • spiritual growth: "a desire to grow closer to God in a personal relationship"
 • honor to God: "a desire to obey and respect God and avoid making him angry"
 • service to others: "a desire to be better able to serve others"
 • social contact: "a desire to meet new friends and acquaintances"
 • identity formation: "a desire to find out who I am in relationship to others in my youth group"
 • cognitive interest: "a desire to learn just for the sake of learning"
 • social stimulation: "a desire to get closer to current friends and acquaintances"
 • integration with life: "a desire to find out how things I learn about church connects with my life"
Other motivators revealed by respondents' were escape ("a desire to get away from unpleasant aspects of my life") and external expectations ("a desire to please significant other people in my life").

10. George Barna, *Today's Pastors* (Ventura, California: Regal Books, 1993), 130; John Harold Beck, "The Effects of the Number of Roles, the Time Spent in Different Roles, and Selected Demographic Variables on Burnout and Job Satisfaction Among Iowa Lutheran Clergy," unpublished dissertation (University of Iowa: 1997), 67; and Samuel W. Blizzard, "The Minister's Dilemma," *Christian Century* (April 25, 1956), 508-510.

cator/enabler, recreator/activities director, counselor, and pastoral worship leader.[11] As with pastors in general, a subtle expectation implied both in this survey and anecdotal evidence from youth workers nationwide seems to be that they should be omni-competent, omni-skilled, and omni-gifted.

As with most other ecclesiological communities, a youth group requires leadership. Given the ongoing intellectual, emotional, relational, and spiritual development that adolescents are experiencing, it is possible that the adult leadership in the youth community may need to function in more distinct, if not significant, roles than the adult leadership in an adult community. Yet in the midst of the multiple roles expected and sometimes demanded of youth workers, it's possible that some roles are more important and maybe more biblically supported than others. Thus the critical research question becomes, *What is the purpose and role of adult leaders in a youth group community?*

The role of the student leader

Many youth ministries describe their attenders as advancing through a sort of progression. While expressed in various diagrams, ranging from a bull's-eye to a pyramid to a funnel, the progression remains fairly constant: from casual attenders, to more committed attenders, to influencers in the ministry. The message that is often implicitly or even explicitly communicated in these diagrams and practices is that there are two different kinds of students: *guests* and *hosts*. What is often assumed is that the *guests* are the less mature and skilled who receive ministry; in contrast, the *hosts* are the more mature and skilled influencers who give ministry. Often the latter are called *student leaders*, or *student ministers*.[12]

While there is almost certainly a continuum of spiritual, psychological, and socioemotional maturity among adolescents, the underlying theory seems to be that some students are *willing* to minister while others are not. In some cases, the subtle theory appears be that some students are *able* to minister and others are not. Thus an important investigative question emerging from this widespread practice is, *What is the purpose and role of a* student leader*, and how is that different than the rest of the students?*

Step 2: theological reflection

While keeping in mind the backdrop of the whole of Scripture, I intentionally focus my exegesis on the Pauline epistles for three reasons. First, Paul, while being a theologian, maintained a strong sociological thrust by paying attention to the social attitudes and structures of his day, even adopting them at times (1 Corinthians 9:19-23). Second, far from being cloistered in isolated theological reflection, Paul was actively engaged in understanding and responding to the Jewish, Greek, and Roman cultures that blanketed the Mediterranean region. Following the practical theology methodology adhered to in

---

11. Martha Jean Woody Minardi, "*The Roles of the Minister of Youth*," unpublished dissertation (Southern Baptist Seminary, 1987), 67-68. Respondents were youth pastors, pastors, chairpersons of deacons, denominational workers, and leaders in Southern Baptist churches.

12. Joe Brown, "Do You Believe Your Students Have Spiritual Gifts? Are You Sure?" unpublished paper, *Talbot School of Theology* (draft dated July 31, 1998), 2.

this chapter, Paul allowed these cultural issues, as well as the problems and questions of specific communities, to direct his creative energy and the topics of his letters.[13] Third, while admittedly far from exhaustive, Paul's writings provide us with a fairly comprehensive biblical doctrine of community immediately following the resurrection of Christ.[14] In seeking resolution to the critical investigative questions from Step 1, I have confined my search to the epistles with the most conclusive historical-critical evidence of Pauline authorship, namely Romans, 1 and 2 Corinthians, Galatians, Ephesians, Philippians, Colossians, 1 and 2 Thessalonians, and Philemon.[15]

What are some purposes for a youth group meeting that seem to be missing from students' current understanding of their youth group involvement?
The definitive nature of the church community can be at least partially understood from Paul's use of the term *ekklesia*.[16] Used over 100 times in the New Testament, 60 of these by Paul, *ekklesia*, while commonly translated as "church" in Scripture, is more generally defined in the Greek language as "assembly."[17] It seems that most often these assemblies were held in private homes (Acts 2:46; 12:12; Romans 16:3-5; and Philemon 1:2). We can logically infer that the size of the gathering was limited by the size of the meeting space; since the entertaining room in a moderately well-to-do home could hold roughly 30-40 people, church membership was likely approximately that size.[18] Not once does Paul employ the term *ekklesia* to describe a building, for such "church buildings" did not exist until the third century; rather, he consistently uses it to describe the gathered believers.

For today's youth group, a baffling element in Paul's description of the purpose of this assembly is not so much what he teaches, but what he does not teach. Paul does not label the primary purpose of the gathered community as teaching or learning. Neither does he describe it as worship.[19] Rather, for Paul, worship is a consuming lifestyle of obedience that can be experienced both corporately and individually at any time and in any location (Romans 12:1-2). Furthermore, Paul never defines the assembly's mission as evangelism and/or social action. Although important to his practical theology, dispersing the gospel and serving others can also occur outside of the gathered church.[20] Of course, teaching, worship, evangelism, and social action can and do happen

---

13. Robert Banks, *Paul's Idea of Community* (Peabody, Massachusetts: Hendrickson Publishers, 1994), 4-6.

14. Luke's writings in the book of Acts, while also portraying community following the resurrection of Christ, take a more narrative approach.

15. Uncertainty seems to persist regarding the authorship of the pastoral letters (1 and 2 Timothy, Titus), which, if not from Paul's own hand, are nonetheless profoundly influenced by Pauline thought.

16. While some might assume that Paul's use of the term *koinonia*, or fellowship, is equally important, Paul more often uses it to refer to fellowship with Christ.

17. Banks, 27; Doohan, 141; Gerhard Kittel, *Theological Dictionary of the New Testament*, vol. III (Grand Rapids, Michigan: Eerdmans, 1965), 503. *Ekklesia* does not occur in Mark, Luke, John, 2 Timothy, Titus, 1 and 2 Peter, 1 and 2 John, and Jude.

18. Banks, 35.

19. Maurice Goguel's claim that the church is assembled for worship, based on 1 Corinthians 11:18, 22, appears to be flawed exegesis of the passage. Maurice Goguel, *The Primitive Church* (London: George Allen and Unwin, 1964), 52.

20. Banks, 89.

when a community gathers, but they are either precursors or consequences of a greater purpose (1 Corinthians 14:25).

The greater purpose for the gathering is the strengthening of the church (1 Corinthians 14:12, 26). In Ephesians 4:13, Paul advocates that the body of Christ should be built up "until we all reach unity in the faith and in the knowledge of the Son of God and become mature, attaining to the whole measure of the fullness of Christ."[21] When understood in its immediate context, Paul's description of *"we all" who become united and mature* implies a communal growth in spirituality and comprehension that takes place in the company of God's people.[22] In any church gathering, other purposes, while potentially contributing to the ultimate purpose of spiritual maturity, are decidedly penultimate to this eventual goal.

In the verses just prior to Ephesians 4:13, Paul gives the means by which the gathered believers grow in maturity: God's people doing "works of service." Paul understood what some youth groups don't, namely that the incarnation inaugurated by Christ did not end at his resurrection. Christ continues to take bodily form by incarnating himself not just in youth pastors, but in the millions of individuals who know him as Savior and Lord.[23] These individual members of the church, regardless of background or spiritual maturity, have been given spiritual gifts to be used for service within the community (1 Corinthians 12:7, 1 Peter 4:10). There is no Scriptural evidence that gifts are given to believers at a certain age. Rather, they are granted when any child, teenager, or adult surrenders his or her life to Christ. The church, Christ's ongoing body, requires its members of all ages to exercise these gifts in order to remain healthy and productive (1 Corinthians 12:14-20). As the members function and cooperate together, transformation occurs, both at an individual and corporate level.

What is the purpose and role of adult leaders in a youth group community?
Because of the transformative power residing in the spiritual gifts of community members, ministry in the community should be *by* the community and *to* the community. In Ephesians 4 as Paul leads up to his description of community ministry and spiritual maturity, he gives a blueprint to help adult leaders build a serving community. In Ephesians 4:11, Paul describes the apostles, prophets, evangelists, and pastor/teachers as those who "prepare God's people for works of service." Note that the apostles, prophets, evangelists, and pastor/teachers do not do the works of service themselves; they support others as they do the work of the ministry. Thus the use of spiritual gifts in a youth group community does not eliminate the position of pastor/shepherds or leaders. On the contrary, the adult leaders assume the role of preparing and equipping all members of the body to minister to one another, as Paul himself modeled in his relationship with the believers at Corinth (Ephesians 4:11-13).

Building community
Much has been written about creating community in a youth ministry setting. Clearly, the theological preference for youth ministry is to gather the disciples in order to build the body. Yet for adolescents the reality of lengthened adolescence and other developmental factors combined with sociological skirmishes between groups, or clusters, of students can make for very difficult youth group gatherings.

What is your experience with trying to build community in youth ministry? Do you think, for example, that it is desirable, or even possible, to create community with Entry Level or Outreach students?

21. Ephesians 4:13. As I will explore in my answer to the subsequent section, the context for Ephesians 4:11-13 is the catalytic role of leadership in empowering others to use their gifts, which in turn builds up the church.

22. Andrew T. Lincoln, *Word Bible Commentary*, vol. 42 (Dallas: Word Books, 1990), 255-257.

23. Ray C. Stedman, *Body Life* (Nashville: Discovery House Publishers, 1995), 57-58.

What is the purpose and role of a *student leader*, and how is that different than the rest of the students?

Although all members are gifted, it is almost inevitable that some members become more visible within the community, either because of their gifts or because of their personalities. However, the uniqueness of students with these gifts is in the visibility and scope of their gifts, not in the fact that they possess gifts. It is theologically incorrect to assume that, and even label, only a portion of Christian students in a youth group as *ministers*. Every follower of Jesus Christ is a minister.

All parts of the body, regardless of the visibility and prominence of their gifts, are to honor each other and treat one another with humility and compassion (1 Corinthians 12:21-26). As Eugene Peterson vividly paraphrases Paul's writings to the church at Corinth,

> You can easily enough see how this kind of thing works by looking no
> further than your own body...A body isn't just a single part blown up
> into something huge. It's all the different-but-similar parts arranged and
> functioning together...An enormous eye or a gigantic hand wouldn't be
> a body, but a monster. What we have is one body with many parts, each
> its proper size and in its proper place. No part is important on its own.
> Can you imagine Eye telling Hand, "Get lost; I don't need you?" Or,
> Head telling Foot, "You're fired; your job has been phased out"? As a
> matter of fact, in practice it works the other way—the "lower" the part,
> the more basic, and therefore necessary. You can live without an eye, for
> instance, but not without a stomach...If anything, you have more con-
> cern for the lower parts than the higher. If you had to choose, wouldn't
> you prefer good digestion to full-bodied hair?
> —*1 Corinthians 12:21-26,* The Message

Thus it would be a theological mistake to assume that *student leaders* have more important gifts or functions than others. They may be more visible, but just like the adult leaders, their role becomes one of ultimate service as they figure out how to help others fully experience the role of priest granted them through their relationship with Christ.

Step 3: a renewed paradigm

I'm aware that many youth workers have discovered at least some of these truths in books and seminars, or in their own study of Scripture, and maybe even taught them in their own classrooms or youth meetings. Despite this, it may be the exception, and not the rule, that youth groups let theories permeate their actual practices. As one of several possible reasons that these theories have not been embraced and translated into concrete behaviors, it may be that although youth workers judge them to be true, they cannot penetrate the dominant stereotype of a *strong and gifted* leader who remains the driving force of his youth group. Or it may be that because these truths are so rarely embodied in actual youth ministries that even youth workers who desire to apply them aren't sure how.

Whatever the obstacle, my third and final step will map out a renewed paradigm for youth group community that I call a *mutually ministering community*. I call it a renewed paradigm and not a *new* paradigm because it has existed, albeit rarely practiced, since the middle of the first century. In order to make this paradigm of mutual ministry understandable in today's context, I will explain it using the image of the football team. In order to make it transferable, I will briefly highlight both guiding principles and concrete practices that can potentially be copied or adapted to fit youth groups in a variety of settings.

Keep in focus what you want to have accomplished when the game ends.

All football team players and coaches know exactly what they want to have accomplished when the whistle blows at the end of the game: they want to have scored more points than the other team. Their ultimate mission could not be more clear.

In alliance with Paul's doctrine, the mission for every youth group is equally clear: to see lives changed by Christ change the world. The mission of a youth group is not to grow bigger, to have fun, or to welcome others, although youth workers (and sometimes students) desire these. The primary purpose for gathering is so people will walk out a little, or a lot, different than when they walked in. Youth workers who recognize this truth should take advantage of the variety of opportunities they have to share it as they stand in front of students in their youth groups, meet with parents, and share proposals with church boards. This will make not only the youth worker and the youth group, but the church and its leadership, more likely to look beyond the more superficial gages of youth group attendance, budget, and staff size to the ultimate standard for evaluation: life transformation.

When I train small group leaders, I ask them, "True or false: the goal of our small groups is to build quality relationships." They usually answer, "True," but as we have seen from Paul, that is not the ultimate purpose for any phase of a youth group community, including its small groups. So then I ask them, "True or false: The goal of our small groups is to build community." They usually answer once again, "True," but once again they have settled for a secondary purpose instead of the primary one. So finally I ask them, "True or false: the goal of our small groups is to see students changed by Christ to change the world." Understandably because of their difficulties in the previous two questions, they hesitate before they answer, but they generally catch on and agree that the final purpose is definitely true.

Ponderable
Kara states that it is rare when "youth groups let theories permeates their actual practices." Do you think professional youth workers would agree with this? Why or why not? Is it possible that, in the midst of the battle—the business, the expectations, the phone calls, the events, the programs—the average youth worker is so busy trying to simply survive that there is little time for theoretical reflection?

Only do what helps you win the game.

No football team would run drills and execute plays that weren't designed to help them reach their end goal of winning the game. If passing the ball isn't working, a wise team adjusts and runs with it instead.

When certain elements of a youth group aren't bringing about life transformation, they should probably be eliminated, at least temporarily. Whether it's because what used to be provocative has been so repeated it is now mundane, or because this year's seniors aren't like last year's, even the previously effective practice of a youth group can become impotent. However, a wise youth worker recognizes the subtle but surprising influence that some youth group elements have in forming students'—especially young adolescents'—image of God. For instance, the crowdbreaker you play will probably teach more about the wild adventure of following God than your well-planned talk. The greeting students receive when they step into the youth group may say more about God's love than memorizing 1 Corinthians 13. [24]

Eliminate the stands.

Like many youth groups, a football game is comprised of a few players on the field who desperately need rest and a crowd of people in the stands who desperately need exercise. Instead of viewing themselves, their adult leaders, and maybe their student leaders as a hard-working team playing in front of the rest of your spectating students, youth workers in a mutually ministering community eliminate the stands and set up a series of adjacent practice fields instead. In other words, they do everything they can to convert *guests* into *hosts*, and spectators into players. It might mean they change their seating arrangement so that students are seated eye to eye instead of shoulder to shoulder. Or it might mean they change their terminology, referring to *all* of their students as *ministers*. Perhaps if they're involved in a larger youth group, they might choose to model their ministry after the early church and regularly divide into smaller groups that allow for more interaction and discussion. The overriding goal shifts from entertainment to active participation.

Remember that a seasoned coach is needed.

When the football team calls a time-out, no matter how talented the quarterback, he always makes his way over to the sidelines to get advice and affirmation from the coach. Most of these football coaches are former players themselves who draw from the good, the bad, and the ugly of their past experience in their present coaching.

Although most students want to be treated like adults, they're not. The youth workers are the adults in the room. They have something to offer students. For instance, although student-led groups are gaining in popularity, there is some evidence that adult-facilitated groups are more effective than student-led groups. [25] A mutually ministering youth group does not mean adults sit on the sidelines. To paraphrase C. S.

Ponderable

One of the most sweeping criticisms of contemporary youth ministry is that it fosters an entertainment mentality. Kara, on the other hand, advocates eliminating "the stands" and transforming youth ministry into a participatory or community experience. Yet what does it mean to entertain? Is a skit by leaders entertainment? What about a competition in which only a few of the group are involved? Is a testimony or special music entertainment? Is an energetically delivered message entertainment? Perhaps before we can ask if entertainment is appropriate in youth ministry, we should determine just how similar or different it is from leading a community.

24. Kara Eckmann Powell, "What Lurks behind Those Fish, Toilet Paper, and Pantyhose Games?" *Youthworker Journal* 16, 1 (September/October 1999), 21.

25. Amy Lynn Meriweather, "The Influence of Self-Led Discussions on the Learning of Problem-Solving Skills with Adolescent Females," unpublished dissertation (California School of Professional Psychology, 1997).

Lewis' view of leadership and influence, "Think of me as a fellow patient in the same hospital who, having arrived a little earlier, could give some advice."

Lots of seasoned coaches are needed.

Although every football team has a head coach, no head coach can supervise all the players, nor can he develop and maintain expertise in all positions. As a result, most teams have additional specialized coaches to give focused attention to the defense, the offense, the passers, and the special teams.

No youth pastor can or should be expected to develop and maintain mastery in all the spiritual gifts. It is a theological and anthropological impossibility. But all youth pastors, regardless of the size of their church or ministry, can and should be expected to recruit other adults to help them in their coaching—especially in their weaker areas. An insightful youth pastor who excels in evangelism will seek out help in areas of pastoring and teaching to ensure ongoing spiritual formation. Similarly, a youth pastor who has the gift of teaching should intentionally pursue fellow coaches who have gifts in service and giving in order to make sure students experience God not only in their heads, but with their hands. Some of these fellow coaches may be *long-distance mentors* who inspire and guide through e-mail, phone calls, or letters.

Every coach's job is to make the players excel.

No matter how the team is doing, deep down in many coaches' hearts, there often beats the desire to run out on the field and join the action. When a team is doing well, the coach might want to have the chance to join in the momentum building on the field. When a team is doing poorly, the coach might want to throw on a helmet and rescue it from its misery. But the rules don't allow them to. Their position is *coach*, not *player*.

If Ephesians 4:11-12 could be rewritten for youth group communities, perhaps it would run something like this: "It was Jesus who positioned some as youth evangelists, some as Sunday school teachers, some as small group leaders, some as youth sponsors, and others as youth pastors to make sure that kids excel in using their spiritual gifts to serve others." Youth workers who aren't sure how this is translated into a language that makes sense in their own context should pay special attention to the next three ideas.

Teach the fundamentals.

Although the wide receiver tends to learn more about catching, the running back generally gains expertise in running, and the quarterback is usually more astute throwing, *all* players are taught the fundamentals of the game. By this I mean how each position functions, what each position hopes to accomplish, and how the positions work together. Without this basic knowledge, several players might try to play the identical position and run into each other, leaving some positions and areas of the field empty.

A prudent youth worker makes sure all members of the extended youth group understand that all believers are priests and have a special and unique part to play. The adult leadership team, the small group leaders, the students, the student leaders, and the students' parents should all be taught about spiritual gifts and mutual ministry. If only the adult and student leadership group is taught these fundamentals, the myth that only some can minister is reinforced and perpetuated.

Figure out the best position for each player.

A good coach never assumes that the positions his players currently occupy are optimal. Instead, he constantly assesses, experiments, substitutes, and improvises with his players, helping them discover their ideal role on the team.

In a youth group, the youth pastor, adult leadership team, small group leaders, students, student leaders, and students' parents all need help in deciphering their ministry gifts and positions. Three common methods of helping people identify their gifts are personal reflection, spiritual gifts inventories, and input from others. It is best to use a combination of all three methods because personal reflection can be distorted, spiritual gift inventories can be impersonal, and input from others can be biased.

Organize the team.

A coach keeps track of which players have which talents, so that he knows who he needs out on the field when it's time to run, punt, or stop the ball. Similarly, a youth pastor in a mutually ministering community tends to organize the group around spiritual gifts. She recruits adult leaders and interns based on gifting, both what they have and what the body seems to need. During leadership gatherings, she may schedule times for separate spiritual gift task forces so those who have the gift of administration can plan events, those with the gift of teaching can develop curriculum, and those with the gift of giving can brainstorm for the upcoming missions fundraiser. She maintains spiritual gift lists of the adults and students that seem to have certain spiritual gifts and calls on them as needs arise. When one of her students is in the hospital, she contacts some members in the body with the gift of mercy; when another is struggling with sin, she involves someone who has the gift of prophecy or teaching; when a student seems interested in becoming a Christian and wants to meet with her, she invites someone along with the gift of evangelism.[26]

All the positions are important; some are more visible.

On most football teams, the offensive players receive more public attention than the defensive players; even still, those offensive players who are immediately involved in scoring touchdowns and field goals, such as the kicker, the quarterback, the wide receivers, the tight ends, and the running backs are more likely to receive either the admiration (or condemnation) of the crowd. Yet a quarterback is generally only as skilled as the protection he receives from his offensive line, and a running back is only as talented as the holes created by the blockers.

26. Brown, 7.

Although some have more visible gifts, such as teaching, prophecy, and leadership while others have the more quiet and less visible gifts of serving, mercy, and giving, in a mutually ministering community, all students and adults are equally important. Either because of personality, gifting, or spirituality, some students will stand out in a youth group, and that's okay. These are often the student leaders, who possibly have the gift of leadership or have a spiritual maturity that influences others.

When the ball gets fumbled, all grab for it.

While a football team will only be successful if the center does his job and hikes the ball to the quarterback, who in turn does what he is supposed to and throws the ball to the wide receiver, who does what is intended and catches the ball—when the ball is fumbled, everything changes. The center, quarterback, wide receiver, and linemen alike, scramble to grab that ball.

Similarly, as youth workers help their students understand and move out in their spiritual gifting, they must be on guard against lopsided spirituality. Most (potentially all) of the spiritual gifts are also practices of discipline and obedience that are universally expected of every believer. While believers excel in their specific areas of gifting, all are to show mercy, give, serve, share their faith, teach, pray, have faith, and exhort others.

Expect a few fumbles and interceptions.

A final word of warning: when youth workers start working with rookie students just learning how to use their spiritual gifts, they need to be prepared for a few fumbles and interceptions along the way. The more they practice, the better they'll probably get. Furthermore, as students leave their benches and begin to handle the ball, they're more likely to realize that it is more difficult than it seemed and possibly become less critical of others ministering.

★　★　★

It seems appropriate when referring to football to quote the most winning NFL coach of all time, Vince Lombardi.[27] "Any man's finest hour—his greatest fulfillment to all he holds dear—is that moment when he has worked his heart out in a good cause, and he's exhausted on the field of battle."[28] What Lombardi realized is that playing a game, whether it be professional football or youth ministry, can be simultaneously draining and exhilarating. What he missed is that your finest hour is not when you've worked your heart out for a good cause, but when you've been part of a team that has.

Ponderable
Everyone agrees that all positions are important, whether in football or youth ministry. But how do we communicate that to those with ministry positions that are not as visible, recognized, or appreciated as others? How do we make those in the background feel as if they are equally as valuable and part of the team as the speakers and musicians?

---

27. Lombardi's career coaching record was 105-35-6.

28. www.southendzone.com/roster/coaches/lombardi/

Focusing Youth Ministry through Innovation
Soren Oestergaard and Simon Hall

One of the few things that doesn't change about our world is the fact that it is constantly changing. We are aware of many discontinuities between the culture of first century Palestine and our own culture, but one that we are less conscious of is the amazing rate of change we live amongst. In the United Kingdom dance music scene, the fashionable style changes from drum'n' bass to garage to big beat within a year. I remember first hearing about the terrible corrupting influence that some yellow cartoon character called Bart Simpson was going to have on the youth of the world, but now Bart seems like an angel compared to Beavis and Butt-Head and the kids from South Park. These aspects of youth culture may seem trivial to the average adult observer, but their place in helping to define the culture of adolescence cannot be underestimated.

In this chapter we hope to address the issue of this rapidly changing culture and our response to it as youth ministers. This is not an academic exercise; it has huge missiological significance. As the cultures of our environment change faster and faster, the church seems to be more and more out of touch. If, then, rapid cultural change leads inevitably to decreasing evangelistic effectiveness, where is God in all of this? And what is our creative response to youth subcultures and their rapid division and regeneration—a cultural phenomenon unique to the last century? Unless we begin to take cultural change seriously, the church is going to become just one more cultural group in the huge supermarket of values, neither understanding those around it, nor being understood. This might be acceptable in the United States, where church attendance can still support an "instant" youth ministry of church kids, but in Leeds, U.K., a city the size of Boston, there are only five youth groups (to our knowledge) with more than 12 members. We must address our terrible failure to reach unchurched[1] young people, and to do that we need to look at the culture issue and reflect on it biblically and theologically.

Cultural change is not a new issue; nor is it one on which the Scriptures are silent. One of the Bible's many miracles is the way in which God's revelation unfolds over hundreds of years and still remains consistent. Yet as we look at the history of God's relationships with humankind, we see that while his purpose has remained the same, his plans have changed according to "the times" (1 Chronicles 12:32). From the calling of Abraham and his nomadic family to the establishing of a foothold in Palestine, from the birth of the royal kingdom to the exile of the two kingdoms and the restoration of Judah, from the life, death, and resurrection of Jesus to the phenomenal

---

1. These terms need definition beyond their use by churches such as Willow Creek Community Church in South Barrington, Illinois. I use the verb *to church* to mean a process of socialization by which an outsider to the church is educated in the unfamiliar cultural forms of church life. I see no particular biblical content in "churching the unchurched."

spread of his followers, God has worked through the people and culture of the time.[2] The Bible witnesses to the ways in which God's redemptive purposes are fulfilled through methods that seem right for the times. The parallels between the stories of Joseph and Daniel (see particularly the dream narratives in Genesis 41 and Daniel 2) indicate that this is not merely about time. For despite the huge time gap, God is calling his followers to live in a similar way when they find themselves in similar situations. In different situations, different solutions are called for: when the early Jewish Christians lay down their beloved law in order to include the first fruits of the gentile mission field (Acts 15), they were led by the Holy Spirit into completely uncharted territory. Their zeal for the law had been supplanted by a zeal for the lost, a miraculous "heresy" that God initiated because the time was right to fulfill God's promise to Abraham (Genesis 12:2-3).

Babel or Pentecost?

The question we must rightly ask this: Is God altering his plans according to how the culture changes, or is he altering culture to fit in with his plans? The story of the Tower of Babel (Genesis 11:1-9) indicates a clear understanding that God's lordship extends to cultural matters, but there are other scriptural witnesses, too. For example, how should we interpret Romans 5:6, in which Jesus' work of salvation is described as having happened at "just the right time" (*kairos*)? Does that mean that God had set up the universe for Jesus' arrival or that he was himself somehow waiting for a moment in history that arrived at exactly the time Jesus was born? We do not think there's any way of avoiding the conclusion that God is working constantly throughout history, but that the exact mechanisms of this are beyond us. Also, we have to admit that God's people frequently fail to perceive what God is doing in the world. Within our own situation, perhaps our attitude should be an eager desire to know the purposes of God within youth culture—humbly accepting that we might get it wrong!

As we look at the fragmentation of Western culture, we are left wondering what God might be doing within it. Are we being punished for our pursuit of power and wealth—our desire to be like God—with a Babel of splintering subcultures and tribes? The imposition of globalization by the multinationals may have created a worldwide market, but it has clearly not created a worldwide community. If such a pessimistic and conservative view of Western culture is accurate, at least we have the hope of a new Pentecost, in which each alienated tribe heard the good news about Jesus in their own language (Acts 2:6). However, we could choose to see within young people a wonderful spirit of creativity, a sign of God's image in them—a sign of hope. Either way, we have the chance to see God at work within the varieties of youth cultures that blossom around the western world.

Is there a global village?
It is clear that we have a global marketplace, a worldwide economy—that we have grown as close in some ways to people on the other side of the globe as we used to feel to people in the next town. Some go a step further, believing that because communication and goods now conveniently cross geopolitical, religious, and cultural lines, that we are becoming a family of happy, compatible, like-minded, and close-knit brothers and sisters.

Or is it more accurate, do you think—and as the authors imply—that things are getting worse between people groups, subcultures, and even clusters of students?

---

2. For more on God and time, see Pinnock, and others, *The Openness of God* (Downer's Grove, Illinois: InterVarsity Press, 1994).

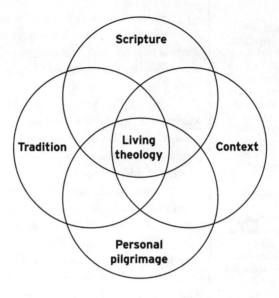

Figure 13.1. Living theology

Theology and praxis in extremis

The situation in Western Europe is calling for radical new approaches in youth ministry if we want to reach out to the many different youth subcultures constituted not by nominal Christians or non-Christians, but by pre-Christians who know nothing of what Christianity is all about. The situation demands what has been called *theology and praxis in extremis*—a process where we reflect critically on some of the core issues about being the church and our current approaches to youth ministry.[3] A process where we dare to ask ourselves tough and basic questions like, *What is the good news for teenagers living at the beginning of the 21ST century? What is the nature and function of the church in a postmodern context? What is the role of young people in youth ministry and the church?*

To dare to begin this process is very much a matter of life and death for the church in Western Europe—this is a task so important that it should not be a process in which only professional youth workers participate. We need to equip young people to get involved in doing *communal exegesis and hermeneutics in* and *of* their specific context. We need to get them involved in doing theology that is relevant and that gives answers to the real questions. We need to create models of ministry that meet the current and future needs of the young people we know as well as their pre-Christian friends. We need to train and challenge them to be the leaders and innovators of the future churches.

Involving young people in doing theology—instead of them simply being influenced by a theology to which they very seldom have any ownership—can be a frightening adventure. Young people ask questions that challenge our thinking and identity as youth workers. It is, however, a necessary process.

---

3. For a short introduction to the thinking behind this term, see Michael Riddell, *Threshold of the Future: Reforming the Church in the Post-Christian West* (London: SPCK, 1998), 26-28.

Accidental church plant: a case study

A youth pastor in a suburban Baptist church, Simon had a heart to reach unchurched young people. He also had a heart to see Christian young people be effective in mission. When both his visions began to be realized and a number of newcomers started attending the youth ministry, problems began. The church young people began to think about the kind of youth group their friends would want to come to. They changed the way they dressed and the music they listened to. Inspired by the new young people, they started complaining about how boring church was and they started to write their own worship songs, which were very different from what the church was used to, both lyrically and musically. Eventually, the young people began meeting in the church sports hall, where more people got caught up in the exciting worship and relevant preaching that was happening in the youth service. Lots of young adults came, who said that this was great for them, too.

The problem was that many of the new Christians who had joined this group, had never been to church and never really wanted to. They liked Jesus, they liked us, and they liked "doing church" with the group. Suddenly everyone realized that the group had become a separate church, almost by accident. Simon approached his fellow leaders with this situation, and 18 months later, Revive was born. Now two years old, it is a church made up almost exclusively of

As youth workers in a European context we very much see ourselves as missionaries to foreign cultures. That's the primary reason we often feel very inspired by the thinking of the mission theologians and the experiences and approaches used by pioneer missionaries reaching the so-called unreached people groups. The following model draws heavily on the insights from missiological thinking and praxis.[4]

As youth workers we can view our current theology and praxis as a result of what we have read in the Scriptures, the influence of the specific church tradition that we are a part of, our personal journey as human beings and Christians, and the influence and needs of the local context that we are a part of. This can give us an understanding of why we think as we think and do what we do. When we're honest most of us will admit that the main sources that influence our way of doing youth ministry are tradition and our own personality, pilgrimage, and preferences. Scripture and the needs of our local setting only play a minor role.

The above model can be used for evaluation of our current thinking and praxis in youth ministry. We've also found it very helpful for getting young people involved in the process of doing theology and rethinking the purpose of the church and youth ministry in a new millennium. The results of such a process in both the United Kingdom[5] and Denmark have been challenging and creative. When asking young people from unchurched backgrounds to reflect on these themes, whole new areas of exploration open up.

Scripture

Our experience is that when young people are challenged to reflect on some very basic and some complex theological questions, they obtain a new platform for dealing with matters concerning church and youth ministry. For example, what are the changeable and the unchangeable elements in the gospel? What is the Good News? What does it mean for us today that the Word became flesh? Being open to these questions with young people can be transformative because over time we begin to discover what really matters. Young people find out that church doesn't need to be static in that our current way of doing church and youth ministry is more influenced by a specific cultural setting than the Scripture. At the same time they find out that God is an active Lord who is so eager to get in contact with his creation that he chose to meet us at our home base, in our specific cultural situation. The significance of the Incarnation grows and grows in this dialogical setting. More and more young people—often inspired by a youth worker who takes on the role of a facilitator, mentor, and project consultant—will frequently choose to act on their communal reflection.

Tradition

Research done all over Europe shows that most of the new churches being planted are so-called new old churches: the same method of preaching, leadership, and structures that didn't work in the old context, are all uncritically reproduced in a new context.

---

4. E. G. Charles van Engen, *Mission on the Way. Issues in Mission Theology* (Grand Rapids, Michigan: Baker, 1996), 23.

5. Iain Hoskins, a mission adviser for the English Baptist Union, has done a great deal of work in facilitating sharing between young people and adults through an event called Quo Vadis.

people aged 18 to 40, which meets regularly in a bar and in homes. God has used the church to reach young adults who were seeking for God but who would never have dreamed of going into a church. Looking back, the team sees God in all that has happened, apart from one moment when it became clear that the music, art, poetry, and dance of the young people was not welcomed by the "adult" church. Although the young people were invited to do "youth services" each term, the young people felt that these were being used to marginalize their contribution to the church and felt forced into creating their own sacred spaces. Revive is a frightening, challenging, life-changing place to be, and to be honest, it feels a lot more like the body of the One who hung around with prostitutes and other "lowlifes" than the average church.

Cutting Edge: case study
In the early 1990s a young new convert got a job at a Christian recording studio. After learning his trade, he started getting some musicians together for a worship band, and within a few years he was leading worship for thousands of young people every month at an event called Cutting Edge. The key to these events (the worship band eventually became the band Delirious) was the leadership of the local church (Arun Community Church) that lead singer Martin Smith belonged to. The church backed his vision, providing support in a variety of ways. This was particularly brave as Martin soon began to write songs using heavier and heavier rock music and lyrics that began to talk about doubt as well as faith. The Cutting Edge events pioneered a whole new wave of worship music in the United Kingdom and, more recently, America.

Club in the 'hood: case study
In 1992 a former black belt karate fighter and professional soldier was converted through the ministry of a new charismatic church

And, naturally, this approach isn't very successful.[6] Consciously or unconsciously we stick to traditional ways of "doing church"—usually because it's the only approach we know. Sometimes it is also the fruit of a misunderstood respect for "the fathers." As youth workers we are often reminded that we have to be sensitive to the tradition of the church, but what does *tradition* actually mean? Usually this means "taking the best of the old and changing it so it fits into a new setting," but often we confuse *tradition* with the term *traditionalism*, which means to take the old things and bring them into a new context without changing a thing.[7] It's been described this way: "Tradition is the living faith of the dead and traditionalism is the dead faith of the living." Young people in Western Europe are fed up with "dead faith and empty rituals." However, if you try to introduce them to the context in which the traditions were developed and the original thinking behind certain practices in the church, they very often get inspired by "the fathers" and begin to develop their own traditions. It's good to be reminded of how we ended up with organs in churches. Once upon a time they were an instrument of the devil that aroused the passions. Primarily used in drinking dens around Europe, the church adopted the organ as a hugely influential vehicle of popular music. The irony is not lost on young people. This is even more true when they discover that the lyrics of many of our favorite traditional hymns were set to drinking tunes.

Young people have the ability to accept the challenge that faced Paul: to communicate a cross-cultural gospel in language that is both understandable and truthful. It's fascinating to see tradition—a word that teenagers are supposed to hate—giving them guidelines on how to reflect on their own situation in a way that "honors" the fathers much more than most of our "traditional" activities in the church!

Personal pilgrimage

A common experience among youth workers today is that teenagers are looking for authentic and transparent role models. People who are not willing to simply play a certain role but who live on the outside what they are inside. People who are appropriately open about their struggles, hurts, and doubts—in other words those issues that young people can identify with. When we introduce teenagers to the wide range of people and personalities that God uses in the Bible, they discover that God takes our personality and experiences seriously. When they realize they don't have to fit into a specific model to be involved in ministry, teenagers receive the freedom to develop a spirituality that reflects who they are—a spirituality that they feel fits them more than "the adult spirituality"—a spirituality that reflects their culture.

The local context

As youth workers we are always looking for new models and concepts that we can use in our ministry. Often quite uncritically we use ideas that have developed in a totally different context and the danger is that we don't meet the real needs and address the questions of the teenagers we are working with. But taking incarnation seriously means

6. See Soren Oestergaard, *Church Planting in the Tension between Tradition and Context* (Copenhagen; 1998), 290-299.

7. See K. E. Skydsgaard, *Traditio et traditiones* (Copenhagen: 1940), 9-19.

in the suburbs of Copenhagen. The church tried its best to "church" him, but after some years he realized that his personality and background didn't fit into the specific style and spirituality of that particular church. He decided not to leave the church but to go back to his roots and share the gospel in his own neighborhood. He bought a basketball and every Saturday for two years, summer and winter, he invited the local teenagers to come and play basketball with him.

Among the teenagers he soon got a nickname—the guy who can't hit the basket—but also received tremendous respect on the street because of his background and the way he communicated with them. They soon found out that he was one of their own, that he understood their problems, fears, and many questions—he talked their language. His home soon became a meeting place for the local teenagers where he and his wife touched many lives.

The ministry began to grow and in 1996 they (together with a team of similar church fringe members) decided to establish an alcohol-free nightclub where the teenagers could hang out with their friends, dance, and build relationships in a safe environment instead of hanging out on the street. The volunteers kept the club open every weekend from 8 p.m. to 5 a.m. This was the start of a ministry that today still has the nightclub as the cornerstone of its work, but also cell groups, services, peer counseling, new converts, and contact with approximately 500 suburban teenagers who would probably never have been exposed to Christ had not "the guy who can't hit the basket" not followed his convictions. In 1998 the Danish Youth Council nominated Power Plant as one of the most innovative youth projects in Denmark.

that we always have to be serious in our search for what kind of "Good News" teenagers in our local context are longing for. For many young people it's an eye-opener to find out that incarnation is very much about God wanting to meet their specific needs and longings and that he wants to meet them in a way that's contextually relevant.

Our experience is that many youth workers base their work on assumptions about the needs of the young people they try to reach—assumptions that often don't match the reality. If we really want to know what's going on out there, we need to be continuously doing research. We need to read about trends within youth cultures, gather data, talk to resource persons like teachers, social workers etc., do surveys and—most importantly—talk with the young people we know and get them involved in the research process: after all, they are in many way the "real experts"! We have to talk to them about values, worldview, and their felt and existential needs. We have to find out about how they make decisions, gather together, communicate their dreams and fears about the future, etc.

We don't need to accept their values, belief, and praxis, but it's crucially important that we understand the background for their thinking and acting, so that we can address both the felt and the existential needs of their lives. For many of us it maybe feels a little bit overwhelming to do this kind of research—we are trained to be youth workers, not sociologists! Yet if we want to be involved in contextually relevant ministry instead of just concept ministry, research should always be a crucial task for us. An introduction to the most basic methods of gathering information and equipping young people to exegete their own culture should probably be an integrated part of our training as youth workers.

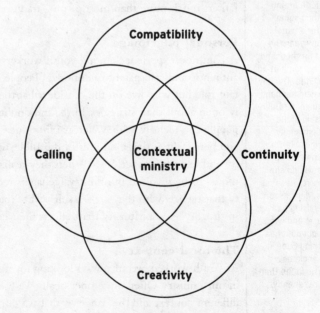

Figure 13.2. Contextual ministry

Inhabiting the story

British theologian N. T. Wright has struggled with new approaches to understanding the authority of the Bible and he has come up with a picture that I find most helpful. Imagine a Shakespearean five-act play.[8] One is the creation of the universe. Act Two is the fall. Act Three is the nation of Israel. Act Four is Jesus. Act Five is the journey of Jesus' followers to the *eschaton* ("final"—refers to the end of time; closely related to *eschatology*, the study of end-time events). The key to this image is the fact that *we* are part of Act Five! The first scene of the final act is written in the New Testament, which also tells us how the story is going to end, but in the Bible we have an unfinished script, a drama that is unfolding before our very eyes. As directors, producers, and actors, it is our role to study the script(ure) that we have and to learn the story and the nature of the characters. We must continue this drama in a way that is true to all that has come before, but which also moves the story on to its conclusion. We learn that this story has boundaries over which we cannot step and opportunities for innovation that we can exploit. The first scene of our final act and the knowledge of the drama's end provide a strong framework for our innovation, but there is still room for the plot to thicken a little. Suddenly we are participants and partners in God's great narrative, rather than mere observers and imitators of his ancient history.

In addressing our present issue, this approach can help us no end. Because God's will for his followers in certain cultural situations is the same, we should search the Bible for the analogues we need. We also need to acknowledge where we are in God's story (between Acts and Revelation and in the early 21ST century). We need to ask ourselves if there is anything unique about our situation that may introduce a new plot twist.[9] Finally, we need to be aware of our own place as actors in the drama. We will now attempt to address these issues from our own Western European context.

Compatibility with Scripture

Ponderable
Are youth ministry programs you know truly compatible with "biblical predecessors"? How tightly should we hold on to historical ministry models in a culture that is changing faster than ever? Are we simply doing what we have always done because it used to work, or are we willing to constantly re-evaluate in light of the biblical witness?

Is what we're doing compatible with our biblical predecessors?

The church in Western Europe has been in serious decline for most of the 20TH century. The decline appears to be slowing, but with only 6 percent of Britons claiming weekly church attendance, that's hardly a surprise—there's no one left to leave! Most European Christians now live in a post-Christian community in which Christianity has formed the culture of a nation but is now largely forgotten or ceremonial. There is still a trace memory in the national psyche, but it is rarely stimulated by the insecure, irrelevant church.[10] Yet the charismatic movement has revived many evangelical churches and over the last 30 years there have been encouraging signs that these churches are "turning the corner." Perhaps the closest analogue within the Scriptures is the return of the

---

8. N. T. Wright, "How Can the Bible Be Authoritative?" *Vox Evangelica* 21 (1991), 11.

9. The invasion of the Americas by the Europeans is a significant plot twist, as is the move of the church's center of gravity away from Western European culture toward the developing world. Both have had huge impacts on the way God's purposes have been moved forward in our own time.

10. For an obvious exception, the U.K. was transformed by the death of Diana, Princess of Wales. Perhaps in a fit of jealousy, the church in the U.K. largely ignored the enormous outpouring of grief and religious longing that this event prompted.

exiles in Ezra/Nehemiah. Here there remained a faithful remnant struggling to survive and maintain its identity. The returning Israelites, attempting to rebuild the temple and the holy city, were under constant attack from neighboring tribes, but the ultimate attack came from within: the temptation to give up the distinctives of Judaism and melt into the cultural milieu of their neighbors. God's solution was a fearsome ethical holiness and a strict adherence to the rituals of the old temple, carried out while the new temple was being built around them.

If this analysis is correct, we should expect the Western European church to be more in danger of assimilation and syncretism than of "ghetto-ization." This is generally true, with the exception of the more extreme charismatic/Pentecostal churches, which tend to take their lead from outside Europe. The Bible speaks to us from this story about the need for radical holiness as an important antidote to our loss of identity. In order to say that our witness is compatible with the biblical witness, we need to be challenging young people about the lifestyle choices they are making.

Continuity with tradition

In what way are we part of God's developing story?

But we are not actually in the seventh century B.C., we are now over 2,500 years away from the return to Jerusalem. We are no longer required to worship daily at the temple, but we are now a worldwide church of followers of Jesus. Not only that but both the authors of this chapter are European Baptists, raised in a Protestant tradition of radical discipleship. This church tradition affects the way we perceive and analyze our situation; it may even restrict the options open to us. We have also been influenced by a variety of theological movements in the 20TH century, including new approaches to mission, spirituality, social engagement, and so on. What is there in our tradition that can help us reflect on our situation?

We would instinctively begin with the insights of missiology, more particularly contextual theology.[11] Over the last 100 years Christians from around the world have been reflecting on the communication of the gospel across cultures. Surely their thoughts will have some bearing on our own work of mission across subcultures? This whole awareness of the significance of culture in shaping our beliefs and practice will hopefully prevent us from repeating some of the gravest errors of the early missions. Likewise the thought that has gone into the sociology of postmodernity and its impact on the way our generation sees and judges must affect our approach to reaching out to young people.[12] We can choose to disparage the increasing significance of experience as the measure of reality, or we can choose to live up to the challenge: is our faith something that can be seen and touched and heard and tasted and smelled, or is it just some dusty old head-knowledge? A young person today doesn't just want to hear you talk your talk, she needs to see you walk your walk. Going back to the Bible with this frame of mind shows us that many of Jesus' words came in response to people's experi-

---

11. See particularly David Bosch, *Transforming Mission* (Maryknoll, New York: Orbis Books, 1991) and Charles Kraft, *Christianity in Culture* (Maryknoll, New York: Orbis Books, 1979).

12. Richard Middleton and Brian Walsh, *Truth Is Stranger Than It Used to Be* (London: SPCK, 1995), is a brilliant analysis of postmodernity from a Christian perspective.

ence. Very rarely did Jesus offer unsolicited advice or comment to the crowds. He would heal someone or perform a miracle or show compassion on someone, and then people would be gathering around him, asking, "What was that?" And he was then in a place to talk about the kingdom.

Creativity of the Spirit

The leader
It is easy to get so wrapped up in working for God that we forget he is way ahead of us, leading the way. How do we open our eyes to what God is already doing?

Is God doing something new here?

Some of the unique elements about our own situation are those already mentioned: the diversity and rapid change of our situation. This means that for the first time in history, a parent and child can belong to two different (and sometimes conflicting) cultures while living in the same house. The extended end of adolescence means that this is no longer about the teenage years: the six main characters from "Friends" could be any age from 18 to 40. Hence we have to take our own cultural situation seriously, because this problem is going to get worse, not better. In simple terms, if youth ministry culture is renewing itself every 50 years, as Mark Senter suggests,[13] and youth culture is renewing itself every five to 10 years (where is grunge/angst now when it spoke for a generation 10 years ago?), then it's easy to see why there is a significant culture gap between the churched and the unchurched. If we add to that the 19th century culture of many of our churches, then the situation gets doubly serious. The time for what we might term *radical discontinuity* may have arrived.

Calling from God

Is this what God wants me to do?

Church growth experts such as Peter Wagner often talk about "pioneers" and "home-steaders" to distinguish between those who plant churches and those who maintain them. The Bible has a much more complicated list of giftings. Undoubtedly a test of a groundbreaking ministry must be the calling of those involved. Youth work practitioners tend to be the pioneer types, but this work is not for all. We all get to a place in ministry when we wonder why we are doing it, and unless you can give yourself a clear answer to that question, you will be out of ministry in double-quick time.

Compatibility, continuity, creativity, calling

Reflecting on these four approaches to our context (analogues with biblical history, an understanding of our place in the fifth act of God's drama, an awareness of our own unique situation both in context and calling), we can perhaps begin to think about ways forward for youth ministry. These ways will need to be true to all that has gone before in the witness of Scripture and the church, but also to speak powerfully to our own generation. In our view, a youth ministry that is going to be effective in reaching young people for Jesus will need to have these characteristics, among many others:

---

13. Mark Senter III, *The Coming Revolution in Youth Ministry* (Wheaton, Illinois: Victor, 1992).

- *Any youth ministry needs to be "in the world and not of it" (2 Corinthians 10:3; 1 Peter 2:11), and needs to check its balance.* Many youth ministries are Christian ghettos that protect their members from harm but that are not impacting their local communities with the radical message of Jesus. Likewise, many youth ministries have lost their identity and distinctiveness in their desire to be accommodated within the world they are reaching. Young people, if they are effective in reaching their peers, need to love the world, but love Jesus even more. That is a dangerous route to take, but the New Testament says nothing if it doesn't tell of the risks that God took to get us back into relationship with him. It means challenging young people to lives of obedience and holiness now, rather than training them to be adult Christians when they grow up.[14]

- *At the heart of God's way of keeping us holy is prayer and worship.* We would expect that there would be a new psalmody of music and poetry that will reflect the heart of this generation. We see a disciplined life of study, prayer, and worship at the absolute center.

- *We see that the mustard seed has more to teach us than McDonald's about Christian community.*[15] The growth of the church in the developing world contexts shows us that in the cross-cultural mission in which we are now engaged, contextual ministry that grows from the bottom up is what will maintain its integrity and last the course. Youth ministry that is shaped, even led, by young people who are part of unchurched youth cultures will redefine the nature of youth ministry over the next few years. Young people who have been brought up in church will need to be unchurched in order to reach the young people of their community who have no interest in being churched, thank you very much.

- *The context of post/late modernity provides youth ministry with a variety of challenges and opportunities.* As mentioned above, it means that Christianity will have to be lived out in all its terrifying, world-changing completeness in order to attract experience-based young people. That means that discipling will become more and more important as young people go out on the edge for Jesus. Relational means of discipling and evangelism, such as mentoring and cells,[16] will form a bedrock of the new youth ministry.

Small, less, insignificant
Long-time youth ministry leader Mike Yaconelli has been telling youth workers for years that youth ministry is more about small, not big…about less, not more…about how the insignificant is significant…about the power of quiet. Some think it's time youth ministry becomes less committed to massive programs and hot models and more committed to building intimate communities of faith. Perhaps the hot idea for the next generation of youth workers will be creating programs that are theologically driven, in which the Spirit leads, where kids are free to love and be loved, and where prayer is central and relationships are genuine.
    What do *you* think?

---

14. Pete Ward, *Growing Up Evangelical* (London: SPCK, 1996) is an fearsome indictment of evangelical churches that protect their young people from the world and render them ineffective in the world by teaching them a neutered gospel of salvation and safety. While written specifically about the British context, it is one of the most significant books on youth ministry ever written.

15. Tom Sine and Ravi K. Zacharias, *Mustard Seed vs. McWorld: Reinventing Life and Faith for the Future* (Grand Rapids, Michigan: Baker, 1999).

16. See particularly Gunter Krallmann, *Mentoring for Mission* (Hong Kong: JENSCO, 1994).

- *We predict that the church will be transformed over the next 30 years.* Either it will accommodate these radical changes in youth ministry, it will quash them and die, or it will force the creation of new churches that will have as much in common with "Friends" and MTV as a traditional church. If youth pastors and senior pastors are both willing to acknowledge the enormous culture gap between their own culture and that of their communities, there is great hope for the future, but if not, we are in for as rocky a ride as an unwanted baby who will probably be born anyway.

Ora et labora

Genuine innovation is hard work that demands careful study, critical reflection, courage, and much prayer! In our approach we need to be balanced and holistic, grounded in Scripture. It's crucial that we get young people involved in both individual and *communal* careful study of the Scripture so that they find out for themselves what the Good News is in their specific context. We should teach them to be sensitive and learn from the traditional global church as well as the local church and challenge them to generate their own meaningful traditions. We need to challenge them to be authentic and use their gifts and the experiences they have gathered through their own personal pilgrimage in their local context, and we should challenge them to see and meet the specific needs of their own cultures.

It is also crucial that we continuously evaluate our motives for getting involved in a process of innovation. It's of the utmost importance that our motivation is based on sound motives, which means that we mustn't get involved in this process because we don't like what's going on in the traditional church or youth ministry. We want to reach out to youth cultures in a contextually relevant way. Mission should always be our main motive!

The last thing we want to mention is that communication is very important if we want our innovative approach to be successful. We have to explain why we are doing the things we are doing, and our experience is that we can get away with a lot of things and get the blessing of our local churches if they understand that our approach is based on careful study and reflection. Another important area of communication is our communication with our heavenly Father. Genuine innovation has to be a Spirit-filled and Spirit-led process where we have the courage to be still and let him direct us, correct us, and challenge us!

And if the results aren't what was expected?

In his book *The Spontaneous Expansion of the Church*, Roland Allan describes how much mission history is often the story of an unexpected result of well-planned mission. Of course it's the same concerning youth ministry. One example from the youth ministry scene in the United Kingdom is the so-called *youth congregation* movement, which for many church leaders was seen as a bridging strategy from youth cultures into the adult church.

The pioneering work of Soul Survivor in Watford is a good example of this approach. The project was set up to be a bridge project where the strategy was to reach out to people through a café ministry and worship celebrations. The people who came to faith were then to be transferred to the "mother church," St. Andrews, Chorleywood, a contemporary charismatic church. The first part of the strategy worked out fine—people got saved—but the second part of the strategy failed totally. The young people didn't want to leave Soul Survivor, and the final result was a youth church plant.[17]

As in Watford many youth congregations that were started as a bridging strategy have now developed into genuine churches with their own leadership, worship, pastoral care, evangelism, and church planting. The output was certainly different from what many had expected and has caused much debate, but more and more church leaders recognize that though youth congregations never became the intended bridge to the "real thing," they are genuine expressions of the church of Jesus Christ. In a time of cultural transition, youth congregations have helped the church to discover the shape of its future.

---

17. Graham Cray, "Youth Congregations—the Best Biblical Bridge?" *Youthwork* (August 1999).

Section 3

The Tasks of Practical Theology:

Detecting Our

Convictions and

Evaluationg Our

Practices

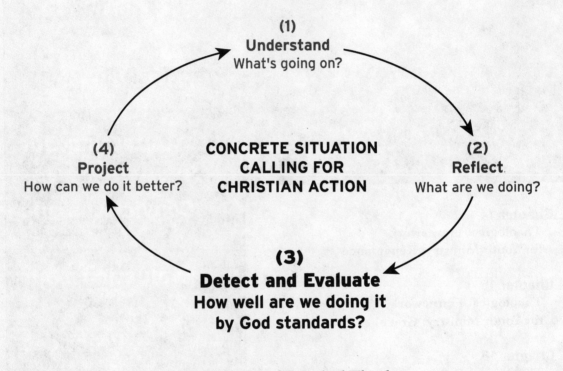

The Tasks of Practical Theology

The Tasks of Practical Theology: Detecting Our Convictions and Evaluating Our Practices
Kenda Creasy Dean

Intro

Greetings to the Faith Church congregation:

As I begin to write this, I'm overwhelmed by God's goodness and faithfulness for the opportunity [to potentially serve as your youth pastor]. Please allow me to take a moment to introduce my wife Hannah and myself to you...I have volunteered and worked in various realms of youth ministry for over 10 years now. Though my philosophy and vision for ministry may have evolved over the years, my passion for youth ministry and Christ is still what makes me tick.

As I sit here, I'm wondering about each of you and what it will be like filtering through all this information about Hannah and me. In particular, my medical condition may have sparked lots of questions that I hope you will find satisfying and correct answers to in these next weeks. However, I would like to offer you some facts up front. Several years ago I was diagnosed HIV-positive. There was a short period during my late adolescence in which I made some poor choices that resulted in me contracting HIV. I'm now 31 years old, and those situations occurred many years ago.

Hannah and I realize that we didn't have to disclose this information, but I wholeheartedly believe that living openly with my medical condition will allow me to be a completely authentic person, free to fully live for God and for others. My medical condition doesn't define me, but it's a part of me. My ministry is about the gospel of Jesus Christ, not about HIV/AIDS, but I do feel a responsibility to live openly so that God may be glorified in the fullness of what I might bring to Faith Church...

Friends, in closing, I'm fervently committed to the gospel of Jesus Christ and to the service of the church. The greatest gift in my life is my loving relationship with Hannah, for whom I would live and die. I wholeheartedly believe that the richest part of what I have to offer a congregation is grounded in the emotional, mental, and spiritual health I strive for in these primary relationships. I'm a man of my word who strives every day to reflect the integrity and truth of the Christian life. I look forward to the possibility of continuing the tradition of excellent youth ministry and being part of what God is doing at Faith Church.

Peace in Christ,
Josh McCormick[1]

---

1. The name of both the candidate and the church have been changed.

This is an excerpt from a real letter submitted by a candidate for a youth ministry position at a wealthy, mid-sized congregation on the West Coast. After several interviews, the nominating committee concluded that Josh was the candidate God had prepared for Faith Church, and they moved his recommendation as associate pastor for student ministries.

Meanwhile, Josh and Hannah agonized over going public with a secret they had kept since before they were married: Josh is HIV-positive.

Josh's diagnosis five years ago seemed like a death sentence, but he had responded well to drug therapy and in many ways had beaten the odds. Although Josh lived under careful medical scrutiny, he and Hannah were convinced, not only that he had a future in youth ministry, but that he had a future, period. They had told the other pastors at Faith Church about Josh's illness midway through the interview process. The pastors' reactions were overwhelmingly supportive. The senior pastor urged Josh to tell the nominating committee. Just before the committee made the recommendation to hire, Josh and Hannah flew to the coastal town where Faith Church is located to tell the committee personally.

It was gut-wrenching weekend both for Josh and Hannah and for members of the nominating committee, who had grown to love and admire them both. The nominating committee wanted some time to think it over. In the interim, the committee consulted countless medical and legal experts to assess the risk of having an HIV-positive pastor working directly with teenagers. A few weeks later, they voted unanimously to recommend Josh as their new youth minister.

Faith Church's polity required a congregational vote to ratify the committee's recommendation before they could actually hire Josh. Everyone knew that revealing Josh's medical condition could jeopardize his nomination, especially in a position working with youth. Several lawyers frankly advised Josh and Hannah not to disclose Josh's illness, fearing legal ramifications. In particular, the question "How did you get HIV?" seemed both invasive and inevitable. It had already come up in the nominating committee.

Josh considered skirting the question if it arose again; he had no legal obligation to share this information, and the senior pastor advised him to just tell people it was none of their business. He drafted a letter that essentially said this, but then destroyed it. Why didn't it seem right to withhold this personal detail?

Finally, Josh concluded that everything he stood for as a Christian—not to mention as a youth pastor—grew out of a life lived in the freedom of God and in trusting God against the odds. All of his references spoke about Josh's rare integrity, his deep self-knowledge, his ability to inspire trust. How could he be free for honest ministry or be trustworthy with other people's pain, without full disclosure now? He and Hannah prayed feverishly over their decision. Just before they flew out for the final interview—where they would meet the entire congregation—he addressed an envelope to Faith Church, slipped in this letter, and dropped it in the mail.

Detecting our convictions and evaluating our practices

Practical theological reflection is the responsibility of faith communities as well as individuals. Brought up short by something that jars our accustomed practice of Christian life, we are forced to look for new ways to live out our faith that communicate the gospel more faithfully. The news that their top candidate for the youth ministry position was HIV-positive shocked Faith Church's leadership. They immediately invested in better understanding the concrete situation calling for their Christian action. They reflected deeply on their Christian practice in calling a new youth pastor: had they left room for the Holy Spirit in this process? Had they prayed genuinely? Had they searched the Scriptures for guidance? Had they invoked their minds as well as their hearts in making this decision? Was calling Josh to serve at Faith Church God's will or just their will? While nothing about the nomination process seemed to contradict Faith Church's understanding of the gospel, the committee wondered how they might communicate this gospel more clearly—to both the congregation and the community—if they called a new youth pastor known to be living with HIV.

Thus they entered the third task of practical theology by setting out to *detect* their theological touchstones for calling a new pastor and to *evaluate* their practice of ministry according to those touchstones. This is different from evaluating a practice according to whether it works or not. There's nothing inherently wrong with something that works—but in practical theology, we are primarily concerned with the radical congruency between God's action and our action, which means we need to find out whether our normative practices of ministry are *faithful*. Does our standard way of doing business in youth ministry reflect who God is and how God works in the world—or does it subtly (or not so subtly) reflect something else? In this task of practical theology, our theological rocks become quite explicit, for we use them as plumb lines against which we evaluate our Christian actions, touchstones for defending—or dismissing—practices of ministry with young people.

Putting detection and evaluation to work

Evaluating Christian practice requires us to detect the theological standards by which we measure these practices. This is more straightforward than it sounds. Until recently, for example, much parachurch youth evangelism considered the *magnet kid strategy* normative for building youth clubs. The magnet kid strategy sought to attract to the club the most popular young person at school, on the premise that this student would draw other youth to the club as well. As a strategy for building Christian youth clubs, the magnet kid strategy worked exceptionally well.

However, when evaluated by standards of faithfulness rather than standards of effectiveness, the magnet kid strategy raised serious questions. For one thing, Jesus called "the least of these" as his first disciples. Whether Peter, James, John, or any of the rest of the Twelve would have qualified as *magnet kids* is highly questionable. Furthermore, the magnet kid strategy tended to suggest that young people should come to Christian youth clubs in order to follow the magnet kids, not Jesus Christ. As parachurch organizations matured and their leadership became more theologically self-aware, the magnet kid strategy began to receive less attention in leadership training manuals.[2]

In the case of Faith Church, the nominating committee first affirmed two theological convictions: God can overcome impossible odds, and God seemed to be calling Faith Church to stand as a witness to this kind of God in the midst of their affluent community. Hiring Josh seemed to underline both of these convictions. Even while Josh lived secretly with HIV for five years, God had used him in ministry despite incredible odds, and—ironically—God now seemed to be calling him to serve in a community where external beauty and economic comfort often forced hardship underground. Given those theological *starting points*, the nominating committee wondered: Should we hire Josh because we have faith in Josh? Or should we hire him because we have faith in *God*?

The committee decided that medical grounds were insufficient cause to withdraw their endorsement of Josh. And they could find no other reason not to hire him. He seemed a natural *fit* in both their church and their community. His youth ministry credentials and references were impeccable, surpassing the committee's highest hopes. The person who asked, "How did you get it?"—as Josh immediately surmised—really wanted to know about his moral character, leading Josh to disclose in brief form the circumstances around his contracting HIV.

In short, when they held up their procedure for calling Josh alongside their practice and mission as a congregation, the nominating committee concluded that hiring Josh reaffirmed their belief in an awesome God, and renewed their sense that Faith Church was called to be a *witness*—to the community, to Josh, and now to the broader church that struggles with issues related to HIV. On these grounds, they defended Josh as their candidate of choice, and their procedure for arriving at this decision.

Now it's your turn

The third task of practical theology (detecting our convictions and evaluating our practices) asks, *Given our theological commitments, how can we defend the norms of youth ministry in this concrete situation?*

The point here is not defensive—to counter charges against our practices of

---

2. To be sure, the "magnet kid" strategy—most often associated with Young Life's "key kid" strategy but used in other organizations as well—is still in place in parachurch and congregational youth programs alike. When used in concert with other forms of youth evangelism, it can be theologically defended. In the 1950s, however, the magnet kid strategy received near canon status in some parachurch leadership training materials, an emphasis that has faded in recent years. The current Young Life training handbook directly addresses the key kid concept, including its critiques. Under Procedures in Contact, the handbook offers the following Guiding Thoughts: "2. We must be aware of influential kids within different groupings. If we touch these kids, we may have the potential of touching others. If we ignore them, we may automatically ignore many who would have been influenced by them. The key kid concept was based on a sound missiological principle. It has also been the target of much criticism over the years. Our call first and foremost is to every kid and we must use whatever strategy possible to reach every kid for Christ. In some schools the kids who traditionally would have been Young Life key kids are actually the objects of ridicule and scorn. We should love kids unconditionally, and offer Christ to all. 3. Most important of all, we must seek to be led of the Holy Spirit. The Lord will often lead us to people who do not seem to be key kids. Many times these will turn out to be the real disciples." (*Leadership 1*: Foundations for Relational Ministries, 119.)

youth ministry against charges levied by complaining parents, queasy congregations, or hyper-critical higher-ups. The purpose of the third task of practical theology is evaluative: In which of our normative practices of youth ministry can God's truth be heard most clearly? Which practices have the most static? Which practices are evidence of a radical congruency between God's action and our action?

The next four chapters offer examples of theological *starting points* that make a difference in the way we defend what we do in youth ministry. Starting points are not ending points; theology is an interconnected discipline, and one doctrine leads to another and another and another. Emphasizing one theological theme as a foundation for youth ministry does not necessarily exclude others.

But we do have to start somewhere, and where we begin makes a difference in how we proceed. Each of the following authors has chosen a theological starting point for youth ministry—repentance (chapter 14, Robin Maas), grace (chapter 15, Rodger Nishioka), redemption (chapter 16, Darrell W. Johnson), and hope (chapter 17, Evelyn Parker). They demonstrate how to use such theological rocks as benchmarks, standards by which our practices of youth ministry may be defended because they are faithful, and not merely effective.

An avalanche of welcome

Prior to Josh's final meeting with the Faith Church congregation, the nominating committee circulated a booklet introducing Josh to every member of the congregation. It included a letter from the nominating committee, theologically defending the committee's procedures and why they viewed Josh as the person God had called to this position. The booklet included a summary of Josh's résumé, a review of his credentials, and excerpts from Josh's recommendations pertaining to his admirable moral character. A schedule of opportunities to meet Josh and Hannah on their visit to Faith Church was included.

The booklet also included Josh's letter to the congregation, followed by a lengthy question-and-answer section on HIV and AIDS, tailored to the concerns of Faith Church. The nominating committee had developed the Q-and-A section in consultation with numerous experts in the medical, counseling, and pastoral fields (who were cited in the document). Furthermore, the booklet assured the congregation that their concerns would be taken seriously, listing many opportunities for members to raise questions, with obvious care taken to acknowledge anxiety and protect anonymity:

> We encourage you to consult one of the following resources for answers to any questions you may have:
> 1. Educational forums are being offered to provide information and answer questions.
> 2. Answers to questions we anticipate congregation members may

have are provided [in this booklet].

3. The senior pastor and associate pastor will be happy to meet with any congregation members regarding questions or concerns [phone numbers and e-mail addresses listed].

4. National HIV/AIDS Hotline, operated by the Centers for Disease Control and the American Social Health Association, that answers questions on a 24-hour, anonymous basis [phone number and email address listed].[3]

5. A box will be available on the church office counter. You may deposit your questions in the box along with your name and phone number. You will receive a phone call with a response to your question.

Finally, the booklet contained enthusiastic letters of endorsement from both the senior and associate pastors.

Josh was overwhelmed by the document's generosity. By the time Josh and Hannah arrived at Faith Church, an avalanche of welcome awaited them. So did a unanimous vote of approval and an invigorated congregation, convinced that with Josh as their new associate pastor, God would lead them into a new era of ministry.

---

3. The National HIV/AIDS Hotline can be reached at 1-800-342-2437 or www.ashastd.org.

Theological Framework for Youth Ministry: Repentance[1]
Robin Maas

14
Chapter

Christ and the adolescent: piper or prophet?

There is a legend, told now as a charming nursery tale, that must chill the heart of every parent who reads it. It is a story of seduction and enchantment; a story in which children disappear—*forever.*

You know the tale I mean. It comes to us in the form of a long narrative poem by Robert Browning, "The Pied Piper of Hamelin." Most children today probably encounter bowdlerized versions—retellings that may try to mitigate the horror. (One such retelling asserts that all the adults of Hamelin, and not just the city fathers, were greedy and ungrateful, implying that these parents deserved to lose their children.) What you may not know is that the legend is rooted in an actual historical event, recorded by some ancient, unknown hand on the city walls of Hamelin, Germany.

Something awful happened in Hamelin. We will probably never know precisely how it happened or why. But it did happen and that, I believe, is why this story is at the same time so strangely fascinating and repulsive. The writing is on the wall. It happened.

Just what does the writing say? That on July 22 of the year 1284, some 130 children were led out of town by a Pied Piper and were lost in (not on) Koppen Hill.[2] Some believe the Piper was an agent of a Bishop Olrnutz who, in the late 13TH century, drew many of Hamelin's youth to Moravia, where they were permanently resettled. Others claim that the children were kidnapped by landowners to replace serfs who had died in recent epidemics. A more elaborate theory proposes that the children of Hamelin suffered from the purple fungus ergot, which grows on rye grain during rainy seasons. Anyone who consumed the contaminated grain was likely to be afflicted with severe muscle spasms and hallucinations. The poison acted to constrict blood vessels, causing burning sensations in the victim's hands and feet, could be relieved by strenuous physical activity, such as dancing; hence, the hiring of musicians, such as the Piper, to play for the afflicted so that they might dance. This explanation is a particularly poignant and intriguing one, since ergot is the source of the modem drug lysergic acid diethylamide, or LSD—the poison of choice for many of today's youth.[3]

Another even more interesting hypothesis connects the legend to the bizarre and infamous children's crusade, which occurred in the year 1212. Close to 100,000

1. This chapter originally appeared as "Christ and the Adolescent: Piper or Prophet?" in The 1996 Princeton Lectures on Youth, Church, and Culture (Princeton, New Jersey: Institute of Youth Ministry, Princeton Theological Seminary), 35-48. Adapted with permission of the author.

2. This date is supplied by the *World Book* entry on Hamelin. The poem by Robert Browning gives the date as July 22, 1376.

3. Gloria Skurzynski, *What Happened in Hamelin* (New York: Four Winds Press, 1979), 176.

youths—most of them boys around the age of 12—set off from both France and Germany to recapture Jerusalem from the Muslims by entirely peaceful means. Against all reason, rejecting all adult pleas to the contrary, these idealistic but deluded and ignorant children—led by other idealistic, ignorant, and deluded children and accompanied by a motley crew of both well- and ill-intentioned adults—set off to put right what the adult crusaders had gotten wrong.

While the majority of clergy and almost all other adults looked askance at the project and tried to dissuade the young idealists, there were some, including the father of the boy who led one of the German contingents, who found either personal or professional advantage in encouraging the unlikely project. The lad who led the French contingent claimed that Jesus himself appeared to him and handed him a letter commanding him to organize the crusade. One popular explanation of what really might have happened proposes that the boy was duped by an ambitious and unscrupulous priest, pretending to be the Lord.[4]

At any rate, there was no stopping them once the ball got rolling; and, in the end, many thousands of them perished or disappeared. Of the lost, those who did not die from cold, exhaustion, and starvation en route to the Mediterranean either perished at sea or were sold into slavery and prostitution in North Africa. The lucky ones straggled home, bitterly disillusioned.

Wanted: deliverer, money no object

Piper or prophet?
Look at a youth ministry job description. (If you don't have ready access to these, you can find some online at www.youthspecialties.com/jobbank) Is the congregation or sponsoring organization looking for a piper or a prophet to fill this position?

Whatever happened in Hamelin, the fact remains that the young are always easy targets—especially when somebody comes along who will protest adult incompetence and injustice, make great music, and hold out the utopian promise of a perfect world—somebody like the Pied Piper.

A plague of vermin has a chokehold on the town of Hamelin. Destroyers of both public and private peace, these countless rats, harbingers of deadly plagues, fought the dogs and killed the cats,

> And bit the babies in the cradles,
> And ate the cheeses out of the vats
> And licked the soup from the cook's own ladles,
> Split open the kegs of salted sprats,
> Made nests inside men's Sunday hats
> And even spoiled the women's chats
> By drowning their speaking
> With shrieking and squeaking
> In 50 different sharps and flats.[5]

The beleaguered citizens of Hamelin are ready to throw their ineffective government out of office when an improbable savior suddenly appears. The poet Browning describes

---

4. See George Zabriskie Gray, *The Children's Crusade: A History* (New York: William Morrow & Co., 1972).

5. Robert Browning, *The Pied Piper of Hamelin* (London and New York: Frederick Warne & Co., no date), 6-11.

him as a tall, thin, ethereal character, swarthy but beardless, and quaintly garbed in a brightly colored, long robe—half yellow, half red—hence, the designation *pied*. He claims to be an expert *terminator*, a professional rescuer; and so the politicians, desperate for any kind of a solution, hire this strange-looking fellow. Besides, his résumé looks good:

> "Please your honours," said he, "I'm able,
> By means of a secret charm, to draw
> All creatures living beneath the sun,
> That creep or swim or fly or run,
> After me so as you never saw!
> And I chiefly use my charm
> On creatures that do people harm."

Of course it will cost. They promise him 1,000 guilders to do the job, and then watch with astonishment as the Piper pipes thousands of rats out of town, leading them to their doom as they plunge, like lemmings, into the river Weser.

You remember the rest. Freed of the plague of rats, the mayor reneges his promise and offers the Piper only 50 guilders in place of the original 1,000. The Piper, a man not to be trifled with, gets his revenge. He changes his tune, and this time it is the youngest citizens of Hamelin who dance after him in droves, only to be swallowed up, not by a river, but by a magic mountain, wherein the Piper promised a veritable garden of delights. None are left to tell the tale except a single child, a little lame boy who could not keep up the pace and was left to his lonely fate in a town full of grown-ups:

> "It's dull in my town since my playmates left!
> I can't forget that I'm bereft
> Of all the pleasant sights they see,
> Which the Piper also promised me;
> For he led us, he said, to a joyous land,
> Joining the town and just at hand,
> Where the waters gushed and the fruit trees grew,
> And flowers put forth a fairer hue,
> And everything was strange and new.
> The sparrows were brighter than peacocks here,
> And their dogs outran our fallow deer,
> And honey-bees had lost their stings,
> And horses were born with eagle's wings;
> And just as I became assured
> My lame foot would be speedily cured,
> The music stopped and I stood still,

Ponderable
The Pied Piper exercises personality-based leadership, something to which all ministry—and not just youth ministry—is extremely vulnerable. Why is this? Is this necessarily a bad thing? Have you ever been part of a personality-based ministry? What are the advantages of this kind of leadership? What are the dangers? Some experts say that a particular youth ministry must be in place for six years or more if it is to outlive the personality of its leader. Does this ring true to you?

And found myself outside the Hill,
Left alone against my will
To go now limping as before,
And never hear of that country more!"

Because of his physical imperfection, this boy misses out on the delicious paradise promised by the Piper, where everything would be strange and new—a place that sounds remarkably like that wonderful "holy mountain" envisioned by the prophet, where "the wolf will live with the lamb, and the leopard will lie down with the goat, and the calf and the lion and the yearling together…and the young child put his hand into the viper's nest. They will neither harm nor destroy…" (Isaiah 11:6-9). This bereft and damaged child, who knows he is not perfect, is the only one of his generation fated to remain behind in the mundane and bourgeois little hamlet filled with anguished adults who, try as they might to find him, cannot pay the Piper what they owe and whose beautiful children, bound for an unearthly paradise, are lost to them *forever*.

Browning appends a word of advice at the conclusion to this cautionary tale:

So, Willy, let me and you be wipers
Of scores out with all men—especially. pipers;
And whether they pipe us free from rats or from mice,
If we've promised them aught, let us keep our promise.[6]

There, but by the grace of God, go youth ministers

I suspect that those of you who are preparing to be full-time youth ministers may feel a profound empathy for the Piper. If you have served in youth ministry, perhaps you even envy him. You, too, may have felt manipulated by ungrateful adults who, for a pittance, wanted you to keep their children out of mischief and out of their hair, who expected you to work miracles by ridding the local environment of all its toxic elements, but who certainly did not wish you, in any sense of the word, to work miracles with their children.

You, too, may have fantasized about a showdown with the senior pastor or the parish council about craven compromises and fundamental injustices in the running of the youth program; and you have probably dreamed of having 130 teenagers hanging on your every word, taking what you have to offer with utmost seriousness, and showing up—without fail—for every meticulously planned meeting and event your program had to offer.

Perhaps you'd give anything for that secret charm and, like the Piper, you'd chiefly use it "on creatures that do people [*especially young people*] harm." You, too, may be ready to pipe a different tune—because it's easy to be seduced, even when you're not so young. So be warned! The Piper remains a dangerous man, not just for the young but also for those who minister to them.

---

6. Browning, 47.

Repentance: time to pay the piper

Ponderable

Robin Maas frames her description of repentance around a passage from the gospel of Luke, that carries forward an Old Testament view of repentance as having both personal and public dimensions. How is repentance viewed by your religious community? Do you talk about it much? Is repentance considered a private matter, or does repentance carry public consequences as well? What does a ministry that takes repentance seriously imply for the way youth leaders conduct themselves? What does it mean for youth?

Cause for repentance?

Would you ask for repentance in any of the following scenarios? What might that look like? Would you consider repentance entirely personal, between the party involved and God, or would it have public consequences as well?
- Two volunteer leaders (a man and a woman) for the senior highs are living together as boyfriend and girlfriend.
- Two girls in the youth group have been arrested for shoplifting. Their parents bring them to you for a meeting.
- The single mom of one of your most active junior high girls has been having her (the mother's) dates spend the night. The girl comes to you to make sense of her mother's edict to never have sex before marriage.
- Marijuana showed up in the bedroom of a ninth grade boy in your congregation. He does not participate in youth activities but shows up occasionally for worship.
- A kid you know who is not a Christian, but who hangs out with many of the youth from your church, admits to you that he has stolen a test and sold it to most of the junior biology class.

But take heart. There is another historical figure who, though he shares many of the Piper's exotic and engaging qualities, offers a model of spiritual leadership that will lead neither you nor the young astray.

> A voice of one calling:
> "In the desert prepare
> the way for the Lord;
> make straight in the wilderness
> a highway for our God.
> Every valley shall be raised up,
> every mountain and hill made low;
> the rough ground shall become level,
> the rugged places a plain.
> And the glory of the Lord will be revealed,
> and all mankind together will see it.
> For the mouth of the Lord
> has spoken."
> —*Isaiah 40:3-5*

This voice—urgent, piercing, insistent—penetrates hearts and either stirs or shakes them. The sound of this voice is not seductive, but compelling. We cannot ignore it, for it speaks words of both warning and promise. It is the voice, not of the Piper, who says, "I can deliver you—and the goods," but of the prophet, whose role it is to prepare us for reality, and who says, "It's time. Get ready. He's coming."

The young listen to this voice with excitement, the old perhaps with fresh hope, the powerful with suspicion, and the wicked with disdain or despair. But it is a sound, a message, that cannot be shut out: Wake up! Put your house in order! All your bills are falling due—*it's time to pay the Piper!* Yes, something wonderful awaits those who are faithful to the God of Israel, but first there is something you must do. And it will not be fun. You will not go dancing to this task.

The people who first listened to this voice had some sense of what he was talking about. The prophet told them not only what to expect, but what to do about it: Clear a path, a straight, level path, a *highway* for your God. He is going to come barreling through in a way that cannot be mistaken for anything but what it is meant to be. The glory of the Lord carries with it beauty, terror, and power—the power to move mountains, to level them, if need be, and the will to lift up whatever has sunk into the depths. Is this the path to paradise? And if it is, do we want to be on it? Do we want our kids on it?

This is not a route that leads through the land of good grades, high SAT scores, careers, babies, and minivans. The prophet is talking about God. God is coming, and our little dreams—our modest hopes and plans—may all come to naught. The voice that makes this radical claim is a voice crying out about the transformation of a waste-land—the restructuring of an entire landscape. God is coming, and nothing will ever again be the same. Everything will be strange, and everything will be new.

This voice, the one that urges us to hurry up, to get ready, to prepare a highway for our God, is always the voice of the prophet—the one through whom the Lord speaks. Although these words first appear in the book of Isaiah, Christians have learned to associate them with the voice of a prophet named John, who did indeed announce the coming of God.

The ministry of pointing and prodding

John was a young man who was all about getting ready for God. He embodies readi-ness for God in much the same way Mary does. Each one was bringing something *to light*. In the darkness of Mary's womb, the light was taking flesh. Through this very young woman, "the true light that enlightens every [living soul] was coming into the world" (John 1:9). She neither piped nor prophesied. She was the instrument through which God blew; not the Piper, but the pipe.

John does not bear the light within, but points beyond himself toward the light. John's words, his works, and his life all testify to the light that is coming into the world (John 1:7). The prophet is always herald, witness, and guide. His words, his works, and his *person* all bear witness to a reality that is beyond him, to something, someone, *else*. Any power he exercises is borrowed, derivative. His role, first and always, is to speak the truth and in this way to warn, console, and prepare. It is the prophet John the Baptiz-er—and not the mysterious Piper—who best serves as a model for youth ministers. Where the Piper enchants, the prophet prods and pokes. He is follower first, leading only where he is led. His testimony, because it is true, compels but cannot coerce.

What do we know about John? First, that he was kin to Jesus, son of a priest and a very pious but previously barren woman. Like so many great figures in biblical histo-ry, the circumstances of his birth mark him out as a special gift from God. The angel Gabriel tells John's father, Zechariah, that his son will drink neither wine nor strong drink. He will not need these intoxicants because he will be filled, *inebriated*, with the Holy Spirit—even from his mother's womb where the as-yet-unborn prophet recog-nizes the presence of the Messiah and leaps for joy (Luke 1:44). The Spirit has bestowed upon this child a special mission. John, says the angel, is coming to turn many of the people of Israel to the Lord their God, "and he will go on before the Lord in the spirit and power of Elijah, to turn the hearts of the fathers to their children and the disobedient to the wisdom of the righteous—to make ready a people prepared for the Lord" (Luke 1:16-17).

Can it possibly be that our own calling mirrors that of this new Elijah? Do we find in John's commission any clues to an authentically prophetic ministry with the young?

Incarnational ministry
Because of the relational nature of our work, we like to say that youth ministry is *incarnational ministry*—ministry in which God enters the world through human beings, the way God entered the world in the person of Jesus Christ. On the one hand, incarnational ministry points to youth ministry's theological char-acter, and helps to keep it from devolving into nothing more than good interpersonal relationships. After all, anybody can have a rela-tionship, but only God can be Incarnate.

On the other hand, the term *incarnational ministry* has been abused by youth ministers who interpret it to mean that they are the incarnate ones. These leaders say to youth, in effect: "Follow me, because I follow Jesus Christ."

True incarnational ministry, however, is never about "following me." It is always about following Jesus Christ, the true Incarnation of God. We do better to say that we point to the true Christ, as wit-nesses (as Karl Barth suggested) or that we are windows or icons through which the true Christ may be glimpsed (as Martin Luther taught). But in no case are we the One youth should follow. While we want our lives to be faithful exam-ples, faithfulness is not an educa-tional strategy. We live faithfully in order to be more Christlike—not to be prototypes young people will imitate.

Incarnational ministry involves primary, not secondary, encoun-ters between young people and the God of Jesus Christ. In incar-national ministry, youth follow their ministers only to the extent that we are transparent to Christ, allowing them to see Christ beyond us, and therefore follow him even if our footsteps stray from the path.

◼ Clue: prophetic ministry tells young people the truth

> And he will go on before the Lord, in the spirit and power of Elijah...
>
> —*Luke 1:17a*

The child's name, chosen by Elizabeth in obedience to the angel Gabriel and in defiance of family tradition, means "Yahweh has shown favor." The God of Israel loves his people. He takes pity on them and sends them prophets. John is the last of these remarkable gifts from God to God's people. He comes when things are in a desperate state. He is Israel's last chance—to change.

Those of us who read the Gospels centuries later would like to think that we would have heeded the preaching of this remarkable young man—that we would have recognized him as the true messenger of God. Maybe. Maybe not. Mark's account suggests he was on the eccentric side. He camped out in that very same wilderness the prophet Isaiah had said would have to be transformed—leveled—for the highway of God. Like his spiritual predecessor Elijah, John wore a (camel's) hair garment with a big leather belt. He ate bugs sweetened with honey (Mark 1:6). John, descended from a line of priests, was irritatingly noisy and odd—as odd in his own way as that other strange messenger of God, Elijah.

I think of Elijah as the prototypical Hebraic prophet: a morose loner—cranky, eccentric, irascible, and meddling. A seasoned "smiter," his word "burned like a torch" (Sirach 48:1). Using curses as his favorite weapon, he could call down fire and famine. He did indeed attack injustice; but his driving passion was combating idolatry—the vicious practices associated with the loathsome worship of Baal.

By John's day, nearly nine centuries later, Elijah was an ancient memory—a symbol loaded with Messianic significance, and with hope. At the appointed time, it is written, Elijah will be the one "to calm the wrath of God before it breaks out in fury, to turn the heart of the father to the son, and to restore the tribes of Jacob" (Sirach 48:10).

In Malachi we see another instance of how the association of John with Elijah's spirit comes to be made: "See, I will send you the prophet Elijah before the great and dreadful day of the Lord comes. He will turn the hearts of the fathers to their children, and the hearts of the children to their fathers; or else I will come and strike the land with a curse" (Malachi 4:5-6).

John, who like Elisha now wears the mantle of Elijah, is sent to tell Israel—and us—what to expect and what to do before that great and terrible day when we stand revealed for what we really are in the light that is Christ. John, as the new Elijah, is sent to *turn hearts*—to turn the hearts of fathers to their children and the hearts of children to their fathers. And there is, we should recognize, only one way to turn hearts—and that is through repentance.

That is why John comes preaching a baptism of repentance for the forgiveness of sins. Repentance is the hard, not-so-fun work of spiritual path—clearing or moral

Sirach

Robin cites Scripture taken from the Book of Sirach, an intertestamental ("between the testaments") book. Intertestamental books, sometimes called the Apocrypha, are not part of Protestant Bibles but are canonical have Scriptural authority) for Catholics.

Sirach, an upper-class Jew with liturgical interests, probably wrote his book as poetry around 180 B.C. It is considered wisdom literature, and teaches that fulfilling the law of Moses means showing great wisdom. Like other intertestamental literature, Sirach is excluded from the Protestant Bible because it is unclear whether the book is revealed" by God or serves primarily as an ethical book. Often criticized for its harsh treatment of women, the Book of Sirach shows similarities to Proverbs but has more of a historical tilt.[1]

1. John E. Rybolt, *Sirach* (Collegeville, Minnesota: The Liturgical Press, 1986), 5-7.

roadwork. It is a heart-turning, stomach-churning, mind-burning experience that actually changes people; and contrary to popular and current Christian opinion, forgiveness is not offered prior to repentance.

It is not enough, as you probably know, to be a show-stopping preacher. Strong words seize our attention—for as long as their sound lingers in the air. Real change requires a death; and that is what baptism is. Even the baptism of repentance is a slayer; and what we expect to find in the wake of dying is grief. And *tears*. These are the real change agents. The prophet always demands change; and this demand, though often experienced as harsh, is rooted in compassion; for the unpleasant dousing we receive in the baptism of repentance is a painful but effective way of staying out of hot water.

It is always the prophet's responsibility to tell people this, especially young people who today scarcely know what sin is and whose culpability is perhaps mitigated by adult unwillingness to reveal this truth to them. Better they be smitten by the torch of John's word now than—sooner or later—to meet their Lord unprepared. How foolish we are when we think the young will reject outright a righteous rebuke when many of them are yearning for precisely this sign of love—for this prophetic witness to their worth.

Clue: prophetic ministry shows young people how to change

> And he will…turn the hearts of the fathers to their children and the disobedient to the wisdom of the righteous…
>
> —*Luke 1:17b*

The prophet John the Baptizer makes a dramatic appearance in the church lectionary during the season of Advent; and just as Advent signifies a special time of preparation in the church calendar, adolescence represents a special time of preparation in the life cycle of each individual. For the teenager, there is light just over the horizon. The teen calls this light *freedom* and equates it with adulthood. But while the light is in sight, the teen still needs a lot of adult guidance in preparing for adult responsibilities. High schools and colleges are places where youth prepare themselves for the adult responsibilities our society has identified as necessary for personal success.

The church has the responsibility for preparing youth for something much more momentous, however. Like John, the light to which we bear witness is Christ himself. We bear the heavy responsibility of announcing his coming to youth, of convincing them that he is indeed on the way, and that they can and must do something about it. We must do this, so that they have the chance to *change*.

The kind of change we most often expect from youth is the kind of change we call *development*. It is change that is bound to come, so to speak, and the issue is how well each individual will navigate the shoals of certain types of necessary change. But that's not the only kind of change youth ministers need to be concerned about. The

---

Ponderable

Since the earliest research on adolescence a century ago, adolescence has been considered a uniquely spiritual phase in the life cycle. Psychologists in the early 20TH century assumed conversion was necessary for a healthy transition from childhood to adulthood (although not all agreed that it needed to be a religious conversion). For most of the 20TH century, churches assumed that most conversions took place during adolescence; a common statistic cited (though undocumented) is that 85 percent of commitments to Christ come before the age of 18.

Recently, George Barna's research found that only 4 percent of those surveyed said they had had religious conversions as teenagers.[1] This statistic has caused a stir among youth ministry professionals; it not only flies in the face of common assumptions, but it also contradicts generations of anecdotal evidence.

What's going on here? Does Barna's research ring true to you? Is conversion common during adolescence? Is it important that what Robin calls a "personal moral conversion" happen during adolescence?

1. George Barna, *Third Millennium Teens* (Ventura, California: Barna Research Group, 1999), 66.

Bringing youth to repentance and tears

Anybody who has been part of a youth camp or conference knows the role tears play in the event. Typically, the momentum of the week builds to some kind of a commitment service on the last night, which is often an emotional—and significant—experience for youth. Youth returning year after year to the same event look forward to this night. On the last day of the event, young people cry at the thought of leaving each other to go back to their daily routines.

Developmental theorist Erik H. Erikson has pointed out that adolescents need to be moved, existentially as well as physically, and that this is important to their developing need for transcendence.[1] Robin suggests that "bringing youth to repentance—to tears" is a way to prepare them to meet Christ. Some Christians who look back on their experiences at emotional worship services as youth remember them as life-changing events. Others remember them as shameless emotional manipulation of tired, hyped adolescents who want to fit in.

Pay attention to the link Robin draws between repentance and tears. To Robin, tears are not part of an emotional high; on the contrary, they suggest the depth of remorse that accompanies true repentance. Is repentance the reason for the tears you see at youth events? If not, what is their purpose? Are these tears indications of real change on the part of young people? How can youth ministry address the adolescent need to be emotionally moved, especially to be moved toward repentance, without resorting to manipulation?

1. See Erik H. Erikson, *Identity: Youth and Crisis* (New York: W. W. Norton, 1968).

kind of change John the Baptist is asking for is personal moral conversion. It can happen when you're 15, five, or 50. And while I imagine you think often about certain changes you would like to see affected in your youth, including moral change, you may not have thought much about your role in terms of bringing them to repentance—*to tears*—as a way of preparing them to meet Christ, the Lord of the Universe who is asking to be Lord of their hearts.

A great deal of energy is expended by youth leaders and program developers in the interest of social justice. Certain aspects of American society, our culture, and "the establishment" are regularly excoriated for perpetrating injustices. This is fine as far as it goes. But we must be careful that we adults are not sending our kids off on fruitless and dangerous crusades for which they remain spiritually under-equipped. It is a form of adult exploitation to train our youth to sniff out these corporate moral failures from miles away while allowing them to remain blissfully ignorant of their personal moral failings because we have forgotten, or choose not to remember, that the prophets confronted individual sinners as well as nations.

We may all deeply regret the injuries suffered by those who occupy the lower social and economic rungs of the ladder; but the wounds that actually bring us to *tears of repentance* are those for which we recognize our own personal culpability—when the person we've hurt has a face and a name.

We know John the Baptist did not neglect the larger moral horizon in which he lived; it was one of his favorite sermon topics. But he baptized people one by one. To each one who came to him he said, "Own up to your sins, name them, repent, be cleansed in the waters of baptism—*and change your ways*. If you have been dishonest, hypocritical, selfish, a cheat, or indifferent to the poor, *change your behavior*."

We religious professionals hear these words, and we think about the complacent and comfortable-but-faceless adults who, although they sit in the pews of our churches, remain indifferent to human suffering and go on consuming this world's goods as if there were no tomorrow. Think again.

Remember, the new Elijah was to turn hearts—in particular the hearts of parents and children. The human family is the nursery of virtue *and vice*, and anyone who has spent more than 10 sessions with a therapist has been forced to recognize how many bruises on the heart first appear in disappointing and destructive struggles with family members. *I* remember—you remember—how anxious we were as youth to be rid of our tiresome siblings, our meddling mother, our embarrassingly inept or overbearing father. *I* said, *you* said, when *I* am grown up, when *I* am married, when *I* am a parent, *I will not be like that*…If I could just get away from this mess, I could be happy—I could even be good! You and I, because we expected our families and our world to be perfect, were easy bait for the Piper.

So what are we saying—that the youth minister's job is simply to whip up a lot of adolescent guilt and remorse, to make the girls cry and the boys blush with shame? By no means! Back to John.

Although the prophet profoundly disturbs people, he also gives them hope, because he tells them the truth—not the false hope of a paradise without pain, but the real hope of conversion, of *personal change*. This is how the two-edged sword of truth works. It cuts to the bone; but truth is a surgeon, not a slayer. It is the ax laid to the root of the tree. It removes only that which is dying or already dead.

John gave his hearers hope because he told them there was something they could do to change themselves. He said: *You can do something now that will make this future encounter with the Lord a "fruitful" one.* And what he asked of those who wanted to prepare themselves was nothing heroic. It was doable. "Produce fruit in keeping with repentance....The man with two tunics should share with him who has none, and one who has food should do the same" (Luke 3:8, 11). Nothing here about trouping off to liberate the Holy Land or being burned at the stake. Just the cheerful, unrelenting performance of duty, simple kindness to the neighbor, the generous impulse unhesitatingly indulged.

Youth ministers are in a unique position to confront youth on immediate problems of personal morality, as well as trying to sensitize them to macro- and long-term issues of social justice. This is where we have a golden opportunity to "turn the disobedient to the wisdom of the just." Turning the hearts of the young should begin with the place where their hearts are most vulnerable: the home, first, and then the school. These are places where personal accountability, courage, self-restraint and self-respect, honesty, and generosity are either nurtured or starved to death. These are the places where kids are not only vulnerable but where they are powerful as well—where *they* can hurt and destroy. These are the places where teenagers can most effectively begin to produce the kind of fruit that will testify to their repentance.

Youth ministers, insofar as they are prophets and not pipers, can say what a parent wants to say but is often afraid to say. We can offer warnings that will be heard where voiced parental forebodings are ignored. We can witness to the coming of Christ not simply as a consoling personal encounter, but as an *acutely clarifying event*, first in our own life and then in theirs. Don't be surprised if this opportunity is not immediately embraced. Some kids would rather be swallowed up by a magic mountain than exposed to the light—especially if they are sinning and lack the courage or even the concepts and the language to acknowledge this.

The coming of God in the flesh *to our flesh* is a time when the light gets turned on. When the light gets turned on we can *see everything*, including the things we'd rather not see. When the light gets turned on, other people see things we'd rather not have them see. That's the thing about light: It's ruthless, because it reveals *whatever* is there, roadkill and all.

Fruits of repentance: go home and go to school

Robin suggests that youth ministers have a "golden opportunity" to turn disobedient youth "to the wisdom of the just" by helping them contribute to righteousness in their families and schools. This involves not only confronting youth on issues of personal morality, but sensitizing them to issues of social justice that impinge on their family or their school. The fruit that testifies to adolescent repentance should first be evident in these places, where teenagers are most invested.

To do this would require that youth themselves be in ministry to their families and classmates. In your experience, does youth ministry treat young people as agents of ministry or only as objects of ministry? How might young people learn to be ministers of righteousness (justice) at home and at school? What does that look like in families or schools that are engaged in patently unrighteous behavior?

Clue: prophetic ministry knows when to let go

Many of the people of Israel will he bring back to the Lord their God...to make ready a people prepared for the Lord...

—*Luke 1:16, 17c*

When we have done what we can, when we have told youth the truth about what to expect and what they can do right now—right where they live—to prepare for the coming of God, when we have instructed the disobedient in the wisdom of the just, when we have exhorted them to turn their hearts—with tears of repentance—back to their families and schoolmates; then we will have done much to prepare them to confront what is wrong in our imperfect world, without their being tempted to give up on it in despair or disgust when the changes they want to see happen are slow in coming—or do not come at all.

When we have done all this, and if we have not tried to co-opt immature youth by enlisting them prematurely in our own pet adult crusades, we will have "made ready a [young] people prepared for the Lord." They will be prepared for whatever grand and challenging new missions the real rescuer—the master piper—has destined for this particular generation. When we have done all this, we will have done as much as we can *properly* do.

That you will often pipe in your ministry to those who will not dance is to be expected. Jesus himself complains that he and John both have come to a generation who will not hear, no matter what kind of tune the piper plays (Matthew 11:16-18). That you will sometimes be plagued with faith-threatening doubts about the Lord and the claims you make for him is also to be expected. John himself did not escape these doubts (Matthew 11:2-6); and no doubt, the Lord will answer you as he answered John: "What changes have you seen? What evidence of the Spirit is at work in the lives of those you serve? Wisdom is justified by her deeds" (Matthew 11:4-6, 19). Neither of these problems need defeat you. But there is something else that could.

John the Baptist ministry: go to *him*, go to *him*

Several years ago, while on a trip to Peru, I met a Jesuit priest involved in youth work. He said something very interesting and very important about his work that I have never forgotten and that has provided the seed for what I am saying here. "Youth work," he said, "is very appealing because young people are so responsive, so appreciative, and so easily idolize their leaders." The great temptation of the youth leader, therefore, is to say: "*Come to me, come to me*." What they should be saying, of course is, "*Go to him, go to him.*"

Because the kind of people who tend to be drawn to youth ministry are usually caring, compassionate, and idealistic, they can easily fall into the trap of trying to be pipers instead of prophets—they can be seduced into thinking that they have what these kids really need, and that they are personally responsible for saving them from themselves.

When this happens, what the trade calls *burn out* is not far behind. The distressingly rapid turnover of people in youth ministry has much to

Not here—there
This painting, Christ on the Cross with the Virgin, Saint John the Evangelist, Magdalen, and Saint John the Baptist, by Grünewald (1515), allegedly hung above Karl Barth's desk throughout his career as a theologian. It shows John the Baptist pointing to the crucified Christ, drawing our attention away from the Baptizer and directing us to look toward the cross. Barth was intensely uncomfortable with anything that seemed to suggest that humans played a role in God's saving work. For him, Christians are "witnesses" who point to the cross, where God's salvation takes place.

do with failing to be content simply with *witnessing* to the light. We are not the light. Youth ministers who cast themselves in the role of piper are not entirely unlike those well-intentioned but naive adults who accompanied the brave but deluded child crusaders on their impossible journey over the Alps. And what a burned-out youth minister often leaves in her wake are disappointed, sometimes disillusioned young crusaders.

So hear, all ye who are burned out, the words of the prophet to his disciples: "*Look the Lamb of God, who takes away the sin of the world!*" (John 1:29). Behold, the one who can remove the impossible burden from your weary shoulders by relieving you of your illusions.

"*Look!*" says John the Baptizer, to those who are searching. "*There* is the one you should follow—not me." John admits he didn't know whom the great one coming after him would be. That he now recognizes Jesus as God's own anointed is due to the visible manifestation of the Spirit. The same Spirit with which John is filled descended on the Lord like a dove when John baptized his cousin; and because he has seen this revelation with his own eyes, he can say with authority, "*He* is the one—follow *him*." When Jesus inaugurates his own ministry and quickly gains a following, this news is communicated to John the Baptizer by his disciples: "Rabbi, the one who was with you across the Jordan, to whom you testified, here he is baptizing and everyone is coming to *him*." Instead of feeling threatened by this development, John replies,

> You yourselves can testify that I said, "I am not the Christ, but am sent ahead of him." The bride belongs to the bridegroom. The friend who attends the bridegroom waits and listens for him, and is full of joy when he hears the bridegroom's voice. That joy is mine, and it is now complete. He must become greater; I must become less.
>
> —*John 3:28-30*

He must become greater; I must become less. *He must increase, I must decrease*, is the way another translation puts it. These words should be engraved on the heart of every youth minister. We must never forget that the children of God are meant to walk in the light. If we are not the light, then when the light appears the ones we love must be on their way—on his way.

This, of course, is the hard part of being a youth minister, but also the best part. It is closely related to the understanding that we are not the light but only witness to it. If we are in fact faithful and effective in witnessing to the light, then sooner or later, the young people we work with are going to go after it. And if we are like John, this is when we will feel most rewarded, when our joy will be full.

Repentance: holy road work

Here is the true measure of John's greatness as a spiritual leader. He knows when to let go; he knows that if he is true to his calling, he will indeed diminish in importance to his disciples. They will be increasingly attracted, not by him and his radical witness, but by the radiant beauty—*the light*—to which his radical witness points. He cannot hang on to the wonderful young people who follow him for a while. To be true to his calling he must constantly point beyond himself to something more. Something better. *Someone else.*

How hard this is! It is so good to be needed, so good to be adored—or at least appreciated! But for this, John was born. For this, he leapt in his mother's womb, foreswore strong drink, wore camel's hair, and ate bugs—not to pipe his followers into an earthly paradise, but to help each person prepare a way, a broad and beckoning highway, over which the Lord may pass, into her life, into his heart.

The valleys that must be filled, the mountains that have to be leveled, the rough country that must be smoothed over, are apt metaphors for our own inner terrain. This is where the serious roadwork of repentance has to begin. It is an equally apt description of the unfinished state of adolescence—peaks of exhilaration, valleys of despair, rough and rugged ways of thinking, speaking, acting—a real wilderness of confusion and rebellion.

Into this rough and not-yet-ready place comes the prophet, the new Elijah, looking a little rough and ragged himself, but filled with unshakable faith in the truth of God's promise to deliver—both us and the goods; filled with a healthy fear of God's wrath and an immense hope in God's mercy; filled with a hatred of sin and the injustices that are its inevitable fruits; and filled with boundless compassion for the sinner. *Filled to the brim* because he is inebriated with the Spirit, who blows his own tune, and who never fails to enchant. This new Elijah is not someone who will have to go looking for young listeners. They will come flocking—because they are looking for the light. And they are ready to do something about it.

Theological Framework for Youth Ministry: Grace
Rodger Nishioka

"I'm not sure I need to be in your class," said the student as he walked into the first session of the course on ministry with youth and young adults. "But I needed an elective so I took this one."

"Why do you think you might not need to be here? Aren't you studying to be a pastor?" I asked, somewhat perplexed.

"Well, yes. But I think I have good instincts in doing youth ministry," he said. "And I have a lot of fun with kids, and they seem to like me. I guess it's a no-brainer."

"Explain to me why your instincts work," I asked him.

"What?" he replied.

I said it again. "Explain to me why your instincts work."

He shrugged his shoulders. "I don't know," he said. "They just do."

"That's why you need to be in this class," I replied.

"What do you mean?" he asked.

"Instincts are great," I told him, "especially when they work in your favor. But as a youth director or pastor or church educator, your job is to not only depend on your instincts, but to be able to help others who don't have such instincts develop them. You have to be able to teach others—and to do that, you have to know *why* you make the choices you do. And you have to be able to articulate all of that in ways that young people and adults can understand. Otherwise you end up doing a Lone Ranger-style of ministry that's of little value to anyone. That's why you need to be in this class."

It's a common indictment of youth ministry professionals: too often we appear to be flying by the seat of our pants or just running on instincts without taking the time to articulate why we are doing what we are doing. Too often we are so busy jumping from activity to activity that we appear more concerned with entertaining young people than engaging them in the gospel of Jesus Christ.

That's why this conversation about grace as a theological framework for youth ministry is so important. We owe it to young people, parents, stepparents, church leaders—whomever—to be able to articulate the theological framework in which we carry out the ministry to which we have been called. It's one of the key reasons burn out is so prevalent in youth ministry—because we neglect to construct a theological framework upon which we can build the various programs and events that make up a balanced ministry with youth and their families.

To my thinking, the first theological framework for Christian ministry with youth is *grace*. This framework is primary because it separates Christians from other belief systems. This framework begins not with our measuring up but with a remarkable decision by the God of the universe to reach out to us.

Understanding grace

Calvin and Hobbes is a comic strip about a young boy named Calvin and his stuffed tiger named Hobbes. Hobbes comes to life only in Calvin's experience. The author of the strip named the characters for the Reformed theologian John Calvin and the English philosopher Thomas Hobbes.

Hobbes, a soporific sort of feline, settles in for an afternoon's nap. Calvin, who spots his friend sleeping, comes over and scratches him behind the ears, rubs his belly, pets his back, and so on. Hobbes stretches luxuriously and gives a sigh of bliss. In the last frame Calvin says, "*That* sigh ought to get me out of a few years' purgatory." As we consider grace as a theological framework for youth ministry, we must acknowledge that most young people think of grace as Calvin does. For Calvin, God's saving grace is only possible if we do good things like scratching our pet tiger's back. Thus, God's grace is dependent upon our being good or faithful. In truth, this is not at all what the doctrine of grace is about.

Augustine and the doctrine of grace

The doctrine of grace came to its fullest understanding through the writing and thinking of Augustine, one of the great fathers of the Latin Church. For Augustine, grace was "unmerited divine favor." Grace was not a human idea. Grace came from the mind of God and was accordingly bestowed upon God's people. One of the great theological debates during Augustine's time set the doctrine of grace against the doctrine of human free will. If God is sovereign and decides to offer us God's grace, where does human free will fit? Some theologians argued that while God does offer grace to us, human nature already is predisposed to serve and love God. Others said God has given humankind the power to choose to be saved or not be saved.

Augustine rejected these ideas and cited the fall of Adam as an example that humankind was indeed able to turn away from God. Therefore, salvation was not our own doing or even our own choosing—all salvation came from God. For Augustine, even the so-called *decision* to follow God came at God's invitation, and the ability to believe in God (let alone choose God) was a gift of divine grace to the believer. Augustine's doctrine of grace dominated the church for several centuries. But by the Middle Ages, the late medieval church viewed grace more as a quality flowing from the church's authority rather than as a gift from God. Further, the church had drifted so far from Augustine's doctrine of grace that priests began to teach that the ability to believe at all, and to persevere in the faith, were fruits of human will rather than signs of God's grace. Thus, persons turned to the church to purchase "indulgences" for the forgiveness of sins and the insurance of salvation.

The Reformation called the purchase of indulgences *theological malpractice*, and brought about a revival of Augustinian theology with the key phrase: *sola fides, sola gratia, sola scriptura* (faith alone, grace alone, Scripture alone). Martin Luther, Jan Hus, and

---

Where does grace come from?
Dutch theologian Edward Schillebeeckx points out that the New Testament contains "the beginnings of a theology of grace," rather than a full-blown religious doctrine.[1] Jesus never talks about grace. The concept is altogether absent from the Gospel of Mark and is used only as a greeting in the Gospel of John. Matthew and Luke use the term sparingly, usually without a theological meaning. Perhaps this was because the Greek terms *charis* (something that brings joy, favor, and grateful response) and *eleos* (gracious mercy) originally were associated with the favor of Greek gods, but were not central to either Greek religion or philosophy.

Paul, on the other hand, gave the term *charis* a thorough Christian baptism. The word *charis* occurs about 100 times in the Pauline corpus, 60 of them in the authentic letters of Paul.[2] Paul found the concept of grace useful in many ways that still influence our vocabulary. Grace could mean thanksgiving (we say grace before meals), works of mercy on behalf of the poor (being gracious to others), or a demonstration of God's favor (as in gifts and graces). It wasn't until Augustine used the concept of grace to disarm Pelagius—who incensed Augustine by teaching that good works led to salvation—that a theology of grace began to take shape. Theologically, grace represented a new way God saves us, by divine favor, not by human action.

---

1. Edward Schillebeeckx, *Christ: The Experience of Jesus as Lord*, trans. John Bowden (New York: The Seabury Press, 1980), 84.
2. Schillebeeckx, 84.

John Calvin are important theologians who helped the church reclaim Augustine's doctrine of grace. Their work was continued by modern theologians like Karl Barth, who reminded the church that salvation is God's gift from beginning to end, and it is not dependent upon works or the church or the sacraments.

Scripture and grace

Vehicular grace
Somebody once described the different traditions of grace stemming from Wesleyan, Presbyterian, and Baptist traditions as a car racing to save a man who was about to commit suicide from a bridge. The Wesleyan grace car races up to the man, throws the door open, somebody reaches out a hand, and then waits for the man to get in. The Presbyterian car races up to the man, somebody leaps out, throws the man into the car, buckles him up, locks the door, and speeds off. The Baptist car races up to the man, somebody leaps out and preaches a sermon, and then asks the man if he wants a ride.

The point of these (admittedly distorted) descriptions of grace is that Christians have debated for centuries whether God's gift of grace is something we can refuse. Is God's grace irresistible? Can we lose God's grace once we accept it? What difference do your answers make in your approach to teenagers?

Grace upon grace
John Wesley—the Anglican priest who started the Methodist movement in the mid-1700s, and who described himself as "only a hair's breadth away from Calvin"— believed that regeneration, or recovering the holiness God intends for us, was made possible by three kinds of grace, given to us one on top of the other, "grace upon grace": prevenient, justifying, and sanctifying grace.

Wesley had a different view of grace than Luther or Calvin. He thought conversion was both a conscious awakening to God and a

In the Old Testament, grace is viewed first as divine favor toward humankind. God's grace is shown through the creation, through the redemption and election of the Hebrew people, through the freedom from slavery in Egypt to the discovery of the Promised Land to the establishment of the kingdoms. But grace is also viewed as favor between humans. It is an undeserved gift or favor that is freely and unilaterally given and not coerced. In most human interactions in the Old Testament where the Hebrew word for *grace* is used, grace is characteristically given for a specific occasion from a person of greater authority to a person of lesser authority. In the Old Testament, the Hebrew words that occur most often are *hesed* and *hen* meaning *mercy* and *favor*. In the New Testament, the Greek word most often used is *charis*. *Charis* appears most often in Acts and in Paul's letters.

Throughout the Old Testament, grace comes from God to humankind and from humankind to each other. In the New Testament, grace is exclusively descriptive of God and God's relationship to humankind. For instance, in the New Testament, grace is only seen as an attribute of God or of Jesus Christ. Perhaps the best example of this comes in John 1:14 where Jesus is described as full of "grace and truth." Then the writer quotes John the Baptist in comparing Moses and Jesus: "For the law was given through Moses; grace and truth came through Jesus Christ" (John 1:17). Only God and Jesus Christ, then, exhibit the characteristic of grace. Grace is not a human invention. In the old way, people were saved through the law of Moses by keeping the law. In the new way, people are saved through grace—an undeserved gift in the person of Jesus Christ. Obviously this is a huge shift in the culture and mindset of the Hebrew people. This verse summarizes well the battle between theologians. Can we be saved through keeping the law, or are we saved simply through the grace of God?

The letter to the Church at Ephesus gives a clear answer, reflecting the thinking of the early church that grace is a divine gift, completely undeserved: "For it is by grace you have been saved through faith—and this is not from yourselves, it is the gift of God—not by works, so that no one can boast" (Ephesians 2:8-9). Paul's letter to the Romans notes that sinners are "justified by his grace freely through the redemption that came by Christ Jesus" (Rom. 3:24). And the author of Acts likewise focuses on God's grace as salvation. At the Jerusalem council, Peter clearly states a new order has been established for Christians (even Gentiles!), setting aside the need for Mosaic law: "We believe it is through the grace of our Lord Jesus that we are saved, just as [the Gentiles] are" (Acts 15:11).

lifelong process that actually begins before repentance, through prevenient grace. Wesley thought that even before we turn to God, the Holy Spirit is at work in us, tilling the soul-soil, readying us for reconciliation with God.

When we repent, or wake up to our need for God's forgiveness and justification, God imparts a second kind of grace—justifying grace. Justifying grace pardons sinners and receives us into God's favor. At the moment of justification, God bestows upon us yet a third kind of grace—sanctifying grace. Sanctifying grace is what makes it possible for Christians to resist sin and do good. Sanctifying grace, is what gives us the strength to lead a holy life.

As a result, Wesley insisted that holiness—the state of avoiding all known sin and doing all possible good (which he also called perfection or entire sanctification)—was not only possible in this life, but that every Christian is called to it. Furthermore, Wesley contended that, thanks to sanctifying grace, we have no excuse to live otherwise.

Take a stand: Is conversion a moment or a process? Does regeneration begin before repentance? Does grace make holiness (or "perfection") possible in this life?

For Peter and for all of the new believers, God's grace through Jesus Christ is the focus for salvation. These texts point out the huge transformation taking place among these Jewish Christians. At first the thinking was that people earn salvation by keeping the Jewish laws—which made salvation possible only for Jews. Then, through Jesus Christ, the Messiah, the church began to view salvation as God's freely offered gift; keeping the law no longer would save people. Finally, amazing as it may seem, salvation through the Messiah was no longer limited to Jews. We see Peter, Paul, and others being led by the Holy Spirit to recognize that God's grace is for all people. Again, it is Paul who seems the most concerned that the reader understand that salvation is only by God's grace, and not in any way merited by works. In Romans 4:16, Paul writes, "the promise comes by faith, so that it may be by grace." And again, Paul writes in Galatians 2:21, "I do not set aside the grace of God, for if righteousness could be gained through the law, Christ died for nothing."

Paul goes to great pains to remind the reader that it is God's grace made known to us through Jesus Christ that saves us. We are not saved (or justified) by keeping the law or by various works. If that were the case, then why did Jesus Christ die for us? As if to remind his readers of this key idea, Paul uses *grace* in every salutation and benediction throughout the New Testament. In each case, Paul wants to emphasize that it is God's grace, not Paul's, bestowed upon those to whom Paul is writing.

Characteristics of grace

So then, having looked at the historical and biblical viewpoints of grace, let's summarize by looking at the characteristics of grace.

Grace is undeserved. There is nothing you can do to earn grace. Grace happens when you receive a gift you did not deserve. Nothing is paid back here. Nothing is owed here. You cannot do anything to be worthy enough of the gift. You simply receive it.

Grace is given by God. Grace is given *only* by God. Can human beings be kind and gracious to one another? Of course. But the nature of grace described in the New Testament is made even more extraordinary because it describes a relationship between the divine and humanity. God does not need to save us. God does not have to sacrifice God's only son. But God chooses to do so out of a love and kindness that we cannot grasp or understand.

Grace is unexpected. Clearly this kind of grace is completely unexpected. There is no logic and no reason as to why God, who is the maker of the universe, should love us so incredibly that God would send Jesus to die for us. There is no logic and no reason—no explaining—except to say that God, out of God's amazing love, chose to give us this remarkable gift.

Grace is irretrievable. There is nothing in Scripture to indicate that God ever removes God's gift of grace from us. If this were so, then God would be capricious and fickle. This is not the nature of God. It appears that God's decision to offer grace to

Costly grace

"Cheap grace is the deadly enemy of our church. We are fighting today for costly grace.

"Cheap grace means grace sold on the market like cheap-jack's wares. The sacraments, the forgiveness of sin, and the consolations of religion are thrown away at cut prices. Grace is represented as the church's inexhaustible treasury, from which she showers blessings with generous hands, without asking questions or fixing limits. Grace without price, grace without cost! The essence of grace, we suppose, is that the account has been paid in advance; and, because it has been paid, everything can be had for nothing…

"Cheap grace means the justification of sin without the justification of the sinner…Cheap grace is the preaching of forgiveness without requiring repentance, baptism without church discipline, Communion without confession, absolution without contrition. Cheap grace is grace without discipleship, grace without the Cross, grace without Jesus Christ, living and incarnate.

"Costly grace is the treasure hidden in the field; for the sake of it a man will gladly go and sell all that he has. It is the pearl of great price to buy which the merchant will sell all his goods. It is the kingly rule of Christ, for whose sake a man will pluck out the eye which causes him to stumble, it is the call of Jesus Christ at which the disciple leaves his nets and follows him.

"Costly grace is the gospel which must be sought again and again, the gift which must be asked for, the door at which a man must knock.

"Such grace is costly because it calls us to follow, and it is grace because it calls us to follow Jesus Christ. It is costly because it costs a man his life, and it is grace because it gives a man the only true life. It is costly because it condemns sin, and grace because it justifies the sinner. Above all, it is costly because it cost God the life

humankind through Jesus Christ is the final word to us that defines our relationship to God.

Grace is costly. Dietrich Bonhoeffer, a 20TH-century martyr and theologian, coined the phrase *cheap grace* when he described Christians who saw little cost in Jesus dying for believers.[1] After all, while Jesus was fully human, he was also fully divine. Some people conclude that this must mean that Jesus didn't really suffer or hurt because he knew God would be victorious in the end. As a result, we take sin lightly, since God apparently overcame it with ease. Bonhoeffer warned against such *cheap grace* by reminding us that we have been saved through the very real suffering, death, and resurrection of God's only son. Jesus felt every pain we have ever felt and even more—felt the ultimate pain in being rejected by his father.

Grace begets other gifts. "Each one should use whatever gift he has received to serve others, faithfully administering God's grace in its various forms" (1 Peter 4:10). Peter reminds us that just as we have each received God's grace (*charis*), we have also received gifts for ministry (*charisma* or *charismata*). These gifts seem to be a consequence of God's grace. Our task is to use them to build up the body of Christ. It's important to remember that we use these gifts in grateful response to God's grace, not in order to earn or be worthy of God's grace.

Grace is never finished. John Calvin wrote—

It behooves us to consider the sort of remedy by which divine grace corrects and cures the corruption of nature…God begins his good work in us, therefore, by arousing love and desire and zeal for righteousness in our hearts; or, to speak more correctly, by bending, forming, and directing, our hearts to righteousness. He completes his work, moreover, by confirming us to perseverance.[2]

Calvin reminds us that God's gift of grace does not happen once in our lives and is over forever. Rather, God's gift of grace is a continuing work in us, calling us to be more righteous and even to persevere. This is in keeping with Calvin's emphasis not only on the act of salvation, but even more on the life lived in response to God's grace—a life of righteousness and piety.

The challenge of grace for youth ministry in the 21ST century

While the word *grace* appears to float freely through conversations and song lyrics these days, careful readers and listeners will discover it means different things to different people. Furthermore, few young people seem to believe that they've ever experienced grace at all. Therefore, the great challenge for leaders who choose to take grace seriously as a theological framework for youth ministry is that few young people will be able to relate to it.

---

1. See Dietrich Bonhoeffer, *The Cost of Discipleship* (New York: MacMillan, 1948).

2. John Calvin, *The Institutes of the Christian Religion*, Book II, chapter III, section 6, trans. Ford Lewis Battles (Grand Rapids, Michigan: Eerdmans, 1986).

of His Son…Above all, it is grace because God did not reckon His Son too dear a price to pay for our life, but delivered Him up for us."[1]

In your experience, has youth ministry been more likely to offer youth cheap or costly grace?

---

1. Dietrich Bonhoeffer, *The Cost of Discipleship*, trans. R.H. Fuller (New York: MacMillan Co., 1949), 37-39. Bonhoeffer, who was executed by the Nazis in 1945 for his role in a plot to assassinate Hitler, began his ministry as a youth. As the 28-year-old leader of the German youth delegation to the Universal Christian Council for Life and Work in 1934, he presented eight theses to the convention concerning youth work and the church. Taken together, his theses urged a form of costly discipleship for young people.

Ponderable

Rodger Nishioka claims that young people today are rather skeptical about the idea of grace. Do you agree? Why or why not?

Ponderable

Tony Campolo once told youth leaders in a seminar, "We will not lose this generation of young people because we ask too much of them. We will lose them because we ask too little." Stack this up beside Rodger Nishioka's claim that young people are too performance-oriented. Are these statements contradictory? If so, who is right? If not, how does the church ask more of young people without reducing their importance to how well they perform?

Ponderable

Is there a difference between self-esteem and God's esteem? Is one more important than the other for healthy adolescent development? Is one more important than the other for youth ministry?

In fact, most young people today are rather skeptical about the idea of grace. We minister to a generation that believes they have experienced very little grace. Most postmodern young people are driven by issues of performance.[3] Most have tied their self-esteem, whether they know it or not, to how well they do on tests, report cards, recitals, and games. The link to performance is easy to understand. Many young people today, from very early on, have been rewarded most when they perform. Many have been paid for receiving A's and B's on report cards. Most are part of school systems that use standardized testing as a key determination for graduation from high school. Teachers, coaches, administrators, parents, stepparents, and others in their lives all reinforce this.

If you cannot measure up, many believe it's best to drop out and stop trying. These dropouts find little reason for hope in their lives. No one seems to care about them. Some school administrators and teachers are just as ready to write them off, as they are to suspend or expel them.

Remarkably, many parents and stepparents are convinced that too little is asked of this generation of teenagers. Ironically, while their children and stepchildren are caught up in a performance orientation for their self-esteem, most parents and stepparents think their children know they are unconditionally loved and that more often than not they take advantage of that.

For a healthy self-esteem to be formed, young people need a sense of performing well on various tasks *as well as* a sense of unconditional love in their lives. Young people base their entire self-esteem on how well they perform at tasks when no one in their lives is delivering a consistent message of unconditional love. As youth ministers, we must be careful about how we talk with young people. Unknowingly, we may be contributing to a fragile form of self-esteem based only on performance. When youth ministry leaders only ask, "How did you do on your paper?" we inadvertently reinforce the idea that a young person's value depends only upon how well they perform.

The same message is sent when churches create youth ministry bulletin boards with only clippings from the local paper about who scored highest on their Scholastic Aptitude Tests or who is a National Merit semi-finalist or who won at last week's track meet or basketball game. When winning or achieving is the only way to be noticed by the church, then the not-so-subtle message is that the church also only values you as much as you perform. The decision to focus on grace as a key theological framework means ministry with young people and their families must look radically different from the culture.

Leading from a doctrine of grace

The doctrine of grace forms a key theological basis for youth ministry because it is the basis for our relationship with God and the cause for our discipleship in Jesus Christ. Salvation is God's gift. Our job is to live a life in response to that remarkable gift. Fur-

---

3. See Barbara L. Schneider, *The Ambitious Generation: America's Teenagers, Motivated but Directionless* (New Haven, Connecticut: Yale University Press), 1999.

1. James E. Loder, *The Logic of the Spirit: Human Development in Theological Perspective* (San Francisco: Jossey-Bass, 1998), 174-175.

thermore, the doctrine of grace serves as a key theological basis for youth ministry because adolescents, more than people at any other age, desperately need to know they are loved for who they are without ties to performance or condition. When young people experience unconditional love, they are strengthened to face life's struggles and to endure in the face of pain and suffering. The doctrine of grace does this. The very idea that God loves you not because of how you perform but rather because you are a child of God is a relief.

This is the essence of the gospel message. You are loved! You don't have to do anything or *not* do anything! In a world that seems to measure, compare, and rank you from the moment you are born, the good news is that you belong to God and are loved by God, and there is nothing you can do to remove yourself from God's love. If this message is not the reason for our ministry, then what is? Why else do we gather? Anyone can get together to play games, watch movies, cook in soup kitchens, go on retreats, and even read the Bible. But if we are not gathering to tell each other and to live out the good news—the news that we are loved unconditionally by the God who made the whole universe—then what *is* our message?

Certainly young people need community and care, but more importantly, they need to know that they are loved unconditionally. It is important to their very survival as a human being. With the rising violence in schools in particular and culture as a whole, many researchers have been looking more intensely at how young people emerge from their adolescent years with a relatively healthy self-esteem and positive outlook on life. Scholars call this the *resilience factor*—the degree to which young people can bounce back from disappointment and risk as mature, responsible, and healthy adults.

This *resilience factor* asks that a young person think about the worst possible thing she can imagine herself doing. For some, this means robbing a store; for others it means shooting someone or beating up someone. Then the young person is asked to identify the adults in her life whom she knows she could tell that she did this horrible thing and the adults would still love her. Most studies agree that the minimum number of adults needs to be five. The young person must name at least five adults in her life that would love her unconditionally. These five adults seem to act as the foundation for the young person's life. They seem to form the ground upon which these young people can grow and build their lives. They act as mentors and guarantors for the young person's very survival. What happens to those youth who cannot name at least five adults in their lives? Many either die or are in jail before they reach the age of 21.

This idea of grace, then, is not simply some important theological paradigm. This idea of grace is a matter of life and death. If the church is to take the doctrine of grace seriously, we will have to place more emphasis on loving young people than on how well they perform.

Practices of grace

A ministry with young people that grows out of a foundational doctrine of grace looks very different from the culture that places more value on performance than on unconditional love. These eight practices provide youth ministers with a place to begin:

The practice of acceptance

Acceptance takes hard work. Using grace as a theological framework for youth ministry means first and foremost that everyone practices acceptance. This does not mean that anyone who shows up is automatically a part of the ministry. That's not acceptance. Acceptance is active rather than passive. Practicing acceptance means we invite people to become part of us and we become part of them. It means we resist judging their makeup, hairstyle, clothes, tattoos, and body piercings. It means, at first and last glance, we see a child of God in each human being and we treat them accordingly. Practicing acceptance means we are aware of our own biases, prejudices, and nonverbal cues. Unconditional love means just that—unconditional.

The practice of welcome

Most groups who use grace as a theological framework have developed a process of welcoming people to their group. They do this in such a way that all persons are affirmed for who they are as children of God. Some groups use rituals of welcoming words. One youth group I know has a "welcoming wall," and throughout the year anyone who visits the group is invited to autograph the wall and to add something about themselves. Other groups use their bulletin board space to take digital photos of group members and visitors. They download the photos, print them up on their color printer, and post them for all to see—and then follow up by using the photos as the basis for a prayer chain.

The practice of remembering

Being accepted into a group of people can be especially difficult because newcomers do not know the rituals, expectations, or the history of the group. Not knowing the group can be a barrier to experiencing the grace of unconditional love. In every group of young people, some do better than others at bringing new persons to the group, or reminding the group of its foundational goal to live out the grace God offers to us in Jesus. When someone new enters the group process, pair the newcomer with a veteran who takes time to explain some of the group's norms and history. Each time the group gathers, take time to "re-member"—to join together again by sharing what has happened since you were last together. In this way you continue to build a history together, a history that includes new persons as well as long-time members.

The practice of solidarity

There are times when unconditional love must be demonstrated. In one youth group,

Ponderable
Can you name five adults from your own adolescence who still would have loved you, even if you did something unspeakably wrong?

"Take, eat. Do this in remembrance of me."
—Jesus, at the Last Supper

when a member testified before a school board committee on school violence, the whole youth group made a point to attend the meeting as a sign of pride and solidarity. They sought to show support to their group member on an issue that was important to her. She knew that not everyone in the youth group agreed with her; that wasn't the issue. The issue was solidarity and unconditional love. Because she was part of the group, they were with her. They were indeed proud of her, but they did not attend to approve her performance. They were proud of her because she belonged to them, just as they belonged to her.

The practice of justice

A theology of grace calls us to focus on each person as an individual human being with particular concerns, hopes, and needs. Sometimes leaders, seeking justice, make decisions on the basis of treating everyone in the same way. This, after all, is a common notion of fairness in our culture. Thanks be to God that God does not treat us fairly. Justice and fairness are not the same thing. God looks at each heart to know what we need. Grace is not bound by precedent or the need to view everyone the same way. Grace applies to each person individually as the Holy Spirit works with us in our uniqueness. One common complaint from young people is that adults often fail to see the individuals; they just see a group of "kids." As youth ministers, we must take time to appreciate and consider the needs of each young person as an individual.

The practice of humility

Sometimes our own well-meaning structures can hinder grace as a theological framework in our own programs. Experiencing grace means every person experiences acceptance for who they are. One church had an elaborate system of privileges and chores for the group. The older you were, the more privileges you had. The younger you were, the more chores you had assigned to you. Yet grace ignores human divisions of classes, age levels, or even experience in the church. Jesus Christ showed us the ultimate model of humility by taking on our sins. The radical call for grace is a call for humility of the most privileged to become "as the least" so that everyone shares in the privileges and chores together.

The practice of self-control

Grace as a theological framework for youth ministry does not mean that we accept everything and anything anyone wants to do. An important practice of youth ministry and of each individual is self-control. Doing whatever you want and then demanding that you be accepted no matter what is not grace—it's selfishness and manipulation. Even grace—even unconditional love—involves important elements of self-control. Unconditional love does not allow people to hurt themselves or others, or to be abusive or mean. God accepts us for who we are, sin and all. That is true. But in this divine acceptance—in God's grace shown to us in Jesus—we are transformed. We are given

What if there is no youth group? Rodger assumes the presence of a stable youth group as a context for ministry with young people. Youth ministry does not require a youth group, however. Can you think of an example of ministry with young people that is not based in an ongoing youth group? What do practices of grace look like in this setting?

the grace necessary for self-control. People who seek total acceptance by a group also need to practice self-control.

The practice of witness

It's important that we remember that grace is a gift from God—a fact true for everyone in the church, young and old alike. The ability for ministry to accept young people with unconditional love is a gift from God and it is God who is to be thanked and praised; not just the participants in the group. This is an important witness. Throughout the Old and New Testaments, the Hebrew people are reminded that God is the giver of community and God alone is the giver of grace; we as Christian people are to bear witness to God's power in our lives. We are not witnessing about ourselves. We are witnessing about God.

The challenge for youth leaders

In my mind, a ministry predicated on divine grace brings with it at least two particular challenges for youth leaders. First, if we truly believe that salvation is offered as a gift from God, then we must also believe that it is God who saves, not us. Further, if we believe that grace is the primary theological paradigm for our work, then we must temper the temptation to judge. All too often I hear youth ministry leaders talking as if they are the ones who "saved" this person or that person. To my mind, such talk is idolatry. No one can save but God. Surely we can be the instruments—the empty vessels—for God to use, but the subject in the story of salvation is always God. We are not the ones who save. We are the ones who are saved by God.

I am often troubled by how I hear youth ministry leaders talk about others and especially their young people. Judgment comes easily and quickly. This person is bound for trouble, or that person is a bad kid, or she is so selfish and he is such a manipulator. If grace is our theological framework, we must think differently and act differently toward those with whom we minister. If grace is our theological framework, then every interaction with our young people is new and fresh. We are not called to be naive. But nor are we called for our preconceived judgments that cloud our vision of God's grace. The second challenge that a doctrine of grace presents youth ministers is the fact that many of us are rescuers by nature. We want to make "everything right." If something is wrong between young people, we'll get in there and try to make it better. We'll drop whatever we're doing to step in. If grace is our theological framework for youth ministry, we have to learn at times not to step in but to step aside. If we are honest with ourselves, many of us trust ourselves more than we trust God.

Several years ago I received a phone call from a pastor. She was distraught over one of her brightest and best young people. The young woman had fallen in love with a young man six years older. They were sexually active, getting married in a month, and moving across the country. She had dropped out of the youth group entirely and was

Ponderable
Does youth ministry predicated on the doctrine of grace allow youth to fail? Why or why not?

going to leave high school early. She fought with her parents until they threw her out of the house.

The pastor and I talked about keeping communication lines open. We talked about words to use and words to avoid. Then she said something that chilled me. She said: "I'm just so worried. I'm afraid we're going to lose her forever."

"Who is 'we'?" I asked.

"You know, we...the church...God....we're going to lose her," said the pastor, exasperated.

"But she belongs to God," I said. "You told me that years ago she received Christ as her Lord and Savior."

"I know," said the pastor. "But I'm so afraid."

"I am, too," I confessed. "I'm afraid because I worry she's making some bad decisions that will affect the rest of her life. But one thing I am not afraid of: she is not going to be lost to God. God will never let her go. God's grace knows no boundaries—no limits. There will come a time when she will need God desperately and God will be there."

"I hope you're right," said the pastor.

We prayed together that day, and I sent a follow-up note of encouragement. It is hard for us to see beyond young people's immediate decisions, but if grace truly is the theological framework for youth ministry, then we must trust that the God of grace will sustain us—all of us, youth and youth leader alike. We must trust and live with the conviction that God cares for all and that no one can be lost to God. We must trust more in God than we do in ourselves.

Theological Framework for Youth Ministry: Redemption
Darrell W. Johnson

16

Chapter

Every human being wears a set of glasses, regardless of his vision test score. These glasses were not given to us by the ophthalmologist, but by our parents and grandparents, schoolteachers, childhood experiences—by the culture in which we were raised. No one sat down with us and deliberately, intentionally, lens by lens, shaped the glasses we wear. They became ours as we grew up. They continue to be shaped and will change as we change.

This set of glasses is also known as our *worldview, frame of reference, mind-set,* or *vision of reality.* In his helpful little book, *Fully Human, Fully Alive: A New Life Through a New Vision,* Father John Powell makes this observation: "It has been generally agreed upon that true and full living is based on three components like the legs of a tripod: intra-personal dynamics, inter-personal relationships, and a frame of reference." Powell goes on to argue that our set of glasses controls the quality of our participation in a truly human life:

> Through the eyes of our minds, you and I look out at reality...However we see things differently...Both of our visions are limited and inadequate, but not to the same extent. We have both misinterpreted and distorted reality, but in different ways. We have each seen something of the available truth and beauty to which the other has been blind. The main point is that it is the dimensions and clarity of this vision that determine the dimensions of our worlds, and the quality of our lives. To the extent that we are blind or have distorted reality, our lives and our happiness have been diminished. Consequently, if we are to change—to grow— there must first be a change in this basic vision, or perception of reality.[1]

Our worldview serves as the lens through which we interpret reality. Historian and biblical scholar N. T. Wright argues that every worldview speaks to at least five questions:

• Who are we?

• Where are we?

• What's wrong?

• What's the solution?

• What time is it? (Where are we in the flow of God's saving work in the world?)[2]

Theological opthamology: constructing a Christian worldview
According to N. T. Wright and James Sire, our worldviews are made up of those assumptions that govern our responses to certain perennial questions about life.

Answer either Wright's or Sire's five questions in the main text, then find someone to share your answers with. Reflect back to each other the kind of worldview these answers suggest. Are you surprised by your responses? Do they contradict each other, seem isolated from one another, flow one from the other?

---

1. John Joseph Powell, *Fully Human, Fully Alive: A New Life Through a New Vision* (Niles, Illinois: Argus Communications, 1976), 3.

2. N. T. Wright, *Jesus and the Victory of God* (Minneapolis, Minnesota: Fortress Press, 1996), 138.

James Sire, editor of InterVarsity Press, frames his understanding of worldviews with a similar set of questions. Sire defines *worldview* as the set of conscious or unconscious assumptions we hold about reality that allow us to answer:

- What is prime reality?
- What or who is a human being?
- What is the basis for morality?
- What happens to human beings at death?
- What is the meaning of history?[3]

As a disciple of Jesus Christ and as a youth worker, you also wear a set of glasses. As you interact with young people, you look at them through a particular frame of reference. Your approach to each young person depends upon the way you answer questions like the ones posed by Wright and Sire. You may not always be able to articulate the answers, but you have them. And you automatically live them. I could follow you around for a week or so, watching you interact, listening to the way you speak, hearing you pray, and then tell you your answers.

Viewing ministry through the lens of redemption

If I were to suggest that Christian youth workers should approach ministry through the lens, or worldview, of *redemption*, just what might that mean? Specifically, what would it mean for young people if we were to approach ministry through a *biblical* understanding of redemption?

Right away we have a challenge—there is no single biblical view of redemption. Right away we are dealing with a multi-dimensional reality—the challenge of a youth worker is to grow in the biblical understandings of redemption so that we are approaching young people *wholly* redemptively. Wearing "redemption glasses," we must begin by asking, What do we see? How do those glasses affect the way we minister?

The bad news: there's a worldwide web, and it's not the Internet

A worldview based on a Christian understanding of redemption knows that something is wrong. And it's worse than we thought. This *wrong* is not just a problem of poor self-image. It is not just a problem of profound relational estrangement. It is not just a problem of cultural upheaval and displacement. Every person we meet is caught in a terrible web. We're all caught in it. The web is huge and ubiquitous. And we cannot free ourselves from its presence and captivity. The web is made up of many strands, many fibers, many threads. In truth, they are more than strands. They are chains. They are what the Bible identifies as *sin, evil, the lie, the curse, death*, and *vanity*. And every human being on this planet is caught in the complexity of this horrible web.

Is sin original?
Original sin is the Christian doctrine that maintains two facts about humans' relationship to God: (1) sin is inevitable; and (2) every person is responsible for his or her sinfulness. Augustine formulated the classical explanation of original sin in terms of Psalm 51:5: "I was brought forth in iniquity, and in sin did my mother conceive me." Augustine concluded that human rebellion against God, or sinfulness, therefore must be biologically inherited, and concluded that sex must be the root of sin.

Many contemporary theologians blame Augustine's doctrine of original sin for the church's historically conservative stances on sexual intercourse and for much of the church's sexism throughout the centuries.

What do you think? Is Augustine's biological explanation of original sin convincing? If not, how would you explain the concepts this doctrine is designed to uphold? Does original sin matter Christian faith? Is there an inherent relationship between sin and sexuality?

The matrix of sin
If you haven't already seen it, rent *The Matrix* after you read this chapter. How does Hollywood's conception of *The Matrix* compare with Darrell Johnson's description of the interrelationship of sin, evil, the lie, the curse, death, and vanity? How does a Christian lens change the way you watch this movie? How is the Christian understanding of redemption like—and unlike—the resolution to the matrix portrayed by the movie?

---

3. James W. Sire, *The Universe Next Door: A Basic World View Catalog* (Downer's Grove, Illinois: InterVarsity Press, 1988), 17.

The bad news about sin

Somewhere along the way in our ministry, we have to use the S word. Or at least face and deal with the S reality. The Bible has three words for the reality: *sin, transgression,* and *iniquity.* They are often used together. Read Psalm 51, for example. *Sin* means "missing the mark." The Hebrew word *hatta't* is used for an archer who shoots the arrow at the target and misses the bull's-eye. So the apostle Paul says, "For all have sinned and fall short of the glory of God" (Romans 3:23). *Transgression* goes deeper. The word refers to the deliberate crossing of a line. We come across a sign that says, No Trespassing, and we keep going. The word refers to the deeply rooted rebellion in our souls. *Iniquity* goes even deeper. The word refers to "that thing in us" that makes us want to rebel—that causes us to consistently miss the mark. *Iniquity* could be translated as "perverted twistedness." And it has a hold on every one of us.

While ministering in Beijing, China, I had the privilege of meeting with a young Chinese psychology student. He was not yet a Christian, he said, but was searching, spending a lot of time reading the Bible. He asked me about sin. "What is this *sin?*" he asked. I told him about the three different words. He understood *missing the mark.* He understood *transgression.* When I told him about *iniquity,* he exclaimed, "Oh, that is what's wrong with China, and why we need a Savior!" Indeed.

The bad news about evil

By *evil* I am meaning what the New Testament means: more than human meanness and madness. *Evil* refers to the *evil one*—that personal embodiment of evil at work in the world. Evil that opposes God and seeks to destroy everything God has made. The whole idea gets distorted into ghosts and goblins. And one of the tasks of ministry is to help undistort things. But evil is real. And evil has a hold on us. When the first human beings declared independence from God (Genesis 3), they did not thereby become free. They became captives of forces opposed to the Creator. It's like smoking: the nicotine gets us. No one intends to become a slave to nicotine. No one starts out by saying, "Hey, I think I'll get hooked." But it happens. Nor did humanity set out to become enslaved to evil. It happened as we chose to live independently from God. "The whole world is under the control of the evil one," says the apostle John (1 John 5:19).

The bad news about the lie

Sin and evil keep humans from thinking clearly. The apostle Paul tells the Romans that once we left the living God out of the equation—out of the center of life—our "thinking became futile" and our "foolish hearts were darkened" (Romans 1:21). In Ephesians, Paul speaks of "the futility of their thinking." They are "darkened in their understanding" (Ephesians 4:17-18). Since we do not have an accurate center (the living God), the circumference of our lives is inevitably distorted. We buy the lie that we are our own masters; that our destiny is in our own hands; and that we must take charge of our lives. And we buy into the lie that this is good.

or accurate, then we live a lie.

Christians agree that Jesus is important, but is he the center of our lives? If not, where do you think your outer circumference—your public life and ministry—may be buckling a little? Can you think of an example when the outer circumference of a youth leader's life revealed an inner life that was off center? What happened? How do you stay centered in Jesus Christ as you prepare for ministry with young people?

Ponderable
Darrell contends that Generation X does not soft-pedal death, as previous generations have. Is that true from your experience? How does the reality of death affect Generation X's spirituality? Does death play a role in the spirituality of millennial youth as well?

The bad news about the curse

Terrible word. Terrible reality. To curse means to condemn—to consign them to death, to ban them from the presence of God. The world simply does not work the way God created it to work. Worse than that, our disobedience and transgressions have horrible consequences. The apostle Paul speaks of the most horrible curse of all: "the curse of the law." Working with Deuteronomy 27:26, Paul says, "All who rely on observing the law are under a curse, for it is written: 'Cursed is everyone who does not continue to do everything written in the Book of the Law'" (Galatians 3:10). Paul is referring to the curses that Moses said would come with breaking the law (see Deuteronomy 27 and 28). Breaking the law, Moses warned, would unravel everything, and he was right. Nature does not work as it was designed to work, human bodies no longer work as they were designed to work, and relationships come apart. Since the law of God describes the integrated way God intended us to live with creation, disobedience—by definition—leads to the dis-integration of human life. The curse involves confusion, alienation, emptiness, and finally death.

The bad news about death

Death is both physical and spiritual. The whole planet lives under the cloud of death. Death is all around us. No technology can stop it. The so-called Generation X does not play the games previous generations played denying the reality of death. They do not try to soft-peddle it, as previous generations have, by using euphemisms like *pass away* or *expire*. Death. Everywhere.

The bad news about vanity

Because of the other strands of the web, the whole leads to the experience of vanity. Nothing lasts. Nothing heals the aching in the soul. We seem to just keep going around and around. So we grab for anything that promises pleasure. The void is so painful, we choose to fill it with anything that offers hope of relief.

Every young person we serve is caught in the web, just as we are. One of the tasks of youth ministry is to help young people grasp this fact. It involves a lot of relational work, getting close enough to help them put on a new set of glasses, to see things as they really are. Every kid, every parent, every teacher and counselor, every rock star and super athlete and political leader is caught in the web.

The good news: the gospel is more than good advice

Gospel means "good news," not "good advice." Besides, what good advice is there for people hopelessly entangled in the web with no way out? What we need is Good News, the gospel of redemption. And that we have! Jesus Christ comes to dismantle the web and set us free.

Jesus speaks of giving his life as "a ransom for many" (Mark 10:45). Paul speaks of "the redemption that came by Christ Jesus" (Romans 3:24). Although we tend to

Premodern or postmodern?
The word *redemption* originally had a secular ring to it. Darrell points out that the early church used the term for this reason. Early Christians wanted people to associate God's activity in Jesus Christ with drama in real life: freeing slaves, releasing prisoners, paying off somebody's debts. In a world where Christians were in the minority and few people knew about God's plan of salvation, claiming that God was in the redemption business was like saying that God is in the business of paying off student loans, or helping undocumented immigrants shake the INS.

As Christianity spread, redemption began to be associated with the church more than with the marketplace. But today the church is a minority institution once more. Fewer and fewer people in postmodern society know about God's plan of salvation.

How do postmodern young people hear the word redemption? Does it have a secular sound to it, as it did to premodern people; or does it sound churchy, as it did to modern people? What meanings does redemption have for youth today? (Think of the prize counter at Chuck E. Cheese, video games, guns-for-money exchange programs, and so on.) Is the word still a good one to describe God's work in the death and resurrection of Jesus?

Ponderable
Do young people you know identify a purpose for Christian redemption? How would they answer the question, "Redemption from what?"

use the word *redemption* as a synonym for *salvation*, the New Testament uses it of a particular kind of salvation. Australian theologian Leon Morris points out that, while people in our century hear the word *redemption* and immediately think in religious terms, people of the first century heard it and "immediately thought in non-religious terms. Indeed, that was the reason the word came to be used by the early Christians. People in general knew quite well what 'redemption' was. Therefore, Christians found it a convenient term to use."[4]

The word for redemption, *lutroo*, basically means, "to loose." In particular, *to redeem* means to loose people from captivity of one sort or another, and to do so by paying a price. The word *redemption* comes from the slave market, the prisoner-of-war camp, or the savings and loan office. When first-century people heard the word, they immediately thought of slaves being purchased from their owners and then set free, of prisoners-of-war being purchased and then released, or of debts being paid and the debtors unchained. If Jesus Christ comes to redeem us, then he comes to set us free from whatever binds us—to release us from whatever prevents us from being the person God created us to be.

Jesus Christ enters the web with us. And then he starts messing with the strands and threads. More specifically, he does something to the strands and threads. He draws them all to himself and then breaks them. As a result, he opens the possibility of a different way of life—a life free of the web, unconstrained by sin, evil, the lie, the curse, death, and vanity. Before the death and resurrection of Jesus, these phenomena were woven together one way. After the death and resurrection of Jesus, sin, evil, the lie, curse, death, and vanity, are unraveled and re-woven in another way.

The good news about sin

Something has happened to sin. As a result of the death and resurrection of Jesus Christ, sin remains present in human life but it works differently. Notice the way the apostle Paul speaks of sin in Romans 6, not as specific actions or attitudes, but as an independent power or force. Paul almost gives sin a *personality*, which suggests to me that we get at the good news of Romans 6 by at least setting it in print this way: SIN

Paul tells the Roman church: "Even so consider yourselves to be dead to sin, but alive to God in Christ Jesus" (Romans 6:11 NASB). That *good advice* about SIN is grounded in *good news* about SIN. At the cross and through the empty tomb, Jesus Christ has done something *to* SIN; not just *about* SIN, but *to* SIN. And what Jesus does alters the very structure of reality in the direction of setting captives free!

The apostle Paul's declaration and exhortation in Romans 6 emerges out of his preaching of the gospel in Romans 1-5. That preaching culminates in one of the most exhilarating verses of the Bible: "Where sin increased, grace abounded all the more" (Romans 5:20 NASB). Here the word *abounded* literally means "super-abounded." Where sin increased—where human unbelief and rebellion and rejection of God increased—the grace of God increased faster, super-abounded. As Dietrich Bonhoeffer put it, in

4. Leon Morris, *The Apostolic Preaching of the Cross* (Grand Rapids, Michigan: Eerdmans, 1955), 11.

Ponderable
What is at stake in Darrell's decision to talk about post-resurrection SIN (instead of sin)? Does your reaction to reading it this way suggest anything about the way SIN works in our lives?

Jesus, "God's grace outruns the avalanche" of SIN.[5]

Now everywhere the apostle Paul preached that scandalously good, good news, a question arose. Paul quotes it at the beginning of Romans 6: "Are we to continue to sin so that grace might increase?" (Romans 6:1 NASB). Good question. If God's grace outruns SIN, why bother trying to stop sinning? If the living God delights to shower mercy and grace on sinners (which God does!), why not give God even *more* opportunity for delight by continuing to sin? If I have been justified freely by the hugely merciful grace of God; if, when I sin again and again, God will forgive me again and again; if the more I sin the more God gets to manifest his amazing and praiseworthy grace by forgiving me; why not continue in SIN that grace may abound?

It is not just a theoretical question. People in Paul's day actually reasoned this way and acted on it. God's free justification of sinners was used to justify sinning freely, and people since Paul's day have also reasoned this way and acted upon it. Philip Yancey, in his book, *What's So Amazing About Grace?,* tells of a group of devout martyrs in the third century who devoted their last nights in prison to drunkenness, revelry, and promiscuity. And he tells of an extremist group in England known as the Ranters who developed a doctrine of the "holiness of sin" and acted on it by sinning as wildly as possible to experience more grace.[6] Why not sin again that grace might super-abound? "Are we to continue in sin that grace may increase?" (Romans 6:1 NASB).

Paul's answer is a thunderous "*No!* May it never be!" Paul exclaims—which is his way of saying, "Are you out of your mind?" And the reason for his *no* is the gospel, the good news: "How shall we who died to sin still live in it?" (Romans 6:2 NASB). The good news is that SIN is not the same as it was before Jesus' death and resurrection. SIN lacks the relationship with us it once had. An even better way to put it might be to say, SIN does not have the kind of claim on us it once had.

The good news about evil

Jesus Christ has overcome evil in a surprising way: by walking into the face of evil and letting it have its way with him. At the cross, Jesus let evil unleash its full force on him. And thus he overcame it—at the cross. Not in the empty tomb? No, Paul reminds us: at the cross. "And having disarmed the powers and authorities, he made a public spectacle of them, triumphing over them by the cross" (Colossians 2:15). Evil is still evil, but now it has been mastered, overcome. We can, therefore, say to evil, "You have no authority over Jesus. You must submit to him. And because I am his, you have no final authority over me either."

The good news about the lie and the curse

Jesus Christ exposes the lie by virtue of who he is. He walks into our situation, and simply by being there, sheds light on it: he reveals the truth. He *is* the truth. He *is* the light. He speaks, and in speaking sets us free from the debilitating power of deceit. Likewise, Jesus Christ has "redeemed us from the curse" (Galatians 3:13), released us from our condemnation to death and our banishment from God's presence. How? By

---

5. Dietrich Bonhoeffer, *Creation and Fall* (New York: The MacMillan Company, 1959), 85.

6. Philip Yancey, *What's So Amazing About Grace?* (Grand Rapids, Michigan: Zondervan, 1997), 185–186.

taking the curse upon himself. We will never experience "the curse of the law" when we break the law. Consequences, yes. Curse, no. The curse intended for us has been borne by him. God's promise is clear: "There is now no condemnation for those who are in Christ Jesus" (Romans 8:1).

The good news about death

Jesus Christ defeats death at the cross. Not through the empty tomb? Yes—but first, at the cross. Matthew tells us that in the moment Jesus died, tombs were opened (Matthew 27:52). What? Shouldn't that have happened when Jesus rose from the dead? No, the Scripture writers describe his death as the defeat of death. As the writer of Hebrews puts it, Jesus Christ partook of our flesh and blood, "that by his death he might destroy him who holds the power of death—that is, the devil—and free those who all their lives were held in slavery by the fear of death" (Hebrews 2:14-15). As an older pastor friend of mine, Peter Joshua, used to say to me when I first started doing youth ministry, "When death stung Jesus Christ, it stung itself to death." Death is still around. But it no longer has the last word. It only has the second-to-the-last word.

We can, therefore, look in the face of death, and say: "You have no grip on Jesus. And because I am his, you have no final grip on me. I am not going to be intimidated by you."

The good news about vanity

Jesus Christ comes to give us life: "I have come that they may have life and have it to the full" (John 10:10). Having freed us from the binding power of sin—from the curse, from the lie, from the ultimate power of death—he frees us for life that is no longer empty, but full. Jesus Christ "gave himself for our sins to rescue us from the present evil age" (Galatians 1:4). This is what Paul meant when he wrote that God has "rescued us from the dominion of darkness and brought us into the kingdom of the Son he loves" (Colossians 1:13).

Key questions for youth workers with good news in mind

"How shall we who died to sin still live in it?" (Romans 6:2 NASB). Died to sin? *I* died to sin? What gives? If youth ministry is to take redemption seriously, then we must structure ministry in such a way as to help young people ask and answer three questions:

When did I die to SIN?

Ponderable
How important is baptism to youth ministry? Can you be a Christian without being baptized? Will your ministry focus more on baptized or unbaptized young people—and what difference does that make in how you do ministry?

Paul's answer is that you died to sin when you were baptized into Christ Jesus (Romans 6:3). Note the preposition *into*: through baptism we were immersed into a *person*, into the Creator, Redeemer, and Re-creator. Through baptism we were transferred from the old humanity that was headed by the first Adam—into the new humanity that is headed by the last Adam, Jesus Christ.

We need to make two qualifications. First we need to remember that for Paul, baptism is not a magical rite that automatically actualizes the reality it symbolizes (see 1 Corinthians 10, for example). The issue for Paul is not the *rite* but the *reality* the rite portrays—and that reality is placing our lives *into Christ*. The decision to place my life into Christ is what baptism is all about. Secondly, we need to remember the setting in which Paul wrote. In his day, baptism ordinarily took place at the time a person came to faith. On the Day of Pentecost, 3,000 people came to know Jesus as Savior and were immediately baptized (Acts 2:41; Acts 8:34–38). Today, even among the youth you work with, baptism might occur long before the decision of faith or sometime after coming to faith. If Paul were writing to us today, he would answer the question *When did I die to SIN?*, by saying, "When you placed your life into Jesus Christ, an act symbolized and sealed by your baptism."

How did I die to SIN?

Did baptism bring about this death? Paul saw baptism, or making a decision to fully trust Christ, as more than an event involving water. It is an immersion into *Christ himself*. Other religions and philosophies call their members to follow their great leader or to imitate their leader. Christians are called to follow Jesus and to imitate Jesus, but we are also called to go *beyond* following and imitating, to participating in union *with* Jesus. We not only walk behind him and live under him; we live with him and in him (and he in us)!

Now, here is the powerful point Paul is making in Romans 6: our participation and union with Christ is total. We participate in and are united with the totality of Jesus' life and work. Through baptism we are united with him in his death, and through baptism we are united with him in his resurrection. Through baptism we are also united with Christ in Christ's present existence in a life lived to God (Romans 6:10). How, then, do I die to SIN? By being baptized *into Christ Jesus*; which means being *unified* with him in his death. And because Jesus' death was a death to SIN, those who are unified with Jesus Christ die to SIN also.

Paul drives home the objectivity of this death with two bold words. In Romans 6:6 he says, "our old self was *crucified* with him" (italics added). And in Romans 6:4 he says, "We were therefore *buried* with him" (italics added). Crucified and buried. As New Testament scholar Charles Cranfield notes, the word *buried* makes the point most boldly: "Burial is the seal set to the fact of death—it is when a man's relatives and friends leave his body in the grave and return home without him that the fact he no longer shared their life is exposed with inescapable conclusiveness."[7] Baptism, therefore, is a kind of funeral. It is also a type of resurrection. "Died with Christ, raised with Christ." We're talking good news, not just good advice!

What Paul means is that since we have been crucified and buried with Christ, it is flat out inconsistent to continue to live in SIN. But not impossible; Paul makes clear

---

7. Charles Cranfield, *Romans,* vol. 1 (Edinburgh: T. & T. Clark Limited, 1979), 304.

Funerals and resurrections
"I baptize you in the name of the Father, and of the Son, and of the Holy Spirit. Amen."

The rite of baptism—whether you sprinkle, douse, or dunk—literally symbolizes death (going under water) and resurrection (coming up for air). In this way we do more than believe in Jesus' death and resurrection; in baptism we actually participate in it. Some preachers even like to hold baptismal candidates' heads under water, to make the experience of dying and rising to life a little more vivid!

The rite ends with laying on hands to denote that the gift of the Holy Spirit has been conferred, and that this candidate is now ready to be brought into a life of discipleship, which is to say, a life of Christian ministry. Membership in the body of Christ is not like being a member of the band or the drama club or the tennis team, where you play your specified part only when the group gets together. Membership in the body of Christ means ministry—which involves playing our part in God's plan of salvation wherever we are, when we gather with the body of believers and, especially, when we don't.

You take ministry to youth very seriously, or you wouldn't be reading this book. How seriously do you take the ministry of youth, to which they are called on account of their baptism? Does your congregation consider baptism an invitation to church membership or to ministry?

that, as long as we are in this world, we will struggle with the tension between our death and resurrection in Jesus Christ, and our human sinfulness: "The good that I wish, I do not do; but I practice the very evil that I do not wish" (Romans 7:19 NASB). Paul's point is not that it is now impossible for me to SIN; his point is that—in union with Jesus' death and resurrection—it is now *logically* and *morally* incongruous to SIN.

In what sense did I die to SIN?

This is the critical question. Because Paul uses the phrase *died to sin* three times (twice in reference to believers, and once in reference to Christ), the key to knowing in what sense you died to sin is to understand the sense in which Christ died to SIN. Christ died to SIN because he paid the penalty for SIN. The penalty for SIN is death (Romans 6:23). And here is Paul's major message, the Good News: since the penalty or debt has been paid, SIN no longer has any claim on Christ, or on anyone in Christ. Let's look at it this way: say you owe Sears $2,000 for new carpeting. As long as you owe the $2,000, you are alive to Sears—you are obligated to Sears. But once the debt is paid, Sears has no more claim on you. You are dead to Sears. Say I owe the IRS $30,000. As long as I owe that debt, I am alive to the IRS—I am their slave, so to speak. Imagine Jesus coming and paying the $30,000. Because the debt is now paid, the IRS has no more claim on me. I am dead to the IRS.

That is the good news! The debt of SIN has been paid. Jesus Christ paid it on the cross. He is, therefore, dead to SIN because SIN has no claim on him; and in union with Christ we are dead to SIN too—SIN has no more claim on us either. That does not make us insensitive to SIN. What Paul is declaring is that we no longer *have* to respond to SIN's appeal, for we are no longer *beholden* to SIN. If the debt has been paid by Christ, then in his name, SIN has to let us go! Through the death of Jesus, SIN's hold on the world has been broken—SIN has been deprived of its ultimate power. We no longer have to respond to SIN. We do respond, and there is grace when we do. But the good news is we do not have to. We are no longer SIN's slaves.

Here's the practical consequence for ministry: we must teach students how to look SIN in the face and say, "I do not have to give in to you." SIN says to me, "Oh yes you do...and besides you know you *want* to give in to me." To which we can now say, "You are right. I do want to give in to you, but you are also wrong; you are lying to me. I do not have to. Jesus Christ is dead to you, and I have been baptized into him. I am united to him in his death and his resurrection and his present existence. You have no claim on him. And because I am his, you have no claim on me either. Therefore, SIN, I am going to present the members of my body to him and not to you. I present my hands to him and not to you. I present my feet to him and not to you. I present my eyes to him and not to you. I present my ears to him and not to you. I present my mouth to him and not to you. I present my brain to him and not to you. I present my needs and drives and longings and glands to Christ and not to you."

Youth ministry: a redemption center

Ponderable

"When did I die to SIN? How did I die to SIN? In what sense did I die to SIN?"

What difference do these questions make for youth ministry? What might ministry look like that focuses on these questions with young people? Did youth ministry ever ask you these questions?

Ponderable

Is ministry that uses redemption as its theological starting point easier with churched kids or with unchurched kids?

Therefore, when you as a youth worker encounter any young person, you know that (a) she is, by virtue of being human in a broken world, caught in the web; but (b) by virtue of the redeeming work of Jesus Christ, the web has been rearranged in the direction of freedom; and (c) any young person who then enters into relationship with Jesus Christ, begins the journey into greater and greater freedom.

Our task in ministry, therefore, is to walk with young people in a way that helps them walk in the direction of freedom because of Jesus Christ. We do this as those who are also learning what it means to be redeemed. We do it by being honest about where we are in the process, by being vulnerable, by accepting them where they are, by declaring the Good News again and again, and by trusting Jesus Christ to do his redeeming work—to untangle the strands that still hold us back.

What Jesus said of himself at the beginning of his public ministry, he says of youth workers: the Spirit of the Lord is upon you "to proclaim freedom for the prisoners" (Luke 4:18).

Theological Framework for Youth Ministry: Hope
Evelyn Parker

> Despair inheres in the [painful] conclusion...that our yearnings—for ourselves or our wider communities—will never be fulfilled.
> —*Mary L. Bringle,* Despair: Sickness or Sin?[1]

Case study: Nikki

> God! Please hurry to my rescue!
> God, come quickly to my side!...
>   I've lost it. I'm wasted.
> God-quickly, quickly!
>   Quick to my side, quick to my rescue!
>   God, don't lose a minute.
>
> —From Psalm 70 *(The Message)*

Yearning for the presence of a loving parent, 14-year-old Nikki allowed a 25-year-old man to crawl through her bedroom window at night for days, even months. On one occasion her brothers caught the man, who was one of their friends, and told their mother who worked from midnight to eight in the morning. Nikki made excuses about her "boyfriend," saying that they did not engage in sexual intercourse, but only talked. Months later the baby growing inside her revealed the truth. In some ways the conception was the result of statutory rape—an adult male with a 14-year-old girl. In other ways the sequence of events indicates Nikki's conclusion that love—the kind that listens and comforts—was futile, and that moving beyond poverty was only a fantasy.

Case study: Bruce

> "I don't know much about how to deal with my own evil, but I have learned to recognize that sometimes all I can do is pray."
> —Kathleen Norris,
> *Amazing Grace* (New York: Riverhead Books, 1998), 179.

Yearning for the companionship of his best friend, grief-stricken Bruce Corwin from Plano, Texas, committed suicide.[2] During the summer that Bruce and his parents moved to Plano from Rochester, Michigan, he spent his time alone watching television and playing on the family computer. When school started that fall at Plano Senior High, he became friends with Bill Ramsey. Everyone referred to them as The Two B's because the inseparable duo brought energy to every party and restaurant they walked into. It was on the night of February 19, 1983, that The Two B's met another friend, Chris Thornsberry, at the Chuck E. Cheese—a pizza parlor complete with animated Elvis and video games. While in the parking lot Bruce and Chris agreed to drag race, Bruce in his Skylark and Chris in his Corvette. Bill would wave the flag, signaling the start of the race. However, the race scarcely started when Chris's Corvette veered and hit Bill, who was dead by 5:30 the next morning at the Plano Emergency Center. After the accident Bruce kept to himself, telling schoolmates that he would see Bill again. The day after Bill's funeral, Bruce's mother, Lucy, surprisingly found his car in the garage. Parking it there was not Bruce's usual pattern.

His mother recalled:

---

1. Mary Bringle, *Despair: Sickness or Sin? Hopelessness and Healing in Christian Life* (Nashville: Abingdon, 1990), 20.

2. David Gelman, "Teen-age Suicide in the Sun Belt," *Newsweek* 102 (August, 1983), 70-73.

His feet were sticking out the window and I remember thinking, "Oh,
Bruce is so tired he fell asleep in the back seat." But the motor was on,
there was a smell of gas and in the car's cassette player was a Pink Floyd
tape, spun down through its last song, "Goodbye Cruel World." [I] stood
in the driveway screaming, "My son is dead, my son is dead…"[3]

Nikki and Bruce's stories are true. Only their names and some of the events have been
altered for confidentiality. Nikki's story is an example of a hopeless young adolescent
girl, living in poverty, repeatedly making choices about her life that cause her to sink
deeper into poverty and deeper into despair. Bruce's story is an example of the ultimate
act of hopelessness—suicide—committed by this 17-year-old upper-middle-class boy.

Nikki's choice to become pregnant is common among teenage mothers today.
Unlike the teen mothers of the '50s and '60s, today's teen mothers face more obstacles.
Developmental psychologist Judy Musick states:

They [teen mothers] are more likely to lack both a family to instill high
expectations and a community environment to provide a vision of a
productive future, two time-honored pathways for getting up and out of
poverty.[4]

Nikki's series of choices leading to pregnancy indicates one form of hopelessness: she
did not expect to move beyond the circumstances of her poverty.

Bruce, on the other hand, experienced the loss of a close friend during a tragic
accident. Perhaps Bruce not only grieved for his friend; perchance he also experienced
the guilt of his choice to stage a drag car race. We can only speculate, since in the evidence he left, his stated desire was to see Bill again. No doubt, Bruce, grieving the loss
of his friend slipped into another form of hopelessness: the abyss of depression that led
him to kill himself.

We don't know Nikki's or Bruce's religious beliefs. Although as a child Nikki
attended Sunday school in the Methodist church where her mother and grandmother
were members, she rarely attended church after she turned 12. Other than this bit of
contextual information concerning Nikki's church attendance, her beliefs and Christian
practices are unknown. We have no contextual information concerning Bruce's religious
life, only the method of burial for his body. Newsweek recorded the words of Bruce's
mother, who explained why she and her husband chose to have Bruce cremated:

"Where would we bury him?" says Lucy. "Where is home?" They knew
the [family] moves were the biggest thing in Bruce's life, but they had
believed he was happy in Plano. "I guess," Lucy speculates, "Bruce hurt
so bad. And maybe he just couldn't bear to start all over again and find a
new best friend."[5]

3. Gelman.

4. Judith S. Musick, *Young, Poor, and Pregnant: The Psychology of Teenage Motherhood* (New Haven, Connecticut: Yale University Press, 1993), 8.

5. Gelman, *Newsweek*, 74.

Does prosperity create despair?
According to a CDC study cited by Evelyn Parker, the suicide rate of African-Americans between ages 10 and 19 has increased 114 percent since 1980. In Southern states, the rate of increase is even higher—214 percent. The CDC concludes that rising prosperity and social integration for blacks over the last few decades has caused a loss of racial identity and distance between families, children, and community. These factors, according to the study, contribute to a rising sense of despair among African-American youth.

Some African-American leaders disagree. They say the bureaucratic welfare state has caused the skyrocketing suicide rates among young blacks by eroding families and educational systems in black communities.[1] One member of the African-American leadership network, Project 21, noted: "Unless a commitment is made to strengthening the basic family unit, reforming our urban schools and reenergizing the spirit of our communities, these awful numbers will only increase."[2]

How do you interpret the findings of the CDC study? Keep in mind the following:
- Teen suicide affects every race, gender, and socioeconomic class.
- Suicide among white males has increased more sharply than in any other group.
- The ratio of male to female suicides is four to one—although girls attempt suicide three times more frequently than boys.

Do you find the CDC explanation convincing? What kinds of stress might contribute to despair in various racial/ethnic communities, in white males, in girls of all races?

Although we are unaware of Nikki's or Bruce's religious lives, their experiences echo those of youth in our church groups. These stories are examples of hopeless youth—just the tip of the iceberg of stories behind the statistics of adolescent despair.

A litany of hopelessness in youth

Hopelessness is a constant refrain in the life stories of many teenagers today. Regardless of their race, class, gender, or sociocultural context, when teenagers speak of the present or the future, despair is a common motif. On January 4, 1993, the *Atlanta Journal-Constitution* noted, "If there is one group who needs that touted and tenuous thing called hope, it's today's adolescents."[6] Ruby Takanishi, former executive director of the Carnegie Council on Adolescent Development, indicates that anxiety and depression among teens are the chief health concerns of teachers and pediatricians.[7]

The most startling result of adolescent despair is the high suicide rate among teenagers. A Gallup Poll survey in 1994 found that almost half (44 percent) of teenagers polled said they knew someone who actually tried to commit suicide.[8] In 1990, the United States Centers for Disease Control and Prevention (CDC) survey of 16,000 teens indicated the suicide death rate among 15- to 19-year-olds increased from 2.7 cases per 100,000 in 1950 to 11.1 cases per 100,000.[9] In other words, the suicide death rate among teenagers has quadrupled over the last 40 years.

The CDC also reported high suicide rates among black teens in the U. S.—doubling from 1980 to 1995 when 3,030 blacks between the ages of 10 and 19 killed themselves. These are the ones that were reported to authorities and confirmed. In 1995 the rate was 4.5 suicides per 100,000 blacks ages 10 to 19, up from 2.1 in 1980.[10] In addition to factors such as drugs and the breakdown of the family, the CDC suggested African-Americans in upwardly mobile families are dealing with more stress and may adopt the coping behaviors of the larger society, in which suicide may be more commonly used to deal with hopelessness and depression. Carl Bell, an African-American mental health expert who works with black youngsters in Chicago, points out that middle-class blacks feel alienated at a young age. "You don't belong in any world," he said. "You don't belong in the white middle-class and you don't belong among poor blacks. There is an alienation that occurs."[11]

In 1991 and 1994 the Gallup International Institute conducted two landmark studies with teenagers ages 12 through 17 asking them about their experience with peers who considered suicide or actually committed suicide. The 1,500 teens interviewed in the 1994 survey listed drug abuse (86 percent), not getting along with parents (84 percent), peer pressure (82 percent), and problems in growing up (81 percent) as the most significant fac-

---

1. Phyllis Berry Myers, president, Black America PAC's Leadership and Training Institute, "Black Teen Suicide Study Alarming," March 20, 1998 (www.project21.org/21TeenSuicide398.html).

2. Robert George, cited in "Black Teen Suicide Study Alarming, Yet Misleading," March 20, 1998 (www.project21.org/21TeenSuicide398.html).

6. "Future Looks Bleak to Anxious, Pessimistic Adolescents," *The Atlanta Journal-Constitution* (January 4, 1993), B-9.

7. "Future Looks Bleak to Anxious, Pessimistic Adolescents," B-9.

8. George H. Gallup, Jr., *The Spiritual Life of Young Americans: Approaching the Year 2000* (Princeton, New Jersey: George H. Gallup International Institute, 1999), 62.

9. George Gallup, *Growing Up Scared in America* (Princeton, New Jersey: Morehouse Publishing, 1995), 51.

10. "Blacks' Rising Suicide Rate, Middle-class Ties Linked," *Richmond Times-Dispatch* (March 29, 1998), A-6.

11. "Blacks' Rising Suicide Rate, Middle-class Ties Linked," A-6

Suicide signals
Suicidal young people tend to
demonstrate several of the following symptoms. Naturally, these signals are not foolproof. The key to
distinguishing between normal
adolescent turbulence and danger
is the time and degree of the
behavior, and the amount of deviation from usual personality and
behavior. If you suspect that a student is in despair, save the
sermon and intervene.
    For detailed information
about suicide signals that
teens send, see www.
adolescentservices.com/
desk/suicidal.html.

**What do I do
if a student is suicidal?**
There is simply no question that
you will deal with suicidal young
people in the course of your ministry. It is not a matter of if, but
when.
    If you think a young person
may be thinking about
suicide, say to them: "I'm
worried about you. Are you thinking about killing yourself?" Be
direct—suicidal youth drop clues
so that someone will ask this question. If she says yes, ask, "Do you
have a plan?" All suicidal comments must be taken seriously—
but youth who can outline a plan
for carrying out a suicide are in
imminent danger.
    If a teenager opens up to you
with a problem, take time to listen
immediately. For strategies to prevent teen suicide, go to
www.uky.edu/agriculture/
sociology/suicide.html.

tors contributing to adolescent suicide. Other factors included alcohol abuse (71 percent), satanic cults (65 percent), problems with school (64 percent), teen pregnancy (62 percent), AIDS (56 percent), teen gangs (53 percent), and copycat teen suicides (42 percent).

This research underscores the hopelessness affecting youth across cultures. Asian, African-American, European-American, Hispanic, and Native-American youth cry out for deliverance from the evils that cause them to spiral down from cynicism to pessimism—down to despair and nihilism.[12] They cry for the church to proclaim a relevant Christian hope for teenagers of North America, and perhaps for the global Christian community as well.

Spiritual resistance: the essential missing ingredient

The stories and statistics of teenagers in despair, or who are dangerously at risk for hopelessness, indicates their struggle with understanding evil that affects their lives. Evil can be either intentionally perpetrated by human agents with the intent to harm, or it can be the harmful consequence of natural disasters.[13] Divorced parents, death of a loved one, drive-by shootings, poverty, hate violence, HIV/AIDS, and sexual abuse are all evils that teenagers may face. Whenever evil impacts the lives of teenagers—and adults as well—hopelessness may occur. However, given adolescents' newfound ability for abstract thought—and their appropriate efforts to form a coherent ideology during this stage in the life cycle—negotiating the contradictions and ambiguities of life experienced and observed through suffering and evil can prove insurmountable. When overwhelmed with the realities of an imperfect world, teenagers who weather the storms of life usually have a strong religious ideology.[14]

When less spiritually resilient adolescents experience evil, however, they can become profoundly pessimistic or depressed. In addition to genetic factors, clinical depression may stem from environmental influences such as "having dysfunctional relationships within the family, learning helpless or hostile explanatory styles from a parent, having a depressed mother, lacking the skills to make close friends, and experiencing a loss."[15] When an adolescent is incapable of managing evil manifest by life's tragedies and setbacks, depression can often lead to suicide.

Years ago, adolescents might have turned to adults to help them confront evil at this stage in the life cycle. But people and institutions capable of offering teenagers hope in the face of evil and suffering are no longer readily available. Parents and other significant adults, youth organizations, and the church increasingly seem to sidestep serious engagement concerning the role of evil in the world. In addition to being unavailable to listen to teenagers,[16] North American adults tend to reinforce the pre-

---

12. Nihilism is often used in describing the severity of hopelessness in the African-American community. Nihilism is the combination of hopelessness, meaninglessness, and powerlessness. For an extensive discussion of nihilism, see Cornel West's *Race Matters* (New York: Vintage, 1993).

13. This understanding of evil is adopted from Patricia L. Wismer, who conceptualizes "Evil" in Donald W. Musser and Joseph L. Price (eds.) *A New Handbook of Christian Theology* (Nashville: Abingdon Press, 1992), 173–175.

14. The work of James Garbarino makes a strong case for this aspect of identity development. In his book, *Lost Boys: Why Our Sons Turn Violent and How We Can Save Them* (New York: The Free Press, 1999), a chapter focuses on spirituality as a source of resilience in violent boys.

15. Linda Nielsen, *Adolescence: A Contemporary View* (New York: Harcourt Brace College Publishers, 1996), 594.

16. Patricia Hersch discusses the absence of parents in the lives of teens in her book *A Tribe Apart* (New York: Fawcett Columbine, 1998).

vailing gloom and doom when they speak of global warming; pollution of the air, rivers, and lakes; no jobs after college; and the end of Social Security.[17]

The problem of evil and the church

The Christian church is one of several institutions due this indictment. The church, in its ministry with youth, tends to sidestep issues arising from the problem of evil, as mentioned above. In some ways the church has adopted a type of *don't ask, don't tell* approach to events that cause disappointment or grief to youth. At best, the church, in its ministry with youth, will only name the evil, leaving it hanging ominously in the air in need of honest dialogical process, prayer, and resolution.

The church has promoted an impotent spirituality with youth regarding evil and despair. *First, this impotent spirituality is empty of significant discussion with youth about the activity of God in the midst of evil.* Where is God when death steals a loved one and hate maims and paralyzes your best friend? What is God doing to ease the pain when crying will not wash it away? Why does God allow such misery and suffering? Youth need to explore these and other related questions in the biblical text, in the lives of patriarchs and matriarchs of the Christian faith, and in the lives of Christians in their communities of faith.

Second, the church has promoted a spirituality that is void of relevant coping skills sufficient for confronting youth's disappointments and tragedies. Spiritual disciplines offered by the church, which include prayer, meditation, fasting, solitude, and worship are the foundations for coping with crisis and disappointment.[18] Yet a more integrative approach to the practice of spiritual disciplines and the dialogical process needs to be considered. Youth need spirituality of sufficient substance to anchor them when religious beliefs are challenged. The Christian church is challenged to engage in spiritual formation with youth that offers a spirituality replete with a relevant hope to fortify teens when they encounter evil and suffering.

A relevant Christian hope

Why should hope be the starting point for youth ministry? Given the state of hopelessness among teenagers in North America, an emphasis on Christian hope shifts the theological lens of youth ministry to eschatology as we consider the theory and practice of ministry with youth. *Eschatology*, or the doctrine of the last things, is reflection on the Christian hope for the consummation of God's purposes for all creation and for the completion of our lives in perfect fellowship with God."[19] Significant words and phrases that hold meaning for this doctrine are *expectation*, *assurance*, *certainty*, *confidence*, and *God's promises*. Classical symbols of Christian hope are the *parousia* or expectation of the

Spirituality with teeth
Evelyn suggests that authentic spirituality requires potency, from the Latin word for *power* or *lord*. A potent spirituality, then, conveys lordship—specifically, the Lordship of Jesus Christ—as the One with power in the world.

IMPOTENT SPIRITUALITY
Avoids discussing God's activity in the midst of evil
Lacks coping skills for confronting disappointment and tragedy

POTENT SPIRITUALITY OF HOPE
Points to Triune God who is present in suffering and despair
Relies on spiritual disciplines that sustain teenagers in times of sorrow and joy
Integrates young people into concrete Christian communities where they can develop coping skills for disappointment.
What do you think of Evelyn's criteria for a potent spirituality of hope? Why would a trinitarian faith, spiritual disciplines, and integration into concrete Christian communities make a difference in helping young people develop spiritual resilience?

---

17. *The Atlanta Journal/Atlanta Constitution* (January 14, 1993), B-9.

18. My partial list of spiritual disciplines is informed by Richard J. Foster in *Celebration of Discipline* (San Francisco: Harper San Francisco, 1998-78).

19. Daniel Migliore, *Faith Seeking Understanding: An Introduction to Christian Theology* (Grand Rapids, Michigan: Eerdmans, 1991), 231.

Why hope?

Christians approach the end times, or the eschaton, knowing that all people will "appear before the tribunal of Christ to give an account of their thoughts, words, and deeds; and to receive according to what they have done in the body, whether good or evil" (Westminster Confession, XXXIII, 1). If someone is going to judge us for our purity or our piety, then we should be talking about Christian dread, not Christian hope.

However, it turns out that we have an in with the judge. The judge will be Jesus Christ, the Son of God who loved us sinners enough to give his life for us, and that fact completely changes the eschatalogical scenery. We may eagerly, not fearfully, look forward to the future, because it is being chosen by Someone who loves us! That isn't just good news—that is *great* news!

This is why hope is linked with Christian eschatology. Christian eschatology contains two kinds of hope: hope for the world and hope for the individual.

Christ's judgment will create a new heaven and a new earth, where justice will finally triumph over injustice, love over hatred and greed, peace over hostility, humanity over inhumanity, the Reign of God over the Reign of Evil. This is the Christian hope for the world.

But the final judgment also brings hope to individuals. We confess our belief in "the resurrection of the body and the life everlasting." We don't know how this happens; centuries of Christians have been tempted to keep score on who is in and who is out in the final countdown. A more reliable method would be to remember who Jesus is and what he did while he was here. And what he did was turn the world upside down, inverting the human order of things at every turn.

What does that mean for Christian eschatology? Reformed theologian Shirley C. Guthrie points out that the Good News of Jesus Christ does have two sides to it,

return of Jesus Christ, the resurrection of the dead, and the final judgement.[20] Theologian Jurgen Moltmann defines hope in this manner:

> [T]he biblical texts understand hope as a positive, divine power of life. It is expectation of a good future that is awakened through God's promise and supported by trust in God. It does not detach the human spirit from the present through delusions, but rather the opposite; it pulls the promised future into the present and places the experienced present in the dawn of God's future.[21]

In the trinity of divine powers, Paul places hope and faith second only to love. "And now these three remain: faith, hope and love. But the greatest of these is love" (1 Corinthians 13:13). Paul also connects *hope*, the noun, to our salvation: "Not only so, but we ourselves, who have the firstfruits of the Spirit, groan inwardly as we wait eagerly for our adoption as sons, the redemption of our bodies. For in this hope we are saved" (Romans 8:23-24a). Paul offers a word of caution concerning this *positive, divine power:* "But hope that is seen is no hope at all. Who hopes for what he already has?" (Romans 8:24b).[22] Paul goes on to define *hope*, the verb, and the conditions under which the act of hoping must take place: "But if we hope for what we do not yet have, we wait for it patiently" (Romans 8:25). These passages illumine the power of hope and its connection to vital aspects of Christianity: salvation, faith, and love.

Ingredients for a potent spirituality

Christian hope is the expectation of a future rooted in the promises of God, which motivates us to live in the present with certainty and confidence. Central to a relevant Christian hope for ministry with youth, is a potent spirituality sufficient for the lives of 21st-century youth. An impotent spirituality leads to the two problems mentioned above—a lack of significant discussion on the problem of evil and inadequate coping skills in the face of tragedy and disappointment. Yet these problems point us to several possibilities in forming a potent spirituality for adolescents.

A God who promises to be present in the midst of suffering and despair

Teens need to discover God who suffers with us when our minds and bodies throb with pain in illness, disappointment, death of loved ones, and abandonment by those we love. God promises never to leave us regardless of the circumstance—to be present with us even during the worst of times. When Joseph's brothers sold him to the Ishmaelites, he no doubt felt betrayed, abandoned, and afraid. Seventeen-year-old Joseph knew that his older brothers had grown to hate him because he was their father's favorite son. Perhaps Joseph didn't help matters by sharing his dreams and adorning

---

20. Migliore, 242-247.

21. Jürgen Moltmann, "Hope," in Donald W. Musser and Joseph L. Price's (eds.), *A New Handbook of Christian Theology* (Nashville: Abingdon Press, 1992), 239.

22. Moltmann.

warning and promise. But it is warning to good people and promise to sinners.[1] Christians live in the confidence that heaven is for sinners, and for this reason we can come humbly before God—now, and until the end of time—in hope, not fear.

_____

1. Shirley C. Guthrie, *Christian Doctrine* (Atlanta: John Knox Press, 1968), 400.

40 developmental assets

For decades, social science research on young people tried to identify factors detrimental to healthy adolescence. Search Institute changed its perspective to approach adolescence differently. Instead of asking "What goes wrong during adolescence?," Search asked, "What goes right?" After years of testing, they identified 40 developmental assets—building blocks that help young people grow up healthy, caring, and responsible, regardless of their family background, socioeconomic status, or educational experience. This research has launched an array of youth curricula, leadership training, and educational programs designed to help churches, synagogues, schools, and communities foster developmental assets in adolescents.

See the list on pages 275-276.

What do you think of an assets approach to youth ministry? Should youth ministry focus on helping young people grow up healthy, caring, and responsible (in which assets play a central role), or should we focus on helping youth form a relationship with Jesus Christ? Are assets part of faith formation—or is faith formation asset enough?[1]

_____

1. For a comprehensive approach to developing assets through family-based ministry with youth, see Merton P. Strommen and Richard A. Hardel, *Passing On the Faith: A Radical New Model for Youth and Family Ministry* (Winona, Minnesota: St. Mary's Press/Christian Brothers Publications), 2000.

himself in the colorful royal coat his father Jacob had given him. But had their jealousy come to this? They were his brothers, those with whom he played and worked, yet they discarded him like a slave for 20 pieces of silver. Joseph must have cried the entire journey to Egypt, wondering if he would ever see his family again. Perhaps the memories of his father's love eased his pain. Perhaps the stories of Yahweh's presence with his father Jacob, his grandfather Isaac, and his great grandfather Abraham when they were strangers in foreign lands, restored his confidence. Perhaps Joseph experienced the assurance that Yahweh was with him. In any case, once in Egypt, Potiphar—Pharaoh's captain of the guard—purchased Joseph. "The Lord was with Joseph and he prospered, and he lived in the house of his Egyptian master" (Genesis 39:2). Spiritual resilience saw Joseph through the worst of the crisis and brought him into a hopeful future.

Stories of God's presence in the lives of men and women through the ages sustained Israel and still sustain the church. God, known in Jesus Christ, came to save the world. Matthew echoes Isaiah's Messianic prophecy: "'The virgin will be with child and will give birth to a son, and they will call him Immanuel'—which means, 'God with us'" (Matthew 1:23). Throughout his ministry, Jesus Christ was the incarnate presence of God with the sick, downtrodden, and the oppressed. Beyond his ministry, through his death and resurrection, Jesus is *Immanuel*, God with us: "And surely I am with you always, to the very end of the age" (Matthew 28:20). No doubt these words assured—and still assure—dejected disciples of Jesus' presence as we go forth to make disciples of people around the globe.

Jesus, the ground of our hope, continues to assure us of his presence through the promise of the Holy Spirit. "I will not leave you as orphans; I will come to you…But the Counselor, the Holy Spirit, whom the Father will send in my name, will teach you all things and will remind you of everything I have said to you" (John 14:18, 26). Just as Jesus promised, the Holy Spirit came on the day of Pentecost while the disciples waited hopelessly together in the Upper Room. Today, God the Holy Spirit dwells with us, comforts us when we suffer, sustains us when in despair, and fortifies us with truth. Christian hope for ministry with youth requires the triune God who promises never to leave us in times of suffering and despair.

Spiritual disciplines that are sufficient for sustaining teenagers in seasons of sorrow as well as joy

Practicing the spiritual discipline of lament during seasons of sorrow is the prelude to hope.[23] As Richard Foster writes, "The spiritual disciplines are an inward and spiritual reality," an attitude of the heart that fortifies us for life in the present age so that our living ushers in "God's promised future."[24] Of course, merely practicing spiritual disciplines alone cannot help us live out the hope that God has promised—but they do prepare us to receive God's gift of grace that helps us live hopefully. Foster states:

_____

23. For more on the concept of lament, see Emilie Townes, *Breaking the Fine Rain of Death: African American Health Care and a Womanist Ethic of Care* (New York: Continuum, 1998).

24. Foster, 3; Moltmann, 241.

Lament as a spiritual discipline
The depth of sorrow expressed in much of the music, poetry, and conversation enjoyed by adolescents sometimes seems morose to adults. In Scripture, lamenting begins in despair and turns toward God in hope. How does this compare with laments found in popular culture? Why is lament—the expression of grief or regret—so appealing to adolescents? Should the church encourage adolescents' use of lament through popular culture, or do these expressions of grief contribute to adolescent despair?

A farmer is helpless to grow grain; all he can do is provide the right conditions for the growing of grain. He cultivates the ground, he plants the seed, he waters the plants, and then the natural forces of the earth take over and up comes the grain. This is the way it is with the Spiritual Disciplines—they are a way of sowing to the Spirit. The Disciplines are God's way of getting us into the ground; they can only get us to the place where something can be done. They are God's means of grace. The inner righteousness we seek is not something that is poured on our heads. God has ordained the Disciplines of the spiritual life as the means by which we place ourselves where he can bless us.[25]

We are fallow grounds with rituals, mantras, and creeds alone. It is when God's grace transforms us in the process of practicing these disciplines of the spiritual life that we become cultivated soil for Christian hope.

Relevant coping skills sufficient for confronting youth's spiraling from pessimism to despair.

Internal disciplines of the spiritual life such as prayer, fasting, meditation, and Bible study, in conjunction with corporate disciplines such as worship, are rudimentary for developing coping skills that resist evil. When integrated with other spiritual disciplines, the discipline of service, for example—not "self-righteous service" but day-to-day "active helpfulness"[26]—helps teenagers realize their agency in transforming hopeless situations into relevant Christian hope, thereby becoming agents of God in the transformation of the world.

Christian educator Charles Foster writes: "Church education nurtures hope if it equips children, youth, and adults to participate in the congregation's vocation in the world."[27] Foster argues that congregations focusing on the "transformation of structures and attitudes in the larger community that threaten and demean human life" rather than focusing on preserving their "traditions and congregation's heritage," are about the business of educating for hope. Education that nurtures hope with young people recognizes them as equal participants in the vocation of their congregations. This recognition facilitates the integrative process of service as a spiritual discipline. Together youth and adults prayerfully discern their call to ministry, determining those institutions that help and hinder justice for their neighbors. The unique talents of youth and adults are intentionally utilized for the common purpose of ministry. Not only are the activities of ministry formal in the sense of being intentional, but they are informal in the sense that they involve daily activities of personal decision-making and acts of kindness that promote the hope-giving vocation of the congregation.

In summary, the essential ingredients for a potent spirituality for young people include—

---

25. Foster, 7.

26. Foster, 7.

27. Charles Foster, *Educating Congregations: The Future of Christian Education* (Nashville: Abingdon Press, 1994), 125.

---

1. Barbel Inhelder and Jean Piaget, *The Growth of Logical Thinking,* translated by A.Parsons and S. Milgram (New York: Basic Books, 1958), 343.

2. Robert Kegan, *In Over Our Heads: The Mental Demands of Modern Life* (Cambridge: Harvard University Press, 1994), 39-41

3. David Elkind, *All Grown Up and No Place to Go: Teenagers in Crisis* (Reading, Massachusetts: Addison-Wesley Publishing, 1984), 33-36.

• the acknowledgement of a relevant triune God.
• the practice of spiritual disciplines.
• the development of coping skills resulting from spiritual disciplines that integrate youth into the vocation of the Christian community.

Some cautions

When considering a ministry with youth that promotes a potent spirituality of Christian hope, several cautions should be considered. First, in a broad sense, one might conclude that youth ministry under this framework is only for youth who are suffering in some way, whether psychologically, socially, or economically. A false assumption could be made that youth ministry that begins with Christian hope is for *at-risk* youth. If we examine the factors that place an adolescent *at risk,* we find that, in addition to the usual criteria of drug and alcohol abuse, sexual promiscuity, and smoking other more subtle factors contribute to risky behavior in adolescents as well. Biological changes such as puberty, environmental changes such as the transition from middle school to high school, familial stresses such as divorced parents, even parental psychiatric disorders can place an adolescent *at risk.*[28] Simply stated, being *at risk* is a reality of all adolescents living in North America. Therefore it is all the more essential for the church to make Christian hope the central doctrine of our ministry with youth.

Secondly and more specifically, youth ministry that promotes a potent spirituality of Christian hope may appear to promote an egocentric spirituality. By this I mean a spirituality that emphasizes more of what God does for the individual—a type of self-centered perspective about the expectation of a good future based on trust in God and the promises God has made to us. This egocentric spirituality leads to a "What is God going to do for me?" mentality. Egocentric spirituality stands in opposition to hope experienced by the corporate body of Christ, as the congregation brings hope to despairing humanity. David Elkind argues that the advancing cognitive capabilities of young teenagers gives them the new ability of taking the perspective of others, which leads to *adolescent egocentrism.* During this time young teenagers tend to believe that they are the center of everyone's attention.[29] As a result, I am suggesting that young adolescents—middle adolescents to a lesser extent—are prone to an egocentric spirituality if youth ministry fails to continually remind youth of God's activity in bringing hope to the corporate body of Christ as well as to individual believers.

Here again Charles Foster is instructive for addressing egocentric spirituality among youth. It is important to keep in mind that all of the educational tasks of a congregation nurture hope in children, youth, and adults—in all members of the congregation—as the congregation serves as God's agent bringing hope to all humanity. The church nurtures hope by equipping all members for participation in the vocation of the church in the world, but there are three other tasks as well:

---

28. The various aspects of placing youth at risk are termed normative and nonnormative stresses by Stuart Hauser and Mary Bowlds, "Stress, Coping, and Adaptation" in Shirley Feldman and Glen Elliott's (eds.) *At The Threshold: The Developing Adolescent* (Cambridge, Massachusetts: Harvard University Press, 1990).

29. See David Keating, "Adolescent Thinking," in Shirley Feldman and Glen Elliott's (eds.) *At The Threshold: The Developing Adolescent* (Cambridge, Massachusetts: Harvard University Press, 1990).

• The congregation nurtures hope in children, youth, and adults when they are given intentional opportunities to practice transformative service for those in society who suffer from dehumanization.
• The congregation nurtures hope as it begins to realize its mission in the world.
• The congregation nurtures hope in the community of faith when it dreams and envisions possibilities for itself and all humanity. This aspect of imagination yields reality.[30]

Using Foster's typology I am suggesting that youth ministry can avoid egocentric spirituality—or hope that focuses only on the individual teenager—if ministry with youth is placed in the context of the congregation's vocation, practice, mission, and imagination for the community of faith and broader humanity.

Finally, what is the role of adult leadership in youth ministry that promotes a potent spirituality for Christian hope? What cautions might we consider for ourselves? The primary concern is that adult leaders avoid the temptation to alleviate anxiety, pessimism, pain, and despair in youth by offering quick solutions. It is natural for pastors to assuage pain. We live in a culture where instant gratification is demanded of and by us. Adult leadership must be cautious about falling prey to such demands. Perhaps a more fruitful approach would be adult leaders becoming vulnerable enough to admit helplessness in knowing the answers to evil in the world. Our presence during times of despair—as listeners and as dialogue partners—is the best posture we can offer youth as their adult leaders.

* * *

Hopelessness touches the lives of many North American teenagers whether they are rich or poor, white or black, Asian or Hispanic, male or female. A cultural milieu of anxiety, cynicism, and pessimism informs teens' decisions about their lives and their communities. The Christian church is charged with the responsibility of transforming the milieu of despair into one of hope in light of the eschatological promise of God. Emphasizing hope as a starting point for youth ministry offers a spirituality for youth that confronts this milieu with a positive, divine power necessary for living into the promises of God.

---

30. Charles Foster, 125–128.

Forty Developmental Assets

Search Institute has identified the following building blocks of healthy development that help young people grow up healthy, caring, and responsible.

External Assets
Support
1. Family support—Family life provides high levels of love and support.
2. Positive family communication—Young person and her or his parents(s) communicate positively, and young person is willing to seek advice and counsel from parent(s).
3. Other adult relationships—Young person receives support from three or more non-parent adults.
4. Caring neighborhood—Young person experiences caring neighbors.
5. Caring school climate—School provides a caring, encouraging environment.
6. Parent involvement in schooling—Parents(s) are actively involved in helping young person succeed in school.

Empowerment
7. Community values youth—Young person perceives that adults in the community value youth.
8. Youth as resources—Young people are given useful roles in the community.
9. Service to others—Young person serves in the community one hour or more per week.
10. Safety—Young person feels safe at home, at school, and in the neighborhood.

Boundaries and Expectations
11. Family boundaries—Family has clear rules and consequences and monitors the young person's whereabouts.
12. School boundaries—School provides clear rules and consequences.
13. Neighborhood boundaries—Neighbors take responsibility for monitoring young people's behavior.
14. Adult role models—Parent(s) and other adults model positive, responsible behavior.
15. Positive peer influence—Young person's best friends model responsible behavior.
16. High expectations— Both parent(s) and teachers encourage the young person to do well.

Constructive
17. Creative activities—Young person spends three or more hours per week in lessons or practice in music, theater, or other arts.
18. Youth programs—person spends three or more hours per week in sports, clubs, or organizations at school and/or in the community.
19. Religious community—young person spends one or more hours per week in activities in a religious institution.

20. Time at home—Young person is out with friends "with nothing special to do" two or fewer nights per week.

Internal Assets
Commitment to Learning
21. Achievement motivation—Young person is motivated to do well in school.
22. School engagement—Young person is actively engaged in learning.
23. Homework—Young person reports doing at least one hour of homework every school day.
24. Bonding to school—Young person cares about her or his school.
25. Reading for pleasure—Young person reads for pleasure three or more hours per week.

Positive Values
26. Caring—Young person places high value on helping other people.
27. Equality and social justice—Young person places high value on promoting equality and reducing hunger and poverty.
28. Integrity—Young person acts on convictions and stands up for her or his beliefs.
29. Honesty—Young person "tells the truth even when it is not easy."
30. Responsibility—Young person accepts and takes personal responsibility.
31. Restraint—Young person believes it is important not to be sexually active or to use alcohol or other drugs.

Social Competencies
32. Planning and decision-making—Young person knows how to plan ahead and make choices.
33. Interpersonal competence—Young person has empathy, sensitivity, and friendship skills.
34. Cultural competence—Young person has knowledge of and comfort with people of different cultural, racial, or ethnic backgrounds.
35. Resistance skills—Young person can resist negative peer pressure and dangerous situations.
36. Peaceful conflict resolution—Young person seeks to resolve conflict nonviolently.

Positive Identity
37. Personal power—Young person feels he or she has control over "things that happen to me."
38. Self-esteem—Young person reports having a high self-esteem.
39. Sense of purpose—Young person reports that "my life has a purpose."
40. Positive view of personal future—Young person is optimistic about her or his personal future.

Section 4

The Tasks of

Practical Theology:

Projecting a More

Faithful Ministry

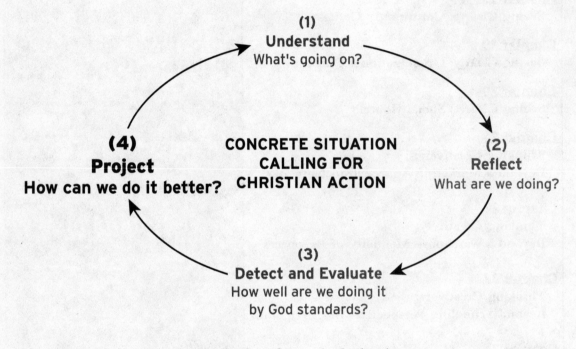

The Tasks of Practical Theology

The Tasks of Practical Theology: Projecting a More Faithful Ministry
Kenda Creasy Dean

Sharon Daloz Parks tells the story about a friend's daughter, Barbara, who suffered a serious accident playing basketball as a teenager.[1] The accident forced this bright, gifted young woman to become dependent on a wheelchair. While still in high school, Barbara was invited to attend a national gathering of Lutheran young people. Barbara was dubious about attending; she knew little about the event itself, and she had a lot of reservations about the church in general. To Barbara, the church seemed oppressive and hierarchical, and as far as she concerned it had completely missed the boat on teenagers. Still, Barbara knew that this conference was making a special effort to include differently abled young people like herself, and so she decided to attend.

The conference scheduled a Christian dance for the last evening. Barbara and another young woman, who also uses a wheelchair, debated whether to attend. They didn't know what they would do at a dance, but in the end they decided to go. As music blared and the festivities swirled around them, Barbara and her friend watched the dancers from the edge of the gymnasium floor. They began to wonder just what they were doing there. Nobody seemed to know how to include them; they weren't sure they knew themselves.

Practical theology begins and ends in practice. *Understanding* the concrete situation calling for Christian action, *reflecting* on current practices of youth ministry, *detecting* the theological assumptions guiding our practices of youth ministry—and holding up these practices to see where they do, and do not, bear out those guiding theological assumptions—are not enough. These aspects of practical theology all point to the fourth task: *projecting* a more faithful practice of youth ministry, reconstructing our practices for a more faithful witness as we live out our faith alongside youth.

The fourth task of practical theology addresses these questions: *What means, strategies, and forms of persuasion best communicate the gospel in this concrete situation? How shall we reconstruct our action so it is more transparent to God's action on behalf of young people in this particular case?* You will notice that the fourth task is not only focused on strategies of professional youth ministry, but also on strategies of living faithfully in the presence of young people.

The spiral of *practical theological reflection* culminates in practice itself. A spiral is never complete; each practice begins a new spiral of *practical theological reflection* as we reflect again on our Christian actions and move toward detecting our assumptions, evaluating actions, and reconstructing those actions again. We never return to precisely the same place in our journey of faith. But *practical theological reflection* does move us to live our faith in new ways, to recast Christian practices according to new norms, to

---

1. Barbara is not her real name. I heard this story as part of a lecture given at Princeton Theological Seminary in 1997; the written version of the story appears in Sharon Daloz Parks, "Home and Pilgrimage: Deep Rhythms in the Adolescent Soul," in *The 1997 Princeton Lectures on Youth, Church, and Culture* (Princeton, New Jersey: Institute of Youth Ministry, Princeton Theological Seminary), 61.

come a little closer to radical congruency between God's action and our actions. Every task in practical theology looks toward *faithful judgments*—decisions both congruent to our theological convictions and uniquely appropriate to the concrete situation calling for Christian action. The first task of practical theology asks, What's going on?; the second task reflects, What are we doing?; the third task discerns, Are we doing it well by God's standards?—and the fourth re-creates by asking, What will it take to do it better? The fourth task of practical theology helps youth ministry evolve and risk new directions and practices that are appropriate to the time and place into which God has called us to ministry.

Putting projection to work

Barbara and her friend's reaction to the dance was understandable. It takes courage to attend an event where you know you'll be sidelined—to assert your presence even when there's no space for it. Marginalized people from every generation, in every culture, share this experience; as a group, adolescents share it as well. Young people we serve in ministry often watch mature faith from the sidelines, even though well-meaning adults like us often invite them to participate. We're glad they came, but we often don't know what to do to make the church hospitable to teenagers—and as a result, even teenagers who come to church often wonder what they're doing there. How we approach Barbara and her friend at the dance says a lot about the way we approach young people in our congregations as well.

What *would* be a faithful, appropriate response to Barbara and her friend at the dance? Ignoring them would certainly be easiest but hardly faithful in light of divine hospitality. Furthermore it would play right into Barbara's impressions of the church back home—missing the boat where her needs as an adolescent were concerned. Involving the girls in some auxiliary capacity—maybe helping out at the punch bowl—might seem less awkward; on the other hand, Barbara and her friend had come to have fun, not to work, and consigning differently abled young people to helper roles not shared by other youth could communicate that they are not fully human enough to participate in the dance. Such an impression would be insulting as well as theologically untenable.

Canceling the dance so that Barbara and her friend would not be excluded would certainly make a political statement, but it also *uses* Barbara and her friend's physical conditions to make a policy point—not exactly the way most young people want to be singled out. And anyway, canceling the dance wouldn't be much fun.

If you were a young person at the dance with Barbara and her friend, what would you do?

Now it's your turn

In this final section, you will have a chance to probe the *faithful judgments* of youth ministers who have arrived at a number of norms, strategies, and practices for communicating the gospel with young people that address concrete situations facing ministry in the 21ST century. If we are to arrive at faithful judgments and reconstruct our practices of youth ministry so they are more transparent to Jesus Christ, then we must see clearly, think creatively, act wisely, and assess honestly our practices of ministry.

Steve Gerali, Dave Rahn, and Patricia Davis will help you see more clearly the community, organizational, and social contexts of your ministry (chapters 18, 19, and 20); Mark Dodrill, Ed Trimmer, and Duffy Robbins will give you guidelines for thinking creatively in terms of networks, resources, and curriculum (chapters 21, 22, and 23); and Charles N. Neder, Karen Jones, and Marv Penner will offer some normative ways for acting wisely in concrete situations of ministry requiring programs, events, and counseling (chapters 24, 25, and 26). Finally, Dave Rahn and Chap Clark will help you find ways to honestly assess your ministry's improvement and your own spiritual readiness to respond to God's call to serve in ministry with young people (chapters 27 and 28).

Dancing sitting down

There is no question: practicing praise and fellowship through dance poses problems for young people who use wheelchairs. But reconstructing Christian practice, whether on a dance floor or in a Sunday school lesson, always requires creativity and vision—and no small amount of courage—as we reconceive Christian action in ways that are both faithful and uniquely appropriate to the particular situation.

Remember how Barbara and her friend were feeling as they watched the action from the edge of the gymnasium floor? Just as they began to wonder what they were doing at a Christian party that so obviously separated *us* from *them*, a young man from Latin America came over to Barbara and asked her to dance. Surprised—and curious—Barbara said, "Okay." The young man wheeled Barbara to the center of the room, grabbed a chair for himself, and then sat down facing Barbara in the middle of the gymnasium. Then the two of them began to dance.

Another young man went to Barbara's friend and invited her to dance as well. When she accepted, he wheeled her out onto the dance floor as well, grabbed a chair, and sat down—and they too began to dance, facing each other in their chairs. Suddenly the remaining youth on the dance floor went for chairs of their own, and within moments, all 500 teenagers in the gymnasium were *dancing sitting down*. It should come as no surprise, Parks notes wryly, that Barbara—while still cautious—has a renewed respect for the possibilities of the church. That evening, says Parks, *us* and *them* became *we*.[2]

Reconstructing our practices of youth ministry faithfully and appropriately takes creativity, vision, and courage. As you enter this final task of practical theology, bring the ministry you envision for young people along with you—along with everything else you have gained from your *practical theological reflection* throughout this book. Now

---

2. Parks, 61.

the rubber meets the road. What ministry will look like that is appropriate both for the situation in which you serve, and for the person God has created you to be—and how that ministry is both faithful to your theological convictions and appropriate to the circumstance to which God calls you—is about to unfold.

Seeing Clearly: Community Context
Steve Gerali

18
Chapter

Ministry to adolescents has come a long way over the course of the years. We have formulated strategies, philosophies, and theological perspectives to make youth work effective. We have even created some "effective-ministry" labels that may identify a youth ministry. One such label is *relational-incarnational ministry*. Many youth ministries today would classify themselves as relational-incarnational youth ministries. Despite this fact, these ministries fail to hit the mark. This phrase has come to mean everything from strategic programming to hanging out with kids.

I was asked to train some denominational youth leaders who categorized their ministries as relational-incarnational youth ministries. It became evident that while their ministries may have been relational in some aspects, they were far from being incarnational. These youth workers were attempting to do ministry out of their frame of reference—combining archaic ideologies with the newness of a program or principle that was working in some other part of the country. They thought they knew students but, in fact, they were ministering out of their biases, needs, values, norms, and practices in accordance to what effectively worked when they were adolescents. This approach to youth ministry is not incarnational; it is only transferable.

Out of context
Steve Gerali is suggesting something provocative here: because these youth ministers didn't understand the theological realities behind incarnational ministry, they misconstrued and misapplied the term. To the contrary, all they had done was transfer their own context-bound approaches to youth ministry into their current settings.

Incarnation and community

Incarnation is a cornerstone of God's program for the world. God took on flesh. Without incarnation we have no salvation, no relationship with God, no church, and no ministry. We cannot attempt to create strategies around incarnation without clearly seeing that incarnation—for those already clothed in flesh—is about invading, understanding, and becoming a part of a social context known as a community. Incarnation cannot be understood apart from the context of community.

The apostle John gives us a key verse on incarnation. He says, "The Word *became flesh* and made his *dwelling among us*. We *have seen* his glory, the glory of the One and Only, who came from the Father, full of grace and truth" (John 1:14, italics added). Christ became one of us and invaded the human community so that we might know (see his glory) him. This text becomes an outline that will help us clearly see youth ministry in the context of community.

Becoming flesh: the first incarnational youth ministry initiative

When Christ took on flesh, he began a good work. He became one of us to reach us and show us how we can minister to each other. Becoming flesh for Christ meant that he covered himself in *our* flesh. Becoming flesh for us has different implications since we are already clothed in flesh. For the youth minister it means to *become like*. Young youth ministers have two common misconceptions about this concept. First, it does not mean *become like* in immaturity. It is a mistake to think that we must *act like* an adolescent to reach an adolescent. The second misconception is that *becoming like* means being lik*ed*. Compromising authority for the sake of establishing rapport only ensures that the youth worker will be perceived as a peer and not a role model. Youth workers who operate from this premise are ministering out of their personal need for acceptance and will fail to reach adolescents.

In 1 Corinthians 9:19-22, Paul addressed what it means to *become like*. Paul became a student of the community and culture of those that he was trying to reach. "I have become all things to all men so that by all possible means I might save some"   (v. 22). Our goal is to become all things to all adolescents so that we might reach them. The practical implications are simple.

Understand the social science of community

A community is a collection of individuals—families and smaller groups with similar experiences, norms, values, beliefs, biases, traditions, ethnicity, ideals, language, gender and societal roles, and attitudes. Within a community there might be a subgroup or a smaller population that embraces the aforementioned list with slight deviation, interpretation, or modification as it fits their groups' needs. Thus a Western-cultured, middle-class, Anglo-American, educated, white-collar, Christian (I use the word generically), suburban group of people would be a community. To change any one of those labels would change the community. For example if we changed Anglo-American to African-American or Hispanic-American, we would have a different community. If we changed middle-class to lower-income, we would have an entirely different set of values and standards that would change the context of community.

Each community is also defined by the uniqueness of its problems, values, ideals, needs, etc. This means that solutions, strategies, assessments, etc., must be as unique as the community.

An individual is shaped by the community in which she lives. As that individual searches for meaning and significance to life, she will align with subgroups or smaller communities within the larger community. The larger community transfers and perpetuates the distinctives of the community, whereas the subgroup lends itself to the development of uniqueness. If my community is Western-cultured, middle-class, Anglo-American, educated, white-collar, Christian, suburban; I will inevitably buy into many of the distinctives of that community, but my uniqueness will also be defined by the smaller community, like church, school, age group, etc. We have all been part of a group that—while it embraced the larger community—had its own ideals, slang, norms, and trends. The population of adolescents who form a community are a subcommunity within the larger community. A youth worker must know the broader community before she can minister to the subcommunity of adolescents.

We can gather a lot of information about the broader community by studying its demographics—the statistical facts about the community. An Internet search of a community census would yield information about the socioeconomic make up; the average educational status; the ethnicity and gender ratios; the types (intact, single-parent, blended, adoptive, etc.) and percentages of families; and number of adolescents in a community. Youth workers can secure additional demographic information from school district boards.

Be a student of culture and community

Too often youth workers jump into a ministry setting without doing the right homework. Like the denominational youth leaders mentioned earlier, many youth workers operate from the perspective of the community in which they experienced youth ministry. An effective youth worker must understand that observation precedes practice. It takes a lot of work, but a youth worker must become an *ethnographer*—someone who observes, studies, defines, and describes a cultural community and subcommunities within the broader community. Youth ministry is different from community to community. Adolescents on the East Coast of the United States are drastically different from the adolescents on the West Coast or in the Midwest, not to mention urban or rural youth, or youth in an entirely different ethnic culture. The youth worker as ethnographer must invade the community and observe—and in the process answer strategic questions that define needs, norms, values, biases, etc., of that community. Two very strategic questions are *what* and *why*. What do these kids need and why? What do they like and why? Why do they go where they go? What is important to them and why? What do their parents value and why? What other adolescent specific organizations exist in that community and why are they there? What are the more powerful influences on this community's adolescents and why do they gravitate toward those influences? Ethnography involves continuous observation with the intent to understand the core issues of the community. It's not enough to have a handle on the trends, fashions, and tastes that kids buy into. Anybody can do that. An ethnographer seeks the deeper meanings and reasons in an attempt to understand the kid, not just the surface. In doing this, the youth worker is becoming like the community and the kid.

Observation also means that we seek to see what God is already doing in the lives of kids before we assert our ministry agendas. It is an error to think that God has not started a work in a group of adolescents' lives prior to our coming into their community. If we are to understand kids, we will see the work that God is already doing. When we read through the history of Israel in the Old Testament, we find that while God is active in the life of that nation, he is not absent in the nations around Israel. One of the greatest pictures of Christ in the Old Testament is Melchizedek the King and priest of Salem. Genesis 14:17-24 records his encounter with Abraham.

Melchizedek appears on the scene to meet with Abraham. Abraham has had no prior knowledge or encounter with him. All we know about Melchizedek is that he is a priest of the Most High God and that he is from a foreign land (Salem) where he also serves as king. This passage indicates that while God was active in the life of Abraham, he was equally as active in the lives of people outside the influence of Abraham and the nation of Israel.

The Holy Spirit is doing a great work in the lives of adolescents even as you read this sentence. He is the one who draws kids into relationship with Christ (John 16:13–14). He is the one who convicts them of sin and righteousness and judgment (John 16:8). He regenerates lives with completeness and newness (John 3:5–6; Titus 3:5). He builds and protects youth ministry in the church (Psalms 127:1–2; Matthew 16:18). Effective youth workers understand that God is not beginning his presence in the community of adolescence with the arrival of a youth ministry, but that it is a privilege to be a part of a great thing God has already begun in that community. When a youth worker internalizes this truth, he becomes truly humble and teachable. It is at this point that the youth worker is an effective learner of the culture and community.

Become part of the community

Being like adolescents involves immersing oneself in their culture. When missionaries go to foreign fields, they learn the languages, customs, practices, traditions, and values of the people they are trying to reach. To fully understand the community, they must bring those practices into their home. They speak the language within the context of their family so that they adapt to the community. They practice the customs and traditions so that they can relate to the people. They become all things to all men so that they might save some.

The missiology of youth ministry requires the same thing. A youth worker must understand that she is entering into another (foreign) community. *Cultural immersion* means that the youth worker must have the experiences that the adolescent community experiences. It means to be plunged under or saturated by whatever affects adolescence. It means thinking, feeling, and knowing adolescents better than they do themselves. This concept of cultural immersion will be a bit more developed in the next section of this chapter when we discuss what it means to dwell among adolescents. Cultural immersion involves *being like* concurrent with *dwelling among*. It is relatively easy to figure out that one must go where kids go to have the same experiences. School sporting events, activities, the local mall, or restaurant all provide an opportunity for cultural immersion, but these just scratch the surface. We should also study current research on adolescents.

A youth worker should read professional journals of adolescence to stay in tune with hard-core problems on everything from medicine to education as it intersects the lives of adolescents. Research on generational studies; marketing strategies to adolescents; adolescent developmental issues and disorders; technological interface

---

Know thy turf

Steve has done a great job explaining how a Christian ethnographer can be different from others. And it seems that the difference is precisely in the sort of theological awareness that this book is trying to raise. As a follower of Jesus, Steve is saying, you have access to truth that others do not have—which helps you set a more ambitious investigation agenda with regard to *what* and *why* than others might set. Yet don't claim that you know enough about a community until or unless you understand something of the work of God in the particular locale in which you're ministering.

Walking a tightrope

It sounds like Steve is suggesting that one's personal convictions may conflict with the need to immerse herself in the world of teens. When this does indeed happen, Steve is calling us to find a way to respect our own areas of vulnerability without giving up the (apparent) ministry essential of becoming part of the community. Even if one is generally successful in walking this tightrope, aren't there dimensions of a community that he may have to avoid because personal holiness is a higher value than ministry effectiveness—even if his "culture-learning" grade suffers?

and its effects on teens; and so on. all immerse one in the adolescent community. Watch the movies, listen to the music—not just the music you like—and read the material (magazines, school newspapers, underground publications, etc.) that kids ingest. Some may need to wrestle with their own personal struggles before they can do this. Seek out accountability relationships to deal with the struggle. Effective youth ministry is more than great games and a Bible study. It involves the hard work of being like adolescents by studying them and knowing them better than they know themselves.

Cultural immersion also involves constant clarification of terms. Don't assume that you know what kids mean when they use slang and other conceptual terms. The community of adolescents is constantly changing. Young youth workers often make a mistake of thinking that because they are close in age to adolescents, they have a full understanding of them. I often remind young youth workers that the community (high school) changed as soon as they left. The trajectory of meaning for things may have changed so slightly in the course of a year, that it could put the youth worker outside the community.

Try an experiment. Have a conversation with a high school sophomore or junior. In your conversation, don't assume that you know the meaning of the concepts that the student is talking about. Ask the student to define the meaning of phrases like *cool*, *going out*, *partying*, *popular*, etc., as they come up in the conversation. You may be surprised that your concepts and ideas about things like *acceptance*, *normal*, and *moral* are often assumed and the meaning can be different enough that we can easily misunderstand. I have my youth ministry students do this exercise and record their observations. Inevitably they are jolted into a fuller awareness of how inaccurate their assumptions are or could become. If a young youth worker makes assumptions where the trajectory is off, imagine how out of touch that youth worker will become years later if he doesn't practice the art of challenging personal assumptions immediately. By doing this, the youth worker compares his cultural ideologies against the cultural ideologies of adolescents. This makes the youth worker an *ethnologist*. While *ethnography* is the study of a culture, *ethnology* is the comparative study of two or more cultures. A youth worker can stay effective, regardless of age, if he stays immersed in the culture of that adolescent community, while continuously comparing that culture's perspectives against his personal cultural perspective.

Understand the process of contextualization

Contextualization, simply stated, is a process of change. The evangelical community sees contextualization as "a way to develop authentic and relevant responses to the Christian message that would lead to significant and beneficial changes among individuals and groups as well as to the confirmation of the worth and value of the message."[1] This represents a mighty struggle of effective youth ministry: How do we make the gospel *culturally relevant* to kids? We continuously look for ways to present Christ and his

---

1. Henry Lazenby, *God, Change and Chaos: The Contextualization of Religion and Society*, unpublished manuscript (1990).

gospel in a way that students will understand and embrace him without compromising the integrity of that gospel.

The contemporary church growth movement was born to embrace this view of contextualization. It largely challenged the values, norms, and practices of the traditional church. It took from the traditional church that which reached a new generation of individuals and reshaped the context by allowing the values of the new generation to form the new context of the gospel.[2] This is often very threatening to the faith community because the church has tended to blur the lines between biblical principle and its cultural interpretation of that biblical principle. In essence, it makes cultural values equal to biblical principle. Youth ministry can and will often come under fire because the attempt to stay culturally relevant can be seen as an attempt to compromise or water down the principles of Scripture.

If the process of contextualization is to be effective, there must be a change within us that precedes the change in how we communicate Christ to kids. That change involves the continuous, internal, personal reassessment of the youth worker whereby the youth worker changes without compromising her personal value and integrity. The youth worker must be culturally relevant before her message can be culturally relevant. This internal process of change (contextualization) becomes part of an incarnational approach to reaching kids.

Philippians 2:1-11 is described as the great *kenosis* passage in Scripture. This passage gives insight into the union of the nature of Christ as being fully God and fully man. This is where we see the change resulting from incarnation. Christ who, being in very nature God does not find "equality with God something thing to be grasped, but made himself nothing, taking the very nature of a servant, being made in human likeness" (v. 6). While Christ does not renounce his divinity, he does renounce the exclusivity of inhabiting the God-form.[3] His divine attributes are not abandoned nor are they unavailable to him, rather they are concealed in the weakness of human flesh.[4] Jesus Christ changed in order to be a servant. He did not change from being God to become man. He changed in the form of God to the form of man as a bond servant. His service was so great that he humbled himself by dying on a shameful cross (v. 8). An incarnational approach to youth ministry demands that we embrace the same servant attitude demonstrated by Christ (v. 5). That attitude starts with a willingness to change.

An effective youth worker is aware that he is in a context that intersects, interacts, and sometimes interferes with the community of adolescents. Youth workers live out the gospel before students, therefore contextualization—while it results in change within the community—also requires change in the individual youth worker. Internal change is difficult and involves various levels of cognitive dissonance, internal realignment, getting out of one's comfort zone, challenging one's personal frame of reference (including personal beliefs and values), thinking outside the box, and living in a constant state of some level of chaos.

2. Steven Gerali, "Paradigms in the Contemporary Church that Reflect Generational Values," in P. Ward (ed.), *The Church and Youth Ministry: How Does Youth Ministry Fit with the Life of the Church?* (London: Lynx Communications, 1995).

3. Karl Barth, *Church Dogmatics, IV, 1* (Edinburgh: T. & T. Clark, 1957).

4. Donald Bloesch, *Essentials of Evangelical Theology*, vol. 1 (Peabody, Massachusetts: Prince Press, 1998).

Pete Ward recognizes not only that the external paradigm shift that takes place in the church is difficult, but that there is also the difficulty of the internal paradigm shift that must take place within the youth worker. He states,

> The evangelical subculture is resistant to relativizing tendencies. It is therefore, something of a shock to find that the context within which you yourself found faith and were nurtured will not similarly help the young people you have come to know. The relativizing of the evangelical subculture involves a major paradigm shift on the part of the youth minister. Suddenly what was seen as a universal answer to the problems of the world becomes one approach amongst many others to Christian truth.[5]

Ward suggests that this internal paradigm shift in the belief structure and spirituality of the youth worker is often accompanied by a need to distance oneself from the subculture and paradigms of the church. He suggests three reasons why this is required.

First, it is difficult to understand that the expression of the gospel, as it is contextualized by the faith community, is only one among many ways to express that message. Distancing, while it creates turmoil in the youth worker, is needed for the youth worker to think outside the box.

Second, many Christians (church leaders, friends, etc.) steeped in a cultural perspective, will find the new approaches, ideas, and questions raised by the youth worker to be threatening. Distance allows for the grassroots movement of an emerging paradigm to relatively solidify. While this may occur, being culturally relevant will always make waves with someone.

Third, those who live in the cultural and social context of the church operate in a different paradigm than kids outside the church. If we are to be like Christ, we must change and step into their world because they will not invade our world. It is also important to note here that while distancing is a necessity to effective contextualization, distancing does not mean that the youth worker abandons either the church or the wisdom of godly leadership. It also does not mean that we become Lone Rangers, intent on establishing a self-contained youth ministry. This distancing is a healthy check and balance where the youth worker constantly evaluates, at arm's length, the culture of the faith community against the culture of the adolescent community. It is in this distancing space that we will experience the personal change—pain, tension, alienation, turmoil, chaos, challenge, and resolve—that will make us all things to all men so that we may win them.

Contrasting imperatives
The contrasting imperatives are fascinating. On the one hand, it seems we have the need to immerse ourselves in the community of those with whom we minister—a call to incarnational closeness. This theological imperative is necessary for us to really know the kids of our ministry. On the other hand, we have a personal need to distance ourselves from our own comfortable cultural zones. This theological imperative is necessary for us to distinguish the timeless truths of Scripture from those context-bound expressions that have likely contributed to our own spiritual formation. Without such theological reflection we may inadvertently pass on our experiences as universal truth and hinder the work of God.

◼ Dwell among: the second incarnational youth ministry initiative

Would Jesus do youth ministry like we practice it? Certainly Jesus could have pulled off a spectacular outreach event. He could have had an unprecedented light and media

---

5. Pete Ward, "Distance and Closeness: Finding the Right Ecclesial Context for Youthwork," in P. Ward (ed.), *The Church and Youth Ministry: How Does Youth Ministry Fit With the Life of the Church?* (London: Lynx Communications, 1995), 42.

show—a supernova experience. Can you imagine the band that Jesus could have had at his outreach event? Hark Harold and the Angels! And talk about an outrageous super-charged activity—everyone-walks-on-water games. This would have made Jesus so much more effective. No! Without discrediting large outreach events, clear thinking helps us realize Jesus modeled a different way of ministry. Jesus came to dwell among those he wanted to reach.

It involves hard-core truth

The Pharisees and religious leaders of the day had a difficult time with this. To them it looked as if Jesus was compromising and participating in or condoning the sin of the rabble. They doubted his deity because of this, for surely God would not get into the center of a sin circle (Luke 5:30; 7:39). Jesus' primary method of outreach was to go where sinners were—to dwell among them (Luke 5:29-32; 7:36-50; 19:1-10; John 4:1-26). Jesus hangs out with sinners. He touches sinners and eats with them, all the while violating every sense of internalized righteousness to which the faith community of the day held dear. We read about the Pharisees and we loath their wickedness but that is because Jesus brings their wickedness to our attention. We forget that these were men who valued rightness with God. Many of them sincerely believed they were pleasing God and never intended to get so far away from God's plan and heart. They had dedicated themselves to godly living so much so that they could not put themselves in the place where they would be tempted to sin or associated with the sin. In short, they separated themselves from sinners. They ceased to dwell among those who needed to be reached as the result of their cultural ideology of pleasing God. They even supported their premises with Scripture, often confronting Jesus with the Law. We would do well to note that, throughout the gospels, Jesus reserves more condemnation for the concepts of righteousness held by the faith community than for the immorality of the sin-living community. We sanctimoniously separate ourselves from kids because we don't need to "hear that kind of language" or "see what they're doing to know they're doing it" or "guard ourselves from making a weaker brother stumble."

Though we never intended it, we may have become modern day Pharisees. Many youth ministries expect that kids should to come to them. It's easier to count heads if we have them come to our events. Additionally, many youth ministries expect students to change behaviors before they will be embraced. We don't want our core kids to be wrongly influenced or offended by certain T-shirts, cigarettes, or language. We even train our Christian kids not to engage with "the world," citing 2 Corinthians 6:17, "Therefore come out from among them and be separate." Ward says,

> A separate subculture lessens the need to engage with "the world." The
> result is that Christian young people are in danger of becoming more
> and more isolated. The separation of Christian teenagers from their
> peers, however, seems to be one of the chief aims of the Christian sub-

culture. Outreach is then limited to brief forays into the outside world to encourage non-Christians to join the youth group.[6]

Rolling Stone magazine published an article by Kevin Heldman[7] entitled "Welcome to the Jungle." The article describes the lifestyle of street teenagers living in the Montrose section of Houston, Texas. These kids are immersed in every kind of sin that could be imagined. Their world is a total antithesis to that of the faith community. The article describes a social service (Houston Institute for the Protection of Youth—HIPY) and a Christian-based organization (Covenant House) that is attempting to reach these kids. Covenant House condemned what HIPY was doing because it was boundary-less, while HIPY blasted Covenant House for being too rigid with their insistence on kids adhering to mainstream values. As I read the article I couldn't help but wonder where the local church youth ministries were. Then it dawned on me that youth workers would have to go down to that bad part of the city at night and walk the same street as a male prostitute or junkie. *Dwelling among* might mean being associated with wickedness, risking our safety, or feeling grossly out of place.

The stark realization is that the majority of the world's adolescent population lives in an entirely different world than ours. Unless we dwell among these kids, we ignorantly assume that we can reach them. We may have a cognitive idea of what's going on in the adolescent community, but we're relatively clueless about reaching them unless we step into and inhabit, reside, make our home in, *dwell* in their world. We become like Christ when we dwell among kids.

It involves invading their world

Invading a kid's world doesn't just mean that we minister to students. It also means that we minister to those within the sphere of that student's influence. In other words it means that youth ministry involves ministry to the people who touch the lives of teenagers as well as teenagers themselves. An effective youth minister cannot dwell among teenagers without ministering to parents, families, teachers, employers, and youth professionals in community-based programs.

Youth workers need to network with area schools and social service agencies (juvenile court, counseling and youth centers, park and recreation districts, etc.) that work with adolescents. One of the first tasks of a youth worker who moves into a new position is to introduce himself to and arrange to meet with area junior and senior high administrators and organization directors as a professional courtesy. A youth worker can invade a kid's world on a professional level by networking with teachers and administrators who oversee student activities and services. While schools protect the separation of church and state, many school administrators see the value of networking. This can often lead to the youth worker's involvement in extracurricular school functions as a volunteer. Schools look for available, reliable adults to help chaperone events and field trips, assist coaches, sponsor club activities, etc. I've known youth workers who have run for school board, been involved in parent and teacher organizations, and

Ponderable
Are there any theologically acceptable reasons for not dwelling among those living in sin?

---

6. Pete Ward, *Growing Up Evangelical: Youthwork and the Making of a Subculture* (London: SPCK, 1996), 181.

7. K. Heldman, "Welcome to the Jungle," *Rolling Stone* (September 7, 1995), 60–97.

even served as security for senior proms. I've also known youth workers who have led 12-step support groups at area hospitals, been police chaplains with juvenile crime units, and run summer sport camps for the park district. All of this allows the youth worker to have an active presence in the kids' world.

One overlooked area of invasion into a kid's world is ministry to parents and adolescents' primary care givers. Many youth ministries do a great job at keeping parents informed about activities and even use parent volunteers from time to time, but they are not proactive about ministry to parents of adolescents. Youth workers can invade a kid's world by providing competent resources that will assist a parent in their task of raising a teenager. Young youth workers often don't initiate this because they feel inadequate to tell a parent how to parent teens without having that experience themselves. This lack of attention to parents can become, and often does become, a ministry pattern. Youth workers must mobilize resources by bringing in parenting experts, counselors, and educators to do parent workshops and interactive sessions with parents and teens. Part of the regular youth ministry program should include series, classes, retreats, and workshops for parents on adolescent-related issues and parenting skills.

It is important to remember that dwelling among adolescents is not just limited to their activity but involves penetrating their sphere of influences. Effective youth work demands that we take Christ into those influences.

It involves going where kids go

The concept of hanging out where kids are, as I mentioned earlier, is the most common way that youth workers associate with dwelling among kids. We know that our presence at sporting activities, plays, and concerts is usually standard protocol. While we tend to put our efforts into these standard activities, we can overlook some strategic points of contact.

Kids hang out at malls, certain favored restaurants, coffee shops and in their bedrooms and their cars. A youth worker should work her way into these areas. It's risky to have students drive you somewhere, but by doing this you dwell among them. Their car is the equivalent of a condo on wheels. Think about it. Kids' cars are fully equipped with surround-sound digital CD players, a cell phone to keep in touch with friends, mobile access to any drive-thru, fast-food vendor (like having the kitchen close by, only you don't have to leave your room). It's not hard to see how this makes a perfect environment to hang out with three or four of your closest friends.

Kids today tend to have different values and experiences than kids of past generations. Their ideas of hanging out will be shaped by those values. For example, hanging out can become a virtual experience. Youth workers should host and become a part of student Internet chats. We tend to think this lacks the relational intimacy we are accustomed to in our world. We forget that we need go where adolescents are; "online" is a location. Cyberyouth ministry may be becoming the cresting wave in incarnational youth ministry.

Weighing the risks
This kind of personal contact is worth the risk, Steve writes, because of the larger theological value that comes from dwelling among kids. Yet we may need to understand the nature of the risks more explicitly if we're going to make judgments about the value of hanging out with our students in this fairly intimate way. Perhaps we can do something that helps us to reduce the risk and still allows us to hang out in these important ways—like ensure that we're never *entirely* alone in very personal settings. Or is this overreacting?

Glory beheld: the result of incarnational ministry

Jesus became like us and dwelt among us for the expressed purpose of allowing us to see his glory. The incarnational ministry that Christ entrusts to the church is for the same purpose. Youth workers are allowed to cross the boundaries of the adolescent community when they become like kids and dwell among them so that the reflection of Christ's glory may be seen through the youth worker. The Apostle Paul tells us that we are to be imitators of Christ (Ephesians 5:1). Christ lives through us, and his glory is seen by kids. When we contextualize Christ in our lives by allowing ourselves to be culturally relevant to kids without compromising the integrity of Christ's character, we become his arms, his feet, his wisdom, and his heart to adolescents. So powerful should be our invasion into the community that we can challenge adolescents to be the same. Paul does this with the church at Corinth when he tells them to imitate him just as he imitates Christ (1 Corinthians 11:1).

Incarnational ministry means that we are entrusted to be the reflection, representation, and tangible expression of Jesus to kids. We do this initially when we submit to personal, Christ-like change—the kind he did when he wrapped himself in flesh and humbled himself. We need to become like those we are attempting to reach. Only then can we dwell among them. Our incarnational ministry task involves stepping into the world of adolescents. God gets the glory—he is revealed—when we leave our communities of comfort in order to bring Christ into teenage communities.

Seeing Clearly: Organizational Context
Dave Rahn

After directing Campus Life clubs for eight years, I decided it was time to pursue my master's degree. The decision made for an easy escape from the gnawing dissatisfaction I had been experiencing as our ministry was growing. My history with Fort Wayne's Youth for Christ chapter had included being part of a rebirth of this organization. A new executive director had come to town at the same time I started college down the road. It was natural for me to connect my own efforts to begin Campus Life with the larger organization, and I grew professionally under the direction of a capable and caring veteran. After leading clubs for four years while attending school, I immediately accepted the full-time responsibility of coordinating Campus Life in the area when I graduated. After a few years we had established a solid ministry focused on helping teens that were not church-oriented to discover the hope of new life through Jesus Christ.

Our organization had grown significantly larger, but the expansion didn't always feel right. When I began as a part-time club director, about 20 of us—almost all volunteers—would meet regularly for training and encouragement. We met in our executive director's home, enjoying the camaraderie of that personal setting. It wasn't unusual to be belly laughing about the antics of Rody's overly stimulated poodle one minute and immersed in misty-eyed prayer about the difficult situations of kids in our clubs the next. Such experiences helped us feel like we were part of a team, that our mission was great, and that each one of us mattered deeply.

By the time I became full-time, our work had expanded to include Youth Guidance, an evangelistic effort targeted at kids in trouble with the law. Our professional team was now a trio, as I joined Rody and Larry, our Youth Guidance division coordinator. Ministry volunteers had grown to around 50, and a couple of office location moves helped us all feel more stable as an organization. The sense of pride in who we were, how we were expanding, and what God was doing through us, helped us develop confidence in our future. We could squeeze our professional staff meetings around a booth near an Azar's breakfast bar; we were very comfortable with one another.

Over the next few years we began more aggressive expansion efforts. Both Larry and I added full-time staff to our respective divisions of the ministry, and our total volunteer numbers doubled. We became a little more sophisticated in our training efforts and a little more specialized in how we worked with those under us. Policies, paperwork, and accountability became more important as the operation grew. Systems were created to ensure that we took care of audio-visual equipment, vans, camping gear—all resources we felt fortunate to have. It became trickier to get people together for meetings if there wasn't advance notice. We locked formal planning days and goal-setting retreats into our schedules early each year. Much of my time was spent in organizational strategy meetings and problem solving. I had to track the progress of our youth evangelism efforts and develop new staff while still working in direct ministry myself. My job had changed in some significant ways, but my awareness that more kids were being reached with the gospel made the extra burden well worth it.

Except for the grumblings.

I first learned that our aggressive organization wasn't as healthy as I thought when some staff complained that they didn't feel a part of the decision-making process. Mistrust began to creep into our workplace environment, as junior staff would frequently see the leadership team huddle in an office for a meeting, or grab exclusive lunches together. "What was the agenda all about, and why can't we join in?" they would wonder.

Our volunteers felt like they were part of a big system; it seemed impossible for all of the professional staff to know everyone who was part of our mission, let alone care for everyone. This was especially true for our harried executive director, who had his hands full trying to raise the money to keep our operation moving forward. To be fair, some volunteers appeared well cared for by their ministry staff leader; others grew disenchanted. Volunteer turnover became a huge problem. I was personally quick to write them off as not dedicated and began to wonder if volunteer recruitment, training, and development were worth the considerable effort. I couldn't understand why they had such difficulty owning the mission and ministry to which I had so obviously committed myself.

That's when I left for grad school. I was feeling more frustration than fulfillment and couldn't clearly understand what was going on. Within a month after leaving I was introduced to the concept that every organization, large or small, has a distinct culture of its own. I learned that such cultures could be explored and analyzed using skills of observation and research.

In particular, I could identify the reasons for my recent ministry frustrations. Fort Wayne YFC's growth had resulted in an organizational structure, communication patterns, and a goal-setting process that undermined the kind of Christ-honoring operation we wanted to be. These insights brought about an immediate transformation in my attitude toward my YFC experience; they allowed me to return to Fort Wayne 15 months later with a surprising optimism about our chances to correct ourselves. I realized that we had not become ugly Christians while we were leading our organization. We were simply naive about the fact that our organization's culture had changed—inevitably—during our growth and, in so doing, had *hindered*, rather than *furthered*, our most important values.

It is understandable that many volunteers and staff who were part of our youth ministry during those days left disappointed with the degree of Christianness they had experienced in our organization. I have since learned just how common it is for per-

Our underminded values
The simple fact that many Christians experience a disconnect between clearly Christian values (as described in the Sermon on the Mount, or the "one anothers" of the New Testament) and their organizational home base ought to sound the alarms on our theological sensors. We have *issues* that need exploring! And before moving to the host of organizational gurus (Covey, Senge, Peters, Maxwell, etc.) for an explanation, we'd be smart to reflect more specifically on what theological values seem to be undermined. We may discover that there's more than *effectiveness* at stake in our practical ministry designs.

sons in churches and parachurch settings alike to experience considerable disenchantment with their organizations. Churches are torn apart over power struggles, changes in methods, and leadership styles.

My own experience has led me to consider the ministry leadership in such places with considerable charity. It's often unfair to question the depth of their Christian faith. It may, however, be fair to wonder about the extent of their understanding about the nature of their organizational culture, and whether they've engaged in the theological reflection necessary to shape the ministry's structures toward greater faithfulness.

As Howard Snyder explained in *The Problem of Wineskins*,[1] the church has often been slow to adjust our man-made organizational structures to the fresh work that God wants to do in our lives. As is true in Jesus' parable, the wineskins of our own design sometimes become too inflexible to accommodate the wine of the always-renewing gospel of Jesus Christ. When clear theological thinking is married to insightful sociological analysis we can identify the changes that need to take place and ensure that our organizational cultures serve the purposes of God nobly.

On the continuum between organizational innovators and traditionalists, those of us who are in youth ministry likely lean toward the creative and flexible side. Without insights about what's at stake in our structural revisions, we may unwittingly employ ministry strategies, programs, and operations that result in undesirable outcomes. Organizations-as-culture are educational powerhouses, tapping into the transformational nature of socialization to help us catch values. I have such genuine respect for the Clydesdale nature of the learning that takes place in organizational cultures that I have sometimes wondered if a youth ministry graduate's first full-time job couldn't undo much of the educational good that I am committed to as a professor. That's why we must be alert. If we don't see potential outcomes clearly, we may unintentionally misrepresent the Christian faith through our organizational culture.

> **Ponderable**
> Can organizations be faithful? If it's possible to lay such a designation on an organization, it will be because its people recognize the places in the organizational culture that are vulnerable to biblical corruption. When we do accurate sociological analysis it's more likely we can do penetrating theological reflection about our organizations.

Ingredients in the mix of an organizational culture

Whether we're trying to understand the culture of our overall youth ministry, or that of a particular small group of teens, there are certain elements to which we may want to pay attention. Analyzing each of these individual parts will give us a picture of the ministry structure that is sharper than what we might derive by thinking about the operation as a whole. It's not unlike how we determine our health status. Symptoms convince us that something is wrong, perhaps because we have less energy than we once did, feel unusual aches or pains, or notice uncommon variations in our digestive system, etc. In order to understand the true picture of our health, we may need to scrutinize parts of our body—including the various systems that form our physical make-up. Those who have tried to understand the development of organizations have found it useful to examine values, beliefs, goals, history, environment, leadership styles, methods

---

1. Howard Snyder, *The Problem of Wineskins: Church Structures in a Technological Age* (Downer's Grove, Illinois: InterVarsity Press, 1976). Though this book is out of print, it has been re-released as *Radical Renewal: The Problem of Wineskins Today* (Touch Outreach Ministries, 1996).

or technologies, and various forms of power.[2] Taken together, these different aspects of a ministry offer a pretty good picture of its organizational culture.

Values

An organization's values can be understood as that which is considered important by those within the ministry. Sometimes these values are openly identified, as in the case when a group chooses to promote their core values through training and other forms of public declaration. In other settings values may not be openly championed, but are nonetheless woven throughout the observable behaviors of the ministry.

For instance, a youth group might explicitly state that worship is a central value in their ministry, but implicitly choose to value the quality of the worship *programming* over, say, the broad *participation* of lots of kids during their meeting times. Both explicit and implicit values contribute to the organizational culture and, as can be seen by this example, both need to be reflected upon so they can be measured against biblical values.

Beliefs

How are an organization's beliefs different from its values? Beliefs are operational assumptions that are building blocks for ministry strategies. Some youth ministries are built around the belief that there is nothing adults do that can't be done better by well-trained students. It's easy to see how significant this *single belief* might be to the organizational culture of the ministry. The same can be said for all kinds of operating beliefs that inform ministry practices.

Note that beliefs may or may not be rooted in an accurate understanding of truth and can often even reflect the nuances of a group's particular theological orientations. Consider the difference between youth groups from Pentecostal and Presbyterian backgrounds. It would be a mistake to underestimate how important the Pentecostal youth ministry's *beliefs* about the activity of the Holy Spirit would likely contribute to the distinctiveness of their organizational culture.

Goals

Like both values and beliefs, an organization's goals can be either explicitly or implicitly pursued. In addition, it's possible for one's personal goals to conflict with the group's goals, having relevant impact upon a ministry culture. However, one of the most telling observation points about goals is when we see the process by which goals were formulated and distributed throughout the organization. Sometimes youth ministers operate like Moses coming off the mountain (or out of their study) with goals revealed to them by God and already written in stone. The only thing that others are expected to do, in such situations, is dutifully pursue these divinely ordered directions.

---

2. For example, see Robert Worley, *Dry Bones Breathe!* (The Center for the Study of Church Organizational Behavior, McCormick Theological Seminary, Chicago); Robert Worley, *A Gathering of Strangers: Understanding the Life of Your Church* (Louisville, Kentucky: Westminster John Knox Press, 1976); Edgar H. Schein, *Process Consultation: Its Role in Organization Development* (Reading, Massachusetts: Addison-Wesley, 1969); Wendell L. French and Cecil H. Bell, *Organization Development* (New York: Prentice-Hall, 1978); Richard Hall, *Organizations: Structure and Process* (New York: Prentice-Hall, 1977); Paul Lawrence and Jay Lorsch, *Developing Organizations: Diagnosis and Action* (Reading, Massachusetts: Addison-Wesley, Reading, Massachusett: 1969).

Whether the goals are worthy or not is beside the point I'd like to make. The organizational culture that results from this type of goal-setting process is very different from that which is felt when the group participates in formulating the goals they will subsequently be asked to achieve. As participants in the body of Christ, spiritually mature people can be expected to help understand the Lord's directives for their ministry.

History

A church youth ministry in our area has been rocked in recent years by the successive hiring of two youth pastors convicted on charges of molestation. With such a traumatic history as an example, it shouldn't be a surprise that this element can be—at times—a dominating influence on an organizational culture. Of course, a ministry's history doesn't have to be catastrophic to impact the overall culture of the youth group. While conducting research about student leader effectiveness,[3] I asked small groups within larger leadership teams to agree on the most significant experience of their youth ministry's previous three years. It was enjoyable and insightful to hear these clusters—without benefit of interacting with other groups—identify the same important experiences. Clearly these collective memories had made a positive impact on the culture of these youth ministries.

Environment

Is there any question that a youth ministry that operates in a wealthy suburban context has a different organizational flavor than that which is nestled in a more impoverished urban area? We will help ourselves if we reflect about how the environment in which we minister may, at the same time, be both a strength and a limitation to our work. If a youth ministry is located in the 'burbs, it may be difficult to attend to the priority of ministry among the poor. The environment will have contributed a natural, though not insurmountable, barrier that is a significant factor in the organizational culture of the ministry.

Socioeconomic status is not the only demographic worth paying attention to. Some youth ministries are located in rural settings where kids live miles away from one another. There are no common or convenient hang-outs where kids comfortably collect. This environmental reality also contributes to a youth ministry's culture.

Leadership styles

Youth pastors and others who serve in leadership roles exercise an impact on the culture of an organization that dare not be underestimated. At one end of the continuum, leaders may exercise an authoritarian leadership style; others are more laid-back and laissez-faire. In between are styles that may be characterized as participatory, consulting, and democratic.[4] Each style adds a distinctive imprint on the ministry's culture. Just yes-

---

3. Dave Rahn and Terry Linhart, *Contagious Faith: Empowering Student Leadership in Youth Evangelism* (Loveland, Colorado: Group Publishing, 2000).

4. While there are a number of sources that speak to a leader's style and instruments that may be used to clarify one's style, this particular continuum is borrowed from Em Griffin's *Getting Together: A Guide to Good Groups* (Downer's Grove, Illionois: InterVarsity Press, 1982), 53–56.

terday I had a conversation with an adult youth ministry volunteer at a local church. She was frustrated to the point of quitting. Her description of the part-time youth director, a young man in his early 20s, painted the picture of a guy who would tell his team what they would each do without inviting any participation in the planning. (This style is almost always frustrating to competent people.) Add to this particular authoritative style the fact that this young man was also poor in his preparation and still developing his own skills, and it's not hard to see the source of frustration for this 35-year-old mother of three. If I would have asked her to color the culture of their youth ministry, I'm not sure she could have reported anything different than the red she was seeing right then! And the rookie youth director's leadership style was supplying scads of scarlet for her vision!

Methods or technologies

Some youth ministries are designed around small cell groups that grow and multiply as their outreach is effective. Others are committed to frequent retreats or mission trips. Still others employ an aggressive strategy of alternative worship forms. Some have begun to develop Internet-based ministry strategies. The list is practically endless when we think about methods used in various youth ministries: concerts of prayer; car wash fundraisers; lock-ins; outreach parties; inductive Bible studies; confirmation classes; newsletters; student leader training; altar calls. Each of these methods or ministry technologies wield influence on an organizational culture.

Some ministries have found it useful to list every method they employ in their work with youth, whether it relates to their direct ministry or the organization of their work. They might then circle the five methods that seem to have the greatest impact on their collective experience. For example, though Campus Life staff insist that there are nine points of concentration to their ministry, one program may be dominated by the weekly large group meetings while another program emphasizes interpersonal appointments. The differences in the resulting organizational cultures are worthy of consideration.

Forms of power

One of the more fascinating considerations of any ministry comes about when we take a closer look at one of the five ways (at least?) power is located in organizational forms.

If we look at the organization's formal *structure*, we are typically checking out a chart that describes lines of authority and accountability. Some charts point to a classic pyramid structure, and others look like a 20th-century matrix variation of this model.[5] In each case it's not hard to locate the power in the organization. Others, in order to diffuse this power, have advocated a cellular organizational structure. In the case of Larry Richards, it is his theological commitment to servant leadership, the priesthood of all believers, and the exclusive role of Jesus as head of the church that has led him to advocate this more responsive and consensual structure for the church.[6]

---

5. Worley, *A Gathering of Strangers*, 36–39.

6. See Larry Richards and Clyde Hoeldtke, *A Theology of Church Leadership* (Grand Rapids, Michigan: Zondervan, 1981), especially chapters 20–23.

Communication patterns are also a form of power within an organizational culture. Imagine that you were an invisible researcher, recording every instance of communication that took place within your ministry. Who talks to whom? How often? Over what topics? Who seems cut off from communication patterns? After some time you would be able to draw these patterns and locate the persons who wield the most power as a result of their place in the communication process. For example, many youth ministries employ prayer chains. If the strategy is designed so that everyone passes the info on to one person who also passes it on to another, then those at any place in the chain have the power to disrupt accurate communication to those who follow. On the other hand, if five persons are called and each of these is also responsible for calling five others, the communication power is more concentrated in these first recipients of information.

The first is a *grapevine*; the next is a *gatekeeper*.[7] Locating the power points through these patterns need not be confined to the ministry's formal communication agenda to be instructive. When gossips are well-connected, their power—and destructive impact—on the organizational culture is important to understand.

Rules and procedures can be standardized in many youth ministries, often resulting in a manual that is intended to govern common, or tricky, situations. The power in this instance is located with those who know, or can change, these standard operating procedures. When a youth minister friend called earlier this week for counsel on how to confront the key distribution policy at his church, he was really experiencing the unwelcome use of power by some who used standard procedures to keep him from giving building keys to some of his youth leadership. Part of the embarrassment for him was that he hadn't realized he was in violation of a policy when he handed out church keys. For those new to a ministry, this is called *learning the ropes*. I watched a veteran youth minister stumble in the first year of a new responsibility because he did not realize the relationship between his reporting procedure, planning, and the budget process. His organizational power—along with his budget—grew the next year when he learned the system.

Paying attention to *decision-making processes* can also be useful in locating power. What decisions—large or small—are made related to youth ministry? Who makes them? How are they made? Listing these three headings (What? Who? How?) at the top of a paper and filling in the columns may help map the decision-making processes and serve to locate those with power. This can also help leaders understand ways they may unthinkingly exclude others from the process. For example, if real plans take place at the "informal" breakfast after early-morning small groups, then the more formally designated times for making decisions can be extremely frustrating for those who weren't part of the bacon-and-eggs strategy sessions. Sometimes our favorite kids wield power in ministry because they actively lobby us in our decision-making. We can't decide if this is a good thing or a bad thing if we don't recognize its existence.

Control of resources is yet another way that power can be located, and like decision-making processes, *mapping* is a useful way to see where the power resides. List

The key to faithfulness
How can getting keys to adult volunteers be a theological issue? It's certainly true that it doesn't *have* to be. On the other hand, if we are missionally focused on empowering others for ministry, distributing church keys to our team makes perfect sense. When a policy (or person) insists that limiting key distribution is central to organizational effectiveness, the ensuing power struggle may contain some actual theological dimensions. Granted, we're not talking about Micah 6:8 here, but there are still faithfulness issues at stake.

7. Worley, *A Gathering of Strangers*, 60–65.

every organizational resource you can think of—from expertise to gifts to money to time—down one column and try to put the name of the person who exercises the most control over that resource in an opposite column. This exercise can help us see who holds this form of power within the organizational culture. It can be enlightening to learn just how much power one person in a small group holds because of the number of resources he or she controls (location, meeting time, biblical expertise, food distribution, etc.). Do you see how this information could help you understand why the particular group has yet to cultivate healthy interdependence?

Why is it so difficult to be aware of the impact of organizational culture? Culture in general is like the air we breathe. We are often unaware of its quality unless there are problems. The same is true for the atmosphere of the youth ministries in which we are immersed.

Intentional eyes and minds
The fact that culture is so often unexamined is one reason that theological reflection—an underused discipline itself—is seldom applied to our organizational life. We don't have much hope at all unless we're intentional in both our *seeing* and our *thinking*.

Seeing organizational culture clearly and theological usefulness

When we see clearly, we have an opportunity that is not otherwise available to us. We can reflect upon what we see. Armed with solid theological grounding, such reflection can help us uncover areas where our organizational efforts are getting in the way of our faithfulness. We can understand the connection between what God wants to do and the organizational (in)flexibility that may hinder him.

Consider the historical example of John Wesley. While his perseverance, godliness, discipline, and passion for Jesus Christ were quite remarkable, there are others in history possessing similar qualities who did not achieve what he did. His organizational creativity was an additional genius he offered the Lord. He preached in the fields because that's where the masses could be reached. He empowered lay preachers because there was so much to do. Class meetings provided settings for accountability and discipleship. Love feasts were celebrations that the common people could understand.[8]

When we're overly pragmatic...
The statement that "organizational vision was driven by theological necessity" really affirms the priorities for which this book was written. Unfortunately, our organizational designs are often exclusively shaped by pragmatic concerns, without regard for the theological implications. We end up stumbling away from faithfulness, ignorant of not only the damage that was done, but the opportunities that may have been lost.

None of these innovations were sanctioned by Wesley's Anglican Church. He proceeded to innovate because he recognized that the organizational forms of the church could not be bent to the work to which God had called him. His organizational vision was driven by theological necessity. Like many of us, he realized that his previous ministry was simply not meeting the expectations of faithfulness that the Lord has for us. Seeing clearly paved the way for his radical changes. Jim Petersen has said that Christians ought to always be revising our organizational structures for the cause of Christ.[9]

To help you see your organizational culture more clearly, try using the following 10 questions to reflect upon the youth ministry that you know the best. Ask the Lord to guide the response to what you discover.

1. What are the three most important values that can be deduced from your behavior, and how do they align with the most important biblical values for ministry?

---

8. Explore each of these topics through the helpful index in Howard Snyder, *The Radical Wesley* (Downer's Grove, Illinois: InterVarsity Press, 1980).

9. Jim Petersen, *Church without Walls* (Colorado Press: NavPress, 1992), 216ff.

2. What three core beliefs seem to have the greatest impact on your approach to ministry? What faith-based beliefs need to have a greater impact than they currently do?

3. Who participates in setting goals? Are they openly reported for all to see? How does the goal-setting process reflect your uniquely Christian identity?

4. What stories in your youth ministry's history are you proudest of? What stories are sources of sorrow? What has God been doing in your history?

5. How does your environment contribute to how your ministry has been formulated? Are there any biblical priorities—perhaps not natural to your environment—that may need to be recovered for your ministry?

6. What three methods or technologies are most deeply connected to how this ministry operates? Is change possible? How could you contextualize Psalm 20:7 for your ministry?

7. What is the testimony of the leadership? What are the conflict management styles of those who lead? Is it clear that Jesus is head of this organization by their leadership styles and patterns, or does he seem to be a figurehead?

8. What does the organizational chart look like? Is it more of a tribute to biblical faithfulness or organizational efficiency?

9. Who communicates to whom? How does Jesus want this to be answered?

10. Where is the power in your ministry? Do those who hold the power honor the Lord with the way they use it? How can you influence this balance of power without violating biblical values in the process?

Theological truth compels us to order our lives and ministries around God's priorities. None of us want to thwart God's agenda by failing to see how our organizational cultures hinder his work.

Seeing Clearly: Social Context
Patricia Davis

Dr. Evil is easily the most memorable comic character of Mike Myers' *Austin Powers* spy-adventure movies. He feebly attempts to gain control of the world by demanding one *million* dollars from the United Nations. His tiny double, Mini-Me, has to be restrained from nibbling the ears of his cat ("We don't gnaw on our kitty! Not even just a little bit!"). His son, Scott Evil, can barely contain his contempt for Dr. Evil's inept and overly elaborate plans ("Aren't you even going to watch them? They could get away!"). But Dr. Evil does one thing very effectively—he knows how to silence Scott.

One of the funniest running jokes of the movies is Dr. Evil's ability to utterly quiet Scott by interrupting him, talking over him, pointing, motioning, and totally drowning him out—"Zip it!… Shhhh….Ziiiiiiip!….All right, zip it!" "When a problem comes along we must zip it!" "Ladies and gentlemen of the jury, Exzip-it A." Over and over again Scott is prohibited from speaking, and part of the humor of the moment is watching his totally frustrated eye-rolling response to his goofy and totally out-of-touch evil father.

For the joke to be funny, Mike Myers counts on the audience to identify with Scott. Myers counts on us to remember the feelings from those maddening moments in our own lives when we have been silenced—especially when we knew we understood a situation more clearly or had a better idea than the one keeping us quiet.

Most youth ministers think of ourselves as the opposite of Dr. Evil—we are the ones to whom adolescents can come to tell us their problems and share their pains. And we are the ones they can count on for respectful listening. Most of us wouldn't like to think that at times we are more like Dr. Evil the silencer than Scott the frustrated son. Unhappily, though, we often function as unintentional *silencers* to the very kids who need our care and our listening ears the most.

All of the youth with whom we work are susceptible to being silenced (despite the incessant noise of any particular youth group meeting). This is true because of something happening in their psychological development at this time in their lives: they are beginning to relinquish their childhood outlooks and identities and attempting to try to establish stable adult identities for themselves—to leave behind childish ways and to become adults.

Silence isn't golden
Can you feel the tremendous difference—in theological values, anyway—between ministry that *listens and hears* and ministry that *silences*? While one hopes that much of what effectively silences young people is done unwittingly, it's hard to think of any defendable reason to silence someone before they are even listened to.

Identity development

Adolescents are at a crisis point in their lives. Their bodies are becoming more and more like women and men; their minds are becoming more and more capable of thinking in mature ways; and their emotions are beginning to get more and more complex. Adolescence is a truly stressful time of constant change. The psychological goal for adolescents is to try and establish some kind of adult stability for themselves—to figure out who they are, what they believe, who they want as friends, and who they want to become. For boys this may be mostly about trying to become the independent and autonomous man the culture tells them they should be.[1] For girls this will probably be a time of entering complex relationships that will teach them who they are.[2]

For both boys and girls, this period is about taking risks. Children who are becoming adults choose parts of their childhood to cling to and parts to reject. They watch adults to see what they might want to emulate and make part of their own lives. No adolescent can feel secure while this sorting-out process is taking place. Every morning a new person might appear in the mirror; every night new dreams take the place of yesterday's dreams. Every day is a challenge. In each piece of clothing, each telephone call, each class period, and each worship service, new things are being added and subtracted. Most importantly, new things are being tested.

In our culture—a culture that demands perfection—most teenagers feel inadequate. It's hard to make a perfect presentation of one's self to the outside world even after we've attained adulthood. Adolescents make different presentations of themselves depending on where they are and whom they are with. They are different at home with their families than they are at church. They are different in worship than they are on retreat. They are different this year than last—different this afternoon than this morning. Each presentation is an important experiment with identity. But our culture provides a cruel stage for experimentation. Where nothing less than perfection is required, kids are reluctant to stray very far from what seems to them to be perfect (or at least "normal"—which is as close as most can come to perfection).

Adolescents need *oases*—places where they can go and make mistakes and be imperfect—places where they can test themselves in the presence of safe, caring, and accepting adults and peers. An adolescent who is given the zip-it silencing treatment, learns quickly not to experiment or trust himself. But silencing can also be manifest in more subtle ways than the physical restraining of someone's voice—a room can be full of noisy teenagers who are silenced nevertheless. How is that so?

Kids are susceptible to being silenced, because they are unsure that they are worthy—unsure that they even are *real* people. Anytime a teenager, or anyone, feels that his inner world does not match with his outer world—that his deepest feelings are not valued by those in his outer world—that his views are not acceptable or interesting to those with whom he associates (especially people he admires)—he will be more likely to be quiet about his real self and his real beliefs. If he attends a youth group or a church where one point of view prevails all the time—where one way of doing things always wins, where there is no encouragement to question and to be different—he will more than likely *act* as if he agrees, or believes the same, or doesn't have questions. Eventually, if he doesn't quit or act out (Columbine is an extreme example) he will

---

1. See Eric Erikson, *Identity: Youth, and Crisis* (New York: W. W. Norton, 1968), part III. See also William S. Pollack, *Real Boys* (New York: Random House, 1998).

2. See Carol Gilligan, *In a Different Voice: Psychological Theory and Women's Development* (Cambridge, Massachusetts: Harvard University Press, 1982), chapters 1–3.

forget the real part of himself that isn't valued. He will forget his real feelings, questions, and desires in order to be a person who is treated with what appears to be respect. Being silenced means being shut down psychologically—being forced to stop growing and changing, forced to give up on the project of becoming the person God intends him to be.

Silencing a teenager is almost equivalent to asking her to forego salvation—how can she present her*self* to God when she has been prevented from developing the *self* she needs to be?—when she has been forced to adopt a style instead of a true identity?

Ponderable
Does there have to be a clash between a theological commitment to absolute truth that is significantly, if not entirely, knowable and a desire to help students develop their own sense of identity? Say, for example, you're convinced that unless students build their identity around the exclusive claims of Jesus Christ to be the way, the truth, and the life, their identity construction will be fatally flawed. You come to that conclusion based upon your theological convictions. Does this mean you're a silencer of kids who are working out their identity formation because you don't consider all options to be equally worthy?

To what degree should you respect the intensity and personal nature of the identity task that young people must engage in? How can you hold your theological convictions and, at the same time, be genuinely supportive to them in their process?

Kids at special risk of being silenced

Some youth are particularly susceptible to being silenced because they are, by definition, not a part of what is considered normal. These include: most girls, youth from outside the majority race or ethnicity (especially if they are attending mixed-racial/ethnic fellowships), youth from lower-income families, youth who are lesbian or gay, and youth who are in other ways different, quiet, or odd. Sadly these kids tend to be silenced even when their youth leaders and teachers are not particularly sexist, racist, classist, or homophobic.

Silencing doesn't take place because the youth leaders or teachers are evil—more often it is because the leaders have accepted the hurtful cultural norms without thinking about them. Silencing happens naturally because the leaders *are* who they *are*—with their own identities at stake, points of view, ways of looking at the world, theologies, and ways of judging what is and is not important and true. Unhappily the leaders themselves—along with the rest of the culture—have been taught to be in compliance with the norms, and even to forget that the norm is an artificial set of potentially and probably hurtful rules.

It is very hard to listen to someone who seems different—and hard to give respect to the ideas of someone we feel has less valid ideas than our own (even if we wouldn't admit we feel this way). It goes against the grain even to notice those who do not fit the norm—the ones who don't behave—dress, speak, walk, look—in the ways we are all taught to expect from important people. One example of silencing is the way in which the culture, and even the church, refuses to hear adolescent girls. Similar dynamics take place for kids who are black, Asian, Hispanic, poor, gay, lesbian, or just different in any other major way.

How girls are unintentionally silenced

Silencing a girl is another way of telling her she's not smart, that her ideas are not good, that her ways of looking at the world aren't valuable, and—at the deepest level—that she doesn't really matter. No one who loves kids would intentionally do this to any girl—yet, studies show that we silence girls unintentionally all the time. Adolescent girls live in the same world as their male counterparts, but they experience it much differently. Among other things they are more likely to be depressed, to try to commit suicide, to be the victim of violent sexual assaults, and to experience the consequences of sexual activity (becoming pregnant and losing their social standing). They are less likely than boys to be called on in any class in school, less likely to find role models in their textbooks, and more likely to be told to be content with traditionally female career choices.[3]

Many girls become confused and depressed around the time they enter high school when gender roles become very rigid and pronounced. They discover that although they used to have the run of the playground, they are now expected to be young women—more sedate and polite. They learn quickly that to attract a boyfriend they must appear to be less intelligent, lose weight—in fact, they must pay excruciating attention to every detail of their appearance, and stuff anger deep inside themselves so that it doesn't ever show. They must learn to compete with their friends and other girls for boys. They must take care of others' feelings. Above all they must be nice and perfect.

All of these rules serve to teach girls that they must not talk—at least not about anything that really matters to them. Their emotions may be too intense, and they may actually place themselves in danger by revealing their inner lives. I've never met a youth leader who intentionally silenced girls. But youth groups often serve to silence girls by reinforcing the two most powerful cultural messages: girls must be nice and they must be perfect. When a girl hears these messages at church, they seem to be sent to her from God. Does God really value niceness and perfection, as the culture defines it, above all else in girls? Does God expect girls to swallow their anger when it is often a sign that they are being abused or are in compromising situations? Does God want girls to value their appearance to the point that they stop eating and caring for their bodies? Do we send a message to girls that they aren't important when we call their agonizing over relationships *silly*, and tell them that they don't really know what love is? Do we reinforce the cultural sexual double standard for girls when we insist in our sex education classes that the girls should be the gatekeepers and upholders of sexual morality?

Most of us would never intentionally silence girls—or any other member of our youth groups—yet we seem to send them messages that tell them not to speak. Where do these messages originate? How do we learn them? How can we unlearn them?

How we learn to silence others

At a recent youth seminar where a friend of mine was a leader, she was approached by a young man—a youth leader—who wanted to discuss the problem of hypocrisy in his group. He was extremely frustrated with his senior high students, because the ones he called the *good kids*—the natural leaders, good-looking, good students, well-respected by the adults, and socially-involved—were also the kids who were partying, taking drugs, drinking, and having dangerous sex on the weekends. He was particularly mad that some of them were coming to church on Sunday mornings drunk.

---

3. See Patricia H. Davis, *Counseling Adolescent Girls* (Minneapolis, Minnesota: Fortress Press, 1996), chapter 1.

When my friend suggested that perhaps these weren't really the *good kids* in his group, and that he might want to consider removing them from positions of leadership, he was shocked. She told him that, in fact, it sounded like the other kids—the ones with less polish and sophistication, less-stylish clothes, not the best grades, and less adult approval—probably had a better chance of deserving the description *good* than the first group. It seemed as if these more invisible kids were being silenced in his church, and they were learning a hard and bad lesson: those who present themselves in the perfect mode are more likely to be heard and appreciated despite their self-destructive behaviors.

Ironically, in accepting the cultural picture of who is good and important, this youth group leader was hurting the first group as well as the second. In overlooking the first group's dangerous, dishonest, and ultimately self-destructive behaviors, he was giving his unspoken approval to it. In allowing them to function as leaders in the youth fellowship, he was teaching them that appearances are more important than reality. Isn't this the opposite of what we should be trying to teach adolescents about their relationships to each other, the church, and to God?

Where did this youth leader learn to silence the *invisible* kids in his group? Indeed, why were they invisible to him? And why did the other group—the group he called *good*—seem so important to him?

These kinds of lessons are not taught by our parents or our schools directly. They are not learned like we learned how to tie our shoes, match our clothes, use forks and knives, write in cursive, or take SAT tests. If our shoes don't stay tied we can return to our father to demand more instruction. If we don't get a high enough score on our SAT's, we return to our prep course teachers and demand a refund. But the kind of learning that teaches us to silence others seems almost to come from the air we breathe. Philosophers of knowledge tell us that this kind of learning takes place without specific teachers and without our even being aware of it; this unexamined and unnamable knowledge is called *tacit knowledge*.[4] It's taught to us in many ways—all of them indirect. It is knowledge overheard in our grandparents' and parents' houses, on the street, on television, and in church. It tells us what is true and not true about our lives on the most basic levels—the levels we are taught never to question. We learn such things as: it's okay to eat meat, not bugs, and never peanut butter sandwiches that have fallen to the ground; that churches are holy buildings; that women need to wear shirts or blouses at all times, but men don't; that we ring bells when people are married and when they die; that raising our lips at the edges and showing some teeth (smiling) usually is a signal of happiness, but sometimes of threat; that it is a good thing to be married and to have children.

Some of these may seem like silly examples; most of us have probably even violated the peanut butter on the ground rule. But the most powerful tacit knowledge doesn't seem like knowledge at all—it seems more like "the way things really are and ought to be." Tacit knowledge as a whole is a vast collection of these kinds of rules and

4. Michael Polanyi, *The Tacit Dimension* (Gloucester, Massachusetts: Peter Smith, 1983).

"truths" that shapes and guides the ways we live our lives. Without this kind of very basic knowledge, the world would be chaotic, unmanageable, unintelligible, and essentially meaningless. Children are allowed several years to learn tacit knowledge; adults who don't seem to have learned it are often considered crazy.

Not all tacit knowledge is harmless or beneficial. Some of the tacit knowledge of this culture includes such harmful beliefs as: the more important gender is male; the most favored race is Anglo; the best body shape is thin; the cultural expectation for its members is perfection; lower economic status is despised; violence is to be tolerated; and silence is to be expected from all those who are not male, Anglo, thin, perfect, rich, and successful. These evil cultural tacit beliefs are harmful for everyone, because they produce oppression and violence—and they are powerful because, for many, they just seem to be true.

Christians have a call to be resisters of these evil tacit beliefs. In Jesus' last prayer for his disciples, he says: "As thou didst send me into the world, so I have sent [the disciples] into the world. And for their sake I consecrate myself, that they also may be consecrated in truth" (John 17:18-19 RSV). Jesus is not asking that his followers be taken out of the world; in fact, the opposite is true. But, he asks that the disciples be "consecrated in truth," freed from the kinds of tacit "knowledge" that produces sin, hatred, and oppression. The ultimate goal is "that they may all be one" (John 17:21 RSV) and "that the world may know that thou hast sent me and hast loved them even as thou hast loved me" (John 17:23 RSV). Christians are called to uncover tacit beliefs that work in opposition to God's will, hurt others, and cause violence. Christians are called to resist this kind of evil cultural tacit "knowledge" to bring glory to God's name.

Part of what it means to resist harmful and untrue forms of tacit knowledge, is to uncover those kinds of accepted beliefs that lead to the devaluing of girls; to racist actions and thoughts; to the devaluing of the poor; to the oppression of gay and lesbian people; and to the disapproval of anyone who seems different from normal. Once these beliefs are uncovered, it's easy to see that they are false by the standards of God's love. God empowers us to uncover these beliefs so that we can "all be one." To uncover falsity, however, is also to uncover our own accountability. We have not often listened to those the culture has devalued; in fact, most often we've contributed to silencing them, even though we try not to be sexist, racist, etc.

The youth group leader mentioned above was shocked and saddened to think that he might have contributed to the pain of both groups of youth in his church by unthinkingly affirming what seemed normal to him. The handsome, thin, rich, white kids just seemed better. By the time he left my friend, he had been encouraged— reminded that he wasn't totally blinded by the cultural tacit belief system. He had at least taken the first step in uncovering some harmful tacit beliefs—he had gotten angry and frustrated by the kids' behaviors. In the end he was able to see that he also needed to resist and challenge the cultural norms that had hidden the hard truths about his

A theological spring cleaning
This discussion is key to the central purpose of this book. Patricia Davis writes that we may have to do some massive spring cleaning regarding our theological thinking and identify previously unexamined tacit beliefs, dragging them out in the open for closer scrutiny and submitting them to rigorous tests in the light of God's word. That's a lot of work, not naturally or easily done; few things are more important for our lives or ministries.

youth fellowship. He left with the hope that when he is able to refocus his attention on the invisible group, they will undoubtedly feel more free to speak and be themselves. Removing the previous leader group from the privileges of leadership will probably help them understand the necessity of changing their behaviors; at the least, it will show them that their actions have consequences. Both groups will have been encouraged to move toward what God intends for them, through the courage of this youth leader who was angered by hypocrisy.

★ ★ ★

Very few among those of us who call ourselves youth ministers or leaders would intentionally silence any adolescent based on gender, race, sexual orientation, or the economic status of her family. Most of us, however, unintentionally silence some of our youths because we have not adequately uncovered and resisted some of the harmful and hurtful tacit beliefs we've inherited from our culture. God calls us to the work of resisting these harmful messages for the sake of our own souls, our youth, our churches, and ultimately for the glory of God. Our goal should be the creation of fellowships where every member can feel free to speak, test, grow, and become what God intended that individual to be.

Thinking Creatively: Beyond a Marketing Approach to Networks
Mark Dodrill

Something was bothering Juan as the worship band played the final song at the annual event organized by the Barcelona Youth Coalition he had helped found. Originally the idea of a united front between area church and parachurch youth ministries had seemed quite attractive. But the reality of making program decisions in a group with highly diverse philosophies of ministry was taking its toll. While one leader was intent on doing a theological analysis of the lyrics of the worship songs, another was thrilled by the impromptu conga dance that had started during an upbeat praise number. The result was often a consensus program based on common denominators that lacked the creative edge Juan liked to see in his own group's events. He thought for a moment of how incredibly unspiritual it would sound for him to propose that the coalition be discontinued. "Of course a united front is an important goal," he mused, "but at what price?"

Sometime during the 1970s a new verb came into use in the English language. In the face of rapid technological advances and globalization, many business leaders began to talk about *networking*. "More than we ever anticipated, alliances among companies are changing the way business is conducted today," says business consultant Larraine Segil. In her best-selling book on the subject, she goes on to note that alliances are "today's most important strategic tool." However, far from being an international expression of peace and brotherhood, business alliances are pursued for mutual advantage and often for competitive advantage over a key rival. The title of another book clearly underlines this purpose, *Collaborating to Compete: Using Strategic Alliances and Acquisitions in the Global Marketplace.*[1] Despite the enthusiasm over this new trend, Segil cautions that "an alarming 55% of alliances and 78% of mergers and acquisitions fall apart within three years of conception. And only 23% recover the costs of walking down the corporate aisle."[2]

But what does this business trend have to do with youth ministry? Strategic alliances or the development of networks, as it is sometimes called, are also becoming more common in youth ministry. One of the first groups to highlight this concept was the National Network for Youth Ministries in 1981. The reasons cited for advocating greater cooperation in youth ministry have not only been practical but also theological. No one, at least openly, advocates cooperation with other youth ministries as a way of gaining strategic advantage for one's own. Sometimes such efforts have produced a true synergy and a more effective ministry for all the groups involved. On other occasions however, the time and energy invested have led to disappointing results, sometimes

---

1. Joel Bleeke and David Ernst (eds.), *Collaborating to Compete: Using Strategic Alliances and Acquisitions in the Global Marketplace* (New York: John Wiley & Sons, 1993).

2. Larraine Segil, "Strategic Alliances for the 21ˢᵗ Century," www.larraine.segil.com (1999).

yielding less than any of the participating groups would have on their own. What biblical and theological principles can provide orientation for this aspect of youth ministry?

A theological framework for strategic alliances in youth ministry

The word *alliance* and its various synonyms, such as *pact, agreement, relationship,* and *covenant* are central to the entire message of the Scriptures. The major divisions in the Bible are called the Old Covenant and the New Covenant because a major theme of the Scriptures is the relationship between God and humankind. Jesus said that second only to loving God with all one's heart, soul, and strength was loving one's neighbor as one's self. A theological basis for building networks for youth ministry must start with the basic obligations of love and respect that Christians should have for all—and especially for all other Christians. However, the kind of relationship involved in a strategic alliance goes beyond this basic foundation of love and respect since it is also a working relationship where the differences between people can either facilitate or frustrate the achievement of the shared goal of bringing young people to spiritual maturity in Christ.

God's plan for unity and diversity

The Scriptures teach that God's plan for humankind contemplates both the need for unity and diversity. Many human civilizations have wanted to homogenize groups of people into a large melting pot for more effective centralized control—just like the early Babylonians attempted to do at the Tower of Babel. But in response, God introduced immediate cultural, ethnic, and linguistic diversity to mix things up a bit. While some interpreters have seen such diversity as a curse, it actually works toward the fulfillment of God's original purpose and would have occurred as a natural result of carrying out the creation mandate to "fill the earth." God's idea of unity is not an artificial uniformity but one that reflects his own triune nature where the parts are neither confused nor divided—where unity coexists with diversity. As Old Testament scholar Walter Brueggeman puts it in discussing Genesis 11:

> Thus what may be discerned in our text as the judgment of God may also be another way of forming a community genuinely loyal to the creator and dependent upon God's gifts and purposes. In such a community there may be different languages attending to distinctive needs, yet the community is not divided in its primary loyalty.[3]

Diverse networking
This is significant to a discussion about networking, which often becomes basically doing the *same something in the same way.* To the contrary, Mark Dodrill is suggesting that the only *sameness* we must insist upon is our commitment to the Lord in the midst of whatever we do. Other than that, diversity should actually be embraced—a distinctly different approach from typical networking experiences.

Sin alienates and divides

In the face of human diversity, only God can bring a unity that respects individuality. Sin is the great divider. Although theologians have advanced several suggestions regarding the essential nature of sin—including unbelief and disobedience—the one that most directly affects our relationships with others is that of pride. Pride is com-

---

3. Walter Brueggeman, *Genesis* (Atlanta: John Knox Press, 1982), 100.

petitive by definition. It tolerates no rival; its goal is total supremacy. It breaks up friendships, causes divorces, foments rivalries, and delights in winning an open war. Human sin takes natural differences based on race, sex, or family or social backgrounds and turns them into reasons for exclusion and claims of superiority. Sinful pride is capable of immense subtleties, refinement, and self-discipline if only a sense of superiority can be maintained. If left unchecked, it can turn any "ministry" into a project for self-promotion.

In his fascinating theology of church structure, James F. Cobble explores the social dimensions of sin and demonic powers. He traces the relationship between human institutions that give order and structure to social relationships and the "basic principles of this world" as well as the "principalities and powers" discussed by the Apostle Paul in Galatians 4:8-11 and Colossians 2:14-16; 20-23.[4] The organizations and ministry structures created by individuals within the church can be changed and influenced by them in their initial stages, but as the process of institutionalization sets in, these structures take on a life of their own and begin to regulate and control the lives of those who participate in them, including the lives of their creators.

One of the ways in which such powers manifest themselves is in their ruthless quest for growth and self-preservation. Personal salvation does not necessarily dismantle structural sin. Such powers operate not only in the larger economic and political systems in society but also in church and ministry structures. Youth ministers often discover the strength of these powers through what someone has called the seven last words of the church: "We have always done it this way." But neither are they exempt from the controlling influence that their own youth ministry structures can exercise upon them.

Christ reconciles people and breaks down barriers

The salvation that comes through faith in Jesus Christ strikes a deathblow to sin since it requires sincere confession and repentance. The Apostle Paul states that it comes through faith "not by works, so that no one can boast" (Ephesians 2:9). In the same passage he goes on to outline some of the social implications of the gospel to the most important cultural and ethnic division of his time, that between Jews and Gentiles. "For he himself is our peace, who has made the two one and has destroyed the barrier, the dividing wall of hostility" (Ephesians 2:14). In Galatians 3:28, oneness in Christ is seen to abolish the discrimination based on ethnic, cultural, economic, and sexual differences.

The body of Christ

Despite the clarity of the gospel message in regard to the nature of relationships among Christians, it is clear from the Acts of the apostles and the Epistles that the early Christians were not exempt from tensions in their working relationships with each other. Sanctification is progressive and the New Testament is filled with exhortations to "live

---

4. James F. Cobble, *The Church and the Powers: A Theology of Church Structure* (Peabody, Massachusetts: Hendrickson Publishers, 1988).

by the Spirit" so as not to "gratify the desires of the sinful nature" with this specific application in mind (Galatians 5:16). The Corinthians used not only natural distinctions like economic background (1 Corinthians 11:17-22), but also the preference for the teaching of certain leaders (1 Corinthians 3), and the use of particular spiritual gifts (1 Corinthians 12) as a basis for rivalries and distinctions between them.

In response to the latter problem, Paul appeals to the principle of unity in diversity as pictured in the illustration of the body of Christ. "The body is a unit, though it is made up of many parts; and though all its parts are many, they form one body. So it is with Christ" (1 Corinthians 12:12). In an atmosphere of conflict in which many were intent on making everyone else's experience conform to their own, Paul said it's all right to be different. In 1 Corinthians 12:4-6, he talks about different *gifts (charismaton), services (diakonion)*, and *workings (energematon)*. This detail is helpful because it shows that legitimate differences occur not only on an individual level, but also in regard to groups of Christians within the church and different kinds of activities. Specialization is a necessity and a fulfillment of the unique gifts God gives to each one. What the unity of the body of Christ forbids is prideful independence from or exclusion of other members.

Partnership in the work of the ministry

Paul sought to apply these principles to the relationships between different churches and his own apostolic ministry. Missiologist Ralph Winter notes that this apostolic band developed a certain independence from the local churches both in terms of economic support and direct supervision, and thus represents a kind of prototype of mission societies and other specialized parachurch ministries.[5] However one interprets this historical precedent, it certainly represents a case study in conflict and cooperation between groups in Christian ministry. For example, the Council at Jerusalem (Acts 15) was called to deal with a theological issue that threatened to hinder Paul's preaching to the Gentiles. The resulting decision allowed for Jews to continue to keep the ceremonial law, but did not obligate the Gentiles to do so as well. It left Paul free to continue his specialized ministry.

Later in the same chapter, Paul has to deal with conflict within his own apostolic band. Barnabas had a more inclusive and forgiving policy in regard to giving a second chance to John Mark. Since they could not reach an agreement on the matter, Paul and Barnabas decided to go their separate ways. The writer of Acts simply reports this event without taking sides one way or the other. He leaves the reader wondering, Who, if anyone, was at fault here? Does the principle of Christian unity obligate them to work together or was it all right for them to go their separate ways, at least for a time?

In other conflicts, the reporting is not as neutral. In Paul's struggle with the "false apostles" of 2 Corinthians, there is little room for doubt about who the bad guys were. The key issue seems to have been that these other apostles were not simply in disagreement with Paul, they were distorting the essential nature of the gospel.[6]

---

5. Ralph P. Winter, "The Two Structures of God's Redemptive Mission," *Missiology: An International Review* (January 1974), 121–139.

When this was not the case, Paul responded in a different way. In Philippians 1:15-18 he reports on some who "preach Christ out of envy and rivalry" but his response is without defensiveness or self-pity. "But what does it matter? The important thing is that in every way, whether from false motives or true, Christ is preached. And because of this I rejoice."

So it seems that while Paul valued the collaboration of others in the task of ministry, he picked his potential partners with care. Robert Banks points out that the expansion of the Roman Empire in the first century led to a decline in the ability of both the family and the city-state to effectively organize social life at the local level. As a result, voluntary associations began to be formed to advance the common interests of such diverse groups as craftsmen, herders, women, youth, and religious groups.[7] The key principle for the formation of such a voluntary association was that of *koinonia*— a relationship based on voluntary sharing or partnership. J. Paul Sampley goes even further and sees the term as equivalent to the legally binding verbal contract of the Roman *societas*. In this light, when Paul speaks to the Philippians of *koinonia*, he is not referring to some kind of vague superficial relationship, but rather to a serious partnership in which both parties were committed to common goals. In the lists of personal greetings to individuals at the end of Paul's epistles, he commends those colaborers who have sacrificed much, worked hard, and loved deeply, but he also warns against partnership with some who like Alexander, the metal worker, have done "a great deal of harm" (2 Timothy 4:14).

Two main applications grow out of this theological overview of strategic alliances for ministry: some youth workers may need to broaden their perspectives and adopt a more open attitude toward working together with other ministries. Others may need to leave behind an all-inclusive ideal and think more critically about the strategic alliances in which they are involved.

Changed attitudes for a broader perspective

Historically youth ministry has been a highly entrepreneurial activity, based on the creative individual. It was invented as an updated version of "normal" ministry as a better ministry mousetrap in increasingly industrial, consumer-oriented societies. The results have been creative, innovative, and often effective. Mark Senter documents this historical tendency among parachurch groups and suggests that a megatrend for the future is for churches to become even more entrepreneurial in their ministry to youth.[8] In the best light, this tendency reflects a fervent desire to see the message of the gospel communicated to each new generation of young people. Thus it is no surprise that the current interest in networking follows a major business trend.

However, a theological analysis of personal and corporate sinfulness must make us suspicious of our own empire-building tendencies. For those who accept the logic of consumerism uncritically, networks will only be covert ways of enhancing their

---

6. Donald A. Carson, *From Triumphalism to Maturity* (Grand Rapids, Michigan: Baker Books, 1984).

7. Robert Banks, *Paul's Idea of Community* (Homebush West, New South Wales, Australia: Anzea Books, 1979).

8. Mark H. Senter III, *The Coming Revolution in Youth Ministry* (Wheaton, Illinois: Victor Books, 1992).

Confessing corporate sin
"Confessing our corporate sin" may require corporate processing. At the end of 1999, for example, YFC/USA (the ministry that Mark works with) invested themselves collectively in a period of reflection about what they've historically done well and poorly over the years. They acknowledged that the sort of pride the author writes of here often kept them from forming strategic partnerships with others who could help them more effectively accomplish youth evangelism. They signaled a desire to no longer compete for credit, money, or access to the brightest kids; this for the sake of the kingdom. If organizations have a heart, theirs seems to be tenderized for new levels of cooperation. Their example may represent the sort of pre-networking reflection that will help us enter into honest and meaningful partnerships.

Ponderable
Why do you suppose that networking with your own church members—a kind of "intra-networking"—is so often overlooked? Why shouldn't this be the home base of integrity when it comes to networking any further afield?

Ponderable
However theologically grounded and faithful Youthfront may be, might this organization be falling for the same old parachurch pride? The rushing to establish *the* tent under which everyone else gathers? Doesn't "hosting" confer a sort of temptation of status upon the host? All these questions just to say that the practical reasons Dodrill gives for parachurch groups leading the way in coalition-building don't automatically address some of the theological concerns the author raised earlier.

competitive edge over other ministries. They will trivialize life issues and water down the gospel in order to reach a wider market.

It might be well to begin by confessing our corporate sin, by admitting that our youth ministries have often been conducted out of a good deal of pride and self-sufficiency—that we have often failed to cooperate with others either because we have not taken sufficient awareness of their existence, or because in a bizarre inversion of the biblical perspective, we have considered them as inferior to ourselves. If our networks are to go beyond a mere pragmatic business trend, we must realize our need to build relationships with other ministries in order to give *and* receive. We must realize that life together is costly and that it will involve denying ourselves.

A first practical step toward building networks, once we have repented of our self-sufficiency, involves a more careful look at who else is involved in youth ministry in our context. The following are six types of relationships that definitely need to be strengthened:

Youth ministries/host congregations

The first group with which a youth ministry needs a stronger partnership is the host congregation (and its leaders and the families of youth). As the tendency of complex societies to separate into increasingly narrow age groups accelerates, there is greater alienation between age groups. Many youth ministries function as parallel churches and some have broken away to establish independent youth churches. At a recent conference in England, a large group of youth workers were discussing research data that indicated a serious decline in church attendance, especially among children and youth. In the search for solutions, one young leader made a popular suggestion that perhaps the church as we know it should die. While many of us have perhaps sympathized with that sentiment at times, the Scriptures tell us that God's desire is for intergenerational reconciliation (Malachi 4:5-6).

Church youth ministries/parachurch youth ministries

"One of our young people is going into full-time youth work," a pastor confided recently. He didn't seem excited about the idea. When I asked why he responded, "Well, he says he's called to the ministry in a certain parachurch group. His leaders didn't tell us about the idea ahead of time. We have no input in regard to the training he needs or the design of the ministry. They supervise him, but we will end up paying for it because this is his home church." It was a sad example of how not to build a network. The apostle Paul would have been horrified. More than ever before, church and parachurch youth ministries need to take maximum advantage of the resources that each has to offer, but the feasibility of such collaboration depends on the skill with which strategic alliances are built. Given their inherent flexibility, parachurch groups will need to take the lead in this area. One excellent example comes from Kansas City where a fairly traditional Youth for Christ program has been completely reorganized to effectively serve a large coalition of youth leaders under the name Youthfront.[9]

Youth ministries of different churches

Perhaps the most common kind of strategic partnership involves an area meeting for different youth leaders that begins with a sharing of common concerns and can evolve into the planning of joint events or other kinds of partnerships. In the past the strength of denominational lines made such networks difficult, but the situation is changing rapidly in an increasingly post-denominational age. This trend has been quite helpful for overcoming irrelevant or peripheral distinctions, but it is also possible that some denominational distinctives should be maintained. This is another area where God's design for unity in diversity needs to be applied.

Adult-led youth ministry/student initiatives

In spite of television-inspired passivity, some youth ministry initiatives rise up from the grass roots. They may include student-led Bible studies, school prayer groups, and independent music groups. Recognizing, nurturing, and guiding such groups can be a ministry in itself.

Christian youth ministries/community youth services

Many adults are concerned about young people in a given community. Often community youth services touch sectors of young people with which the church has little or no contact. When a congregation begins to develop a genuine service orientation, networks with these groups become essential.

Local ministries/international ministries

A great number of youth ministries use short-term mission trips as part of their program for discipleship of young people. Very few go beyond a hit-and-run approach to the development of mid- or long-term partnerships with the international ministries that host them. The potential benefits of a more stable relationship are enormous.

A need for clearer thinking

An openness to building strategic alliances does not mean that we must go over to the other extreme of a romantic, blind, cooperation with everyone all the time. Jesus gave the following counsel to his disciples before he sent them on their first short-term mission that depended on their receiving some local hospitality and resources. "I am sending you out like sheep among wolves. Therefore be shrewd as snakes and as innocent as doves" (Matthew 10:16). Personal and corporate sin affects not only ourselves but also those with whom we will build strategic alliances. Thus we need to take our heads out of the clouds and think clearly about the kinds of activities we try to do together. Just as the apostle Paul did not establish strategic alliances with every possible

---

partner, we need to be selective about our partnerships in ministry as well. In this sense, a good deal of the literature from the business field can be applied to strategic alliances in ministry.[10]

A partnership is built on a common relationship. As we have noted, in Greek, the same term, *koinonia*, is used for both ideas. Three major reasons are commonly noted for both the failure and success of strategic alliances:[11]

Personal characteristics and interpersonal skills of the leaders

Just as personal and spiritual integrity are prerequisites for leadership in any Christian group (1 Timothy 3:1–13), they are also essential for partners in any strategic alliance. In light of these standards, we should be concerned about such matters as the family life, personal character, and overall stewardship of our potential partners. Unfortunately these aspects are often overlooked—especially when particular speaking or musical abilities are the key point of collaboration. In long-term relationships, personal transparency and the ability to communicate values and feelings on a regular basis also helps to ensure that misunderstandings can be cleared up as soon as possible. Flexibility is a requirement for any ongoing strategic alliance. A generous margin of error, especially in the initial stages, allows for fine-tuning of the entire system.

Differences between the philosophies and organizational cultures of each group

To establish effective alliances, we need to know who we are—our unique identity, calling, gifts, and ministry resources. We also need to have a clear understanding of those aspects of our potential partners. Just as in a marriage, a strategic alliance is not only between two leaders, but between their respective ministry families as well. Without accurate knowledge of the other group involved, too many unpleasant surprises can occur.

Differing levels of commitment to the joint project

Partners need to have similar levels of reliability and commitment to the project, or at the very least, if levels of commitment differ, there needs to be a clear communication of mutual expectations. Many well-meaning partners have failed to plan their use of time and resources carefully. Trust is based on keeping promises. Time must be dedicated not only to the part that each partner plays but often in larger alliances to the organization of joint projects as well. Time and again interchurch projects fall into mediocrity due to a lack of a shared infrastructure.

Person-centered networks
Should even *this* assumption—that networking is project-centered—be challenged by healthy theological reflection? When we see ministry as program-centered, it's natural to find expressions of networking in common programs. But if we see our youth ministry as *person-centered,* doesn't that lead us to think about our outcomes in more personal and kid-specific ways?

Here's what a person-centered network might look like: a coalition of local youth ministers meet together to talk about the kids they know in common, what their needs are, and who seems to be best equipped through gifting and opportunity to exercise a ministry of influence with those particular kids. *That* seems to be strategic networking of an entirely different stripe, and one where the temptations of pride don't seem to be quite as strong.

10. While only a brief summary of some of these ideas is offered in the text, this reference list contains resources for further reading: Robert Banks, *Paul's Idea of Community* (Surry Hills: Anzea Books, 1979); J. Paul Sampley, *Pauline Partnership in Christ* (Philadelphia: Fortress Press, 1980); Larraine Segil, *Intelligent Business Alliances: How to Profit Using Today's Most Important Strategic Tool* (New York: Times Books, 1996); Mark H. Senter III, *The Coming Revolution in Youth Ministry* (Wheaton: Victor Books, 1992).

11. Larraine Segil, "Strategic Alliances for the 21ST Century," www.larraine.segil.com (1999).

★ ★ ★

Building effective ministry alliances is difficult but also essential for maximum impact in youth ministry. For this reason, there are no easy answers to the dilemma Juan faced in relation to the Barcelona Youth Coalition. Sticking with the united front might seem like the more "spiritual" option, but it might not be the best one, especially if it means that individual creativity has to be suppressed. Ideally, these leaders need to work harder to gain the freedom to speak the truth in love and take best advantage of their individual strengths. Jesus foresaw that there would be difficulties in the relationships between his disciples, but he was willing to pay the price to make them possible anyway. (John 17). Visible, sincere unity, in spite of diversity, is a powerful witness to the reality and active presence of God. Networking is worth the effort (or the pain, as we say in Spanish) not only because it often works well, but also because it is very close to the essence of the gospel in which giving is more blessed than receiving.

22 Chapter

Thinking Creatively: Beyond a Warehouse Mentality of Resources
Ed Trimmer

There is an abundance of resources being produced in youth ministry today—but this was not always the case. In the 1960s, as mainline Protestant youth ministry collapsed for a variety of reasons, the number of resources produced by denominational publishing houses dropped dramatically. Into this breech stepped Youth Specialties and Group Publishing. They began to produce a wide variety of youth ministry resources and are still flourishing today. In the 1990s and now into the new century, denominational resources for youth ministry are once again being published in growing quantity as well as quality. From 1994 to 1999 the United Methodist Church, the second largest Protestant denomination, more than doubled the youth ministry resources it published. Additionally, new groups, as well as some old established nondenominational publishers, like Cook Publishing and Gospel Light, continue to turn out youth resource after youth resource.

The overabundance of youth resources has led to dubious habits for many youth ministries. Rather than toil with advanced planning and cautious scrutiny of resources, they simply seize whatever is at hand and off they go. Others appear lost at having so many options available and are paralyzed, wondering which resource is the most useful. Having so many alternatives, while terrific for those who labor in the field of youth ministry, means that extra attention must be devoted to complex choices. Where should we begin? We need time dedicated to planning with God, youth, and the youth ministry team as we assess the congregation's youth ministry. If we don't set aside time to think creatively about what resources we will use or develop in our work with young people, we'll quickly fall into urgency traps.

Several simple principles are essential in this process of resource consideration.

Advance planning

There is an adage that one should plan at least six months ahead for youth ministry or Christian education programming. This allows time to find the best possible resources and to have them available where most needed for God's ministry with youth. Unfortunately, many people in youth ministry do not plan ahead. Two reasons are often identified to explain this lack of advance planning. First, some feel they need to allow room for the Holy Spirit to move; advance planning may "cramp" the style of the Holy Spirit. Second, the culture is changing so rapidly that we cannot predict ahead of time what is needed in youth programming. Both of these concerns deserve some attention.

A few years ago I attended a funeral service for a wonderful Christian woman who had died after a long bout with cancer. The pastor told those assembled that as she

Ponderable
How has advanced planning come to represent resistance to being led by the Spirit? Maybe it's an overreaction to the sort of self-contained arrogance behind some long-range planning. This seems to be what James has in mind when he trashes those of us who act like our plans are sufficient (James 4:13-16). Or perhaps it's a generalized misapplication of Jesus' instructions to the Twelve about defending themselves if arrested (Matthew 10:17-20). But it's hard not to see planning everywhere in Scripture. In fact, we're not to even follow Jesus until we count the cost (Luke 14:25-33). Certainly, we should be careful to not shift our dependency from God to our excellent planning disciplines, but that doesn't justify *not* planning. And, as Ed Trimmer clearly points out, some of the best resources we may want to use in ministry aren't available to us unless we plan ahead.

and he were preparing for this service, she asked him to speak extemporaneously so that he would rely on the Holy Spirit. From my perspective, the Holy Spirit was not present as the pastor rambled all over the place in his remarks and made little sense. She and he both held the odd notion that somehow the Holy Spirit is not available to us in the planning process but is available only when we do not plan. Nothing could be further from the truth. Often it is by allowing plenty of planning time that the Holy Spirit is able to creatively guide us in developing abundant resources.

At times, things happen in the lives of youth that are of such significance that one needs to address them with a sense of urgency. In these situations advance planning must be put aside to address the concerns of youth. However, this happens much less often than those who do not like to plan would suggest. It may be just an excuse to cover up for a lack of planning. Indeed, it is through careful planning that we can address the deepest needs of young people and not just grab whatever program helps are at hand. Those who do not understand the vital role of planning clutch at these two excuses. By doing so they deny youth the opportunity to have the best and most creative alternatives. Naively, they resist God's working in their lives over a period of time, perhaps expecting a miracle from God to make their program vibrant and alive.

Planning over time allows God to be at work in our lives and allows us time to discern God's leading and nudging. Simply utilizing a canned program without appropriate review could be considered reckless at best and potentially harmful or useless at worst.

Time to be creative

Having been the acting academic dean of a theological school on two different occasions, I've been amazed at how many creative people stop being creative in their approach to problems when they're being pushed for time. It's as if they go from meeting to meeting without taking or making the time to think creatively about whatever issue they are facing. To think creatively we need to provide ourselves space and time to reflect on various issues that need to be addressed. We must take enough of a breather to allow God to speak and deal with us as we are in ministry. Too many of us have fallen into the trap of acting as if salvation will come about from being busy or always having something to do. This is simply not the case. If we allow ourselves a daily moment of reflection with God and are attentive to the ministry in which we are involved, often the Holy Spirit will work with us as we plan and think creatively about programmatic resources.

Helen R. Neinast and Thomas C. Ettinger[1] report on a study of seminary students who were divided into three groups. Each group was given the task of getting to a certain place across campus. One group was given 10 minutes, another a half-hour, and another several hours to make the journey. Along the way were drama students acting the part of a person in difficulty. Not one of the group with only 10 minutes to get across campus stopped to help any of the students they encountered. In the more leisurely group every one of the students stopped at least once to offer help

1. Helen R. Neinast and Thomas C. Ettinger, *With Heart and Mind and Soul* (Nashville: Upper Room Books, 1994), 70.

and assistance. The implications of this small experiment are enlightening. Those of us who feel compelled to hurry through our days, hours, and minutes deny ourselves the necessary time required to unlock creativity and develop stronger relationships with God and others.

Drive time, to and from the office, has become an opportunity to spend some time thinking about the ministry of which I am a part. I used to spend the time listening to music as I drove back and forth—trying to keep up with what youth listened to—but then I switched to sports talk radio. Now I often turn off the noise and focus on thinking about the issues of our ministry. During this period of time, I often have—or if your theology prefers, the Holy Spirit gives me—an insight that I would not have had, had I not made time to think deeply into various issues. I believe when we find time every day to work on our walk with God—reflecting about ministry with God—we will discover creative resources available to us.

People

In 1994 I wrote that "people are the best and the worst resource in the world."[2] Today I believe even more strongly that people are the best possible resource available—that God loves to use God's creation of human beings to spread God's message of love to youth. Often, however, we are reluctant to use other people in God's youth ministry for at least two different reasons. First, we are uncertain of the person's theology and don't want them communicating with our youth. Second, we like to be in control and thus we do not want to turn our ministry or our youth over to others. Let me attempt to address these familiar issues.

I have always been, and still remain, wary of letting others speak to or lead *my* youth. Over time, however, I have begun to see how God uses other people in ministry to bring another perspective—maybe even God's perspective—into focus. Even when the speaker has not met my standards of quality, either in terms of presentation or theology, we ought to use the situation creatively and positively.

One of the goals of our youth ministry ought to be to help young people learn to discern God's voice in the midst of a propensity of voices calling out for the attention, response, and devotion of youth. (One way this had been stated in the past is by saying, "Youth will be converted! But to what?" Will youth be converted by the gospel of Jesus Christ or the gospel according to Madison Avenue or someone else's gospel?) Some of those voices are very good in catching the attention of youth. So a practice I have found helpful is to have a time of reflection after every sermon, youth talk, or program. A time when we can ask together, *Was God present? What did that program say to you? Do you believe what you heard? Is that message faithful to God's revelation?* Indeed it is when I am not the main speaker in a program, that youth find a voice and we really dialogue about what is troubling them and how God may be dealing with them. In doing this I am often surprised how well some students filter what they hear or how they hear something—through the aid of the Holy Spirit—that I didn't pick up on.

---

2. Ed Trimmer, *Youth Ministry Handbook* (Nashville: Abingdon, 1994), 94.

Many of us think about youth ministry as *our* ministry rather than being in a partnership with God and with God's people. As such, we are reluctant to allow others into our personal ministry arena, fearing their intrusions. Unfortunately, the ordained leadership of God's church is not providing a model of cooperation in using the people resources of a congregation. So we too fail to identify ways to bring the gifts and graces of others into the congregation's youth ministry. We want control. But God provides an abundance of creative, exciting people as resources who bring a new approach and different frame of reference in explaining God's revelation to youth. All that is required is that we relax our grip of wanting control and that we use them.

Several other issues around people ought to be raised. The first is how little we make use of the people resources in our communities. For example, many communities have small colleges associated with them where resources abound. Additionally, one may be able to bring in a nationally recognized speaker or resource by joining with other groups and simply extending the person's stay by a day or two. This can make the most of limited expenses and help people resources become affordable. And finally there is the issue of youth doing programs themselves. Youth must be encouraged to plan, lead, and evaluate programs. This can be a primary way youth grow in their faith and explore their gifts for ministry.

Finding ways to bring God's people and their gifts and graces into our congregation's youth ministry is essential. Giving up our private control of the ministry to God, to God's people, and to God's church is imperative. Ultimately it is not "our" ministry; it is the ministry of each congregation and a ministry in which God may use us. But we are neither the focal point nor the justification for a ministry. We are not God, although we often act as if we are the only ones who know what God wants.

Places

While we believe that since God created everything, every place has sacred worth, we rarely act out that belief. This does not mean we are pantheists. However, there are indeed special locations that can become sacred places, holding special and religious significance in a congregation's youth ministry. Moses found a special place on Mount Sinai. Often outdoor camps have a special fire bowl where worship takes place after the sun goes down. Can you think of a special place that could be a useful resource for your congregation's ministry with youth? Could you develop a place for the youth of the church? Even ordinary places can become sacred grounds, places where we want to take off our shoes because we know we are in the presence of God (Exodus 3).

A sacred space for younger youth can sometimes assist their emotional transition from play space or eating space to one of worship. Look around and develop those special places that can aid in the congregation's youth ministry.

Ponderable
Are planning, leading, and evaluating programs really the best ways to use young people as resources? Or the best ways for them to grow in their faith? Many would challenge this programmatic assumption biblically. In fact, the more ministry is identified with programs, the less it is identified with the kind of natural, transformational opportunities for influence that Jesus seemed to model. And if programs were not inherently necessary to the practice of biblical ministry, how quick should we be to embrace them as non-negotiables today?

Accidental discoveries
The examples given here for a special or sacred place seemed to be almost accidental discoveries on the part of Moses. They became sacred only as they became the location of a significant encounter between God and Moses. Should we predesignate such locations, or do we simply need to be alert to the possibilities of sacred places as we move through our ministry patterns? In other words, does our deliberate choice of space help to bring about a meaningful encounter with God, or should we seek a meaningful encounter with God and celebrate the special nature of the location after the fact?

Organizations

All around us, wherever we are in ministry, there are a multitude of organizations. Many of them employ people to educate others about services they offer or issues they are concerned with. These can be valuable resources for the congregation's youth ministry. From Planned Parenthood (I know someone is going to get upset about me even mentioning them) to Habitat for Humanity (will someone also get upset about them?), organizations can help in providing resources for youth ministry. Local funeral homes, organizations that deal with addictive behaviors, local schools, public libraries that provide free Internet services, and extension services of land grant institutions are but a few of a long list of such organizations. In fact, in most communities, even small rural communities, there are so many organizations that are willing to come and speak to your group that care must be utilized about who will be invited.

I have often found it helpful to ask the following question as a foundation for sorting out the contributions an organization might make to the ministry: What are God's or the congregation's intentions for this youth ministry? When I have a sense of this, then I can ask whether this organization or speaker helps meet those intentions. When purposes converge, I invite the organization to partner with us; if not, I don't. Our task is too important to get bogged down inviting every organization that wants to speak to us.

What organizations exist in your local community that could assist in your youth programming? What church organizations can you partner with? What theological commitments will allow or restrict you from entering into such cooperation?

My own perspective is that of an ordained United Methodist pastor (chances are that this label—all by itself—puts me in good standing with some and causes others to dismiss me). I have a good United Methodist friend who works at a Presbyterian university. She teases that she is doing, "missionary work among the Presbyterians." Contained in her jest is a deep truth for many of us in youth ministry: we have forgotten the larger picture and are bogged down in the particulars. Can we get beyond our own dogma—our own set of theological imperatives—to embrace the vastness of God's kingdom and those who are working with us (not against us) to help usher in or bring about God's kingdom? We of the Christian faith have so much more in common than those who have rejected or neglect God. Can we find and discover ways to work together instead of competitively? Whether in small, rural churches or urban settings, when we cooperate by using, creating, and discovering youth ministry resources, the youth we touch may move closer to God. We should strive to work with God and all the saints as we endeavor to follow God's leading; we'll help our youth follow our example and be all the richer for it!

Let us not forget the inroads that need to be made to the various professional counseling services available in local communities. Too often I have observed youth workers getting in over their heads in counseling situations where a teen has a very serious problem and the youth worker thinks with a little prayer everything will be all right.

We must know to whom, and when, we must refer a young person. Further, we need this information before a problem exists so that we are ready when the situation arises.

Technology and entertainment

This past year I asked several of my students to try to find a list of youth resources that were available on the Internet. Three of them handed me pages and pages of resources, many times not even duplicating themselves. The available resources not only seem endless, they're growing every day. Add to this the number of resources available on movies (a colleague has a bibliography of over 25 pages on groups that provide resources for movies alone), music, TV, and more. I have a list in my office of catalogs for film rental that's over a foot high.

The growing use and availability of computers will only increase resource availability. But I am not without a caution in this area, as well. Those who are computer literate sometimes act as if computer-accessed information is inerrant. Statements considered suspect in a book or publication may be looked upon as fact when located on the Net. We must remember that the Internet is only a delivery service, not a source of God's revelation speaking directly to us.

★ ★ ★

The availability of resources for youth ministry continues to grow. The tough task in youth ministry is to find ways to evaluate these resources. We need to take the time to plan ahead, find the space to think creatively, and use the resources that God has blessed us with in terms of people, places, organizations, and even the World Wide Web. We dare not forget that young people themselves are among our most important resources. St. Paul was uncanny in his ability to use his contemporary culture to point to God. He often would take a common term or concept popular in the modern culture and turn it or alter its meaning slightly so that it would point to God. With God's help, we too can find ways to bring God's message of saving love to youth in this culture. By God's grace may it be so this day and every day.

Thinking Creatively: Beyond Schooling Perspectives in Curriculum
Duffy Robbins

Do your best to present yourself to God as one approved, a workman who does not need to be ashamed and who correctly handles the word of truth.

—*2 Timothy 2:15*

The task of the modern educator is not to cut down jungles, but to irrigate deserts. The right defense against false sentiments is to inculcate just sentiments. By starving the sensibility of our pupils we only make them easier prey to the propagandist when he comes. For famished nature will be avenged and a hard heart is no infallible protection against a soft head...

—C. S. Lewis, *The Abolition of Man*[1]

Anyone who has had more than a month of youth ministry experience knows the drill: a group of largely disinterested teenagers walk into a typically bland room, listen to an all-too-often hastily prepared Bible lesson, and walk away from the experience sighing in complaint that the whole affair was boring and too much like school. And one more youth worker who graduated from seminary or college thinking, "I have the gift of teaching," finishes out the evening wondering, "Why don't my kids have the gift of learning?"

Just like school

Not exactly a recruiting poster for youth ministry, is it? After all, let's be honest—*boring* and *just like a schoolteacher* are not the two phrases we youth workers hope to build into our résumés. And yet, it may well be that behind the words of this adolescent critique is a more serious question: Is there anything distinctive about our mission of teaching the Bible to teenagers? Maybe *Christian* education, at least in its assumptions, *is* just like school. Or is there some sense in which teaching Matthew and Mark is wholly different from teaching math or Marx?

If we take seriously the call of God, the Word of God, and the work of God, it seems quite clear that there is a uniqueness in our mission of teaching Christian truth to teenagers. As Zuck explains it, "Christian education is unique because of its *subject matter*—the Bible, God's written revelation; because of its *goals*—spiritual transformation of lives; and because of its *spiritual dynamics*—the work of the Holy Spirit." In other

---

1. C. S. Lewis, *The Abolition of Man*, quoted in Clyde S. Kilby (ed.), *A Mind Awake* (New York: Harcourt, Brace, 1968), 241.

words, we are in this enterprise beginning with a distinct and essential set of *foundation stones*[2] that make our task distinctive.

- We believe that these kids are creations of God, made in his likeness (Genesis 1:26), body and mind, not simply brutes manipulated by bodily impulses or physical and cultural realities, but moral agents with the capacity to think, know, and will.
- We believe that this God-given capacity has been tragically marred and damaged by sin (Romans 1:18-32), an inherent flaw that affects both the way we learn and what we do with what we learn, especially with respect to truth about the God who made us (1 Corinthians 2:14-16).
- We believe that the great need of our students is not just information, but transformation, a Spirit-transacted change that comes through a relationship with Jesus Christ (Romans 12:1-2). Apart from this life-giving work of God, the most knowledgeable person on the planet is no more than an educated fool (1 Corinthians 2:12-14).

In short, what we are talking about is a strategic and critical alliance between the youth worker and the Spirit of God. It is the teacher who teaches, but without the Spirit to "guide (our students)...into all truth" (John 16:13), to convict our students of sin (John 16:8), and convince them of righteousness (John 16:13), our effort is bankrupt—no more capable of igniting the fires of passion for God than plastic logs in an electric fireplace. The lesson may look good; it may even provide a little light, but don't expect a lot of warmth from it.[3]

Do these basic theological presuppositions affect what happens when 25 junior high kids stumble into the room for Wednesday night Bible study? Unquestionably. Is what happens just like school? By the power and promise of God, no.

Boring in Jesus' name

We need to be challenged, though, that our involvement in a God-given mission does not give us license to ignore good sound teaching technique. What we are doing is not just like school, and hopefully the way we do it will not produce an experience that's boring. Just as our mission grows out of the Word of God, our methods must be informed by the works of God. And God was not, is not, and will never be boring.

> The people who hanged Christ never, to do them justice, accused him of being a bore—on the contrary; they thought him too dynamic to be safe. It has been left for later generations to muffle up that shattering personality and surround him with an atmosphere of tedium. We have very efficiently pared the claws of the Lion of Judah, certified him

Ponderable
Might God not actually call us to walk through the Valley of the Shadow of Boredom on occasion as we follow him? Doesn't God want to teach us to navigate life's normalcies, which include boring times? And if he does, shouldn't we expect that boredom might actually be an important tool to use, explore, and probe now and then in our curriculum? Do I ever need to facilitate Boredom As Learning? Or are these questions just too boring?

---

2. Mark Fakkema, *Christian Philosophy: Its Educational Implications* (Chicago: National Union of Christian Schools, 1952).

3. The Apostle Paul gives a thorough explanation of the Spirit's essential work in our teaching ministry in 1 Corinthians 2:9-14. See also his prayer in Ephesians 1:18 "that the eyes of your heart may be *enlightened in order that you may know* the hope to which he has called you, the riches of his glorious inheritance in the saints..." (emphasis mine).

"meek and mild," and recognized him as fitting a household pet for pale curates and pious old ladies. To those who knew him, however, he in no way suggested a milk-and-water person; they objected to him as a firebrand...he was emphatically not a dull man during his human lifetime, and if he was God, there can be nothing dull about God either.[4]

Teaching that reflects the image of our creator

The challenge, of course, is to present biblical truth to our students in a way that is neither boring, nor does it stoop to the level of what David Poling describes as "the spiritual babes-in-joyland approach."[5] As Elton Trueblood reminds us, "Holy shoddy is still shoddy."[6] Part of our heritage as people created in the image of God is that we can give glory to our maker through our creative work. Bruce Lockerbie puts it this way:

> We are told that God ceased from all his work and rested on the Seventh Day; but with the dawning of the Eighth Day, the Artist of the Beautiful, the Master Potter, set his Apprentice to work, teaching him to copy the Master's originals, summoning her to image forth new benedictions of praise.[7]

To paraphrase Lockerbie, every time we teach—whether it be through small groups, object lessons, melodramas, lecture, initiative games, role plays, computer graphics, poetry, music, or video, we must view our work as that of a steward rightly using the gifts of God to render him glory. It is a task that brings together new combinations of novelty (thinking in a new way), appropriateness (an approach that does justice to both the topic and the student), transformation (taking something old and making it new), and condensation (taking that which nourishes and serving it in bite-sized, digestible portions).[8]

In light of this challenge, it is no wonder that we so often hear—and perhaps voice ourselves—the complaint of the unfaithful servant, "...I was afraid and went out

---

4. Dorothy Sayers, *Creed or Chaos?* (New York: Harcourt, Brace, 1949), 5-6.

5. David Poling, quoted in Bruce Lockerbie, *The Timeless Moment* (Westchester, Illinois: Cornerstone Books, 1980), 49.

6. Elton Trueblood, quoted in Bruce Lockerbie, *The Timeless Moment* (Westchester, Illinois: Cornerstone Books, 1980), 49.

7. Lockerbie, 23.

8. Philip Jackson and Samuel Messick, "The Person, Product and the Response: Conceptual Problems in the Assessment of Creativity," in Jerome Kagan (ed.), *Creativity and Learning* (Boston: Beacon Press, 1970), 1-19. I have used the four categories suggested by Jackson and Messick. But I have taken some liberties with my brief explanations of these categories, particularly the latter two. For a fuller explanation, as described by Jackson and Messick, see the original article.

and hid your talent in the ground" (Matthew 25:25). There is a risk and a cost to the creative process. In her book, *The Eighth Day of Creation*, Elizabeth O'Connor warns:

> When we have not exercised our own capacity to create, we do not know what it is to wrestle with the angel[9]...If your daily life seems poor, do not blame it: blame yourself, tell yourself that you are not poet enough to call forth its riches; for to the creator there is no poverty and no poor indifferent place.[10]

Jesus' own teaching ministry gives us vivid examples of this sort of creative approach. He used such diverse teaching techniques as—

* object lessons (John 4:1-42)
* relational ministry (John 1:35-51)
* problem-solving (Mark 10:17-22)
* conversation (Mark 10:27)
* questions (the Gospels record over 100 questions posed by Jesus in various situations)
* lecture (Matthew 5-7; John 14-16)
* parables (John 10:1-21; 15:1-10)
* teachable moment, teaching through experience (John 4:5-26)
* contrast (Matthew 5:21-22, 33-34, 38-39, 43-44)
* illustrations, examples (Matthew 6:26-34)
* simulation, symbols (John 13:1-20)
* large and small groups (as many as 5,000 or as few as three)
* modeling (Luke 18:15-17)[11]

And he did all of this without sacrificing content or calling. Jesus was sent by his Father with an explicit curriculum (John 6:38; 17:6-8), and he was faithful to that task. What an awesome sense of fulfillment he must have felt when he prayed in that high priestly prayer, "I have brought you glory on earth by completing the work you gave me to do" (John 17:4).

A curriculum that brings glory

But how do we design a curriculum that is faithful to our content, our calling, and our Creator? Good question.

Perhaps we should begin by establishing what we mean by *curriculum*. Originally, the Latin word *curriculum* meant, among other things, "a racecourse or prescribed path." In more modern usage, the word has come to mean (1) a prescribed academic program

---

9. Elizabeth O'Connor, *The Eighth Day of Creation: Discovering Your Gifts and Using Them* (Waco, Texas: Word Books, 1971), 5; quoted in Marlene Lefever, *Creative Teaching Methods* (Colorado Springs: David C. Cook, 1985), 18.

10. O'Connor, 64; in Lefever, 18. This is a citation from Rainer Maria Rilke's *Letters to a Young Poet*.

11. Robert Joseph Choun, Jr., "Choosing and Using Creative Methods," in Kenneth O. Gangel and Howard G. Hendricks (eds.), *The Christian Educators Handbook on Teaching* (Wheaton, Illinois: Victor Books, 1989), 166-168.

("The core curriculum of our college includes two Bible courses"), (2) a written plan outlining which topics will be taught within a specific subject area or over a given course of time, and (3) the printed handout materials used to teach the lesson.[12] For most youth workers, the major concern with curriculum will be in those latter two areas.

Essentially, what we're talking about is the plan by which we intend to approach our teaching task. Indeed, it is this definition of the role of curriculum that Larry Richards believes has been underestimated and underemphasized in the church.[13] Richards argues that curriculum is about much more than just the content to be learned. It is about structuring a teaching/training experience—whether that be in a Wednesday night Bible study, a Sunday night fellowship, a discipleship camp, a mission trip, or a Sunday school—in such a way that the process of learning be given as much attention as the truths to be taught.

Jesus and experiential teaching
It is every bit as fascinating to study how Jesus *structured* his teaching experiences as it is to study the explicit *content* of his teaching. For example, there was probably something significant at stake when our Lord chose to use nonformal learning experiences as much as he did. Most agree that the learning closest to the natural patterns of one's life has the greatest chance to be genuinely transformational.

Setting the course: curriculum design

It is a basic rule of navigation, and appropriate to the teaching task as well: the best way to begin charting the course is by determining the destination. In the lexicon of teaching, we're really talking about objectives. How do we define our goals and aims for a given teaching opportunity? Before we can design a curriculum, we must ask ourselves, Where do we want to take this lesson?

The church's traditional answer to that question has been the transfer of some set of facts:

- The students will be able to recite all four gospels
- The students will understand that God accepts them as they are
- The students will be able to describe in vivid detail how the left-handed Ehud stabbed the obese King Eglon
- The students will be able to recite from memory each of the Song of Solomon passages that refer to the sex act

This *schooling* approach was essentially based on the general assumption that changed minds lead to changed behaviors.[14] Typically, it featured Sunday school classrooms in which all the chairs were facing one way, classrooms in which the vital signs included

12. David Edwards, "Designing Biblical Instruction," in Kenneth O. Gangel and Howard G. Hendricks (eds.), *The Christian Educators Handbook on Teaching* (Wheaton, Illinois: Victor Books, 1989), 52. In *Teaching for Reconciliation* (Grand Rapids, Michigan: Baker Books, 1992), 135-136, Ron Habermas actually identifies a curricular approach in Jesus' training of the 12 that begins with a Phase One teaching focus: "I am the Messiah"; then shifts into a different focus with Phase Two: "The Messiah must suffer, die and rise again"; and then concludes with yet another focus in Phase Three: "You are my witnesses to all nations."

13. Larry Richards, *A Theology of Christian Education* (Grand Rapids, Michigan: Zondervan, 1975), 320. Richards identifies two ways of thinking about curriculum: (1) a structure of "those things which can best be learned in a formal educational setting," and (2) a way of "structuring roles and relationships" within the "teaching/learning situation."

14. In *The Shape of Religious Education* (Mishawaka, Indiana: Religious Education Press, 1971), 7-8, James Michael Lee characterizes this schooling approach as "a system of complex, planned, organized, systematic, purposive, deliberative and intentional learning experiences which in concept bring about behavioral changes in the person."

quiet, attentive students listening to an intent teacher who in a fit of passion might occasionally gesture to a map of the Holy Land.

Richards summarizes this approach with the following chart:[15]

Primary emphasis	Subject matter and skill development primary; academic subjects have priority
Learning decided by	Learning developed sequentially by experts and professionals
Content determined by	Curriculum content dispensed by teachers and texts and workbooks
Curriculum organization	Curriculum organized around subjects, courses, or disciplines
Criteria for learning	Evaluation of learning largely by paper-and-pencil…tests

Figure 24.1. Richards' summary of the *schooling* approach

The intent of the approach is a good one. We certainly cannot ignore basic Bible content and be faithful to the one who described himself as *truth* (John 14:6). The teaching task is much bigger and deeper than merely seeking not to bore. Too many youth workers, fearful of the B-word, fixate only on the process of teaching and lapse into a kind of spiritual vaudeville that leaves students only mildly entertained and acutely (spiritually) illiterate. Curriculum involves more than simply content, but neither should it involve less.

Ratcliffe and Davies cite research by William McCready (1985) in which he found that religious educators who "identified their work as ministry tended to have unclear goals and unformulated objectives about their work. In marked contrast, those Catholic religious educators who identified their work as education tended to have clear goals and well-formulated objectives about their work."[16] We don't need more youth workers who know how to communicate "nothing" in an engaging way.

In fact, it has been the education establishment's abandonment of this traditional *schooling* approach that has led to a catastrophic decline in academic performance in America's public schools, well-documented by Charles Sykes in his fascinating book *Dumbing Down Our Kids: Why American Children Feel Good about Themselves but Can't Read, Write or Add.*[17] E.D. Hirsch does a remarkable job of describing how present-day education "reformers" have so disparaged content learning and what is described as *factory-model* schools[18] that we have become infatuated with what is now called *higher-order skills*, *discovery learning*, or the *student-centered approach*: "*less* whole-class teacher-directed

---

15. Richards, 18.

16. James Michael Lee, "Procedures in the Religious Education of Adolescents," in Donald Ratcliff and James A. Davies (eds.) *Handbook of Youth Ministry* (Birmingham, Alabama: Religious Education Press, 1991), 237.

17. Charles Sykes, *Dumbing Down Our Kids: Why American Children Feel Good About Themselves but Can't Read, Write or Add* (New York: St. Martin's Press, 1995), 17-24.

18. See for example, Kieran Egan, *Teaching as Story Telling* (Chicago: University of Chicago Press, 1986), 31-37. This book has some wonderful insights about using stories to teach, and how to construct a lesson using story techniques like "binary opposites" (e.g., Good vs. Evil), but he overplays his hand in his critique of content learning.

instruction, *less* student passivity, sitting, listening, receiving, *less* student time reading textbooks, *less*...rote memorization of facts and details"[19]

As one very progressive high school principal put it: "It is more important for me to have students know how to read a map than for them to have any one bit of information about that map. Rather than knowing where Nepal is, it's more important that they know how to find Nepal." In other words, students can be taught something called *map reading skills* or *geographical thinking.*[20]

It's an interesting analogy, because it is reminiscent of C. S. Lewis' comment about a conversation he once had with an old crusty RAF officer who complained that he had little need for Lewis' discussions of theology and doctrine for *he had felt God's presence* (emphasis mine). Out alone in the desert at night, he had sensed this mysterious, tremendous presence.

> Now in a sense I quite agreed with that man. I think he had probably had a real experience of God in the desert. And when he turned from that experience to the Christian creeds, I think he really was turning from something real to something less real. In the same way, if a man has once looked at the Atlantic from the beach, and then goes and looks at a map of the Atlantic, he also will be turning from something real to something less real: turning from real waves to a bit of colored paper. But here comes the point. The map is admittedly only colored paper, but there are two things you have to remember about it. In the first place, it is based on what hundreds and thousands of people have found by sailing the real Atlantic. In that way it has behind it masses of experience just as real as the one you could have from the beach; only, while yours would be a single isolated glimpse, the map fits all those different experiences together. In the second place, if you want to go anywhere, the map is absolutely necessary. As long as you are content with walks on the beach, your own glimpses are far more fun than looking at a map. But the map is going to be more use than walks on the beach if you want to get to America.[21]

Hirsch cites a good deal of research[22] demonstrating that in our repudiation of *content learning* we may have thrown out the baby with the bath water. As Richards argues, process is an important and critical element of curriculum design.[23] But *how* is no more important than *what*. We must not forsake *schooling*, we must go beyond it.

Process versus content
Those who want us to choose between either process or content are forcing a choice that need not be made. Aren't we bound to teach biblical truth as content and help persons experience biblical truth as reality? Neither one is sufficient on its own. If you are one who believes that teaching can be content *and* process, you probably use some form of cooperative learning methods. And if you're successful at teaching through interdependent collaboration, then the structure *alone* teaches something important about the way we are to relate to one another in the body of Christ.

---

19. S. Zemelman, H. Daniels, and A. Hyde, *Best Practice* (Portsmouth, New Hampshire: Heineman, 1993), in E. D. Hirsh Jr., *The Schools We Need and Why We Don't Have Them* (New York: Doubleday, 1996), 129–143.

20. Sykes, 3

21. C. S. Lewis, quoted in Walter Hooper (ed.), *The Business of Heaven* (New York: Harcourt, Brace, 1984), 226.

22. The research Hirsch cites includes Nuthall and Church, 1973; Stallings and Kasowitz, 1973; Brophy-Evertson, 1973, 1979; Good-Grouws, 1977; Rosenshine and Stevens, 1986. See Hirsch Jr., 160–167.

23. Richards, 22.

The Hebrew word for *to know* helps us understand that *knowing* goes deeper than mere cognitive learning. The verb *to know* has a richer, wider meaning that ranges from recognizing good and evil (Genesis 3:22; 39:9; 1 Samuel 28:9), to the ability to perceive accurately (Genesis 19:33, 35; 1 Samuel 12:17), to the ability to discriminate and discern (Jonah 4:11), to growth that comes through experience (Joshua 23:14, Psalm 51:5; Isaiah 59:12).

Research has shown that teaching religious ideas to teenagers as a mere exercise of passing along knowledge has very little impact on their lives.[24] A study of one secondary school in England at which students are given regular classroom religious instruction reported that "relatively few pupils thought that it helped them in self-understanding or regarded it as a personal quest for values and meaning, but most saw it as concerned mainly with the transmission of knowledge, in which they were involved in a passive manner, reading, writing, and listening. *Knowledge was indeed acquired, but few saw any use for it in the future*" (emphasis mine).[25]

An approach to teaching that gives us this fuller range of *knowing* is reflected in Robert Gagne's five varieties of learning capabilities,[26] listed below with examples of how these varieties of learning experiences might be relevant for a junior high Bible study:

- Impart basic intellectual skills *(John 3:16—What do the components of this Bible reference mean? Is this a man's name, his birthday, or a bathroom on the third floor?)*
- Extend verbal information *(Where is the Gospel of John? How do I find other Bible verses?)*
- Facilitate development of cognitive strategies *(How can I understand these verses when I find them?)*
- Develop attitudes *(What difference does God's love make for me?)*
- Enhance life change *(How would my behavior change if I took seriously God's love for me?)*

The significance of this approach is that it reminds us that different kinds of curriculum are suited to different kinds of learning.[27] There is a sense in which it is completely appropriate to define our teaching objectives in very basic terms: *ownable* (we might expect the student to be willing to receive this objective—to respond to this truth or lesson), *reachable* (the student is able to accomplish this response), and *measurable* (we will be able to evaluate whether or not we have accomplished our objective). Or to put it another way, lesson objectives should be "(1) brief enough to remember, (2) clear enough to write down, and (3) specific enough to achieve."[28]

---

24. Kenneth Hyde, *Religion in Childhood and Adolescence* (Birmingham, Alabama: Religious Education Press, 1990), 142-143.

25. Hyde, *Religion in Childhood and Adolescence*, 142.

26. Robert M. Gagne, *The Conditions of Learning and Theory of Instruction*, 4th ed. (New York: Holt, Rhinehart & Winston, 1985).

27. David Edwards, "An Evaluation of Contemporary Learning Theories," in Kenneth O. Gangel and Howard G. Hendricks (ed.), *The Christian Educators Handbook on Teaching* (Wheaton, Illinois: Victor Books, 1989), 98.

28. Edwards, "Designing Biblical Instruction," 50.

On controlling outcomes
How in-charge are we really in our spiritual-formation roles? Most Christian teachers realize they are frankly *not* in control of the most important transformational outcomes that God may want to accomplish in a young person's life. Which is why some teachers use *process-oriented* objectives— believing the results of their efforts will be good and assessing the value of the strategy *after* the learning experience takes place. When you ask students to reflect on how a certain passage of Scripture relates to their relationships at home, for example, you're shifting from attempting to *control the outcome* to *managing the learning activities*.

For example, consider this basic lesson plan objective: "Students will identify three ways they can exercise an attitude of servanthood in their homes over the next week." This kind of basic objective keeps us focused on the fact that our mandate is not simply to hear, but to do (James 1:22). We do not want just to teach; we want the students to learn. But it also keeps us honest. If we never define our objective in measurable terms, we will never know if we have missed it. Perhaps that's why we don't!

On the other hand, defining our objectives strictly in these terms is to possibly miss a significant portion of the teaching process because it doesn't sufficiently account for the variety of ways that the kids in our youth groups might respond to a truth from God's Word. Egan hints at this in his book, *Teaching as Story Telling*:

> If we reflect not just on the diversity of things a teacher might hope to have happen in an average class, but the ways in which all kinds of associations of ideas, particular hobbies or interests, wonder and humor, that might purely incidentally be stimulated, we may consider whether the reality of educational engagements is inappropriately represented as planned means working carefully along a prespecified path to precisely delineated objectives. Of course we can organize our curricula and lessons this way. But such a process seems not to fit some obvious features of education.[29]

Nor does it adequately account for the ways the Holy Spirit moves in our midst when we open our lessons to his presence, enlightening, encouraging, convicting, convincing, revealing, confirming, surprising, applying, and clarifying.

A simple and yet more wholistic approach to the task of designing the Bible study would incorporate all the different facets of the learning/knowing experience:

- Cognitive (receiving): *What content, facts, and ideas do I anticipate my students will learn in this study?*
- Affective (feeling): *What sort of feelings might I anticipate this study will invoke in my students?*
- Behavioral (doing): *If the students take seriously this truth from God's Word, how might their behavior be different on a daily basis?*
- Existential (being): *How do I anticipate this study might impact the basic values and inner core of individual students?* [30]

To be sure, even these broad objectives will have to be adjusted from time to time, even during the course of the lesson. As Habermas and Issler point out, the Scripture gives us at least one occasion when that seems to have happened with Jesus and the disciples (Matthew 16:5-12), and it clearly happened when Paul overestimated the ability of the Corinthian believers to receive some of what he planned

---

29. Egan, 35.

30. John Dettoni, *Introduction to Youth Ministry* (Grand Rapids, Michigan: Zondervan, 1993), 67.

to teach (1 Corinthians 3:2).[31] But this approach to curricular design will give us the best opportunity to incorporate the intriguing, mysterious, miraculous mix of teacher, student, and Spirit of God.

It is a dynamic combination that students are rarely exposed to in most schools, and hopefully, if we are diligent in our creative task, it won't just be one more boring night at youth group.

---

31. Ron Habermas and Klaus Issler, *Teaching for Reconciliation* (Grand Rapids, Michigan: Baker Books, 1992), 141.

Acting Wisely: Programs, Routines, and Disciplines
Charles N. Neder

There is no more exciting and challenging ministry than God's call to youth ministry—and no gratification richer than the week-to-week work with young people and their parents. Yet it must be remembered that there are many pitfalls and potential areas of danger in the daily tasks to which the youth minister is called, especially in light of the fact that most youth workers are inadequately trained for their calling. This lack of training is in both the professional and personal areas. This situation can often lead to confusion in roles, errors in judgment, and discouragement in ministry. It is not uncommon for youth workers to play many different roles and perform many different tasks in any given week. For example, they may be administrators planning a weekend retreat, counselors comforting grief-stricken parents, a friend of kids hanging out at the mall, or accountants justifying money they have spent. Many times youth workers do not have the appropriate skills for performing these tasks. This can lead to personal and team tensions and stresses, often resulting in a bitter break in the youth ministry team.

In light of these variables, it is absolutely critical that youth ministers learn the skill of acting wisely in the many different roles they are called to play. In doing this they will mature in the following areas. They will begin to—

- think more theologically (by bringing Scripture to bear on their personal and professional lives).
- act more professionally (by gaining the tools to be more effective leaders and managers).
- grow more personally (by keeping their faith strong in order to avoid the pitfall of not living what they teach).

To assist the youth minister in developing in these three areas, this chapter will seek to demonstrate that acting wisely in youth ministry is a skill that can and must be learned and to indicate the four skill areas in which a youth minister must function well on a weekly basis to be effective in building disciples for Jesus Christ: relationships, programs, administration, and time management. The following methodology will be used in developing each of these two areas. First, we will *reflect* on theological foundations (the biblical implications for every area of youth ministry). Then we will *investigate* the transferable concepts of Scripture (those universal principles of Scripture that can be uniquely applied in any given context). Finally, we will seek to help the youth worker to *apply* these principles in his unique situation.

If any of the above methodological steps are neglected, aberrant youth ministry

Applying wisdom
Acting wisely is a skill that revolves around the ability to reflect about how Scripture must connect to our routine practices. As this chapter progresses, it will be interesting to see if Neder derives *each* of the four skill areas from a timeless biblical foundation with regard to acting wisely. For example, do *programs* carry the same nonnegotiable weight in the Bible as *relationships* do? And why these four areas, and no more or less? Do they reflect theological assumptions or modern ministry savvy (which isn't altogether bad but is certainly less compelling)?

is sure to follow, resulting in the practice of searching for the best program and hunting for the latest youth ministry guru and his bag of tricks. Then these tricks are dropped on a local situation without theological reflection about what is truly needed in one's particular context, with the result often doing damage to kids and the cause of Christ.

Acting wisely in youth ministry

The definition of acting wisely

In biblical theology, acting or living *wisely* is a skill for living life so that the end result is a thing of beauty and harmony.[1] The biblical portrait of the world of reality is more like a dangerous minefield than a cultivated rose garden. If ever youth workers and young people needed to learn to live and act wisely, it is surely in our present postmodern world, with all of its hidden mines and traps. We must develop the skill of navigating through the morass of moral relativism, worldly materialism, and sexual destruction. We must then, by precept and example, walk with our kids and their parents as, together, we journey through life.

The development of acting wisely

The skill of acting or living wisely is not learned quickly or easily. It is nurtured over a lifetime. Even when one attains some degree of wisdom, there is no guarantee that she will continue to live wisely (Solomon, etc.). All of us start off life as anything but wise (cf., Proverbs 22:15), but we can all move in the direction of wise living, even though we may fail many times along the journey (John Mark).

How do we develop into wise youth ministers? First, we must have a heart for God and a teachable spirit (Proverbs 1:7; 13:13, 20). God does not nurture fools and unteachable persons. Presupposing a hunger for God's kingdom and his righteousness (Matthew 6:33), we learn to live and act wisely in the following ways:

1. The primary source of wisdom is God himself (Job 28; Proverbs 2:1-8; Ecclesiastes 12:9-11; Ephesians 5:15-17; James 1:5-8).
2. God gives his wisdom to those who diligently seek it (Proverbs 2:1-5ff; 4:5-7; 18:15; 23:23).
3. God gives his wisdom to those who fear him (Job 28:28; 1:7; 9:10; 15:31-33; Ecclesiastes 12:12:13-14; 2 Corinthians 7:1).
4. God gives his wisdom to those who live in the company of other wise people (Proverbs 13:20; 1 Corinthians 15:33).
5. God gives his wisdom to those who live in daily fellowship with Jesus Christ, who is the very wisdom of God personified (Matthew 11:19; 12:42; Luke 7:34-35; 11:31; 1 Corinthians 1:18-25, 30; cf., Isaiah 11:1-2ff; etc.).

---

1. The Hebrew term for *wisdom* is *hokmah*, which is used 153 times in the Old Testament. The term always means a *skill*. For example, the builders of the Tabernacle and the Temple were "wise" men, in that they had a skill for architecture and construction (Exodus 31:1-5; 35:30-33; 1 Chronicles 22:15ff.; 2 Chronicles 2:7-18). Likewise, the weavers of Aaron's high priestly garments and sailors who had a skill for navigating the seas were said to be men of wisdom. In each of these cases, and others, the end result or product was a thing of beauty and harmony. For more on this, see Robert Hicks, *In Search of Wisdom* (Colorado Springs: NavPress, 1995) and David Wyrtzen, *Raising Worldly-Wise But Innocent Kids* (Chicago: Moody Press, 1990).

All of this is to say that wise-acting young youth workers should be ministering with older wise men and women who will model, teach, and love them enough to hold them accountable to God's righteous standards of wisdom. These mentors can be volunteers. The implication is that if younger youth workers are to progressively move toward maturity in wisdom, they must be nurtured by God through older and wiser mentors, teachers, pastors, parents, etc. Churches should seek to provide mentors for youth workers to walk with them in their ministries. Youth workers should also be part of fellowship groups with peers that meet on a regular basis.

As youth ministers grow in wise living and serving, they will have to learn how to function well in at least four major skill areas on a weekly basis to effectively disciple young persons.

Ponderable
Acting wisely has implications for the selection of these mentors. Are we to assume that these older mentors must have reached a certain level of competence in the four priorities of youth ministry (to be explained below)? Or could wise coaches who are skilled in the art of mentoring—with or without the four skills—actually help us to act more faithfully in areas of life that are not necessarily their own priorities?

Four priority skills of youth ministry

Because no week is the same for youth workers, the question must be asked: *what must a youth worker do each week no matter what events press in on him or her?* In other words, when everything is disrupted and in chaos, what are the foundational and priority skills that must be maintained to effectively deal with whatever events the week may bring? These four areas of skill development are working with people, programs, administration, and time management. These skill areas demand that the youth worker be wise, thoughtful, and theologically sound.

Acting wisely in relationships

Theological reflection. It is clear that the Bible is a book about relationships—with God, others, and the earth (Mark 12:28-31). Youth ministry is a ministry of building relationships of grace, compassion, and truth (Romans 12:9-21; Ephesians 4:15). Throughout Scripture we see an emphasis on maturing relationships. This is because God has created us in his own image, which is a reflection of the triune nature of the Godhead (Genesis 1-2, etc.). And although sin and death entered the world through the Fall, the image of God in man has not been erased, only defaced (James 3:8-10). Therefore, it is imperative that, without condoning sin, we still affirm innate dignity and worth. This is further confirmed by the fact that Christ died for all people, making possible not only a restored relationship with God, but also with others (2 Corinthians 5:14-21). Added to this is the biblical reality that when one trusts in Christ as Savior and Lord, the Holy Spirit not only indwells that person but also places them in the body of Christ, a living and eternal community of growing relationships (Romans 8:9; 1 Corinthians 12:13).

Relationships are so important in the heart of God that Jesus himself prayed for the unity of all of his disciples (John 17:20-23) and that we would love each other in such a way that the world would know that we were his disciples: "the living apologetic" (John 13:34-35).

Transferable concepts. The Bible lays out a clear priority of relationships for the youth worker. First and foremost is his relationship with the Lord (Matthew 6:33; Mark 12:28–31). Under his lordship all other human relationships are aligned: family, church, staff, parents, and kids.

When considering this universal principle, the youth minister must ask hard questions as they relate to his ministry. For example, is the person more important than the task? This might well mean that we might have to let individuals fail in certain tasks so that they might grow and mature in their faith. It is, therefore, critical for the youth minister as he acts as a mentor to know when to intervene and salvage a situation and when to lay back and let the youth worker learn from his mistakes. Interventions are mandatory when issues involve physical danger, sexual or emotional abuse, financial irregularities, and doctrinal errors.

In light of these kinds of matters, it is important in dealing with relationships that the youth minister be willing to confront issues on a personal and program level. This will require a theology of confrontation that is appropriate to his particular situation (cf., Matthew 18:15–20; Galatians 6:1–2). To not confront a situation can, in many instances, do more harm than good. Behavior has natural consequences, and those consequences produce growth and peace (Hebrews 12).

Practical application. There are a number of practical applications that emerge from our theology of relationships. First, the youth worker must not fall into the trap of emphasizing program over relationships. It is much easier for some people to plan a program than to interact on an honest level with another person. The youth minister is no longer acting wisely when she falls into the program trap (i.e., the trap of thinking that programs build disciples). To be sure, as we shall see, programs are important, but they are not the foundation of effective youth ministry.

Second, if the youth ministers are going to be effective in these kinds of ongoing relationships, they will have to act wisely in the following matters: (1) quality time with the Lord in the Scriptures on a *daily* basis, (2) quality time with one's family, (3) truthful and honest relationships with staff and volunteers, and (4) quality time with kids and parents on a *regular* basis.

When youth workers' relationships are growing and healthy, then they can think more clearly and act more wisely in all areas of ministry.

Acting wisely in programs

Theological reflection. A key passage in the Old Testament on the theology of programming is Deuteronomy 6:4–7. God's program for ancient Israel was to first hear, know, and love him, and then to obediently serve him as well as passing on his truth to the children. In other words, the program was a vehicle for relationships with God and each other.

In the New Testament, Jesus and his approach to programming stands out as the biblical example of true relational ministry. In Mark 3:14, he personally selected his 12 disciples that "they might be with him and that he might send them out to preach." The key word here is *with*, which describes Jesus' method of discipleship: relational programs must always precede ministry programs. This is what Jesus meant when he assigned the Great Commission to his church (Matthew 28:16-20): make disciples by baptizing them (enfolding them into his body) and teaching them (instructing them in his Word). This is still his program for the church—including youth ministry.

Transferable concepts. The Apostle Paul laid down at least two transferable principles in his ministry and teaching that are relevant to youth ministry. First, youth ministry must seek to program in such a way that kids will become equipped "for the work of service, to the building up of the body of Christ..." (Ephesians 4:12 NASB). This means that programs aimed at youth leadership must point in this direction. If kids cannot do "the work of service" in the long run, then the program has failed—no matter how flashy it was. Second, the most effective youth ministries are those that are reproducing themselves, that is, when (at least in theory) the youth minister has worked himself out of a job. Paul emphasized this transferable concept in 2 Timothy 2:2, "And the things you have heard me say in the presence of many witnesses entrust to reliable men who will also be qualified to teach others." The key terms here are: *heard*, *entrust*, and *teach*. This is the true ministry pattern of multiplication for youth ministry.

Practical application. It is crucial in youth ministry that programs be designed in such a way that they are used as discipling tools for the committed kids (cf. Matthew 28:18-20). For example, if a social is planned and the committed kids have an ownership in it, they will bring their friends. By bringing their friends, they are in fact learning how to evangelize and reach out to their friends. Thus, the program has become a two-edged sword: It helps disciple the Christian kids and it reaches the non-Christian kids with the gospel.

A key word in programming is *indigenous*. Indigenous programming is seeking to understand what God is doing in a particular situation and becoming part of what he is doing. In practical terms, this means attempting to discern what unique factors are at work in any particular situation and then designing programs that flow out of this discernment. Indigenous programming can prevent youth workers from imparting successful programs without theological consideration of its suitability for a particular situation.

A final applicational point is that programs must be need-based. If a program is not meeting a particular need, then one must question the rationale undergirding it. A simple way to determine needs is through a *needs assessment*, which can be conducted in the following manner. The participants conducting the assessment should include staff and volunteers who work with families. First ask the question, What are the primary needs of our families? These needs should be written down. Then ask, What kinds of programs are needed in our particular situation to build maturing disciples?

After asking and answering these two questions, youth workers can begin to establish goals that meet these needs. They then design specific programs that will

Learn to discern

The term *indigenous* describes the concept of youth ministry programming well, largely because it is loaded with theological richness. The clear implication is that before you start rummaging through Ideas books, you need to be in reflective prayer, trying to understand what program God has already set in motion. This priority will make your hunt for resources both focused and fruitful.

Are needs all we need?

Should needs assessments be taken on as focused research projects rather than solo reflections in the youth pastor's study? Certainly, just thinking about needs independently is an improvement on how much youth ministry programming is done; yet our relational presence among those with whom we minister is critical to our accurate determination of real needs. This squares nicely with the incarnational value discussed in chapter 18. Furthermore, we can ensure that our assessment is on target when we practice some of the disciplines that researchers employ when they try to get reliable data.

accomplish these goals. Having done this, they make the necessary assignments with dates for completion. This is where all of the details are determined. Finally, after the program has been completed, the youth team meets to evaluate the program on the basis of whether it addressed the perceived needs. It is important to note that the actual designing of the program was not conducted until the needs were determined. A common mistake in youth ministry programming is to implement a program without a needs-assessment. Determining need and programming to meet need should be a regular part of the youth minister's schedule.

If youth ministers are to be successful in programming, they must be both leaders and managers. The degree to which youth workers can accomplish these tasks will determine their effectiveness in youth ministry. In other words, successful programming is based on successful administration.

Acting wisely in administration

Theological reflection. Behind every administrative task is the reality of the sovereignty of God—that is—the sovereign placement by God of each youth worker in their own unique calling, with their own unique gifts (cf. Psalm 19; Acts 17:24-28). This theological truth, when understood and embraced, will buttress each youth minister when the storms of ministry hit. Youth ministers must know they are where God wants them and that he has something to teach them; whether in the valley or on the mountaintop.

Another theological reality is that God gives spiritual gifts to each of us for accomplishing his tasks for his glory (cf. 1 Peter 4:10-11; Romans 12:1-8; 1 Corinthians 12-14; Ephesians 4:11-16). In particular, the Holy Spirit gives the gift of leadership to many—"if it is leadership, let him govern diligently" (Romans 12:8). Thus, in any given youth ministry, the wise youth worker should pray and look for individuals, staff, or volunteers who have this gift and therefore can be delegated certain administrative responsibilities.

Transferable concepts. The reality in many youth ministries is that the youth worker must be both a leader and a manager. He is a *leader* in that he must see the over all vision for the ministry and articulate that vision to those who work with him. He is a *manager* in that he must insure that the details are accomplished. Basically this means that effective leaders lead from their strengths, staff to their weaknesses, and leave room for the oddball (the individual whose crazy idea may be exactly what the ministry needs). The Scriptures are replete with many examples of how leading and managing come together to form effective ministry. The two most prominent examples are Jethro's wise counsel to his son-in-law Moses on how to lead and manage in a very difficult situation (Exodus 18) and the 12 Apostles delegating leadership and management responsibilities to the first so-called deacons (Acts 6).

Practical applications. Each particular youth worker should assess her own ministry situation to determine how much time to spend on administration. Time should be set aside each week to handle the administrative details of the ministry. There is always ten-

Ponderable
God is sovereign and he gives gifts as he chooses. Yet how does one administrate around this reality?

sion in this area of youth ministry; therefore, a conflict-resolution model should be put in place. Learning to resolve conflict increases communication and effectiveness in ministry. Unresolved conflict leads to alienation and a breakdown in communication.

It should be pointed out that churches are generally unclear in their expectations of the youth minister in the administrative areas. The church, therefore, should give the youth worker written, clear, specific instructions on what is expected in the daily administrative areas (finances, office hours, lines of authority and accountability, dress codes, etc.). General, non-specific expectations will only lead to trouble for the youth worker and the youth ministry. Administrative inexperience is often the undoing of youth ministers, resulting in lack of trust from parents, frustration in kids, and confusion in the church.

Having looked at the youth ministers relationships, programs, and administration, we now need to turn to the vital area of time management. Positive concepts of time management, properly understood and implanted into the youth worker's daily schedule, can only enhance the possibilities of a successful ministry.

Acting wisely in time management

Theological reflection. The Scriptures give abundant evidence of a theology of time. For example, we are called to walk wisely by redeeming the time in the midst of evil days (Ephesians 5:15-17). God desires us to "be wise in the way [we] act toward outsiders; make the most of the opportunity" (Colossians 4:5).

Time is such a precious gift that we are called "to number our days aright that we may gain a heart of wisdom" (Psalm 90:12). Even Jesus Christ, the Son of God, had only 24 hours a day to accomplish all the Father gave him to do. No wonder he could say, "My food…is to do the will of him who sent me and to finish his work" (John 4:34). "I seek not to please myself but him who sent me" (John 5:30). "For I have come down from heaven not to do my will but to do the will of him who sent me" (John 6:38).

This theology of time will focus the youth minister's prayer and planning on those choices and unique moments when God is about to do a special work (i.e., a *kairos* moment in time). In other words, biblical time management is our partnering with God in what he wants to do and when he wants to do it.

Transferable concepts. Once again Christ's own use of time becomes our model for godly time management. He determined his schedule; his schedule did not determine him. It's the difference between being led and being driven. For example, even though Christ was busy with people's demands, he always found time to spend with his Father. On a number of occasions, he found time to rest. He always found time to be with and instruct his disciples. He found time to visit the synagogue, to study the Scriptures, to walk among the people, and to reach out to the needy. It was often said that he did things "as was his custom," which implies that Jesus was deliberate in his use of time and lived according to his God-ordained priorities. The youth minister can learn much about time management from the master of time himself.

Practical application. It is important that the youth worker manage his time according to divine priorities. The youth minister's schedule will reflect his priorities. It's important that once a weekly schedule is determined, what is set for Thursday is not done on Tuesday. Work the schedule—don't let the schedule work you. We must remember that each night some time must be prayerfully given to determining what must be done the next day.

Finally, a youth minister's schedule must be flexible enough to adjust for emergency interruptions. But careful thought must be given to what constitutes an emergency. There will always be good things that interrupt our schedules. The wise youth minister never forgets that the good is often the enemy of the best. Her schedule will allow for both structured time and spontaneous time.

★ ★ ★

No week is typical in the life of the youth worker—the nature of the tasks and responsibilities makes the unexpected and unplanned commonplace. Therefore it is essential that wise youth ministers plan time to include the basic tasks to be done each week, regardless of interruptions. This means prioritizing that which forms the foundation of the youth ministry.

We have suggested that these foundations (relationships, program, administration and time management), when maintained, will increase the effectiveness of the youth worker's ministry. Growth in these areas will increase professional competence. If an unexpected crisis occurs, it will be in one of these four areas—hopefully, the youth worker will be prepared to effectively deal with the situation. We have further suggested that the Scripture is very clear that the skills of acting wisely can be learned and developed. If these skills are not learned and developed, the conclusion is that the youth worker chose not to do the necessary hard work to increase his ministry competence. If, on the other hand, the youth worker chooses to do whatever is necessary to grow in wisdom, he will not only bring glory to God, but will also participate in equipping young people to face the stresses and demands of the world in which they live.

Acting Wisely: Retreats, Trips, and Events
Karen Jones

Students often describe and evaluate their own youth ministry experiences in terms of those major events that punctuate their calendars—summer camp, mission trip, weekend retreat, youth conference, lock-in. Face-to-face encounters with God are likely to occur at just such times, and many youth have established internal spiritual markers at these pages in their life stories. It may also be, however, that these pages/events have been bookmarked because a significant face-to-face encounter with a member of the opposite sex took place on that hallowed occasion. The reality is, God sometimes has to intrude and squeeze himself into a packed schedule just to make his presence known among youth group members.

Regardless of the ministry value of specific individual trips or events, it is clear that they are viewed as mandatory happenings if a youth ministry is to be considered a valid enterprise. Parents, church leaders, and community observers often make judgments about the vitality of a ministry based on how many times the youth are taken out of their homes for extended periods of time. Youth ministers know this, and many even conduct self-evaluations based on their ability to involve large numbers of youth in multiple major events.

Busyness: your enemy
Busyness bears little inherent connection to faithfulness, and in fact is often the enemy of the kind of focus necessary for keeping pace with God's perfect stride in our lives. What would a youth ministry trip or retreat look like—*feel* like— with this purpose?

This pressure to promote and produce can lead to a disproportionate expenditure of resources, with no guarantee that the kingdom of God is advanced or the mission of a particular youth ministry fulfilled. Time demands on youth schedules are already enormous. They continue to escalate as schools seek to increase academic standards, communities create more opportunities for athletic and civic involvement, colleges raise acceptance expectations, and economic pressures lure more youth into the work force. What youth do not need from a ministry are more claims on their time that do not impact their lives in a significant way.

Intentionality versus serendipity

How can a youth minister distinguish between calendar-cramming and purposeful planning when it comes to scheduling? The secret is to plan with intentionality. This requires an understanding of the role the minister is called to fulfill. The Great Commission (Matthew 28:18-20) and the Great Commandment (Luke 10:27) outline God's expectations for all Christians, and Ephesians 4:12-13 explicitly describes the additional purposes to which vocational ministers are called:

To prepare God's people for works of service, so that the body of Christ may be built up until we all reach unity in the faith and in the knowledge of the Son of God and become mature, attaining to the whole measure of the fullness of Christ.

A serendipity occurs when something wonderful and totally unexpected crosses your path while you were headed somewhere else. Youth ministers cannot rely on these serendipitous situations, or *God-moments*, to emerge in the midst of their activity calendars. Intentional and purposeful planning is required if youth are to be reached for Christ, prepared for service, and matured in their faith.

Youth ministers are called to seek out young people; to love them enough to confront them with the gospel; to help them discover their identity in Christ; and to continue to help them mature as disciples, discovering and utilizing their gifts as members of his body. If this is to be realized, then youth ministry planning should emanate from an articulated philosophy that balances evangelism and edification, group-building and God-exalting. To neglect this is to reduce youth ministry to social or community work, which just happens to be directed by persons who are Christians. Pete Ward, professor at King's College, London, suggests that "to be truly Christian, youth work must carry within it the essential dynamic of the gospel story," and this should always be the motivation for the ministry.[1] In his axioms of youth ministry, Mark Senter takes the position that "youth ministry happens as long as a Christian adult is able to use his or her contact with a student to draw that student into a maturing relationship with God through Jesus Christ" and it ceases to exist "when the adult–student relationship is broken or no longer moves the student toward spiritual maturity."[2] This suggests that a ministry can be replete with activities, trips, and events that entertain and occupy, and still not be accomplishing ministry goals.

Doing big events for event's sake is not legitimate ministry. There are scores of life-changing, must-attend, unlike-any-other, deeply spiritual, ultimately challenging, once-in-a-lifetime activities promoted by youth ministry entities, as well as hundreds, if not thousands, of resources available to ministers that offer assistance and suggestions for planning major events, camps, and retreats. The challenge for ministers is not to discover places for their youth to go or things for their youth to do—the ultimate challenge is to answer the question, Where should my youth go and what should my youth do if I want them to experience the fruits of a ministry that is both faithful and effective by kingdom standards?

Who's in charge?
Karen Jones makes it sound as if the ultimate burden of choosing timely theological purposes for ministry must be left in the hands of youth ministers, not in those of trip/event/retreat vendors/planners. Youth ministers are the ones charged with the direction-setting agenda for their teens because their reflective, God-dependent life among kids is the key to knowing how to answer the solid questions raised here.

The compass and the ruler

There are two tools that all youth ministers need to have: a compass and a ruler. When faced with a multitude of possible ministry directions, the compass keeps it on the right course. The ruler is then used to measure the results: *Did we choose wisely? Did we actually accomplish what we intended?* These two figurative tools are embodied in a philosophy of ministry. James Wilhoit identifies the two tools as a *to-do list* and a *measuring stick*. In the form of a ministry philosophy, they allow ministers to conduct a discrepancy analy-

---

1. Pete Ward, *God at the Mall* (Hendrickson Publishers, 1999), 34–35.

2. Mark H. Senter III, "Axioms of Youth Ministry: The Context," in Richard R. Dunn and Mark H. Senter III (eds.), *Reaching a Generation for Christ* (Chicago: Moody, 1997), 125, 127.

sis, looking "at what one is seeking to accomplish (the goals in one's philosophy statement) and what one is actually accomplishing."[3]

A ministry philosophy is a well-developed way of thinking about ministry that is used to guide the practice of ministry. Both right thought (orthodoxy) and right practice (orthopraxy) are necessary components of a theologically sound youth ministry. Ministers must have a clear understanding of what a biblically faithful ministry *looks like* and they must also have a sense of how that ministry is to be lived out in their unique settings.[4]

A series of questions can be useful for formulating a ministry philosophy. Norman DeJong suggests that these questions include such things as the purposes and goals of the ministry, the structural organization in which they will be implemented, the resources and methods that will be utilized to accomplish them, and a means or standard of evaluating their impact.[5]

While not all youth ministers have taken the time to thoughtfully develop a philosophy, many have likely attempted to develop a mission statement, or a vision statement, or a key objective, or purpose for their ministry. There are slight differences between each of these *compasses*, but all of them are useful in helping to plot the course for a ministry. Unfortunately the youth calendar is rarely planned with any of these statements in mind.

Covey describes this same dilemma in terms of time management. He describes the problem as a struggle between the clock and the compass. One's actual schedule and activities—the things that fill the calendar—are depicted by the clock. Those things that are deemed important—the vision, mission, and direction—are represented by the compass. The struggle comes when the clock and the compass are not in sync; there is little or no connection between what is identified as the mission and what is actually being accomplished.[6] It is this discrepancy between purpose and programming that must be overcome in youth ministry.

Doug Fields addresses this need for aligning practice and purpose in his popular book, *Purpose-Driven Youth Ministry*. His principles are not necessarily new or even revolutionary, but they are built upon a philosophical foundation that is theologically sound—a winning combination many youth ministers are rediscovering, after abandoning them in their search for the cutting edge. Fields advocates planning based on purpose, as opposed to creating a purpose for activities and events ex post facto (after the fact). Often youth ministers attempt to *proof-text* their events by filling a calendar with events, then justifying their presence by assigning a spiritual purpose to each. The labels of *fellowship* or *outreach* can easily be attached to anything that does not appear to have any other rationale for appearing on the schedule.

Debunking the Law of Perpetual Events

Karen is onto something with the notion of how we tend to proof-text our events. There must be some sort of Law of Perpetual Events at work in ministry—one that suggests that once we do something and it brushes with success, it will be done forever and ever, amen.

We can get away with this practice if we insert our purposes *after* they've been burned into our calendars, but this is rather backwards. The possibility of *not* doing an event must be numbered among the scheduling decisions that deserve our theological reflection.

---

3. James C. Wilhoit, "Developing a Philosophy" in Robert E. Clark, Lin Johnson, and Allyn K. Sloat (eds.), *Christian Education: Foundations for the Future* (Chicago: Moody, 1991), 63.

4. Stone and Duke refer to this in their discussion of the meaning of faith, "all elements of the Christian life: belief, action, and heartfelt devotion to God as object of ultimate concern in a living faith." Howard W. Stone and James O. Duke, *How to Think Theologically* (Minneapolis, Minnesota: Fortress Press, 1996), 10.

5. For a complete discussion of DeJong's views, see Norman DeJong, *Education in the Truth* (Nutley, New Jersey: Presbyterian & Reformed, 1974), 61-63.

6. Stephen R. Covey, *First Things First: To Live, to Love, to Learn, to Leave a Legacy* (New York: Simon and Schuster, 1994), 19-20.

Fields proposes to guide ministry with purposes derived from the Great Commandment and the Great Commission: evangelism, worship, fellowship, discipleship, and ministry.[7] These same purposes have been expressed by others in a variety of ways, all representing the biblical mission of the church.[8] *Form follows function* is another way of describing this same process of intentional planning. It advocates identifying the key objective, or function, of a ministry or program, then fashioning the ministry into a form that holds the greatest possibility for fulfilling that function.[9] When trips and events are planned on this basis, the ministry takes on a balance. Instead of an over-abundance of fellowship events, there is a greater likelihood that evangelistic, discipleship, ministry, and worship opportunities will also be calendared on a regular basis.

This need for intentional youth ministry planning should not be interpreted as advocating more formally structured events and trips over those that are less structured. Intentionality and structure are not the same; intentionality refers to the goals and objectives of an event, and structure refers to how that event will be carried out. If youth ministry is *to go somewhere* instead of merely *going,* then each calendared activity must serve to fulfill a ministry purpose. According to Lee, this need for intentionality is a fundamental reason why youth workers should view themselves as youth religious educators rather than youth ministers. He argues that "ministry is an amorphous term having no real parameters and therefore having no inbuilt axis of intentionality."[10] Regardless of the title, those ministering with youth need to thoughtfully consider the outcomes they desire from their ministries before they commit their resources to any major event or activity.

In or out? Christ and culture

Another key consideration when planning youth ministry activities, events, and trips is the church's or ministry's view of cultural interaction. Will events be planned to protect youth from, or engage them with the world? Jesus' prayer for his disciples shortly before he was arrested has posed a *protect or engage* dilemma for Christians down through the ages:

> I have given them your word and the world has hated them, for they are not of the world any more than I am of the world. My prayer is not that you take them out of the world but that you protect them from the evil one. They are not of the world, even as I am not of it:
>
> —*John 17:14-16*

7. Doug Fields, *Purpose-Driven Youth Ministry* (Grand Rapids, Michigan: Zondervan/Youth Specialties, 1998), 17.

8. Evangelism and edification are often identified as the two purposes of the church, with edification used as an umbrella term for four separate aspects: worship, instruction (Fields's "discipleship"), fellowship, and expression (Fields's "ministry"). These are often referred to as the WIFE acronym, with reference to the church as the "bride of Christ." Michael J. Anthony and the Christian Education Faculty of Biola University, Talbot School of Theology (eds.), *Foundations of Ministry: An Introduction to Christian Education for a New Generation* (Wheaton, Illinois: Scripture Press, 1992), 214.

9. Wilhoit, 58.

10. James Michael Lee, "Procedures in the Religious Education of Adolescents," in Donald Ratcliff and James A. Davies (eds.), *Handbook of Youth Ministry* (Birmingham, Alabama: Religious Education Press, 1991), 237.

How can Christian youth be in the world, but not of it? Even if youth ministers have not consciously wrestled with this theological question and articulated a stance, they have certainly formulated an opinion about it. Their embedded beliefs about Christ and culture shape their ministry plans, even without their awareness. Niebuhr's descriptive paradigm for assessing one's cultural attitude has become a classic, and many have reinterpreted his work, assigning their own labels to each of his four positions.[11]

- **Christ *against* culture.** Culture is viewed as totally corrupt and any interaction with it is totally avoided by youth ministers. Youth are provided with Christian alternatives to worldly events to protect them from evil. Often youth are forced to choose between school and church activities when this view is operating. While its emphasis on purity is laudable, this approach can also produce unnecessary guilt on the part of teens heavily invested in school and community groups.

- **Christ *of* culture.** Youth ministries with this understanding embrace culture and utilize it to entertain and capture the attention of the youth. The focus is on nurturing young people so that they feel good about being a part of the youth group. There is often little substantive difference between this type of youth ministry and any other school or civic youth group.

- **Christ *above* culture.** This view takes the position that the *sacred* and the *secular* are distinctly different; there is a place for each in the life of the individual. Youth ministry strives to provide opportunity for the sacred side of life to develop and does not concern itself with attempting to impact how youth live their lives at school or home. There are ritualistic events with assigned "religious" functions, but no attempt is made to compete with or provide alternatives for other non-church activities.

- **Christ *transforming* culture.** Culture is corrupt, but there is still hope that it can be salvaged. Ministry can take place within this corrupt culture and some of its forms may actually be useful for effective ministry, but they should only be used with discrimination. Because God is concerned with every facet of a person's life, ministry with this view actively plans opportunities to impact all areas of the lives of youth with the gospel, and seeks ways for the youth ministry to be a catalyst for spiritual transformation in the surrounding culture.

11. For three interesting applications to youth ministry, see Leonard Sweet, "Living an Ancient Future Faith," *The 1997 Princeton Lectures on Youth, Church, and Culture* (Princeton, New Jersey: Institute of Youth Ministry, Princeton Theological Seminary); Anthony Campolo and Donald Ratcliff, "Activist Youth Ministry," in Donald Ratcliff and James A. Davies (eds.), *Handbook of Youth Ministry* (Birmingham, Alabama: Religious Education Press, 1991); and Doug Stevens, *Called to Care* (El Cajon, California: Youth Specialties, 1985).

Youth ministry planning that does not flow out of a clear philosophical foundation may reflect any one of the cultural views. A philosophical approach to planning may also reflect any of the four cultural views. Regardless, the view becomes apparent when the youth ministry calendar is analyzed. If a youth minister desires to give leadership to a theologically informed ministry, both the purposes for ministry and the cultural strategies employed to implement the purposes should be carefully considered.

A biblical rationale

Some truths are best learned in transit, away from home, in unique surroundings, and sometimes even accompanied by amazing, entertainment-quality productions. God modeled this with the Children of Israel, and Christ built upon this principle during his earthly ministry. Instead of sitting everyone down around a campfire, laying down all of his indisputable truths and pouring out all of his eternal wisdom; he chose to take his children on trips and produce marvelous spectacles and involve them in a big-screen-quality spiritual journey. The life of faith is a lifelong, covenant relationship, more field experience than traditional classroom. Because faith learning is developmental and there is educational value in repetition, God included some events on the "calendar" multiple times.

Think about the big events and ministry trips recorded in the Bible, such as the many prescribed feasts and festivals with food, fun, and fellowship celebrated on a regular basis; the extended journeys and short trips taken by people such as Abraham and Isaac—up a mountain, Moses—on a river, into the desert, in and out of Egypt, and into the wilderness; the dedication of the first and second temples; the prayer-walk by Joshua and his men around Jericho; the great fireworks display by Elijah; the calling of the Twelve to a short-term missions trip with lifelong implications; the cross-country road trips that Jesus led; the hillside "revivals" with masses of people and lunch provided; lock-ins in prison cells; and spiritual retreats and prayer vigils in gardens.

As the master teacher, Jesus modeled the value of experiential and service learning long before it was promoted by John Dewey in the early part of the 20TH century. Dewey believed that the purpose of education was the growth of an individual, and this could only come about if students were involved in real-life problems taking place in real-life settings.[12] Many other educators and psychologists have built upon this idea since that time, all emphasizing the benefits of joining conceptual learning with concrete experience.

This is at the heart of intentional planning for youth ministry events and projects. Youth ministers who are able to articulate their ministry objectives can then implement strategies for realizing these goals in the most effective means possible—by planning concrete experiences that support conceptual learning. For example, youth ministers who want their students to gain an understanding of the value and beauty of God's creation and commit to living as responsible stewards of all that he has created

---

12. John Dewey, *Experience and Education*, Kappa Delta Pi Lecture Series (Kappa Delta Pi, 1938); (Collier Books, 1963), 35–48.

may plan nature-based trips, such as camping, backpacking, floating, or climbing. While these experiences would be nice fellowship or entertainment additions to any calendar, the youth minister who plans such a trip to *intentionally* fulfill a ministry objective might structure the experience in a manner that will draw youth into an appreciation for the Creator God. This does not happen automatically, however, by simple participation alone. The learning is assured only when there is a reflective strategy employed. Youth can float a river with an ecology class or a group of friends on the weekend without ever considering the wonder of God's creative powers or the awesome responsibility Christians have for managing his creation.

This same principle holds true for service activities. Schools, civic clubs, and even businesses involve participants in volunteer service. When the service is performed in the name of Christ, however, and this motivation is reflected upon, the benefits to the participants are multiplied. They can include such outcomes as deepening religious faith, integrating faith and social ministry, increasing leadership abilities and self-confidence, contributing to church and missions commitment, helping participants understand the role of the church in society, building a sense of community with other Christians, developing cultural sensitivity and appreciation, enhancing self-esteem and self concept, developing values, and increasing one's dependence on God.[13]

In addition to specifically designing events that fulfill a stated ministry goal or objective, when opportunities arise for youth ministers to attend events sponsored by other churches or organizations, they may choose whether or not to participate based upon their ministry purposes or objectives. While the purposes of a ministry should never change, objectives may. For example, discovering ministry gifts and utilizing them in service should always be a ministry purpose, but one year this purpose might be fulfilled through an objective of involving all youth in community ministry. The next year this purpose might be carried out through an objective that targets international ministry efforts. The focus on a stated objective might lead a youth minister to involve the group in a work camp sponsored by an international organization one year and pass on the opportunity the next.

Acting with wisdom

There are additional considerations that should be given when planning major events and trips. Activities can be planned for the right reasons and still be carried out in an unwise manner. The following questions may serve as an informal check on the soundness of any event or trip on a youth ministry schedule.

- Is the context "Christian"? Will it detract from the intended purpose?
- Does the event allow for good stewardship of God's resources: time, money, talents, and possessions?
- Will the event connect students with or alienate them from the collective body of Christ?

13. Karen Jones, "A Study of the Difference between Faith Maturity Scale and Multidimensional Self-Concept Scale Scores for Youth Participating in Two Denominational Ministry Projects," dissertation (Southwestern Baptist Theological Seminary, 1998).

- Who will serve in positions of leadership? Are they worthy mentors and spiritual examples?
- If youth are being sent out "into the world," will they be spiritually prepared so as to advance God's purposes and not hinder them?
- Has time been allowed in the schedule for youth to reflect and integrate the experience with scriptural principles, if appropriate?
- Is there a sound rationale for the event, or has it been justified because it has popular appeal?
- Is this event allowing young people to join God in his work?
- Will our actions create obstacles for non-Christians?
 Will this event cause divisions within the body or promote harmony?
- Will this activity place burdens on families or disrupt family unity?
- Will this provide a context for moving youth forward on their faith journey, or will it simply fill their calendar?
- Will some youth be left out or alienated due to their social status, family or economic conditions?
- Will youth be given opportunities to use their spiritual gifts?
- Will their good experiences translate into meaningful encounters with the God who loves them and created them for himself?

This list is not exhaustive, but it does represent the type of theological thinking that should be undertaken by youth ministers when planning for major events in the life of the group. Some activities may be planned with the sole intention of attracting non-Christian youth, but the same scrutiny should be given to them as to the most spiritually intense retreats. The advice of Paul and Timothy to the Christians in Colosse summarizes the wisdom needed by youth ministers to act wisely in their planning.

> Let the peace of Christ rule in your hearts, since as members of one
> body you were called to peace. And be thankful. Let the word of Christ
> dwell in you richly as you teach and admonish one another with all
> wisdom, and as you sing psalms, hymns and spiritual songs with grati-
> tude in your hearts to God. And whatever you do, whether in word or
> deed, do it all in the name of the Lord Jesus, giving thanks to God the
> Father through him.
>
> —*Colossians 3:15-17*

Acting Wisely: Counseling and Crises
Marv Penner

Jennifer's voice sounded so matter-of-fact, it was impossible to imagine the life-changing significance of her phone call. What had been a routine Wednesday afternoon of preparation for the Senior High Bible Study that night, was about to turn into a terrifying race for a student's life.

The church secretary had told me it was Jenn on the line, and I was glad to hear from her. It had only been a few months since she had started attending our youth group. She had come with a friend and seemed to plug into the life of the group easily. Because of her great sense of humor and cute pixie face, most of the guys in the group had welcomed her instantly. The girls had rallied around her, too, but for different reasons. Jenn's family was a mess and the girls sensed she needed their support and friendship. Both her parents were alcoholics and there were whispers about abuse—certainly verbal, physical, and emotional, and probably sexual, too. One thing was true—she had experienced more pain in her life than most 15-year-olds I knew.

Lots of students would call at the office, but she never had. It didn't seem at all unusual until we got past the "hi-how-are-ya's" and she told me her reason for calling. "I'm calling to say goodbye," she said, "and to tell you thanks for all you've done for me. You guys have been awesome."

"What do you mean 'Goodbye?'" I asked, dreading a confirmation of what I feared she was trying to tell me between the lines.

"I'm just saying goodbye and thanks," she responded with an uncharacteristically emotionless voice.

"Jenn, are you trying to tell me that you're planning to hurt yourself somehow?"

"So what if I am?"

"It's a huge 'so what' if you are. You're part of our group, and we need you to stay a part of us. What have you planned, Jenn? How are you hoping to do this…and when?" I tried to keep my voice calm as my gut was screaming with fear.

What do you do as a youth worker when you're faced with the despair of a kid who has reached the end of her hope? What are the right questions to ask? You can't exactly put her on hold for a few minutes and call a crisis hotline for advice in the middle of it all. What if you blow it and say the wrong thing at a critical moment like this? If the responsibility feels huge, that's because it is.

To make a long and complex story much shorter, Jenn told me that afternoon that it was her plan to leave where she was calling from immediately to go to the nearest subway stop and jump in front of the first train that came into the station. It was one of the common suicide methods in our city, and after having spent a few years on the fire department before going into full-time youth ministry, I knew it was lethal. As I heard her begin to cry quietly, she hung up the phone. The last word I heard before the click was "sorry."

She hadn't told me she was calling from home but I had a hunch, and you know I was praying a lot harder than I had been when I began preparing my Bible study a half-hour earlier. I was right about the route she had chosen to walk and as I rounded the corner onto her street, she saw me coming. I was amazed when she got into my car as I stopped across the street from where she was walking. My mind was racing as she looked hopelessly at me.

Where do you start in a case like this? What's the right thing to say? Do you lock the car doors and rush her to the nearest hospital? Do you let her talk or make her listen? Do you give her some helpful Scripture or ask her why? Where do you go with the confusion and intensity of these sorts of youth ministry moments?

Jennifer's story is true and sadly not all that unusual. If you're going to work with students, you *will* face overwhelming circumstances at some point in your ministry. I realized that Jennifer had called me on that day, not because of my expertise in suicide intervention (I had none). Neither was it because of my deep understanding of the theological issues that surround suicide (I still don't have very good answers to some of those questions). Jenn also didn't know that I could refer her to the kind of professional counseling she would need to help her out of her deep hole of despair (I had a few names and numbers.) She called me because somehow she knew I cared about her and her friends in the youth group, and for some mysterious reason she trusted me with her deepest moment of hopelessness.

Youth ministry, in the middle of complex counseling situations and crisis, is fundamentally no different than any other time in youth ministry. Certainly the stakes can be much higher and there is no room for carelessness. What we're talking about is still simply a basic commitment to loving students with integrity and a willingness to share our lives with them for the sake of pointing them to Jesus. Loving Jennifer was a costly commitment. It turns out that she had just found out that she was pregnant, and with all the other junk going on in her life, the news had pushed her over the edge. The next seven months, and the first few years after the baby was born, could only be described as intensive care. But Jenn made it, and as I look back on it, I was honored to be part of the group that represented Jesus in her life.

This is what Paul is talking about in the opening thoughts of 2 Corinthians when he encourages us to comfort others out of the comfort that we have received from God. For reasons we can't fully understand, God chooses to use us in the lives of kids to be his voice of encouragement and his touch of healing. According to Paul's instructions, our point of connecting with hurting students does not come from the pain we have in common with them but from the confidence we have in our healing heavenly Father. You can't minister to children of alcoholics simply because your dad drank to excess. That might give you some rapport, but ministry will come from how

Forewarned is forearmed?

Marv Penner mentions that he doesn't have very good theological answers to suicide. What other issues are just as theologically complex, which you may not always have worked out before a crisis hits you? Marv waded into the suicide situation armed with theological certainty on at least one point: because Jesus was represented in Jennifer's life, he felt committed to get involved.

The difference is...

Is this to say that our ministry to others will depend, not so much on our particular skills and training, but on the experience of God's work in our own lives? The difference between experiences that give us empathetic insights or rapport and the historical reality of God's grace in our own formation is critical to understand as we evaluate our own level of preparedness for crisis ministry.

you've experienced God's grace in the reality of that pain and your ability to communicate his grace. I'm not talking about simplistic platitudes that say, "Just trust Jesus and everything will be fine in the morning." Acting wisely when we're surrounded by pain and crisis requires careful thought, personal integrity, spiritual sensitivity, and a clear sense of our mission.

Basic presuppositions

Several important assumptions underlie everything else that follows in this chapter. These fundamental realities must be taken into account each time we get involved with a young person for the sake of bringing healing and hope.

Most adolescents are hurting much more deeply than they (or we) are willing to admit.

Things are generally worse than they appear. We don't need a long list of statistical evidence to confirm that life is tough for kids growing up today. Very few adults would argue that contemporary adolescence is marked by pressure, stress, and pain unlike any known in recent history. Broken families, uncertain peer relationships, addictions, abuse, fear of the future, terror in the present, confusion about the past—these are the realities our young people live with.

Sadly, the issues are not dramatically different for church kids. Yet most of the students you know are experts at covering up what's really going on inside. They are cautious about deciding whom they will allow to peek behind the carefully constructed masks they've perfected over the course of their childhood. We know from our own lives that a happy-go-lucky exterior often camouflages a deeply hurting heart, or that an angry outburst may be rooted in fear. That cocky senior, who seems to have everyone eating out of his hand, may be terrified that someone will get close enough to see how insecure he really feels. The life-of-the-party cheerleader who seems so comfortable with her sexuality, might very well be living with the shame of abuse that has left her feeling scarred and betrayed.

Why are adolescents so afraid to admit what's really going on and to let adults know that they could use some help? In many cases the answer is simple. They've shown people how they've felt before, and no one has ever taken them seriously. The sense of rejection that came when they took the risk of being vulnerable and found themselves ignored was simply too painful. The logical response for most kids is to pretend that everything is all right and hide the reality from everyone else.

So what? The responsibility we have as youth workers to listen carefully and deeply to the heart of a hurting teen cannot be overstated.

In addition, some young people feel that if they admit a problem, they aren't adequately handling their transition to adulthood. The notion that normal adulthood is a problem-free existence is a myth that has been perpetuated—especially in the church by adults unwilling to face the reality of their own lives. If being an adult means "having all your ducks in a row," it follows that the shortest path to adulthood is to make sure everyone thinks that's the case.

So what? We must learn to live honestly in front of our students so they can see that the relevance of the gospel is most profoundly felt in the midst of reality, even when that reality is painful. Seeing this kind of integrity will give them hope.

It should be noted that an often overlooked reason adolescents don't share how they're feeling is that they legitimately don't have any idea. The confusion of raging hormones, cognitive transitions, and emotional upheaval may just feel too intense. They may not have a name to put on the intense feelings they're experiencing, even though the effect is very real.

So what? Avoid the temptation to tell adolescents what they are feeling. Giving them permission to feel something deeply without having to put a name on it may be an important first step toward emotional honesty and healing.

Perhaps a more important question to ask is why we as spiritual leaders are so reluctant to acknowledge the seriousness of a kid's pain. So often we find ourselves pretending that everything is fine, avoiding the students we know are hurting, and changing the subject when it feels like they want to take us to a deeper place in their lives. The spiritual leaders of Jeremiah's day must have done the same thing: "From the least to the greatest, all are greedy for gain; prophets and priests alike, all practice deceit. They dress the wound of my people as though it were not serious. 'Peace, peace,' they say, when there is no peace" (Jeremiah 6:13-14) Dressing the wounds of people as though they aren't serious is rooted in selfishness and dishonesty. Applying a Band-Aid when surgery is needed will cause far more damage in the long run. But it is costly and often terrifying to go to the painful places in a student's heart. It often feels inadequate to provide only our presence when the situation seems to call for answers.

So what? Don't underestimate the power of your presence when a young person has trusted you with a hidden corner of his life. You might need to refer him to someone who can provide answers, but your presence may be the basis for healing because he trusts you.

Resources for healing exist in the body of Christ that exist nowhere else.
Sadly these resources are often unacknowledged and underused. The power of community is something the early church understood and is something this millennial generation has embraced as no recent age group has. Perhaps it is the collective pain of contemporaries abandoned by family and misunderstood by the church that has driven them to the depth of interdependence they seem to experience so deeply. In the midst of crisis it seems that people are driven to deeper relationships with each other. It amazes me that we have failed to better harness the power of community. Like Larry Crabb, I have "strong reason to suspect that Christians sitting dutifully in church congregations for whom 'going to church' means doing a variety of spiritual activities have

been given resources that if released could powerfully heal broken hearts, overcome the damage done by abusive backgrounds, encourage the depressed to courageously move forward, stimulate the lonely to reach out, revitalize discouraged teens and children with new and holy energy, and introduce hope into the lives of countless people who feel rejected, alone, and useless."[1] It seems as though youth groups have often grasped this concept better than others in the church. The reality of Paul's body metaphor in 1 Corinthians 12 is something young people seem to understand intuitively. Perhaps if we celebrated the resources of community more consciously during adolescence when the concept seems natural, our young people could become Christian adults who know how to apply the "one another's" of the New Testament more consistently.

We have observed over and over in recent years that when crisis hits a community of adolescents, their strength as a group increases instantly. The consistent story coming out of Jonesboro, Arkansas; Littleton, Colorado; Fort Worth, Texas; and other communities where violent crisis has hit groups of young people is that their deepest comfort came from one another. The youth ministry implications are obvious.

So what? We must cultivate a climate of true Christian community in our youth groups where mutual ministry and spiritual interdependence are the norm so that when times of crisis occur, the relational framework for intervention is already in place.

Healing and change will always be a mystery and can't easily be reduced to a formula or series of steps to victory.

Adolescence is, by definition, a time of developmental disequilibrium. With one foot reluctantly holding on to a place to stand in the familiar world of childhood, and the other searching for solid ground in the strange world of adulthood, it is no wonder teenagers often describe their lives as chaotic, confusing, and stressful. Perhaps this is why we often feel such a strong compulsion to provide simplistic solutions for the complex realities they live with.

Our natural attraction to formula solutions and steps to victory may be more tied to our lack of trust in God than our desire to see a young person experience deep healing. Formulas give us the illusion that we can control the outcomes. "If I follow the recipe carefully enough I can guarantee the results." How many times have we realized in our own lives that these step-based approaches don't always produce the outcome we desired?

Scripture often gets misused in counseling dilemmas because of our need for formulaic quick fixes. Passages taken out of context lose their intended power. Furthermore, verses meant to deliver healing and hope are impotent when quoted mindlessly without acknowledging the depth of pain they are meant to address. Romans 8:28 ("And we know that in all things God works for the good of those who love him") is a powerful declaration of God's sovereignty in the midst of confusing circumstances. However, all too often it's given to young people without taking the time to understand what's really going on in their lives. This is in no way meant to minimize the

First thing first
The depth of need adolescents have for counseling make one immediately conclude that youth ministry professionals need more and better skills and training. Marv doesn't deny us that route, but as the first line of response, he calls our attention to the theological design of the body of Christ.

---

1. Larry Crabb (1997).

Ponderable
Is it possible that even caring relationships can be reduced to a cookbook solution during crises? In other words, God's whole plan for healing is not likely caught in either *Bible Verses R Us* or *Relationships R Everything*, but in some combination that guarantees a supportive person will be present to guide a teen into life-changing interaction with God's Word.

importance of allowing the Scripture to speak into the life of a hurting teenager but to remind us of the importance of providing a relationship in which the Scripture can take hold. The central hope of Christianity is the assurance of Christ's presence in whatever circumstances we find ourselves. He is our example in the work we do with hurting kids.

So what? It is always more costly to provide our presence to a young person in crisis than to impose a cookbook solution and walk away. In most cases God chooses to work through relationships.

Wholeness and healing truly are available in relationship with Christ.
Contemporary psychology has become more and more adept at naming and classifying disorders and less effective in suggesting trustworthy solutions. With each release of a new edition of the *Diagnostic and Statistical Manual,* the American Psychiatric Association adds dozens of new diagnoses. There is a name for virtually every behavioral, relational, or emotional quirk people can dream up. In the meantime, the proliferation of apparently acceptable therapeutic strategies increases. A widening range of methodologies are being proposed with little consensus emerging about what really is effective. With all these conflicting voices, it is encouraging for the Christian youth worker to lean confidently on Christ's words in John 10:10, "I have come that they may have life, and have it to the full."

When we affirm that wholeness and healing are available in Christ, we do so realizing that it will still surely require work on the part of both the counselor and counselee. We recognize that healing may take time and could involve substantial pain along the journey. Pointing young people to Jesus is never a cop-out if we commit to staying engaged in the relationship while they experience his help. Our confidence comes in knowing that healing is his specialty.

So what? Christ's life provides us with a model for dealing with crisis and counseling and the power to be the change agent in the lives of those with whom we work.

The Christ of crisis and counseling

When we read the stories of Jesus in the Gospels we see his healing touch expressed over and over. We imagine blind people tossing away their white canes, cripples using their crutches for kindling, and lepers auditioning for complexion commercials. It's no wonder crowds chased him everywhere. It's not a surprise that the religious leaders of his day felt more than just a little threatened by this healer who had chosen their neck of the woods to set up shop.

We can learn countless lessons from Christ's interaction with hurting people. The gentleness of his touch is evident when he works with children. The boldness of his confidence in the power of his heavenly Father is seen when he confronts the insidious power of evil. The sensitivity of his spirit is obvious when he deals with those damaged and victimized by the actions of others. His acceptance is unconditional even when he knows that the mess the hookers and tax collectors are in is because of their own choices. The amazing thing is that in most of these cases he weaves spiritual solutions into the conversation and models what it means to deal with a whole person. Reading the stories gives us a picture of what it means to be like Jesus as we represent him in the lives of the students we care about.

There is an earlier biblical reference to the kind of healer Christ would become, and it, too, gives us some insights from which we can learn. The prophet Isaiah, speaking prophetically hundreds of years before Christ's birth, describes Jesus' mission in a series of names he uses in Isaiah 9:6. In this familiar Christmas passage, we get a look at the kind of people Christ was destined to touch by hearing the names he would go by: Wonderful Counselor, Mighty God, Everlasting Father, and Prince of Peace. His incarnation appears to be a direct response to the nature of the brokenness of those he came to save. Since we are committed to an incarnational ministry in the world of adolescents, we would do well to pay attention.

Who needs a counselor? Is it not someone who is hurting, confused, unsure, wounded, and at the end of their own resources? What about a strong and Mighty God? People who feel weak, helpless, powerless, and alone long to know the strength Christ brings. The Everlasting Father Isaiah describes stands in sharp contrast to the deadbeat dads and detached workaholics a lot of kids today live with, and a Prince of Peace is what people who are stressed, fearful, and anxious need. The words *hurting, confused, unsure, wounded, weak, helpless, powerless, alone, abandoned, stressed, fearful,* and *anxious* could certainly be used to accurately describe the generation of young people God has called us to serve on his behalf. Our greatest privilege is to point them to that counselor, strong one, father, and prince.

Isaiah goes on at the beginning of chapter 61 to outline God's call on his life. The parallel between Isaiah's call and Christ's character is clear. "The Lord has anointed me to preach good news to the poor. He has sent me to bind up the brokenhearted, to proclaim freedom for the captives and release from darkness for the prisoners" (Isaiah 61:1). The words *broken* and *bound* are so accurate in describing life apart from Christ, that to attempt to bring healing through any means that does not involve him is to overlook the reason he came.

So what? The healing ministry of Jesus is the template by which we model and evaluate our work with hurting students. To suggest that true wholeness is available in any way that eliminates Christ is to declare the cross irrelevant to the struggles of life in this broken world.

Acting wisely in counseling and crises

How, then, does this all look in the real world of working in youth ministry? How do we respond to the barrage of crises that seems to mark the lives of kids today?

qualifications. She was looking for someone she could trust. Certainly she needed some professional help along the way when she started dealing with the deeper issues, but before any of that could happen she needed someone in her life who cared about her and was willing to get involved. We can all be those kinds of people in the lives of hurting young kids if we are willing to start now. Here are some steps you can begin immediately to increase your effectiveness as a helper.

Cultivate the character of a healer

Certain characteristics of Christlikeness show up again and again when effective helpers are described. These character qualities are worth cultivating whether or not we see ourselves in the role of a helper. They include—

- *integrity*—a walk that lines up with the talk, a person true to their word, someone who has faced the reality of their own weaknesses and struggles
- *humility*—a recognition that God is in control, an absence of arrogance, a determination to keep pointing people toward Jesus rather than becoming all they need
- *acceptance*—a willingness to love people no matter who they are or what they've done, a non-judgmental spirit
- *warmth*—a genuine care for the individual, a positive encouraging presence, an ability to project undivided attention without patronizing
- *empathy*—an ability to feel deeply with another person. The Bible takes it to another level when it talks about bearing one another's burdens.
- *a growing walk with God*—a conscious commitment to avoiding spiritual stagnation, an increasing dependence on him based on a willingness to increase relational risks and choose costly obedience.

As these qualities increase, our trustworthiness with hurting students will increase as well—and the level at which they share will become deeper and more meaningful.

Define desired outcomes

What is the goal of your work with hurting teenagers? It's easy to fall into the trap of measuring effectiveness purely on the basis of changed behaviors, more pleasant emotions, or altered circumstances. While each of these may be desirable in their own way, they do not necessarily represent spiritual growth in an individual. Movement toward health can be best understood in directional terms. Ask yourself, *Is this young person trusting God more deeply today than last week? Is she willing to take risks based on obedience rather than creating a safe path through relationships? Is she able to define her feelings more accurately now than before? Does she have a clearer sense of who she is and how events of her life have shaped her to this point?* Healing is always a journey. It may involve the participation of many different people all working together under the Wonderful Counselor's ultimate supervision.

The Chinese have an interesting insight into the nature of crisis. In their colorful language they have designated a compound word to portray the concept. The two words that make up the word for *crisis* are the words *danger* and *opportunity*. We must recognize that in the face of the danger that every crisis brings, there is also great opportunity. We have the opportunity to see God at work in difficult circumstances, the opportunity to use the comfort we have experienced from God to help someone, and the opportunity to grow in our own faith as we are stretched beyond the range of our personal skills and resources. The students we work with have great opportunity to grow in the midst of adversity as well. The nature of God is to meet us most personally in our darkest times, and for young people who want to know God deeply, there may be experiences of overwhelming pain to provide that opportunity.

Counseling adolescents is one of the biggest challenges of youth ministry. It seems that just when we think we've heard it all, a new story emerges that makes us shake our heads and wonder why we didn't pursue a career in retail. What is it about counseling kids that makes it so challenging?

- It's a unique kind of counseling because the stakes are often so high. The choices made by kids in crisis often have immediate and seriously destructive consequences. We feel an urgency that is very real.
- It's a lonely kind of counseling because we often endure the anger and disdain of a kid who doesn't want help, and we live with the pressure from parents or social agencies who just want the behavior to change.
- It's a discouraging kind of counseling because so often we see the kids we work with going right back into the situation that caused their pain in the first place—a home that is no more functional now than it was before the crisis, or a relationship that will continue to do damage as long as they are involved. As a friend of mine once said, "It's a game where batting .100 is considered high."
- It's a frustrating kind of counseling because often the kid we're working with is healthier than the parent who sent her.

But in spite of all that's just been said, the strategic potential of counseling teenagers must be appreciated. There is no better time in the human developmental process to come alongside someone than during their teen years. We can connect with them at a critical moment in their lives—when their childlikeness still leaves them open to the input of others who genuinely care, and their adultlikeness allows them to deal with the tough realities of choices in a way that can be mature and life-changing.

Getting started in counseling and crisis intervention

Some people seem to think that, without a Ph.D. and years of experience, they can't do much to help a teenager in crisis. Remember Jenn? She wasn't looking for academic

Practice interactive skills

Although who you are is probably more important to your work with kids than what you know, it is wise to develop the expertise necessary to work with people who are hurting. In fact, if you want to make counseling and crisis intervention a key part of your ministry, it will be critical that you receive training in the skills that will maximize your effectiveness. A good first step is to begin consciously practicing some of the components of good counseling. Learn to listen. This may be the most important skill of all to practice. Listen beneath the words for the feelings that are being expressed. Listen to the non-verbal language of the body, facial expressions, and tone of voice. Practice reflecting back to people what you are hearing them say. Learn ways to make it safe for them to say more. Develop your spiritual sensitivity so that you can more accurately determine what is going on for a person in that area. Use open-ended questions (those that require a thoughtful answer rather than just yes or no) in your conversations with friends to draw out their thoughts.

Don't become an amateur psychologist in all of this. There's nothing more obnoxious! Just work at being a better friend. As these skills become natural, you will be more effective in your counseling interactions and more confident in your ability to help people.

Recognize your own limitations

This chapter is not intended as training for professional therapists. It is aimed toward people who love kids and desire an opportunity to help them when they're hurting. As a lay person, there are specific limitations to what you can and cannot do. Some of these limitations are legal and others are based in common sense. It is not your job to replace parents and family. It is wise to involve a young person's parents wherever possible in recognition of their spiritual role of leadership in the lives of their children.

When you are dealing with issues of abuse, criminal activity, and other serious matters, you should be aware of the legal obligations in your area. They can be reviewed at the police department or at one of the child protection or social service agencies in your community. Even though you are not a professional counselor, you are bound by laws in these areas, and it is your obligation to understand and apply them as needed.

Also beware of your personal limitations. These will be different for every person, but it will be important for you to discover yours. There is a limit to the number of hurting students you can be involved with. There are certain topics you will feel less qualified to talk about than others. When you reach your limit in some of these areas, get help for yourself. A basic principle of lifeguarding is that there is no point in two people drowning. The rescuer must take responsibility for his own safety. The same principle applies in people-helping. It is easy to become overwhelmed with the needs of hurting kids all around us, but we are finite creatures with limits on how much we can offer.

Be ye faithful
Not only have most youth ministry vets realized they can't do everything, but they've also realized that God never *intended* them to do it all. We can relax by accepting our limitations as a theological reality; faithfulness is doing what *God* expects us to do—no more or less.

Be careful not to tell kids that they can call you whenever they need you or that you'll be there for them anytime. Reserve that privilege for rare and very extreme circumstances. Create a safe and healing place that you can retreat to so that your soul can be replenished.

Prepare for the unanticipated

Some people thrive on imagining worst-case scenarios. They seem to enjoy the possibility that a disaster is just around the corner waiting to crush them. We tend to look on folks like this with some suspicion. Rightly so! Without becoming chronically pessimistic about the future, it is important that we take a realistic position on the matter of crisis in our world of ministry. If we truly care about adolescents and surround ourselves with them for the sake of ministry, we will encounter crisis. The best way to prepare is to maintain a close relationship of dependence with the Wonderful Counselor we talked about earlier in the chapter. After all, our role is simply to be apprentices in his ministry plan. When we are familiar with his ways, sensitive to his voice, and responsive to his guidance, we can confidently embrace the most severe crisis knowing that we do not need to carry the burden alone. He is faithful. His grace is sufficient for any ministry circumstances we may face.

★ ★ ★

When I began my life in youth ministry over a quarter of a century ago, I imagined the thrill of having hurting kids pour out their souls to me. I envisioned myself as a hero to parents who couldn't deal with the complications of raising an adolescent without my valuable insights. The novelty has long since worn off.

I remember standing in the shower one evening after a long and sweaty day of working in the yard. As I watched the dirty water swirling down the drain at my feet I found myself wishing I could wash my soul as easily after a day of working with hurting kids and their families. The stories of abuse, anger, violence, and victimization I heard so often left me feeling contaminated and stained. And yet there was always a joy in seeing God's healing at work in the lives of his children.

The experience of working with hurting teenagers is bittersweet. It is not for the faint of heart. If the novelty of seeing into the secret corners of someone's life or a curiosity about the sordid details behind a story you've heard is what draws you to this ministry, I would suggest you look elsewhere. If the need to be needed energizes you in pursuit of kids to counsel, it will be a disappointing journey. But if God calls you to it and you understand what it means to be in partnership with him, there is no life like it. You'll see miracles the likes of which you couldn't have imagined.

Assessing Honestly: Continuous Improvement
Dave Rahn

At the end of each week, we must find ways to make peace with the worth of our work. If we don't, we can get chased out of youth ministry by our insecurities and bewilderment. And so we routinely figure out ways to assess our ministries. Some of our efforts are formal; others are private mental exercises. These patterns suggest that the most pressing question is not typically *whether we will do ministry assessment*, but rather *what kind of ministry assessment we will do*. This question, and numerous derivatives, is profoundly connected to our theological commitments.

Some of us find it hard to *not* evaluate our ministries; we seem to be constantly working out our nearly involuntary judgments about how well a particular program, lesson, or even conversation went. Youth pastors cut from this cloth mentally replay their ministry encounters over and over, looking for the slightest indicators of health or sickness, strength or weakness, success or failure. Even subtle nuances of activity are scrutinized with microscopic diligence. Too many yawns during the evening's talk are instantly interpreted as a testimony to our ineffective communication. A first-time smile becomes the magnificent relational breakthrough we've been working toward—holding promise to usher in the next Great Awakening. Those of us in this camp assess our ministries through observable *outcomes*. Sure, we make too much meaning of too little information, but we can't help it. Like some sort of result-driven junkies, we feel the need for more and more reliable data, believing that such information can offer us certainty and peace about how we're *really* doing.

Others of us have achieved a remarkable, transcendental bliss about the whole notion of ministry assessment. We can immerse ourselves fully in ministry moments, concentrate on giving our best, and not be bothered by concerns about outcomes. Since our effectiveness indicators come from within, we are liberated from the need to be ever vigilant about what's happening *out there*. We gauge a ministry's worth by checking the pulse of our own efforts. Rather than monitoring results, these assessment strategies pay close attention to the processes of ministry. The worth of our efforts is judged on the merits of our efforts themselves. Many times these judgments can be made on the spot, in the "here and now" of ministry.

Even our reasons for doing ministry evaluation vary. Sometimes we're driven by *external obligations*. A board, senior pastor, supervisor, or accountability partner is waiting to hear our assessment of how things are going. The year-end report is due, or a presentation needs to be made in order to secure funding. For someone—or something—*outside of ourselves*, we need to give an accurate report of our ministry.

At other times we may be interested in evaluation for the noblest of reasons. We feel the need to learn all we can about what works and doesn't work in our ministries. Years ago I learned that, for me to be fulfilled in my work, I need conditions that allow me the chance to do the best and be the best I can be. It's really important for me to have feedback loops that help me constantly assess and improve whatever it is I'm doing. Those of you who are put together like me would agree we "owe it to ourselves" to get accurate feedback about our ministry. Such an *internal obligation* represents a powerful motivation in our lives.

Let's reflect on our personal ministry assessment preferences. By meta-thinking our way through this, we may benefit from considering which of the preceding descriptions most accurately describe us. Are we primarily concerned with our ministry's outcomes, or does the process of ministry get our closest attention? Is our sense of obligation for assessment primarily a response to others' requests or are we addressing our personal need for integrity? If we locate the quadrant (see figure 27.1) that combines our chief orientation with our number one assessment motivation, we can concentrate on exploring the theological reflection questions that will yield the greatest personal benefit.

Assessment
We can certainly turn an assessment eye on other things. For example, many persons do a *needs analysis* before formulating ministry strategies—a type of assessment that focuses neither on an outcome nor a process, but on helping youth workers get an accurate picture of what ministry needs they should address.

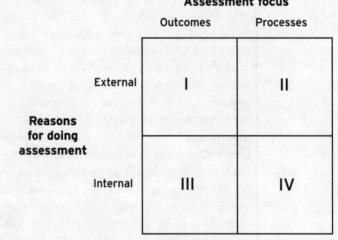

Figure 27.1. Assessment: personal motivation and targeted focus

Try this on. Jan is a youth minister in quadrant I who cares about ministry assessment largely because of the biweekly meeting she has with the senior pastor. It may also follow that this senior pastor is a bottom-line type of person, and so wants to hear exclusively about ministry results. The questions bomb away at Jan: How many kids have been attending? Have there been any significant spiritual decisions lately? Who has completed the discipleship program? How are camp sign-ups coming? A youth minister working in this setting very quickly learns what is important to her supervisor, and can be tempted to pay exclusive attention to those outcomes that are most measurable. That's where our "nickels and noses" bias come from with regard to ministry assessment. As Larry Richards has pointed out, it's not as easy to record clear observations about life change as it is to see how many showed up for Wednesday's meeting.[1] When we've got to point to immediate outcomes to keep the boss happy, it's not hard to sympathize with the tendency to grab our data from the most accessible shelf in the store.

Rich's "results orientation" is a little different from Jan's. He sometimes wishes he were held accountable by a senior pastor—or anyone who knew *anything* about youth ministry. He's a quadrant III person, driven to figure out what outcome measures will signal to him that he's on the right track in all of his efforts. Sometimes his difficulty sleeping traces back to the fact that he can't yet see the fruit that he wants so desperately in his ministry.

There are cautions we must attend to if we're going to use ministry assessment to weigh outcomes—regardless of our motivation. The Bible makes it clear that the outcomes that ultimately matter the most are those that are attributed to God's efforts, not ours. The psalmist writes, "Unless the Lord builds the house, its builders labor in vain" (Psalm 127:1a). Jesus indicated that each of us depend on God's initiating activity to be drawn to him (John 6:44, 65). When we believe that we bring about uniquely God-based results through our ministry routines, we have fallen for the mechanical/technocratic myth of ministry.[2] Paul rebuked the Corinthians for giving undue (and divisive) credit to the ministers of their formative past when it is clear that only God is responsible for growth (1 Corinthians 3).

Ponderable
This is the lie? Which of us doesn't honestly have a vision of God-glorifying results in mind as we struggle to persevere in ministry? Isn't the exercise of writing one's vision statement, in fact, an exercise in painting a picture of desirable, measurable outcomes?

Some of our approaches to ministry evaluation belie our cause and effect misconceptions. Kenda Creasy Dean and Ron Foster illustrate this in a short case: "Eric's relationship with youth will 'cause' them to develop an interest in Christ; the youth's involvement in Sunday school will 'cause' them to know the Bible; their experience in youth group will 'cause' them to mature in their faith, and so on."[3] Here's the lie in a nutshell: If we can count on the fact that our right efforts will bring about desired results, it should be fair to target outcomes as the focus of our ministry assessment.

So we shouldn't pay any attention to results when we evaluate our youth ministries, right? Hold that thought. Luke reported on the early church in ways that have caused many of us to aspire to greater dedication, richer fellowship, a common life, reputations of integrity, and explosive numerical growth (Acts 2:42-47). These were observable outcomes, and the early church understood that they had received God's blessing as a result of them. When the Holy Spirit interrupted Peter just as he was getting into the meat of his message to Cornelius' and company, Peter drew upon this experience in a way that helped to untether the early church from its restrictive moorings (Acts 10:24-11:18). Paying proper attention to the right results can actually guide us to greater faithfulness!

What if you're not necessarily inclined to look at results in ministry assessment? For example, Joey works at South Northville Community Church and thinks of him-

---

1. Lawrence O. Richards, *Christian Education: Seeking to Become Like Jesus* (Grand Rapids, Michigan: Zondervan, 1981), 25-28.

2. Christian Scwartz, *Natural Church Development* (ChurchSmart Resources, 1996).

3. Kenda Creasy Dean and Ron Foster, *The Godbearing Life: The Art of Soul Tending in Youth Ministry* (Nashville: Upper Room Books, 1998), 33.

self as a quadrant II type. He also has a biweekly accounting with his supervisor, but the kind of questions he has to answer have very little to do with outcomes. His senior pastor wants to see weekly goals, asks how the youth pastor's time was spent, and even explores how he (the head honcho) might assist the youth pastor with his current urgent projects.

Joni, on the other hand, doesn't let ministry assessment keep her awake at all. She's also highly motivated, but she has the overall sense that she can't control the outcomes that will really matter 200 years from now, so she concentrates on trying to be the right person doing the right things by the kids she serves. Daily disciplines of journaling and reflection help her explore her own degree of faithfulness in ministry. Joni's a quadrant IV person—self-motivated to evaluate and focused on improving herself.

There is a lot to commend process assessment to us as we minister. For one thing, as we've already observed, our partnership with God in ministry means that we do as we are told and leave the results up to him. This frees us to really pay attention to the details of our obedience. If you need a reminder of how important the little things are in our faithfulness to God, try arranging for an interview with Moses about why he didn't get to go into the Promised Land. At the end of Israel's desert training experience, God told him to speak to the rock for water. This must have been a little déja vu for Moses. "Wasn't this the same place where thirsty grumblings resulted in a rock faucet appearing 40 years ago?" he might have thought. Of course, *then* he was instructed to strike the rock with the big stick God had given him (Exodus 17:1-7). Seems reasonable that he could do an encore this time. But God had asked Moses to *speak* to the rock this time, not strike it. Moses' actions constituted a disrespect for God insofar as he wasn't attentive to doing precisely as God wished. Details, details. Apparently, they were important enough to God that he benched Moses, keeping him from leading the Promised Land Victory Parade even after his distinguished run of faithful service (Numbers 20:1-13; 27:14; Deuteronomy 32:51). If ministry assessment helps us honor God by correcting our "good enough" ministry tendencies to conform to more exacting standards of holiness, it has served us well.

There's a further consideration that suggests the way we approach ministry is an important ingredient in ministry evaluation. God is not simply sovereign over the outcomes of ministry; he also rules in matters of timing. As followers of the crucified Christ, we are aware that doing the right things in the right way doesn't always result in immediately positive results. An evaluation of Jesus' ministry effectiveness conducted on Good Friday would have yielded disastrously wrong conclusions. Similarly, if you were scouting Jesus' team for future promise on the evening of their Last Supper, I'm not sure you would have concluded that Peter was the kind of person on which the new church could be built. Timing is a theological issue that must be accounted for in our assessment strategies.

God graciously personalized this lesson for me in my first few months of full-time ministry with Youth for Christ. While backpacking in the Smokies with me and a dozen others, a charismatic high schooler named Dave made an unusually strong commitment to follow Jesus Christ. His growth curve after that trip was almost as remarkable as the impact he seemed to be having upon his friends. The day we returned from the trip he convinced a friend to join him in his newfound faith. Troi and Dave forged an inseparable bond in Jesus, and I saw them at least once a day. We shared Scripture, prayed, laughed, and dreamed together about how God was going to rock their school through them.

Three and a half weeks after returning from the Smokies, everything changed. Dave and Troi were involved in a tragic accident at our office where they were both electrocuted. Dave was killed instantly; Troi was burned severely and would take months to recuperate.

Student body president and vice-president, co-captains on the football team, white and black best buddies…what a waste! The senselessness of this tragedy overwhelmed me. I remember asking—accusing—God if he really knew what he was doing. The Lord allowed me to vent—to pour out my pain. He then reminded me that he had never let me down and it wasn't in his nature to do so now. I had to be patient. In the meantime I stumbled through the first funeral of my ministry. I met parents and tried to offer comfort when I was desperate for healing myself. The first time I met Dave's father we cried in one another's arms. In a remarkable show of personal grace, he *thanked me* for my investment in Dave over the past month! He had noticed the change in Dave since our trip together.

Here's the real kicker. For the next four years I ministered through Campus Life in that school community. Each year I met someone I had not previously known who testified that his life was profoundly changed by the personal impact Dave made on them during the three-plus weeks that he walked with Jesus on planet Earth. Assess that.

So which is it? Should we evaluate processes or outcomes? It's possible to infer that I believe one's approach to ministry assessment is simply a matter of personal preference and style. I certainly *do* believe that our natural and circumstantial orientations become the *default* assessment strategies that we employ. But if our *evaluation* efforts aren't rooted in biblical ministry *values*, then what values are we serving?

Look again at the matrix constructed for earlier reflection, but this time concentrate on the consideration of motives for assessment. Are there biblical ministry values that transcend the practical worth of doing assessment in order to meet someone else's accountability demands? Connecting our ministry evaluations to external obligations testifies to the reality of interdependence of which the Scripture speaks. It suggests that we appreciate the call of Scripture to submit ourselves to one another, particularly to those who have authority over us (Ephesians 5:21; Hebrews 13:17; 1 Peter 2:17). We recognize the kingdom value of having our work scrutinized today, because we know it will be judged in the future (1 Corinthians 3:12-14).

The practical reasons we assess our youth ministry may include the need to meet external obligations, but submission is healthiest when it reflects an internalized value. We must be convinced that interdependence is a two-step reality. Unlike independent and self-reliant structures, the metaphor of the body suggests that we truly do need one another. Unlike dependent and other-reliant structures, it suggests that we have been uniquely designed to make original and meaningful contributions, without which others will genuinely be impoverished.

The highest forms of assessment can take place only when honesty and humility blaze a trail that honors truth above all else. This isn't always easy; it's the same sort of posture that earned Socrates the label as the *gadfly of Athens*.[4] In the service of the truth, any question was fair game for this ancient philosopher. Douglas Hyde reported that this kind of attitude provided the climate for critical evaluation among Communist Party members as they critiqued their various campaigns.[5] Knowing the truth was more important than protecting someone's ego from being bruised. The nice thing is that caring for others and loving the truth are not incompatible in the economy of the Christian faith. Paul insisted that the Ephesians should contribute to one another's growth by "speaking the truth in love" (Ephesians 4:15).

Honest evaluation can help us understand the true state of health in our youth ministries. It can also reveal something about our own biases and ill preparedness to make important judgments about ministry effectiveness. We can always see what needs cleaning up better when the lights are on. Assessment helps us make sure we've got enough candlepower pointed in the right direction to really improve our ministry effectiveness. Continuous improvement is a worthy, even holy, goal. As John Wesley wrote, "It is a great thing to seize and improve the very now."[6]

So what does good assessment look like? For one thing, it probably appreciates the multiple ways of knowing that are available to us. Rick Yount points out that there are at least six different lenses through which we understand the world around us.[7] When applied to youth ministry assessment, these various approaches describe familiar practices. For instance, we use *common sense* to determine that the retreat we planned around winter sports had trouble attracting kids because the unseasonably warm weather didn't produce any snow. At another time, we deferred to professional *authority* to help us understand something beyond our own expertise—that a kid's psychiatric disorder was the major influence in his bizarre behavior. Many times we'll draw assessment conclusions informally, while we're in the middle of the action, listening to our Holy Spirit aided *intuition* as to whether a particular time might be right for a particular confrontation with a young person. Of course, most of us lean on our past *experience* to help us evaluate current situations. Youth ministry veterans may have difficulty getting beyond this "been there, done that" version of ministry assessment. When logic or

4. For a great picture of this holy irritating quality, see Peter Kreeft, *Socrates Meets Jesus* (Downers Grove, Illinois: InterVarsity Press, 1987).

5. Douglas Hyde, *Dedication and Leadership* (Notre Dame, Indiana: Notre Dame University Press, 1992).

6. As reported in Dean and Foster, 55.

7. This excellent discussion is introduced in a wonderful resource for the technically challenged and advanced student alike in William R. Yount, *Research Design and Statistical Analysis in Christian Ministry* (self-published for classes at Southwestern Baptist Theological Seminary), 1–4.

deductive reasoning are used to help us evaluate our ministries, we have reasoned our way from a true principle to an understanding of specific situations. For example, if we know that crowding has a positive effect on persuasion,[8] and that a particular meeting was in a cavernous hall, we may conclude that the impact of the message was not as great as it could have been. Finally, the scientific or *inductive* method may be used in assessment. This approach requires us to make a number of different observations (perhaps using a survey) and come to our ministry judgments based upon what we've discovered through various samples.

None of these approaches are entirely sanctified, just as none of them need to be godless. The following 10 questions may help us drag our ministry assessment practices into compatibility with our theological convictions. There's no reason that we can't honor God by continuously improving our ministries through assessment.

1. What evidence is there that the results you currently monitor matter to God?

2. How do you ensure that the way you measure your ministry outcomes, places this data in proper perspective relative to God's role and timing in bringing about those results?

3. What are some outcomes highly valued by God that you are not currently trying to assess? (For example, consider how the unique sequential structure of 2 Peter 1:3-8 may provide biblically valid indicators of Christian growth.)

4. Identify five ministry practices that seem to be a priority of the earliest church in the book of Acts. How well do you assess the strength of these practices in your youth ministry?

5. How has ministry assessment actually helped you become more faithful and effective in your ministry?

6. What do your current disciplines and attitudes related to ministry assessment say about your interdependence, accountability, and submissiveness within the body of Christ?

7. What could you do to gain more benefit from your currently natural and infor mal practices of ministry assessment?

8. What formal ministry assessment patterns could you put into place that would help you continuously improve your ministry?

---

8. Emory Griffin, *The Mindchangers: The Art of Christian Persuasion* (Wheaton, Illinois: Tyndale, 1976), 57-60.

9. Study Revelation 2 and 3 and notice how the Lord Jesus assessed each of the seven churches. Invite your leadership team to pray with you as you discern what he might have to say to your youth ministry.

10. Under what conditions could ministry assessment disregard the lordship of Jesus? Under what conditions does ministry assessment reflect a faithful response to Jesus' lordship?

28 Chapter

Assessing Honestly: Spiritual Readiness
Chap Clark

"Youth workers never die...they just get a new T-shirt!"

I saw this slogan on an elderly counselor at a conference, and I had to smile. There's something about this thing called youth ministry that, after you have been in it a while, is like a vaccine that stays forever in your blood.

I've been in and around youth ministry for three decades—as a student, a junior high leader, a Young Life staff person, a director of student ministries in a church, and a professor. I have seen programs and models come and go. I have heard the great speakers and danced to the hottest bands. I've been hit with a pie, and I've cried in the mud. I can't drive by a 7-11 without wondering aloud who is loving those kids to Jesus Christ. I cry when I see precious ballerinas and seven-year-old Joe Montanas, because I know what the next 10 years will do to their souls. I am, and will always be, a youth worker.

Modern perceptions of youth workers include ideas that we are a fun-loving, wild, mildly irreverent (but appropriately so), passionate, energetic, and a hip bunch. And there is a great deal of truth to that. We are typically not hired because of our effervescent spirituality, and in fact the majority who read this will never be asked in an interview about their interior walk with Christ or what spiritual disciplines they use. People *want* and *expect* us to be a bit different—a bit odd. We are hired, after all, to run a program, ensure some semblance of perceived spiritual growth in a group of students, and basically keep the congregants happy. Strategy, vision, and experience are sometimes also valued, at least a little, in choosing and evaluating a professional youth worker, but for the most part, the bottom line in this vocational calling is we will always be measured against the perceived response of the students. And adults and students alike want us to be the one happy-go-lucky, on-the-edge person on a church staff. It's the name of the game.

But there is also a frightening cancer lurking just beneath the surface of that youthful facade of youth work. For youth ministry is ultimately not about running events or casting a programmatic spell over students and their parents. Ministry in a missional context, of penetrating a disenfranchised and disconnected subculture, goes far beyond and far deeper than program planning and implementation. Our ministry is not just knowing the latest songs, hanging out for hours at the high school, and being the most proficient *Webmeister* in the church. Youth ministry is not a game. It's a strategic calling of God's church.

Youth ministry that makes a difference is theologically driven youth ministry. The intense kind of incarnational ministry that youth ministry requires (see chapter 18) is fundamentally not something we *do*, but rather something we *are*. Youth ministry ultimately emanates from the very core of the youth worker's life. In God's economy, it really doesn't matter much what you know about youth culture, programmatic philosophy, or modern technology. As the culture around us cranks up the music and throws life into overdrive, more than ever a ministry to and about adolescents needs to be simple, direct, and straightforward. Our message and our motive is the same as it was for Paul and the Corinthian church:

> So from now on we regard no one from a worldly point of view.
> Though we once regarded Christ in this way, we do so no longer.
> Therefore, if anyone is in Christ, he is a new creation; the old has gone,
> the new has come! All this is from God, who reconciled us to himself
> through Christ and gave us the ministry of reconciliation: that God was
> reconciling the world to himself in Christ, not counting men's sins
> against them. And he has committed to us the message of reconciliation.
> We are therefore Christ's ambassadors, as though God were making his
> appeal through us. We implore you on Christ's behalf: Be reconciled to
> God. God made him who had no sin to be sin for us, so that in him we
> might become the righteousness of God.
>
> —*2 Corinthians 5:16-21*

This is the essence of our message, and therefore needs to be at the core of our life in ministry. We must be constantly on the lookout for anything and everything that would seek to divert us from the beauty of God's plan of reconciliation. You as a youth worker are God's *ambassador*, and you therefore are called to *implore* those students and families you serve to be reconciled to the God who loves them. This is the essence of our message, and this is the central mandate and motivation for the youth ministry task.

Cultivating spiritual readiness

So how does one cultivate a vibrant, or even adequate, *spiritual readiness* in youth ministry? How can a youth worker keep her heart and life cleanly devoted to Jesus Christ, and at the same time run an efficient, popular program that is universally valued? Even the framing of this question, however, brings the issue into the programmatic realm, which implicitly misses the point. When all is said and done, authentic ministry is an *inside-out* sense of focus and calling. The *how* is not nearly as important as having the *will* to go after it. The mystery of our faith, "Christ in you, the hope of glory" (Colossians 1:27), is the seedbed of our ministry, indeed our very lives. Cultivating a spiritual readiness for the task of youth ministry is to see that you are committed to ensuring that your ministry comes from someplace deeper than your history, training, and experience. Ministry must come from deep within in order to sustain the focus necessary to be labeled *ministry*. As Len Kageler writes—

> If we are going to successfully survive our first five or 10 years in youth ministry, we must learn the secrets of renewal. A renewed heart and spirit make it possible for us to not be blown away by criticism. A renewed heart keeps us going when we are starved to see results and go hungry instead. A renewed heart makes it possible to keep perspective when it seems like our world is falling apart.[1]

Doing and being
Does this make you wonder if our greatest enemy is the assumption—the first, biggest rock—that we have to *do* something before we can *be* somebody? After all, it's a lot easier to monitor someone's job effectiveness than it is to get a handle on her life faithfulness. Training, interviews, assessment—all of the socializing determinants of our profession—push us toward *doing* ministry. Chap Clark is saying that we can't *do* identity; high achievers among us need to let that truth wash over them.

But more importantly, our ministry must flow from our deepening walk with Christ in order to continually remind ourselves that God is far more concerned about our character than the number of students who like our program. It is not so much about how many quiet times we schedule, or whether or not we regularly fast, but rather the condition of our hearts. Paul Borthwick, in *Feeding Your Forgotten Soul*, entreats us to pursue a tenacious honesty in taking spiritual inventory of our lives: "We need to ask questions (of ourselves) about matters of character, because fulfilling external disciplines (reading the Bible, personal worship time, and service) can become mundane and empty if they are not penetrating our spirits."[2]

Five areas of focus for healthy spiritual readiness for ministry

The following five areas of focus for the healthy spiritual readiness of the authentic youth worker are summed up in the Great Commandment:

> "The most important one," answered Jesus, "is this: 'Hear, O Israel, the Lord our God, the Lord is one. Love the Lord your God with all your heart and with all your soul and with all your mind and with all your strength.' The second is this: 'Love your neighbor as yourself.' There is no other commandment greater than these."
>
> *—Mark 12:29-31*

These words of Jesus provide the definitive and final job description for the youth worker—and for anyone in Christian ministry. We are to be guided by love, and *only* guided by love. What is our role with students? To love each one as we would be loved. What, then, is our job concerning leaders and staff? To love each one as we would be loved. What is our calling with respect to the senior pastor, elder board, or school principal? To love each one as we would be loved. As Werner Kummel points out, these two related commandments represent the summation of the call to Christ:

> [The] coordination of [these two commands] by Jesus unmistakably has the intention of naming all that [humanity] has to do in the sight of

1. Len Kageler, *The Youth Minister's Survival Guide* (Grand Rapids, Michigan: Zondervan/Youth Specialties, 1992), 167-8.

2. Paul Borthwick, *Feeding Your Forgotten Soul* (Grand Rapids, Michigan: Zondervan/Youth Specialties, 1990), 89.

God: the response to the encounter with God in Jesus and to the promise of the kingdom of God can only be love for God which is actualized in love for one's neighbor. If love for one's neighbor grows out of the encounter with God's love and is inseparable from the love for God, then such love for one's neighbor knows no limits.[3]

So what does this mean when it comes to *spiritual readiness* for youth ministry? How does loving God and loving others *summarize* a youth worker's job description? This is explored by looking at the terms Jesus uses in these two commandments from the viewpoint of the youth worker.

"With all of your heart"—readying the heart

As is true today, the word *heart* (*kardia*) in the Bible is used to describe not only the physical organ, but also is seen as "the center of the physical, mental, and spiritual life of humans."[4] The Bible declares that the heart is the source of understanding (Matthew 13:15) and of thinking (Proverbs 23:7), and it is somehow involved in introspective meditation and reflection (Luke 2:19), the will (2 Corinthians 9:7), and even in our propensity to worry (1 Samuel 9:19-20). "The word came to stand for (humanity's) entire mental and moral activity, both the rational and the emotional elements. In other words, the heart is used figuratively for the hidden springs of the personal life."[5]

But in both the Old and New Testaments, and for many contemporary believers, the heart is the most appreciated metaphor for describing the emotional aspect of our faith. The Psalms alone, for example, are filled with dozens of emotional references of the heart.[6] Throughout the Scriptures emotions like joy (Psalm 4:7; Isaiah 65:14), fear (1 Samuel 25:37), depression (Proverbs 12:25), hate (Leviticus 19:17), and love (1 Timothy 1:5) all are described in terms of the heart.

So how does one cultivate a *spiritual readiness* in loving God with the heart? One way to think about readying your heart is to *allow enough space for the spiritual romance God wants with you as his beloved child*.[7] Although few talk about the intimacy of faith in these terms, in both the Old Testament (Isaiah 62:5) and the New (Revelation 19:7) our relationship to God and to Jesus Christ is spoken of in romantic terms.[8] Our devotion to God is an *emotional* devotion: "Go and proclaim in the hearing of Jerusalem: 'I remember the devotion of your youth, how as a bride you loved me and followed me

---

3. Werner G. Kummel, *The Theology of the New Testament*, trans. John E. Steely (Nashville: Abingdon, 1973), 56-7.

4. "Heart," *Holman Bible Dictionary*, CD-ROM (Parson's Technology).

5. W. E. Vine, *Expository Dictionary of New Testament Words* (Grand Rapids: Zondervan, 1952), 206-7.

6. A sampling of Psalms of the heart expressing emotion: "How long must I bear pain in my soul, and have sorrow in my heart all day long?" (13:2); "But I trusted in your steadfast love; my heart shall rejoice in your salvation" (13:5); "the precepts of the Lord are right, rejoicing the heart..." (19:8); "Relieve the troubles of my heart, and bring me out of my distress" (25:17); and "Insults have broken my heart, so that I am in despair" (69:20).

7. For more on this life-changing idea, see the works of Henri J. M. Nouwen, especially *In the Name of Jesus* (New York: Crossroad, 1988) and *Life of the Beloved* (New York: Crossroad, 1992).

8. Throughout the Scriptures we are called the "wife" of God and the "bride of Christ." To many cultures that may have the emotional sense of a "marriage by contract," but clearly in the Hebrew context this romantic relationship is filled with passion, celebration, and emotion.

through the desert, through a land not sown'" (Jeremiah 2:2). And this emotional aspect of the faith journey is not just the one-sided expectation of a distant-yet-powerful deity. The all-loving, supreme, and mighty architect of Creation also experiences powerful and overwhelming emotion toward those he loves. The Scriptures consistently affirm the Great Romance of the cosmos—God *longs* to *woo* us to himself:

> "For your Maker is your husband—the Lord Almighty is his name—the Holy One of Israel is your Redeemer; he is called the God of all the earth. The Lord will call you back as if you were a wife deserted and distressed in spirit—a wife who married young, only to be rejected," says your God. "For a brief moment I abandoned you, but with deep compassion I will bring you back. In a surge of anger I hid my face from you for a moment, but with everlasting kindness I will have compassion on you," says the Lord your Redeemer.
>
> *—Isaiah 54:5-8*

In response to this rush of passion and longing, we are invited into the intimacy of the Trinitarian fellowship. That is the central theme of the Christian journey—allowing ourselves to encounter the incredible love that God personifies. This is the final and only source of true life.

To be equipped and prepared for the various demands of adolescent ministry, then, the primary focus of love you cultivate must *never* be primarily a love of the students. Rather, love for students, and leadership, and parents must flow out of a healthy, authentic, inside-out romantic affection for the Savior. Youth work is not youth ministry without this being the focus. Many people who love students do not make room for a relationship with God as the motivating and sustaining force. Loving Jesus is the central, most fundamental calling in the life of every believer (John 8:32; 14:15). Loving others flows from this emotive fountain of an intimate joyful relationship with the God who created you.

To make space to love God with the heart, then, is the key. For some the classic daily devotional is sufficient to remember that a wildly romantic dance is just a brief prayer away. For most of us, however, we need to be shaken out of our routines by setting time aside for a half day a month or more. But the point is for ministry to be authentic and to maintain perspective, you must never allow the demands of the job, the excitement of the event, or the response of the students to crowd out your intrinsic thirst for a lover to comfort you by satisfying the deep longings of your heart.

"With all your soul"—readying the soul

In the Scriptures there is an intrinsic link between the body, the spirit, and the soul. To the Hebrew mind there is no mistaking that all three are clearly woven together into an intimate tapestry called the human person. W. E. Vine describes the distinction this

Mortal danger
We who have been professionally employed in youth ministry can't let professionalization squeeze out our first love. (Professional lovers, after all, are whores, right?) Our love for Jesus should lead us to daily put our job on the line, to be willing to give up the career move in order to be authentic lovers of the Lord Jesus. Whenever one can be bought and sold by those who want to define the priorities of the job, that person's heart is in mortal danger.

way: "The spirit (*pneuma*) may be recognized as the life principle bestowed on (humanity) by God, the soul as the resulting life constituted in the individual, the body being the material organism animated by soul and spirit."[9] The soul is the essence of the unique person, what John Calvin called the "best part."[10] For our purposes, then, the soul (*psuche*) can be described as the core of the human person. The soul is what receives salvation (1 Peter 1:9) and is the emanating source of praise from the deepest part of who we are: "Praise the Lord, O my soul; all my inmost being, praise his holy name" (Psalm 103:1).

Because the soul makes up the center of who we are, we cannot separate our souls from our work. The soul of the youth worker belongs to God, and it is therefore central to our calling to *ready our souls* as we assess honestly what it means to serve in Christian ministry to adolescents. Loving God with *all my soul* implies a willingness to reach into the depths of my being and surrender all that is there to the God who first loved me. This type of responsive love means that I am willing to go to any lengths, or depths, no matter how difficult, uncomfortable, or painful that search may be, to place at the feet of the Creator anything and everything that is buried within me. This can be what is in my past or what is in my present. It can affect the thoughts I carry as well as the plans that I make. In readying my soul to love God, I must be willing to do the work it takes to be honest with who and what I am. For some reason, this kind of call to honesty has been an Achilles heel for many in youth ministry.

Few youth ministers are open to input about the areas of their lives that get in the way of ministry. Whether it's because we tend, as a lot, to be overly insecure about our jobs, or in our youthful zeal the thought of perceived organizational interference seems stifling, or because we are frankly unsure of how we are doing and that makes us nervous, youth ministers are seldom known for their teachability. But loving God with *all* my soul means that I must be willing to regularly and freely take who I am to the throne of God, appealing to his mercy for my failures and receive his "grace to help in the hour of need" (Hebrews 4:16 *Phillips*). This means that I must not only be open to—but proactively seek out—critique and input about both my job and my character. It means we must be willing to go to counseling if needed, and, at the very minimum, to allow a few friends, supervisors, and co-workers into the core of our lives.

"With all your mind"—readying the mind

The mind (*dianoia*) "represents the intellectual, reflective faculty" of humanity.[11] To love God with the mind is to meditate and carefully consider our life and faith. This involves one of the significant reasons for this book—we (the editors) carry a deep conviction that youth workers are far better at emotively and programmatically reacting

---

9. Vine, 54.

10. Institutes 1. 15. 2., as quoted in Justo L. Gonzales, *A History of Christian Thought*, vol. III (Nashville: Abingdon, 1975), 128. See also Revelation 6:9.

11. Connell, J. Clement, "Mind," in Everett F. Harrison (ed.), *Baker's Dictionary of Theology* (Grand Rapids: Baker Book House, 1960), 355.

in our lives and ministries than theologically reflecting on who we are and what we are about subject to the lordship of Jesus Christ.

For example, a few months ago I asked a junior high worker seminary student who had just gotten his lip pierced, "What was your theological motivation for getting the lip ring?" Because we have a great relationship, he knew I was not intending to trick or insult him, but rather wanted to see where he was coming from. As we talked, he admitted that he got it because it was cool and he had always wanted one and his parents had finally given in. Clearly, this is not exactly a prime example of loving God *with all your mind*.

The lack of theological thinking and decision-making has been one of the most destructive markers of youth ministry over the past several decades. Many programs, games, events, illustrations, shirt designs, and any number of other youth ministry staples have been advanced and promoted without the slightest nod given to theological reflection—and sometimes these have inadvertently hurt people in the process. My friend ultimately admitted that his work with junior high students had only been considered as a side issue in deciding to pierce his lip, and only the positive side at that. ("Kids will trust and like me more.") It had never occurred to him to consider what this might model for the students or how this may impact legitimate family concerns in the church. These are but examples of how we are called to love God with our mind.

To love God with our mind we must continually ask the three most foundational questions relating to all theological decision-making:

• What does God think about this?
• What has the church historically believed about this issue?
• Will the consequences of this decision hurt anyone?

It is possible that someone could do a careful theological reflection around those three questions and still come to the same kind of conclusions they would have reached had they *not* done the work of *loving God* with their mind. But just the disciplined commitment to *caring* about these questions leaves the Holy Spirit room and time to work. Readying your mind to love God in your life and ministry means committing to the discipline of thinking before acting.

"With all of your strength"—readying the strength

Youth ministers are often perceived as lazy by people who do not understand their world. In my experience this is too sweeping a generalization, for youth workers typically work hard at the tasks that they deem vital or most important. But in our decision-making regarding such mundane and "nonspiritual" tasks as time management, informing the office support staff of our schedule, keeping good expense records, and driving safely, the perception that is out there may be closer to the

Ponderable
Is Chap suggesting that when we love God with all of our minds, every action (thought, etc.) will be intentional, deliberately chosen with a theological motivation in mind—even for an expression of, say, personal fashion? Is this reasonably ambitious or unfeasible? What do you find in the Bible that permits or forbids such practices?

truth than we would like to admit. It is almost always in our power to be diligent in *all* aspects of our job. For the person who longs for a ministry that flows out of an intimate love for Jesus Christ, self-discipline and responsibility are important components of our devotion.

Loving God with *all my strength* describes an individual's willful decision to do her part in pursuing a love relationship with God. Strength (*ischus*) is concerned with follow through and has to do with the "ability to enforce one's will."[12] It is not just *wanting* to love God with my heart, soul, and mind, it is about accessing and then implementing the Holy Spirit's indwelling power to live out my convictions.

"The second commandment is like it"—loving others as we would like to be loved

It is here in this second command where Jesus puts our personal devotion for him into action. The Apostle Paul picks up on this and goes straight to the heart of issue of love when he states, "The entire law is summed up in a single command: 'Love your neighbor as yourself'" (Galatians 5:14). The word used for love here and in Mark 12, *agape* (*agapao*), is the highest form of the word in the Greek. This love, "whether exercised toward the brethren, or toward (people) generally, is not an impulse from the feelings, it does not always run with the natural inclinations, nor does it spend itself only upon those for whom some affinity is discovered. Love seeks the welfare of all."[13]

Each of us is called to love anybody and everybody, whether or not they agree with us, threaten us, help us, make us look good or bad, or deserve our love. We are *not* called to destroy ourselves in the process, or to deny when we have been hurt or unjustly treated. But, even with those who seek to harm us, we are still called to love.

The *source* of this kind of love is the intimacy we experience with God. It is not an *either/or* love, where we have to choose between loving God and loving others, but rather a *because of* love. As I love God, so I love others, as I am called to love myself. Love is therefore a package where the power and motivation is fueled by God's initiative to first love us (1 John 4:19). This is the definition of ministry—to love others.

The bottom line: the theological task of youth ministry

Jesus Christ has redeemed and called men and women into intimate relationship with himself. He is the consummate romantic, in that his love is piercing, penetrating, and forever seeking out the object of his love. We in youth ministry, then, are invited to participate in God's redeeming work by responding to his love for us, and in so doing to nurture those who are placed in our care, including ourselves. This summarizes the theological task of youth ministry.

---

12. L. E. H. Stevens-Hodge, "Might," in Everett F. Harrison (ed.), *Baker's Dictionary of Theology*, Grand Rapids: Baker Book House, 1960), 351.

13. Vine, 21.

A *practical* theology of the youth ministry task, then, involves putting together a careful and decisive set of vocational parameters for staying personally healthy and spiritually vital as we engage in the difficult task of ministering to and caring for students and families.

10 keys to healthy living in youth ministry

The following keys to healthy living in youth ministry represent a practical response to many of the issues presented in this chapter. This is not an exhaustive list, but rather it is intended to help the student put practical wheels on the concepts offered.

1. **Your ministry is God's ministry.** The reality of Christian ministry is that it is ultimately not your ministry—it's God's ministry in which you get to participate. This is not your student, your program, your leaders, your situation, your church, or your world. You are called to be a steward of those responsibilities you have been given, but God's foremost concern is your life and character, and your ministry is a far cry below that.

2. **Learn to draw boundaries.** To survive over the long haul of ministry, you must learn that God is not asking you to give your life away to the ministry, but rather to Jesus Christ himself. Boundaries are healthy, theologically appropriate relational devices that ensure that you are able to stay the course of loving God, self, and others. Boundaries may involve such programmatic day-to-day issues as what kind of limits you put on use of the telephone, how accessible you are on days off, and whether or not you take your full vacation. If you are married, and have children, healthy boundaries are necessary for all of you—for you need your family as badly as they need you. If you are single, most churches will subtly expect you to have more time and energy than a married employee. But beware of buying into this pressure, for you need boundaries every bit as much as a married person. No matter what your personal situation, build in a system of self-protection so that you are able to develop friendships, cultivate a hobby, take walks, and play games.

3. **Make a few good friends.** Most youth ministers are lonely, especially if they have been doing it awhile. Being the relational animals most of us are, people think that we are never in need and never feel alone. But many youth ministry people have hit a major wall in their 30s and 40s because they never took the time to cultivate peer friendships. It is vital that you spend time developing an adult community where you can experience mutual soul-feeding relationships. Intimate friendships with peers is not just a need of middle adolescents, it is an integral aspect of God's plan for all his children—even those who are in ministry!

4. **Be strategic with your time and energy.** Youth ministry is seasonal, so make sure that you are spending time planning and rebuilding during the down times and pacing yourself during the hectic times.

5. **When it is time to work, work hard.** The perception of the lazy youth worker is usually more due to the youth worker's tendency to work hard at some things but let others slide instead of raw laziness. This is a tendency that others may overlook in your 20s, but as you age this will cause many to take you less and less seriously as a committed, capable Christian leader. Avoid allowing a lack of preparedness and planning cause people to discount and thus hinder your ministry. "Don't let anyone look down on you because you are young, but set an example for the believers in speech, in life, in love, in faith and in purity" (1 Timothy 4:12).

6. **The practice of spiritual discipline is essential for those in vocational ministry.** As a minister of the gospel, it is *your job* to take time to pray, to be quiet, to walk, think, read, and meditate. This should be scheduled along with all of the other duties of your calling.

7. **Use technology wisely.** Pagers, cell phones, the Internet, PowerPoint, and video technology can be useful (and even fun) tools for connecting with and communicating to adolescents. But there is also the great danger that these will eventually hurt your ministry. Your primary calling is to love people, and that means taking time to be with people—adults and students. Technology can keep us in the office too long, up too late at night, and even overwhelm a program or meeting. Students in today's culture yearn to connect, with you, other adults, and each other. Make sure you don't allow technology to overshadow the fundamental theological goal of youth ministry.

8. **Find a mentor.** The idea of mentoring scares many people because there is a common misconception that it needs to function just so—weekly meetings, commit to a year, etc. But committing to a mentor has less to do with the structure of the relationship than it does the relationship itself. Find someone, or a few people, who will promise to get to know you, tell you the truth, and be your friend on a deep, non-job-related basis. There is such a wealth of love and joy waiting for the youth worker who will connect with one or two older people who love her.

9. **Never stop learning.** No matter what level of schooling you find yourself, never consider yourself finished in terms of training or schooling. The most potentially destructive youth worker is the one who has taken a few classes in college or seminary, gone to one or two conventions, and now "knows" youth ministry. God never wants to stop teaching you, so commit to being a lifelong learner.

Ponderable

What Chap prescribes here makes some Christians nervous. It's like saying that humans really ought to eat, sleep, exercise, and rest—not exactly a *job* issue, it it? Rather essential for life itself, right?

By the same token, *everyone* who names the name of Jesus needs to pray, be quiet, etc.

On the other hand—and perhaps more to the author's point—vocational ministers of the gospel *do* have leadership obligations that heighten the consequences if they do *not* practice spiritual disciplines.

10. **When it's time to quit, quit graciously.** When it becomes obvious that it's time to move on from a ministry, maintain a commitment to loving even as you turn to walk out the door. Great work has been undone by a messy or contentious exit. If the ministry belongs to God, then even if it's not our choice to move on but we must, God is still faithful to take care of us. Even in the midst of a difficult situation, do your best to be kind and also to be committed to relationships as well as the existing ministry. Do whatever you can to provide smooth continuity for the next leader. This will be a lasting gift to both the community and the Lord.

Thinking Theologically as a Right Start
Dave Rahn

Epilogue

During a high-adventure training session in Jackson Hole, Wyoming, one of the guys in our group kept sidling up to me, whispering suggestions that we wouldn't learn the really *important* stuff until we got in the wilderness.

He was wrong.

Among the instructors was a fairly unsociable bearded man who expressed his disdain for us cityfolk by fixing his coal-eyed stare on some point deep within our skulls. He talked about the perils of hypothermia, proper responses to bears and moose, what to wear if we expected to survive—and I gradually realized that this was more than an adventurous romp.

Maybe I grew sober because it seemed like every teaching point our mountain man made ended with the phrase "…or you could die." My comfortable blue jeans were actually death traps, and my hope for a chance to stroke a moose's velvety antlers was now a death wish. I wasn't just stupid, I was *dangerously* stupid.

After that session my buddy and I went back to our cabin, fell into our cots, and stared at the ceiling, prayer-whimpering softly for our safety, begging God to take care of all of those loved ones we'd leave behind. I was transformed from a carefree, fun-loving frolicker on Mister Mountain to a cautious, awe-inspired climber.

Veteran and beginning youth ministers alike need the same sort of upheaval in attitude. Young pups who see youth ministry as a fun-loving frolic must learn to bring a sense of respect and humility to the task. Others who may have reduced youth ministry to a convenient set of practical categories need to be sobered by embracing the importance of theological thinking. We all need to be subdued by the reality that what we *do* in the practice of youth ministry is powerfully shaped by how deeply and faithfully we *think about* those practices.

That's why this book was written—that it might be read, studied, discussed, and debated so as to facilitate such thinking.

As you read books like this one and reflect on youth ministry, some will doubtlessly come alongside you, whispering during your ruminations that if you *really* want to learn youth ministry, you simply need to get out where the action is—get out of your book and hit the streets, the schools, the courts, the juvenile centers, the ball fields. Their inference is that the only worthy way to improve youth ministry's practice is *by* practicing. Unfortunately they don't appreciate the value of Learning in the Lodge. They're dangerous frolickers on Youth Ministry Mountain.

And they're not ready.

Youth ministry will include a future that continues to see exponential growth in human knowledge. It's easy to be numbed in the face of what's unknown. No one can study or know all that's currently relevant to youth ministry, let alone what *will* be relevant.

But we can learn to practice the discipline of integration, building reflective bridges between life and God's word. The Bible contains principles of ministry that have been true for thousands of years. We ought to study and learn them. We must learn how to faithfully contextualize them in the world to which God has called us. Such foundational knowledge and skills are well suited for study in the academy—our version of the mountain lodge—and they will be valuable for a lifetime of ministry, well into a tempestuous future.

Since youth ministry's future will undoubtedly include circumstances we cannot predict, our most critical preparation needs to be based on timeless, transferable principles rather than the new, hottest whatever:

• *Discipleship* will never be outdated, and biblical principles will always be foundational to the task of contextualizing those truths in particular settings.

• Methods come, go, and continuously improve, but youth *evangelism* principles—that are not method-dependent, that are rooted in biblical theology and historical faithfulness—can be taught.

• Even something as seemingly pragmatic as curriculum development has a theological nut at its candy core. When we understand the task as helping students move from point A to point B in their faith journey, we must reckon with what we as youth ministers have control of and what is exclusively God's responsibility.

★ ★ ★

After El Beardo's warnings about the perils of the great outdoors, my buddy and I were very alert to the consequences of any action we took during our time in the wild. After the tongue-lashing he gave to one careless fellow in our group whose foot happened onto the perlon coil, we were careful to *never* step on the rope. We learned the art of checking the rope for small abrasions that might weaken its support strength. After all, that rope was our lifeline.

We also learned to read mountain conditions. We once aborted a climb up the Middle Teton because of observable avalanche conditions. No matter that we had driven 32 hours for such an adventure—one does not mess with an avalanche.

I did not learn such life-preserving lore and humility and caution by surviving an avalanche; I learned it in the lodge. What I learned *inside* myself changed the way I related to the wilderness.

Once we see the youth ministry world through theological lenses, we may wonder what illusion of faithfulness we were operating with before. We will be changed in the way we relate to God, the task he calls us to, and the young people we serve.

This is where this book's contribution to understanding youth ministry's future peaks. The writers herein do not see themselves as reservoirs of untapped, expert knowledge. They are guides. They know how to learn, where to look, what knowledge to draw upon as they solve problems. Trained as theological thinkers, they have trouble *not* reflecting on biblical values. I think they're a lot like me in this respect: I tend to ask *why* until I get answers I wouldn't be embarrassed to present to Jesus. As a "So what?" specialist, I love applying new insights toward timeless biblical purposes. Even as in, *How can we do this goofy game in a way that somehow glorifies God?* (I can be a pain at parties.)

Thinking theologically provides me with a grounding that helps me sleep well at night. It will also sustain me in the future. It is a testimony to the transformation that God has and is bringing into my life—the one where my mind is being renewed, and I get a clear reading of God's will. Because, like most youth ministers, I am one who really wants to do the job like God wants it done.

So there—we've offered our best. Now our prayer is that this book will help you and many like you **start right** on your youth ministry adventure.

Index

Youth Specialties Resources

Youth Ministry Programming

Camps, Retreats, Missions, & Service Ideas
(Ideas Library)

Compassionate Kids: Practical Ways to Involve Your
Students in Mission and Service

Creative Bible Lessons from the Old Testament

Creative Bible Lessons in 1 & 2 Corinthians

Creative Bible Lessons in John: Encounters with Jesus

Creative Bible Lessons in Romans: Faith on Fire!

Creative Bible Lessons on the Life of Christ

Creative Bible Lessons in Psalms

Creative Junior High Programs from A to Z,
Vol. 1 (A-M)

Creative Junior High Programs from A to Z,
Vol. 2 (N-Z)

Creative Meetings, Bible Lessons, & Worship Ideas
(Ideas Library)

Crowd Breakers & Mixers (Ideas Library)

Downloading the Bible Leader's Guide

Drama, Skits, & Sketches (Ideas Library)

Drama, Skits, & Sketches 2 (Ideas Library)

Dramatic Pauses

Everyday Object Lessons

Games (Ideas Library)

Games 2 (Ideas Library)

Good Sex: A Whole-Person Approach to Teenage
Sexuality & God

Great Fundraising Ideas for Youth Groups

More Great Fundraising Ideas for Youth Groups

Great Retreats for Youth Groups

Holiday Ideas (Ideas Library)

Hot Illustrations for Youth Talks

More Hot Illustrations for Youth Talks

Still More Hot Illustrations for Youth Talks

Ideas Library on CD-ROM

Incredible Questionnaires for Youth Ministry

Junior High Game Nights

More Junior High Game Nights

Kickstarters: 101 Ingenious Intros to Just about Any
Bible Lesson

Live the Life! Student Evangelism Training Kit

Memory Makers

The Next Level Leader's Guide

Play It! Over 150 Great Games for Youth Groups

Roaring Lambs

So What Am I Gonna Do with My Life? Leader's Guide

Special Events (Ideas Library)

Spontaneous Melodramas

Spontaneous Melodramas 2

Student Leadership Training Manual

Student Underground: An Event Curriculum on the
Persecuted Church

Super Sketches for Youth Ministry

Talking the Walk

Videos That Teach

What Would Jesus Do? Youth Leader's Kit

Wild Truth Bible Lessons

Wild Truth Bible Lessons 2

Wild Truth Bible Lessons—Pictures of God

Wild Truth Bible Lessons—Pictures of God 2

Worship Services for Youth Groups

Professional Resources

Administration, Publicity, & Fundraising (Ideas Library)

Dynamic Communicators Workshop for Youth Workers

Equipped to Serve: Volunteer Youth Worker
Training Course

Help! I'm a Junior High Youth Worker!

Help! I'm a Small-Group Leader!

Help! I'm a Sunday School Teacher!

Help! I'm a Volunteer Youth Worker!

How to Expand Your Youth Ministry

How to Speak to Youth...and Keep Them Awake at the
Same Time

Junior High Ministry (Updated & Expanded)

The Ministry of Nurture: A Youth Worker's Guide to
Discipling Teenagers

Postmodern Youth Ministry

Purpose-Driven Youth Ministry

Purpose-Driven Youth Ministry Training Kit

So That's Why I Keep Doing This! 52 Devotional Stories
for Youth Workers

Teaching the Bible Creatively

A Youth Ministry Crash Course

Youth Ministry Management Tools

The Youth Worker's Handbook to Family Ministry

Academic Resources

Four Views of Youth Ministry and the Church

Starting Right: Thinking Theologically about
Youth Ministry

Discussion Starters

Discussion & Lesson Starters (Ideas Library)

Discussion & Lesson Starters 2 (Ideas Library)

EdgeTV

Get 'Em Talking

Keep 'Em Talking!

Good Sex: A Whole-Person Approach to Teenage
    Sexuality & God

High School TalkSheets

More High School TalkSheets

High School TalkSheets from Psalms and Proverbs

Junior High TalkSheets

More Junior High TalkSheets

Junior High TalkSheets from Psalms
    and Proverbs

Real Kids: Short Cuts

Real Kids: The Real Deal—on Friendship, Loneliness,
    Racism, & Suicide

Real Kids: The Real Deal—on Sexual Choices, Family
    Matters, & Loss

Real Kids: The Real Deal—on Stressing Out, Addictive
    Behavior, Great Comebacks, & Violence

Real Kids: Word on the Street

Unfinished Sentences: 450 Tantalizing Statement
    Starters to Get Teenagers Talking & Thinking

What If...? 450 Thought-Provoking Questions to Get
    Teenagers Talking, Laughing, and Thinking

Would You Rather...? 465 Provocative Questions to Get
    Teenagers Talking

Have You Ever...? 450 Intriguing Questions Guaranteed
    to Get Teenagers Talking

Art Source Clip Art

Stark Raving Clip Art (print)

Youth Group Activities (print)

Clip Art Library Version 2.0 (CD-ROM)

Digital Resources

Clip Art Library Version 2.0 (CD-ROM)

Ideas Library on CD-ROM

Youth Ministry Management Tools (CD-ROM)

Videos & Video Curricula

Dynamic Communicators Workshop for Youth Workers

EdgeTV

Equipped to Serve: Volunteer Youth Worker Training
    Course

Good Sex: A Whole Person Approach to Teenage
    Sexuality and God

The Heart of Youth Ministry: A Morning with
    Mike Yaconelli

Live the Life! Student Evangelism Training Kit

Purpose-Driven Youth Ministry Training Kit

Real Kids: Short Cuts

Real Kids: The Real Deal—on Friendship, Loneliness,
    Racism, & Suicide

Real Kids: The Real Deal—on Sexual Choices, Family
    Matters, & Loss

Real Kids: The Real Deal—on Stressing Out, Addictive
    Behavior, Great Comebacks, & Violence

Real Kids: Word on the Street

Student Underground: An Event Curriculum on the
    Persecuted Church

Understanding Your Teenager Video Curriculum

Student Resources

Downloading the Bible: A Rough Guide to the
    New Testament

Downloading the Bible: A Rough Guide to the
    Old Testament

Grow For It Journal

Grow For It Journal through the Scriptures

So What Am I Gonna Do with My Life? Journaling
    Workbook for Students

Spiritual Challenge Journal: The Next Level

Teen Devotional Bible

What (Almost) Nobody Will Tell You about Sex

What Would Jesus Do? Spiritual Challenge Journal

Wild Truth Journal for Junior Highers

Wild Truth Journal—Pictures of God